ROME, FLORENCE & VENICE

ALEXEI J. COHEN

Contents

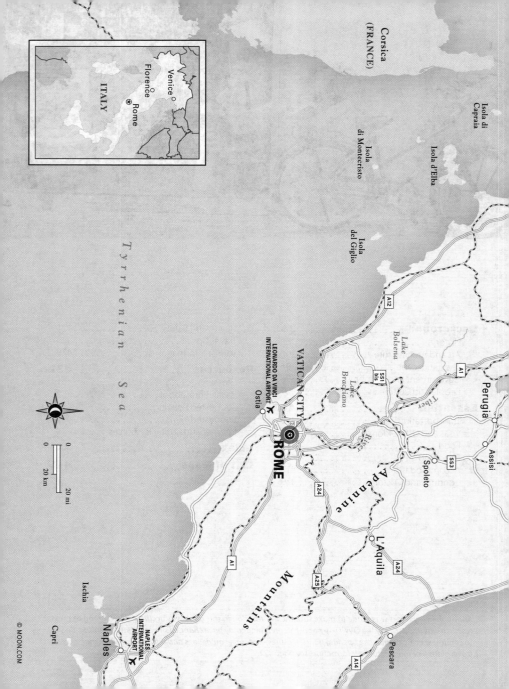

Corsica
(FRANCE)

ITALY

Venice
Florence
Rome

Isola di
Capraia

Isola
di Montecristo

Isola d'Elba

Isola
del Giglio

Tyrrhenian Sea

Lake
Bolsena

A12

A1

SS1
bis

Lake
Bracciano

Perugia

Tiber River

Assisi

SS3

Spoleto

VATICAN CITY

LEONARDO DA VINCI
INTERNATIONAL AIRPORT

Ostia

ROME

Apennine

A24

L'Aquila

A24

A25

Mountains

A1

A14

Pescara

Ischia

NAPLES
INTERNATIONAL AIRPORT

Naples

Capri

© MOON.COM

0   0
20 km   20 mi

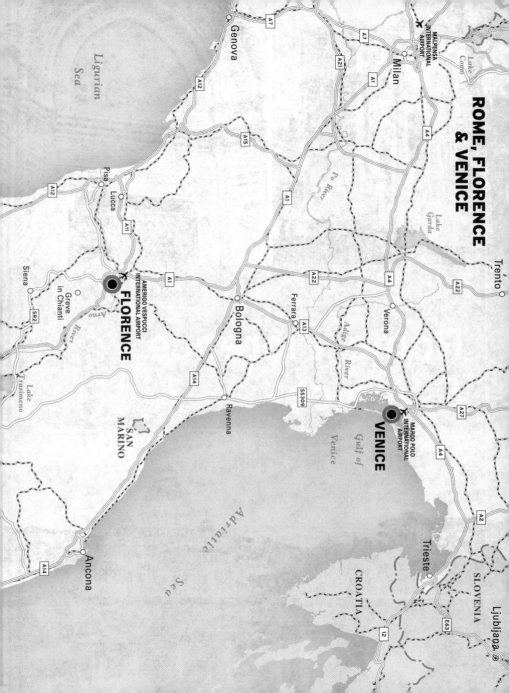

Rome, Florence & Venice

R ome, Florence, and Venice are no ordinary cities, and visiting them all is no ordinary journey.

You may diligently plan a must-see itinerary of museums, churches, and monuments—and the Colosseum, statue of *David,* and Doge's Palace certainly won't disappoint. However, you'll soon realize there's more to satisfy the senses than you ever imagined, and a lot of it is unexpected, from the scent of freshly baked bread to the sounds of children playing soccer in city squares.

Go beyond the stereotypes and treat yourself to an Italian adventure you'll never forget. Cycle up Tuscan hillsides, browse lively leather markets, and relax at neighborhood cafés. Greet shop owners with *buon giorno* and order espresso confidently at bar counters. Sample traditional flavors in local *trattorie*, bite into tripe sandwiches, enter unexpected alleys, and turn strangers into friends. Every moment here is worth savoring and offers an opportunity to soak in the creativity of the past and energy of the present.

Clockwise from top left: Arch of Constantine in Rome; detail of Duomo entrance in Florence; statues in Villa Borghese, Rome; Villa Borghese gardens, Rome; *cicchetti,* Venice; Vatican with bridges over the Tiber River in Rome

Italy will reward you. All it takes is a little determination combined with a dash of curiosity, and you'll soon discover the characteristics and customs that make Rome, Florence, and Venice unique. You'll begin to distinguish Roman-esque churches from Renaissance *palazzi*, Florentine Negroni cocktails from Venetian spritz, and superb gelato from average ice cream. The experience will change you and is likely to leave an indelible mark on mind, stomach, and soul.

Enjoy the journey!

Clockwise from top left: St. Peter's Square, Vatican City; Italian *ribollita* vegetable soup; Trastevere neighborhood, Rome; Ancient Roman ruins

16 TOP
EXPERIENCES

1 Gazing up at Michelangelo's **Sistine Chapel**—the greatest fresco ever painted (page 76).

2 Taking in the thousands of golden mosaics that decorate **St. Mark's Basilica,** Venice's holiest site, where the city's patron saint is buried (page 289).

>>>

3 Savoring **local specialties** like *cacio e pepe* in Rome (page 88), *pappa al pomodoro* in Florence (page 208), and *fritto misto* in Venice (page 320).

<<<

4 Getting a close-up look at **Michelangelo's David,** the world's most famous statue, at the Galleria dell'Accademia (page 186).

>>>

5 Exploring the **Colosseum** by day—then returning to see it illuminated at night (page 51).

6 Cruising **Venice's canals** by gondola, *vaporetto*, or *traghetto* (page 312).

7 Joining locals for *aperitivo* (page 223), the Italian version of happy hour. Venice has a distinct version, accompanied by snacks known as *cicchetti* (page 324).

8 Climbing to the top of Florence's **Duomo,** Brunelleschi's iconic and innovative dome that's become a symbol of the city (page 175).

<<<

9 Discovering your favorite flavor of **gelato,** one of Italy's greatest gastronomic contributions (page 214).

>>>

10 Cycling down **Via Appia Antica,** an ancient road flanked by Roman monuments (page 146).

<<<

11 Hiking to **Basilica San Miniato al Monte,** the highest spot in Florence, for undisturbed views of the city skyline. Take the back route up secluded paths to escape the crowds (page 238).

> > >

12 Learning the techniques of **Venetian glassmaking** at the working furnaces of Murano (page 371).

> > >

13 Admiring the **Ponte Vecchio** at sunset with Florentine locals (page 199).

14 **Ordering espresso—** in Italian—at a neighborhood bar (page 218).

>>>

15 Waking up early to wander the cobblestone labyrinth of **Trastevere** (page 79).

16 Watching boats sail up and down Venice's Grand Canal from **Punta della Dogana** (page 301).

Planning Your Trip

Where to Go

Rome

Italy's capital and largest city is an heirloom of art, history, and culture. Its vast historic center contains some of the world's most iconic monuments. The **Roman Forum** and **Palatine Hill** are the focal points of antiquity, where ancient Romans once debated, worshipped, and played. Many sights including the **Colosseum** and **Pantheon** are remarkably intact. Across the Tiber River lies the **Vatican.** The world's smallest state packs an artistic punch with the Vatican Museums, **Sistine Chapel,** and **St. Peter's Basilica,** which houses Michelangelo's *Pieta* and attracts thousands of visitors every day.

Rome is more than a collection of famous sights. A vibrant population proud of their past and their soccer teams animates this busy metropolis day and night. The city stays up later than either Florence or Venice, with clubs and *aperitivo* **bars** hosting the Italian version of happy hour. Wandering the medieval alleys of **Trastevere,** sipping **espresso** at outdoor cafés, or enjoying *pizza al taglio* are all excellent opportunities for acquainting oneself with the Eternal City.

Florence

The **birthplace of the Renaissance** is a grand city on a human scale. Stepping off the train in Florence feels like entering a different era, where artisans practice age-old traditions and handmade jewelry is still sold in boutiques along the **Ponte Vecchio.** Visitors flock to Florence to admire *David,* the world's most famous statue;

view of Florence

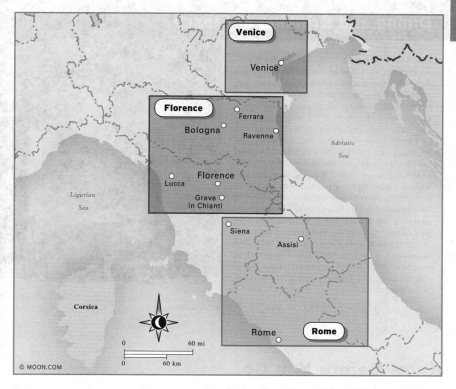

glimpse artistic masterpieces inside the **Uffizi Gallery;** and climb Brunelleschi's **Duomo,** an engineering triumph that rises majestically above the terra-cotta skyline. Experiencing the city also means sampling **Tuscan food** and uncorking bottles of locally produced **Chianti.** Outside the lively center, hillsides are dotted with sumptuous **villas** and **gardens** where travelers can escape the heat and get a unique perspective on the city.

Venice

It's hard not to feel romantic in Venice. Founded after the fall of the Roman Empire, this island city's glorious past is still evident within mosaic-encrusted **St. Mark's Basilica** and inside the **Doge's Palace,** where *doges* ruled over much of the Mediterranean. Geography forced the city to look outward and prosper by trading with the world. The result of this commercial and cultural exchange is still evident in art, architecture, and cuisine.

Today, the **gondolas** that glide across the **Grand Canal** infuse the city with otherworldly charm. Flavors and smells inherited from the Orient enrich local kitchens. Venetians toast with *prosecco,* snack on delectable finger food known as *cicchetti,* and regularly dine on **seafood.** Artisans keep the traditions of **glassblowing** and **lacemaking** alive, and the city's ferries put the lagoon islands of **Murano** and **Burano** enticingly within reach.

Dining and Drinking *al Fresco*

In Rome, Florence, and Venice, nearly every *osteria, trattoria,* café, and restaurant has tables set up outdoors to accommodate locals and visitors, and warm Roman weather makes outdoor dining nearly a year-round affair. (Florence and Venice are rainier and colder in the winter months.) The best seats are along pedestrian streets and quiet squares—and **away from major monuments** where the views may be good but the food poor and pricey. Getting a table at peak lunch hours (1pm-2:30pm) and peak dinner hours (7:30pm-9pm) often requires a reservation, especially as the demand for outdoor dining has increased during the coronavirus pandemic. Learning the phrase *Un tavolo all'aperto per favore* (an outdoor table please) will come in handy over the phone or in-person. Without a reservation, show up before 7:30pm, since Italians tend to dine late. Still, there's enough supply to go around, and a short stroll is usually all it takes to find a great table.

dining *al fresco*

Know Before You Go

When to Go

Rome, Florence, and Venice are among the most popular cities in the world. Deciding when to go will have a significant impact on your experience.

SUMMER

Summer sees a dramatic increase in arrivals, with **July** and **August** the apex of the tourist season. Airlines and hotels take advantage of demand to raise their rates, and temperatures rise to sweltering. Avoid visiting in July and August if you can. If you can't, book ahead and purchase **sightseeing passes** like the **RomaPass** (Rome), **Firenzecard** (Florence), or **Venezia Unica** (Venice) to speed up entry to monuments. The majority of Italians take their vacations in

August, which means many small businesses close and tourists may outnumber locals.

SPRING AND FALL

Late spring and early fall are the best times to visit all three cities. **May** and **September** are especially pleasant. Not only are there fewer visitors, but temperatures are comfortable, daylight is long, and precipitation low. Hotels charge mid-season rates and locals are engaged in their usual routines. Autumn is also harvest season, when food-related festivals are held and newly picked grapes are transformed into wine.

WINTER

November and **December** are relatively mild in Rome, but they are the rainiest months and can be very cold in both Florence and Venice. Christmas and New Year festivities attract a wave of visitors over the holidays, as does *Carnevale,* which each city celebrates in its own way. Apart from during the holiday season, accommodations and airfare are more affordable in winter, and accessing the Vatican or Uffizi in January can take minutes rather than hours.

Passports and Visas

EU citizens can travel visa-free to Italy. Travelers from the **United States, UK, Canada, Australia,** and **New Zealand** do not need a visa for visits of less than 90 days, but a passport is required. For travelers from **South Africa,** a visa is required. There is a fee, and the application process takes two weeks.

Transportation

Within Europe, all three cities are easily reached by quick flights. Travelers outside Europe will likely arrive at Rome's **Leonardo Da Vinci Airport,** also known as **Fiumicino** (FCO; Via dell'Aeroporto 320;

tel. 06/65951; www.adr.it), an international hub. Venice's **Aeroporto di Venezia** (VCE; Via Galileo Galilei 30; tel. 041/260-6111; www.veniceairport.it) also receives some flights from outside Europe, including North America. Florence's airport, **Aeroporto di Firenze-Peretola (Aeroporto Amerigo Vespucci)** (FLR; Via del Termine 11; tel. 055/30615; www.aeroporto.firenze.it), is the smallest of the three, with no direct flights from anywhere outside Europe.

Traveling between Rome, Florence, and Venice by **train** is fast, easy, and convenient. **Buses** are a cheap alternative, with several companies operating daily between Rome, Florence, and Venice. Travel time, however, is longer than by train and offers less flexibility than a car. If you prefer to drive, reserve a **car** before departure and specify automatic transmission if you're unfamiliar with manual. Get the maximum insurance, as driving in Italy has its risks and fender benders are frequent. An international license is not required but can resolve confusion if you are pulled over.

eating *al fresco* in Rome

drinks with a view in Florence

view of Castel Sant'Angelo in Rome

Final Tips

Most Italian businesses accept credit and debit cards, although some restaurants remain proudly cash-only. **Tax** is already included in all prices and you should keep receipts on major purchases if you plan on VAT reimbursement. **Tipping** is never required. Monuments offer discounts for under 18s and over 65s. Transportation is free for kids 6 and under and most museums are free for preteens.

The **coronavirus** has changed how Italians live and how travelers experience the country. Whether the rules implemented during the emergency will remain in place in 2021 and beyond is uncertain. At the time of writing, many museums and monuments had compulsory online booking and allowed only a limited number of visitors at one time. Book at least a week or two in advance to secure visits to major sights, including the **Colosseum** and **Vatican Museums** in Rome and the **Uffizi** in Florence. For more information on traveling during the pandemic, see the Pandemic Travel sections of each chapter, and Italy and the Coronavirus (page 422).

Best of Rome, Florence & Venice

Rome is a convenient starting point for a three-city tour of Italy. Most transatlantic flights land directly in the Italian capital and tickets are less expensive than to Florence or Venice, which may require connecting flights. The 327 miles (526 kilometers) that separate the cities are covered by high-speed trains, which are the quickest and easiest way of getting between destinations. A Rome-to-Florence-to-Venice itinerary also allows you to travel from most populated to least populated and from oldest to newest, which can facilitate appreciation and understanding of the cities.

Seeing everything is impossible, and visiting one museum after another will leave you exhausted and unable to enjoy anything. You're better off taking it slow and balancing your days with a mix of sights and everyday activities, like lingering in *piazze,* searching for the best gelato, and partaking in *aperitivo* time (happy hour). Using local travel cards like **RomaPass, Firenzecard,** and **Venezia Unica** help get the most out of your journey without wasting precious hours in line.

ROME
DAY 1

Walking is the best cure for jet lag, so after you settle into your room, head out for lunch and a stroll. The *pizza al taglio* parlors in the center provide a good introduction to Roman pizza. Point to the variety you want and have it wrapped up to go. Wander through **Campo De' Fiori** and observe the comings and goings in this busy square. At the first sign of a yawn, enter a bar and order an **espresso.** Although most Romans drink at the counter, outdoor table seating is common. Afterward, ride the number 23, 44, or 280 bus or 8 tram to Aventino and Testaccio. If it's close to *aperitivo* (happy hour), order a cocktail at

the Pantheon, Rome

In Italy, romance awaits around every corner, inside every *trattoria*, and along every canal.

WATCH THE SUNSET

Watching the sunset is a summertime ritual in Florence. It's best viewed from the Ponte Santa Trinità bridge just west of the Ponte Vecchio, where you can sit on the stone siding next to other couples watching the final rays of sun transform the pastel colors of the city (page 199).

SPLURGE ON A MEAL

The way to your lover's heart is through the stomach, and at Florence's Il Nugolo (page 211), love costs less than you think. Trattoria da Enzo (page 99) in Rome and Antiche Carampane (page 327) in Venice may not have as many stars but are still very seductive.

SIP *PROSECCO*

A lot of people swear *prosecco* is better than champagne, and there's only one way to find out. This sparkling wine is available throughout Venice and can be ordered along with *cicchetti* appetizers at canal-side *bacari* bars throughout the day (page 324). You can also purchase *prosecco* from a historic *cantina* and improvise a happy hour for two.

TAKE A STARLIT STROLL

Nighttime is the best time to explore and forget what century you're in. Venice has an entirely different vibe once the sun sets, and the possibility of getting lost heightens a feeling of excitement. Walking hand-in-hand through empty streets without a destination is a wonderful aphrodisiac.

gondola ride, Venice

GLIDE DOWN VENICE'S CANALS

Nothing is more romantic than a gondola ride along Venice's canals (page 312). Just make sure to start your journey in one of the city's less-crowded neighborhoods like Dorsoduro or Cannaregio, where you can exchange sweet words in solitude. You don't have to spend €80 to quicken the pulse. Any *vaporetto* ferry will do; just make sure to score an outdoor seat and let the views do the rest.

Porto Fluviale and enjoy the buffet that doubles as dinner. The longer you resist sleep the easier it will be to adopt Italian time.

DAY 2

The Colosseum cannot be missed. Walk to the ancient stadium, or ride Metro B to the Circo Massimo subway station and approach from the south. Spend an hour exploring the interior with the audio guide. Then, head next door to the Roman Forum, where you can wander through ruins and get a feel for ancient Rome. To see more artifacts, climb the nearby Capitoline Hill and visit the Musei Capitolini. Michelangelo designed the square outside and there's a great view of the city from the adjacent Vittoriano monument.

Walk down to the Jewish Ghetto for a taste

of deep-fried artichokes prepared Jewish style at **Nonna Betta** or any of the kosher restaurants lining **Via del Portico D'Ottavia.** Alternatively, ride the number 8 tram to Piramide and swap ancient ruins for 19th-century history. Pay your respects to Keats in the **Protestant Cemetery** before heading to the covered **Testaccio Market.** Pick a stand and create an improvised picnic with a beef sandwich, cheese, and bread, washed down with local wine served in plastic cups. On the way back, explore the residential streets of **Aventino** and the shaded **Giardini degli Aranci** (Orange Garden) with a surprising view of the Vatican. Return at night to **Monte Testaccio** via Metro B for dancing and Roman **nightlife,** or dine *al fresco* at one of the informal kiosks along the Tiber River and let your feet have the night off.

DAY 3

Zigzag along pedestrian streets toward **Campo De' Fiori.** Search the market for household souvenirs and order *pizza bianca* from **Il Forno** on the northwestern corner of the square. There's a regular flow of tourists on their way to **Piazza Navona,** but plenty of scenic side streets leading to the oblong square. Take the long way and once you arrive admire the fountains and street painters with the help of a **gelato** from **Frigidarium.** Musicians play near the fountains and the colorful canvases make for good browsing. Avoid cafés where waitstaff bait passing tourists, and order your espresso at an authentic **neighborhood bar.**

The **Pantheon** is less than 10 minutes away and remains free to enter. After a visit, browse the boutiques along **Via del Corso** as you head toward the freshly scrubbed **Spanish Steps,** which lead to **Villa Borghese.** If you tire, hop aboard the electric **119 minibus** on a scenic loop of the area. Otherwise, escape the summer heat by **cycling** or strolling through the city's largest park and visit the **Borghese Gallery** (reservations required). Afterward, walk down to **Piazza del Popolo** and follow **Via di Ripetta** to the **Ara Pacis Museum,** then dine at **Gusto.** End the day sitting in front of the **Trevi Fountain.** The later you arrive, the more likely you'll score a travertine seat and get a clear shot of the fountain.

the Roman Forum

Villa Borghese, Rome

DAY 4

Ride Metro A to Ottaviano or walk and follow the pilgrims to Vatican City. Remember to dress appropriately, and arrive early to the **Vatican Museums** and make reservations. Inside you can choose from several itineraries and could easily spend an entire day here. Most visitors beeline to the **Sistine Chapel,** but there are plenty of underrated sections of the museum such as the first-floor **antiquities collection** near the entrance. Once you've gotten your fill, take the guided bus tour of the Vatican gardens or enjoy a drink outside at the museum café before entering **St. Peter's Basilica.** Light a candle and descend into the crypt to pay homage to past popes, then climb your way to the top of Michelangelo's **cupola.** The elevator only goes so far and you'll need some stamina to reach the highest point in the city. If you arrive on Sunday morning you can join the faithful in the square below and receive the pope's blessing.

The nearby streets of **Borgo Pio** and **Borgo Vittorio** have catered to pilgrims since the Middle Ages and are lined with eateries and souvenir shops. Follow either of these parallel roads to **Castel Sant'Angelo.** There's a good view from atop the ancient mausoleum and a convenient rooftop bar serving cold beer. Walk or catch a bus to **Trastevere** and mingle with the evening revelers in **Piazza Trilussa.** Order *cacio e pepe* pasta at **Da Giovanni** or any Roman *trattoria* and explore the streets of this lively neighborhood packed with bars and clubs.

WITH MORE TIME

Via Appia Antica takes a morning or afternoon to visit. It's a 15-minute bus ride on the 118 from Circo Massimo or a 45-minute trek on foot to this ancient highway. When you get there, rent a bike from the park office or saddle up and set off on a leisurely trot down the Queen of Roads.

FLORENCE
DAY 5

The journey from Rome to Florence on board an Italo or Trenitalia train takes less than two hours. Both operators run frequent departures from Termini and Tiburtina stations. Depart

Via Appia Antica, outside Rome

midmorning so you can enjoy lunch in Florence. There are taxis and buses waiting outside Santa Maria Novella station, but the historic center of Florence is small and flat enough to navigate on foot, with no two monuments more than 20 minutes apart. If you're driving, consider stopping in **Assisi**, burial site of Saint Francis, or **Siena**. Florence's historic rival is famous for its shell-shaped *piazza*, annual horse race, and enormous cathedral.

After you've checked-in, find a small *trattoria* like **Trattoria Mario** and discover the difference between Florentine and Roman gastronomy. Order *pappa al pomodoro* or T-bone *fiorentina* steak from Chianina cattle raised along the Tuscan coast. The two covered markets in the center are good places to learn about local culinary traditions. The second floor of **Mercato Centrale** is a food emporium, while downstairs you can sample **tripe sandwiches,** a Florentine specialty. Otherwise, grab a booth at **Trattoria da Rocco** inside **Mercato di Sant'Ambrogio.**

You can work off any meal by **hiking to Basilica San Miniato al Monte** via the less-traveled footpath, which has a panoramic payoff. Just cross **Ponte alle Grazie** bridge and follow the brown signs through the old city gate before turning right and up the grassy path. On the way back follow the **medieval walls** to **Forte Belvedere,** where free outdoor sculpture exhibitions are organized on the terrace overlooking the city, and enter the **Pitti Palace** gardens from the back entrance. If there's time, catch the sunset over **Ponte Vecchio** from nearby **Ponte Santa Trinità.** Otherwise, order a Negroni cocktail, first mixed in Florence in 1919, at any of the bars lining **Piazza Santo Spirito.** During the summer, head to the riverside **beach Spiaggia sul Arno,** where DJs play lounge music until late.

DAY 6

Start the day with an espresso from either of **Ditta Artigianale's** two locations, then head to the **Duomo.** There are 463 steep steps to the top of the **Cupola,** but seeing the inside of Brunelleschi's masterpiece is worth the effort and culminates in a 360-degree view of the city. Next door is the **campanile** bell tower and beautifully

Monumental Architecture

The ancient Romans left their traces everywhere with remarkable feats of engineering that are as impressive now as they were 2,000 years ago. But the collapse of the empire did not signal the end of architecture in Italy. These cities abound with iconic monuments, palatial estates, gravity-defying domes, and humble homes. All of these form an improbable patchwork of architecture that spans the centuries and has served as a model for buildings worldwide.

ROME

- **Pantheon:** Two thousand years after being built, the Pantheon still features the largest unreinforced concrete dome in the world (page 59).

- **St. Peter's Basilica:** It's not just the scale of this cathedral that's impressive; it's the fact that so many different architects (including Michelangelo and Bernini) working in different centuries were able to create so harmonious a structure (page 69).

the dome of St. Peter's in Rome

- **Colosseum:** The Roman Empire's largest arena set the standard for stadium design. It was equipped with features many modern arenas lack—such as retractable roofs and underground storage facilities—and its 50,000 occupants could be seated in under 10 minutes. Incredibly, it took only eight years to build (page 51).

- **Trevi Fountain:** This baroque masterpiece was meant to impress. It does that through its size and dramatic positioning of statues that look good from every angle of the *piazza* (page 66).

- **MAXXI:** Rome isn't only about ancient architecture. New structures like this, designed by Zaha Hadid, have become contemporary urban classics (page 68).

renovated **Museo dell'Opera,** where you can learn how Florence's cathedral was built. Just a few blocks south is **Piazza della Signoria,** the political center of the city, where **Palazzo Vecchio** imposingly stands and you can set off on another bell tower ascent.

Florentine pizza or thick local steaks at **Cucina Torcicoda** can satisfy appetites before visiting the **Museum of San Marco,** filled with colorful frescoed cells where monks once reflected. Nearby, the **Accademia** houses the statue of *David,* along

with a number of Michelangelo's unfinished works. Here again you'll need reservations as the number of visitors allowed in at a time is capped.

You can pay homage to Michelangelo, who grew up in Florence, and visit his tomb inside **Basilica di Santa Croce.** Then, take a short detour to **Vivoli** for **gelato.** Try their *crema de' Medici* (cream-flavor) gelato in a cone or a cup. At night, wineries offer cellars full of local **Tuscan vintages,** served with cured meats and cheese. **Coquinarius** and **Le Volpe e L'Uva** are both

FLORENCE

- **Duomo:** Filippo Brunelleschi's ingenious dome design resolved an architectural problem that had puzzled the city for decades. His solution relied on a double shell and eight ribs bound together by horizontal rings that can be seen on the climb to the top (page 175).

- **Campanile:** Few bell towers are as graceful, elegant, or tall as this one. It's also one of the rare towers not attached to a church, which symbolized the city's independence from the Vatican (page 179).

- **Ponte Vecchio:** The oldest bridge in Florence is no ordinary bridge. This one is lined with shops and a private second-story corridor for getting members of the Medici family across the river to their residence in Palazzo Pitti (page 194).

- **Palazzo Davanzati:** Not quite medieval, not quite Renaissance, this modest palace sits on the cusp of two eras. It was equipped with indoor plumbing and dumbwaiters used for moving goods between the four floors centered around an open-air courtyard (page 185).

VENICE

- **St. Mark's Basilica:** This one-of-a-kind church is an early example of architectural multiculturalism and a result of Venice's ties with the Orient. Domes, mosaics, and exotic sculptures were the work of Middle Eastern craftsmen hired to decorate the elaborate exterior and stunning interior over several centuries (page 289).

- **Ca' d'Oro:** Of all the Gothic Venetian palaces along the Grand Canal, this is the finest. The delicately carved facade looks made of linen rather than stone and little expense was spared on the high-ceilinged interiors (page 311).

- **Rialto Bridge:** Mocked by many who predicted it would crumble into the Grand Canal, the Rialto has passed the test of time. The elegant arch connecting the embankments was a revolutionary solution in its day, and the newly renovated bridge remains an undisputable symbol of the city (page 296).

- **Cottages of Burano:** Good architecture combines practicality and beauty. In Burano all the houses are brightly painted in different pastel colors, creating a wonderful rainbow effect meant to guide fishermen back to their homes (page 374).

cheery options with appetizers that can substitute for dinner.

DAY 7

Mornings are the only time to see the city's *Last Supper* frescoes, which were painted inside small churches like **Cenacolo di Ognissanti** and **Cenacolo di Sant'Apollonia** and are often overlooked by tourists. It's a unique opportunity to come face-to-face with a masterpiece. After you've seen a handful, enjoy your own supper with an enormous sandwich from **All'Antico Vinaio.**

Take your time wandering the rooms of the **Uffizi** and gazing upon Botticelli and Michelangelo. At the end of the second-floor galleries, step out on the **terrace** of the museum café overlooking Piazza della Signoria and enjoy a coffee break. The Uffizi is considerably smaller than the Vatican Museums and you can see it all in a couple of hours. Afterward, if you want to discover the city's most underrated museum, head to

Rome, Florence, and Venice can feel like vast, unde-cipherable mazes from the ground, but climb up a hundred meters and you'll gain an entirely different perspective. There are plenty of church domes, bell towers, fortifications, and hillsides to choose from, and each comes with sweeping panoramas of the landmarks below. Getting a great view, however, isn't always easy. Most monuments don't have el-evators and require the energy to overcome steep steps, narrow passageways, and claustrophobic in-teriors. Many vantage points have become popular tourist attractions, while others are in remote areas where you can reflect on each city and grasp its true shape undisturbed.

view of Florence from Fiesole

ROME

The Optical Illusion
Most days there's a short line of tourists waiting to look through the **Buco di Roma** (page 83) on the Aventine Hill. The city's famous keyhole offers a surprising view of the Vatican that causes a lot of double takes. Nearby in the **Giardini degli Aranci** (page 121) you can get a wider view from the terrace overlooking the Tiber River.

Past Made Perfect
The Forum can appear like an archeological disaster when you're in it, but climb to the top of the **Vittoriano** monument (page 56) to get a clearer picture of ancient Rome.

A Holy Ascent
It doesn't get higher than **St. Peter's Basilica** (page 69) and there's no better view of the square below and the city stretching out in all directions. It's also one of the toughest climbs, which can be made less strenuous with the aid of the elevator that goes halfway up.

Long and Arduous… But Worth It
Gianicolo Hill (page 80) may not be the most accessible view, but once you complete the 15-minute hike from Trastevere it's clear why it's the most popular. All the domes and bell towers of the city are at your fingertips, and the cannon fired every day at midday is the icing on the cake.

Continuous Panorama
The pathways and terraces above the **Spanish Steps** (page 64) leading to **Villa Borghese** (page 121) provide a view of the city that changes with every step.

View and Brew
What **Castel Sant'Angelo** (page 77) lacks in height it makes up for with its location. Views of the historic center can be accompanied with draft beer or cold drink from the rooftop bar.

FLORENCE

View *from* the Duomo
The cupola atop the Duomo (page 175) isn't just an opportunity to get a great view of Florence but also to step inside history and discover one of the greatest feats of Renaissance engineering. It's a tough climb, with long spiral staircases and cramped passageways that regularly cause bruises and bumps on visitors who forget to use the handrails.

Views *of* the Duomo
The Duomo is an essential part of the Florentine skyline and can be admired from many angles. The best are on the hillsides of Oltrarno. Tourists flock to Piazzale Michelangelo (page 199), but if you keep climbing to San Miniato al Monte (page 199) you'll get an even better view of the city.

The Campanile (page 179) is right next to the Duomo and easier to climb. It's often crowded but tends to be quiet in the late afternoon when you can catch the sun setting and get a close-up of the Duomo.

The highest public tower in Florence was erected inside Palazzo Vecchio (page 183) where lookouts once scanned the surrounding countryside for trouble. It's a steep, narrow climb to the top, past tiny cells where medieval criminals were imprisoned.

Drinks With a View
For something more relaxing, ride an elevator up to Empireo (page 222), on the rooftop terraces of Plaza Luchese hotel, and enjoy the view with a cocktail.

Florence from Afar
Fiesole (page 256) lies 20 minutes outside the city on a hillside from where all of Florence and the Arno Valley are visible.

VENICE

Bird's-Eye View
Venice has fewer panoramic options, but both bell towers open to the public are equipped with elevators. Campanile di San Marco (page 293) is by far the busiest, and limited numbers on the terrace means lines are slow. Alternatively, five minutes away by *vaporetto* ferry lies Isola di San Giorgio (page 316) where a similar tower attracts a trickle of visitors.

Panoramic Toast
The Skyline Rooftop Bar (page 339) on the island of Giudecca is a little out of the way but sits atop the tallest building in Venice with a pool and lounge where you can spend the evening gazing at the city.

Grand Canal Drama
Views from the four bridges spanning the Grand Canal are good, but to get a close-up of the busy maritime traffic, nothing beats Punta della Dogana (page 301). This historic entry point to the city is the ideal spot to sit and admire the city.

Venice from Afar
Getting to the *campanile* in Torcello (page 379) is an hour-long trek by ferry and foot, but it's one adventure few regret. The view of Burano, lagoon islands, and Venice in the distance makes the journey worthwhile.

the Duomo facade, Florence

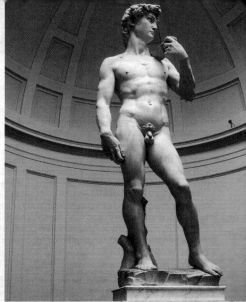

Michelangelo's *David* in the Accademia, Florence

the **Bargello National Museum** and be blown away by another *David* with far fewer admirers. For a pick-me-up, stop into a local bar, or pull up a lounge chair at **Amblé** and start the evening with a fruit cocktail. The rustic **Osteria Antica Mescita** is a reliable choice for lunch or dinner, but if you prefer to sample Michelin-starred flavors and dine in a romantic interior, reserve a table at **La Bottega del Buon Caffè**.

WITH MORE TIME

Fiesole is a half-day excursion overlooking the city with stunning views of Florence. You can get there on the number 7 bus from the train station in around 20 minutes or rent an e-bike from **Florence by Bike.** During the summer there's a musical festival and evening concerts are held in the ancient **Roman amphitheater.**

VENICE

DAY 8

If you're driving from Florence to Venice, consider stopping in **Ferrara** or **Bologna,** two cities famous for their food. Both are also on the same high-speed train line that connects Rome, Florence, and Venice, which make them convenient detours. Journey time by train from Florence to Venice is around two hours with several stops. Venice is the end of the line, and Santa Lucia station is located on the city's doorstep. You can reach accommodation on foot with the help of porters who will cart your bags or via water taxi on the **Grand Canal,** which is more expensive but also a lot more fun.

After you've settled into your hotel, follow the yellow signs to **St. Mark's Square** and take the secret tour of the **Doge's Palace** to discover why they call it the **Bridge of Sighs.** Enter **St. Mark's Basilica** next door and listen to the audio guide explain the meaning behind the mosaics. Restaurants are expensive in Venice, but snacking at local bars is affordable and offers a chance to sample lagoon fish transformed into tapas-like appetizers called *cicchetti.* Try **All'Arco** across the **Rialto Bridge** and near the animated fish market. From there you can hitch a €2 ride over the **Grand Canal** in a **gondola** ferry and spend the evening in **Campo Santo Stefano** listening to Vivaldi.

DAY 9

Purchase a ferry pass and go island-hopping on the 4.1 or 4.2 *vaporetto* from Fondamente Nuove. Get a window seat or stand on deck for the best views. Get off at the first stop on **Murano.** From there, you can visit **workshops** and watch a **glassblowing** demonstration at **Vetreria Artistica Emmedue.** Some furnaces charge visitors a small fee while others are free.

Continue on the 12 *vaporetto* from the Faro station to **Burano.** It's a 45-minute ride past lagoon wildlife, and you can order fried calamari and beer at **Fritto Misto** near the main dock. Afterward, circumnavigate the island on foot and put your camera to good use. Along the way are **colorful houses** and **galleries** where locals create and sell textiles and glassware of all kinds.

Just north of Burano is the sparsely inhabited island of **Torcello.** There's only one path to follow unless you decide to cross the **Ponte del Diavolo** (Devil's Bridge) and follow the dirt trail to **Santa Maria Assunta** cathedral. On the way back stop at **Locanda Cipriani,** where Hemingway wrote, drank, and slept, before returning to Venice by *vaporetto* as the sun sets over the lagoon.

DAY 10

Wake up early to watch fishmongers and greengrocers under the colorful **Rialto market** and **shop for masks** along the adjacent streets. **Atelier Pietro Longhi** is a good place for finding costumes and getting into the *Carnevale* spirit. Head to any of the traditional *bacari* bars nearby and accompany every meal with locally produced sparkling *prosecco* wine. If you don't want to wander unknowingly past Marco Polo's house or the oldest ghetto in Europe, spend a couple of hours with a **certified guide** who can provide an insightful perspective on the city. Take a break inside a **pastry shop** and sample as many delicacies as your appetite can handle. There's a different sweet for every season, but *burranei* are baked all year long.

Hop a *vaporetto* to the **Galleria**

Doge's Palace, Venice

Rialto Bridge, Venice

dell'Accademia for a glimpse of Venetian Renaissance art. Alternatively, if you prefer contemporary canvases, keep walking to the **Guggenheim Foundation** and **Punta della Dogana** at the very tip of Dorsoduro. Escape the narrow streets of the center and stroll along the sun-drenched **Fondamenta Zattere** promenade and enjoy a gelato from **Da Nico.** At night the squares near the university fill up with revelers. **Campo Santa Margherita** is the most animated, with street musicians and improvised parties that spill out into the square on weekends. If you haven't tried Venetian *risotto* yet, make your way to **Osteria da Codroma.**

WITH MORE TIME

It's difficult to tire of Venice, but if you long for a different landscape spend a morning cruising up the **Brenta Canal** with **Il Burchiello** and take the train back. You could also ride a *vaporetto* out to the **Lido** and lie on the beach or rent a bike near the main landing and cycle to the nature reserve where Goethe was inspired and Mussolini played golf. Otherwise, try kayaking through Venice with **Venice by Water** or take a stand-up paddling tour with **SUP in Venice.**

BACK TO ROME

DAY 11

It takes a little over 3.5 hours to get back to Rome by train. Leave Venice early enough to enjoy a last supper in the capital. Take the subway, tram, or bus to **Trastevere** for a tasty farewell, and if you haven't ordered *amatriciana* or *carciofi alla romana* yet, this is the time to do it. Before heading off to the airport, climb the nearby **Gianicolo Hill** for a last look at the Eternal City and final *arrivederci* to Italy.

Rome

Rome isn't a single city; it's many cities built on top of one another over thousands of years. These layers blend together into a collage of art and architecture that makes it possible to travel from antiquity to the Middle Ages, from the Renaissance to the present, and back again within a single neighborhood. Every street, facade, fountain, and fresco has an invisible history and a unique splendor that dazzles the senses.

Even before you set foot in the city, it's hard not to have an idea of what to expect. Monuments in Rome are global icons. The Colosseum, Spanish Steps, Trevi Fountain, Piazza Navona, and Sistine Chapel are ingrained in the collective imagination and attract millions of travelers

Highlights

Look for ★ to find recommended sights, activities, dining, and lodging.

© MOON.COM

★ **Colosseum:** Circle it, touch it, stand above it, go inside during the day—return to see it by moonlight. Rome's ancient amphitheater exceeds all expectations (page 51).

★ **Roman Forum:** Politics, commerce, and justice were all centered here from the rise of the Roman Republic to the fall of the Empire. A treasure trove of ancient Roman artifacts tell the tale (page 53).

★ **Pantheon:** Rome's largest temple has survived 2,000 years and counting. Its immense portico columns still influence architects today (page 59).

★ **Trevi Fountain:** This baroque fountain is one of Rome's most popular photo ops. Throw a coin into the water and guarantee yourself a return visit (page 66).

★ **Borghese Gallery:** Masterworks by Bernini, Botticelli, and Caravaggio are displayed in this sumptuous villa (page 67).

★ **St. Peter's Basilica:** Bernini, Michelangelo, and Raphael all contributed their talents to design and decorate the largest church in the world (page 69).

★ **Sistine Chapel:** These 3,000 square feet (279 square meters) of frescoes by Michelangelo are arguably the greatest work of art ever made (page 76).

★ **Gianicolo Hill:** Escape the crowds as you wind among the narrow streets and hidden squares of Trastevere on your way up to the terrace that overlooks the entire city (page 80).

★ **Palazzo Massimo:** View one of the finest collections of Roman mosaics at this modern museum (page 83).

★ **Via Appia Antica:** Walk, cycle, or ride a horse along an ancient road lined with pine trees and dotted with ancient ruins (page 145).

every year. Experiencing these wonders first-hand is what a visit to Rome is all about.

The past is fundamental, but it's not everything in Italy. Rome is alive with a contagious energy that pulsates through its streets, markets, and squares. You feel it the moment you enter an *osteria*, smell freshly baked *pizza bianca*, taste the bitter sweetness of Roman espresso, or get stuck in rush-hour traffic. The city's nearly three million residents may appear oblivious to the magnificence that surrounds them, but a few days here is all it takes to realize there's nowhere else quite like it.

If you remain on the well-trodden tourist trails, you'll only catch a glimpse of Rome. Getting a wider picture requires wandering Trastevere's village-like streets and elegantly elbowing through crowded bars. It means not only observing grand monuments and masterpieces, but meeting friendly locals who love talking, especially when the conversation revolves around family, food, or their city.

Old-timers in Testaccio and Trastevere may gripe that things have changed, but globalization cannot eliminate Rome's age-old routines. Most shops still close at 1pm and reopen at 3pm, the Pope still blesses pilgrims every Sunday morning, and daily fruit and vegetable markets still feed the masses. Artichokes appear in spring, peaches ripen in late summer, and grapes are pressed in autumn. There is an underlying rhythm to the city from *Carnevale* to Christmas, with resilient traditions and perennial dishes that have whet appetites for generations.

Once you cross the tourist divide and enter the everyday reality of the city, you will start to understand local body language and may even learn a few phrases of Roman dialect. At the very least, you will know how to order pizza by the slice and defend your place in line. The learning curve may be steep but it is endlessly gratifying for mind, stomach, and spirit.

HISTORY

Rome has been making history for nearly 3,000 years. It was the first city with a population over a million, the first to have running water, and the first to build apartment buildings. It developed the Latin alphabet and spread a language that influenced the letters and words spoken today by billions. Romans transformed the calendar and the perception of time, built roads that altered the concept of distance, established laws that regulated behavior, and designed stadiums that standardized entertainment.

Rome didn't start out as an eternal city, nor was it built in a day. It started out as a quiet place near a river with a few hills and no roads. It was an attractive spot for Iron Age settlers searching for food and safety. The first buildings were not the marble and travertine ruins of the Forum but timber huts on the Palatine Hill. Time passed, numbers grew, tribes merged, and before long clash of clans evolved into age of empires.

The early civilized centuries were influenced by Etruscans, who ruled the town until 509 BC when they were forcibly expelled, and the Roman Republic founded. The next 500 years saw the steady growth of the city. One by one the peoples of the Italian peninsula were conquered or absorbed before attention was turned to overseas colonization. It was during this period that Rome's first roads were built, Hannibal was defeated, and Spartacus's revolt nearly changed the course of history.

Caesar's assassination in 44 BC marked the beginning of a new age, and it took 17 years of civil war before his adopted son Augustus eliminated the competition and declared himself emperor of Rome. The Roman Empire increased the city's size in territory and splendor. The brick of the Republican age was replaced with marble and the city took on new dimensions. Subsequent emperors used architecture to influence public opinion and ensure a legacy that has survived to this day.

Previous: Piazza Navona during fall; Colosseum; view of St. Peter's Basilica

Rome

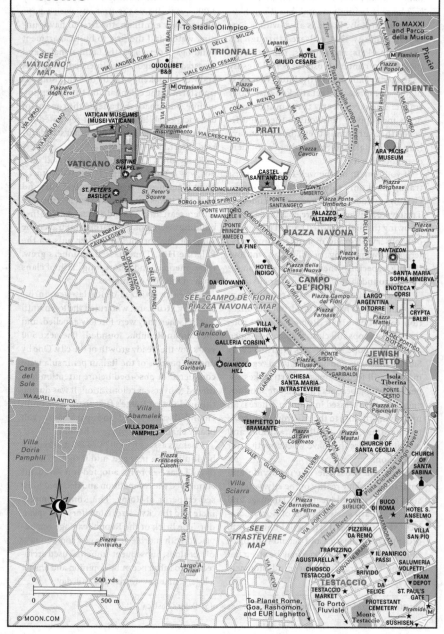

To Stadio Olimpico

VIA BARLETTA

VIA ANDREA DORIA

VIALE DELLE MILIZIE

TRIONFALE

VIA MARIA COLONNA

Lepanto

M

HOTEL
GIULIO CESARE

T

To MAXXI
and Parco
della Musica

M Flaminio

Pincio

VIA FLAMINIA

Tiber River

Pista Ciclabile Lungo Tevere

SEE
"VATICANO"
MAP

QUODLIBET
B&B

VIALE GIULIO CESARE

M Ottaviano

Piazza
dei Quiriti

Piazza
del Popolo

TRIDENTE

VIA DI RIPETTA

VIA DEL CORSO

Piazzale
degli Eroi

VIA CIPRO

VIA ANGELO EMO

VIA OTTAVIANO

VATICAN MUSEUMS
(MUSEI VATICANI)
★

Piazza del
Risorgimento

VIA COLA DI RIENZO

VIA CRESCENZIO

PRATI

Piazza
Cavour

ARA PACIS/
MUSEUM
★

VATICANO

SISTINE
CHAPEL
★

CASTEL
SANT'ANGELO
★

Piazza
Borghese

ST. PETER'S
BASILICA

St. Peter's
Square

VIA DELLA CONCILIAZIONE

PONTE
UMBERTO

Piazza Ponte
Umberto I

Piazza
Colonna

BORGO SANTO SPIRITO

PONTE
SANT'ANGELO

PALAZZO
ALTEMPS
★

VIA DELLA SCROFA

PONTE VITTORIO
EMANUELE II

PIAZZA NAVONA

PANTHEON

Piazza
Navona

SANTA MARIA
SOPRA MINERVA

VIA DELLA STAZIONE
DI SAN PIETRO

VIA PORTA
CAVALLEGGERI

VIA DELLE FORNACI

PONTE
PRINCIPE
AMEDEO

LA FINE

HOTEL
INDIGO

DA GIOVANNI

CORSO VITTORIO EMANUELE

Piazza della
Chiesa Nuova

VIA GIULIA

CAMPO
DE'FIORI

Piazza Campo
del Fiori

LARGO
ARGENTINA
DI TORRE ★

Piazza
Mattei

ENOTECA
CORSI

CRYPTA
BALBI

VIA DEL PORTICO
D'OTTAVIA

SEE "CAMPO DE' FIORI/
PIAZZA NAVONA" MAP

Parco
Gianicolo

VILLA
FARNESINA ★

GALLERIA CORSINI ★

Piazza
Farnese

Tiber River

Casa
del
Sole

VIA AURELIA ANTICA

Piazza
Garibaldi

GIANICOLO
HILL

VIA GARIBALDI

Piazza
Trilussa

PONTE
SISTO

JEWISH
GHETTO

PONTE
GARIBALDI

Isola
Tiberina

CHIESA
SANTA MARIA
IN TRASTEVERE

PONTE
CESTIO

Piazza in
Piscinula

Villa
Abamelek

VILLA DORIA
PAMPHILJ

TEMPIETTO DI
BRAMANTE ★

VIA DI SAN
FRANCESCO A RIPA

Piazza
di San
Cosimato

Piazza
Mastai

CHURCH OF
SANTA CECILIA

CHURCH
OF
SANTA
SABINA

Villa
Doria
Pamphili

Piazza
Francesco
Cucchi

VIALE DI TRASTEVERE

VIALE GLORIOSO

TRASTEVERE

Pista Ciclabile Lungo Tevere

LUNGOTEVERE

VIA GIACINTO CARINI

Villa
Sciarra

Piazza
Bernardino
da Feltre

PONTE
SUBLICIO

T

BUCO
DI ROMA

HOTEL S.
ANSELMO

VILLA
SAN PIO

Piazza
Fonteiana

SEE
"TRASTEVERE"
MAP

VIA PORTUENSE

Tiber River

MARMORATA

PIZZERIA
DA REMO

VIA NICOLÒ

Largo A.
Oriani

VIA GIACINTO

TRAPIZZINO ▼

AGUSTARELLA ▼

VIA GIOVANNI BRANCA

IL PANIFICO
PASSI

SALUMERIA
VOLPETTI

TRAM
▼ DEPOT

0   500 yds

0   500 m

© MOON.COM

CHIOSCO
TESTACCIO ▼

TESTACCIO
MARKET

TESTACCIO

To Planet Rome,
Goa, Rashomon,
and EUR Laghetto

BRIVIDO

DA
FELICE

To Porto
Fluviale

ST. PAUL'S
▼ GATE

PROTESTANT
CEMETERY

Monte
Testaccio

SUSHISEN ▼

Piramide

M

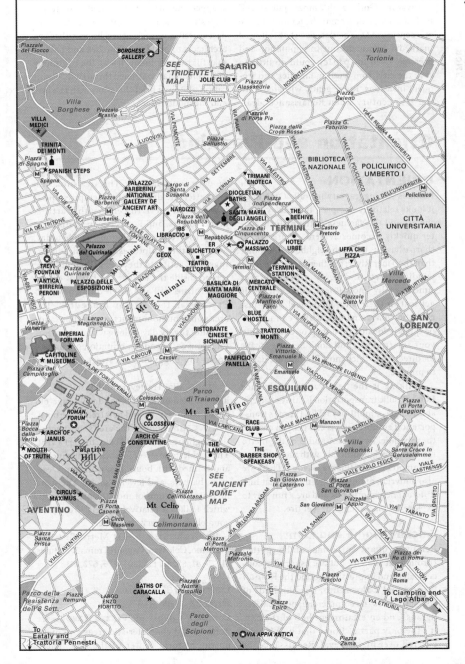

Invading Goths and Vandals put an end to 1,200 years of Roman hegemony in the 5th century AD. The decades that followed marked a drastic decline in population and prestige. Even the papacy could do little to save the city from feuding families and frequent invasions. Rome gently withered until the 15th century when Renaissance ideals snapped the city out of its medieval stupor. Popes and aristocrats began to value the city's past as well as its present and hired artists and architects to build the churches and palaces that fill the city today. It was the beginning of a rebirth that continued through the unification of Italy, a brief flirtation with fascism, and the modern age.

Orientation and Planning

ORIENTATION

Rome is the biggest city in Italy. On a map, it looks relatively compact, but once you hit the ground the vastness of the historic center quickly becomes evident. There are no sharp divisions between neighborhoods other than the Tiber River; but there are seven hills, winding streets, and plenty of stairs. It takes time to really know Rome, and even locals get lost in their city. Don't feel bad—just check for *piazza* names, which can usually be quickly located on a map or entered into your smartphone, and don't hesitate to ask for directions, which most Romans are happy to provide.

Walking is the best way to experience Rome. Public transportation is fairly efficient, and a single or multi-day **ATAC** (Rome's transportation authority) pass can get you around the city quickly. Lines A and B of the metro reach most neighborhoods, with the exception of Campo De' Fiori/Piazza Navona. There are also a myriad of bus and tram lines that link different neighborhoods and are a fun way to explore the city when your feet tire.

Ancient Rome and Monti

Remnants of ancient Rome can be spotted throughout the city but are especially concentrated and impressive around the **Roman Forum** and **Colosseum**. For hundreds of years, this was the commercial, political, religious, and entertainment hub of the city. It's the only part of Rome that hasn't been covered over by medieval, Renaissance, or modern constructions. The area sunk into ruin after the decline of the empire, and it wasn't until the 17th century that artists, archeologists, and Popes began to discover and preserve the foundations visible today. Many of the sculptures, personal belongings, and artifacts they unearthed are preserved inside the **Musei Capitolini** on the **Capitoline Hill** and **Museo Gregoriano Profano** in the **Vatican Museums.** The area's ancient monuments attract thousands of visitors every day—along with tour operators, souvenir vendors, imitation gladiators, horse-and-buggy drivers, street artists, and beggars.

Monti, like Trastevere and Testaccio, is a historic Roman neighborhood where age-old habits are preserved and new trends are born. **Via Urbana** is one of the area's most active thoroughfares and a good place to start a visit. The cobblestone street follows a gentle incline and is lined with boutiques, workshops, eateries, barbers, and jewelry shops. There are no major museums or monuments in Monti, which makes it relatively tourist-free and a good place to observe local life.

Public transit lines: Metro B: Circo Massimo, Colosseo, Cavour; Trams 3, 8; Buses 51, 75, 81, 85, 87, 118, 204, 175, 673, C3.

Campo De' Fiori/ Piazza Navona

Campo De' Fiori and **Piazza Navona** are Rome's most characteristic areas and make up the historic center of the city. These neighborhoods flanking the Tiber River are home to the finest **Renaissance** and **baroque buildings** and a maze of streets ripe for exploration. Both are vibrant and filled with **animated squares** where locals get their freshly baked pizza and kosher treats. Rome's highest concentration of **wineries** and **eateries** are in these neighborhoods, though they can veer toward touristy. During the day, Campo De' Fiori fills up with market stalls selling flowers, food, and souvenirs. At night partygoers congregate around the lively square enjoying *al fresco* happy hours.

The area is divided by Corso Vittorio Emanuele II, which runs from the Tiber River to Piazza Venezia. Campo De' Fiori and the **Jewish Ghetto** lie south of this busy avenue, while Piazza Navona and the **Pantheon** are north.

The Piazza Navona area is not served by metro; however, there are many convenient bus options for reaching the neighborhood.

Public transit lines: Tram 8; Buses 23, 40, 46, 62, 63, 64, 70, 80, 81, 87, 280, 492, 628, 780, C3.

Tridente

Tridente is the result of 17th- and 18th-century urban planning. Artists were commissioned to gentrify and bring architectural order to this corner of Rome. Under successive popes and the will of Napoleon, medieval neighborhoods were demolished and **Piazza del Popolo,** the **Spanish Steps,** and the **Trevi Fountain** were constructed along with imposing palaces and elaborate churches. Today, this neighborhood constitutes Rome's most glamourous **shopping district,** with luxury brands flaunting their goods on the pedestrianized Via Condotti and Via del Corso. From the top of the newly restored Spanish Steps there's a wonderful view of the city and access to the shaded **Villa Borghese** park.

Public transit lines: Metro A: Barberini Fontana Trevi, Spagna, Flaminio Piazza del Popolo; Tram 2, 8; Buses 51, 53, 62, 63, 71, 80, 83, 85, 160, 301, 492, 628, C3.

Vaticano

Whether you are a believer or not, it's difficult not to be impressed by the grandeur of **St. Peter's Basilica,** the view from its cupola, and the works on display within the Vatican Museums—not to mention the **Sistine Chapel.** The Catholic world has been governed from here for over a thousand years and the art collection and antiquities amassed within the walls of the Vatican (the smallest state in the world) attracts six million visitors per year.

The Vatican is easily reached by bus, tram, or subway, but the only way to appreciate its monumental size is on foot. **Via Della Conciliazione** was built to provide a grand entrance to the square and is packed with pilgrims and visitors throughout the day. If you want to see Pope Francis in person, you can watch him bless crowds from his balcony on Sundays at noon or attend a free Papal Audience Wednesday mornings at 9:30am.

Public transit lines: Metro A: Ottaviano San Pietro, Lepanto; Tram 19; Buses 23, 32, 34, 40, 49, 62, 70, 81, 87, 280, 590, 982, 990.

Trastevere

Trastevere literally means "across the Tiber," and this neighborhood's proximity to the river once attracted sailors and fishermen. Later, wealthy Romans built their villas here, the remains of which can be found underneath **Villa Farnesina.** During the Middle Ages the population increased and the neighborhood grew haphazardly. Much of Trastevere's **medieval character** remains and there are plenty of labyrinthine passages to explore. Residents have always been slightly secluded from the rest of the city, and the neighborhood offers a vibrant and characteristic slice of Roman life. Trastevere has a high concentration of *trattoria*-style restaurants and cocktail bars that makes it popular with locals, university students, and visitors.

Unless your hotel is in Trastevere, you'll probably have to cross a bridge to get to there. The most scenic and convenient options are **Ponte Sisto** if approaching from Piazza

Navona, or **Ponte Cestio** from the Forum. The neighborhood is split by the busy Viale Trastevere avenue and the eastern half, opposite Tiberina Island, is the one that often gets overlooked by visitors heading toward **Piazza Santa Maria**. The **Gianicolo Hill** that borders the neighborhood provides some of the best views of Rome.

The closest metro station (Circo Massimo) is a 20-minute walk from Trastevere, and it's easier to reach the area by tram or bus.

Public transit lines: Metro B: Circo Massimo; Trams 3, 8; Buses 23, 115, 125, 280, 780, H.

Aventino and Testaccio

Testaccio and Aventino lack major tourist attractions—but that's arguably what makes them worth exploring. Both areas have maintained their Roman identity and provide an authentic feel of daily life in the city.

Testaccio is a working-class neighborhood with a grid-like street pattern that was laid in the 1930s under the orders of Mussolini. Tucked between a bend in the Tiber, the Aurelian wall, and Via Marmorata, it's populated with spirited residents who are proud of their neighborhood and their soccer team. On weekday mornings the streets are alive with locals going about their business. Especially animated are the small parks and covered market where residents shop and socialize. Most businesses are concentrated around these areas. After dark, the **nightclubs** and restaurants at the base of **Mount Testaccio** attract a young crowd.

Aventino lies on one of Rome's famed seven hills adjacent to Testaccio. Unlike its gritty neighbor, Aventino is well heeled and predominately **residential.** Streets are lined with trees, and elegant apartment buildings are interspersed with luxurious 19th-century villas. Most points of interest are concentrated along **Via di Santa Sabina.** Here you can get the famous keyhole view of the Vatican through the **Buco di Roma,** visit a Franciscan church or Dominican basilica, and look out over the city from the intimate

Giardini degli Aranci (Orange Gardens). What you won't find are shops or restaurants, so come before or after lunch or pack a picnic.

Public transit lines: Metro B: Piramide; Tram 3; Buses 23, 75, 81, 83, 118, 160, 170, 175, 280, 628, 673, 715, 716, 719.

Ostiense

The Ostiense neighborhood lies south of Testaccio and was once home to factories, warehouses, and the city's largest food market. Today, it's become a hub for artists, students, and young professionals. There's a university, startups, restaurants, and an enormous **Eataly** emporium. The area is being gentrified but remains gritty and rough around the edges with giant murals and graffiti art along the walls of **Via del Gazometro.** It's a fun destination that's distinct from other parts of Rome and worth exploring if you want to experience local **nightlife.**

Public transit lines: Metro B: Piramide, Garbatella, Basilica S. Polo; Buses 23, 280, 716

Termini

Termini train station is Rome's main **transportation hub,** where high-speed and commuter trains arrive, two subway lines (Metro A and B) intersect, and dozens of buses depart. The streets around the station are full of **hotels** and **fast-food joints** catering to commuters and tourists. It's been cleaned up in recent years but some seediness remains and the immediate area is best avoided. The exception to that rule are the **Diocletian Baths** and **Palazzo Massimo** where some of ancient Rome's finest mosaics and paintings are on display.

PLANNING YOUR TIME

While you can hit the highlights in two days, it's worth spending three or more to really appreciate Rome. With that much time you will be able to explore much of the historic center as well as several major museums. You can also venture into the outskirts towards Ostia Antica or Appia Antica and discover what lies beyond the center. But whatever you do be careful of overscheduling, and make sure to leave time for chance encounters with the unexpected. Go with the Roman flow, which means enjoying everything calmly without the agonizing feeling you should be somewhere else.

Daily Reminders

Many museums close on **Mondays,** and box offices stop selling tickets an hour before entry. The Vatican closes on **Sundays,** except the last Sunday of every month when it's open and free, and churches restrict visiting hours during masses. Some monuments like the Baths of Caracalla and many parks have different closing times according to the season and amount of daylight. All public institutions close on December 25 and January 1, and some smaller museums also take national holidays off. Roman monuments and museums are free on the first Sunday of every month while the Vatican Museums are free on the last Sunday of every month. Many sites offer informative audio guides in English that are vital for understanding the art and history on display.

Advance Bookings and Time-Saving Tips

Most monuments and museums, including the **Vatican, Colosseum,** and **Borghese Gallery,** offer convenient online prebooking services that can save you the frustration of waiting in line. There's a small fee and reservations should be made a couple of weeks in advance to ensure a spot. Note that during COVID outbreaks, **advance reservations** are not only recommended, but required, at a number of sights.

The Colosseum, Roman Forum, and Palatine Hill share a single ticket. If you haven't prebooked, get it at the San Gregorio ticket office (near the aqueduct) instead of the Colosseum entrance, which is very crowded.

Many museums now require visitors to check large bags and backpacks, which can lead to further waiting. If you don't want to stare at the back of someone's head for 20 minutes, travel light and avoid a trip to the Vatican and Borghese cloakrooms.

Sightseeing Passes

RomaPass (tel. 06/0608; www.romapass.it) is Rome's official visitor card that includes a map, museum entry, unlimited travel on public transport, and discounts. The 72-hour option (€52) includes free entry to two museums or archeological sites, while the 48-hour pass (€32) is good for a single visit. Both will save you time and money, especially if you plan on moving around by bus, subway, or tram. Pass holders have access to a dedicated entrance at the Colosseum, Castel Sant'Angelo, and Capitoline Museums. Reservations are still required if you plan on visiting Galleria Borghese. Passes can be purchased online or at any of the five Tourist Information Points located around the city and Fiumicino airport (online purchasers must still visit an info point to pick up their pass). The 72-hour pass can also be purchased at all participating museums and major subway stations. There are no discounted passes for children or seniors.

The Full Experience Pass (tel. 06/3996-7700; www.coopculture.it; €16 + €2 online reservation fee) provides entry to the Forum, Colosseum, Palatine, and seven lesser known ancient sites in the area, including Casa di Livia on Palatine Hill. It's valid one day and can be purchased directly at each of the monuments, by telephone, or online.

The Omnia Card (tel. 06/6989-6375; www.omniakit.org; Mon.-Sat. 9am-5pm, Sun. 9am-1pm) is the Vatican visitor pass and comes in a 24-hour (€55) or 72-hour (€113) version. Both options provide a map, direct entry to Vatican Museums, an audio guide to St. Peter's, and a 16-stop, hop-on hop-off, bus tour of Christian monuments around Rome. The 72-hour version includes the **RomaPass,** making it the most comprehensive card available. If you do everything it offers you can save 15 percent; if you don't, you are better off buying single entries. Both passes can be purchased online and operate with a dedicated app but the rest of the kit must be picked up at one of four

Omnia Collection Points (Piazza San Pietro, Piazza Pio XII; Mon.-Sat. 9am-4pm and Sun. 9am-1pm) listed on the website. Discounts for children are available.

A **combined ticket** (€12) is available to visit the four National Museums of Rome: Palazzo Massimo, the Diocletian Baths, Crypta Balbi, and Palazzo Altemps. The ticket can be purchased from any of the museums and is valid for three days. A single ticket to either of the museums is €10, so it's worth paying an extra €2 if you plan to visit two or more.

Crowd Control

Tourism is a year-round reality in Rome that peaks in August and during the Christmas and Easter holidays. In summer, lines to popular sites can stretch for hours, making sightseeing passes and advance bookings essential. The Vatican Museums alone require at least a half day to visit. Getting up early can help avoid tour groups that generally don't leave their hotels until midmorning. Staying up late gives you a chance to admire fountains and squares undisturbed, and partake in Roman nightlife.

Pandemic Travel

During COVID outbreaks, some sights employ reservations-only policies in which visitors must select specific visiting dates and times in advance. This includes the **Vatican Museums,** the **Colosseum, Roman Forum,** and **Borghese Gallery** (whose reservation-only policy was in place before the pandemic). It's best to reserve a week or two ahead of arrival during the summer and a few days the rest of the year. Reservations must be made on each sight's website. In addition, all of the city's museums and monuments measure the temperature of visitors, enforce social distancing, and require **masks** to be worn during outbreaks. **Sightseeing passes** are still valid during outbreaks.

The latest COVID regulations are available from the Italian Ministry of Health (www.salute.gov.it/portale/nuovocoronavirus/homeNuovoCoronavirus.jsp). U.S. travelers can also check the U.S. embassy (https://it.usembassy.gov/covid-19-information) for updates and advice.

SAFETY AND SECURITY

The coronavirus and terrorist attacks in the last decade have led to tighter security. Military personnel are stationed around monuments, embassies, airports, train stations, and many subway stations. Checks at popular sights are routine and metal detectors frequently used to control visitors. Checkpoints have also been put into place at Termini station where travelers must now show their tickets before accessing platforms.

Itinerary Ideas

Rome is a big city with more World Heritage Sites than anywhere else in the world. You can get a memorable introduction in a weekend, but you won't see everything, and that's okay. Pizza and *aperitivo* hour are just as important as sightseeing in this dynamic city.

If it's your first time in Rome, you may want to stay in the Aventino or Monti neighborhoods, close to all the ancient sights. **The Inn at the Roman Forum** is a good choice. The **RomaPass** is useful for saving on museum tickets and public transportation.

ROME ON DAY 1

Check out the Colosseum and other major sights of Ancient Rome, ending your day with a sunset from Villa Borghese.

1 Head to the **Colosseum** for an eyeful of ancient Rome's largest amphitheater.

2 Cross the street and explore the ruins of the **Roman Forum** and **Palatine Hill.**

3 Descend into the **Jewish Ghetto** along the Via del Portico d'Ottavia and explore the labyrinth of medieval Rome.

4 Follow Via dei Giubbonari west to the lively market stalls of Campo De' Fiori and enter **Il Forno di Campo De' Fiori** to sample *pizza bianca.*

5 When jet lag strikes or it gets too hot, do as the Romans do and take a quick nap back at the hotel. Afterward, walk through the enormous bronze doors of the **Pantheon.**

6 Follow Via dei Pastini to the **Trevi Fountain** and toss a coin in (legend has it that this will ensure a return trip to Rome).

7 Grab a gelato topped with *panna* whipped cream from **San Crispino.**

8 Navigate your way to the Spanish Steps and climb up to **Villa Borghese** to watch the sun set over the city.

9 For dinner, every Roman knows where to order the best *cacio e pepe* or *amatriciana* pasta. Start your education with traditional fare from **Da Gino,** and order a carafe of house wine to wash it down. End the meal sipping *limoncello* or *grappa* liquor.

ROME ON DAY 2

Cross the river to Vatican City, leaving Rome—and Italy—behind. This day is dedicated to the Vatican, with a jaunt to Trastevere after lunch.

1 Admire the immensity of **St. Peter's Basilica** and climb to the top of the cupola for a unique 360-degree view.

2 Enter the **Vatican Museums** and follow the flow of visitors to the Sistine Chapel.

3 Have lunch at **Arlu** on the long, narrow street of Borgo Pio for a taste of Roman pasta specialties like *cacio e pepe* and *amatriciana.*

4 Walk lunch off with a jaunt along the Tiber River to Trastevere. (It's a 30-minute walk or you can ride the 23 or 280 buses three stops.) Stroll through medieval streets until you reach **Piazza di Santa Maria in Trastevere,** which is the heart of the neighborhood. Peek inside the church at the mosaics, grab a seat in a café, or rest on the fountain steps in the middle of the square, an ideal vantage point for people-watching.

5 Climb to the top of the **Gianicolo Hill** and spot all the places you've been.

6 Head to an authentic *trattoria* with outdoor seating like **Trattoria da Enzo** and enjoy a three-course dinner.

7 Hang out in Trastevere's quieter side and enjoy a cocktail among locals at **404 Name Not Found.**

ROME LIKE A LOCAL

Head off the beaten path on your final day in Rome. Spend the morning in the working-class neighborhood of Testaccio, popping back over to the city's historic center after lunch, before ending the day with drinks on Isola Tiberina.

1 When in Rome, start your morning at a neighborhood bar. **Tram Depot** is a good outdoor option between Aventino and Testaccio. Resist being escorted to a table next to

Itinerary Ideas

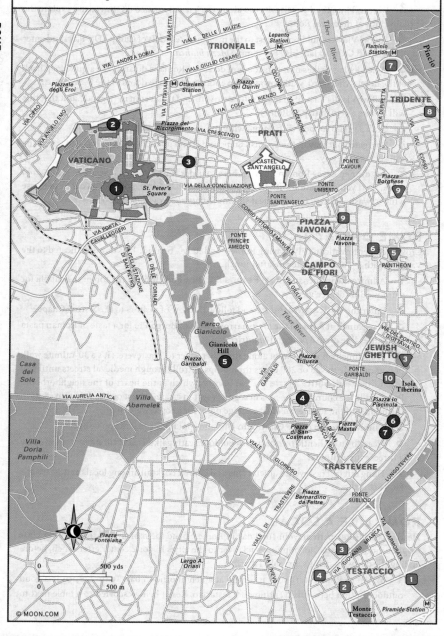

© MOON.COM

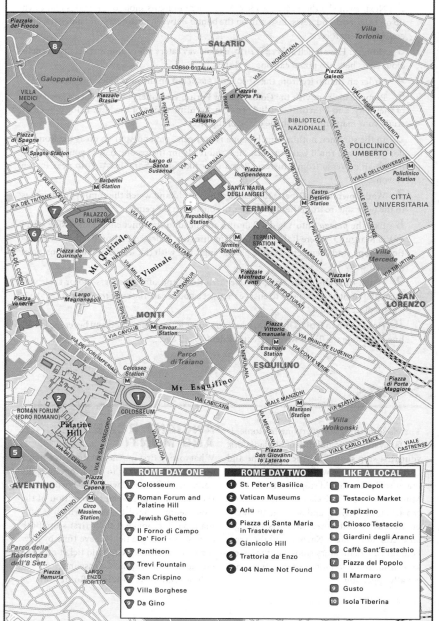

ROME DAY ONE	ROME DAY TWO	LIKE A LOCAL
1 Colosseum	1 St. Peter's Basilica	1 Tram Depot
2 Roman Forum and Palatine Hill	2 Vatican Museums	2 Testaccio Market
3 Jewish Ghetto	3 Arlu	3 Trapizzino
4 Il Forno di Campo De' Fiori	4 Piazza di Santa Maria in Trastevere	4 Chiosco Testaccio
5 Pantheon	5 Gianicolo Hill	5 Giardini degli Aranci
6 Trevi Fountain	6 Trattoria da Enzo	6 Caffè Sant'Eustachio
7 San Crispino	7 404 Name Not Found	7 Piazza del Popolo
8 Villa Borghese		8 Il Marmaro
9 Da Gino		9 Gusto
		10 Isola Tiberina

the other tourists and join the locals at the counter, where the coffee is cheaper and tastes just as good.

2 Next, swing by the **Testaccio Market,** where Romans shop for groceries and catch up on neighborhood news. Listen in on the banter between customers and butchers, bakers, and greengrocers.

3 Hungry? Have lunch at **Trapizzino,** a takeaway eatery whose house specialty is a delicious cross between pizza, calzone, and stew.

4 Order an Italian ice from the **Chiosco Testaccio** on the next block.

5 Romans may not visit the Colosseum or Forum very often, but they love a good view of their city, and **Giardini degli Aranci** in Aventino is one of the best. Bring a book or study your map under the shade of the orange trees.

6 In the summer, nothing much happens between 2pm and 4pm, so do as the Romans do: Take a nap. You'll wake up refreshed and ready for the second half of your day. Start it with an espresso from a historic Roman bar like **Caffè Sant'Eustachio** near Piazza Navona.

7 Walk down Via di Ripetta to **Piazza del Popolo** and watch the comings and goings in the busy square from the steps under the obelisk in the center.

8 Exit the *piazza* onto Via del Babuino and head to the quiet cobblestone side street of Via Margutta, where Italy's greatest film director, Federico Fellini, lived. Browse antique shops, and then get a marble plaque engraved with the words of your choosing at **Il Marmaro.**

9 When the bells strike 6pm, it's *aperitivo* time, and office workers motor their way through the city at top speed to ensure they get a good seat. The cozy *trattoria* at **Gusto** is a good place to find it.

10 Head south to **Isola Tiberina,** where, on summer evenings, food and beverage kiosks lined up along the Tiber River attract residents of all ages.

Sights

There's something for everyone in Rome. If you fancy antiquity and dream of gladiators, your first stop should be Ancient Rome and Ostia Antica; anyone with a passion for painting or sculpture should stop into the Vatican Museums or Borghese Gallery. There's modern art at the MAXXI and baroque throughout the city. Architecture enthusiasts will get an eyeful, and Piazza Navona and the Trevi Fountain are mandatory stops, but the lesser-known squares and fountains in between are equally appealing.

ANCIENT ROME AND MONTI

What to visit first in Ancient Rome is a tough question. If you want to be chronologically correct, you'll start with the Forum—but the monumental size and reputation of the Colosseum is hard to resist, which is why many visitors make it their first stop. Both sites share a single ticket. Save time by buying yours at the San Gregorio ticket office or online instead of at the Colosseum.

The center of ancient Rome can be

approached from several directions. The traditional route along **Via dei Fori Imperiali** leads directly to the Colosseum. This road was recently pedestrianized (except for buses and taxis), but ongoing work on the Metro C subway extension leaves eyes sore. For an instant impression, take the Metro B subway to the **Colosseo station.** Get out and be wowed. **Via di San Gregorio** from Circo Massimo is less crowded and provides a subtler entrance.

★ Colosseum
(Colosseo)

Piazza del Colosseo; tel. 06/774-0091; www. coopculture.it; daily 8:30am-7:15pm summer and 8:30am-4:30pm winter; €16 combined with Palatine Hill and Forum, valid 24 hours, €22 with access to underground or third tier, valid 48 hours, audio guide €6, video guide €6; Metro B: Colosseo, Trams 3, 8, Buses 75, 81, 85, 87, 175, 673, 204

The Colosseo was ancient Rome's largest amphitheater, where citizens came to be entertained. It's nearly as impressive today as it must have been in AD 80 when it was inaugurated before a crowd of 50,000 eager spectators. Remarkably it only took eight years to build and survived pillaging by generations of architects and builders for which it was a convenient quarry. Restoration began in the 19th century when pioneering archeologists and the Vatican recognized the building's historical significance and began safeguarding the area.

Today, the Colosseum towers over visitors and looks like many of the modern sporting stadiums it inspired. The monument consists of three levels of stone archways that have been stripped of their original marble but remain impressive. Archaeologists added a platform on the ground level to partially cover the passageways and storerooms underneath the arena where wild animals and gladiators waited their turn to entertain the masses. From here, you can get to the second tier, which can be entirely circumnavigated and provides the best views of the monument.

The Colosseum teems with visitors (along with those hoping to make a euro off them) most of the year and is especially packed throughout the summer months. Lines to visit the interior, which was a cow pasture in the Middle Ages and once housed a barbershop, are long, and there is only one entrance. **RomaPass** provides easy access as well as transport and discounts to other museums. The **ordinary ticket** (€16) gets you inside and up to the first two tiers, while the **Full Experience** (€22) option provides access to the third tier or underground passages. There are also a variety of small group tours to follow. **Official English-language tours** of the Colosseum (€5) depart daily every 30-45 minutes 9:15am-5:15pm and last 45 minutes, while 60-minute **Full Experience** tours (daily 9:20am and 4:20pm; €9) recount the history of the underground and third tier of the monument. All tours depart from the ticket office are organized by **Coop Culture** (www.coopculture.it), and reservations are recommended.

Only 3,000 visitors are allowed into the Colosseum at any one time. It's worth visiting in the early morning and evening when crowds thin and the stadium's travertine surface is bathed in sunlight. All visitors must go through metal detectors. Although the combined tickets are valid over two days, you can only enter each sight once.

During COVID outbreaks, reservations may be required, tours suspended, and visitor numbers limited.

Arch of Constantine
(Arco di Costantino)

Via del Velabro 5; tel. 060608; 24/7; free; Metro B: Circo Massimo

Triumphal arches were common in ancient Rome and erected whenever a consul or emperor had something to celebrate. That usually meant winning a war and gaining new territorial conquests. One of the best-preserved examples is the Arco di Costantino next to the Colosseum. It commemorates Emperor Constantine's victory over a rival in 312 BC and incorporates sculptures plundered

Ancient Rome

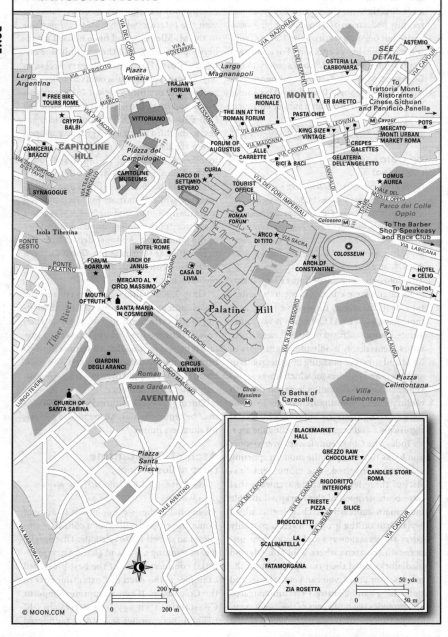

VIA DEL CORSO

VIA 4 NOVEMBRE

VIA NAZIONALE

VIA DEI SERPENTI

VIA CAVOUR

ASTEMIO

SEE DETAIL

OSTERIA LA CARBONARA

Largo Magnanapoli

To Trattoria Monti, Ristorante Cinese Sichuan and Panificio Panella

Piazza Venezia

VIA PLEBISCITO

Largo Argentina

S. MARCO

TRAJAN'S FORUM

MERCATO RIONALE

MONTI

ER BARETTO

FREE BIKE TOURS ROME

VIA D'ARACOELI

VIA ALESSANDRINA

THE INN AT THE ROMAN FORUM

PASTA CHEF

Cavour

MERCATO MONTI URBAN MARKET ROMA

POTS

CRYPTA BALBI

VITTORIANO

VIA BACCINA

KING SIZE VINTAGE

V. LEONINA

CAMICERIA BRACCI

CAPITOLINE HILL

Piazza del Campidoglio

FORUM OF AUGUSTUS

VIA MADONNA ALLE CARRETTE

VIA CAVOUR

CREPES GALETTES

VIA DEL PORTICO D'OTTAVIA

VIA TEATRO MARCELLO

CAPITOLINE MUSEUMS

CURIA

BICI & BACI

GELATERIA DELL'ANGELETTO

SYNAGOGUE

ARCO DI SETTIMIO SEVERO

TOURIST OFFICE

VIA DEI FORI IMPERIALI

DOMUS AUREA

VIALE DEL MONTE OPPIO

VIA TERME TITO

Parco del Colle Oppio

Isola Tiberina

ROMAN FORUM

Colosseo M

PONTE CESTIO

KOLBE HOTEL ROME

ARCO DI TITO

VIA SACRA

COLOSSEUM

To The Barber Shop Speakeasy and Race Club

VIA LABICANA

PONTE PALATINO

FORUM BOARIUM

ARCH OF JANUS

CASA DI LIVIA

ARCH OF CONSTANTINE

HOTEL CELIO

MERCATO AL CIRCO MASSIMO

VIA SAN TEODORO

To Lancelot

MOUTH OF TRUTH

SANTA MARIA IN COSMEDIN

Palatine Hill

VIA DI SAN GREGORIO

VIA CLAUDIA

VIA DEL CERCHI

Tiber River

GIARDINI DEGLI ARANCI

VIA DEL CIRCO MASSIMO

CIRCUS MAXIMUS

Circo Massimo M

Piazza Celimontana

Roman Rose Garden

AVENTINO

Villa Celimontana

LUNGO TEVERE

CHURCH OF SANTA SABINA

To Baths of Caracalla

Piazza Santa Prisca

VIA DEL CAPOCCI

BLACKMARKET HALL

VIALE AVENTINO

GREZZO RAW CHOCOLATE

CANDLES STORE ROMA

VIA DI CIANCALEONI

RIGODRITTO INTERIORS

VIA MARMORATA

TRIESTE PIZZA

SILICE

BROCCOLETTI

VIA URBANA

VIA CAVOUR

LA SCALINATELLA

FATAMORGANA

ZIA ROSETTA

0   200 yds
0   200 m

0   50 yds
0   50 m

© MOON.COM

from monuments around the city. The arch spanned the Via Triumphalis where military parades once passed; it's now protected from overeager sightseers by an iron fence. The arch's proximity to the Colosseum makes it look small, but the closer you get the more imposing it becomes.

★ Roman Forum
(Foro Romano)

Via dei Fori Imperiali; tel. 06/3996-7700; daily 8:30am-7:15pm summer and 8:30am-4:30pm winter; €16 combined with Colosseum and Palatine Hill; Metro B: Colosseo

The Foro Romano is a narrow strip of land beneath the Palatine and Capitoline Hills that was once the epicenter of the Roman Empire. Today its temples, government buildings, triumphal arches, shops, and monuments are in various states of decay, but walking along the **Via Sacra** path into the Forum still feels like a monumental step into history. Deciphering the ancient foundations, staircases, and columns isn't easy, but remember that for hundreds of years this was the center of Western civilization.

Arco di Tito (Via Sacra), easy to spot near the entrance of the Forum, is one of several arches still standing. It was commissioned by the Roman Senate to honor victories over rebellious Jews. Scan the sculptured relief carefully to spot a menorah and other spoils Emperor Tito brought back from his conquest of Jerusalem. The **Arco di Settimio Severo** (Via Sacra) at the other end of the Forum was built to celebrate Emperor Severo's 10th year in power. Although the decorative bronze sculptures have disappeared, the arch is in excellent condition and provides welcome shade from the hot summer sun.

Next-door is the **Curia,** where the Roman Senate convened. It's a faithful reconstruction of the building begun by Caesar and completed by his adopted son in AD 29. The replica is based on Diocleziano's plans. Although the original bronze doors were moved to the Basilica of San Giovanni in Laterano, the mosaic flooring, which illustrates daily Roman life, is the original. It's a good place to see what the Forum was like in its heyday.

There are three entrances into the Forum; the least crowded is on Via di San Gregorio beneath the aqueduct.

During COVID outbreaks reservations may be required, tours suspended, and visitor numbers limited.

Palatine Hill
(Palatino)

daily 8:30am-7:15pm summer and 8:30am-4:30pm winter; €16 combo ticket with Colosseum and Roman Forum, audio guide €5.50 ,video guide €6; Metro B: Colosseo or Circo Massimo

Palatino, one of Rome's seven hills, is less crowded than the Forum below. It is dominated by the remains of palaces, once inhabited by Rome's ancient elite, and covered with wildflowers where stray cats like to sun themselves. At the top, there are terraces offering excellent views of the Forum on one side and the Circus Maximus on the other.

One of the most interesting villas on Palatine Hill is **Casa di Livia** near the site where Augustus, Rome's first emperor, lived with his extended entourage. The home is one of the hill's best-preserved dwellings. Time has raised the ground level above the house, and a short flight of steps leads to the rooms. The original mosaic paving and religious frescoes provide insight into Roman decorating tastes. Many of the same colors and patterns used here can be seen throughout the city.

Nearby is a small **stadium** Emperor Domiziano built inside his estate. Though its exact use is unknown, it may have served as a garden, riding track, or outdoor gym. Thinking that it might make a good place for footraces, an Ostrogoth king added a circular enclosure at the southern end in the 6th century. There's enough room for an impromptu 50-yard dash, but the baths next to the track have been out of order for centuries.

Many of the individual sights on the Palatine are numbered and visitors equipped with the audio guide can listen to detailed descriptions of the ruins. There is also a small

museum (Via San Gregorio 30; daily 9am-6pm; free with admission to the Palatino) near the center containing relics uncovered on the hill. Bathrooms are located around the back of the museum and there are a number of drinking fountains marked on the free map included with your ticket.

You can reach the Palatine Hill directly from the Roman Forum or Via San Gregorio, the entrance beneath the arches of the aqueduct that provided running water to residents.

During COVID outbreaks, reservations may be required, tours suspended, and visitor numbers limited.

Imperial Forums

Caesar wasn't satisfied with just one forum. What is now known as the Roman Forum had become cramped and overcrowded in his day so he decided to expand. First, he had Cicero purchase nearby land for a small fortune. Then, on the battlefield of Pharsalus in 48 BC, he vowed to build a temple in honor of Venus. What was initially intended as a simple structure soon laid the pattern for the Imperial Forums, which lie on the northern side of Via dei Fori Imperiali.

The Forum of Augustus (Foro Augusto) is adjacent to Caesar's and was built to mark the defeat of his stepfather's assassins Brutus and Cassius. The centerpiece is a temple dedicated to Mars the Avenger, of which a short flight of stairs and four Corinthian columns are visible today. Nearby is the high wall Caesar built to protect his forum from the densely packed neighborhoods nearby and the constant menace of fire. The area is rarely open to the public, but can be observed from the street or small footbridge that runs behind the site.

After successful military campaigns in Dacia, Trajan used his vast booty to build a forum next to the others. Trajan's Forum was the last and greatest, designed by a Syrian architect who dispersed 30 million cubic feet (849,505 cubic meters) of soil to make way for

1: Roman Forum 2: Colosseum

a semicircular market, the largest basilica ever built in ancient Rome, and Greek and Latin libraries. It became the center of political and administrative action where laws were passed and wars declared. At the end of the complex, Trajan's Column tells the story of the emperor's two campaigns in Dacia (modern-day Romania). The column is wrapped with sculpted reliefs that show Roman troops in action defeating local chieftains. It also includes over 60 portraits of the emperor so no one would forget his achievements. The statue of Trajan at the top, however, was removed by Pope Sixtus V and replaced with St. Peter. The column also marks the height of the hillside, which was removed to make way for the market and has survived nearly intact except for the emperor's gold funeral urn. Small slits on the walls allow light to reach the spiral staircase inside.

Neither Trajan's Forum nor his column are open to the public; however, you can get a good look from Via dei Fori Imperiali or Via Alessandrina.

Domus Aurea

Via del Domus Aurea 1; tel. 06/3996-7700; www. coopculture.it; Sat.-Sun. 9:15am-4:15pm; €16; Metro B: Colosseo

Nero's palace, Domus Aurea, stretched across three of Rome's seven hills and was lavish even by Roman standards. The complex was entered directly from the Forum and contained a small lake and monumental bronze statue of the emperor nearly as high as the Statue of Liberty. The villa was built over land that was vacated after the great fire of AD 64—a disaster for which Nero was blamed by ancient Romans. Needless to say, the villa wasn't popular, and after Nero's death it was gradually dismantled, covered over, and forgotten.

It was accidently rediscovered in the 15th century and had an immediate impact on Renaissance artists like Raphael and Michelangelo, who were among the site's earliest visitors. The delicate frescoes on the interior walls have been in a state of renovation ever since. The villa wasn't opened to the public until 2014, when 32 of its 150 rooms were restored.

The entire villa is underground and can only be visited with a guide who explains the ancient uses of each room. English language tours can be reserved on Saturdays and Sundays at 9am and every 30 minutes onward until 3pm. A VR film and video projections also help to bring the past to life.

During COVID outbreaks, the Domus Aurea may close entirely.

Piazza Venezia

Metro B: Colosseo

Piazza Venezia is one of the busiest squares in the city and difficult to cross at rush hour when cars from five different streets fight for the right of way. Watching traffic cops in the center tame unruly drivers is a treat. On the southern side of the chaos is the massive **Vittoriano** (daily 9:30am-7:30pm; free) monument also known as the Altar of the Republic. This is where Italy's unknown soldier is buried. If you're wondering what the Forum looked like in its heyday, this building completed in 1925 is a decent rendering of classical ancient style. It overshadows everything in the square below and is not particularly loved by locals, who refer to it as "the wedding cake." A dramatic set of stairs, which are free to climb, leads to the altar where an honor guard is permanently stationed. There are three terraces with increasingly better views; however, the best look at the city is from the **Terrazza della Quadrighe** terrace at the very top, which can only be reached by elevator. Inside is the **Complesso del Vittoriano** (Via di San Pietro in Carcere; tel. 06/871-5111; www.ilvittoriano.com; Mon.-Thurs. 9:30am-7:30pm, Fri.-Sat. 9:30am-10pm, and Sun. 9:30am-8:30pm; €15 or €24 for two shows, audio guide included) exhibition spaces where temporary shows dedicated to Andy Warhol, Jackson Pollock, and other icons of art are regularly staged. Free visits of the Roman era underground passages below the complex are organized every Saturday and Sunday. These were used as air raid shelters

during World War II and are equipped with a small hospital and running water. Next to the monument is the **Museo del Risorgimento** (Via dei Fori Imperiali; tel. 06/679-3598; daily 9:30am-6:30pm; €5, audio guide €3) that recounts Italy's mid-19th-century struggle for unification led by Giuseppe Garibaldi.

Piazza del Campidoglio

Metro B: Colosseo, Buses 30, 44, 46, 51, 63, 81

The Capitoline Hill, the smallest of Rome's seven hills, was the most revered. It's here that the Temple of Juno once stood and where Roman coins were minted. Piazza del Campidoglio lies at the top and is a sharp contrast from the ruins below. Michelangelo designed the marble paving of this elegant square as well as the well-proportioned facades of the Renaissance buildings (Palazzo Nuovo, Conservatorio, and Senatorio) that now house city hall and the **Musei Capitolini.**

The stairs to the right of Palazzo Nuovo (the one with a clock tower) lead to the **Vittoriano** monument and great views of the forums. You can enter by way of the monumental steps from Piazza Venezia or take the back way from Piazza Campidoglio. There's a bar at the top with a scenic terrace that makes a pleasant stop.

Capitoline Museums
(Musei Capitolini)

Piazza del Campidoglio 1; tel. 06/3996-7800; daily 9:30am-7:30pm; www.museicapitolini.org; €12 or RomaPass, audio guide €4 video guide €6; Metro B: Colosseo

Musei Capitolini is the oldest publicly owned museum in the world. It was founded in 1471 when Pope Sisto IV donated a collection of ancient statues to the city. Subsequent popes contributed relics dug up in the area and an art gallery was added in the 18th century.

The museums are located inside Palazzo Nuovo and Palazzo dei Conservatori. The ticket office is in the latter building along with the original bronze equestrian statue of Marcus Aurelius (the one in the square is a copy). There's a mix of ancient and Renaissance art including Bernini's marble version of Medusa (room 10) and a bronze statue of Rome's legendary twin founders, Romulus and Remus (room 9). Upstairs in the painting gallery are works by Caravaggio, an outdoor terrace with panoramic views, and a decent café.

Palazzo dei Conservatori is connected to Palazzo Nuovo by an underground corridor; the perpendicular passageway near the end leads to the oldest part of the complex overlooking the forum. This side of the museum is smaller and contains ancient statues including *The Dying Gaul* (room 53) and the Hall of Emperors featuring busts of ancient Roman VIPs.

Circus Maximus
(Circo Massimo)
24/7; free; Metro B: Circo Massimo

Circo Massimo is where ancient Romans cheered their favorite charioteers, and present-day locals jog or walk their dogs. Most of the stone structure was stripped away over the centuries, but the original shape of the immense oval racetrack is still clear and provides plenty of atmosphere.

The Circus Maximus accommodated up to 250,000 spectators, including the emperor, who watched races from the comfort of the Palatine Hill. Chariots were released from 12 gates at the northern end of the track. Drivers attempted to complete seven laps and races lasted around 10 minutes. Not everyone finished in one piece, which may be why horse racing was so popular in ancient Rome. Gambling was another reason, and successful charioteers became wealthy and famous.

Today the area is a pleasant refuge from traffic and a good place to exercise or rest. You can walk along the former track or the raised *spina*, which divided the course and was decorated with obelisks and other spoils of conquest that were removed over the centuries to decorate other parts of the city. The southern end of the Circo Massimo is a small outdoor **museum** (Piazza di Porta Capena;

tel. 06/0608; Tues.-Sun. 9:30am-7pm summer, 9:30am-4:30pm winter; €5). Although not much remains compared to the Colosseum, the flagstones, brick walls, and vaulted corridors provide a feel of what the stadium was like. If that isn't enough, you can pick up the **Circo Maximo Experience** (€12, €22 family) headsets and take a virtual tour of the arena. There are nine viewing points on the itinerary, which culminates with an exciting digital remastered chariot race.

Baths of Caracalla
(Terme di Caracalla)
Viale delle Terme di Caracalla 52; tel. 06/3996-7700; www.coopculture.it; Tues.-Sun. 9am-7:15pm summer and 9am-5pm winter, Mon. 9am-2pm all-year; €8 or RomaPass; Metro B: Circo Massimo

Ancient Romans generally didn't have running water in their homes and visited public baths daily. Hundreds were built throughout the city and used free of charge. Terme di Caracalla is one of the largest and best-preserved imperial spas in Rome.

They accommodated up to 1,600 bathers simultaneously who moved from *tepidarium* (warm room) to *caldarium* (hot room) to *frigidarium* (cold room) and back again. Facilities included pools where citizens relaxed, washed, and socialized; changing rooms; libraries; and a courtyard for exercising that's still visible. Hundreds of slaves manned the underground furnaces below the complex to maintain the right temperature, while servants massaged, cleaned, and attended to wealthier patrons. The water needed to run the complex was transported along an aqueduct that stretched for dozens of kilometers into the Roman countryside.

Forum Boarium
Before the Roman Forum became the center of the ancient world, business was conducted in the Forum Boarium (Piazza della Bocca della Verita) close to the Tiber River. This forum was adjacent to Rome's first port, which explains the presence of the **Temples of Hercules** and **Portunus**. Portunus was

the god of rivers and ports and Hercules was the protector of trade and livestock. The temple celebrating the former is circular in shape and was commissioned around 120 BC by a wealthy merchant who belonged to the oil guild. Both temples show the influence of Greek tastes on early Roman architecture and were recently restored. Neither is open to the public.

Arch of Janus
(Arco di Giano)

Via del Velabro; free; Metro B: Circo Massimo
The Arco di Giano, a rare four-faced arch, lies across a busy street from the temples and was erected in the 4th century. Although the statues of the gods that once adorned the 12 niches on either side are missing along with the marble covering, the monument is still imposing. Today it lies slightly off the beaten path, but once marked a busy crossroads where herders brought their cattle to market and merchants took cover whenever it rained. During the Middle Ages it was converted into a fortress and the structure on top that once decorated the arch was dismantled. The **Anima Mundi** (Via del Velabro 1; daily 11am-2am) bar nearby is the ideal spot to sit and admire the arch.

Santa Maria in Cosmedin

Piazza della Bocca della Verità 18; tel. 06/678-7759; daily 9:30am-6pm; free; Metro B: Circo Massimo
Santa Maria in Cosmedin, an 8th-century church built by Byzantine monks, is famous for the ancient drain cover that hangs in the portico and supposedly distinguishes between fact and fiction. There's usually a long line of tourists waiting to put their hand into the "mouth of truth" (*bocca della verità*) and many forget to enter the church. That's too bad, considering the quality of the colorful mosaic flooring inside. The wooden ceiling is flat rather than arched (making it cheaper to build) and priority was given to prayer rather

than embellishments. There's a small souvenir shop in the lobby and seven-story bell tower, which is still operational.

Crypta Balbi

Via delle Botteghe Oscure 31; tel. 06/3996-7700; www.coopculture.it; Tues.-Sun. 9am-7:45pm; €10 or €12 combined ticket; Tram 8 or Buses 30, 40
Crypta Balbi is located on a street named after the Middle Age craftsmen who transformed blocks of marble (removed from the forum and other ancient Roman buildings) into lime used for construction. The museum displays artifacts illustrating how the city has changed over the ages. It's small and often overlooked by tourists, but the well-organized and informative itinerary helps visitors discover different layers of the city's past. Afterward you should be able to recognize different eras and distinguish between antiquity, medieval, and baroque. The museum is part of a group of four sites that also includes Palazzo Massimo, Altemps, and the Diocletian Baths. The combined ticket allows entry to all four museums over a three-day period.

CAMPO DE' FIORI/ PIAZZA NAVONA

To visit this neighborhood, you can stick to the busy routes visitors use out of convenience or you can begin a visit from the **Isola Tiberina** or **Ponte Sisto** bridges. The former takes you through the Jewish Ghetto and then continues on Via dei Giubbonari toward Campo De' Fiori, while the latter is a more direct route to the major squares. If time isn't pressing, walk along less-frequented, largely pedestrian streets such as **Via Giulia, Via del Pellegrino,** and **Via del Governo Vecchio.**

★ Pantheon

Piazza della Rotonda; tel. 06/6830-0230; Mon.-Sat. 9am-7:15pm and Sun. 9am-5:45pm; free; Buses 30, 40, 62, 64, 81, 87, 492
The Pantheon is the best-preserved ancient Roman building in the world. This former temple's first incarnation dates from 27 BC when it was dedicated to Jupiter, Mars, and

1: Circus Maximus 2: the dome of the Pantheon 3: inside the Capitoline Museums 4: Piazza Navona

Venus. Three gods meant pulling out all the stops, and Emperor Hadrian completely rebuilt the structure less than 100 years later. The 16 monolithic columns his architects used to support the portico are 39 feet (12 meters) high. The darkest one was recently traced to a forced labor camp that the Romans operated in Egypt and was shipped to the city at great expense and effort.

After the empire fell, the building was consecrated as a church in AD 663 and survived centuries of repurposing. It was used as a fortress and poultry market, and bell towers were added and removed, but no misuse or abuse managed to cause permanent damage. The 20-foot-thick (6-meter-thick) walls, one of the keys to the building's longevity, continue to support the largest dome ever built in antiquity. It weighs over 5,000 tons and became a model for churches, mosques, museums, and universities around the world. Even today, the dome is one of the largest in the world and is wider than St. Peter's and the Duomo in Florence.

Light enters the Pantheon through an oculus 30 feet (9 meters) in diameter embedded in the coffered vault. Most of the colored marble is original, as is Hadrian's inscription on the frieze outside. Italy's first two kings are buried inside as is Renaissance artist Raphael who specifically requested to be entombed here.

An **audio guide** (€7) itinerary is available from the help desk and touch-screen totems are located around the site. There's also an official **Bit of Pantheon App** (iOS and Android) with details about the interior and a **guided tour** (roma.pantheon@duvaws.com; Mon.-Fri. noon; €18, children under 10 free, cash only) in English that lasts one hour. You can reserve in advance or show up 10 minutes early to guarantee a spot.

During COVID outbreaks, audio guides and tours may be unavailable.

Piazza Navona
Buses C3, 40, 81, 87, 492

Piazza Navona is not a typical square—in fact, it's not square at all. The *piazza* inherited its oblong shape from when it was an ancient Roman track. Inaugurated in AD 86 the stadium held up to 30,000 spectators who came to watch athletic competitions rather than horse racing. Piazza Navona can be entered from six streets and is free of automotive threats, allowing fountains, churches, musicians, street artists, and pigeons to be enjoyed in peace. Bernini's **Fontana di Quattro Fiumi** in the center is the most intricate of the three fountains and was installed in 1651 after the pope of the time became enamored with his scale model of the fountain. Four mythical figures representing the Nile, Ganges, Danube, and Rio de la Plata rivers support a Roman obelisk that once stood in Circo di Massenzio on the Via Appia Antica.

The church in front of the fountain is **Sant'Agnese in Agone** (Piazza Navona; tel. 06/6819-2134; www.santagneseinagone. org; Tues.-Sun. 9am-1pm and 3pm-7pm; free). According to legend, Agnese was stripped naked in an attempt to make her renounce her faith. The hair she miraculously grew to cover her body is depicted in a marble relief near the altar. Borromini (who had wanted to build the fountain) completely restructured the church in 1657, giving it a unique concave appearance and adding twin bell towers. The underground **crypt** is reached through a passage along the left wall that leads to remains of the original church, foundations of the stadium, a mosaic floor from the same period, and medieval frescoes. It is one of the holiest stops for pilgrims, and there's often a line to enter. The crypt, however, was undergoing restoration at the time of writing and expected to reopen in 2021.

Palazzo Altemps
Piazza Sant'Apollinare 46; tel. 06/3996-7700; www. coopculture.it; Tues.-Sun. 9am-7:45pm; €10 or €12 combined ticket, audio guide €6; Buses 70, 81, 87, 116T, 186, 492, 628

Palazzo Altemps is a branch of the Museo Nazionale Romano and houses Egyptian, Greek, and ancient Roman sculptures within a magnificent Renaissance palace begun in

Campo De' Fiori/Piazza Navona

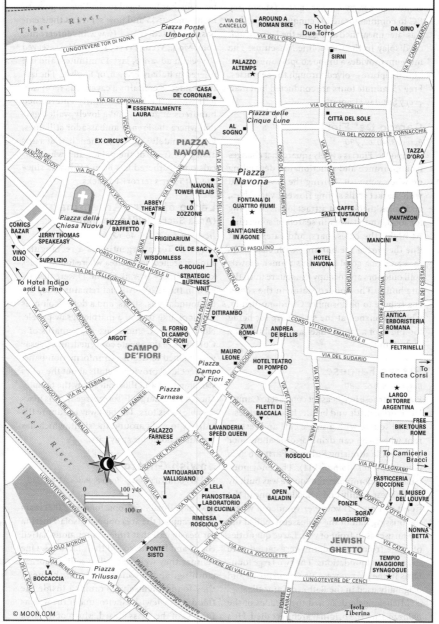

© MOON.COM

1477. The most noteworthy statue in the collection is *Galata Suicida* (Galatian Suicide), commissioned by Caesar in the 1st century BC to commemorate his conquest of Gaul. It was later unearthed alongside the *Dying Gaul,* on display in the Capitoline Museums. The museum provides a unique opportunity to see how sculpture evolved through the centuries. Free 75-minute tours are conducted in Italian every Sunday at noon.

Campo De' Fiori

Buses 23, 40, 62, 280

Campo De' Fiori is a lively square that changes its appearance and functionality depending on when you visit. During the day it's filled with market stalls selling flowers, vegetables, and knickknacks that attract locals shopping for food, and visitors in search of souvenirs. At night, the cafés, bars, and eateries that line the *piazza* are bursting with customers in search of a good time. In summer, crowds spill outdoors and occupy the square until the late hours. The hooded statue in the center is a tribute to philosopher Giordano Bruno, who was burned at the stake here for being too much of a free thinker and doubting the Holy Trinity.

Piazza Farnese

Buses 23, 40, 62, 280

Piazza Farnese is a pleasant contrast to Campo De' Fiori's hustle and bustle. It is a quiet residential square with a single café and restaurant where you can drink or dine at outdoor tables while admiring **Palazzo Farnese** (Via Giulia 251; tel. 06/686-011). The enormous palace that dominates the square was built by the Farnese family and considered one of the finest in Rome. If you ever wondered where the missing half of the Colosseum ended up, the answer is in front of you. Large quantities of stone from the stadium were carted here to build the foundations. The two large fountains in the *piazza* were also repurposed and originally used in the Baths of Caracalla.

Michelangelo designed the facades of the *palazzo* after the original architect died. He's responsible for the cornice, central balcony, and the third floor of the courtyard. The building has belonged to the French government since 1635 and now serves as their embassy. Guided **tours** (www.inventerrome. com; Mon., Wed., Fri.; €9) should be reserved a week in advance, last 45 minutes, and are offered in Italian, French, or English. The lavish residence contains a cavernous reception hall where the Farnese family entertained hundreds of guests, and a lovely walled garden where the French ambassador still does. Unfortunately, the stone bench that runs along the front of the palace and where locals once gathered has been off-limits since the 2015 Paris terrorist attacks.

Largo di Torre Argentina
(Area Sacra dell'Argentina)

Tram 8, Buses 30, 40, 46, 62, 64

Largo di Torre Argentina is a rectangular sunken archeological area where four temples known simply as A, B, C, and D were discovered in the 1920s. All that remains today are the foundations, stairs, and a dozen columns that look like part of a marble jigsaw puzzle. Near temples C and D are the remains of a Curia where the Senate convened, and Caesar was stabbed to death. An information panel at street level provides details about the relics still standing and illustrates how the temples once looked. Largo di Torre Argentina is inaccessible to visitors. The best way to admire the ruins is to walk around the sight, which has become a home for stray cats.

Jewish Ghetto

Via del Portico d'Ottavia; Tram 8, Buses 23, 63, 280, 780

Jews have inhabited Rome for over 2,000 years and occupied the area opposite Isola Tiberina for nearly half that time. As religious hatred ebbed and flowed, so did their fortunes. One century they were limited to selling fabrics, clothing, and secondhand iron; the next, they found themselves cramped inside the flood-prone Jewish Ghetto, under the watchful eyes of the Swiss Guard. Much of the area was demolished after the unification of Italy in 1860 to make way for the synagogue and 19th-century residential buildings that give the area a sense of grandeur.

The Ghetto is small but lively and most of that life is concentrated around **Via del Portico d'Ottavia.** It's the heart of the neighborhood and what locals refer to simply as the *piazza*, an oblong-shaped square where local drama transpires. In the morning it's filled with children on their way to school, at lunch it's packed with tourists and locals eating at dozens of kosher restaurants and bakeries, and in the afternoon it's a peaceful setting for old-timers to relax on benches and catch up with neighbors.

If you look down you may spot gold cobblestones on the streets of the neighborhood. These commemorate residents who were deported from the Ghetto during World War II and were installed by a German artist throughout Europe.

TEMPIO MAGGIORE SYNAGOGUE

Via Catalana/Largo 16 Ottobre 1943;
tel. 06/6840-0661; www.museoebraico.roma.it;
Sun.-Thurs. 10am-6pm and Fri. 10am-4pm summer,
Sun.-Thurs. 9am-5pm and Fri. 9am-2pm winter; €11

Tempio Maggiore Synagogue, or Great Synagogue, is one of the most important synagogues outside Jerusalem and the first to be visited by a pope. It was built by Christian architects, which explains the Greek cross design, and has an innovative square dome that makes it easy to spot. The museum displays ancient manuscripts and recounts the history of Roman Jews. There's also a 30-minute video and a 3-D reconstruction of the Ghetto as it once was. Guided tours (Sun.-Thurs. 10:30am, 11:15am, 12:15pm, 1:15pm, 2:15pm, 3:15pm, 4:15pm) of the Great Synagogue and adjacent Spanish Synagogue are available in English and included in the ticket price. Police have been stationed outside since a terrorist attack in 1982 but have had very little to do since then.

Isola Tiberina

Tram 8, Buses 23, 63, 125, 280

Whoever said the more things change the more they stay the same was probably thinking of Rome, and the Isola Tiberina in particular. This small island of volcanic rock played a crucial role in putting Rome on the map. It's here that Aesculapius, the god of medicine, was worshipped, where ancient Romans waited to be healed outside his temple, and where a hospital has been operating since 1548. The island itself was altered to resemble a ship in the 1st century AD, and the **Ponte Fabricio** bridge that links the island to the Jewish Ghetto is the oldest in the city. It's a popular crossing point into **Trastevere** and often lined with street vendors and musicians entertaining passing crowds. During the summer locals sun themselves on the embankment below, an open-air cinema is set up, and food and drink kiosks line the riverside.

TRIDENTE

Looking down on Tridente, it's clear how this part of Rome got its name. The neighborhood is made up of three main streets that radiate out from **Piazza del Popolo** in a trident-like shape. **Via del Corso,** the longest and partially pedestrianized, lies in the center and leads to the Vittoriano monument. It's lined with shops and is a popular place for locals to take a weekend stroll. Each of the outer streets of the trident is narrower and less trafficked. **Via Babuino** was the traditional home of antiques dealers that have been gradually replaced by luxury boutiques. It connects Piazza del Popolo with **Piazza di Spagna** and runs parallel to the picturesque and often overlooked **Via Margutta,** where Federico Fellini lived and travelers can get a unique marble souvenir. **Via di Ripetta,** the third prong, is the least explored and contains historic shops and low-cost eateries where students from the nearby art school go for lunch. It leads to the **Ara Pacis** and ends near the Pantheon.

Piazza del Popolo

Metro A: Flaminio Piazza del Popolo

Rome is a dense city, which may be why the wide-open space of Piazza del Popolo is so

Tridente

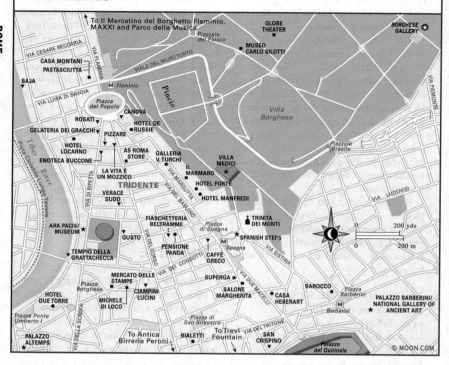

To Il Mercatino del Borghetto Flaminio, MAXXI and Parco della Musica

Piazzale del Flacco

GLOBE THEATER

BORGHESE GALLERY

VIA CESARE BECCARIA

CASA MONTANI PASTASCIUTTA

BAJA

VIA FLAMINIA

VIALE DEL MURO TORTO

MUSEO CARLO BILOTTI

M Flaminio

Pincio

VIA LUISA DI SAVOIA

Piazza del Popolo

CANOVA

ROSATI

HOTEL DE RUSSIE

GELATERIA DEI GRACCHI

PIZZARE

HOTEL LOCARNO

AS ROMA STORE

GALLERIA V. TURCHI

Villa Borghese

VIA PIEMONTE

Piazzale Brasile

ENOTECA BUCCONE

IL MARMARO

VILLA MEDICI

Tiber River

Pista ciclabile Lungo Tevere

LA VITA È UN MOZZICO

VERACE SUDD

TRIDENTE

HOTEL FORTE

HOTEL MANFREDI

VIA LUDOVISI

VIA DI RIPETTA

VIA DEL BABUINO

VIA MARGUTTA

ARA PACIS/ MUSEUM

FIASCHETTERIA BELTRAMME

GUSTO

Piazza di Spagna

TRINITA DEI MONTI

0   200 yds

TEMPIO DELLA GRATTACHECCA

VIA DEL CORSO

PENSIONE PANDA

SPANISH STEPS

M Spagna

VIA SISTINA

0   200 m

CAFFE GRECO

VIA DEI CONDOTTI

MERCATO DELLE STAMPE

SUPERGA

VIA DUE MACELLI

BAROCCO

Piazza Borghese

CIAMPINI LUCINI

SALONE MARGHERITA

CASA HEBERART

Piazza Barberini

M Barberini

PALAZZO BARBERINI/ NATIONAL GALLERY OF ANCIENT ART

HOTEL DUE TORRE

MICHELE DI LOCO

VIA DELLA SCROFA

Piazza Ponte Umberto I

PALAZZO ALTEMPS

To Antica Birreria Peroni

BIALETTI

Piazza di San Silvestro

To Trevi Fountain

SAN CRISPINO

VIA DEL TRITONE

Palazzo del Quirinale

© MOON.COM

refreshing. Here in this circular cobblestone square commissioned by Napoleon, there's room to breathe and admire the twin **Santa Maria** churches. All three Tridente streets begin here, and the *piazza* is a major thoroughfare for local pedestrians and tourists on their way to work or the next monument. In the middle of the *piazza* is a giant Egyptian obelisk flanked by enormous lions. Concerts are organized here during the summer, and crowds gather for national holidays and spontaneous soccer celebrations.

Piazza di Spagna

Metro A: Spagna

Piazza di Spagna is one of the most elegant and refined squares in the city. The luxury shops nearby add to its luster, as do the ingenious fountain, remarkable steps, and church

overlooking the city. The area gets its name from the Spanish embassy to the Vatican that was once located nearby. In the center is the **Fontana della Barcaccia,** credited to Gian Lorenzo Bernini, who overcame the lack of water pressure by sculpting a half-sunken boat that collects the water. The fountain is supplied by ancient Rome's last working aqueduct and was completed in 1629. It's a working fountain, so you can drink directly from the spout located at the bow. The stone bees and suns decorating the fountain are identical to those on the coat of arms of Pope Urban VIII and a reminder of who financed the project.

Spanish Steps

Metro A: Spagna

1: Trevi Fountain 2: Spanish Steps, Piazza di Spagna

It's hard to miss the Spanish Steps, located directly in front of Fontana della Barcaccia in Piazza di Spagna. This majestic outdoor staircase was actually built by the French, who wanted to connect their church with the square below in the 17th century. Wrangling between popes and French monarchs delayed the project until a design was found that satisfied both parties. The result is a stunning combination of terraces, curves, and balustrades.

The steps were renovated in 2018 and have never looked better, especially in spring and summer when they are decorated with flowers. Although technically you aren't supposed to sit here, that doesn't stop tourists, who attract nomadic sellers hawking roses, selfie sticks, and a variety of gadgets. Every so often the municipal government takes a hard line on flaneurs and assigns vigils to ensure the stairs are only used for their original purpose.

TRINITA DEI MONTI

Piazza della Trinita dei Monti 3; tel. 06/679-4179; www.trinitadeimonti.net; Mon-Sat. 10am-8pm, Wed. noon-8pm, Sun. 9am-8pm; free; Metro A: Spagna

The view gets better the higher you climb up the Spanish Steps, reaching perfection at the entrance Trinita dei Monti. The panorama can easily distract visitors from this 15th-century church, which was also recently restored, and whose interior includes paintings by Daniele da Volterra, a pupil of Michelangelo. Volterra was chosen to cover up his master's *Last Judgment* nudes, deemed too racy by the pope, inside the Sistine Chapel. The muscled bodies in his *Deposition* show clear signs of his teacher's influence. Mass is held every day except Mondays in French and Italian.

The church includes a monastery that can be visited by guided **tours** on the first and third Wednesday of each month at 5pm. Reservations must be made by email (secretariat.tdm@emmanuelco.org) at least two days in advance. Tickets cost €12 for adults, €6 for teens, and are free for children under 12.

★ Trevi Fountain
(Fontana di Trevi)

Piazza di Trevi; 24/7; free; Metro A: Barberini Fontana Trevi

Fontana di Trevi is the largest fountain in Rome and probably the most famous fountain in the world. Like many in the city it's linked to an ancient aqueduct that's been supplying water from miles away since Augustus was emperor. Over the years different basins were erected here and it wasn't until 1732 that things got fancy. That's when Pope Clement XII decided to forgo modesty and create a triumphal fountain. The resulting baroque masterpiece took Niccolò Salvi 30 years to complete and dominates the small square in which it was built.

The fountain rises up against the side of an elegant *palazzo* and is framed by four imposing columns representing the major known rivers at the time. Oceanus, god of the sea, occupies the central niche and stands in a shell-shaped chariot guiding two horses (one agitated and one calm). On his right is a statue representing *health* and on his left is *abundance*. Water gushes from the center and flows over jagged travertine rocks into an immense pool around which hundreds of visitors gather.

It's a spectacular scene that sounds and looks even better at night when the fountain is illuminated, and crowds have thinned. If you can't make it then, at least avoid noon (especially in August), when the small *piazza* is crammed with visitors and peddlers selling trinkets. Legend (and Gregory Peck) has it that tossing a coin into the water with your back turned ensures a return trip to Rome. The origin of the habit is unknown, but wishing wells were an ancient tradition that modern visitors have eagerly adopted. Every year over €1 million worth of wishes lands in the fountain. Coins are collected twice a month and donated to charity.

Villa Medici

Viale della Trinita dei Monti 1; tel. 06/676-1311; www.

villamedici.it; Wed.-Mon. 9:30am-5:30pm; €12, half off with RomaPass; Metro A: Spagna

Villa Medici, one of the best-preserved villas in Rome, provides an idea of how Italian nobles liked to live. The Medici family acquired the immense *palazzo* in the 16th century and added the austere facade that was fashionable at the time. Lightheartedness was reserved for the rear of the building, which is much more ornate and overlooks a garden complete with hedged pathways, secret alleys, and fountains. In 1804 Napoleon moved the French Academy into the villa, where such talents as Berlioz and Debussy temporarily resided. Artists are still granted residencies and applications are open to all.

Tickets include entry to contemporary art exhibits and **guided tours** that recount the history, art, and architecture of this remarkable dwelling. Visits are offered from Wednesday to Monday and cover everything from the symbolism of the facade to the private chambers of the cardinal who once called the villa home. The standard apartment and gardens tour in English departs at 11am, 3pm, and 5:30pm from the inner courtyard. There are also a number of themed tours including one for children (€6) on Sundays at 10:30am; however, some of these are only available in French or Italian. A pleasant cafeteria with wonderful views of Rome serves light snacks on the second floor. Security has been beefed up since recent terrorist attacks and soldiers are now permanently stationed at the entrance.

During COVID outbreaks, reservations are recommended, and visitors must fill out a COVID prevention form.

Villa Medici contains several **historic apartments** (€230/garden view or €350/city view), which are rented out to visitors and provide a unique stay. They can be reserved by writing to standard@villamedici.it.

★ Borghese Gallery
(Galleria Borghese)

Piazzale del Museo Borghese; tel. 06/32810; Tues.-Sun. 9am-7pm; www.galleriaborghese.it; €15 +

€2 booking fee or RomaPass, audio guide €5; Metro A: Spagna

Galleria Borghese is one of Rome's finest art galleries. It's located inside the villa of the same name, built in the 17th century, that once belonged to the influential Borghese family whose members included popes and cardinals. They were passionate about art and amassed a unique collection of sculpture and painting that was purchased by the Italian state in 1902.

The two-story villa is elaborately decorated with frescoes, stucco, and marble detailing that recount the family's glorious past. The ground floor is devoted to sculpture, and paintings line the walls upstairs. There are two extraordinary depictions of David: a marble statue by Gian Lorenzo Bernini portraying the hero a moment before striking Goliath, and a vivid canvas by Caravaggio of David holding the giant's severed head. Both artists are well represented in the gallery.

Getting into the gallery isn't straightforward and requires advance booking. A maximum of 80 visitors are allowed in at a time and you can choose from two-hour time slots that start at 9am, 11am, 1pm, 3pm, and 5pm, which can be reserved online (www.galleriaborghese.it) from one day to five months in advance. Guided tours (€8.50) lasting 90 minutes are available in English and should be reserved at the same time as the tickets. Anyone wanting to use their RomaPass must also reserve in advance by telephone (tel. 06/32810) and pick tickets up 30 minutes prior to entry.

Ara Pacis

This monumental stone altar was commissioned by the Roman Senate in 13 BC to celebrate Emperor Augustus and mark a new era of peace after years of civil war. Part temple, part archway, it's adorned with figures showing the city's legendary past and present and was an ancient example of the propaganda and self-promotion at which the Romans were masters. There are finely carved images of the imperial family including Caesar, Tiberius, and Augustus and his wife Livia, along with a frieze showing how the Roman state functioned.

ARA PACIS MUSEUM

Lungotevere in Augusta; www.arapacis.it; daily 9:30am-7:30pm; €10.50 or €17 with entry to exhibition or RomaPass; Buses 30, 70, 81, 87, 280

The glass-roofed Ara Pacis Museum was designed by Richard Meier to house the altar and an exhibition space located on the lower level. Initially criticized by traditionalists, the building has become popular with visitors who can walk through the altar while listening to the multilingual **Ara Pacis app** (€5) that vividly deciphers the monument's limestone reliefs. A standard audio guide (€1.50) is also available.

Palazzo Barberini

Via delle Quattro Fontane 13; tel. 06/481-4591; www.barberinicorsini.org; Tues.-Sun. 8:30am-7pm; €12 or RomaPass, audio guide €3; Metro A: Barberini

Palazzo Barberini, home to the **National Gallery of Ancient Art** (Galleria Nazionale d'Arte Antica) is as stunning as the artwork it holds. The palace was purchased in 1625 by Pope Urban VIII for his nephews and transformed into one of the finest residences in the city. Gian Lorenzo Bernini and Francesco Borromini both worked on the project and are responsible for the stunning square shafted and oval helicoidal staircases that are a must to climb.

Here you can witness the evolution of Italian painting from the 12th century all the way to neoclassicism. The vast gallery is the permanent home of over 1,500 works of art including Caravaggio's bloody *Judith Beheading Holofernes* and poignant *Narcissus*. Paintings are labeled with Italian and English descriptions, and it's hard not to get caught up admiring the frescoed ceilings. A ticket to Palazzo Barberini includes entry to its sister museum, **Galleria Corsini** (Via della Lungara 10) in Trastevere.

MAXXI

Via Guido Reni 4A; tel. 06/320-1954; www.maxxi.art; Tues.-Sun. 11am-7pm; €12 or RomaPass, audio guide free; Tram 2 or Bus 168

MAXXI is the Italian abbreviation for National Museum of XXI Century Arts, and the museum displays contemporary creativity in many forms. The building alone is worth a visit and was one of Zaha Hadid's last projects. It's split into temporary exhibitions and a permanent collection of art, architecture, design, photography, and fashion. Many of the artists on display are unknown, but there are plenty of imaginative drawings, models, photographs, and video to contemplate inside this sleek concrete-inspired museum. It's the perfect balance to antiquity and a nice place to spend a couple of hours admiring the present rather than the past.

MAXXI is located north of the Tridente but can be easily reached by tram or bus. Gallery 4 of the permanent collection is free Tuesday-Friday and entry to the entire museum is complimentary on your birthday as long as you can prove it. The bookshop and cafeteria in the courtyard opposite the entrance make for a nice light lunch or happy hour stop.

VATICANO

It's easy to forget that Rome contains two states in one. There's Italy and there's the Vatican, which is the smallest state in the world but big enough to mint its own coins and issue its own stamps. The Vatican City of today dates from the Lateran Treaty of 1929 when the present boundaries were recognized. Fortunately, no visas are required to enter and pilgrims can come and go as they please. Although the geographic area is small and the population doesn't exceed 1,000 full-time residents, the religious and cultural impact of the Vatican is immense.

St. Peter's Square
(Piazza San Pietro)

Metro A: Ottaviano

Walking through the crowds at St. Peter's

Square feels like a marathon, and it takes about five minutes to cross the square. *Square* is actually the wrong word for what Bernini began building in 1656—it's more of an ellipse superimposed on a trapezoid. The *piazza* was designed for outdoor masses and can accommodate 80,000 pilgrims. Bernini intended the space to symbolically embrace the world, and that's what it looks like from the cupola above St. Peter's. The semicircular colonnades are made up of four rows of columns and topped with statues of 140 saints. Stand on either of the marble discs near the fountains and the columns disappear behind one another. Pope Sixtus V ordered the granite obelisk placed in the center, and it's the only visible reminder of the ancient Roman racetrack that once occupied the site.

Every Sunday morning at midnight from September to June thousands of worshippers gather in the square to hear Pope Francis deliver his weekly *Angelus* in a half-dozen languages. The ceremony lasts 15-20 minutes and ends with a blessing. Papal Audiences are longer and take place on Wednesdays at 9:30am. They require a free ticket, available from the Vatican website, and you need to arrive early to get a good seat. The square is quiet at night and worth a second visit when the dome is lit up and tourists have retreated to their hotels. Note that blessings and audiences with the Pope do not take place during COVID outbreaks.

★ St. Peter's Basilica
(Basilica San Pietro)
Piazza San Pietro; tel. 06/6988-3731; daily 7am-7pm; free; Metro A: Ottaviano

Basilica San Pietro was built on the site of a Roman racetrack and the spot where St. Peter was supposedly buried in AD 64. Early Christian pilgrims began visiting almost immediately after his death, which made it the obvious place for newly converted Emperor Constantine to build the first incarnation of the basilica in AD 324. That building was expanded and remained standing until 1503, when restoration proved impossible and Pope

Julius II opted for demolition. Bramante was chosen to design a new basilica, and the next century and a half saw the church slowly take its current form. Michelangelo engineered the cupola, Carlo Maderno constructed the facade, and Bernini designed the *piazza*. The result is remarkably uniform considering how many different hands worked on the building.

The gargantuan interior leaves no doubt that this is the largest church in the world and is as impressive as the outside. Measuring 614 feet (187 meters) from entrance to apse and 446 feet (136 meters) to the top of the cupola, the basilica contains 11 chapels and 45 altars. Popes didn't cut corners when it came to interior design, and only the finest materials were used. Immediately on the right behind bulletproof glass is Michelangelo's *Pietà.* Completed when he was 25, the sculpture is his only signed work, and he only did so after he overheard someone mistake its creator. It depicts Jesus shortly after his crucifixion in the arms of his mother. It was a recurrent theme for Michelangelo, who sculpted several others in his lifetime.

In the center of the basilica is Bernini's sculpted canopy, **Baldacchino,** that covers the Papal Altar, where only popes are permitted to celebrate mass. Four twisting columns directly under the dome support the sculpted bronze canopy. Nearby is the entrance to the grottoes where relics of the original basilica, including fragments of Giotto's mosaic, can be seen. This is where popes including John Paul II are buried and a mandatory stop for pilgrims. The original Christian necropolis is also open to visitors and provides insight into the origins of modern religion.

One of the greatest challenges in building St. Peter's was completing the **cupola** (daily 7:30am-6pm in summer and 7:30am-5pm in winter), which needed to express the grandeur of the Pope's ambition while withstanding the laws of gravity. By the time of his commission Michelangelo already enjoyed an indisputable reputation and was a master of both expression and form. He was also a native of Florence, where an impressive dome had

Vaticano

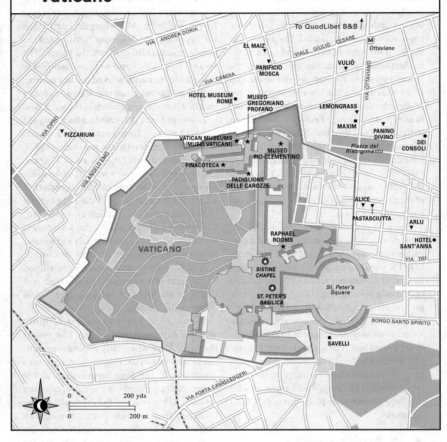

already been built. When the Pope called, he accepted the challenge. The solution, which he never saw realized, consists of two domes, one fitted inside the other. The best way to appreciate this engineering marvel, which kept hundreds of skilled workers busy for decades, is by climbing to the top. The quicker route to the circular outdoor terrace of the cupola is by elevator (€10) followed by 320 steps, while the long way (€8) is strictly on foot and 551 steps that require some stamina to reach the summit and one of the best views in the city.

Mass is said daily in Italian on weekdays at 10am, 11am, and noon at the S. Giuseppe altar and on weekends 9am, 11:15am, and 12:15pm. You don't have to wear your Sunday best, but a dress code is enforced to enter the basilica. Shoulders, knees, and midriff must be covered by both men and women. Flip-flops are another no-no, as is any offensive slogans or branding appearing on T-shirts.

Vatican Museums
(Musei Vaticani)

Viale Vaticani; tel. 06/6988-4676; www.museivaticani. va, help.musei@scv.va; Mon.-Thurs. 10am-8pm (last

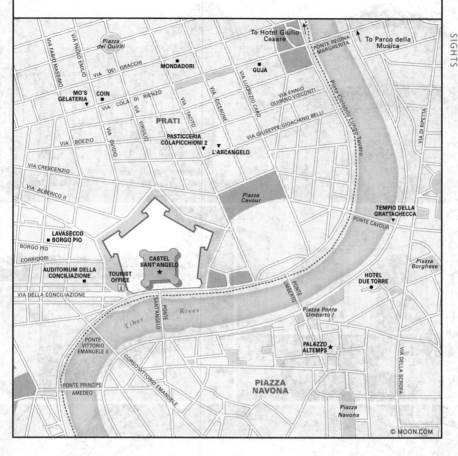

To Hotel Giulio Cesare

To Parco della Musica

PONTE REGINA MARGHERITA

Piazza dei Quiriti

VIA FABIO EMILIO

VIA PAOLO EMILIO

VIA DEI GRACCHI

MONDADORI

GUJA

VIA LUCREZIO CARO

VIA CICERONE

VIA ENNIO QUIRINO VISCONTI

Pista Ciclabile Lungo Tevere

MO'S GELATERIA

COIN

VIA COLA DI RIENZO

VIA TACITO

VIA GIUSEPPE GIOACHINO BELLI

VIA RIPETTA

VIA DI

VIA COLA

VIA VIRGILIO

PRATI

VIA OVIDIO

PASTICCERIA COLAPICCHIONI 2

L'ARCANGELO

VIA BOEZIO

VIA CRESCENZIO

Piazza Cavour

VIA ALBERICO II

TEMPIO DELLA GRATTACHECCA

PONTE CAVOUR

LAVASECCO
BORGO PIO

BORGO PIO

Piazza Borghese

CORRIDORI

CASTEL SANT'ANGELO

AUDITORIUM DELLA CONCILIAZIONE

TOURIST OFFICE

HOTEL DUE TORRE

VIA DELLA CONCILIAZIONE

VIA SANT'ANGELO

PONTE SANT'ANGELO

Tiber River

PONTE UMBERTO

Piazza Ponte Umberto I

PONTE VITTORIO EMANUELE II

PALAZZO ALTEMPS

VIA DELLA SCROFA

PONTE PRINCIPE AMEDEO

CORSO VITTORIO EMANUELE

PIAZZA NAVONA

Piazza Navona

© MOON.COM

entry 6pm), Fri.-Sat. 10am-10pm (last entry 8pm); €17, audio guide €7, free last Sun. of every month 9am-2pm (last entry 12:30pm); Metro A: Ottaviano or Cipro

The Musei Vaticani are really 26 museums, galleries, collections, pavilions, chapels, and rooms in one extraordinary museum exhibiting over 20,000 works of art. The six million visitors who arrive every year soon realize that visiting them all in a day is impossible.

Instead, focus on what you like, and make a plan. The most popular destinations are the Raphael Rooms and Sistine Chapel, but there's also ancient and modern art, Etruscan

and Egyptian relics, papal vehicles and apartments, and a whole lot more. Fortunately, there's a good **audio guide** (€7) that can be reserved in advance and a range of official tours conducted by enthusiastic guides. Perhaps the most spectacular of these is the **Vatican Full Day Tour** (Sat. 8am-5:30pm; €41) of the museum and Pontifical Villas in Castel Gandolfo. Participants ride a special train from the Vatican City station and visit the gardens and estate on the outskirts of Rome where the Pope spends his summer holidays. Another original option is attending

the **Night Visits** (7pm-11pm, reservations required; €21 or €28 with audio guide) held every Friday April-October, and includes a classical music concert. An open **bus tour** (€20) of the Vatican gardens is also available.

Getting into the Vatican Museums is like entering a small airport, with long lines, security checks, and metal detectors. The general line stretches around the Vatican walls and can keep visitors waiting for over an hour. Avoid it by reserving your ticket (€4 reservation fee) and audio guide, if you want one, in advance. In line, you're likely to be approached by ticket touts offering to save you time. Their markup is double or three times the museum reservation fee.

The Vatican Museums have a strict **dress code.** Low-cut or sleeveless clothing, shorts, miniskirts, and hats are not permitted. Food and drink cannot be consumed inside, and large bags, umbrellas, and selfie sticks must be checked at the cloakroom (free). There are several outdoor gardens where visitors can seek refuge from the crowds and enjoy a snack or drink at one of two cafés. Video registration and photography are not allowed inside the Sistine Chapel, but you can take pictures of everything else as long as you don't use a flash. Maps are available at the upper entrance and a food court with five dining options on the ground floor.

There's a lot to see, and tourists on a tight schedule head directly to the Sistine Chapel rather than exploring other parts of the museum. If you have time, start with the **Museo Profano** on the ground floor and explore the **Museo Pio Clementino** on the first before getting drawn into the procession toward the Raphael Rooms and Sistine Chapel. Later, relax on the terrace or in the gardens, and take a break from art in the underground **Padiglione delle Carrozze** where popemobiles and carriages are kept.

During COVID outbreaks, reservations to the Vatican are mandatory, and visitors must arrive within 30 minutes of their scheduled entry. Masks must be worn at all times and minibus tours of the gardens are limited to 12 passengers to facilitate social distancing. Some snack bars will be closed and opening hours may be altered.

MUSEO GREGORIANO PROFANO

The Museo Profano (Profane Museum, so-called because Greek and Roman art were viewed as unholy by the Catholic church), near the entrance to the Vatican Museums, is often overlooked by visitors in the rush toward the museum's more glamorous possessions. That's a shame since it houses one of the best collections of Roman antiquity in the world. These aren't fragments of statues with heads or arms missing like you might see in the Forum but pristine works of ancient art that reveal how Romans looked and how they wanted to be remembered. There are busts of emperors, statues of gods, elaborate sarcophaguses, and colorful ancient mosaics. Many of the sculptures were carefully studied by Michelangelo and his contemporaries and helped establish the artistic aesthetics on which the Renaissance was founded. Their historic value is beyond calculation, and visitors can sit on benches to contemplate their beauty. This section of the museum opened in 1844 and includes a restoration workshop upstairs where visitors can watch restorers at work.

MUSEO PIO-CLEMENTINO

Museo Pio-Clementino is on the second floor and far less crowded than the Sistine Chapel. It's a museum unto itself with several large rooms, galleries, and an immense corridor containing the classical Roman sculpture that formed the nucleus of the Vatican's initial collection. The most famous piece is the *Laocoön* located in an octagonal courtyard. The 1st-century AD work was unearthed in Nero's villa near the Colosseum and depicts a Trojan priest punished for warning his fellow citizens about a large wooden gift horse. The collection is filled with mosaics and portraits

1: St. Peter's Basilica 2: the Round Room inside the Vatican Museums 3: Ponte Sisto 4: spiral staircase at the Vatican Museums

Mission Michelangelo: Rome

Sculpture, painting, urban planning, and architecture: Michelangelo Buonarroti (1475-1564) could do it all. He was recognized as a genius nearly from the moment he picked up a chisel, and spent his long life executing high-profile commissions for cardinals, popes, and princes. Not only did he have a monumental reputation, but he was also prolific in many different fields and combined frenetic periods of nonstop creativity with long bouts of idleness. What he produced has captivated viewers for half a millennium and inspired generations of artists. The majority of his works are in Rome and Florence, which makes a Michelangelo pilgrimage possible.

THE VATICAN

The Sistine Chapel contains the mother of all ceilings, a project that took Michelangelo four years to complete and recounts man's ascent to heaven. Two decades after the frescoes were finished, Pope Clement VII recalled the artist to paint *The Last Judgment* in the same chapel. It's a rare opportunity to compare Michelangelo's creative evolution and witness how changing politics influenced his brushstrokes (page 76).

One of Michelangelo's earliest sculptures, the *Pietà,* is now safely behind glass after being vandalized in 1972. The figure of the lifeless Christ in the arms of Mary still makes a big impression. Although commissioned as a funeral monument, it was later moved to St. Peter's and is the only work signed by the artist (page 69).

Michelangelo wasn't just paid to decorate the Vatican; he also had a hand in its physical expansion. He was appointed chief architect in 1564 and spent most of his time planning the dome. Although he died before its completion, his designs served as the blueprint for what was later built.

PALAZZO FARNESE

To see a building that Michelangelo had a hand in completing, cross the Tiber and head to Palazzo Farnese. The building's third-floor facade and its elaborate cornices are all his doing, along with the renovation of the inner courtyard that can be visited upon request from the French embassy, which occupies the palace today (page 62).

PIAZZA DEL CAMPIDOGLIO

Pope Paul III commissioned Michelangelo to renovate Piazza del Campidoglio and give what was then a dilapidated part of Rome new splendor. The resulting urban plan took four years to complete and required realigning the square with St. Peter's, constructing a *palazzo,* and adding new facades to the existing buildings. Michelangelo also looked after the smaller details and it was his idea to place the equestrian statue in the center of the square (page 56).

of emperors who have surprisingly contemporary faces. The ornate ceilings are nearly as stunning as the artwork.

RAPHAEL ROOMS

While Michelangelo was busy painting the Sistine Chapel, Pope Julius II put Raphael to work decorating his personal chambers, known today as the Raphael Rooms. It took the artist 12 years to paint large sections of the four interconnecting rooms, and he died

before completing the project. What he left behind rivals the Sistine Chapel in brilliance if not size.

The largest room is Sala di Costantino, which was used for formal receptions and completed by students of Raphael after the artist's death. The main theme on the walls and ceiling is the life and times of Constantine, Rome's first Christian emperor. Stanza di Eliodoro was reserved for private audiences with the Pope and the second room

Michelangelo's *Pietà* in St. Peter's Basilica

SAN PIETRO IN VINCOLI

Anyone who was someone wanted Michelangelo to build their funeral tombs, and Pope Giulius II chose the great artist to construct his. Unfortunately, the pontiff died before the project's completion and the work was moved to San Pietro in Vincoli (Piazza di San Pietro in Vincolo 4a) rather than the Vatican where it was originally intended. Michelangelo sculpted a muscular Moses (1513-15) who sits in the center of the tomb and is notable for its anatomical perfection and long, lifelike beard. Michelangelo famously altered the statue years later so that Moses looks pensively to the side.

SANTA MARIA SOPRA MINERVA

Michelangelo also undertook a private commission for a statue of Jesus inside Santa Maria sopra Minerva (Piazza della Minerva 42), a small Gothic church near the Pantheon. The 7-foot (2-meter) statue of *Cristo della Minerva* (1518) is actually a second version, as the first suffered from a crack in the marble and forced the artist to start over. The second version was hastily delivered from Florence and suffered from the journey. Michelangelo offered to sculpt a third version, but the impatient client refused. The statue, originally intended as a nude, is notable for its intricate posture and lifelike nature—the bronze loincloth was added later.

Raphael painted. The pictures have a political undertone and illustrate key episodes of the Old Testament and God's relation to the Catholic Church.

Stanza della Segnatura, the first room Raphael painted, contains the most stunning works. *La Disputa* portrays saints, doctors, and laborers debating the meaning of the Bible while Christ offers himself as a sacrifice for sin. *The School of Athens,* on the opposite wall, depicts a meeting of philosophers

and includes Plato and Aristotle in the center of the fresco as well as a self-portrait Raphael included at the extreme right of the fresco. Raphael also painted a tribute to his artistic rival (Michelangelo) in the bottom left after seeing the Sistine Chapel for the first time.

The last room is **Stanza dell'Incendio di Borgo,** which was used as a meeting and dining room. Raphael had his students do most of the work here, and the paintings symbolize the aspirations of Pope Leon X. They tell the stories of his papal predecessors and depict the coronation of Charles the Great.

All four rooms are extremely crowded. Parts of the first room are currently undergoing restoration scheduled for completion in 2022.

★ SISTINE CHAPEL
(Cappella Sistina)

The Sistine Chapel is where cardinals gather to elect new popes and up to 15,000 visitors a day come to see the greatest fresco in the world. The chapel is long and narrow with a ceiling that's 65 feet (20 meters) high. Skipping it is like leaving the Louvre without seeing the *Mona Lisa*. When it comes to frescoes, nothing is bigger or more impressive.

The chapel owes its magnificence to the single-minded determination and back-breaking effort of Michelangelo. He wasn't supposed to paint it, though. One of his jealous contemporaries who thought the artist could only sculpt convinced the pope to give Michelangelo the commission hoping he would fail. Genius, however, has no limits, and the masterpiece fresco instantly increased Michelangelo's fame.

The ceiling consists of more than 300 figures and took four years of near constant work to complete. A special theological committee determined what scenes to depict and chose episodes from the book of Genesis to make up the central spine of the vault where the *Creation of Adam* and *Temptation* are portrayed. Michelangelo did the rest and worked alone on special scaffolding that allowed him to cover every corner of the 12,000-square-foot (1,115-square-meter) ceiling.

The fresco was an immediate hit and resulted in Michelangelo being appointed the Vatican's chief architect, sculptor, and painter. Pope Paul III later commissioned him to paint the two walls on either end of the chapel; however, only *The Last Judgment* was completed. It covers the entire altar wall and depicts humanity lining up to be condemned or saved by an athletic-looking Jesus flanked by his mother and various saints. Down below are the flames of hell and desperate sinners escorted to their fate by grotesque demons, while angels point to pages of the Bible and trumpet the word of God. It's powerful and took the master even longer to complete than the ceiling. Some of the nudity was later covered up but the work remains stunning by any standard.

Reaching the Sistine Chapel is a small journey, and once you start following the signs, you'll be caught up in a current of visitors all headed to the same place. Along the way you'll pass dozens of rooms (including the Raphael Rooms) and head up and down stairs until you reach a small door leading to the extraordinary chapel.

The Sistine Chapel is the climax of the Vatican Museums and doesn't disappoint. What is slightly disheartening are the museum guards mechanically ushering tourists forward, reminding everyone that photography is prohibited, and periodically using the PA system to silence crowds. There is no time limit for visiting the chapel, so spend as long as you like gazing on a masterpiece. Try to snag a seat on the benches along the side walls to avoid craning your neck.

PINACOTECA

The Pinacoteca houses 460 paintings, tapestries, and statues arranged chronologically from the 12th to the 19th century in 18 elegant rooms. The picture gallery is a relatively recent addition to the Vatican Museums and only opened in 1932. The collection includes works by all-time greats like Giotto, Beato Angelico, Perugino, Raphael, and Tiziano. Many of the paintings in the first nine rooms were created on wood and are highly religious in nature, while canvas and perspective dominate the rest of the gallery.

Room 8 is entirely devoted to Raphael and where his vibrantly colored *Transfiguration* hangs. This was his last work and destined for France, but Cardinal Giulio de' Medici changed his mind after the artist's death. Like many paintings in the museum it was confiscated and moved to Paris during Napoleon's brief reign of Italy and returned after his defeat. In the small room next door is Leonardo da Vinci's unfinished *St. Jerome*, which has puzzled art historians for decades. The second-to-last room contains the clay models Bernini made before casting the larger bronze versions that now decorate St. Peter's Square.

PADIGLIONE DELLE CARROZZE

This underground collection of pontifical vehicles is one of the most interesting parts of the museum, especially for younger visitors. Here you'll find every form of transportation ever used by popes, starting with handheld carriers and evolving to elaborate papal carriages, the first automobiles, and modern popemobiles including the model Pope John Paul II was riding during his attempted assassination in 1981. The underground entrance to the pavilion is outside near the museum café.

Castel Sant'Angelo

Lungotevere Castello 50; tel. 06/681-9111; www. castelsantangelo.com; daily 9am-7:30pm; €15 or RomaPass; Buses 23 or 40

Castel Sant'Angelo didn't start out as the castle, prison, or papal safe house it later became, but as a mausoleum for Emperor Hadrian. Respect for the dead did not outlive the fall of the empire, and the castle was repeatedly modified over the centuries. The walls were enlarged in 1277 and the **Vatican Corridor,** which allowed popes to quickly and safely reach the castle in times of unrest, was added.

The monument gets its name from the Archangel Michael, who allegedly appeared in AD 590 and whose statue now adorns the tower on top. There are many rooms to explore around this six-story monument, including the prison cell where Florentine sculpture Benvenuto Cellini was locked up and more comfortable apartments where popes slept and Vatican fortunes were stored. The terrace provides a 360-degree view of the city and there's a nice rooftop bar serving soft drinks and beer. Lines to enter are short and there are three distinct itineraries to follow.

Hadrian built the bridge known as **Ponte Sant'Angelo** to connect his mausoleum with the city. Pope Clement VII added statues of Peter and Paul, and Bernini lined the parapets with musically inclined angels. Today, itinerant salesmen hawk fake designer bags to passing tourists on their way to and from the Vatican.

TRASTEVERE
Ponte Sisto

Ponte Sisto is one of the oldest bridges in Rome and connects Trastevere with the rest of the city. It was named after Pope Sixtus IV, who opened the bridge in 1474 and financed the endeavor by taxing prostitutes. The Renaissance were boom years for the oldest profession in a city of barely 50,000. Flooding destroyed previous bridges on this site and the remains of the ancient Roman Pons Auerelio were incorporated into the medieval version. The round hole in the center served as a flood alert—if water reaches that level, it's time to head for the hills. On most days someone is playing music, drawing, or selling fake Gucci on the pedestrian bridge spanning the Tiber.

Piazza Trilussa

Piazza Trilussa lies across the street from the Ponte Sisto bridge and is named after the Roman poet Carlo Alberto Salustri (1871-1950), who wrote under the pseudonym Trilussa. There's a sculpture of him on one side of the square and an elaborate fountain on the other reached by a short flight of steps. The square is the main entrance to the neighborhood and a popular weekend meeting place. It starts filling up with locals most afternoons and remains lively until well after midnight.

Villa Farnesina

Via della Lungara 230; tel. 06/6802-7268; www. villafarnesina.it; Mon.-Sat. 9am-2pm, second Sun. of the month 9am-5pm; €10 with audio guide; Buses 23, 125, 280

Trastevere

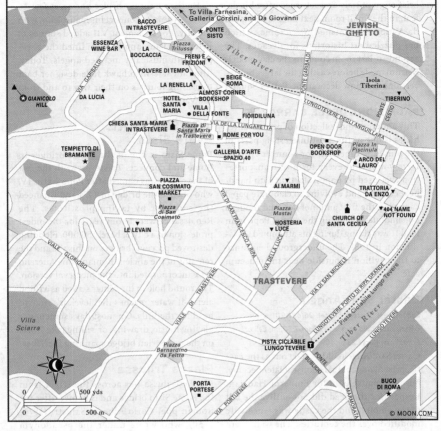

To Villa Farnesina, Galleria Corsini, and Da Giovanni

JEWISH GHETTO

BACCO IN TRASTEVERE
PONTE SISTO
ESSENZA WINE BAR
Piazza Trilussa
LA BOCCACCIA
FRENI E FRIZIONI
POLVERE DI TEMPO
BEIGE ROMA
LA RENELLA
ALMOST CORNER BOOKSHOP
GIANICOLO HILL
DA LUCIA
HOTEL SANTA MARIA
VILLA DELLA FONTE
FIORDILUNA
CHIESA SANTA MARIA IN TRASTEVERE
Piazza di Santa Maria in Trastevere
ROME FOR YOU
VIA DELLA LUNGARETTA
TEMPIETTO DI BRAMANTE
GALLERIA D'ARTE SPAZIO 40
OPEN DOOR BOOKSHOP
Piazza In Piscinula
ARCO DEL LAURO
PIAZZA SAN COSIMATO MARKET
AI MARMI
TRATTORIA DA ENZO
Piazza di San Cosimato
Piazza Mastai
404 NAME NOT FOUND
LE LEVAIN
HOSTERIA LUCE
CHURCH OF SANTA CECILIA
VIALE GLORIOSO
VIA DI SAN FRANCESCO A RIPA
VIA DELLA LUCE
TRASTEVERE
VIA DI SAN MICHELE
Villa Sciarra
VIALE DI TRASTEVERE
LUNGOTEVERE PORTO DI RIPA GRANDE
Pista Ciclabile Lungotevere
Tiber River
Piazza Bernardino da Feltra
PISTA CICLABILE LUNGOTEVERE
SUBLICIO PONTE
PORTA PORTESE
VIA PORTUENSE
MARMORATA
BUCO DI ROMA

Tiber River
PONTE GARIBALDI
Isola Tiberina
TIBERINO
LUNGOTEVERE DEGLI ANGUILLARA
PONTE CESTIO
LUNGOTEVERE

0   500 yds
0   500 m

© MOON.COM

When the wealthiest banker in Rome decided to build himself a villa in 1506, his goal was to set a new standard in palace design. Villa Farnesina did just that. The building's deceptively simple plan of a central block with two projecting wings is enhanced through the paintings and imagination of its architect Baldassarre Peruzzi, who also worked on St. Peter's. His *Salone delle Prospettive* on the second floor creates the illusion of looking out on 16th-century Rome and changes depending on the viewer's position. Raphael was hired to decorate the **Loggia of Psyche** on the

ground floor, which has a distinctly botanic theme and depicts over 200 different plants including some varieties imported from the Americas.

Only part of the original gardens remains; however, what is present was replanted according to the original designs. There are many ornamental species and a small collection of ancient relics. Garden and villa tours (€12) in English are available every Saturday at 10am while performances of Renaissance era music (€18) are organized on the second Sunday of each month at 12:30pm. Visitors with a Vatican Museum ticket stub receive a

Wandering Trastevere

Trastevere is known for its bohemian medieval charm and uneven cobblestone streets where maps can be set aside and every direction invites exploration. Backtracking and going around in circles are part of the fun of this maze-like neighborhood that doesn't go out of its way to satisfy tourists. Wandering off from the main thoroughfare you'll discover narrow alleys, dead ends, vine-covered facades, and graffiti of all kinds. The colors of the houses are a delightful patchwork of worn-out red, yellow, and orange, and the plants and flowers stationed next to doorways provide the greenery.

a typical street in Trastevere

Trastevere is divided in two by **Viale Trastevere**. The half opposite Isola Tiberina is smaller and less trafficked than the other side where most visitors tend to congregate. The pedestrianized **Via Lungaretta** links both and provides a good introduction to the area, which can also be entered by crossing the **Ponte Sisto** bridge. Both lead to **Piazza di Santa Maria** in the center of the neighborhood, around which many restaurants and bars are clustered and from where there are plenty of streets to explore. If you arrive in the morning you can shop for vegetables or watch locals getting their groceries at the **Piazza San Cosimato market** south of Piazza Santa Maria. If you walk uphill, you'll eventually reach the Gianicolo terrace overlooking the city and can visit **Tempietto di Bramante** along the way or come back at night and join the crowd of locals socializing in **Piazza Trilussa**.

---

discount. Flash photography and video are not permitted inside the palace.

Galleria Corsini

Via della Lungara 10; tel. 06/6880-2323; www.barberinicorsini.org; Wed.-Mon. 8:30am-7pm; €12; Buses 23, 125, 280

Before housing Galleria Corsini, Palazzo Corsini was a residence for cardinals and noblemen, including Cardinal Neri Corsini, for whom the palace was named. Over the course of its long history the building has hosted Michelangelo, Erasmus, and Queen Christina of Sweden. Today the gallery is part of Rome's National Galleries of Ancient Art and filled with a first-rate collection of 17th- and 18th-century Italian and European paintings including Rubens, Van Dyck, and many more. The elaborate frescoed interiors

of the *palazzo* are nearly as interesting as the artwork hanging on the walls. The ticket also provides entry to **Palazzo Barberini** (Via delle Quattro Fontane 13).

Piazza di Santa Maria in Trastevere

Piazza Santa Maria, which fronts the church of the same name, is the heart of Trastevere, and the fountain in the middle is one of the oldest in the city. Carlo Fontana, who also designed the fountains in St. Peter's Square, gave it a makeover in the 17th century. Street musicians, tourists, and local children often occupy the steps around the fountain. There are several outdoor cafés lining the square from where the church and street life can be observed in comfort.

According to legend, the church, **Chiesa**

Santa Maria in Trastevere (Piazza Santa Maria in Trastevere; tel. 06/581-4802; daily 7:30am-9pm, Aug. 8am-noon and 4pm-9pm; free; Tram 8, Buses 23, 125, 280) dates back to a dispute early Christians had with tavern keepers in the area. One party wanted a place to worship and the other a place to drink. The matter reached the attention of Emperor Alexander Severus, who sided with the fledgling religious order, preferring faith over revelry. This church was built, rebuilt, remodeled many times since the 3rd century, and its present form dates from Pope Innocent II in 1140. It's notable for the external mosaics, added in the 13th and 14th centuries, which represent the Virgin Mary and Child. The mosaics continue inside with a series illustrating the life of the Virgin Mary.

Church of Santa Cecilia
(Chiesa Santa Cecilia)

Piazza di Santa Cecilia 22; tel. 06/589-9289; daily 10am-1pm and 4pm-7pm; free; Tram 8, Buses 23, 125, 280

Chiesa Santa Cecilia lies on Trastevere's less-visited side and was commissioned by Pope Pascal I in 821 in honor of a martyred saint who resisted her torturers through song before being beheaded. The church complex includes a convent, bell tower, cloister, and the immense *Last Judgment* fresco by Pietro Cavallini (weekdays 10am-12:30pm, weekends 11:30am-12:30pm; €3) located in the choir of the nuns. The fresco is one of the finest examples of medieval painting in existence, and the church is rarely crowded. Guided tours are available during morning opening hours.

Tempietto di Bramante

Via Garibaldi 33; tel. 06/581-3940; Tues.-Sun. 10am-6pm; free; Bus 115, 125

The Tempietto di Bramante was designed by Bramante between 1502 and 1507 and commemorates the site where St. Peter was martyred. The circular temple set a new standard for proportions and became a model for countless other buildings in the 16th century. Gian Lorenzo Bernini built the entrance of the

crypt more than 100 years later. Inside stands a statue of the saint dating from the same period. The temple is entered through the adjacent Spanish Academy and hosts frequent art exhibitions and events.

★ Gianicolo Hill
(Colle del Gianicolo)

Buses 115, 870

Trastevere is generally flat, but the farther you walk from the river, the steeper it gets. Gianicolo Hill flanks the western edge of the neighborhood and is a popular panoramic gathering spot for locals and visitors. At the top is a long terrace with one of the best views of the city, from where the Pantheon, Vittoriano monument, and the historic center are visible. Nearby is a small café and amusement area for kids. A cannon is fired daily at noon just below the terrace. Pope Pio IX started the tradition in 1846 to synchronize Roman church bells. It's a 15-20-minute walk to Gianicolo up the back streets of Via Garibaldi and Via Porta di San Pancrazio with plenty of stairs along the way and several water fountains from which to rehydrate.

AVENTINO AND TESTACCIO
Protestant Cemetery
(Cimitero Acattolico)

Via Caio Cestio 6; tel. 06/574-1900; www. cemeteryrome.it; Mon.-Sat. 9am-5pm, Sun. 9am-1pm; free; Metro B: Piramide

The Protestant Cemetery is a romantic escape from the city. Located on a quiet side street, it's an oasis of tranquility, filled with stray cats and tombstones. A small visitor center provides maps of the cemetery and other information. On Monday and Wednesday mornings kind volunteers can answer questions or point you toward **Keats's tomb.** *Here lies One Whose name was Writ in Water* appears on the poet's gravestone and is hard to beat as epitaphs go. The cemetery is the best

1: Chiesa Santa Maria in Trastevere 2: the Diocletian Baths

place to observe the Pyramid and Aurelian walls away from traffic and underneath the shade of umbrella pines.

Piramide di Cestio (Piazzale Ostiense; tel. 06/3996-7700) is one of the largest and most impressive ancient tombs in Rome. It's the result of an Egyptian fad that started after Caesar's conquest of Egypt in 30 BC that also explains why there are so many obelisks in the city. The structure was incorporated into the defensive walls, and Latin inscriptions indicate it was built in only 330 days. (Caius expressly stated in his will if it wasn't completed within that time his heirs would miss out on a hefty inheritance, and the incentive worked.) Renovation returned the monument to its ancient splendor. Tours of the inner chamber are organized every second and fourth Saturday of the month and must be reserved in advance by telephone.

Nearby is the **Rome War Cemetery** where British soldiers are interred. The Allies invaded the Italian mainland on September 3, 1943, but the advance was bloody and a breakthrough wasn't achieved until Monte Cassino was captured. Rome was liberated on June 3, 1944, and the cemetery started shortly afterward. It contains 426 Commonwealth soldiers and can be visited any time. The combination to the padlock on the entrance doors is 1221.

Aurelian Walls

Piazzale Ostiense; Metro B: Piramide

The Aurelian Walls, which flank both Testaccio and Aventino, were built during the late empire when foreign invasions became a real threat. Much of the fortifications are still standing and in impregnable condition. **St. Paul's Gate** (Porto San Paolo) was and remains one of the strategic entrances to the city. It consists of two imposing towers with living quarters where soldiers were permanently stationed.

The ancient gateway now contains the small and rarely visited **Museum of the Ostian Way** (Piazzale Ostiense; tel. 06/574-3193; Tues.-Sun. 9am-1pm; free). Walking along the narrow corridors provides a feel for

Roman military architecture and a detailed model shows how the area appeared in ancient times. There's an excellent view of the Pyramid from the terrace at the top.

The next gate east is **Porta San Sebastiano** which contains the **Museum of the Walls** (Via Porta San Sebastiano 18; tel. 06/0608; Tues.-Sun. 9am-2pm; free). It's the only place in Rome where you can stroll along a section of the Aurelian walls and get a feel for what it was like to defend the city from invasion. The museum is a pleasant 25-minute walk or 10-minute bike ride from Piramide.

Monte Testaccio

Via Nicola Zabaglia 24; €4; Metro B: Piramide

Monte Testaccio is an ancient Roman dumping ground. The hill stands 164 feet (50 meters) high and consists of discarded *amphorae* (clay vases), which were used to carry oil from Spain and other Roman provinces to the warehouses lining the Tiber River. Jars could not be reused because of the residue that remained and were smashed after being emptied, then piled up here. The area is now a popular nighttime retreat for young Romans who gather in the bars and restaurants that surround the artificial hill. Visits must be reserved in advance by contacting the **Rome Tourist Office** (tel. 06/0608), and expect a steep climb to the top where there's a decent view and plenty of ancient fragments.

Testaccio Market
(Mercato di Testaccio)

Mon.-Sat. 6am-3:30pm; Metro B: Piramide

Mercato di Testaccio is located across the street from the Mattatoio meatpacking district. The large covered space is clean and airy, with over 100 stalls selling fruit, bread, cheese, wine, housewares, clothes, and more. There's a pleasant bar with outdoor seating near the main entrance and another inside the complex near the remains of the Roman road uncovered during construction. Arrive with an appetite and browse the stalls until you find what you need for an impromptu picnic. **Box 15** is run by Sergio and Giuliano, who prepare traditional beef sandwiches for €4. Sandra Dominici serves local red and white wine at **Box 7** by the plastic glass (€0.50) or bottle (€3).

Entrances to the market are at Via Beniamino Franklin, Via Alessandro Volta, Via Aldo Manuzio, and Via Lorenzo Ghiberti.

Buco di Roma

Piazza dei Cavalieri di Malta; Metro B: Piramide or Circo Massimo

Most of the sites and curiosities of Aventino can be found along Via di Santa Sabina. One of the most popular is the Buco di Roma or Hole of Rome. At first glance, it appears to be an ordinary keyhole in a big door, but wait your turn to look through it and you'll get a surprising close-up view of a certain church dome. Lines can be long during the summer, but they move quickly and the optical illusion doesn't disappoint.

Church of Santa Sabina
(Chiesa Santa Sabina)

Piazza Pietro d'Illaria 1; tel. 06/575-0675; daily 7:15am-8pm; Metro B: Circo Massimo

Chiesa Santa Sabina dates from the 5th century and is one of the best-preserved early Christian churches in Rome. The outside gives little hint of the enormous space within, which is pleasantly cool on hot summer days. The flat roof covers two rows of giant columns recycled from the Roman Temple of Juno on the same site. The only ornate part of the basilica is the small chapel on the far side, which has colorful frescoes that were added during the Middle Ages.

Entry is through the side door, which was customary in ancient Roman architecture. The main entrance that links the church with the adjacent monastery was added later and is rarely opened. The large doors are covered in glass to protect some of the oldest wooden Christian carvings (AD 430-432) in existence. One of the 18 surviving panels features an early depiction of Christ's crucifixion. Mass is held on Sundays at 8am, 10:30am, and 11:30am (sung).

TERMINI
★ Palazzo Massimo

Largo di Villa Peretti 1; tel. 06/3996-7701; Tues.-Sun. 9am-7:45pm; €10 or €12 combined ticket, audio guide €5; Metro A or B: Termini

Palazzo Massimo contains the finest collection of ancient Roman mosaics in the world. It's not just fragments but entire pavements recovered from local villas and mounted in special casings hung on the walls. Mosaics were a prized art form and wealthy Romans used them to decorate their homes. They provide colorful clues about the owner's interests and daily life. Republican- and Imperial-age frescoes and statues are also on display inside this modern, easy-to-navigate museum. Start from the top floor and work your way down. The staff is friendly and eager to explain how archeologists recovered relics, and the techniques used to create the ancient images. Perhaps the most stunning of these is the 360-degree garden painting, reminiscent of Monet's water lilies, recovered from a nearby villa. The basement houses a small collection of jewelry, the mummified corpse of a young girl, and an extensive coin collection. Videos help visitors imagine how the works of art once appeared, and the audio guide is clear and insightful.

Palazzo Massimo is one of four branches of the **Museo Nazionale Romano** (National Museum of Rome) and a combined ticket allows entry to all four sites.

Diocletian Baths
(Terme di Diocleziano)

Viale Enrico de Nicola 76; tel. 06/3996-7701; Tues.-Sun. 9am-7:30pm; €10 or €12 combined ticket; Metro A or B: Termini

The Terme di Diocleziano are also part of the Museo Nazionale Romano and located diagonally across the street from Palazzo Massimo. They originally covered 32 acres (hectares) and could accommodate up to 3,000 bathers (twice as many as the Baths of Caracalla). The complex was transformed during the 16th century when Pope Pio IV commissioned Michelangelo to build the **Basilica di**

Santa Maria degli Angeli e dei Martiri. Like many ancient buildings the baths were stripped of useful materials during the Middle Ages and partially transformed into a church. Scores of relics and statues did remain and many of these now line the large courtyard. A short film shows how the baths once looked, and although the marble was stripped and the roof gave way long ago, a sense of grandeur remains. The museum also includes a section devoted to communication in the ancient world and a collection of prehistoric relics discovered in the region.

Basilica di Santa Maria Maggiore

Piazza di Santa Maria Maggiore 42;
tel. 06/6988-6817; daily 7am-6:45pm; free; Metro B: Cavour

There are five major basilicas in Rome. St. Peter's gets the most attention, but Basilica di Santa Maria Maggiore is just as breathtaking, and the one locals consider the most beautiful. The front facade doesn't look much like a church and if it wasn't for the medieval bell tower you might mistake it for something else. It was built on top of an older church beginning in AD 423 under the orders of Pope Sisto III and progressively aggrandized over the centuries. That included adding magnificent marble flooring, placing mosaics along the walls, and installing a finely carved wooden ceiling. It is of particular importance to pilgrims who come to

behold the ancient relics dating from Jesus's nativity stored in the crypt and church museum. Bernini, who created several of the statues decorating the chapels, is buried inside. Security has been tightened recently and metal detectors are now used to check all visitors entering the basilica. Mass is celebrated daily at 8am, 10am, noon, and 6pm. Confessionals lining the right nave of the basilica are manned by multilingual priests throughout the day.

Large crowds gather every year on August 5 to celebrate the legendary foundation of the church. According to legend the Madonna appeared in a dream to a wealthy Roman and instructed him to build a basilica wherever he found snow. He found it here, and today locals celebrate the miracle with artificial snow and live music.

Palazzo delle Esposizione

Via Nazionale 194; tel. 06/696-271; www.
palazzoesposizioni.it; Tues.-Thurs, Sun. 10am-8pm,
Fri.-Sat. 10am-10:30pm; €10-15, free audio guide
app; Metro A: Repubblica

There's always something interesting going on at the Palazzo delle Esposizione. It's the largest exhibition space in the historic center and puts on a half dozen shows a year dedicated to contemporary artists and issues. The grand 19th-century building was recently restored, and a rooftop restaurant added that is a pleasant stop before or after a visit. For a quick bite or coffee, check out the café on the lower level.

Food

Eating in Rome is a pleasure. There are thousands of restaurants in the city, from simple take-out only pizza shops to historic *trattorie* serving local specialties. The dining scene, however, isn't stuck in the past. New establishments open every week. The best put a gastronomic twist on old favorites and an emphasis on quality. And although most travelers come to Rome with visions of

pasta and pizza in their stomachs, that is far from all the city has to offer. There is a delicious variety of food from around the world, served in restaurants run by first-, second-, or third-generation families who have established themselves within the Roman culinary firmament.

That doesn't mean you can't have a bad meal in Rome—you can, especially if you stick

Best Food and Drink

★ **Caffè Sant'Eustachio:** Coffee is serious business in Rome, but to understand just how serious you need to order an espresso here (page 93).

★ **Gelateria dei Gracchi:** Ingredients make the difference between good gelato and great gelato, and here they only use the best (page 96).

★ **Trattoria da Enzo:** Eat like a Roman at this no-nonsense *trattoria* and discover what a three-course meal should taste like (page 99).

★ **Chiosco Testaccio:** Watch as blocks of ice are scraped into plastic cups and covered in refreshing fruit syrups at this friendly neighborhood kiosk (page 101).

★ **Er Buchetto:** This miniscule neighborhood institution has been serving famous roasted-pork sandwiches since 1890 (page 103).

★ **Blackmarket Hall:** Sip late-night cocktails next to funky Romans at this retro hangout (page 104).

to main streets around major monuments where tourists gather. Eating well requires curiosity and a bit of nosing about before committing to a restaurant.

Breakfast is not the most important meal for Romans. Locals start the day with an espresso and may have a *cornetto* pastry. *Cornetto* are the Roman version of the croissant, served in the morning at bars and bakeries around the city. They come in many varieties including plain, whole wheat, chocolate, jelly, or cream, and go well with cappuccino. Romans eat them standing at the counter and don't tend to linger over breakfast—the meal is usually over in less than five minutes and a precursor to the main gastronomic events, which are lunch and dinner. These can involve numerous courses and generally begin with an appetizer, followed by a first course of pasta, and second course of fish or meat with a side of vegetables. Dessert and espresso round out a meal, although coffee is rarely ordered after dinner and Romans never drink cappuccino after 11am. Wine can be ordered by the glass, carafe, or bottle, and dinners often end with a digestif liquor.

ANCIENT ROME AND MONTI

Other than a café at the top of the Vittoriano monument and expensive snack bars lining Via dei Fori Imperiali, choices in the Ancient Rome area are limited. Avoid restaurants facing the Colosseum. The view may be good, but the pasta is likely to have been frozen a few minutes before arriving at your table. For authentic flavors, explore the streets of **Monti.** (In particular, there are dozens of tempting options along **Via Urbana.**) The neighborhood has plenty of culinary variety and you'll find noodles, tacos, and crepes along with traditional fare. The local covered market, **Mercato al Circo Massimo,** is also a great destination for foodies to browse fresh ingredients and indulge in local specialties.

Roman
PASTA CHEF
Via Baccina 42; tel. 06/488-3198; daily 12:30pm-9:30pm; €6-8; Metro B: Cavour
Pasta can be fast, cheap, and delicious. If you don't want to sit down for a long lunch and don't mind eating at a counter, this is the place to take your pick from nine different pastas,

including Roman classics like *carbonara* and *amatriciana* along with regional specials like pesto, ragù Bolognese, and vegetarian lasagna. Just get in line, order, and wait for your name to be called. The only drawback is the absence of a bathroom.

OSTERIA LA CARBONARA

Via Panisperna 214; tel. 06/482-5176; www. lacarbonara.it; Mon.-Sat. 12:30pm-2:30pm and 7pm-11pm; €10-14; Metro B: Cavour

When you've been serving food for over 100 years in a working-class neighborhood and haven't had to change your signage in 50, the pasta can't be bad. That's the case with La Carbonara, and the restaurant's namesake is a good dish to order. The Rossi family is a friendly bunch, and the typical Roman plates Simone and Nando bring out from the kitchen are memorable. The small restaurant focuses on flavors rather than décor, notable for the walls covered in scribbled messages from past patrons. Ask for a pen if you want to add your two cents to the comments on the walls.

BROCCOLETTI

Via Urbana 104; tel. 06/9027-1389; Tues.-Sun. 12:30pm-3pm and 7:30pm-11:30pm; €13-16; Metro B: Cavour

Broccoletti serves classic Roman dishes with a dash of fantasy. The modern interior is simple yet cozy and diners are seated fairly close together, but the real star here is the food. Ingredients are fresh and the young chef prepares a new seasonal menu every three months. Fortunately, the homemade tiramisu is available all year long.

Italian

TRATTORIA MONTI

Via San Vito 13a; tel. 06/446-6573; Tues.-Sun. 1pm-2:45pm and 8pm-10:45pm, closed Sun. dinner; €12-15, Metro A: Vittorio Emanuele

Rome is full of restaurants serving regional Italian food, and Trattoria Monti offers a taste of the Le Marche region. The Camerucci clan has successfully imported Adriatic flavors to Rome, and one taste of the *tortello di rosso*

d'uovo (ravioli-like stuffed pasta) is as good as being there. It's a tranquil eatery tucked between Santa Maria Maggiore and Piazza Vittorio. Reservations recommended on weekends.

Pizza

TRIESTE PIZZA

Via Urbana 112; tel. 06/481-5319; daily 10:30am-11pm; €3-4; Metro B: Cavour

At Trieste Pizza, the pizza has been getting better for three generations. Today the round mini pizzas (called *pizzetta*) are prepared with semi whole wheat grain, extra virgin olive oil, and sausage delivered straight from a butcher in the Abruzzo region. Order takeaway or eat in the small dining area.

ALLE CARRETTE

Via della Madonna dei Monti 95; tel. 06/679-2770; Thurs.-Tues. 11:30am-4pm and 7pm-midnight, Wed. dinner only; €8-10; Metro B: Colosseo or Cavour

There's nothing fancy about Alle Carrette, just good pizza served fast and accompanied by fried starters. It's a popular weekend spot, and on summer nights the best seats are outside at the small wooden tables where most diners are speaking Italian and enjoying cold pints of beer. The total on the handwritten check is a pleasant surprise given the location is so close to the Imperial Forums.

International
CREPES GALETTES

Via Leonina 21a; tel. 06/9437-7696; Wed.-Mon. noon-3pm and 6pm-9pm, Tues. noon-3pm; €5-7; Metro B: Cavour

Sweet or savory? That is the question at Crepes Galettes, and the best answer for taste buds is both. Inside this narrow, modern *creperie* stools line one wall and an open kitchen the other. There are all sorts of fillings whatever your craving and you can watch as crepes come to life behind the glass counter. The house special is *la completa*, with egg, cheese, and ham, which can be followed up with a mouthwatering banana and chocolate dessert crepe.

RISTORANTE CINESE SICHUAN

Via di S. Martino Ai Monti 33c; tel. 06/481-4425;
Wed.-Mon. 11am-3pm and 5:30pm-11pm, Mon.
5:30pm-11pm; €6-10; Metro B: Cavour

Chinese is the most prevalent international food in Rome, but quality varies and many offer the kind of all-you-can-eat buffets that inspire little culinary confidence. That's not the case at Sichuan, where noodles, rice, and vegetable dishes are stir-fried to perfection and served still steaming on your table. Waiters are patient and friendly, and menus include English translations and photos. If you like Chinese, you'll like it even more after eating here.

Snacks and Street Food

ZIA ROSETTA

Via Urbana 54; tel. 06/3105 2516; Mon.-Thurs.
11am-4pm, Fri.-Sun. 11am-10pm; €2-6; Metro B:
Cavour

Rosetta, a traditional Roman bun that resembles a rose, is the star ingredient at Zia Rosetta. This micro sandwich bar 10 minutes from the Colosseum offers more than 30 creative fillings served inside mini- or standard-size buns. They also make fresh salads and mix fruit and vegetable shakes in interesting combinations inside their microscopic but elegant shop.

MERCATO AL CIRCO MASSIMO

Via San Teodoro 74; Sat.-Sun. 8am-3pm; Metro B:
Circo Massimo, Tram 3, Buses 81, 118, 160, 715

Mercato al Circo Massimo is around the corner from the Forum and a good place to fill an empty stomach. The former bus depot is crammed with local producers selling vegetables, bread, cheese, meat, and cold cuts. There are dozens of stands to browse and all the ingredients for a picnic that can be enjoyed on the grassy banks of the Circus Maximus. There's also a kitchen serving a fixed three-course meal. It's cheap, satisfying, and popular with travelers and locals who sit at shared tables in the sunny courtyard where a handful of kiosks dispense wine, juice, and desserts.

Bakeries

PANIFICIO PANELLA

Via Merulana 54; tel. 06/487-2435; daily 8am-10pm;
€5-8; Metro A: Vittorio Emanuele

In Rome, bread is nearly a religion, and few places take it more seriously than Panificio Panella. This is where to try traditional local loaves like the rose-shaped bun known as *rosetta* as well as cakes, tarts, and Italian-style doughnuts. The bar also turns out some of the creamiest cappuccino in town using an antique coffee machine. Every day from 6:30pm-9pm they prepare an extensive all-you-can-eat buffet for €15 that includes a cocktail of your choice, which can be enjoyed on the little square outside.

GREZZO RAW CHOCOLATE

Via Urbana 130; tel. 06/483-443; daily 11:30am-7pm;
€6-10; Metro B: Cavour

It's hard to find anyone who takes chocolate more seriously than the chefs at Grezzo Raw Chocolate, where cacao is an art form. It's never heated above 42°C, is both gluten-free and lactose-free, and comes in so many mouthwatering forms that choosing only one is difficult. There are a multitude of tempting energy balls, cookies, bars, cakes, brownies, ice cream, and bonbons. Prices are high but worth it.

Gelato

FATAMORGANA

Piazza degli Zingari 5; tel. 06/4890-6955; daily
1pm-10pm; €1 per scoop; Metro B: Cavour

Fatamorgana doesn't just serve the usual gelato flavors. This little gelato lab 10 minutes from the Colosseum experiments with unlikely combinations like grapefruit and ginger, rum and coffee, or basil and nuts. There are over 30 to choose from. The friendly staff is happy to provide samples and the little *piazza* outside is the perfect spot to enjoy a cone or cup topped with whipped cream. The fountain is also useful for washing chocolate off hands and faces.

Roman Cuisine

Traditional Roman fare is about getting the most flavor from the humblest ingredients. It's a tale of inventiveness and thrift where nothing is wasted. A good example of that is *fiori di zucchini*, in which zucchini flowers are stuffed with mozzarella and anchovies, then fried. Food in Rome is also very reliant on the seasons. Although many dishes can be enjoyed year-round, others appear only during certain holidays or whenever they are ripe. *Pizza al taglio* (page 92) is always available and a delicious option for those seeking a quick and inexpensive meal.

APPETIZERS (*ANTIPASTI*)

Most menus offer a plate of mixed starters, which is a good introduction to the genre and helps identify favorites.

- *Fiori di zucchini:* Zucchini flowers stuffed with anchovies and mozzarella, dipped in batter, and fried. They are generally served in pizzerias or *trattorie* along with *suppli* and potato croquettes.

- *Suppli:* A rice ball mixed with tomato sauce, stuffed with mozzarella, covered with breadcrumbs, and deep fried.

- *Bruschetta aglio e olio:* A thick slice of toasted country bread rubbed with garlic and seasoned with oil and salt or diced tomatoes.

FIRST COURSES (*PRIMI*)

Every town and region in Italy has its own particular pasta shapes and sauces. In Rome, these dishes are particularly famous and originated as working-class meals made from humble ingredients.

- *Cacio e pepe:* Pasta seasoned with a creamy mix of sharp *cacio* goat cheese and pepper.

- *Pasta all'amatriciana:* Pasta with *guancia di maiale* (pig cheek) and tomato sauce.

- *Pasta alla carbonara:* Spaghetti with egg, bacon, and *Parmigiano* or tangy *pecorino* cheese.

- *Pasta e ceci:* A soup-like dish traditionally served on Fridays consisting of pasta and chickpeas.

GELATERIA DELL'ANGELETTO

Via dell'Angeletto 15; tel. 06/487-4760; daily 11:30am-10:30pm; €3-5; Metro B: Cavour

Down the street and around the corner is another *gelateria* vying to be the neighborhood's best. Gelateria dell'Angeletto has a fine pedigree, with an owner who perfected the craft working at one of the city's historic gelato shops. Now that he's on his own there's more room for creativity, and he experiments with gluten-free and vegan flavors. Portions are generous and can spoil an appetite or substitute a meal. Cones (*coni*) or cups (*coppette*) come in small (*piccolo*), medium (*medio*), or large (*grande*). Whip cream (*panna*) is optional and free of charge.

Coffee
ER BARETTO

Via del Boschetto 132; tel. 06/482-0444; daily 7:30am-11pm; €1-3; Metro B: Cavour

Er is Roman slang for "the," and *etto* is the suffix for "little." This little bar on a side street serves up great coffee and a whole lot more. Feel like a midmorning pastry, fresh-squeezed orange juice, light afternoon snack, or happy

SECOND COURSES (*SECONDI*)

- *Trippa alla romana:* Stewed tripe, onions, and tomatoes.

- *Saltimbocca alla romana:* Veal cutlet topped with a slice of prosciutto ham and sage leaf, cooked in butter and wine.

- *Abbacchio alla romana:* Oven-roasted lamb usually served with roast potatoes. The dish is available year-round but is especially common around Christmas and Easter.

SIDES (*CONTORNI*)

The artichoke holds a central place in Roman cuisine. It's in season from January to June and prepared in a variety of ways. Grilled vegetables are also common on menus, and potatoes are nearly always available.

- *Carciofi alla romana:* Artichoke hearts stewed with olive oil and parsley.

- *Carciofi alla Giudia:* An old Jewish recipe of deep-fried artichokes best sampled in the Ghetto neighborhood.

- *Broccoletti:* A leafy member of the broccoli family boiled and sautéed with garlic and oil.

SANDWICHES (PANINI)

The word *panini* derives from *pane* (bread), which is the secret to a great Roman sandwich. In Rome they can be found piled high behind the counters of most bars and are a lunchtime favorite with office workers and tourists. There are a wide variety of fillings and prices are reasonable.

- *Tramezzini:* Triangular sandwiches made of crustless white bread and filled with cold cuts, shrimp, tuna, egg salad, artichokes, or vegetables. They are inexpensive and make a perfect snack. Most bars in the capital serve *tramezzini* from midmorning to late afternoon.

- Mixed panini: Sandwiches made with pizza *bianca* or rolls containing prosciutto and mozzarella, grilled zucchini and mozzarella, or some other appetizing combination.

- *Porchetta:* Several slices of roasted pork in a Roman *rosetta* (little rose) bun. The pork in question is usually on display and often cut while you wait.

hour *aperitivo*? They've got it all covered. Take a seat on the flower-strewn tables overlooking the comings and goings of a cobblestone street, or grab an espresso quickly at the counter where prices are slightly cheaper.

CAMPO DE' FIORI/ PIAZZA NAVONA

Rome's highest concentration of eateries is in these two neighborhoods. Restaurants around Campo De' Fiori are loud and boisterous, and it's been a while since an Italian stepped into those lining Piazza Navona. Authenticity is

often proportional to the width of the street. If you want to taste the Jewish contribution to Roman cooking, head to the Ghetto, where you can decide if you prefer artichokes *alla romana* (stewed) or *alla guidia* (deep-fried).

Roman

FILETTI DI BACCALA

Largo dei Librari 88; tel. 06/686-4018; Mon.-Sat. 5pm-10:45pm; €10; Tram 8, Bus 63

London may have fish-and-chips, but Rome has *Filetti di Baccala*. Here the fried cod is served with *puntarelle* (a traditional Roman green) and the atmosphere is so simple they only accept cash. A very drinkable house wine is offered by the full, half, or quarter carafe.

SORA MARGHERITA

Piazza Delle Cinque Scole 30; tel. 06/687-4216; daily 12:30pm-3pm, dinner Mon., Wed.-Sat. 8pm-11:30pm; €12-13; Tram 8, Buses 23, 63, 280

Sora Margherita has been written up before and they've got the reviews on the walls to prove it. Lucia, Mario, and Ivan haven't let the attention go to their heads, and run this small, unpretentious family restaurant the way they always have. That's one reason it's so popular, the other is the food. Expect no-nonsense décor and a handwritten menu that changes daily. Thursday features *gnocchi,* Friday *baccala,* and *carciofo alla giudia* is a constant. Arrive early or late to ensure a table inside this Roman institution.

DA GINO

Vicolo Rosini 4; tel. 06/687-3434; Mon.-Sat. 1pm-3pm and 8pm-10:30pm, closed Aug.; €12-14; Buses 119, 628

Good pasta never goes out of style, which is why Da Gino is still around. Don't be surprised if your waiter forgets to bring a menu at this old-time *osteria* filled with regulars who already know what they want to eat. Ingredients are fresh, *pasta e ceci* is usually served on Tuesdays, and one of their best seconds is *pollo con peperoni* (chicken with peppers). Da Gino can be a little tricky to find and it's hardly glamorous, but it is authentic and immensely satisfying.

Italian
DITIRAMBO

Piazza della Cancelleria 74; tel. 06/687-1626; daily 12:45pm-3:30pm and 7pm-11:30pm, Mon. dinner only; €10-13; Buses 40, 46, 62, 64, 916

Most restaurants stopped making their own bread a long time ago. That's not the case at Ditirambo, where fresh loaves are baked daily and form a natural partnership with the wide selection of pasta dishes. They also prepare a good range of vegetarian options and offer great wines by the glass or bottle.

PIANOSTRADA LABORATORIO DI CUCINA

Via delle Zoccolette 22; tel. 06/8957-2296; Tues.-Sun. 1pm-4pm and 7:30pm-11:30pm; €12-15; Buses 23, 280

Pianostrada Laboratorio di Cucina isn't interested in serving the usual fare. The kitchen staff here like to experiment. Fortunately, they know what they're doing, and the daily menu can include everything from apple pie to fish burgers. It's all prepared in an open kitchen behind a long metal counter that's often crowded.

ROSCIOLI

Via dei Giubbonari 21; tel. 06/687-5287; deli Mon.-Sat. 9am-midnight, restaurant Mon.-Sat. 12:30pm-3pm and 7:30pm-midnight; €13-20; Tram 8, Bus 63

Roscioli started out as a deli selling cheese and ham from France, Spain, and Italy. A good thing got better when they opened a restaurant in the back and began serving wine. The starters are a tasty introduction to local cured meats and best enjoyed with the house wine. Unfortunately, there aren't enough tables to meet demand and you may have to settle for a spot at the small counter—where you'll still be able to enjoy the gastronomic sights and smells of this *salumeria.* The owners of Roscioli also run **Antico Forno** (Via dei Chiavari 34; Mon.-Sat. 7am-7:30pm and Sun. 8am-6pm; €5) nearby, which serves pizza, focaccia, sweets, and other Roman delicacies.

Pizza
IL FORNO DI CAMPO DE' FIORI

Campo De' Fiori 22; tel. 06/6880-6662; Mon.-Sat. 7:30am-2:30pm and 4:45pm-8pm, closed Sat. afternoons Jul.-Aug.; €5; Buses 40, 46, 62, 64, 916

Il Forno di Campo De' Fiori is a local institution on the northeastern corner of a bustling square. Everything is baked on-site, and you can watch long strips of pizza being prepared and pulled from the ovens before going in to make your selection. The most popular are the white, red, and zucchini, but several other varieties are also available. It can get chaotic at lunch time and may require a little gumption to be served. The pastry counter in the back features breads, cakes, and cookies including a delicious apple tart. Everything is sold by the kilo and paid for at the cashier near the entrance.

PIZZERIA DA BAFFETTO

Via del Governo Vecchio 114; tel. 06/686-1617; daily noon-3:30pm and 6:30pm-1am; €8-12; Buses 40, 46, 62, 64

Pizzeria da Baffetto is a historic pizzeria that's been satisfying locals for over 50 years. Expect eager crowds who come for thin-crust pizza served by veteran waitstaff who are a bit gruff but mean well. Arrive early or late after a visit to Piazza Navona, and make sure to order a portion of their fried *crostini* appetizers.

Kosher

Roman kosher is a unique combination of Italian and Jewish culinary traditions. The dishes that emerged in the Ghetto over the centuries can now be found across the city, but ordering them here provides added authenticity. Newer options include sushi, pizza, and burger joints that are all kosher certified. Restaurants in the Ghetto close Friday afternoons for Sabbath and are open on weekends.

PASTICCERIA BOCCIONE

Via del Portico d'Ottavia 1; tel. 06/687-8637; Sun.-Thurs. 7am-7pm, Fri. 7am-3pm; €4-6; Tram 8, Buses 23, 63, 280

There isn't much variety at Pasticceria Boccione and what they do have isn't appealing to the eye, but their chocolate and honey *mostaccioli* cookies satisfy the stomach, which explains why they sell out so fast. Pastries here are not the dainty kind but the hefty imperfect variety made from dense dough and stuffed with nuts and dried fruit. The small shop can be empty or under siege by tourists and students from the nearby school in search of freshly baked *pizza ebraica* (Jewish pizza), which is actually sweet and deceptively filling.

FONZIE

Via Santa Maria del Pianto 13; tel. 06/6889-2029; Sun.-Thurs. 10:30am-11pm, Fri. 10:30am-4pm, Sat. 7pm-11pm; €6-9; Tram 8, Buses 23, 63, 280

Fonzie is a popular burger joint near the western entrance of the Ghetto. The faux-1950s interior has a counter at the entrance where 20 burgers and the usual sides are grilled and served up fast. All the beef is certified kosher from Italian beef, and the vegetables are organic. Seating is on stools along the walls but many customers opt for takeaway and enjoy their double cheese or chili burgers on the benches outside.

NONNA BETTA

Via del Portico d'Ottavia 16; tel. 06/6880-6263; Wed.-Mon. noon-5pm and 6pm-10:30pm; €9-13, Tram 8, Buses 23, 63, 280

There are a handful of small historic restaurants along Via del Portico d'Ottavia. Like most, Nonna Betta hasn't changed menu or décor in decades. Waiters have the character that comes with a lifetime of experience, and the long, narrow dining room is lined with paintings of yesteryear. Any item with *alla giudia* at the end means it's prepared the Jewish way. Artichokes, pasta, meat, and desserts have all been given the kosher treatment, with delicious results.

Snacks and Street Food

SUPPLIZIO

Via dei Banchi Vecchi 143; tel. 06/8916-0053; Mon.-Sat. 11:30am-4pm and 4:30-9:30pm; €3-7; Buses 40, 46, 62, 64

Fried rice balls, or *suppli,* are a mainstay in Rome, but few restaurants base their entire business around them. Fortunately, that didn't stop Supplizio from specializing in this wonderful finger food. It's perfect for takeaway if there isn't room on the wooden stools or leather couches inside this cozy eatery.

LO ZOZZONE

Via del Teatro Pace 32; tel. 06/6880-8575; daily 11am-10:30pm; €5-8; Buses 40, 46, 62, 64

This place hasn't changed their cheesy

Pizza al Taglio

pizza al taglio

Roman pizza is thin, prepared in long trays, and served by the kilo at hundreds of *pizzerie al taglio* (takeaway pizza shops) around the city. Varieties range from *bianca* (white) and *margherita* (tomato and mozzarella) to potato and sausage, or four-cheese and some creative alternatives. The best thing to do is enter a pizzeria and check out what they have behind the glass counter. If you like the selection, order a few different cuts and indicate with your hands how much you want and if you intend to eat in (*per mangiare qui*) or to go (*per portare via*). Good places to try *pizza al taglio* include:

- **Il Forno di Campo De' Fiori:** There's little variety inside this popular bakery, but their pizza *bianca* is deliciously doughy and warm (page 90).

- **Pizzarium:** Try an original combination of thick Ligurian focaccia and Roman white pizza topped with artichokes, zucchini, gorgonzola, and more (page 97).

- **Alice:** This reliable chain uses minimal yeast and lets dough rise 24 hours prior to baking. The result is a light base covered with quality ingredients (page 97).

- **Ai Marmi:** A historic pizzeria serving classic thin-crust Roman-style pizza and finger-licking fried starters (page 100).

- **Il Panificio Passi:** Famously crunchy pizza *rossa* that locals order for takeaway and enjoy in the nearby park (page 101).

décor—or, more importantly, the way they make their sandwiches—in decades. The key is the pizza bread, which is baked on-site, cut down the middle, and filled with freshly sliced cold cuts. The house specialty is pork with a tuna sauce that is filling, cheap, and tasty.

Bakeries

ANDREA DE BELLIS

Piazza del Paradiso 56; tel. 06/6880-1480; Tues.-Sun. 9am-8pm; €4-6; Buses 46, 62, 64, 916

Gourmet pastry shops are rare in Rome, and none are as enticing as the small laboratory

Preparing a Roman Picnic

Picnics are a fun outdoor dining option, and in Rome, there's no shortage of markets and eateries where you can pick up all the ingredients necessary. Then head to the nearest square or park, locate a bench, and dig in. Markets with picnic supplies include:

- **Zia Rosetta:** Order a handful of flavorful mini sandwiches to go and enjoy them overlooking the Colosseum (page 87).

- **Testaccio Market:** Panini, wine, cheese, and bread are all available from dozens of tempting market stalls and can be taken away to nearby Piazza Testaccio or the lovely Orange Gardens (page 82).

- **Il Forno di Campo de' Fiori:** Discover the simple pleasure of *pizza bianca* (white doughy pizza without any trimmings) and devour it while strolling toward Piazza Navona and the Pantheon (page 90).

Andrea De Bellis, opened near Campo de Fiori. Inside the bakery a colorful array of pastries tempt the eyes and can be enjoyed with a cup of coffee or tea on-site or carefully wrapped for takeaway. *Sablé al cioccolato, millefoglie, cannoli, profiterole,* and croissants are all mainstays and can be enjoyed any time of day.

ZUM ROMA
Piazza del Teatro di Pompeo 20; tel. 06/6830-7836; Sun.-Thurs. 11:30am-11pm, Fri.-Sat. 11:30am-1am; €3-9; Buses 46, 62, 64, 916

There's more than one way to make tiramisu, and they've perfected dozens at ZUM. Besides the classic recipe you'll find fruit, rum, pistachio, lactose, and gluten-free varieties. Everything is produced inside this charming little shop with a handful of stools where you can contemplate the wonders of sugar, eggs, and mascarpone.

Gelato
FRIGIDARIUM
Via del Governo Vecchio 112; tel. 334/995-1184; daily 10:30am-midnight; €3-5; Buses 40, 46, 62, 64

Frigidarium is a standing-room-only *gelaterie* with two refrigerated cases filled with gelato that's made from scratch every morning. Pistachio and chocolate lovers will enjoy the *Mozart* flavor topped with *panna* (whipped cream). You can choose from various sizes

and enjoy the gelato from a cone (*cono*) or cup (*coppa*). If you can't make up your mind the friendly owner or his assistant can suggest the best pairings.

Coffee
TAZZA D'ORO
Via Degli Orfani 84; tel. 06/678-9792; Mon.-Sat. 7am-8pm; €2; Buses 62, 63, 83, 85, 119

Locals and tourists are nearly always lined up at Tazza d'Oro, waiting for what is arguably the best coffee in Rome. People have been making that argument since this caffeine institution opened in 1944. If you agree you can buy a pack of their unique Arabica blend or try a *granita al caffè* (iced coffee) that's only served in summer.

★ CAFFÈ SANT'EUSTACHIO
Piazza Sant'Eustachio 82; tel. 06/6880-2048; daily 7:30am-midnight; €3-7; Buses 30, 70, 81, 87, 492, 628

Caffè Sant'Eustachio is a historic bar that's been serving a blend of locally ground beans since 1938. The yellow uniformed baristas are all veterans and take pride in preparing cups of the presweetened *Gran Caffè* and *Monachella* house coffee with cacao and whipped cream. It's crowded most of the day and wonderfully chaotic. Order at the cashier, then find a space at the u-shaped counter and order with authority. Their cold *shakerato*, *frappe*, and *caffè freddo* are great summertime options.

TRIDENTE

Tridente isn't an obvious dining destination. Most of the stores around Piazza di Spagna are dedicated to retail shopping, and restaurants are rare along Via del Corso or Condotti. Those present are often expensive and not always worth the price. There are exceptions, and south of Via Corso and away from the shopping district culinary options and quality improve significantly. The neighborhood is also known for historic tearooms and bars where poets and aristocrats once drank and elegantly dressed ladies and groups of crumpet-craving tourists still do.

Roasted chestnuts are available on the streets of Tridente from late autumn to early spring. It's an age-old tradition carried on by new faces who operate mobile roasting carts and serve warm unshelled chestnuts in paper cones (€5). There are several vendors stationed along Via dei Condotti and another facing the Spanish Steps.

Italian
PASTASCIUTTA
Piazza Flaminio 10; tel. 06/6933-6353; daily 11am-10pm; €6; Metro A: Flaminio
Romans value quality, which is why there's often a line outside Pastasciutta. This pasta-only joint prepares eight kinds of pasta daily. A heaping plate of *rigatoni cacio e pepe* or *pappardelle al ragù* is only €6, and they do not skimp on portions. Just decide on the dish, order at the counter, and wait for your number to be called. Seating is elbow-to-elbow on stools that are hard to come by at lunch.

GUSTO
Piazza Augusto Imperatore 28; tel. 06/6812-4221; daily 8am-2am; €10-15; Buses 119, 301
Gusto is the cure to gastronomic indecision. This urban food emporium is made up of a *trattoria*, pizzeria, restaurant, rotisserie, vineria, cocktail bar, and bookstore. Whatever Italian flavor you're craving, you'll find it

here. The buffet brunch is the perfect break between the Ara Pacis and Piazza di Spagna. The wine bar regularly features live jazz and the *formaggeria* is stocked with wonderful Italian and French cheese served with honey, fruit, and wine.

FIASCHETTERIA BELTRAMME
Via della Croce 39; tel. 06/6979-7200; daily 12:30pm-3pm and 7:30pm-10:30pm; €10-15; Metro A: Spagna
Fiaschetteria Beltramme mixes the best of the Lazio region with a dash of Tuscany. The *tagliolini* and *penne* dishes are worth the risk of a sauce stain, and meat dishes are cooked in almost every way imaginable. Italians outnumber tourists here and owners Silvia and Arturo keep everyone smiling. As with many restaurants in Rome, you'll be charged a couple of euros for the bread, but it's worth the expense.

Pizza
PIZZARE
Via di Ripetta 14; tel. 06/321-1468; daily noon-midnight; €6-10; Metro A: Flaminio
PizzaRe serves some of the best Neapolitan pies in town. The large dining room is perpetually full of people eyeing the wood-burning oven with anticipation. Fried starters are excellent, and if you have any room left, sample their traditional desserts like *cassata napoletana* or *torta caprese*. Reservations are essential on weekends.

VERACE SUDD
Via della Frezza 64; tel. 06/3938-7518; Tues. 6pm-10pm, Wed.-Sun. noon-3pm and 6pm-10pm; €8-12; Buses 119 or 698
You don't have to leave Rome to get a taste of Naples and discover each city's take on pizza. The difference is in the dough, water, and yeast, which yields a thinner, crunchier crust in Rome and a thicker, softer crust in Naples. Verace Sudd provides an authentic introduction to Neapolitan pizza and a delicious

---

1: Trattoria da Enzo 2: Tempio Della Grattachecca

contrast to the Roman variety. They also serve great fried starters and craft beer. The one-room dining area has a modern bistro feel and fills up fast.

Snacks and Street Food
TEMPIO DELLA GRATTACHECCA

Lungotevere in Augusta/Corner Ponte Cavour; daily 9am-8pm; €5; Bus 628

Grattachecca (Italian ice) was once sold by itinerant vendors who hauled large frozen blocks around the city in search of customers. Those days are gone, but fortunately, Tempio della Grattachecca survived. The historic kiosk opposite the Ara Pacis is one of a handful of specialists selling this simple concoction. Raphael and his mother crush the ice and mix it with fruit (cherry, melon, strawberry, peach, etc.) they prepare themselves. The refreshing treat is served in a glass with a spoon and a straw and can be enjoyed at the counter or one of the tables facing the busy street. Similar kiosks can be found in Piazzale degli Eroi a few blocks north of the Vatican, Lungotevere degli Anguillara on the corner of Ponte Cestio in Trastevere, and Testaccio.

LA VITA È UN MOZZICO

Via Angelo Brunetti 4; tel. 06/323-6644; Mon.-Sat. 8am-6pm; €6-8; Metro A: Flaminio

It doesn't look like much on the outside, but inside this tiny deli you'll find all the ingredients for a memorable sandwich. The concept is simple, fresh *focaccia* stuffed with freshly sliced cold cuts and cheese. There's plenty to choose from and if you're overwhelmed at the counter just ask the friendly proprietors for a *porchetta* and *pecorino* panini (my personal favorite). They'll wrap it up and you can enjoy it on the marble benches of Piazza del Popolo.

Gelato
SAN CRISPINO

Via della Panetteria 42; tel. 06/679-3924; daily 11am-12:30am; €3; Buses 52, 53, 62

If you're serious about gelato, sooner or later you'll find yourself standing outside San Crispino. The owners only serve the flavors they like, so expect lots of hazelnut, cinnamon, honey, and ginger. The gelato is hidden from view in metal vats but each flavor is labeled in Italian and English. There's some seating inside but most customers enjoy their cups outside. There's a second location in Piazza della Maddalena 3 close to the Pantheon.

★ GELATERIA DEI GRACCHI

Via di Ripetta 261; tel. 06/322-4727; Tues.-Sun. noon-8pm; €3-5; Metro A: Flaminio

Much of the gelato sold to tourists along the Corso is second rate. If you want first rate and people who care about quality rather than quantity, head to Gelateria dei Gracchi for a cone or cup. All the flavors at this small *gelateria* are made without additives and strictly according to what's in season. If you arrive in late summer or early autumn ask for a scoop of prickly pear, which comes from a cactus and is hard to find in other *gelaterie*. Their pistachio and chocolate flavors are equally delicious and available all year long.

CIAMPINI LUCINI

Piazza San Lorenzo in Lucina 29; tel. 06/687-6606; Mon.-Sat. 7am-10pm, Sun. 9am-10:30pm; €3-5; Buses 119, 628

Limited selection isn't always a bad thing, and what Ciampini Lucini lacks in quantity it makes up for in quality. As long as the *zabaglione* (hazelnut chocolate) is available, there's no reason to worry. You can order a scoop at the dedicated counter or outside on the terrace where it comes served in a metal bowl by uniformed waiters.

Coffee
CAFFÈ GRECO

Via dei Condotti 86; tel. 06/679-1700; daily 9am-9pm; €5-8; Metro A: Spagna

Caffè Greco was around centuries before the designer boutiques that now surround it. This is where grand tour pioneers like Goethe and Stendhal sipped coffee, and portraits of famous clients can be seen throughout the elegant rooms. It's a great place to write post-cards and get your literary kicks while drinking tea from porcelain cups.

CANOVA AND ROSATI

There are two historic cafés overlooking Piazza del Popolo where celebrities and intellectuals once gathered and paparazzi still occasionally stake out. Today, **Canova** (Piazza del Popolo 16-17; tel. 06/361-2231; daily 7:30am-1am; €10; Metro A: Flaminio) and **Rosati** (Piazza del Popolo 5a; daily 7:30am-11:30am; €10; Metro A: Flaminio) attract tourists who sit at the outdoor tables and watch the constant stream of pedestrians moving through the square. Federico Fellini was a frequent visitor and there's a small gallery dedicated to the director inside Canova. Drinks are expensive at both cafés and you can people watch from the nearby benches for free.

VATICANO

The Vatican attracts a lot of tourists and those tourists eventually need to eat. That explains the anonymous restaurants located temptingly close to the Holy See. Avoid them at all costs and leave the Vatican several blocks behind before searching for an eatery. **Borgo Pio** and **Borgo Vittorio,** long narrow streets parallel to Via della Conciliazione, may be the only exceptions to the rule and have historically been the place pilgrims have sought sustenance.

Roman

PASTASCIUTTA

Via delle Grazie 5; tel. 333/650-3758; daily 10:30am-6:30pm; €6; Metro A: Ottaviano

The latest food trend in Rome is express pasta bars. The pasta and sauces at Pastasciutta are made fresh daily and you can watch dishes being prepared in their compact kitchen. It only takes a couple of minutes before *cacio e pepe* or *pappardelle al ragù* are served up on plastic plates. There are only six options and little space to eat inside, but the prices are unbeatable and the pasta is good. If the lines are

too long try **Egg** (Vicolo del Farinone 25; tel. 06/8901-3927; daily 11:30am-6pm; €5.50-7) a couple of blocks away, which has a similar concept on a quieter street with fewer tourists.

ARLU

Borgo Pio 135; tel. 06/686-8936; Mon.-Sat. 11:30am-4pm and 6:30pm-10pm; €11-18; Metro A: Lepanto

Arlu prepares Roman specialties within a refined setting. Armando and Lucia run the restaurant with their two daughters who serve fresh bread and pasta with a smile. The house wine goes well with everything on the menu, including the *saltimbocca alla romana.*

L'ARCANGELO

Via G.G. Belli 59; tel. 06/321-0992c; Mon.-Fri. 1pm-2:30pm and 8pm-11pm, Sat. 8pm-11pm; €16-18; Metro A: Lepanto

L'Arcangelo is a gourmet *trattoria* with a limited but high-quality menu of dishes combining the city's culinary past and present. Marble-topped tables are arranged around a medium-sized dining room with dark wood paneling and family photos.

Pizza

ALICE

Via delle Grazie 7/9; tel. 06/687-5746; Mon.-Sat. 8am-6pm, Sun. 10am-4pm; €5-8; Metro A: Ottaviano

Alice is perfect for a quick slice of takeaway pizza on the way to or from St. Peter's. From noon onward the counter is filled with long trays of pizza topped with vegetables, sausage, and other ingredients. There's not much space inside and tourists gather on the steps out front.

PIZZARIUM

Via della Meloria 43; tel. 06/3974-5416; Mon.-Sat. 11am-10pm, Sun. noon-4pm and 6pm-10pm; €7-10; Metro A: Cipro

Pizzarium is a *pizza al taglio* shop behind the Vatican where legendary baker Gabriele Bonci and his crew of dough disciples keep the ovens busy. Toppings are generous and creative, and you're likely to find figs, goat cheese, and plenty of vegetables. It's a simple neighborhood pizzeria with no seating and plenty of regulars congregating outside. Prices are by the kilo and the pizza is thick, so expect to pay more than average for pizza that's better than average.

International
EL MAIZ

Via Tolemaide 16; tel. 06/6600-6878; Tues.-Sun. noon-9:45pm; €5-9; Metro A: Ottaviano

If you like plantains and have never tried Venezuelan food, El Maiz will satisfy your culinary curiosity. It's a small eatery run by a family of Venezuelan expats. They specialize in *arepas* filled with beef, chicken, pork, tuna, and vegetables. Plates are served at the counter and the *tradicional* (rice, beef, plantains, and black beans) provides a hearty introduction to Latin American cuisine.

Snacks and Street Food
PANINO DIVINO

Via dei Gracchi 11a; tel. 06/3973-7803; Mon.-Sat. 10am-9pm; €5-7; Metro A: Ottaviano

Panino Divino is an informal sandwich shop with hams hanging from the ceiling and bottles of wine lining the walls. The menu includes over 25 panini as well as cured meat and cheese plates (€10) served on wooden cutting boards. Sandwiches are prepared while you wait by the jovial owners, who chat while they slice. There are half-a-dozen stools inside and a barrel outside that's been converted into a table. There's a good selection of wine by the glass and makes their 6pm happy hour (*aperitivo*) a good time to visit.

VULIÒ

Via deglie Scipione 55; tel. 06/3973-3825; daily 10am-9pm; €8-12; Metro A: Ottaviano

Paposcia is one of those simple Italian creations born from necessity and elevated into an artform. This open sandwich made with crunchy focaccia originated in Puglia where bakers once used it to test the temperature of their ovens, until local cooks began adding toppings and serving it as an appetizer. At Vuliò, *paposcia* is served with mozzarella, capers, anchovies, and southern Italian ingredients. There are counters and stools along both walls of this original eatery that provides a break from Roman flavors.

Bakeries
PANIFICIO MOSCA

Via Candia 16; tel. 06/3974-2134; Mon.-Sat. 8am-2pm and 4pm-7:30pm; €4-6; Metro A: Ottaviano

The smell inside Panificio Mosca, located near the Vatican walls, has been seducing residents since 1916. Locals come for the handmade pastries in the morning and trays of freshly baked white and red pizza at lunch. Although it's crowded and chaotic at noon, lines move quickly, and the ladies behind the counter are in a perpetual flutter.

PASTICCERIA COLAPICCHIONI 2

Via Tacito 76; tel. 06/321-5405; Mon.-Fri. 7:30am-2:30pm, 5pm-7:30pm, Sat. 7:30am-1:30pm; €5; Metro A: Lepanto

Pasticceria Colapicchioni 2 has been baking bread, biscuits, pastries, pizza, and focaccia since 1934 and even created their own unique cake. It's called *Pangill'Oro* and is a variation of an ancient Roman dessert made from dried fruit, honey, nuts, and grapes that's been trademarked by the shop's owner. One side of the bakery is dedicated to oven-fresh ingredients while the other is filled with regional specialties.

Gelato
LEMONGRASS

Via Ottaviano 29; tel. 06/3972-3524; daily 7am-11pm; €3-5; Metro A: Ottaviano

Picking your favorite gelaterie in this neighborhood is like choosing between Michelangelo and Raphael: They're all good. Lemongrass distinguishes itself with chocolate and hazelnut-covered cones along with traditional options. They have a nice assortment of fruit flavors along with original handmade creations like strudel, ricotta and fig, and lemongrass. There's also an air-conditioned seating area, which is rare and a relief in summer.

MO'S GELATERIA

Via Cola di Rienzo 174; tel. 06/687-4357; daily 11am-8pm; €3-5; Metro A: Lepanto or Ottaviano

Their hazelnut is good, but it's the chocolate flavors that have kept Mo's Gelateria on the map. Fruit is delivered fresh weekly and everything is made without preservatives by a friendly staff who let undecided clients sample flavors.

TRASTEVERE

There's no shortage of restaurants in Trastevere but the vast number of choices can be confusing. Most serve classic Roman fare and it's hard to go wrong. Nevertheless, refrain from stopping at the first *trattoria* you pass, and don't be pressured into sitting down by overzealous seaters who stand outside encouraging passersby to enter. Side streets are a good place to find authenticity, and crossing Viale di Trastevere to the quieter side of the neighborhood has its gastronomic rewards. During the summer many bars and restaurants set up temporary locations along the embankments of the Tiber. It's a fun place to enjoy a light meal or cocktail, or just set off on a stroll.

Roman
DA GIOVANNI

Via della Lungara 41a; tel. 06/686-1514; Mon.-Sat. noon-3pm and 7:30pm-10pm; €8-11; Buses 23, 280

Italians have a way of putting people at ease, and it doesn't take long for Da Giovanni to feel like a second home. The menu reads like all the rest of the Roman *trattorie* in the neighborhood, but tastes slightly better—especially when the check arrives. The small dining room is charmingly untrendy and full of 1950s nostalgia. The *carciofi alla romana*

(Roman-style artichokes) and *tonarelli cacao e pepe* pasta are must-tries.

★ TRATTORIA DA ENZO

Via dei Vascellari 29; tel. 06/581-2260; Mon.-Sat. 12:30pm-3pm and 7:30pm-11pm; €10-12; Tram 8, Buses 23, 280

This classic neighborhood *trattoria* is more concerned about substance than appearance. Dishes are Roman to the core, and the single dining room and handful of tables on the cobblestones outside are reassuringly rustic. This is the place to experience a three-course meal that won't break the bank but will widen your waistline. Fried artichokes, *carbonara,* and roast lamb are all on the menu. The wine list is an homage to regional vintages and reasonably priced. Arrive early or prepare for a wait.

DA LUCIA

Vicolo del Mattonato 2; tel. 06/580-3601; Tues.-Sun. 12:30pm-3pm and 7:30pm-11pm; €12-15; Buses 23, 280

The menu at Da Lucia may seem limited—but it's better to perfect a few great dishes than master none. Specials include *gnocchi al pomodoro* on Thursdays and generous portions of *coniglio alla cacciatora* (roasted rabbit) all week long. The *trattoria* has been pleasing locals since 1938 and is located on one of Trastevere's most photogenic streets.

HOSTERIA LUCE

Via della Luce 44; tel. 06/581-4839; Mon.-Fri. noon-3pm and 7pm-11pm, Sat.-Sun. 12:30pm-3pm; €12-17; Trams 3, 8, Buses 44, 75, 115

Hosteria Luce is a hard place to leave. The charming eatery on a quiet, rarely explored street takes traditional Roman dishes to the next gastronomic level. The bright, shabby-chic interior and outdoor terrace are perfect for enjoying unhurried meals with friends and loved ones. The mixed antipasto plate is perfect for sharing and their traditional *carbonara, amatriciana,* and *cacio e pepe* pastas all have a delicious twist. A piano gets played occasionally, and service is impeccable.

Pizza
LA BOCCACCIA

Via di Santa Dorotea 2 and San Francesco a Ripa 22; tel. 320/775-6277; daily 10am-11pm; €5-8; Tram 8, Buses 23, 280

La Boccaccia has two locations in Trastevere and both are standing room only *pizza al taglio* eateries along lively streets. They bake a delicious assortment of thick-crust pizza all day long that includes plenty of vegetarian options. The Santa Dorotea outlet has a few tables outside but if these are taken order some slices and enjoy them in the nearby square.

AI MARMI

Viale Trastevere 53; tel. 06/580-0919; Thurs.-Tues. 6:30pm-2:30am; €6-8; Trams 3, 8

Regulars call Ai Marmi *l'obitorio* (the morgue), due to the white marble tables. The pizza is blue-chip Roman with a thin crust. Starters include *suppli* (mozzarella-filled rice balls), fried olives, and cold cut platters. The menu is listed on a large blackboard. Waiters move frenetically about the no-frills pizzeria and getting their attention can be a challenge. Traffic on the avenue facing the pizzeria makes this more suitable for a quick bite or late-night snack rather than a romantic tête-à-tête.

Bakeries
LA RENELLA

Via del Moro 15; tel. 06/581-7265; daily 7am-midnight; €5; Buses 23, 280

The secret to making mouths water is stone-ground wheat from an antique mill outside Rome and a hazelnut-burning oven. That's what they've been using at La Renella for the last 130 years. They serve bread, pizza, and hearty sandwiches students and travelers eat at a long wooden counter running down one side of this historic bakery. You can watch the baking as it happens and exit out the back entrance to discover another side of Trastevere.

LE LEVAIN

Via Luigi Santini 22; tel. 06/6456-2880; Mon.-Sat. 8am-8:30pm, Sun. 9am-8pm; €4-6; Trams 3, 8, Buses 44, 75, 115

Giuseppe Solfrizzi learned the art of pastry in France under Alain Ducasse and returned to Italy to open Le Levain. Now Romans enjoy his knowledge of baguettes, croissants, *pain au chocolat*, and some tasty inventions of his own. He's usually busy baking away in the lab or restocking the counter with chocolate delights.

Gelato
FIORDILUNA

Via della Lungaretta 96; tel. 06/6456-1314; daily 11:30am-12:30am; €3-5; Tram 8, Buses 23, 280

Fresh, seasonal ingredients and an obsession with quality are what make Fiordiluna so good. You won't find strawberry gelato in winter or additives any time, but you will discover dozens of chocolate varieties and some flavors made with mule's milk. They take the purist approach to the extreme and only serve their thick, creamy gelato in cups.

TIBERINO

Via Monte 4 Capi 17; tel. 06/687-7662; Mon.-Fri. 8am-10:30pm, Sat. 10am-11am, Sun. 10am-10:30pm; €3-5; Buses 23, 280, 63

Tiberino operates a *gelateria* from a dedicated window where tourists and locals gather. Flavors include the classics along with original combinations like basil and lemon, and cream and cinnamon. It's a reliable gelato stop on the island separating the Jewish Ghetto from Trastevere. You can also have a coffee or sit-down meal, but the gelato is the most tempting option and can be licked while admiring the adjacent cobblestone square.

AVENTINO AND TESTACCIO
Roman
AGUSTARELLA

Via G. Branca 100; tel. 06/574-6585; Mon.-Sat. 12:30pm-3pm, 7:30pm-11pm; €10-11; Metro B: Piramide

Agustarella is a classic Roman *osteria* in a quintessentially Roman neighborhood. They prepare simple dishes known as *cucina povera,* or poor food. Recipes originated from necessity and use nearly every cut of beef or pork available. Those with adventurous palates will give *trippa alla romana* (Roman tripe) a try, while the *rigatoni alla pajata* is the perfect option for pasta lovers.

DA FELICE
Via Mastro Giorgio 29; tel. 06/574-6800; daily 12:30pm-3pm and 7pm-11pm; €12-16; Metro B: Piramide
Da Felice is a sleek *trattoria* with a long history of serving great pasta. It's less rustic and more elegant than other options in the area. There are two dining rooms, both of which have black-and-white-checkered paving, brick walls, and carefully set tables. It's always crowded on weekends.

Pizza
IL PANIFICO PASSI
Via Mastro Giorgio 87; tel. 06/574-6563; Mon.-Sat. 7am-1pm and 4pm-8pm; €3-5, Metro B: Piramide
Il Panifico Passi has been baking bread in the same wood-burning oven since 1931. The *pizza bianca* (white pizza) is often still warm and always delicious. It's cut according to your hunger so just indicate how much you want to the patient woman behind the counter. They also bake interesting breads and prepare lasagna fresh daily. Even if you're not hungry it's worth popping in to see a traditional Italian bakery in action.

PIZZERIA DA REMO
Piazza Santa Maria Liberatrice 44; tel. 06/574-6270; Mon.-Sat. 6pm-1am; €8-10; Metro B: Piramide
Pizzeria da Remo, on a corner across from Testaccio's largest park, serves Roman thin-crust pizza. It's a popular place that gets crowded on weekends, when you're better off arriving early or late. Waiters seem to have a lot of fun navigating the crowded

tables, bantering with clients and speaking in heavy Roman slang. Appetizers should not be skipped and the mixed plate with fried zucchini flowers is a highlight.

Snacks and Street Food
TRAPIZZINO
Via Giovanni Branca 88; tel. 06/4341-9624; daily noon-3pm and 6pm-10pm; €2-4; Metro B: Piramide
Most street food vendors serve fast-food classics, but Trapizzino invented a new classic and sells it inside a small takeaway eatery. The item everyone comes for is a cross between pizza, calzone, and stew. It doesn't take much courage to try, and once you've sampled one it's hard not to want more. Fillings include chicken, meatballs, mozzarella, and vegetables.

TRAM DEPOT
Via Marmorata 13, opposite the fire station; tel. 06/575-4406; daily 8am-2am; €5; Metro B: Piramide
Tram Depot is an outdoor destination for light sandwiches, salads, and fruit shakes. There's plenty of seating and the tram-inspired kiosk is open day and night. Food and drinks are ordered at the counter and can be enjoyed on the shaded terrace. They mix excellent cocktails and attract a loyal happy-hour crowd.

★ CHIOSCO TESTACCIO
Corner of Via Giovanni Branca and Via Florio; daily 2pm-1am; €4-6; Metro B: Piramide
Grattachecca (Italian ice) translates to "scratch the ice block"—which is exactly what the couple at Chiosco Testaccio have been doing for the last 20 years. Their little kiosk on a residential corner of Testaccio attracts a steady stream of summertime clients who come for cups of shaved ice covered with fruit-flavored syrups. Lemon is the classic but cherry, coconut, mint, and many others are also available. There are few *grattachecca* left in Rome and this is one of the most authentic. If you're in the neighborhood on a hot afternoon, head here for relief.

Gelato
BRIVIDO

Vial Giovanni Battista Bodoni 62; daily
11am-midnight; €3-5; Metro B: Piramide

This neighborhood *gelateria* isn't part of a chain and can't rely on a steady stream of one-time visitors. Most customers come back for creamy flavors made fresh every day. The woman behind the counter is happy to provide a spoon-size sample before you commit to a flavor. Just ask *posso provare?* (may I try?). There are plenty of benches to enjoy your cone or cup and observe Italian life in Piazza Testaccio around the block.

OSTIENSE

Ostiense has seen a burst of new restaurant openings in the last few years. Japanese eateries are particularly well represented, and Via del Gazometro alone is home to half a dozen sushi joints.

Roman
PORTO FLUVIALE

Via del Porto Fluviale 22; tel. 06/574-3199; daily
noon-3:30pm and 6pm-1am; €8-14; Metro B:
Piramide

Porto Fluviale is on the gritty southern edge of Testaccio within walking distance of Piramide. The restaurant is divided into several sections and resembles a trendy Italian version of an American diner. Food comes in full-size or miniature tapas-like portions that are ideal for sharing. Happy hour attracts a young crowd and the mustached barman makes an entertaining show of mixing cocktails.

TRATTORIA PENNESTRI

Via Giovanni da Empoli 5; tel. 06/574-2418,
Mon.-Thurs. 7pm-11pm and Fri.-Sun. noon-3pm and
7pm-11pm; €10-13; Metro B: Piramide

Pennestri is a modern one-room *trattoria* that opened in 2018. The young organic-obsessed chefs serve traditional Roman favorites along with original gastronomic creations. Ingredients are grade A, from the bread brought to your table to the eggs used in their delightfully creamy *carbonara*. A 10-minute

walk from Piramide, it's a little out of the way, but the roast pork with myrtle and porcini mushrooms is worth the effort.

Italian
EATALY

Piazzale 12 Ottobre 1492; tel. 06/9027-9201; www.
eataly.it; daily 8am-midnight; Metro B: Piramide

Eataly is a large food emporium that was born in Turin and has spread throughout Italy and well beyond. The Roman branch is one of the biggest and a mecca of Italian gastronomy. It's located in a former train terminal and filled with four floors of food, wine, beer, gelato, bars, and a dozen restaurants. Whatever your appetite you'll find something to quench it here including pizza, pasta, burgers, fish, street food, and fine dining. There's also plenty of Italian ingredients to stock up on after your meal.

International
SUSHISEN

Via Giuseppe Giulietti 21a; tel. 06/575-6945;
Tues.-Sun. noon-2:30pm and 7:30pm-9pm; €12-18;
Metro B: Piramide

Long before Japanese restaurants mushroomed in the Ostiense neighborhood, there was Sushisen, which has been serving some of the best sushi in Rome for 20 years. Anyone craving sashimi, tempura, or ramen will be satisfied here. The underground restaurant has an elegant dining room, but the fun place to eat is along the kaiten sushi conveyor where veteran chefs keep crowds of lunch and dinner guests satisfied. Weekday lunchtime plates are all €3.50 and include a free bowl of miso.

TERMINI

The area surrounding Rome's train station isn't very attractive and caters mostly to commuters and tourists who don't have the time or energy to find a nicer area to eat. There are dozens of fast-food eateries inside the station and along the streets south of Termini. If you continue in that direction, you'll enter one of the most culturally diverse neighborhoods in the city, home to low-priced Chinese, Korean, and Indian restaurants. North of the station, toward the university district, is more residential with a higher number of local eateries. The general rule of thumb is that the farther you get from Termini the better the food.

Roman
★ ER BUCHETTO

Via del Viminale 2f; tel. 329/965-2175; Mon.-Fri. 10am-3pm and 5pm-9pm, Sat. 10am-2:30pm; €5; Metro A: Republica

Er Buchetto is a Roman-style tavern famous for *porchetta* (roast pork) sandwiches. The name means "little hole," and that's not an exaggeration. Tables are tiny inside this neighborhood institution that's been feeding locals since 1890. If you do get to sit on one of the stools, order the white wine from the tap; otherwise have your sandwich wrapped and head to the nearest park.

Pizza
UFFA CHE PIZZA

Via dei Taurini 39; tel. 06/4436-2444; Mon.-Sat. noon-3pm and 7pm-11:30pm; €9-11; Metro A or B: Termini

Uffa Che Pizza is on a tree-lined residential street north of the station near Rome's largest university. It's a simple, clean, one-room pizzeria with reasonable prices, air-conditioning, and quick service. Toppings aren't very creative but that doesn't seem to bother the families and students who fill this pizzeria at lunch and dinner.

International
MERCATO CENTRALE

Via Giovanni Giolitti 36; tel. 06/4620-2900; daily 8am-midnight; €5-20; Metro A or B: Termini

This vibrant, gourmet food court inside Termini train station has dozens of quality options and has become Rome's latest culinary attraction. There are dedicated mini restaurants (many of which have larger locations around the city) serving pizza, hamburgers, sushi, ramen, vegetables, fish, cheese, wine, beer, gelato, and more. Tables are spread out everywhere and you can eat anywhere you like once you get your food. Prices are reasonable and it's crowded on weekends. The original Mercato Centrale is located in Florence and also worth a try.

Nightlife and Entertainment

Evenings in Rome start in neighborhood squares and continue inside theaters, clubs, and discos. Romans aren't heavy drinkers, but they are extremely sociable and enjoy conversing until late. *Aperitivo* is usually how they begin an evening. It's the equivalent of happy hour except it can last a couple of hours and usually includes food. It starts on weekdays around 6pm in bars and cafés around the city. Drink and buffet offers are usually posted outside and rarely exceed €10. Some places fill counters with cold pasta, frittata omelets, couscous, cheese, cold cuts, and bread while others simply provide olives and potato chips. Wine is the most commonly ordered drink, but beer and cocktails are always available.

There are many ways to have a good time after *aperitivo*. The city is sprinkled with theaters and concert halls where symphony, opera, and ballet are performed. Talented musicians of all genres play at intimate clubs, and wine bars entertain the palate. There are also month-long festivals dedicated to the arts, and outdoor performances in Piazza del Popolo and the Baths of Caracalla. Pick up Rome's quarterly event calendar at any TIP office, or swing by a newsstand to buy a copy of *La Repubblica*: the entertainment supplement is published on Thursdays and includes a section in English. At bars, pubs, and clubs, drinks generally cost around €8-12.

The city has several popular nightlife districts. Piazza Trilussa is a vibrant outdoor meeting area where locals congregate and plan what to do next. **Campo De' Fiori** is lined with bars filled with foreign travelers and exchange students. **Monte Testaccio** is a reliable late-night destination for all orientations and the hillside is ringed with clubs featuring Latin, lounge, or deep house. Throughout the summer, dozens of temporary bars and restaurants are set up along the **Tiber River walk,** while some establishments close from June until August and relocate to the nearby beaches of Ostia.

BARS AND PUBS

Rome doesn't conjure up images of beer, but maybe it should. Peroni and Nastro Azzurro are the name-brand lagers, but there's also plenty of craft beer being brewed in Italy and many bars at which to try a pint or two. Some resemble Irish pubs and attract foreigners fond of familiarity, but a growing interest in brewing has inspired new locales where a beer can be savored in style.

Aperitivo at these establishments starts at 6pm and can go on all night. Drinks come with finger food or a buffet that often substitutes dinner. Cocktail bars have also made a comeback, and getting a well-mixed drink in the city has never been easier. Most stay open late and a few charge small membership fees of €5-10, which may include a drink.

Ancient Rome and Monti
RACE CLUB
Via Labicana 52; tel. 06/9604-4048; www. theraceclubroma.org; Mon.-Thurs. 10pm-4am, Fri.-Sun. 7pm-4am; Metro A: Manzoni

Looks are deceiving at the Race Club. This modern-day speakeasy could be mistaken for a garage, but once you've gotten past the motorcycles, paid the €3 membership fee, and walked downstairs, it's clear you've come to the right place. This underground lounge down the road from the Colosseum is a popular late-night haunt where you can order original cocktails and hard-to-find craft beers, then relax on cozy armchairs and listen to DJs or live performers entertain the fashion-conscious crowd.

THE BARBER SHOP SPEAKEASY
Via Iside 2; tel. 06/797-5289; Thurs.-Sun. 10pm-5am; Metro B: Colosseo

Located near Race Club, the Barber Shop Speakeasy charges a small membership fee (€5) for the privilege of entering a secret bar where elegant bartenders shake enticing cocktails with names like Fire for Life and Carbost Fjord while vintage jazz plays. There's an international vibe inside with a mix of nationalities and languages that produces interesting conversations. Walking out at dawn and watching the sun rise over the nearby Colosseum is a great way to start a day.

★ BLACKMARKET HALL
Via de' Ciancaleoni 31; tel. 349/199-5295; www. blackmarkethall.com; daily 6:30pm-2am; Buses 71, 117

Locals chill until the late hours at this cozy, dimly lit bar that is filled with mismatched furniture and artwork. Keep walking through the small rooms or up to the second floor until you find a free sofa and wait for the friendly staff to take your order. They can mix just about anything and have a handful of beers on tap, along with an extensive late-night menu that includes veggie burgers, salads, and shrimp tartar. Live music is often organized on weekends with sets kicking off at 9pm.

Campo De' Fiori/ Piazza Navona
EX CIRCUS
Via della Vetrina 15; tel. 06/9761-9258; Mon.-Thurs. 8:30am-8:30pm, Fri.-Sat. 8:30am-2am, Sun. 9am-8pm; Buses 40, 46, 62, 64, 280, 916

Ex Circus is a sprawling bar with an informal interior that attracts a young crowd of expats and locals who surf the free Wi-Fi, browse the international newspapers scattered on the tables in back, or just drink. The daily happy hour (6:30pm-9pm) is hard to beat, and €8 gets you a wine, beer, or cocktail of your choice and access to a counter full of pasta salads, vegetables pies, cold cuts, and more. Brunch (Sun. 11:30am-4:30pm; €16) is also good and includes familiar dishes like cupcakes, pancakes, and smoothies prepared Italian style.

ABBEY THEATRE
Via del Governo Vecchio 51; tel. 06/686-1341; daily noon-2am; Buses 40, 46, 62, 64, 916

Those craving a Guinness can satisfy their thirst at the Abbey Theatre. This intimate wood-paneled pub is fully equipped with Irish stouts and ales as well as some good bourbon. Sixteen flat-screen TVs make it an ideal place to watch *calcio* (soccer), American football, and rugby. The menu includes homemade stew and an Irish Breakfast plate that can help prevent hangovers.

JERRY THOMAS SPEAKEASY
Vicolo Cellini 30; tel. 370/114-6287; Mon.-Sat. 10pm-4am, Sun. 9pm-3am; Buses 40, 46, 62, 64, 916

Jerry Thomas Speakeasy makes some of the best cocktails in Rome. If you know the difference between single malt and blended whiskey, this is where to drink. Getting into the low-lit, cash-only joint with portraits of Al Capone on the walls and bearded barmen isn't so simple. You'll need to make a reservation at least a day in advance between 2pm and 6pm, memorize a password, and join the club (it's worth the effort). Smoking is allowed, flash photography isn't, and there's no vodka.

★ ARGOT
Via dei Cappellari 93; tel. 06/4555-1966; daily 10pm-4am; Buses 40, 46, 62, 64

The trio who opened Argot aren't interested in sleek design or fashionable interiors. Their mantra is retro comfort, and they succeeded in creating a quirky underground space where you can order unique cocktails, relax on vintage furniture, and listen to live music on weekends. The bar is popular with Romans and visitors tired of the mundane drinking holes around Campo De' Fiori.

OPEN BALADIN
Via Degli Specchi 6; tel. 06/683-8989; Sun.-Fri. noon-3pm and 6pm-11pm, Sat. noon-2am; Tram 8, Bus 63

Choosing a beer at Open Baladin isn't easy. The counter is lined with taps, and the wall behind this upbeat bar is covered with bottles that prove Peroni and Nastro Azzurro aren't the only beers brewed in Italy. Whatever you choose, it can be enjoyed with thick burgers served in the busy front room or the quieter rear dining area. It's busy at lunch and the perfect destination for a late-night meal.

Tridente
★ ANTICA BIRRERIA PERONI
Via S. Marcello 19; tel. 06/679-5310; Mon.-Sat. noon-midnight; Buses 62, 63, 83

The crisp, cold beer on tap at Antica Birreria Peroni is perfect for washing down the Tirolese dishes they serve, such as sausage and sauerkraut. Drinkers are merry, and the proximity of the dark wooden tables in this century-old establishment increases the opportunity to socialize. It can get loud, however, so if you're searching for intimacy head somewhere else.

Trastevere
FRENI E FRIZIONI
Via del Politeama 4/6; tel. 06/4549-7499; daily 6:30am-2am; Tram 8; Buses 23, 230

Freni e Frizioni is a vivacious bar with a large outdoor terrace where locals gather on summer nights. Getting a drink on a Friday evening can be challenging, but the crowd is festive and it's easy to meet people. The weekday *aperitivo* (€8) starts at 6:30pm and includes one drink and all you can eat from a long table lined with healthy options.

★ 404 NAME NOT FOUND
Via dei Genovesi 1; tel. 327/094-8005; Sun.-Thurs. 6:30am-11pm, Fri.-Sat. 6:30am-1am; Tram 8; Buses 23, 44, 280

There are fewer bars and drunken foreign exchange students on the other side of Viale Trastevere opposite Tiberina Island. This is where locals hang out and you can actually hear yourself speaking. 404 is a versatile little bar on a scenic corner with a handful of tables outside that are perfect for observing Roman street life. It's open throughout the day and makes an equally good morning cappuccino or evening craft beer stop. The cocktail menu has some interesting tequila, walnut whiskey, and Cointreau combinations, and if you get hungry there's a full menu of first and second courses to sample.

WINE BARS

Vineyards on the hillsides surrounding Rome aren't as famous as their Tuscan cousins, but the volcanic soil and sunny climate provides a distinct flavor that is helping small wineries establish themselves. You can sample these and many others at the *enoteca* wine bars scattered around the city. These range from historic to modern, but all offer food to accompany their regional and international vintages. Romans tend to combine eating and drinking, and there can be little difference between a wine bar and an *osteria*. All wineries provide by-the-glass (generally, around €5-10) or bottle options. Some, including Rimessa Rosciolo, organize tastings.

Ancient Rome and Monti
ASTEMIO
Via Cavour 93; tel. 06/487-3236; Mon.-Sat. 10am-midnight; Metro B: Cavour

Wine rarely goes without food in Italy, and both are on offer at this sophisticated *enoteca* with counter and table service. There's a wide selection of affordable by-the-glass vintages that cover most Italian regions and a handful of wine-tasting options. The food is also very good and ranges from cheese plates for snacking to a full menu of first and second courses. The bilingual staff are happy to make suggestions and can help organize an informal tasting. There's also plenty of Italian and French bubbly to discover.

Campo De' Fiori/ Piazza Navona
ROSCIOLI
Via dei Giubbonari 21; tel. 06/687-5287; Mon.-Sat. 9am-midnight; Tram 8, Buses 23, 63, 280

Avoid Roscioli if you have trouble selecting wine. This *trattoria* carries over 2,800 bottles for takeaway and a fraction of that for immediate consumption. Getting a table at the counter, along the wine-covered wall, or in the back isn't always easy, but it's worth the wait.

★ RIMESSA ROSCIOLO
Via del Conservatorio 58; tel. 06/6880-3914; www. winetastingrome.com; daily 12:30pm-3:30pm, 5pm-8pm; Tram 8, Buses 23, 63, 280

Friday night in Trastevere

If you prefer to drink without the bustle and want to learn about wine, attend a tasting at Rimessa Rosciolo. The dinner option includes 8 wines, 12 food pairings, pasta, and dessert. It lasts two and half mouthwatering hours and is hosted by a team of sommeliers. Dinner tastings (€69) start at 8pm while customized wine tastings (€59) begin at 5pm. Both must be reserved and are conducted in English.

CUL DE SAC

Piazza di Pasquino 73; tel. 06/6880-1094; daily noon-12:30am; Buses 46, 62, 64, 916

Cul de Sac means "dead end" in French, and that's what this place feels like. It's one long corridor lined with bottles and wooden booths where tables are already set with wine glasses. That's a good sign, as is the little kitchen area at the front where cheese and cured meat plates are prepared. The wine list could take an entire evening to read but if you want to cut to the chase order Barbera d'Asti Montalbera (2012).

VINO OLIO

Via dei Banchi Vecchi 14; tel. 339/533-3283; daily noon-midnight; Buses 46, 62, 64, 916

The nice thing about Vino Olio is that it's away from the main drag and prices are reasonable. Before stepping inside, observe the building's facade that looks like it got sliced in half. Inside, décor is simple with wooden tables, wooden chairs, and shelves lined with bottles. A glass of white or red starts at €5 with a dozen options of each written on a chalkboard behind the bar. During the summer the drinking spreads to the street outside.

ENOTECA CORSI

Via del Gesu 87; tel. 06/679-0821; Mon.-Fri. noon-3:30pm, 7pm-10:30pm, Sat. noon-3:30pm; Buses 30, 46, 62, 64, 70

Enoteca Corsi is an old-style wine bar with old-style prices. Nostalgia keeps regulars coming back for a daily menu of Roman specialties. They occasionally run out of some dishes if you arrive late, but they never run out of wine. Over 300 bottles cover the back room from floor to ceiling, with just enough space for a lucky few to sit and admire labels from every region in Italy.

Tridente
ENOTECA BUCCONE

Via di Ripetta 19/20; tel. 06/361-2154; Mon.-Thurs. 9am-8:30pm, Fri.-Sat. 9am-11pm, Sun. 11am-7pm; Metro A: Flaminio

Enoteca Buccone is located on the quietest of the three streets that make up the Tridente and is where locals go to drink wine and dig into a small menu of local dishes. The shelves are full of bottles and there are a handful of small tables where you can sit down with a glass of Amarone, Barolo, or Brunello and whatever brothers Francesco and Vincenzo have cooked up that day. Generous cured ham and cheese platters are always available.

Trastevere
ESSENZA WINE BAR

Via della Scala 27a; tel. 06/6935-9966; Sun.-Thurs. noon-midnight, Fri.-Sat. noon-2am; Buses 23, 280

The Trastevere neighborhood caters more to raucous beer bars than *enoteca*. Finding a place to enjoy a bottle of red in this neighborhood was hard—until Essenza opened. This sophisticated oasis provides a relaxing environment to sip regional vintages accompanied by platters of cheese, cold cuts, olives, and *bruschette*. The by-the-glass selection is limited and you're better off ordering a bottle.

BACCO IN TRASTEVERE

Piazza San Giovanni della Malva 14; tel. 389/948-4855; Buses 23, 280

Bacco is located on a small pedestrian square where locals and international students from the nearby university regularly gather. Grab a table outside and order a bottle from the long wine menu. There are also three red and three white options available by the glass that can be accompanied with light snacks. A full lunch and dinner menu are also available.

Termini

TRIMANI ENOTECA

Via Gioto 20; tel. 06/446-9661; Mon.-Sat. 9am-7pm;
Metro B: Castro Pretorio

Trimani is the oldest *enoteca* in Rome and has occupied the present site since 1876. Back then wine was served from casks, but the shop has evolved with the times and today sells over 6,000 bottles from Italy and the world. If you like to browse labels, you'll have your eyes full here and can have anything shipped directly home. Around the corner is the **Trimani Winebar** (Via Cernaia 37b; tel. 06/446-9630; Mon.-Sat. 5:30pm-midnight) where you can sample Lazio's version of a Super Tuscan along with appetizers or a full meal.

CLUBS

If you're searching for a party in Rome, you'll find it. The city's clubs present a range of musical scenes. Monday nights are generally slow, Thursdays are up-tempo, and weekends always pull in a crowd. You can also discover new genres spun by the Italian and international DJs who liven up the city's nocturnal hours. During the summer many clubs relocate to the beaches of Ostia where the dancing is done in the sand. Most bars also have a house DJ and straddle the bar-disco divide, and many clubs also serve food. The slightly secluded hillside around **Monte Testaccio** is where a lot of the capital's clubbing is concentrated, and lines start forming from 11pm onward. The **Ostiense** neighborhood outside the historic center is also worth exploring if you want to party like a Roman. Via Giuseppe Libetta alone has a handful of clubs and discos. Dress codes vary from none to chic, but keep in mind Italian fashion standards are high by default.

Clubs were the first to close during the 2020 coronavirus pandemic lockdown, and the last to reopen. Many have gone out of business, so it's worth calling before setting off on a night out.

Campo De' Fiori/ Piazza Navona

LA FINE

Largo dei Fiorentini 3; tel. 349/273-9585; Tues.-Sat. 6:30pm-4am; Buses 23, 280, 270

Step inside La Fine (the end) and you could be in Berlin or New York. This small club inside a former theater has an intimate, underground feel and no pretention. There are plenty of nooks and crannies along with a dedicated dancing area and top DJs or live music. Drinks are priced at €10 and entry is free unless there's a special event.

WISDOMLESS

Via Sora 33; tel. 06/6880-1823; Mon.-Sat. noon-2am; Buses 40, 46, 62, 64

Walking into Wisdomless feels like walking into a museum. It's filled with an eclectic assortment of odds and ends that would be at home in a Jules Verne novel. Staff are welcoming and mix wonderful drinks that can be enjoyed on plush leather couches that add to the air of sophistication. The club has its very own tattoo parlor where you can get a souvenir to last a lifetime.

Tridente

BAJA

Lungotevere A. da Brescia; tel. 06/9436-8869; daily 6pm-1:30am; Metro A: Flaminio

Every night the house DJ at Baja presents a different musical genre to middle-age revelers. It's a floating party located directly on the Tiber River featuring a low-lit lounge and American bar that's conducive to conversations. Happy hour is 7pm-9pm, and the restaurant stays open late.

Trastevere

BEIGE ROMA

Via del Politeama 13; tel. 347/389-1974; daily 7pm-2am; Tram 8, Buses 23, 280

Situated down the street from Piazza Trilussa, this compact club is one of the more affordable nightlife options in the area. Just €10 gets you a cocktail and access to an impressive spread of appetizers. The music is also good and spun by the house DJ. They often organize private parties, during which they are closed to the general public.

Aventino and Testaccio
PLANET ROME
Via del Commercio 36; tel. 06/574-7826; www. planetroma.com; Tues.-Sun., 10pm-4am; Metro B: Piramide
Planet Rome is one of the largest discos in the city and can accommodate up to 2,500 revelers. There are seven dance floors and a fairly strict door policy. Commercial, house, hip-hop, and revival keep dancers busy, while the garden allows for conversation. Rock bands perform most Sundays at 10pm, and Saturday nights host a long-standing LGBT event complete with go-go boys and girls. Entry is often free before midnight.

Ostiense
GOA
Via Giuseppe Libetta 13; tel. 06/574-8277; www. goaclub.com; Sept.-May Thurs.-Sat. 11:30pm-5am; Metro B: Garbatella
Romans have been dancing at Goa since it was transformed from a motorcycle repair shop into a disco. It's a no-frills kind of club with veteran DJs intent on making dancers sweat. There are two bars (€8 cocktails) and a balcony to watch the action. The audio system is one of the best in the city and is usually playing house and techno. No VIP rooms or red-velvet ropes here, although large groups of males are likely to be turned away.

RASHOMON
Via degli Argonauti 16; tel. 391/730-7386; www. roshomonclub.com; Wed.-Thurs. 7:30pm-4am, Fri.-Sat. 10pm-6am; Metro B: Garbatella
Whether you're a nocturnal regular or occasional clubber, Rashomon provides deep house and techno grooves that are addictive. This place is packed and people come to dance. There is a garden for taking breathers and letting eardrums recover (it gets very loud) between sets. Kerri Chandler, The

Analogue Cops, and Jeremy Underground have all spun here and the DJ lineup is among the best in Rome. Depending on the night entry is free or €15.

Termini
JOLIE CLUB
Via Velletri 13; tel. 06/841-2212; Tues.-Sun. 11pm-4am; Buses 63, 83, 92
Jolie Club is as close as Rome gets to Ibiza. They recently installed a new speaker system and the two-hall disco never sounded so good. Both are filled with young clubbers who come for the international DJs that regularly appear behind the decks.

PERFORMING ARTS
Culture is king in Rome, and there's no shortage of high-quality music, dance, and theater experiences available each week. Many historic and newly built venues exist with great acoustics and fabulously ornate interiors. The city attracts international artists of the highest caliber performing in front of audiences who appreciate talent.

Music and Dance
PARCO DELLA MUSICA
Viale Pietro de Coubertin 30; tel. 06/802-411; www. auditorium.com; Tram 2, Buses 168, 910, 982
Modern architecture and music harmonize at the Parco della Musica. Rome's largest music venue showcases the world's best classical, jazz, and contemporary performers on three world-class stages. The Renzo Piano-designed halls resemble metallic whales beached in northern Rome. Connoisseurs of acoustics will appreciate the modular wooden ceilings, which are adjusted according to the genre of music played. The outdoor amphitheater holds summertime concerts and the restaurant/bar and café complement any evening.

AUDITORIUM DELLA CONCILIAZIONE
Via della Conciliazione 4; tel. 06/684-391; www. auditoriumconciliazione.it; Buses 23, 34, 40, 280, 982
The Orchestra Sinfonica di Roma

performs regularly at the Auditorium della Conciliazione. Guest conductors and international soloists often join them in an eclectic symphonic program. The 1,700-seat theater is a few blocks from St. Peter's and regularly sells out. The Chorus Café (tel. 06/6889-2774) located inside is an elegant option for dinner or a cocktail before or after a performance.

TEATRO DELL'OPERA

Piazza Beniamino Gigli 1; tel. 06/481-601; www. operaroma.it; €10-100; Buses 40, 60, 64, 70, 71,

Teatro dell'Opera may not be as famous as La Fenice in Venice, but the lavish interior and persistently good productions never fail to thrill eyes and ears. The opera season runs from November to June and includes classics like *La Traviata, Carmen*, and *The Barber of Seville*, performed the way their creators intended. During the summer the stage moves to the Baths of Caracalla and takes on a whole new dimension. A world-class ballet company also performs within the opera house.

GLOBE THEATER

Largo Aqua Felix; tel. 338/910-4467; daily 4pm-7pm; www.globetheatreroma.com; €10-27; Trams 2, 3, 19, Buses 61, 89

Shakespeare loved Italy so much he set 13 of his plays here. It's no surprise then to find a reconstruction of the original Globe Theater in Villa Borghese. The Bard's plays are faithfully performed in English and Italian, and the drama can be followed standing in the pit or from three open-air balconies where spectators are well-spaced and have a great view of the stage.

Dinner Theater

SALONE MARGHERITA

Via dei Due Macelli 75; tel. 392/224-3672; www. miccaclub.com; Thurs.-Sun. 8pm-2am; €25-65; Metro A: Spagna

Salone Margherita has been hosting dinner theater since 1898 and is the only theater in Rome with a kitchen. Shows are popular fare with regular nights devoted to opera

and big band, but the best time to come is Tuesday when a burlesque troop takes the stage. Dinner includes a three-course meal (€65 pp), but you can also opt just to listen. Performances start at 9pm and audience participation is encouraged.

FESTIVALS AND EVENTS

Rome has a rich calendar of cultural, sporting, and religious events that can make a trip even more memorable. Some, like the marathon or summer opera series, require registration or tickets; others like the Easter festivities and anniversary of Rome celebrations are free.

Spring

Pilgrims flock to the city's basilicas during Easter, following the Procession of the Cross at 9pm to the Colosseum on Good Friday and attending the Pope's Sunday morning mass outside St. Peter's.

For two weeks starting in mid-May, Via dei Coronari rolls out the red carpet, candles are lit, and banners fly. It's time for the Antiques Fair, when the dealers who occupy nearly every shop on the street bring out their best merchandise and prospective buyers put on their poker faces.

Rome celebrates its birthday every year on April 21. Concerts and cultural events are organized in the Circus Maximus to honor the legendary anniversary of the city's foundation in AD 753. The highlight is the historic reenactment charting ancient Rome's rise to greatness and the defeat of its enemies. Hundreds of costumed enthusiasts dress up as battle-hardened centurions and their barbarian foes. Spectators surround the mock battlefield and afterward you can get up close to the warriors, who prefer to remain in character.

Summer

Summer brings entertainment and art to unexpected places around Rome. An outdoor cinema projects films nightly on the Isola Tiberina, world-renowned authors recite their works in the Forum, and concerts are held in the Circus Maximus. Bars and restaurants are also installed along the Tiber River.

Throughout the summer, Terme di Caracalla becomes the backdrop for the **Rome Opera Summer Series** (www.operaroma.it) from late June until the middle of August. Classics like *Aida* and *Madame Butterfly* are performed within the ancient baths. Tickets (€20-90) can be purchased online or at the Teatro di Roma box office in Piazza Beniamino Gigli 7.

According to legend, it snowed heavily in Rome on August 5 in AD 352. Since then, with little interruption, the **Festa della Madonna delle Neve** (tel. 06/6988-6800) has been held at Santa Maria Maggiore. Crowds gather throughout the day and white petals are thrown from the dome of the cathedral during an outdoor evening liturgy.

The **Jazz Festival** (tel. 06/0608) in the Villa Celimontana gardens presents two months of nightly concerts in one of Rome's most beautiful parks, moments from the Colosseum. Prices rarely exceed €15 and the intimate outdoor amphitheater is bordered by an assortment of bars and restaurants.

Ferragosto is the midsummer Italian holiday originally created to honor Emperor Augustus in 8 BC. It takes place on August 15 every year and many Romans escape the heat of the city and head for the beach or countryside. Many restaurants and bars close for a week or two and traffic is greatly reduced.

Fall

In mid-November, cinema stars walk down the red carpet during the **Festival Internazionale del Film di Roma** (www.romacinemafest.it). The festival is held at the Auditorium della Musica and has proved quite popular since its debut in 2006. If you are interested in catching a world premiere, book ahead as tickets (€10-20) sell out quickly.

Throughout November and December, the **RomaEuropa Festival** (www.romaeuropa.net) presents avant-garde music and dance in venues around the city. Artists come from all over the world and provide a snapshot of the latest cultural innovations. Tickets cost €15-40 and performances are exuberant and unlike anything seen before.

Winter

Romans get into the Christmas spirit in early December and traditionally decorate their trees on the 8th, the day of the **Feast of the**

annual historical reenactment celebrating the city's foundation on April 21

Immaculate Conception. Sweets and traditional ornaments are sold in the **Christmas Market** erected in Piazza Navona and the smell of roasted chestnuts permeates the streets.

Italian children look forward to the arrival of **La Befana,** a witch-like figure who rides a broomstick and brings candy to the good and coal to the bad on January 6. The carousel (€2) in Piazza Navona operates throughout December and January, and gives parents a chance to treat children before schools reconvene.

Confetti-strewn streets are a signal that **Carnevale** is near. The edible indicator is the *frappe* (thin strips of fried or baked dough covered in sugar), which appear in bars and bakeries from late January until *Martedi Grasso* (Mardi Gras) and go well with cappuccino or hot chocolate (*cioccolatta calda*). Each of the city's neighborhoods organizes events that take place in larger squares like Piazza Navona and Piazza del Popolo. The **Bioparco di Roma** (www.bioparco.it)

prepares a children's carnival on the Saturday before Mardi Gras with an animal parade and face painting.

The number of joggers increases after New Year's Eve, but that doesn't necessarily have to do with resolutions. Many are preparing for the **Rome Marathon** (www.maratonadiroma. it), which takes place at the end of March or early April. Over 20,000 runners participate, and the start and finish line is next to the Colosseum. If you don't feel like running the entire 26.2 miles (42.195 kilometers), register for the 3.2-mile (5-kilometer) fun run.

Rugby fans can catch the **Six Nations** tournament at the Stadio Olimpico. There are two or three matches every year scheduled on Sunday afternoons in February and March. The Italian national team faces off against England, France, Wales, Scotland, and Ireland. Win or lose, there's a great ambience between fans before, during, and after the match, and unlike soccer games where opposing supporters are divided, the seating at rugby is mixed.

Shopping

While Florence has leather and Venice has glass, Rome doesn't have a distinctive specialty product. It has a little of everything and there are many opportunities to be enticed by high and low fashion, shoes, accessories, antiques, art, home goods, and oddities. If you're searching for something unique, you'll find it, as skilled hands are busy in workshops across the city. Handmade ceramics, candles, clothing, jewelry, and paintings make original souvenirs and leave a lasting impression of the city.

Shops are scattered around the historic center but there are some streets with a high concentration of global chains, boutiques, and specialty stores that attract large numbers of shoppers. The pedestrianized **Via del Corso** is the main shopping drag with a succession of international stores. Higher-end

brands are clustered along **Via Condotti** and the surrounding streets near Piazza di Spagna. Antiques can be found along **Via dei Coronari** in the Navona area, while handicraft workshops and small galleries are scattered near **Campo De' Fiori** and **Monti.** Each neighborhood has its own market, and the city's biggest flea market, **Porta Portese,** is held in Testaccio.

ANCIENT ROME AND MONTI

The shops that once lined Trajan's Forum went out of business a long time ago. Today, the sales continue behind those ruins in Monti, which competes with Trastevere and Testaccio for the title of most Roman neighborhood. There is something a little edgier here, though, and the boutiques aren't run of the mill. You'll find young designers and old-timers carrying on ancient crafts inside narrow storefronts.

Via Urbana is one of Monti's characteristic thoroughfares and a good place to start browsing. Here, artisans and merchants go about their business with no concern for the Colosseum. It lies parallel to the souvenir shops and tourist traps of **Via Cavour** but feels miles away. The cobblestone street, which locals successfully petitioned to have pedestrianized, follows a gentle incline and is dotted with boutiques, workshops, eateries, barbers, and jewelry stores. It isn't very long but may lead to backtracking and can easily absorb an hour or two.

Arts and Crafts
SILICE
*Via Urbana 27; tel. 06/474-5552; Mon.-Sat.
10am-7pm; Metro B: Cavour*
Inside Silice, Anna Preziosi transforms glass into small works of art. She doesn't use a blowing technique; instead, she works with sheets that she melts in an oven at the back of her studio. Lamps and decorative pieces are displayed in the front room and temptingly priced. She's happy to explain her process and show visitors around.

RIGODRITTO INTERIORS
*Via Urbana 118; tel. 06/4547-6078; daily 11am-8pm;
Metro B: Cavour, Buses 71, 75, 117*
Brothers Eduardo and Francesco are masters of shaping wood, glass, and metal into original design objects for the home. Their leaning bookcases and cutting boards with integrated knife slots are functional and elegant. Prices are reasonable considering most objects are handmade in the rear of this urban studio. Don't worry if something won't fit in your luggage; they ship everywhere.

CANDLES STORE ROMA
*Via Urbana 21; tel. 06/9027-3263; daily 11am-1pm
and 2:30pm-8pm; Metro B: Cavour*
Brazilian owner Andrea Moraes and her assistant work wax in the front of this enticing shop and are happy to explain the ancient technique they use to form their creations. The candles are colorful and come in many shapes and designs. Prices start at €10 and go up according to size.

POTS
*Via in Selci 64; tel. 335/690-2179; Mon.-Wed.
3pm-7pm, Fri.-Sat. 10am-7pm; Metro B: Cavour*
Sebastiano and his wife are passionate about pottery. They opened Pots in 2010 and have been teaching ceramics and selling their handmade creations ever since. Pieces are functional and the mugs, espresso cups, water jars, candle holders, and affordable knick-knacks make practical souvenirs. The studio is on a quiet side street outside the hustle of Monti and is worth a detour.

Clothing and Accessories
KING SIZE VINTAGE
*Via Leonina 79; tel. 06/481-7045; daily 11am-8:30pm;
Metro A: Repubblica*
This small and well-organized one-room shop sells men's and women's secondhand shirts, dresses, shoes, and accessories dating from the 1940s to 1990s. They have a good selection of leather jackets as well as sneakers from yesteryear. It's located near the center of Monti and many good browsing opportunities.

Markets
MERCATO MONTI URBAN MARKET ROMA
*Grand Hotel Palatino, Via Leonina 46; www.
mercatomonti.com; Sept.-June Sat.-Sun. 10am-8pm;
Metro B: Cavour*
The Monti Urban Market is held in a hotel. It's not kitsch, just comfortable and friendly with lots of interesting stands. Merchants are part of an extended family that encourages new talents like **Annabella Cuomo,** who paints illustrations on T-shirts, and the **COSMOOS** collective, who create one-of-a-kind jewelry out of natural stones and noble metals. There are scores of tables to scan and clothes racks to consider.

MERCATO RIONALE

Via Baccina 36; tel. 345/460-6488; Mon., Wed.,
Thurs., Sat. 7am-3pm, Tues., Fri. 7am-7pm; Metro B:
Cavour

This small indoor market is where locals go for vegetables, meat, fish, bread, wine, cheese, and other edible necessities. It's totally unpretentious and a great place to find all the ingredients you need for a picnic.

CAMPO DE' FIORI/ PIAZZA NAVONA

These virtually chain-free neighborhoods are full of original clothing and jewelry boutiques. **Via dei Giubbonari** is lined with shops from Piazza dei Fiori to Via Arenula. Anyone interested in antiques can get their fill along **Via dei Coronari**. If you prefer your art fresh from the easel, the dozens of street artists in **Piazza Navona** paint oil and watercolor canvases fit to be framed. Prices aren't exorbitant and the best thing to do is browse different canvases until you find a style you like. **Via del Governo Vecchio** is a long, gently winding street dotted with hip shops that don't attract the crowds of Via del Corso. It's a perfect stroll on a hot afternoon. Activity goes on at all hours in **Campo De' Fiori**. During the day, the square fills with stalls selling flowers, vegetables, and knickknacks that attract locals and visitors in search of souvenirs.

Antiques

The number of antiques stores is especially high around Campo De' Fiori, and Via dei Coronari is the center of the trade. Don't expect bargains, and don't hesitate to negotiate if the price seems exorbitant.

ANTIQUARIATO VALLIGIANO

Via Giulia 193; tel. 06/686-9505; daily 10am-1:30pm
and 4pm-7:30pm; Buses 23, 280

For a break from the baroque furnishings that dominate many shops, try Antiquariato Valligiano. It's a sure place to find objects that once populated 19th-century farmhouses. There are plenty of wooden tools and outdated technology that would look great on mantles and shelves.

COMICS BAZAR

Via dei Banchi Vecchi 127; tel. 06/6880-2923;
Tues.-Sun. 9am-1pm and 3pm-7pm; Buses 40, 46,
62, 64

This shop is crammed with books, prints, paintings, lamps, and knickknacks that make bargain hunting fun. Prices aren't always listed so you may have to ask *scusi, quanto costa?* (excuse me, how much does it cost?).

Books

IL MUSEO DEL LOUVRE

Via della Reginella 8a; tel. 06/6880-7725; Mon.-Sat.
11am-2pm and 2:30pm-7pm; Tram 8, Buses 23, 63,
280

How places like Il Museo del Louvre stay in business is a delightful mystery. This combination gallery and secondhand bookstore specializes in Italian literature and no doubt has a loyal following of readers. A signed edition of Neruda is kept under glass and costs €1,200. Next door is a collection of 20,000 photographs organized by subject and crammed with anonymous shots of everyday Rome from the 1960s to the present day as well as works by celebrated photographers.

FELTRINELLI

Largo di Torre Argentina 5a; tel. 02/9194-7777;
Mon.-Sat. 10am-8pm, Sun. 10am-2pm and 4pm-8pm;
Tram 8, Buses 30, 40, 46, 62, 64

Feltrinelli is the Italian version of Barnes & Noble with better coffee and fewer sofas. They also carry music, and if you've never listened to an Italian singer before the staff can fix that. Find CDs for under €6, including music from the legendary Mina, singer-songwriters like the late Lucio Dalla, aging rockers of the Vasco Rossi and Luciano Ligabue variety, sophisticated songs by Manika Ayan, and Jovanotti's Italian pop. There are several branches around the city but this is the largest.

1: handmade candles from Candles Store Roma
2: Pots ceramic studio and store

Clothing and Accessories

STRATEGIC BUSINESS UNIT

Via di Pantaleo 68-69; tel. 06/6880-2547; Mon.-Sat.
10am-7:30pm, Sun. noon-7pm; Buses 46, 62, 64, 916

Strategic Business Unit doesn't sound like it would create comfortable men's clothing, but the originators of this Roman label obviously have a sense of irony as well as a talent for designing sportswear in a variety of fabrics.

SIRNI

Via della Stelletta 33; tel. 06/6880-5248; Mon.-Sat.
10am-7:30pm; Buses 70, 81, 87, 492, 628

Sirni sells pizzazz you can carry. Their bags are all created from high-quality leather that's transformed into every size and shape imaginable. If you don't find what you're looking for on the shelves or extensive catalogue, they are happy create a clutch, shoulder bag, *pochette,* or backpack according to your specifications. Of course, handmade isn't cheap: All the bags here have three digits on the price tag.

CAMICERIA BRACCI

Via dei Funari 18 and Via delle Coppelle 73;
tel. 06/9291-8159; Mon.-Sat. 10am-2pm and
3:30pm-7:30pm; Tram 8, Buses 30, 44, 51, 63, 81

Getting a handmade shirt may sound extravagant, but it is made accessible at men's shops like Camiceria Bracci. The made-to-measure products provide another level of comfort and confidence. It will take longer than buying off the rack and requires you to learn about collar types, thread thickness, and cotton quality, but once you do it's hard to go back to prêt-à-porter. Clerks are patient with newcomers and they'll file your details so you can reorder whenever you like from wherever you like.

Shoes

MAURO LEONE

Via del Biscione 8; tel. 06/6880-4918; Mon.
3pm-7:30pm, Tues.-Sat. 10am-7:30pm, Sun.
3pm-7:30pm; Buses 46, 62, 64, 916

Mauro Leone is a family business with a half dozen stores and a factory in northern Italy where they produce distinctive women's footwear. All the sandals, heels, flats, and boots are rigorously made from Italian leather and look fantastic on the feet. The shop is tiny but well organized and many models are stored in the back room. If you see something appealing in the window, just point to it and ask for your (European) size.

daily market in Campo De' Fiori

Perfume and Herbal Remedies

ESSENZIALMENTE LAURA

Via dei Coronari 57; tel. 06/686-4224; daily
10:30am-7:30pm; Buses 30, 70, 81, 87, 280, 492
Inside Laura Tonatto's boutique you can smell a variety of fragrances and discover how these are transformed into perfumes, lotions, and creams by the friendly staff of olfactory experts. The Rome-inspired perfumes are sold in distinctive bottles and available for men and women.

ANTICA ERBORISTERIA ROMANA

Via di Torre Argentina 15; tel. 06/687-9493;
Mon.-Sat. 9am-8pm; Buses 30, 40, 46, 62, 64
Rome's oldest herb shop has been in business since 1752 and sells over 350 aromatic plants that cure everything from insomnia to indigestion. Just tell them what's bothering you and they'll prepare a personalized infusion. While you're waiting be sure to check out the antique furnishings and painted wooden ceiling that would be familiar to 19th-century customers.

Housewares

LELA

Via dei Pettinari 37; tel. 06/8777-5792; Mon.-Sat.
11:30am-7:30pm; Buses 23, 280
Lela sells Nordic and Italian household goods in an inviting one-room shop near the Ponte Sisto bridge. The friendly owner and charming selection of kitchenware make this a fun place to browse and find memorable gifts. Wooden items are on display along with glass carafes, colorful tin mugs, and honey-scented candles all at reasonable prices.

Leather

MANCINI

Via della Palombella 28; tel. 06/686-1485; daily
10:30am-7:30pm; Buses 70, 81, 87, 492, 628
Leather isn't as closely associated with Rome as it is with Florence, but you can still find places like Mancini where they've been making leather bags, wallets, and belts since 1918. There's a wide range of traditional luggage and briefcases that come in many colors.

Prices reflect the handmade quality of the products, and a small handbag can easily exceed €200.

Toys

AL SOGNO

Piazza Navona 53; tel. 06/686-4198; daily
10am-8pm; Buses 30, 70, 81, 87, 492
Three shops in the vicinity of Piazza Navona will please both parents and kids, though it's a challenge to leave each one empty-handed. Al Sogno is just off the famous square. Inside, it's hard to decide what mask, puppet, car, sword, or medieval pistol to play with first. Many items are wrapped, and the most realistic toy soldiers are safely behind glass, but the salespeople are relaxed and touching is permitted.

CITTÀ DEL SOLE

Via della Scrofa 65; tel. 06/6880-3805; Mon.-Sat.
10am-7:30pm, Sun. 11am-7:30pm; Buses 30, 70, 81,
87, 492
If your offspring aren't into traditional toys, just walk out of Piazza Navona and zigzag over to Città del Sole. This ecofriendly toy chain fosters creative play. Plenty of wood and educational items are in stock and ready to try along with art supplies, musical instruments, board games, outdoor activities, books, and a fun assortment of safe gadgets for children under three.

TRIDENTE

Tridente is the most glamorous place to shop in Rome. It's primarily about women's clothing, though men are catered to as well. The epicenter of high fashion is **Via Condotti,** while international chains are concentrated along **Via del Corso.** The parallel pedestrian streets are filled with boutiques and megastores from Armani to Zara.

Antiques

GALLERIA VALERIO TURCHI

Via Margutta 91; tel. 06/323-5047; Mon.-Fri.
10am-7pm, Sat. 10am-1pm; Metro A: Spagna or
Flaminio
It's getting harder and harder to spot an

antique shop in the neighborhood, but Turchi is one of the remaining pillars of the trade. The third-generation institution deals in Greek and Roman statues that are thousands of years old and cost many times that. Many items aren't allowed out of the country and museum curators from around the world covet those that are. Large groups are dissuaded from entering the dimly lit gallery, but serious visitors are always welcome.

Arts and Crafts
IL MARMARO
Via Margutta 53b; tel. 06/320-7660; Mon.-Sat. 9am-7:30pm; Metro A: Spagna or Flaminio
Sandro is a remnant of a lost age. Most days you'll find him inside Il Marmaro engraving stone or stirring his soup on an open fire. He's been doing both for decades. The little marble plaques displayed in the basket by the window are a unique souvenir. They come with short epithets (€15) or can be personalized with the words of your choosing (€20) in under an hour.

Clothing and Accessories
AS ROMA STORE
Via del Corso 25; tel. 06/6452-1063; daily 10am-8pm; Metro A: Flaminio
There comes a time when you have to declare your soccer loyalty and reveal your team colors. If you make the popular choice you'll support AS Roma, but before buying a cheap acrylic jersey hanging from an outdoor souvenir stand, check out the authentic uniforms, scarves, and gadgets available at the AS Roma Store. Prices are higher for official kit but you're more likely to find proper sizes and the latest home and away uniforms. During the summer, after the season ends, a lot of merchandise goes on sale.

Shoes
SUPERGA
Via della Vite 86; tel. 06/678-7654; daily 10:30am-7:30pm; Metro A: Spagna
Not all Italian shoes have heels. Superga makes casual street sneakers for men and women that regularly come into and out of fashion. Whatever the fad, they are comfortable for walking and very colorful, like an Italian Converse without the branding.

MICHELE DI LOCO
Via del Leone 7; tel. 06/4547-9103; Mon. 3:30pm-7:30pm, Tues.-Sun. 10:30am-7:30pm; Bus 628
If you're not ready for the stiletto edge of fashion, stay away from Michele di Loco. The selection is small and occasionally outrageous, but the craftsmanship is undeniably high—and so are the prices.

Housewares
BIALETTI
Largo Chigi 5; tel. 06/8927-6836; daily 10am-8pm; Buses 51, 52, 53
The scent of pastries and sweet Roman air can't be bottled, but some smells can be reproduced—and coffee is number one among these. It's brewed differently in Rome and the steam coming out of a **moka** filled with a distinct Arabica blend will rekindle images of café terraces and neighborhood bars. You'll find all kinds of coffeemakers at Bialetti that can be easily used at home.

Markets
MERCATO DELLE STAMPE
Largo della Fontanella di Borghese; daily 7am-1pm; Bus 628
If you're searching for magazine covers of Sophia Loren or old Piranesi prints of 17th-century Rome, Mercato delle Stampe is your jackpot. Everything here looks as though it would be the perfect addition to that blank wall back home.

IL MERCATINO DEL BORGHETTO FLAMINIO
Via Flaminia 32; Sun. 10am-7pm; Metro A: Flaminio
Kitsch, curiosities, and the occasional gem are reason enough to visit Il Mercatino del Borghetto. This flea market housed in a former bus depot is more about quantity than quality, but there are bargains to be had. You'll

find vintage bags and shoes from top designers, antiques, books, conversation pieces from past eras, and plenty of clothes to rummage through. The entry fee is €2.

VATICANO

Shopping is a religion to some, so it's no surprise to find stores in the shadow of St. Peter's. **Via Cola di Rienzo** houses the majority of these, including a branch of the **Coin** department store. The lack of parks in the area means the best place to take a break from spending is inside one of the historic cafés that line this busy avenue.

Arts and Crafts
SAVELLI
Via Paolo VI 27; tel. 06/6830-7017; Mon.-Sat. 9:30am-6:30pm, Sun. 9:30am-2pm; Buses 34, 46, 98
Small, very small, and even smaller mosaics are created at Savelli. Find out how these little gems are made by having a look in the studio, where an assortment of religious objects are also under construction.

Books
MONDADORI
Piazza Cola di Rienzo 81; tel. 06/322-0188; daily 9am-10pm; Metro A: Lepanto
There are two kinds of Roman readers: Those who prefer buying their books at Feltrinelli, and those who only shop at Mondadori. Find out what kind you are at this megastore with an extensive English section.

Clothing and Accessories
MAXIM
Via Ottaviano 17; tel. 06/3972-3718; daily 10am-7:30pm; Metro A: Ottaviano
Before you buy a bag anywhere else, check Maxim. Popular labels like Coccinelle, Nannini, and Biasia are all here and they're priced a lot less than at other stores in the area.

Shoes
GUJA
Via del Cola di Rienzo 36; tel. 06/9760-3838; daily 11am-7:30pm; Metro A: Lepanto

Guja is a small chain that stocks lots of brands. The heels come in all heights and are perfect for romantic escapades. Leather quality is good, and prices not excessive. There's a second location near Corso in Via Gambero 9.

TRASTEVERE
Arts and Crafts
POLVERE DI TEMPO
Via del Moro 59; tel. 06/588-0704; Mon.-Sat. 10am-1pm, 2pm-8pm, Buses 23, 280
Polvere di Tempo seems to be a cross between Hobbit's den and Hogwarts stockroom. Find sundials, hourglasses, compasses, globes, maps, and leather-bound notebooks temptingly on display inside. The shop is the realm of Adrian, the Argentinian owner, and Lavinia, his Anglo-Italian assistant, who happily describe how their unique creations are made.

GALLERIA D'ARTE SPAZIO 40
Via dell'Arco di S. Callisto 40; tel. 349/165-4628; Tues.-Sat. 9am-1pm and 3pm-8pm; Buses 23, 280
Fabrizio and his wife opened their gallery on a quiet side street with the idea of bringing art to the masses. Together they create affordable jewelry, paintings, and colorful knickknacks that are fun to wear and are all hand made by the couple.

Books
ALMOST CORNER BOOKSHOP
Via del Moro 45; tel. 06/583-6942; daily 10am-1:30pm and 3:30pm-8pm; Tram 8, Buses 23, 280
The Almost Corner Bookshop is a charming refuge of English-language literature where browsing is encouraged. There are plenty of up-to-date titles and a range of genres from the latest thrillers to historical fiction.

OPEN DOOR BOOKSHOP
Via della Lungaretta 23; tel. 06/589-6478; Mon. 4:30pm-8:30pm, Tues.-Sat. 10am-1pm and 4:30pm-8:30pm, Sun. 12:30pm-6:30pm; Tram 8, Buses 23, 280

Less than 200 yards away from the Almost Corner Bookshop on the other side of Viale Trastevere is the Open Door Bookshop. Shelves are crammed with used English, French, and Italian titles and the friendly bilingual staff are usually spot on with their recommendations.

Markets
PORTA PORTESE

Piazzale Portuense; Sun. 6am-2pm; Trams 3, 8, Buses 44, 75

The biggest flea market in the city, Porta Portese attracts thousands of Romans and tourists every Sunday morning. It's located just outside the old Aurelian walls along Via Portuense. While it isn't particularly scenic, it is animated, with stalls selling clothing, bags, kitchenware, electronics, and a wide range of cheap curiosities. Haggling is customary and can save you some euros. The best deals are had when the market opens and closes. In recent years, made-in-China goods have replaced antiques, and the crowds seem more interested in knockoffs than authentic wares. Still, the market is an experience. The stretch near Piazza Ippolito Nievo is the best place to find stands selling ancient Roman coins, old maps, and vintage Leicas.

PIAZZA SAN COSIMATO MARKET

Piazza di San Cosimato 64; Mon.-Sat. 6:30am-2:30pm; Tram 8, Buses 44, 75, 115

Piazza San Cosimato Market is primarily dedicated to food and is the place to go for fruit, vegetables, cheese, meat, and fish. It's also a great place to observe Romans in their natural habitat.

AVENTINO AND TESTACCIO
Markets
SALUMERIA VOLPETTI

Via Marmorata 47; tel. 06/574-2352; Mon.-Sat. 9am-2pm and 4pm-8pm, Tues. 9am-2pm; Metro B: Piramide

Window shopping at E. Volpetti will affect your taste buds. This gourmet emporium covers nearly every food group from thick-crusted breads and cured meats to freshly made pasta and dessert. Immaculately dressed attendants serve a steady stream of regulars, but you don't need to feel obliged to buy—the smell alone is worth a visit.

Polvere di Tempo

TERMINI
Books
IBS LIBRACCIO

Via Nazionale 254; tel. 06/488-5405; Mon.-Sat.
9am-8pm, Sun. 10am-1:30pm, 4-8pm; Metro A:
Repubblica

Don't judge IBS by the entrance. The nondescript front doors lead to a palatial hall filled with every category of book imaginable. Used books are in the basement, travel and fiction on the ground floor, and design and architecture are next to the bar on the second. There are also few shelves with the latest best sellers in English if you need something to read on the way to Florence or Venice.

Shoes
GEOX

Via Nazionale 232; tel. 06/481-4518; daily
10am-8pm; Metro A: Repubblica

If you like the idea of a shoe that breathes, then Geox is for you. This ever-expanding franchise produces patented casual and elegant models renowned for comfort and durability (€80-120). There's something for men, women, and children, and they design a new line of fashionable footwear every season. U.S. sizes are indicated, and they've recently branched out into accessories and jackets.

Activities and Recreation

There's more to do in Rome than throwing a coin into the Trevi Fountain. The prevalence of blue skies and fine weather means life is lived outdoors and there's no shortage of activities.

Sport in Italy is synonymous with *calcio* (soccer) and Romans are especially mad for the game. Anywhere there's grass there's likely to be people kicking a ball around. Cycling is another common (if occasionally dangerous) pastime, and what the city lacks in bicycle lanes it makes up for in beautiful parks and scenic trails.

There are even more options outside Rome. Take a day trip outside the city to kayak on a volcanic lake, or cycle past ancient monuments along Via Appia Antica.

PARKS AND GARDENS
Villa Borghese

Piazzale Flaminio; tel. 06/0608; www.
sovraintendenzaroma.it; daily dawn to dusk; Metro A:
Spagna or Flaminio

Private gardens of the rich and famous have been bequeathed to the city over the centuries, leaving Romans with wonderful places to spend their lunch breaks or take a Sunday-afternoon stroll. The largest and most accessible of these is Villa Borghese, covered with immense umbrella pines that provide plenty of shade and make natural goalposts for children who play on the grassy lawns in between the trees. It features museums—including **Galleria Borghese,** one of the world's finest art collections (page 67)—a **zoo** (Piazzale del Giardino Zoologico 1; tel. 06/360-8211; daily 9:30am-6pm; €16, €13 kids under 10), playgrounds, cafés, and a small lake. The different areas are well indicated and connected by a series of paved alleys shared by walkers, bikers, and in-line skaters.

Reservations are required for Galleria Borghese, but you can show up unannounced at the **Museo Carlo Bilotti** (Viale Fiorello La Guardia 6; tel. 06/0608; www. museocarlobilotti.it; Tues.-Fri. 1pm-7pm, Sat.-Sun. 10am-7pm; free; Buses 61, 89) also located within the park. The former greenhouse has been transformed into an exposition space and contemporary gallery featuring 17 paintings by Giorgio de Chirico, which make up the core of the small permanent collection.

Giardini degli Aranci
(Orange Gardens)

Piazza Pietro D'Illaria; daily 7am-dusk; free; Bus 75

Rome specializes in romantic spots like the Giardini degli Aranci next to Santa Sabina where couples regularly practice their kissing. It's called the Orange Garden because of the numerous orange trees growing on either side of the gravel walkway that no one ever seems to pick. The terrace at the far end of the garden provides a view of Trastevere and St. Peter's.

Roman Rose Garden

Via di Valle Murcia 6; Apr. 21-June 24 daily 8am-7pm; free; Buses 75, 81, 85, 87, 118, 628

The Roman Rose Garden just down the street from the Orange Gardens features 1,100 varieties and a view of the Circus Maximus. The garden is open in late spring/early summer when the roses bloom. Keen observers may notice the garden's walkways are shaped as a menorah. That's in honor of the ancient Jewish cemetery once located here, and a few gravestones can still be spotted.

Villa Doria Pamphili

Via di San Pancrazio; tel. 06/0608; daily dawn to dusk; Buses 115, 710, 870

Villa Doria Pamphili, located above Trastevere, is populated by dog owners and their pets. The park is full of pickup soccer games on weekends. The villa and fountains in the center were financed by Pope Innocent X and have been inspiring joggers to run that extra kilometer since the park was opened to the public.

Villa Celimontana

Via della Navicella; tel. 06/0608; daily 7am-dusk; Buses 81, 714, 792

Villa Celimontana is a small hillside park a 10-minute walk from the Colosseum. It fills up with families on weekends and children enjoying the slightly dilapidated playground where pony rides are usually available. During the summer a monthlong jazz festival (www.villacelimontanajazz.com) is organized on the grounds and the gravel paths are lit by candle-light to guide the way.

EUR Laghetto

Vialle America; 24/7; Metro B: EUR Palasport

Rome's *laghetto* (little lake) was built to host rowing events during the 1960 Olympic games. Today the artificial lake and surrounding park is a pleasant break from the city. On weekends it fills up with families and couples out to enjoy the day. There's a playground and several pay-to-play areas where children jump on bouncy castles and ride miniature motorcycles around a small track. The cherry blossoms bloom in spring and you can rent a pedal or sailboat (€10 per hour) from **Happy Lake** (Viale Oceania; tel. 06/321-0715) on a little dock near an artificial waterfall. The Laghetto is a 20-minute metro ride from Piramide station. There is no swimming in the lake—except by the turtles and ducks who call it home.

CYCLING

There are plenty of rental shops around Rome where you can pick up a city, mountain, hybrid, or electric bike for an hour or entire day. Rome is generally flat and the weather is usually good, although when it does rain in early spring and autumn the slick cobblestones become quite hazardous. However, bike paths are few and far between. Depending on your level of comfort on two wheels, you can either dodge traffic and pedestrians of the center or play it safer in the city's vast parks. Bikes can be rented directly inside Villa Borghese, where the treelined alleys allow for stress-free cycling. **Villa Doria Pamphili** provides wilder off-road terrain that is more suited for mountain bikes, which must be rented before arriving to the park.

Helmets are not required but are better off worn and can be picked up at all rental shops.

Bike Rentals

There is no shortage of bike shops in Rome, and chances are you'll be staying close to one. Prices are pretty much standardized and it's

---

1: the boat pond in Villa Borghese 2: cycling along Via Appia Antica

Rome with Kids

Rome is enjoyable at any age and will appeal to toddlers, kids, teenagers, and parents. It's hard not to be amused by cobblestones, gladiators, gelato, fountains, bicycles, toy stores, parks, and tech museums. Of course if those fail to engage young attention spans there are always ponies, petting zoos, and amusement parks ready to keep all members of the family happy.

- Many Roman museums have special activities and workshops for children. The **Vatican** has created a **Family Tour** (www.museivaticani.va; tel. 06/6988-1351) for 5-12-year-olds. It includes an audio guide and map that explores 32 stops from the Pinacoteca to the Sistine Chapel. The kit is available in English for €5 and can be rented from the Antena International office near the entrance to the museum.

- Roman parks are full of fun activities, and **Villa Borghese** is the safest bet for keeping children amused. There are **playgrounds** near the entrance at Via Veneto where **bikes** are available to rent and toddlers can go for **pony rides**. The park also has a **zoo, boat pond,** and miniature **carousel.**

- Once they've visited the Colosseum, boys and girls may want to be put to the gladiatorial test. The only way to do that is at the **Scuola Gladitori Roma** (Via Appia Antica 18; tel. 06/5160-7951; www.scuolagladiatoriroma.it, info@gruppostoricoromano) where they'll learn about the everyday life of these ancient heroes and practice wielding weapons in a small outdoor arena. Instructors are part history teachers, part sparring partners who passionately re-create ancient Rome. Classes last two hours and must be reserved several days in advance, and students must be over 7 years old. This is fun for adults, too, and the price decreases the more participants there are.

- Older children may enjoy the challenge of climbing to the top of the **Gianicolo Hill, cupola of St. Peter's,** or the **Vittoriano** monument. All three come with satisfying views.

- Kids can take part in fun, quick traditions, such as sticking a hand inside the **Mouth of Truth,** tossing a coin into the **Trevi Fountain,** and looking through the **Buco di Roma** in Aventino. They can also watch the **changing of the guards** every hour at the **Presidential**

generally cheaper to rent a bike by the day than for just an hour or two. Renting requires an ID and credit card that is photocopied and returned at the time of rental.

AROUND A ROMAN BIKE

Navona, Via del Cancello 16; tel. 06/4550-3576; www.aroundrome.eu; Tues.-Sun. 9am-7pm; €15-24 per day; Buses 30, 70, 81, 87, 492

Alessandro and Matteo rent cool bikes, the kind Gregory Peck or Marcello Mastroianni would love to ride. Their beige vintage models come with stylish saddle bags, baskets, locks, and cell phone holders. They're fun for casual riding around the center, but if you want something more robust they also carry MTB hard Tail 27.5 mountain bikes and electric models. All bikes are in great condition. Multiday discounts available.

ROME FOR YOU

Trastevere, Via di S. Calisto 9; tel. 06/4543-3789; www.romeforyou.net; daily 9:30am-7:30pm; €13-25 per day; Tram 8, Buses 23, 280

There are fewer rental shops in Trastevere, and Rome for You is well positioned for setting off on the Tiber River cycle path or exploring Villa Doria Pamphili. They've got city, hybrid, electric, and specialized mountain bikes available for hourly, daily, or multiday rentals. Chain, helmet, puncture repair kit, and map are included. A second shop is located across the river near Largo Argentina (Vicolo San Nicola De Cesarini 4).

BICI & BACI

Via Cavour 302; tel. 06/9453-9240; daily 9:30am-6pm; €4-13 per day; Metro B: Colosseo

Bici & Baci is one of oldest rental shops in

Palace (Piazza del Quirinale). The ritual lasts about 10 minutes and is more elaborate on Sundays at 4pm when the mounted Corazzieri regiment takes part in the pageantry.

- **Explora** (Tridente, Via Flaminia 82; tel. 06/361-3776; www.mdbr.it; Tues.-Sun. 10am-7pm, closed Aug. 13-19; €8), Rome's children's museum, is located in a former tram depot and filled with hands-on activities about nature and science. Most kids are attracted to the water and fire engine exhibits, and tots can tumble in safety in the upstairs play zone. On weekends reservations are required to ensure a place in one of the designated time slots that last 1 hour and 45 minutes. The museum is less crowded during the week and throughout the summer.

- **LunEur** (EUR, Via delle Tre Fontane 100; www.luneurpark.it; daily 10am-7pm; Metro B: Magliana) amusement park has been entertaining children since the 1950s and a refurbishment in 2016 means a new generation can get their kicks just 20 minutes from the city center. Entry to the park is €4, after which you can pay per ride or buy the €18 pass and have access to a Ferris wheel, mini roller coaster, and 20 other rides. There are some height restrictions and the park is ideal for 6-12-year-olds.

- On **Via Appia Antica,** Rome's ancient road, **bikes** can be rented at the visitors center and **horses** are available to mount from the nearby stable. No previous riding experience is necessary and the stable also provides picnic lunches. **Ostia Antica** is another good half-day excursion that will stimulate young imaginations and help them understand what a **Roman town** was like.

- **Zoomarine** (Torvaianica; tel. 06/91534; www.zoomarine.it; weekends Apr., May, Sept., daily Jun.-Aug. 10am-7pm; €28), on the outskirts of the city, is a combination water park and animal preserve with hourly shows that may not be on par with SeaWorld but still delight young audiences. Dolphins, penguins, and parrots all have their dedicated areas in a park that's easy to navigate but crowded in summer. Shuttle buses depart from the **Visitor Center** (Termini station, Via Marsala) from 9:30am and round-trip tickets cost €10.

Rome. In addition to this location in Monti, there are branches in Termini (Via del Viminale 5) and Tridente (Vicolo del Bottino 8), and between these three convenient locations they have a combined 4,000 vehicles. They've expanded beyond bikes to scooters, Segways, Fiat 500s, and tours. Prices are hard to beat and bikes are available by the hour or day.

Bike Routes

Maps of the city's cycle paths are available from all tourist info points and online.

VILLA BORGHESE

multiple paths

Cycling is a good way to explore Villa Borghese and take refuge from the intense summer heat. Most of the shaded paths are paved and inclines are gentle. Pedal to gardens, museums, and panoramic terraces, like Terraza del Pincio, where you can get a good view of the sunset. You can spend an hour riding around the park with coffee breaks at the many refreshment stands and cafés where locals and visitors like to gather in spring and summer.

Bicycles, quadricycles, go-karts, and Segways can be rented from five locations. **Bici Pincio** (Viale di Villa Medici; 10am-6pm; 2 locations) rents bikes inside the park for €8 an hour, and a passport or ID must be left as collateral.

PISTA CICLABILE LUNGO TEVERE

Distance: *9.3 miles (15 kilometers)*
Duration: *40 minutes*
Effort level: *easy*

Starting points: *multiple entry points*
Bike lanes are rare in Rome. One of the longest routes is the easy Pista Ciclabile Lungo Tevere, which runs through the center of the city along the Tiber River from Castel Giubileo to Ponte Mezzocamino. It's a wide asphalt path with zero combustion traffic, a five-foot embankment on one side, and the river on the other. There are good views and many entry points, but unfortunately bikes must be carried up and down stairs to reach the path. Romans bike and jog here throughout the day, and although you may pass a few unsheltered people camping under bridges, it is safe. The path can be accessed on the western side of the river near the Cavour, Umberto, and Sisto bridges.

Bike Tours
FREE BIKE TOURS ROME
Piazza dei Calcari 4; tel. 328/562-5201; www. freebiketoursrome.com; Tram 8, Buses 30, 40, 46, 62, 64
Nearly all rental companies, including those listed above, offer tours, but Free Bike Tour Rome is the only one that takes a "pay what you want" approach. Tours are led by knowledgeable guides who set off on customized routes that alter according to the interests of participants. Groups number 6-10 riders and reservations are mandatory. There are plenty of stops along the way for photos, and all tours are conducted in English. They start and finish in Piazza dei Calcari near Piazza Navona at 10am Monday to Saturday and last 3 hours. If you enjoyed the tour, a €20-30 gratuity is appreciated. Private tours also available.

HORSEBACK RIDING
There are more stables in Rome than any other Italian city. Most are located on the outskirts, but a few are near the historic center and can be reached by public transportation or taxi.

RIDING ANCIENT ROME
Via dei Cercenii 15; tel. 392/788-5168; www. ridingancientrome.it; daily 7am-8pm; €40 per hour; Buses 118, 660

Riding Ancient Rome is one of the most accessible stables and provides scenic itineraries along an ancient Roman road and parkland. Horses are mellow, and riders of all levels can set off on 1-3 hour tours accompanied by expert guides. Home-cooked lunches and dinners are served in the clubhouse and ready-made picnics are available.

SPECTATOR SPORTS
Roman sporting events in the age of COVID are a pale imitation of the raucous celebrations that usually occur in the city's Olympic stadium. During the pandemic, soccer games are played with zero or limited fans who must abide by distancing rules. Tickets are difficult to obtain and you're better off watching from the comfort of a bar.

Soccer
STADIO OLIMPICO
Viale Gladiatore 2; tel. 06/36851; Buses 32, 69, 168, 200, 226, 280, 301, 628
Rome's two soccer teams play in the Stadio Olimpico. There's a game nearly every weekend. The season runs from late August to late May and most matches are held on Sunday afternoons. **Rome** (yellow and red), the more popular and successful of the teams, was recently bought by a wealthy American businessman. Their hardcore supporters live in Testaccio and Garbatella. **Lazio** (sky blue and white) won the Italian Serie A championship in 2000 and has languished in mid-table ever since. Tickets for *le curve* (the seats behind the goal), where the most faithful fans sit, are €15, while more comfortable seating in the stands costs €25 and up. Games don't generally sell out. Tickets can be purchased at the gates or the **AS Roma Store** in Piazza Colonna.

Rugby
Italian rugby has come a long way in recent years. Although clubs remain amateurish, the national team is now respectable and doesn't lose by the margins it once did. They even manage to beat Scotland or France now

and again. The **Six Nations** (€25-90) tournament runs from January to March and allows the opportunity to watch England, Wales, or Ireland compete at the Olympic Stadium. Unlike soccer, rival fans don't require a restraining order and postgame celebrations go on for hours at pubs around the center.

TOURS AND LOCAL GUIDES

Even people who live here their entire lives only know a fraction of Rome's history. Spending a couple of hours with a knowledgeable guide can transform how you see the city. One of the biggest benefits of a guided tour is skipping lines and having access to areas that may be off-limits to the general public. The best tours are insightful, entertaining, and make you want to learn more. The worst (usually touted around the Colosseum, Vatican, and other popular sites) are monotonous and overcrowded. To make sure your guide is registered and qualified, ask to see their certification card. You can also check with the Lazio Region (www.regione.lazio.it) to obtain a list of certified guides, or choose one of the guides recommended below. Costs vary widely and may or may not include entry to individual sights.

Walking Tours
WALKS OF ITALY

Via Caio Mario 14a; tel. 1-888/683-8670 U.S. or 06/9480-4888 in Italy; www.walksofitaly.com; €39-95 pp; Buses 30, 70, 81, 87, 492

Walks of Italy might transform your perception of the city. One of their most popular tours is the VIP Colosseum option, which leads small groups into the intricate guts of the arena where gladiators and animals waited to enter the fray above. There's little waiting, and participants enjoy access to areas few tourists get to see. The visit lasts three hours and also includes the Forum and Palatine Hill. All participants are equipped with headsets and led by experienced guides.

ANNALISA CINGOLANI

tel. 328/645-8588; www.visitareroma.net; €145/3-hour tour for 1-6 people

Besides the many companies operating in the city, there are hundreds of registered freelance guides—many of whom are passionate lifelong residents—who provide an intimate take on their city. Annalisa Cingolani is one of these and has been leading tours since 2005. All her tours are for single parties and allow greater personalization than the larger agencies can offer. She will customize tours around your interests, whether it's Caravaggio, sculpture, or fountains. The only downside is that participants are expected to get their own tickets, and entry fees are not included.

JEWISH ROMA WALKING TOURS

tel. 393/217-5898; www.jewishroma.com; €50

Art historian Micaela Pavoncello has been running Jewish Roma Walking Tours for over 15 years and leads small groups on fascinating visits of the Roman Ghetto. Her three-hour tours cover 2,000 years of history during which she recounts the ups and downs of the Jewish experience with a contagious sense of humor. She also organizes one-hour visits to the Jewish catacombs on the Appian Way. It's a thrilling Indiana Jones-like adventure that involves flashlights and spider webs.

GUIDE CENTER ROME

Via dei Fori Imperiali; tel. 06/6979-7707; daily 10am-4pm; €150/tour for 1-5 people; Metro B: Colosseo, Buses 51, 75, 85, 87, 118

If you decide to hire a guide once you arrive in Rome and prefer not to join a large group, head to Guide Center Rome. This organization is operated by the city and matches visitors with certified guides. These are primarily intended for families or groups. Seven fixed itineraries include hidden, ancient, and contemporary Rome. Tours last three hours and can be booked directly from the tourist office near the Colosseum. Entry fees are not included.

Segway Tours
ROLLING ROME
Piazza del Gesù 47; tel. 348/612-1355; www. rollingrome.com; daily 9:30am-6:30pm; €20 per hour; Buses 30, 40, 46, 62, 64

Segways are a common sight in the historic center. They combine a fun and convenient mode of transportation with a bit of history and allow travelers to see more in less time. Rolling Rome has a modern fleet of two-wheeled vehicles that set out on prearranged itineraries around the city. Riders must be over 16, less than 250 pounds, and have a decent sense of balance. Tours start with a 15-minute orientation and practice session. After that it's mostly smiles and occasional stops where guides explain sights and answer questions. Tours are popular with families and a sure way to keep older teenagers and adults entertained for hours. They also rent four- and six-seat golf carts (€100 for four hours, €150 for the day). If you prefer the freedom to Segway on your own, head to their Villa Borghese location (€15 per hour).

Ape Tours
DEAR ROMA
Via dei Balestrari 11; tel. 06/4547-6349; www. dearomatours.com; €30-350; Tram 8, Buses 23, 280

There are a lot of ways of touring Rome, and one of the most nostalgic is aboard a three-wheeled *ape* (pronounced *ah-pay*). It's a cross between a scooter and a micro-van that was popular in the 1950s and remains ideal for navigating the narrow streets of the center. It now comes in a convertible electric version that Dear Roma use to give passengers a fun view of the city. You can take one of their Classic Rome, Food, or Rome by Night Tours that last three hours and seat three.

Boat and Kayak Tours
The **Tiber River** may lack the glamour of the Seine or the width of the Thames, but it was essential to the city's growth and the lifeblood of ancient Rome for centuries. If you want to do more than gaze at it as you cross a bridge or stroll along the embankments there are several options.

ARCHEOBOAT
tel. 06/5093-0178; www.gitesultevere.it; Mar.-Sept.; €20 plus entry fees to archeological areas

Hop on board the Archeoboat to discover the city from a different angle. The boat departs weekends at 10am from a pier underneath Ponte Marconi (Metro B: Marconi) and heads downriver to the ancient Roman port of Ostia Antica. (Note that you stay on the boat for this tour; you don't get off in Ostia Antica.) It's a 2.5 hour roundtrip that combines archeology, ecology, and lunch. The service only operates once a minimum number of participants have registered, so call or email in advance.

ROMARAFTING
tel. 391/708-8061; www.romarafting.com; €45 pp

The more adventurous way to experience the Tiber gets you even closer to the water and guarantees fun and an upper body workout. RomaRafting was founded by a group of rafting enthusiasts who wanted to combine their passion for water sport with their love of Rome. Alberto and the team of English-speaking guides start with a safety briefing at either of the two meeting points before setting off on a 2.5-hour trip. Although they operate all year long, the best time is April-October, and both day and evening excursions are possible. The second itinerary along the Aniene River is great for families and offers a bucolic alternative to the Tiber. Neither current is very strong and both rivers are suitable for beginners. The minimum number of participants is four, and children must be 12 or older. Wear light clothing, close-toed shoes, and sunblock and bring a change of clothes. Reservations should be made several days in advance.

Cooking Classes
COOKING CLASSES IN ROME
Via dei Fienaroli 5; tel. 393/563-7527; www. cookingclassesinrome.com; €75 pp, reservations required; Tram 8, Buses 23, 280

Cooking Classes in Rome, located in Trastevere, could be the best part of your journey. Once you've discovered how to make pasta and prepare homemade tomato sauce, dinner will never be the same. Chef Andrea Consoli teaches the basics of Mediterranean cooking in a professionally equipped kitchen and leads participants through the preparation of a classic four-course meal. As everyone rolls up their sleeves, fellow aspiring cooks quickly become friends. The five-hour course starts at 10am and culminates with a meal. Recipes are emailed to participants in case any of the steps or ingredients are forgotten along the way.

Wine-Tasting
VINO ROMA
Via in Selci 84/G; tel. 328/487-4497; www.vinoroma. com; €50 pp; Metro B: Cavour
There are plenty of opportunities to sample wine in Rome, but learning about what you're drinking from an experienced sommelier educates the palate and makes reading wine menus easier. Vino Roma isn't a wine tour around the city. They have their own storefront location where participants learn about local vintages and what to order where. Their introductory course to Italian wines features six bottles from different regions that small groups choose from the well-stocked cellar and uncork at a long tasting table.

Language
SCUOLA LEONARDO DA VINCI
Piazza dell'Orologio 7; tel. 06/6889-2513; www. scuolaleonardo.com; Mon.-Fri. 8am-6pm; €270; Buses 46, 62, 64, 916
Scuola Leonardo da Vinci provides intensive one-week courses for groups and individuals. They also have an office in Florence, so travelers can begin learning the basics in Rome and continue developing language skills at the next stop on the journey. Like most language schools, they also offer a range of single-day cultural activities.

Accommodations

Hotels in Rome have gone through a renaissance in recent years, and many of the faded carpets and soft mattresses have been replaced with modern furnishings. Boutique hotels have helped shake things up, along with B&Bs that were virtually unknown a decade ago.

Rates change throughout the year, but high season stretches from late spring to early autumn with spikes during the Christmas and Easter holidays. Prices must be displayed in every room by law and dip slightly from November to March, with many hotels offering discounts for multiple-night stays. Around €120 usually gets you a decent double with private bath, air-conditioning, and Wi-Fi, although you'll need to spend more for facilities like a sauna or rooftop terrace with a view. Most three-star or higher hotels come equipped with satellite television.

CHOOSING WHERE TO STAY

Ancient Rome and **Monti** are close to the city's major monuments. Hotels in the area are small and there are many B&Bs. Streets and squares are lined with inviting bars and restaurants but the neighborhood is generally quiet.

Campo De' Fiori/Piazza Navona is walking distance from most sights. Accommodations tend to be on the expensive side, but there are reasonably priced apartment rentals. Nightlife around the main squares remains boisterous until late throughout the summer.

Rome's most exclusive hotels are located in **Tridente.** It costs an arm and a leg for four- or five-star treatment at establishments concentrated around Via Veneto and Piazza di Spagna. Many offer luxurious rooftop gardens

Best Accommodations

quiet courtyard inside Hotel Santa Maria

★ **The Inn at the Roman Forum:** Climb down for a glimpse of ancient underground ruins; climb up for afternoon drinks served on a panoramic split-level terrace (page 131).

★ **Casa de' Coronari:** This sleek, industrial-chic boutique hotel is close to all of the sights and sounds of Campo De' Fiori (page 132).

★ **G-Rough:** Get the rock star treatment at this neo-rustic hotel (page 132).

★ **Hotel de Russie:** Take a vacation from your vacation with the spa facilities at this luxury hotel (page 134).

★ **QuodLibet B&B:** Its authentic, warm welcome will make you feel at home in Rome (page 134).

★ **Hotel Santa Maria:** Get a taste of Trastevere village life in this former 17th-century cloister (page 135).

★ **The Beehive:** This hostel/hotel is easy on the eyes and easy on the wallet (page 135).

and fine dining. Renowned shopping draws crowds throughout the day, but there's noticeable depopulation at night.

Trastevere is one of the most vibrant neighborhoods in the city and a good place to stay if you're looking for nightlife. Hotel rooms are small and light sleepers are likely to have their dreams interrupted by the festivities. Some quieter corners offer romantic escapes from the revelry.

There are many mid-priced accommodations near the **Vaticano,** convenient for pilgrims visiting the Vatican Museums and St. Peter's, as well as secular shopping along 19th- and 20th-century streets to the north.

Testaccio and **Aventino** are mostly residential, with few hotels. Both make good refuges for travelers who value peace and quiet and don't mind walking or using public transportation to reach the main attractions.

That said, Monte Testaccio is a popular party zone with many bars and discos where young Romans gather all year long.

The streets around **Termini** are packed with accommodations of all types, catering to business travelers, tourists, and backpackers. Some of the best-priced hostels in the city are near the train station and subway, but the scenery is less attractive.

ANCIENT ROME AND MONTI

€100-200
LA SCALINATELLA

Via Urbana 48; tel. 06/488-0547; www.

lascalinatellaroma.com; €80-140 d; Metro B: Cavour
La Scalinatella is a charming B&B in the Monti neighborhood, near all the antiquities and full of restaurants, bars, and boutiques. The three large rooms have original furnishings, modern en suite bathrooms, Wi-Fi, and safes. The vaulted reception area is equally comfortable. Hosts Elisabetta and Annamaria provide a warm welcome plus all the guidance you could need.

KOLBE HOTEL ROME

Via di San Teodoro 48; tel. 06/679-8866; www.

kolbehotelrome.com; €130 d; Metro B: Circo Massimo
The Kolbe Hotel Rome is a comfortable, down-to-earth hotel located moments from the Forum, Capitoline Hill, and Circus Maximus. Rooms in the back look out on a garden and are all equipped with TV and Wi-Fi. The hotel restaurant serves lunch and dinner in a simple yet welcoming dining room. Guests are primarily young northern Europeans who have come to explore antiquity.

THE LANCELOT

Via Capo d'Africa 47; tel. 06/7045-0615; www.

lancelothotel.com; €100-175 d; Metro B: Colosseo
The Lancelot is a bit of Britain in Rome. The rooms of this small hotel could be set in an Agatha Christie novel with their plush couches, gilded mirrors, and antique desks. Rooms are bright and cheerful, and some have balconies. Breakfast is served on large round tables that make meeting fellow travelers easy. Many guests are return visitors, and the majority are English speakers. The garden is a pleasant place to plan your next sojourn and the hotel restaurant (€25 fixed price) is conveniently right at your doorstep. Airport transfers and car or scooter rental can be easily arranged.

€200-300
★ THE INN AT THE ROMAN FORUM

Via degli Ibernesi 30; tel. 06/6919-0970; www.

theinnattheromanforum.com; €130-300 d; Metro B: Colosseo
The Inn is a luxury retreat hidden down a forgotten street. The 14 superior, deluxe, and executive rooms are plush with extravagant carpets, bed frames, and curtains. An attentive concierge manages all requests with a smile and invites guests to visit the ancient underground ruins below the hotel. Upstairs afternoon drinks are served on a panoramic split-level terrace where couples gaze upon rooftops, towers, and domes.

HOTEL CELIO

Via dei Santi Quattro 35c; tel. 06/7049-5333; www.

hotelcelio.com; €200-275 d; Metro B: Colosseo
Situated in a restored 19th-century *palazzo* two blocks from the Colosseum, Hotel Celio makes an immediate impression. The lounge is elegant and the staff is unusually attentive in a city where customer service is often neglected. Michelangelo and Caesar are the most charming rooms, with high ceilings and comfortable beds. End a grueling day of sightseeing with a swim in the hotel pool.

CAMPO DE' FIORI/ PIAZZA NAVONA

Under €100
NAVONA TOWER RELAIS

Via di Tor Millina 19; tel. 06/6880-9777; www.

navonatowerrelais.com; €80 d; Buses 30, 70, 81, 87, 492
A location next to one of Rome's last medieval towers and barely 40 yards from Piazza

Navona makes Navona Tower Relais hard to resist. It's somewhere between a hotel and a B&B in terms of services, but the five recently refurbished rooms are large, clean, and comfortable. It's not fancy, but the owners are friendly and happy to look after bags after you check-out.

€100-200
HOTEL NAVONA

Via dei Sediari 8; tel. 06/6830-1252; www. hotelnavona.com; €100-155 s/d; Buses 30, 70, 81, 87, 492

Tastefully decorated rooms and 15th-century charm await at Hotel Navona. Gilt-framed paintings of the city hang above the beds and heavy green curtains keep the sunlight out of the 20 rooms. They also have several large apartments with frescoed ceilings and fully equipped kitchens where guests can spend a weekend or more minutes from Rome's most famous square. Breakfast is served on a long table in the communal dining room that encourages conversation among travelers.

HOTEL TEATRO DI POMPEO

Largo del Pallaro 8; tel. 06/6830-0170; www. hotelteatrodipompeo.it; €120-170 d; Buses 46, 62, 64, 916

At Hotel Teatro di Pompeo, guests enjoy a continental breakfast under the original vaults of a Roman theater. The 12 rooms are spacious and clean, and half face a courtyard. You'll have to stick your neck out the window to see the sky, but these rooms are quiet and conducive to late risers. Rooms in front face a small square and have tiled flooring and dark wooden ceilings. A bar near the entrance is open throughout the day and free Internet access is available throughout the hotel. The Spanish Steps, Piazza Navona, and Fontana di Trevi are all within walking distance.

€200-300
★ CASA DE' CORONARI

Via de' Coronari 234; tel. 06/6880-3907; www. casadecoronari.com; €165-220 d; Buses 30, 70, 81, 87, 280, 492

Casa de' Coronari is a small boutique residence on one of Rome's first linear streets close to all the neighborhood action. The industrial chic lounge on the ground floor leads to six minimalist rooms with original wood-beamed ceilings and terra-cotta floors. The modern furniture in white and grayish tones is sleek and stylish. In-room breakfast is provided, and bikes are free to use for guests. The hotel fills up very fast during the summer.

HOTEL DUE TORRE

Vicolo del Leonetta 23; tel. 06/6880-6956; www. hotelduetorreroma.com; €150-230 s/d; Buses 70, 81, 87, 492, 628

It doesn't get much more central than Hotel Due Torre. Parquet floors and antiques give the hotel a distinctive and refined feeling. It's like staying in a museum or 1970s time capsule. All 22 rooms and four apartments have air-conditioning, minibars, and paintings that depict how the neighborhood once looked. English-language newspapers are stacked in the lobby, which is a comfortable starting point before heading out into the thick of the city.

Over €300
HOTEL INDIGO

Via Giulia 62; tel. 06/686-611; www.hotelindigorome. com; €300-350 d; Buses 40, 46, 62, 64, 115, 870

Hotel Indigo is an unpretentious five-star boutique hotel behind Piazza Farnese that's close to all the major monuments. The 64 rooms range from standards to two-bedroom suites. All are equipped with air-conditioning, docking stations, and satellite TV. There's a wonderful view from the rooftop terrace, and spa facilities help guests relax after a day pounding the cobblestones. If you don't feel like exploring the vibrant neighborhoods nearby, the restaurant and bar provide a mix of local and international flavors.

★ G-ROUGH

Piazza di Pasquino 69; tel. 06/6880-1085; www.g-rough.it; €350-500 d; Buses 46, 62, 64, 916

Italian hotels may have a reputation for

cramped rooms and low water pressure, but those days are long past. The 10 rooms at G-Rough are spacious and suited for rock stars. The 17th-century *palazzo* moments from Piazza Navona have been given the stripped-down, neo-rustic treatment. Surfaces have a rough, incomplete look that contrasts with designer 1920s-1940s furniture and contemporary art. Originality permeates the hotel and the ground-floor bar (7am-midnight) is a convenient destination for nightcaps and gaiety.

TRIDENTE
Under €100
PENSIONE PANDA

Via della Croce 35; tel. 06/678-0179; www. hotelpanda.it; €70-100 d; Metro A: Spagna
Sober rooms at sober prices could be the slogan for Pensione Panda. So what if the decoration is dull? Beds are comfortable, and Piazza di Spagna is only a few steps away. Rooms are spread out on two floors of a 19th-century *palazzo* that has preserved some of its original frescoes. A couple of the rooms have balconies overlooking a central courtyard and are quieter than those facing the street. Air-conditioning costs extra and may be worth the euros if you're staying in August.

€100-200
CASA HEBERART

Via Capo delle Case 18; tel. 06/4201-4107; www. casaheberart.com; €100-130 d; Metro A: Spagna
Anyone with an aversion to big hotels will appreciate the intimacy of Casa Heberart. Each of the five rooms is neatly decorated, some with antiques the owner has transported from her Tuscan farmhouse. The Verde Room is especially beautiful. There is a high standard of service, with perks like a Turkish bath and massages available upon request.

BAROCCO

Piazza Barberini 9; tel. 06/487-2001; www. hotelbarocco.com; €130-180 s/d; Metro A: Barberini
Barocco is the essence of elegance. Some of the 41 rooms have balconies overlooking Roman

rooftops. Interiors are on the flowery side, with primary colors favored throughout and lots of marble in the large bathrooms. Digital safes, air-conditioning, and satellite TV are standard and soundproofed windows guarantee traffic won't interfere with your dreams.

€200-300
CASA MONTANI

Piazzale Flaminio 9; tel. 06/3260-0421; www. casamontani.com; €150-250 d; Metro A Flaminio
It's hard to leave Casa Montani. The five deluxe rooms and suites of this contemporary guesthouse on the edge of Piazza del Popolo are all warm and inviting. Furniture is elegant but cozy, and bathrooms are small but stunning. The in-room breakfast encourages lingering. Room service can satisfy most desires from 7am to 8pm, and when you do decide to leave, Piazza di Spagna is only a short walk away.

HOTEL MANFREDI

Via Margutta 61; tel. 06/320-7676; www. hotelmanfredi.it; €170-240 s/d; Metro A: Spagna
One vine-covered entrance on a quiet street, just moments from Piazza di Spagna, leads to Hotel Manfredi and its neighbor, **Hotel Forte** (Via Margutta 61; tel. 06/320-7625; www.hotelforte.com; €160-230 s/d). Both offer comfortable, chic accommodation that isn't over the top and makes no attempt to be trendy. Each provides large beds in silent curtained rooms and professional three-star service. Breakfast can be eaten in your room or one of two pleasant breakfast rooms.

HOTEL LOCARNO

Via della Penna 22; tel. 06/361-0841; www. hotellocarno.com; €220-280 d; Metro A: Flaminio
No two rooms are the same at Hotel Locarno, where a view of the Tiber River is only as far as the roof terrace. You may never want to leave the enchanting garden on the ground floor with its miniature fountain and overflowing vegetation. All 60 rooms have high ceilings and vintage fittings. Room 201 is especially comfortable, as are the two deluxe rooms on

the 6th floor. Bicycles are provided to guests free of charge.

Over €300
★ HOTEL DE RUSSIE

Via del Babuino 9; tel. 06/328-881; www.
roccofortehotels.com; €450-500 d; Metro A:
Flaminio

Hotel de Russie feels like a miniature Club Med, with enough luxury to make guests forget they're in Rome. There are several levels of rooms with city and garden views decorated in contemporary fashion, which may be a refreshing change from rustic. Downstairs you can dine at the fusion-inspired restaurant or relax with a perfectly mixed cocktail in the lively bar. Guests are free to use the extensive spa facilities and state-of-the-art gym. Mercedes-Benz smart bikes and walking tours can be reserved from the professional staff operating the front desk.

VATICANO
Under €100
★ QUODLIBET B&B

Via Barletta 29; tel. 347/122-2642; www.
quodlibetroma.com; €80-100 d; Metro A: Ottaviano

Bed and breakfasts provide a unique way of experiencing Roman culture. The best hosts offer the right balance of hospitality and privacy, are eager to share their knowledge of the city, and make you feel like an honorary citizen. Not only can Gianluca do all that, but he also has a great apartment. QuodLibet B&B is located in a grand 19th-century *palazzo* 10 minutes from St. Peter's and near a convenient Metro stop. You'll get all the advice you want and a rich breakfast served in an immaculate kitchen or one of three colorful bedrooms with private bath, air-conditioning, and Wi-Fi.

HOTEL MUSEUM ROME

Via Tunisi 8; tel. 06/3972-3941; www.hotelmuseum.it;
€80-100 s/d; Metro A: Ottaviano

Travelers looking to make friends from all over the world should book a room at the Hotel Museum Rome. The low cost attracts a youthful crowd that can survive without luxury. Rooms are clean, and conversations can go on until dawn on the spacious rooftop terrace.

€100-200
DEI CONSOLI

Via Varrone 2d; tel. 06/6889-2972; www.
hoteldeiconsoli.com; €125-200 s/d; Metro A:
Ottaviano

A new addition to the area's four-star hotel scene, Dei Consoli distinguishes itself with professionalism, modern furnishings, and the fact that they welcome pets. The 26 rooms are divided into superior, deluxe, and junior suites where whirlpools help weary guest recuperate. Everyone else can count on power showers and lots of Spanish porcelain in the bathrooms.

HOTEL SANT'ANNA

Borgo Pio 134; tel. 06/6880-1602; www.
santannahotel.net; €130-200 s/d; Metro A:
Ottaviano

After facing the crowds of Piazza San Pietro, the tranquility of Hotel Sant'Anna is a godsend. All it takes is a few moments in the garden of this small hotel for serenity to return. If that doesn't work, the minibar in each room should do the trick. Vatican colors of yellow and white predominate. Breakfast is included and rooms on the third floor have a terrace.

€200-300
HOTEL GIULIO CESARE

Via degli Scipioni 287; tel. 06/321-0751; www.
hotelgiuliocesare.com; €170-210 d; Metro A: Lepanto

Hotel Giulio Cesare is as majestic as the name suggests. The lounge and entrance are decorated with antiques and tapestries. A hearty breakfast is served in the garden, and there's free parking. The fireplace is lit in winter and the high-backed leather chairs in the lounge are perfect for reflecting on the day's events.

TRASTEVERE
€100-200
ARCO DEL LAURO

Via Arco de Tolomei 27; tel. 06/9784-0350; www. arcodellauro.it; €90-140 d; Tram 8, Buses 23, 280

Arco del Lauro is a B&B near a medieval arch a short walk from Tiberina Island. Though simple and small by most standards, rooms are cheery and comfortable. A continental or international breakfast is served at a nearby bar. Reception is friendly, but only open mornings.

VILLA DELLA FONTE

Via della Fonte d'Olio 8; tel. 06/580-3797; www. villafonte.com; €110-185 s/d; Buses 23, 280

Villa della Fonte is a five-room hotel run by a friendly mother-daughter team. What the villa lacks in size it makes up for in charm. Rooms are bright and include a minibar and satellite TV. Mattresses were recently replaced and are quite firm. Parking is available nearby for a small fee and chocolate croissants from a neighborhood bakery are served in your room or on the sun-filled patio. The balconies are perfect for watching the Trastevere street scene down below.

€200-300
★ HOTEL SANTA MARIA

Vicolo del Piede 2; tel. 06/589-4626; www. hotelsantamaria.info; €150-220 s/d; Buses 23, 280

Hotel Santa Maria is an oasis of tranquility that will make you forget you're in Rome. That peaceful feeling has to do with the building's 17th-century cloister past. All the bricks, beams, tiles, and cobblestones have been restored and infused with rustic charm. Bicycles are free for guests as is the buffet breakfast, which can be enjoyed in a romantic shaded courtyard. The 20 rooms come in various sizes and the *aperitivo* is a good way to start summer evenings.

AVENTINO AND TESTACCIO
€100-200
VILLA SAN PIO

Via Santa Melania 19; tel. 06/570-057; www. aventinohotels.com; €100-180 s/d; Metro B: Piramide or Circo Massimo

Surrounded by an attractive garden on a quiet residential street in Aventino, Villa San Pio provides elegant rooms with baroque flair. Much of the furniture is antique. Bathrooms are all done up in black-and-white marble and equipped with hair dryers and hydromassage bathtubs.

€200-300
HOTEL S. ANSELMO

Piazza S. Anselmo 2; tel. 06/570-057; www. hotelsanselmo.com; €220-270 d; Metro B: Piramide or Circo Massimo

Hotel S. Anselmo is as memorable as Rome. Each of the 34 rooms in this four-star hotel has its own personality. The *Camera con Vista* (room with a view) boasts a bucolic panorama while the *Renaissance* room could save you a trip to Florence. Downstairs, old and new blend seamlessly into a timeless style. The breakfast buffet includes smoked salmon, fresh fruit, and homemade cakes. It's served in a pleasant dining room or garden where a giant palm shades guests. Uniformed staff provide impeccable service, and the bar specializes in exotic cocktails.

TERMINI
Under €100
★ THE BEEHIVE

Via Marghera 8; tel. 06/4470-4553; www. the-beehive.com; €25 dorm, €80 d; Metro A or B: Termini

The Beehive is a recently remodeled accommodation two blocks north of Termini station that's part hostel and part hotel. It's owned by an American couple who came to Rome and stayed. All the rooms have been redone in bright colors and are easy on the eye and the pocketbook. You can choose from a mix-gender dorm (€25) or private rooms with (€80) and without (€70) bath. There are three neat common areas where guests hang out and an à la carte vegetarian breakfast is served along with eggs, French toast, and Korean rice porridge. The couple also manage the eight-room **Hotel Urbe** (Via dei Mille 27; www.hotelurbee.com; €70) with the same easygoing philosophy.

BLUE HOSTEL

Via Carlo Alberto 13; tel. 340/925-8503; www. bluehostel.it; €75 d; Metro B: Cavour

Blue Hostel has nothing to do with bunk beds or dormitories. Instead it's intimate and cozy, and just far enough from the train station to make it a decent location that's close to Monti and all the sights of ancient Rome. Rooms are small but the curtains, lamps, exposed beams, and parquet floors make it feel like it could be home. If you need more space, they have a bright suite with an eat-in kitchen and foldout bed. Prices start at €49 depending on the season and rarely exceed €150.

€100-200

NARDIZZI

Via Firenze 38; tel. 06/488-0035; www.nardizzihotel. com; €100-145 d; Metro A: Repubblica

Hotels like the Nardizzi only exist in Italy. This family-run operation takes hospitality very seriously. A few minutes on the terrace is all it takes to feel as Roman as the owners. Rooms are spacious and the service goes way beyond the two stars listed at the entrance.

Information and Services

VISITOR INFORMATION

TOURIST INFORMATION POINTS

Via dei Fori Imperiali, tel. 06/0608; www. turismoroma.it; daily 9:30am-7pm; Metro B: Colosseo

The Rome Department of Tourism operates six **Tourist Information Points** (TIP) around the historic center, at both airports, and inside Termini train station. **TIPs** are open daily 9:30am-7pm and operated by multilingual staff. It's where you should go to pick up a **RomaPass,** public transportation tickets, the city's quarterly event guide, and a detailed map (€2).

The main TIP office is situated near the Colosseum, but you'll also find them at: Stazione Termini (Piazza dei Cinquecento), Fontana di Trevi/Corso (Via Minghetti), Castel Sant'Angelo (Piazza Pia), Leonardo da Vinci Airport (Terminal T3), and Ciampino Airport.

The city's **tourist information number** (tel. 06/0608) operates daily 9am-9pm. The call center provides information in English about events, accommodation, restaurants, transportation, and museum tickets. They also manage visitor information and ticketing for smaller sights like Monte Testaccio, Porta Portese, and Villa Borghese, and you can call to get reliable hours, price, and even directions. Tickets to museums, exhibitions, and shows can also be purchased through the call center and picked up on-site. Basically, you can ask the friendly operators anything about Rome and they'll answer.

Tickets and guided tours can also be reserved from **Coop Culture** (www. coopculture.it).

If all you need are directions, *vigili urbana* (urban vigils) in white-and-blue uniforms and on duty near most of the city's attractions can help.

PSTOPS

tel. 06/0608; www.turismoroma.it

PStops were launched in 2020 and are located in major squares. These glass and steel container-like structures provide free **Wi-Fi, water, restrooms, baby changing** facilities, and tourist information. They're open from 10am-4pm and can be found in Piazza di Spagna, Piazza di Porta San Giovanni, Piazza dell'Esquilino, Piazza di Porta Maggiore, and Piazza della Città Leonina.

Business Hours

Shops generally open between 8am and 9am, close at 1pm for the *pausa pranzo* (lunch break), and reopen at 3pm or 4pm. Department stores and boutiques in the center have continual hours, but the farther you get from Piazza di Spagna the more likely you are to find shutters drawn after lunch. Many small shops and restaurants remain closed on Sundays or one weekday and generally shut down for a week or two in mid-August and major holidays. Few eateries provide continual service: Most kitchens operate noon-2:30pm and 7:30pm-10pm. Many establishments have winter and summer hours that are extended as days get hotter.

TRAVELER SERVICES

Luggage Storage

There's nothing worse than lugging heavy bags under a hot Roman sun. If you can't leave luggage at your hotel after checking out, fortunately, there are many secure options around the city.

Stasher (www.stasher.com) and Luggage Hero (www.luggagehero.com) partner with hotels, bars, and certified shops to provide storage space. There are dozens of locations and reservations are made using their applications. Luggage Hero charges €1 per hour per bag with a €2 handling fee and maximum daily fee of €8. Stasher has a flat €6 for the first 24 hours. Location opening times vary considerably and bag insurance is included.

STOW YOUR BAGS

tel. 06/6227-0110; www.stowyourbags.com; daily 7am-11pm

Stow Your Bags runs fully automated lockers close to major tourist sites. Find storage facilities near Termini (Via Filippo Turati 52), Vatican (Via Germanico 29), Navona (Via dei Chiavari 8), Colosseum (Via del Colosseo 2), and the Spanish Steps (Via della Vite 42). Lockers come in two sizes and can be reserved online or onsite via a code, which is sent by email and SMS. Hourly fees are €2 (standard) and €3 (maxi) with discounts for 24-hour stays. Belongings can be accessed during opening hours; however, there is no staff on hand, except at the Navona location.

Laundry

Laundromats are fairly common nowadays in the city center, and getting a load or two washed is easy. If all you need is to remove a stain, you're better off heading to a *tintoria* or *lavasecco* (dry cleaner). They will have you looking spotless and back on the road again in no time.

LAVANDERIA SPEED QUEEN

Vicolo delle Grotte 19a; tel. 333/886-4624; daily 8:30am-7:30pm; Tram 8, Buses 46, 62, 64, 916

Lavanderia Speed Queen is a small self-service laundromat near Campo De' Fiori with a dozen modern washing and drying machines. An 8 kg load costs €5 and drying is €1.50 every 10 minutes. English-speaking staff are on hand, machines accept coins or bills, and seating is available. You can be in and out of here in under an hour.

LAVASECCO BORGO PIO

Borgo Pio 188, Mon.-Fri. 8:30am-7pm and Sat. 9am-1pm, Buses 23, 40, 62, 982

Lavasecco Borgo Pio is a reliable neighborhood dry cleaner that provides professional, prompt service that keeps clients coming back. They also offer a wash-and-fold service in case you need to refresh an entire wardrobe and don't want to wait around watching your clothes spinning.

Public Restrooms

Several new visitor restrooms and **baby-changing stations** have been erected in Testaccio (Piazza Santa Maria Liberatrice) and

Monti (Piazza dell'Esquilino) and will continue to be rolled out around the city.

Lost and Found

There are two lost and found offices at **Leonardo da Vinci Airport** and which you contact depends on where the loss occurred. The **outer office** (tel. 06/6595-5253; Mon.-Sat. 7am-5pm, Sat.-Sun. 7am-3pm) next to the luggage store deals with items misplaced within Terminal 3, while the **inner office** (tel. 06/6595-3313; daily 7am-11:30pm) in front of conveyer belt 11 is for everything else. Should luggage go missing, contact the handling company. Many airlines use the **Alitalia desk** (tel. 06/6563-4965; daily 7am-11pm) located in the baggage claim area to assist travelers. It's also worth alerting your airline in the arrivals hall outside.

Lost items are sent to the city's **Central Lost and Found Office** (Garbatella, Circonvallazione Ostiense 191; tel. 06/6769-3214; weekdays 8:30am-1pm, Thurs. 8:30am-5pm; Metro B: Garbatella). Each line of the subway also has its own lost and found office: **Metro A** (tel. 06/487-4309; daily 9:30am-12:30pm) and **Metro B** (tel. 06/575-4295; daily 9am-6pm). Passports and other documents remain for 15 days before being transferred to police, and consulates are notified if items belong to foreigners. All offices provide information over the phone and there's a small recovery fee at the main office. The people who work in these offices are not especially sympathetic. However, many items are found and being nice to them can facilitate recovery.

Foreign Consulates

If you misplace your passport, lose a friend, or need to declare a birth abroad, your consulate can help. The **United States consulate** (Via Vittorio Veneto 121; tel. 06/467-41; www.it.usembassy.gov; Mon.-Sat. 8:30am-5:30pm; Metro A: Baberini, Buses 52, 53, 61, 160, 590) is near Villa Borghese park, while the **Canadian consulate** (Via Zara 30; tel. 06/854-441; www.canadainternational.

gc.ca; Mon.-Thurs. 9am-noon; Trams 2, 3, 19, Buses 62, 66, 82) is located in the northwest of the city. The **British Embassy** (Via Venti Settembre 80A; www.gov.uk; weekdays 9am-5pm; Metro A: Castro Pretorio) is in a modern building near Termini station. For urgent assistance UK nationals can call 06/4220-0001 24/7. **Australia** (Via Antonio Bosio 5; tel. 06/852-721; www.italy.embassy.gov.au; weekdays 9am-5pm; Metro B: Bologna), **New Zealand** (Via Clitunno 44; tel. 06/853-7501; www.nzembassy.com; weekdays 8:30am-12:30pm and 1:30-5pm; Buses 38, 88, 89), and **South Africa** (Via Tanaro 14; tel. 06/852-541; lnx.sudafrica.it; Mon.-Fri. 9:30am-noon; Trams 2, 3, 19, Buses 63, 83, 92) also operate consulates in Rome.

HEALTH AND SAFETY
Emergency Numbers
Dialing **118** in Italy is like calling 911 in the United States and 999 in the UK. Call that number in any health-related emergency. An ambulance with a unique siren sound will be on the scene in minutes.

Police
There are a lot of uniformed personnel on the streets of Rome and each has its own color uniform. White issues parking tickets, blue chase criminals, and the ones carrying machine guns deter terrorists. The *vigili urbani* (white; tel. 06/888-7620) are the most common in the city and can direct you to the Colosseum or make taxi drivers honest. The *polizia* (blue; 113) will listen to you recount how your phone was stolen and stop speeding vehicles. The *carabiniere* (blue with red stripes; 112) set up roadblocks and guard embassies.

Hospitals and Pharmacies
There are dozens of hospitals in the city center. The **Rome American Hospital** (Via Emilio Longoni 69; tel. 06/225-51; Buses 058, 313) has no shortage of English-speaking doctors. **Policlinico Umberto I** (Viale del Policlinico 155; tel. 06/499-71; Metro B: Castro

Roman Economics

Although most Italians are honest, tourists can be easy targets for unscrupulous business owners who charge one price for locals and another for anyone holding a map. Note that taxis, bars, and shops must openly display their prices. Markets can be murkier, but all food is generally sold by weight. Clothes and other objects should be labeled. If they aren't, inquire about price and ask for a discount if you feel it's too high. A receipt (*ricevuto*) should accompany every transaction (except for cigarettes) and always ask for one if it isn't (*la ricevuto per favore*).

Prices fluctuate slightly depending on neighborhood and location, but the average costs listed below provide an idea of what to expect:

FOOD AND DRINKS

- espresso: €1

- cappuccino: €1.20

- *cornetto* (breakfast pastry): €1

- *tramezzino* (light sandwich): €2-3.50

- other sandwiches: €3-5.50

- fresh-squeezed juice: €2.50-3.50

- small bottle of water: €1

- large bottle of water: €2

- small beer: €3-4

- large beer: €4-6

- bottle of house wine: €7-10

- first course: €8-12

- second course: €12-18

TRANSPORTATION COSTS

- bus/metro fare: €1.50

- unleaded/diesel fuel: €1.45/1.30 per liter

- street parking: €1 per hour

Pretori, Trams 2, 3, 19, Buses 61, 490, 495, 649) is one of the largest facilities.

You'll find well-equipped **pharmacies** on Via Cola di Rienzo 213/215, (tel. 06/324-4476; Metro A: Ottaviano), Piazza Risorgimento 44 (tel. 06/397-38166; Metro A: Ottaviano), Piazza Barberini 49 (tel. 06/487-1195; Metro A: Barberini), Via Nazionale 228 (tel. 06/488-0754; Metro A: Repubblica), and Viale Trastevere 229/229 (tel. 06/588-2273; Trams 3, 8).

COMMUNICATIONS
Wi-Fi

Rome has gone wireless, and anyone with a Wi-Fi-equipped device can access the Internet throughout Villa Borghese and many other locations in the city. The plan is to provide total coverage in the near future. Most of Rome's historic center is covered and the area around Piazza Navona is one continuous hot spot. Registration is quick and a confirmation call is required. Most hotels also provide broadband access, which has led to the disappearance of Internet cafés.

Newspapers

Italian newsstands are crammed with newspapers and magazines on everything from knitting to military aviation. *La Repubblica* and *Corriere della Sera* are the two most popular papers, and both print local editions. Journalists in Italy don't seem to be familiar with objectivity, and most newspapers have some political agenda. For example, *L'Unità* represents the Communist Party, while *La Padania* serves the interest of the right-wing Lega Nord party. Italians care a lot about sport, and the best-selling broadsheets are the *Corriere dello Sport* and the pink *Gazzetta dello Sport.* Several Roman papers have events listings that comes out midweek with a small English section. When in doubt, ask the newspaper attendant.

Transportation

GETTING THERE
Air

Rome has two international airports, Leonardo da Vinci and Ciampino, and both are within close proximity of the city center.

LEONARDO DA VINCI

FCO; Via dell'Areoporto di Fiumicino; tel. 06/65951; www.adr.it

Leonardo Da Vinci Airport, also known as Fiumicino, is located near the sea 16 miles (26 kilometers) from the Colosseum. It's the main intercontinental entry point, with five terminals and scheduled nonstop flights to and from dozens of North American and European cities. Alitalia is the Italian national carrier and provides service to many of these, although it is not necessarily the cheapest option. Alitalia is based in T1, while U.S., Canadian, and most international airlines arrive and depart from the recently opened T3 terminal, which has excellent shopping, food, and lounge facilities. A tourist office is located in the arrivals hall along with currency exchange, bars, newsstands, and transportation services.

Trenitalia (www.trenitalia.com) operates two train services between Fiumicino and Termini station in Rome. The Leonardo Express (€14) is a direct-link shuttle that departs every 15 minutes from the airport between 6:23am and 11:23pm and from tracks 23 and 24 in Termini station between 5:35am and 10:35pm. The trip takes 32 minutes and service is guaranteed even during strikes. FL1 (€8) city service makes frequent departures throughout the day and a half-dozen stops including Trastevere and Ostiense, which is convenient if you're staying in Aventino or Testaccio. Journey time is around an hour and requires a transfer if you're departing/arriving to Termini. Tickets for both are available from the Trenitalia website, automatic ticket machines at the airport, train stations, and many *tabacchi* shops and newsstands in the center.

SIT (www.sitbusshuttle.com; daily 7:15am-12:40pm; €6) and Terravision (www.terravision.eu; daily 5:35am-11pm; €5.80) provide bus service to Fiumicino. The trip is one hour with multiple departures per hour from outside the arrivals hall.

Travelers in groups of three or four may find it convenient to split a taxi. They're white and lined up outside the arrivals hall. Rides into the city center are fixed at €48 from Fiumicino. Bags are included in the fare and the trip takes 40 minutes. Uber exists in Italy and anyone using the app can order an UberBlack (€70), UberLux (€90), or UberVan (€90). Taxi drivers aren't fond of Uber drivers and friction between the two is common. Another alternative is carsharing. Enjoy (enjoy.eni.com) operates a fleet of Fiat 500s in Rome, a dozen of which can usually be found in the parking lot facing Terminal 1. You'll need to register before arriving, download the app, and reserve a car once you land. Payment is through credit card and rides cost €0.25 a minute. Cars are usually all gone by early evening.

CIAMPINO

CIA; Via Appia Nuova 1651; tel. 06/65951; www.adr.it

Ciampino is a smaller, one-terminal airport used by low-cost airlines flying to domestic and European destinations. SIT (www.sitbusshuttle.com; €6) and Terravision (www.terravision.eu; €6) buses outside the arrivals hall shuttle passengers to and from Termini station in the center. Journey time is 40 minutes. Taxi rides into the city center are fixed at €30 from Ciampino and bags are included in the fare.

Train

Trenitalia (www.trenitalia.com) operates the Italian rail network and runs local, intercity, and high-speed services. All types generally have a first- and second-class option and arrive at **Termini station** (www.romatermini.com; Metro A or B: Termini), which is the hub of the rail network and is located 10 minutes east of the city center. The station itself contains many shops and eateries. The large number of travelers attracts some less-than-savory characters and only train spotters should linger; a barrier was recently added near the tracks to keep pickpockets away from passengers and tickets are necessary in order to access the platforms. The A and B lines of the subway intersect downstairs at the station and the main bus terminal is out front in Piazza dei Cinquecento.

There are several other train stations around the city including the ultramodern **Tiburtina station** (Metro B: Tiburtina) 1.2 miles (2 kilometers) east of Termini, where high-speed trains also stop; and **Porta San Paolo station** (Metro B: Piramide) in Testaccio, where commuter trains connect the city with Ostia Antica and the sea.

From Florence: High-speed trains arrive in 1.5 hours from Florence's Santa Maria Novella station. One-way standard fares start from €21.65. There are approximately 50 departures per day with either **Italo** or **Trenitalia.**

From Venice: Trains arrive in under 4 hours from Venice's Santa Lucia station. One-way standard fares start from €49. There are approximately 50 departures throughout the day. Trains departing from Venice stop in Florence.

Car

Drivers arriving from the north on the A1 highway should exit at Rome Nord; those coming from the south should exit at Rome Est. Both lead to the Grande Raccordo Anulare (GRA), or ring road, from where the center can be easily reached via the Aurelia, Flaminia, or Colombo. The GRA also leads to both of the city's airports.

From Florence: There are several ways to reach Rome, and the fastest is also the simplest. Just get on the **A1** highway on the western outskirts of Florence and follow it all the way to the Roma Nord/Aeroporti exit, which leads to the GRA ring road. The 174 miles (280 kilometers) can be covered in around three hours and there's a €20 toll at the exit.

From Venice: The journey from Venice is slightly less straightforward and requires merging onto several highways. Cross the bridge connecting Venice to the mainland and follow signs for the **A57** toward Bologna. On the outskirts of Padova exit onto the **A13** and continue following signs for the A1 Firenze near Bologna. There are a couple of merges to make and then it's all A1 until Rome. The 330-mile (530-kilometer) journey takes around six hours and costs €40 in a single final toll.

Bus

Eurolines (www.eurolines.com), **Flixbus** (www.flixbus.com), **Baltour** (www.baltour.it), and **Megabus** (www.megabus.com) operate daily service between Venice, Florence, and Rome. In Rome, passengers are dropped off in either Tiburtina or Termini stations. Most companies offer special discounts for travelers under 26 years old, and there are multiple-week passes that provide the freedom to board buses whenever you like.

From Florence: Most buses depart from or near Santa Maria Novella station and may make a couple of stops before getting onto the highway. The 174-mile (280-kilometer) journey takes four hours and prices start at around €17 for a one-way ticket.

From Venice: Buses leave from the Tronchetto terminal west of the train station, which can be reached via the People Mover monorail from Piazzale Roma. Times for the 330-mile (530-kilometer) journey vary depending on the company but generally take 8-11 hours. Fares start at €25 and rise to €45.

GETTING AROUND

Rome's concentration of interesting sights makes walking the most convenient and rewarding form of transportation. Many streets in the center are now pedestrian-only. Although pedestrians do have the right of way at crosswalks, play it safe and pay special attention to moped and motorcycle drivers, who often follow their own rules of the road. A boom in bike- and scooter-sharing services have made it fun and easy to navigate the city. It can, however, be dangerous, and accidents are frequent, so be careful when using these to get around. Buses and trams may not provide the same amount of flexibility, but they are reliable.

The ferry that once carried visitors up and down the Tiber is no longer active, and the city's official bike-sharing program failed to gain riders. Luckily, **ATAC Rome** (www.atac. roma.it) offers a variety of transit options including subway, tram, bus, and train service to destinations throughout the city. Rush hour is best avoided and peaks 7am-9am and 5pm-7pm. For safety reasons, it's best to avoid Termini station after dark.

During COVID outbreaks, Roman buses and trams are limited to 80 percent capacity, all passengers are required to wear masks inside metro stations and on board, and night bus service (midnight-5am) may be cancelled. A few tips for staying (and keeping others) healthy: Wash or sanitize hands before and after every journey, avoid blocked-off seats, always allow passengers to exit prior to boarding, and skip public transportation in instances where overcrowding makes social distancing difficult. Find the latest travel restrictions in English on the ATAC website.

Transit Passes

There are a variety of travel passes available from **ATAC** (www.atac.roma.it; tel. 800/431-784). A single **BIT ticket** (€1.50) allows unlimited transfer between subway, bus, and tram for 75 minutes after the ticket is validated. A full-day **Roma24** costs €7, **Rome48** is €12.50, **Roma72** is €18, and the **7-day CIS** version is €24. Tickets can be purchased at automated kiosks within subway stations as well as most *tabacchi* (tobacco shops). All tickets

and passes must be validated upon initial use of the transport network.

Metro

Rome's subway system is made up of two lines, **Metro A** and **Metro B,** which intersect at Termini train station. (There's also a Metro C line; however, this serves residential neighborhoods outside the center and is not useful to travelers.)

Daily service begins at 5:30am and the last train departs at 11:30pm (12:30am Sat.). This two-line subway system doesn't cover all of the historic center, but you can easily reach the Colosseum, Vatican, Spanish Steps, and many other sights underground. Connecting commuter and shuttle trains travel to Ostia Antica and Fiumicino airport.

Most subway stations on the Metro B line are equipped with elevators, which isn't always the case with Metro A. However, **bus 590** follows the same route as this line and is wheelchair accessible.

Bus and Tram

Six trams and hundreds of bus lines operate throughout Rome day and night. Getting on and off city buses and trams provides the freedom to follow your instinct and discover the city in unexpected ways. Just remember to avoid the morning and evening rush hours (7am-9am and 5pm-7pm).

Many public buses travel through the city center, and riding these is less expensive and more entertaining than an organized bus tour. **Bus 40** from Termini to the Vatican, **23** from Piramide to the Vatican, and mini electric bus **119** are all good options. **Bus 119** makes round trips from Piazza Venezia past Trevi Fountain, Spanish Steps, Piazza del Popolo, Ara Pacis, and the Italian parliament. It operates on weekdays and the entire 18-stop loop takes around an hour to complete. You can ensure a seat by getting on at the terminus outside Palazzo Venezia. **Tram 3** from Piramide to Villa Borghese is another pleasant ride passing the Circus Maximus, Colosseum, and newer

19th-century neighborhoods that are often overlooked by tourists.

The square outside Termini station is the starting point for over a dozen bus lines that connect all parts of the city. From here you can catch **Bus H** to Trastevere, which isn't served by the metro; **Bus 40** to Piazza Navona and the Vatican; or **Bus 170** to Testaccio. The H and 40 bus lines, as well as Tram 8, terminate at **Largo Argentina,** which is a convenient stop for visiting the Vatican.

Bicycle

Since the onset of the coronavirus pandemic, there has been a sharp increase in bicycle usage in Rome and throughout Italy. The government has encouraged pedaling by offering monetary incentives to citizens who purchase bikes, and Romans have responded enthusiastically.

Nevertheless, exploring Rome on two wheels remains risky and many drivers aren't accommodating. If you do rent a bike, wear a helmet and ride in parks, along pedestrianized streets, or along designated bike paths. Weekends are the best time to cycle as traffic is lighter, and many locals get on their bikes, too. A route map for cyclists is available from any TIP info kiosk and bicycles are available from rental shops around the city.

There has also been a boom in bike sharing over the last couple years. The latest entries are **Helbiz** (www.helbiz.com; €0.15 per minute), which offers a small electric model, and **Uber Jump** (www.uber.com; €.050 to initiate rental and €0.20 per minute thereafter) whose 2,800 pedal-assisted bikes are identifiable by their bright red color. Both run with an easy-to-use application and are ideal for getting from point A to point B quickly. They are expensive, however, on extended rides, and if you aim to meander for hours you're better off with a traditional rental.

Shared bikes are dockless and "free floating," and riders can leave them wherever they like. Once you register, just locate a bike using the app and unlock it by scanning the QR code on the fender or number plate. Whether bike sharing will succeed this time around remains to be seen.

Scooter

Scooters have also begun appearing on Roman streets, but like cycling, this isn't the safest way to get around. **Helbiz** (€1 start fee plus €0.15 per minute or €30 unlimited) and **Lime** (www.li.me; €1 start fee plus €0.25 per minute or Limepass) both manage fleets of 1,000 modern electric vehicles in the historic center and are fun to ride. It can be tricky to navigate cobblestone streets and riders should be attentive throughout their journey.

Rickshaw

Near the exit of the Colosseum subway station, rickshaw bikes are lined up and drivers await their next fare. These three-wheeled vehicles seat two comfortably and are well adapted to the newly pedestrianized areas around the Colosseum. Prices can be €50 per hour or €10 per monument and should be negotiated prior to departure. If you prefer to do your own pedaling, four-wheeled bikes are available nearby.

Taxi

Cabs can be useful, especially at night, and may be reserved by phone or picked up at taxi stands located in large squares (Piramide, Venezia, Popolo, and Trilussi) or near train stations (Termini and Tiburtina). Most drivers are members of a consortium like **Radio Taxi** (tel. 06/3570) or **Pronto Taxi** (tel. 06/6645) that operate 24/7. Taxis are not generally hailed NYC- or London-style, but that shouldn't stop you from trying. Payment can be made by credit card, and tipping is optional.

Fares are calculated by an initial rate of €3 on weekdays (€4.50 on weekends and €6.50 10pm-6am) plus a combination of distance (€1.10 per kilometer) and time (€0.45 per minute). Journeys to Leonardo da Vinci airport and the center are fixed at €48. Ciampino airport is €30. To contest a fare make sure to

get the receipt, which specifies the route, taxi number, and amount paid.

Car

Driving is the most challenging transportation option and more suited for leaving rather than entering the city. Cars offer little gratification unless you have hired a patient driver as well. Finding parking is time-consuming and expensive, and large sections of the historic center compose a limited traffic zone (ZTL) that requires a residential permit to enter. The ZTL is active on weekdays 6:30am-6pm and on Saturdays 2pm-6pm. Most hotels can provide a pass if you're arriving by car, and cars rented within the ZTL are exempt.

Still, anyone determined to experience life in the Italian fast lane can do it easily and quickly. Rome has four car-sharing and two scooter-sharing services that have become very popular with locals and residents. The blue-and-white Smart cars of ShareNow (www.share-now.com; €0.19 per minute/€9 registration fee) are parked throughout the center. These are two-passenger, so if you need more space use the red Fiat 500s of Enjoy (enjoy.eni.com; €0.25 per minute, €60 per day). Both services require online registration and possession of a passport, driver's license, and credit card. There are hundreds of vehicles parked around the city that can enter the historic center and be left anywhere without the need to pay for parking or gas.

Having a car at your disposal without the hassles of traditional renting is liberating and can help you discover the city. It's also great for short excursions, and the same system operates in Florence. There are now even aggregator apps like Urbi (www.urbi.co) and Free2Move (www.free2move.com) that simplify the registration process and provide access to multiple sharing networks in Rome and beyond.

For longer trips between cities, traditional rental agencies can be found inside Termini (Platform 1, Via Marsala 29) or at either airport. Avis (tel. 06/481-4373), Europcar (tel. 06/488-2854), Maggiore (tel. 06/488-0049), and Sixt (tel. 06/3211-0194) all have large modern fleets with manual or automatic transmission vehicles.

Day Trips

Beyond the Aurelian walls of Rome lie ancient roads, a Roman town that rivals Pompeii, and volcanic lakes. None of these are very far or difficult to reach, and each makes for an interesting half-day excursion that will provide a different perspective on Rome. All are served by public transportation, and it only takes 30 minutes to get to Ostia Antica.

★ VIA APPIA ANTICA

Via Appia Antica is a magnificent thoroughfare, now part of a park, that served as the ancient gateway to Rome. This road lined with pine trees once connected the city with the port of Brindisi, 354 miles (570 kilometers) to the southeast. It's a great place to get lost in history and go back in time. Once you arrive you'll be immersed in Roman countryside and surrounded by remnants of villas, tombs, and racetracks.

A visit can last anywhere from an hour to a half day depending on how much of this picturesque road you decide to explore. Although most of the ruins are clustered near the beginning, the farther you travel by foot, bike, or even on horseback the more scenic the landscape becomes.

Stop at the Centro Servizi Appia Antica (Appia Antica Service Center; Via Appia Antica 58; tel. 06/513-5316; www. infopointappia.it; daily 9:30am-5:30pm;

1: Uber Jump bike-share bicycles 2: see the city on scooters

Cycling Via Appia Antica

Parco Regionale Appia Antica provides one of the most scenic trails in Rome, rolling past pine trees and ancient monuments. Cycling is one of the best ways to experience it.

THE ROUTE

Distance: 6.5 miles (11.5 kilometers) from Appia Antica Park Office to Ciampino
Duration: 2 hours
Effort level: easy-moderate
Starting point: Appia Antica Park Office

The ancient road runs right outside the park office where bikes can be rented. There is light automobile traffic for a kilometer or so until the smooth cobble stones give way to uneven flagstones and the tranquility of the Roman countryside. Riders can choose between smooth cobblestones or dirt paths that run along either side of the path. The great thing about this route are the ancient Roman monuments along the way. There's a gentle incline that takes about an hour to complete either way and gradually peters out into the town of Ciampino. From here it's possible to continue 4.5 miles (8 kilometers) farther up into the Castelli Romani hillside and to the volcanic lakes, but heavily trafficked roads must be used and it's a steep climb suited to expert riders.

BIKE RENTALS

Via Appia Antica technically starts at Circus Maximus, but it's easiest to start cycling from the **Appia Antica Park Office** (Via Appia Antica 42; tel. 06/513-5316; www.parcoappiaantica.it; Mon.-Fri. 9:30am-1pm and 2pm-5pm, Sat.-Sun. 9:30am-7pm) or **Centro Servizi Appia Antica** (Appia Antica Service Center; Via Appia Antica 58; tel. 06/513-5316; www.ecobikeroma.it; daily 9:30am-5:30pm), where city, mountain, and e-bikes bikes (€4-6 per hour or €16-30 per day) can be rented. At the service center, you can also pick up a park map, which highlights several off-road itineraries that stretch for kilometers. Child seats are available for kids weighing up to 45 pounds (20 kilograms). The service center also provides 3-hour tours (€18 pp group or €160 private for 1-2 riders) of the park for beginner riders that cover all the sights. Departures are flexible and can be arranged in advance by phone or email. You can reach either office in 15 minutes on board the 118 Bus from Circo Massimo.

Buses 118, 218) to pick up a map of the area, or to rent a bike, which is an excellent way to explore. Tours of the park on horseback can be organized at **Riding Ancient Rome** (Via dei Cercenii 15; tel. 392/788-5168; daily 7am-8pm; www.ridingancientrome.it; €40 per hour; Buses 118, 660).

Sights

CATACOMBS OF SAN CALLISTO
(Catacombe di San Callisto)

Via Appia Antica 110; tel. 06/513-0151; www. catacombe.roma.it; Thurs.-Tues. 9am-noon and 2pm-5pm; €8

High mortality rates and lack of space led ancient gravediggers to dig kilometers of catacombs in the soft tufa rock underground. There are half a dozen in Rome, and San Callisto, begun in the 2nd century AD, once housed over 500,000 of the deceased including 16 popes and dozens of martyrs.

The catacombs are half a mile (1.2 kilometers) from the park office. Once you get your ticket, wait next to the Union Jack flag for the 40-minute English-language tour that departs every half hour. Volunteers provide a brief explanation of Roman funerary rituals before leading groups down to the first and second levels of this vast subterranean mortuary. Tomb raiders removed most of the valuables and the bones disappeared long ago, but there are still plenty of crypts, statuettes, carvings, and frescoes decorating the narrow passages where ancient mourners regularly came to honor their dead.

CIRCO DI MASSENZIO

Via Appia Antica 153; www.villadimassenzio.it; Tues.-Sun. 10am-4pm; free; Buses 118, 660

On Via Appia Antica, the first monumental ruin above ground is the ancient track of Circo di Massenzio, half a mile (1.2 kilometers) from the catacombs. Private sponsorship of stadiums is another Roman innovation and this one is in better condition, although much smaller, than the Circus Maximus. Here, 10,000 Romans regularly gathered to cheer their favorite charioteers.

CECILIA METELLA

Via Appia Antica 161; daily 9am-4:30pm; €6 combo ticket; Buses 118, 660

Cecilia Metella, located a hundred yards after Circo Di Massenzio, is the first of several monumental tombs. Like the others it has been transformed over the ages according to the whims of its owners. It's now a museum where visitors can examine the open-air interior of a monumental mausoleum.

VILLA DEI QUINTILI

Via Appia Antica 1092, tel. 06/712-9121; Tues.-Sun. 9am-7:30pm, winter 9am-4:30pm; €6

Several ancient residences and tombs on Via Appia Antica can only be seen from the outside but Villa dei Quintili, located 2 miles (3.5 kilometers) past Cecilia Metella, was recently opened to the public. It was built by a consul and was the home of Emperor Commodus during the 2nd century AD. Aqueducts can be spotted from the villa and several of these ancient Roman thirst quenchers are still in use today. The villa is slightly off the main road on a dirt path immediately after a mushroom-shaped mausoleum. Your ticket also covers entry to Santa Maria Nova, a medieval farmhouse with ancient Roman foundations and well-preserved mosaic flooring. Guided tours are available upon reservation.

Food

A bottle of wine, a loaf of bread, cold cuts, cheese, and clementines are all you need for a good picnic along the grassy banks of Appia Antica. If you prefer something less improvised, there are several restaurants lining the road.

TRATTORIA DA PRISCILLA

Via Appia Antica 68; tel. 06/513-6379; Mon.-Sat. noon-2:30pm and 7pm-11:30pm; €10-12

Trattoria Da Priscilla is a rustic eatery that serves traditional Roman dishes in humble surroundings. It's a good place to start or finish an exploration of the ancient road. You can sample a multi-course meal with Amatricana pasta as a first and roast pork and potatoes for a second. House wine can be ordered by the glass, quarter or half carafe and the bathroom is outside next to the park office.

ANTICA HOSTERIA L'ARCHEOLOGIA

Via Appia Antica 139; daily 12:30pm-3pm and 8pm-11pm; €14-18

Antica Hosteria L'Archeologia near the Catacombs of San Sebastiano is one of the oldest restaurants and a good way to start or finish a day on the ancient road. Besides à la carte options, they offer a four-course land (€38) and sea (€48) tasting menu.

Getting There

Buses 118 and **660** are the most convenient public transport to Via Appia Antica and can be picked up at Piazza Venezia or Circo Massimo. It's a 15-minute ride, and buses pass daily 5:30am-11pm. Get off at the Basilica S. Sebastiano stop near the catacombs and head south on the ancient road.

It's a 2-mile (3.5-kilometer) walk from Circo Massimo to the park office that rents bikes and about another mile (1.8 kilometer) to San Sebastiano. Follow Viale delle Terme di Caricalla straight and make sure to carry a bottle of water and be wary of traffic. The Appia Antica officially starts after you cross

the Porto S. Sebastiano gate and gets better and better the farther you go.

LAGO ALBANO

The Roman countryside is dotted with four volcanic lakes where ancient Romans escaped summer heat and modern Romans still do. The closest to Rome is Lago Albano, 15 miles (25 kilometers) southeast of the city center. It's also the deepest, at over 525 feet (160 meters) to the bottom, and the only one of the four that's dormant. Lago Albano is a great escape, surrounded by steep forested hills with views of the town of Castel Gandolfo, which looms high above the western crest. The town was founded by a family from Genoa who later donated it to the Vatican. Popes have been spending summers here ever since.

The northern shore of Lago Albano is lined with bathing establishments that rent pedal boats and kayaks. A variety of aquatic vehicles including SUP boards, pedal boats, and sail boats are also available. Not in the mood for activity? An umbrella and lounge chair will cost you €12, and the water is clear and warm enough for swimming.

Boating on Lago Albano
CANOA KAYAK ACADEMY
Via Spiaggia del Lago 17b; tel. 339/682-6524; www. ckacademy.it

Rent a **single kayak** (€10/1 hour, €15/2 hours) or **double kayak** (€15/1 hour, €25/2 hours) from Lorenzo or Alex at Canoa Kayak Academy near the Saroli beach club and explore the lake on your own, or sign up for their 3-hour **tour** (€40 pp) that departs daily at 10:30am and 3:30pm. The guys recount the lake's illustrious history (ancient Romans once staged mock sea battles here) and stop for a swim and snack on the opposite shore. The guides are fun and friendly. No kayaking experience is required, life jackets are provided, and Lorenzo starts each tour with a brief introduction to rowing. Bring sunglasses, hat,

sunscreen, towel, and water. Kayakers must be at least 12 years old.

Getting There

Canoa Kayak Academy operates a by-request **shuttle service** (€10) to and from the Anagnina Metro A station. Just let them know when you expect to arrive and they will pick you up in the morning or afternoon. It's about a 20-minute ride to the lake. Alternatively, the **Regional 7353** train departs hourly from Termini (€2.10) and it's a 25 minute walk the rest of the way.

OSTIA ANTICA

Viale dei Romagnoli 717; tel. 06/5635-2830; www. ostiaantica.beniculturali.it; winter Tues.-Sun. 8:30am-5pm, summer Tues.-Sun. 8:30am-7:15pm; €10, audio guide €2

The ancient city of Ostia Antica provides an instant sense of how the Romans lived. The ruins here are more extensive than those in the city center, and it's easy to imagine oneself on the way to the forum.

The town was founded as a fort at the mouth of the Tiber to protect Rome from invaders. When threats faded, it evolved into a major port where Egyptian grain and other materials from across the empire were stored. Today, Ostia Antica contains warehouses, apartment buildings, shops, and temples. At its peak, the population numbered nearly 100,000 and might have continued growing if the river here hadn't silted up and a second port been built. The consequence was a slow decline and gradual burial that has yet to be fully excavated.

Sights

The entrance to Ostia Antica is on the Decumanus, the Roman main street that ran from east to west. Immediately on the left are dozens of stone **sarcophagi,** and behind these are small family burial chambers where the remains of cremated relatives were placed and frequently visited. (Death was kept outside the city walls and cemeteries ran along the major roads.) Farther along on the right is

---

1: Via Appia Antica **2:** Ostia Antica **3:** kayaking on Lago Albano

Ostia Antica

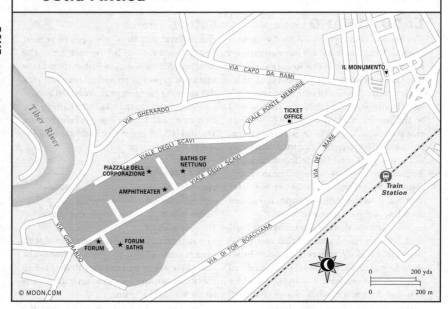

Map labels:
- VIA CAPO DA RAMI
- IL MONUMENTO
- VIA GHERARDO
- VIALE PONTE MEMORIE
- TICKET OFFICE
- Tiber River
- VIALE DEGLI SCAVI
- PIAZZALE DELL CORPORAZIONE ★
- BATHS OF NETTUNO ★
- VIALE DEGLI SCAVI
- VIA DEL MARE
- AMPHITHEATER ★
- Train Station
- VIA GHERARDO
- ★ FORUM
- ★ FORUM BATHS
- VIA DI TOR BOACCIANA
- © MOON.COM
- 0   200 yds
- 0   200 m

the first of several **baths,** a major component of every Roman city. From the top of the steps you can get a good view of the various rooms and the mosaics depicting Neptune. Citizens came here once a day to wash, relax, exercise, or socialize.

Even if actors weren't particularly respected in Roman times, theater was popular and Greek-style plays were regularly performed. Ostia's **amphitheater** is a short distance from the baths. Its surprisingly good condition is a result of restoration during the 1930s. The theater has a semicircular shape, and the three large masks on the stage once formed part of the backdrop. From the last row of the amphitheater **Piazzale delle Corporazioni** is visible directly in front. This large complex once held the offices of importers and the various guilds responsible for keeping ships afloat. The mosaics in front of each doorway were similar to modern-day neon and indicated the origin and business of the traders inside.

The **forum** is located where the Decumanus intersected with the Cardo to form the heart of the city. This is where citizens gathered on religious or civic occasions and where business was conducted. The temple in the center was built by Hadrian in the 2nd century AD. Adjacent to the forum are the largest baths that include a public latrine, which could still function in an emergency. The apartments nearby include the **House of Diana,** which was lined with shops and a bar where antique happy hours were once served.

Ostia Antica is quite extensive. Most visitors turn back after reaching the forum, although much remains to be explored farther south. If you have time, get off the main road and get face to face with history. Most of the time the site is fairly empty except for school groups and adventurous visitors. The museum (daily 10:30am-4pm) near the middle contains the artifacts discovered over the years and offers further insight into daily Roman life. A cafeteria and gift shop satisfy any food or postcard needs.

Food
IL MONUMENTO
Piazza Umberto 8; tel. 06/565-0021; daily 12:30pm-3:30pm and 8pm-11pm; €13-16

It's easy to work up an appetite exploring the past, and Il Monumento has the solution. The *spaghetti monumento* is the house dish for a reason and is served with fresh seafood sauce. Outdoor dining is available in the carefully tended garden. The restaurant is located near a small castle in the pleasant village-like *borgo* opposite Ostia Antica.

Recreation
If you don't feel like heading straight back to Rome after your visit to Ostia Antica, continue to the end of the line and experience a Mediterranean sunset at one of the many beach establishments lining the coast. La Marinella (www.lamarinella.com) rents chairs and umbrellas to nonmembers, and there's a good restaurant serving fresh fish

dishes. Ride the 061 Bus a half dozen stops south along the coastal road to reach wilder dunes where you can lay out for free at Mediterranea or Oasi Naturista (Italy's first nudist beach).

Getting There
Freccia del Mare trains link Rome with Ostia. They depart daily from Piramide station (Metro B) every 15 minutes and take less than half an hour to reach Ostia Antica. From there, it's a 10-minute walk to the entrance of the ancient city.

It's also possible to get to Ostia by a combination of metro and bicycle. Bikes can be transported on the first car of the Rome-Lido di Ostia railway that departs from Piramide station. It takes about 40 minutes to reach the final Cristoforo Colombo stop. From there you can set off on a leisurely ride along Ostia's 6-mile (10-kilometer) promenade. Running close to the beach, it's more of a sidewalk than a bike path. From here, you can take a break to enjoy the sand before heading back to the city.

Between Rome and Florence

ASSISI
As one of the most important artistic and religious centers in Italy, Assisi attracts a crowd. Over six million pilgrims visit every year, many of whom come to see the home and resting place of Saint Francis. To find peace from the rush of pilgrims and tourists along Corso Mazzini, explore the streets behind Piazza del Comune, head to the medieval castle looming above town, or retreat to the hermitage where Saint Francis would get away from it all.

Long before Assisi ever existed there was Asisium. Remains of that ancient Roman town are still present today, and the best place to find them is Santa Maria Sopra Minerva.

Sights
BASILICA DI SAN FRANCESCO
Piazza Inferiore di San Francesco 2; tel. 075/819-9001; www.sanfrancescoassisi.org; Basilica Inferiore daily 6am-6:50pm, free; Basilica Superiore daily 8:30am-6:50pm, free, audio guide available

Basilica di San Francesco consists of two churches built on top of each other. Two booths outside the basilica provide free audio guides to the entire complex. The lower church was begun in 1228 several years after Saint Francis's death. It has a more intimate feel and was intended to accommodate the growing number of pilgrims who venerated Francis. The upper church dates from 1230 and has a grander style. The crypt that houses

Assisi

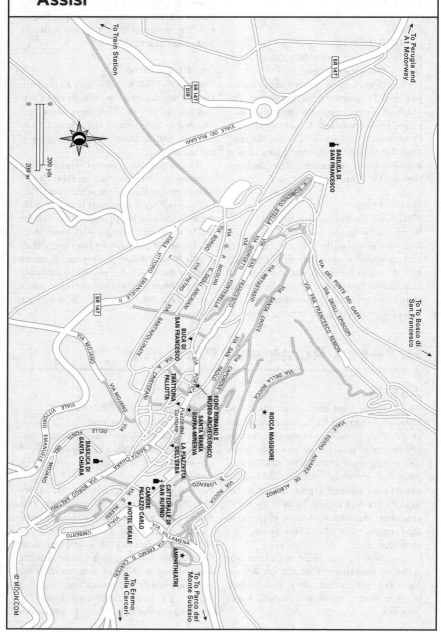

To Perugia and
A1 Motorway

To Train Station

SR 147

SR 147
DIR

VIALE DEI BULGARI

BASILICA DI
SAN FRANCESCO

VIA DOMENICO STELLA

To To Bosco di
San Francesco

VIA G. P. NICOLINI

VIA DEL BORGO

VIA GIORGETTI

SAN FRANCESCO

VIA FONTEBELLA

VIA METASTASIO

VIA DEL PONTE DEI GAFFI

VIA SANTA CROCE

VIA FRA FRANCESCO REMON

VIA DEGLI AFRICANI

VIA PIETRO

VIA VITTORIO EMANUELE II

SR 147

VIA SANTA PIZZAVOLANTE

VIA SAN PAOLO

VIA SAN RUFINO

VIA PORTICA

VIA CAPOBOVE

VIA DELLA ROCCA

BUCA DI
SAN FRANCESCO

VIA A. CRISTOFANI

FORO ROMANO E
MUSEO ARCHEOLOGICO

VIA MOJANO

TRATTORIA
PALLOTTA

SANTA MARIA
SOPRA MINERVA

ROCCA
MAGGIORE

Piazza del
Comune

LA PIAZZETTA
DELL'ERBA

VIA SAN FRANCESCO

VIALE VITTORIO EMANUELE II

VIALE DEL PONTE DEL MOJANO

BASILICA DI
SANTA CHIARA

VIA S. CHIARA

VIA S. LORENZO

LA ROCCA

CATTEDRALE DI
SAN RUFINO

VIALE EGIDIO ALVARO DE ALBOMOZ

VIA BORGO ARETINO

VIA G. ALESSI

CAMERE
PALAZZO CARLO

VIA VILLAMENA

VIALE UMBERTO

HOTEL IDEALE

VIA EREMO D. CARCERI

AMPHITHEATRE

To Parco del
Monte Subasio

To Eremo
delle Carceri

0   200 yds
0   200 m

© MOON.COM

the saint's body was dug in 1818 and is below the lower church.

Both churches attracted the finest artists of the time, and nearly every centimeter of the interior is frescoed. The lower church contains biblically themed frescoes by Lorenzetti and Martini, but the most impressive works are those by Giotto, who nearly singlehandedly invented a new perspective. His paintings gave depth to landscapes and figures that had previously appeared flat. He painted a series of 28 frescoes inside the upper church over five years starting in 1290. The panels illustrate the life of Saint Francis, with the most dramatic panel showing the saint renouncing his father's wealth and stripping himself before God. Giotto's cycle starts on the far right side of the church near the choir. The first painting depicts the future saint in his youth; a man spreads a cloth over the ground where he will step, foretelling his destiny of purity.

SANTA MARIA SOPRA MINERVA
Piazza del Comune 14; free

Santa Maria Sopra Minerva is the most obvious reminder of Assisi's Roman past. The facade of this church is all that remains of the Roman temple, probably dedicated to Hercules, but that's enough. Seven fluted columns are completely intact and form a stunning contrast with the medieval bell tower built next door. Inside is all Renaissance and gold-leafed sculptures.

BASILICA DI SANTA CHIARA
Piazza Santa Chiara 1; tel. 075/812-282; daily 6:30am-noon and 2pm-7pm; free

Basilica di Santa Chiara was constructed from pink stone dug from the nearby mountains. Its 12th- and 14th-century frescoes are particularly well preserved and depict Saint Chiara, who founded the Clarissa order of nuns. In the chapel on the right along the single nave is the cross on which Saint Francis vowed to reform the church.

CATTEDRALE DI SAN RUFINO
Piazza San Rufino 3; tel. 075/812-283; free

The austere 12th-century Romanesque exterior of Cattedrale di San Rufino remains stunning in its proportions and simplicity. The interior, like many churches in Italy, was redesigned during the Renaissance but the baptismal font escaped unscathed and is where Saint Francis was baptized. A crypt (Thurs.-Tues. 10am-1pm and 3pm-6pm; €4) below the church reveals the earliest foundations of the church. The adjacent bell tower is medieval and still in perfect working order.

FORO ROMANO E MUSEO ARCHEOLOGICO
Via Portica 2; tel. 075/815-5077; daily 10:30am-1pm and 2pm-5pm; €5

To find more traces of ancient Rome visit the nearby Foro Romano e Museo Archeologico. It's a small museum but provides a fascinating hint of what the town once looked like. You'll walk underground along Roman foundations and see the tombs, plaques, busts, and vases they left behind.

AMPHITEATRE
Via Anfiteatro Romano; free

Like most Roman towns Asisium had its own amphitheater whose outline is still clearly visible in one of the most charming and least visited parts of Assisi. It's a 15-minute walk through beautiful side streets east of Piazza del Comune. Follow Via Santa Maria delle Rose and turn left at the San Rufino church. Head up the hill, take the last right, and ask for directions if you can't find it.

ROCCA MAGGIORE
Via della Rocca; tel. 075/813-8680; daily 10am-7pm; €8

Begun in 1174, the medieval castle of Rocca Maggiore has seen its share of battles and was destroyed and rebuilt numerous times over the centuries. The fortress is situated on a hillside north of town. Inside the castle are exhibits illustrating daily life in the Middle Ages. It's a steep climb along Via della Rocca and takes around 20 minutes to reach the ramparts from the center on foot. The effortless

Saint Francis (1181-1226)

Born into a wealthy merchant family in Assisi, Giovanni di Pietro di Bernardone (aka Francesco d'Assisi) was expected to follow in his father's footsteps, but destiny took a dramatic turn. He enlisted in a war against Perugia and was captured and spent a year in prison, during which his health declined. After his release he gradually recovered and joined the Crusades but became ill again immediately after departing. That's when he had his first revelation.

It led Francis to act strangely. He continued working for his father and set off on trade expeditions, but instead of returning home with the profits he distributed them to the poor and gave his clothes to beggars. People in Assisi thought he was crazy, including his father, who turned him over to local authorities hoping the threat of punishment would bring the boy to his senses.

The plan backfired and during the trial Francis undressed before the assembly and disavowed his family in favor of God. Later he heard the voice of God instructing him to repair the church, and he began doing so. He lived simply and loved everyone including the lepers he had despised in his youth. He traveled and gained loyal disciples who became recognized as the Franciscans. The order grew even after Francis's death, and dozens of monasteries were founded throughout Western Europe.

Francis left behind many letters, and there are firsthand accounts of his feats including the famed preaching to the birds. The saint's life is illustrated in Giotto's detailed frescoes inside the Basilica di San Francesco where he is buried. Today Saint Francis remains a symbol of peace and an example to thousands of Christians who come to Assisi every year to honor him.

alternative is calling a taxi or grabbing one from the stand in Piazza Chiesa Nuova.

EREMO DELLE CARCERI

Via Ermo delle Carceri 1a; tel. 075/812-301; www. assisiofm.it; daily 7:30am-6pm; free

Eremo delle Carceri was the mountain hermitage where Saint Francis convened with God. Today the small sanctuary attracts pilgrims from around the world. It includes a chapel and monastery where four monks live and share the teachings of the saint. The retreat is reached by a scenic road east of town where travelers can reflect on nature and enjoy the silence. You can also see the grotto where Saint Francis prayed and part of the convent, and attend mass, which is held five times a day. Morning and afternoon tours in English recounting the saint's life must be reserved in advance and last 20 minutes.

Food

TRATTORIA PALLOTTA

Vicolo della Volta Pinta 3; tel. 075/815-5273; www. pallottaassisi.it; Wed.-Mon. noon-2:30pm and 7pm-10pm; €10-12

Every time the bell rings at the Trattoria Pallotta something good comes out of the kitchen. There are three tasting menus for those who can't decide, and the choices include many vegetarian options. Visitors are greeted with a smile as soon as they enter and are given a choice of tables in one of two rustic rooms. The family also runs a small hotel nearby.

BUCA DI SAN FRANCESCO

Via E. Brizi 1; tel. 075/812-204; Tues.-Sun. noon-2:45pm and 7pm-10pm; €10-14

A medieval atmosphere in the center of Assisi is only half the attraction of Buca di San Francesco. The other half is the food, which excels from the appetizers to the desserts. *Fantasia di bruschette* is a good way to start and will arrive on your table within minutes. Trust Giovanni Betti to make the right wine selection to accompany your food.

1: Siena's Duomo 2: steep streets of Assisi 3: Piazza del Campo in Siena

LA PIAZZETTA DELL'ERBA
Via San Gabriele dell'Addolorato 15a;
tel. 075/815-352; Tues.-Sun. 12:30pm-3:30pm and
7:30pm-10:30pm; €12-15

What started out as a hobby among four friends has become La Piazzetta dell'Erba. Their interpretation of Umbrian classics includes a salad of pecorino, pear, nuts, and honey. Meals are served inside amid modern décor or outside on a quiet pedestrian street.

Hiking
Assisi is almost entirely surrounded by nature, with good options for hiking.

PIAZZA DEL COMUNE TO ROCCA MAGGIORE
Distance: *0.8 miles (900 meters) round-trip*
Duration: *35-45 minutes round-trip*
Effort level: *moderate*
Starting point: *Piazza del Comune*

For panoramic views of Assisi and the surrounding Umbrian countryside, follow Via S. Rufino out of Assisi's main square and continue up Via Porta Perlici out the city gates and up along Via della Rocca all the windy way to the castle of Rocca Maggiore. There are a couple of off-road shortcuts and the final stretch provides superb views of Assisi and the valley below.

BASILICA DI SAN FRANCESCO TO SANTA CROCE CHURCH
Distance: *2 miles (3.4 kilometers) round-trip*
Duration: *40 minutes round-trip*
Effort level: *moderate*
Starting point: *Basilica di San Francesco*

The Bosco di San Francesco (tel. 075/813-157; Tues.-Sun 10am-7pm; €6) park lies just outside town. Run by FAI (Italian Environmental Association), it provides 3 miles (5 kilometers) of signaled trails though forests and olive groves, over bridges, past a tower, and to a small cascade where visitors bathe in early summer. From Basilica di San Francesco, a narrow 0.9-mile (1.5-kilometer) road heads up to the lovely Benedictine church of Santa Croce. The inside of the church is as unassuming as the outside and is a quiet place to reflect and take refuge from the summer heat. It's uphill with a dislevel of 300 feet (100 meters). The trail is suitable for novice hikers and children. Wear comfortable shoes.

Osteria del Mulino (Via Ponte dei Galli; tel. 075/816-831; Tues.-Sun. 9am-3:30pm and Thurs.-Sun. 6pm-10:30; €8-12) is opposite the church and a good place to stop for coffee, lunch, or dinner. This is the only place to eat in the area, but the rustic interior and hearty menu mean that's a good thing. The proprietors also prepare picnics (reserved in advanced) that can be enjoyed at outdoor tables within the park.

SENTIERO DEI MORTAI
Distance: *9 miles (15 kilometers) round-trip*
Duration: *1.5-2 hours round-trip*
Effort level: *moderate-strenuous*
Starting point: *Porta Cappuccini (Strada Provinciale 251), a gate on the eastern edge of town*

The mountainous area east of Assisi where San Francesco walked and meditated is now Parco del Monte Subasio (tel. 075/815-5290; www.parcomontesubasio.it; free). There are 14 trails here all managed by CAI (Italian Alpine Club; www.cai.it) and clearly marked with red and white stripes. Trail lengths vary from a couple of hours to half a day. If you're starting out from Assisi, the best one to follow is Sentiero dei Mortai (no. 50). The panoramic trail leads into pine forests, past San Francesco's hermitage, up rocky outcrops, along summit pastures, and—if you walk far enough—all the way to Spello. At 9 miles (15 kilometers) and with a dislevel of over 2,600 feet (800 meters), it is suited for seasoned hikers. The Monte Bilvio peak midway along the trail is 4,170 feet (1,270 meters) above sea level and provides a 360-degree view of Umbria. Pack plenty of water and food for the journey. Maps of the park are available online.

Accommodations
CAMERE PALAZZO CARLO
Piazza San Rufino 3; tel. 075/812-490; www.
camerecarli.it; €47-60 d

For a comfortable bed and warm welcome, look no further than Camere Palazzo Carlo. The *pensione* with three rooms inside a medieval building is a short walk from everything. Breakfast isn't included but there are plenty of restaurants and bars nearby and it doesn't get much cheaper than this.

HOTEL IDEALE

Piazza Giacomo Matteoti 1; tel. 075/813-570; www. hotelideale.it; €120-140 d

This small two-star hotel on the edge of Assisi provides clean comfortable rooms and five-star views. Homemade cakes and a tempting breakfast buffet are waiting downstairs every morning and there's free parking nearby. It's 3.7 miles (6 kilometers) from the train station and only five minutes to the center of town on foot. Make sure to ask for a room with a balcony.

Getting There and Around

Assisi is 114 miles (183 kilometers) from Rome and less than two hours from the capital by car. The fastest route is north on the A1 highway to the Orte exit, after which drivers should follow the E45 and SS3. Flixbus (tel. 02/9475-9208; www.flixbus.it; €13.99) buses depart from Tiburtina station daily at 5:20pm. There are several stops along the way and the journey takes 2.5 hours. Transfers from Perugia may be required depending on the season.

Trains (€11.25) depart from Termini and Tiburtina stations in Rome and some require a transfer in Foligno. It can take 2-3 hours to reach Assisi depending on the service. The nearest train station is 4 miles (6 kilometers) outside town in Santa Maria degli Angeli. Travelers can complete the journey by bus or taxi (€11). APM buses (tel. 800/850-800; www.apmperugia.it) connect Perugia and surrounding towns with Assisi. All journeys start and terminate in Piazza Matteotti.

BusItalia (€1.30 or €2 on board) operates two bus lines within Assisi that connect the principal monuments and squares. It runs every 30 minutes and tickets are available at newsstands or *tabacchi*. Taxi stands are located in Piazza Unità d'Italia and Piazza del Comune, or may be ordered 24 hours a day from Radio Taxi Assisi (tel. 075/813-100; www.radiotaxiassisi.it).

SIENA

Siena offers a refreshing break between the endless monuments of Rome and the extraordinary art of Florence. It feels more like a small town than a city and can easily be navigated in an hour or two on foot. Most of the streets lead to the shell-shaped *piazza del campo* in the historic center. The other essential stop in Siena is the Duomo, which was built in Roman-Gothic style and is one of the great churches of Italy.

Siena first rose to prominence under the Lombards in the 6th century AD. It experienced a population influx during the Middle Ages when wealthy families began building their houses along the Via Francigena on the highest part of town. Prosperity brought about conflict with Florence and the numerous battles that ensued are immortalized in Dante's *Divine Comedy*. Beating the Florentines was one thing, but surviving the plague of 1348 was another. The Black Death brought construction to a halt and began a long period of instability, which ended with Siena's submission to its larger neighbor.

Siena is divided into 17 *contrade* or neighborhoods. They are located within the medieval walls of the city and each has its own colors, coat of arms, and motto. Numbers have special relevance in Siena. The nine sections of the Piazza del Campo represent the Council of Nine, which ruled the city in the 13th and 14th centuries. There are 17 *contrade* (parishes) that inspire loyalty from birth and from which contestants are selected during the two annual *palios* (horse races). Then there are the Terzi, the three districts the town has been divided into since its founding. Terzo di Città is where the Duomo and Siena's oldest buildings stand. The central Capitana dell'Onde borders Piazza del Campo and stretches south of the square.

Sights

PIAZZA DEL CAMPO

Wherever you enter Siena, you are inevitably drawn to Piazza del Campo. The main square has inherited its famous seashell shape from the whims and jerks of medieval urbanization. Fonte Gaie fountain at the northern end is a beautiful replacement for the 15th-century original sculpted by Jacopo della Quercia and now kept safe in Santa Maria della Scala. It's also the location of Siena's famous horse race, the Palio delle Contrade.

PALAZZO PUBBLICO

Piazza del Campo 1; tel. 05/7729-2111; 10am-6pm; €10
Palazzo Pubblico is at the bottom of the sloping Piazza del Campo and was constructed in a Gothic style at the end of the 12th century. The palace is Siena's town hall and has been since the 12th century. Part of the palace is now a museum and visitors can explore magnificent rooms where leaders once gathered. *Sala dei Nove* is the grandest of these and the walls are covered with giant frescoes depicting local history.

Also within the palazzo is the entrance to the **Torre del Mangia** (daily winter 10am-4pm and summer 10am-7pm; €10 or €15 combined ticket), which rises 334 feet (102 meters) and provides great views of the Tuscan countryside. The tower took 23 years to build and was completed in 1348. It's been a symbol of the city ever since and was a useful watchtower during the city's centuries-long feud with Florence. All that separates you from a view reminiscent of the frescoes in the rooms below is 300 steps.

DUOMO

Piazza del Duomo; tel. 05/7728-6300; www. operaduomo.siena.it; Mon.-Sat. 10:30am-5pm and Sun. 1:30-5pm; €5 Duomo only, Opa Si Pass €15
The Duomo is hard to miss. It's the largest building in town and there's a lot to see inside. Built in Roman-Gothic style, it's one of the great cathedrals of Italy and might have been the biggest in the world had the plague not brought construction to a halt. The alternating white-and-black marble is striking and the vast number of columns inside the colorful interior creates many interesting perspectives. The pavement was laid in the 15th century and consists of 56 immense squares featuring mythological and biblical tales. It's covered much of the year to protect the marble and is exposed from mid-August to the end of October. The pulpit, carved by Nicola Pisano, dramatically illustrates the life of Christ. There's also a panoramic **Porta Cielo** (daily 10:30am-6pm; €20) route up the inside of the cathedral that provides an overhead view of the central apse and the city outside. It's a guided tour that leaves every 30 minutes and has a maximum of 18 participants.

There's a lot to see inside the Duomo including the **Piccolomini library** with frescoes by Raphael (he's the one wearing red pants and holding a candle), the **Baptistry** sculpted by Donatello, an ancient underground **Crypt,** and the **Museo dell'Opera** that explains how the cathedral was built. The **Opa Si Pass** (€15) allows you to discover seven sights over three days and is available online, by telephone, or from the **Duomo Ticket Office** (Piazza del Duomo; tel. 05/7753-4511; www.operaduomo.siena.it; daily 9am-6pm) in the square outside. The latter does get crowded in summer. Individual tickets to each sight (€5) are available but if you want to see it all, the pass is the best option. You can also rent a guide (info@guidesiena.com; €150 for three hours), interactive touch-screen tablets (€7) that follow three itineraries or use audio stations (€2) located at different points within the Duomo.

OSPEDALE DI SANTA MARIA

Piazza Duomo 1; tel. 05/7728-6300; Fri.-Wed. 10am-7pm, Thurs. 10am-10pm; €9; €20 family ticket
Ospedale di Santa Maria was the first hospital in the city. It was where pilgrims would get their blisters looked at and anyone with a serious disease might find a little relief. It was operational until a few years ago and now houses a museum. Inside, Sala del Pellegrinaio is a monumental vaulted corridor, built in the

Siena

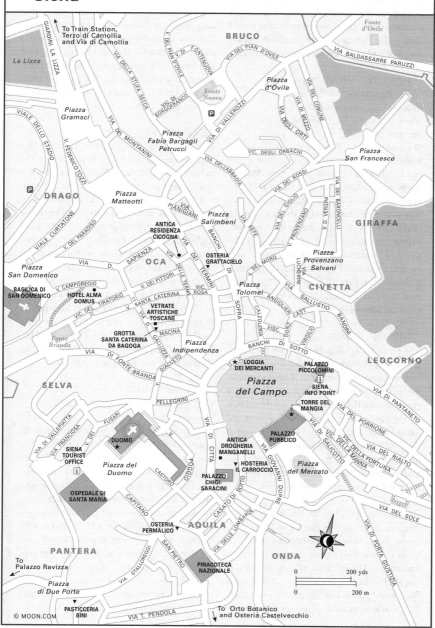

GIARDINI LA LIZZA

La Lizza

To Train Station,
Terzo di Camollia
and Via di Camollia

BRUCO

Fonte
d'Ovile

VIA BALDASSARRE PARUZZI

VIA DELLA STURA SECCA

V. DEL PIAN D'OVILE

V. DEL FONTENUOVA

VIA DEL PIAN D'OVILE

Fonte
Nuova

Piazza
d'Ovile

VIA DEL COMUNE

VIA DI MEZZO

VIALE DELLO STADIO

Piazza
Gramsci

VIC DI
BORGOFRANCO

VIA DI VALLEROZZI

VIA DEGLI ORTI

V. FEDERICO TOZZI

VIA DEL MONTANINI

Piazza
Fabio Bargagli
Petrucci

VIC. DEGLI ORBACHI

Piazza
San Francesco

VIA DELL'ABBADIA

VIA DEI ROSSI

VIALE CURTATONE

DRAGO

Piazza
Matteotti

VIA
PIANIGIANI

Piazza
Salimbeni

VIA DEL GIGLIO

VIA DEI BARONCELLI

V. B. PERUZZI

GIRAFFA

V. DEL PARADISO

ANTICA
RESIDENZA
CICOGNA

BANCHI

VIA REFE

V. PROVENZANO

Piazza
San Domenico

VIA D.
SAPIENZA

OCA

VIA DELLE TERME

OSTERIA
GRATTACIELO

V. DEL MORO

Piazza
Provenzano
Salvani

VIA LUCHERINI

BASILICA DI
SAN DOMENICO

V. CAMPOREGIO

HOTEL ALMA
DOMUS

V. DEI PITTORI

VIC.
ROSA

Piazza
Tolomei

ANGIOLIERI

SALLUSTIO BANDINI

CIVETTA

V. DEL TIRATOIO

V. SANTA CATERINA

VETRATE
ARTISTICHE
TOSCANE

SOPRA

CALZOLERIA

CAST.

VIRGILIO

LEOCORNO

Fonte
Branda

GROTTA
SANTA CATERINA
DA BAGOGA

MACINA

Piazza
Indipendenza

VISC.

BOIDO

BANCHI DI SOTTO

VIA DI FONTE-BRANDA

DIACCETO

CALUZZA

PELLEGRINI

LOGGIA
DEI MERCANTI

PALAZZO
PICCOLOMINI

SIENA
INFO POINT

VIA DI PANTANETO

SELVA

Piazza
del Campo

TORRE DEL
MANGIA

VIA DEL PORRIONE

VIA DI VALLEPIATTA

VIA FRANCIOSA

V. DEI FUSARI

SIENA
TOURIST
OFFICE

DUOMO

V. DI
CITTA

ANTICA
DROGHERIA
MANGANELLI

PALAZZO
PUBBLICO

VIA DI SALICOTTO

VIC. DELLA MANNA

VIA DEL RIALTO

VIA DELLA FORTUNA

Piazza del
Duomo

POGGIO

HOSTERIA
IL CARROCCIO

Piazza
del Mercato

OSPEDALE DI
SANTA MARIA

CASTORO

PALAZZO
CHIGI-
SARACINI

CASATO DI SOTTO

VIA GIOVANNI DUPRE

VIA DEL SOLE

CAPITANO

OSTERIA
PERMALICO

AQUILA

VIA DELLE LOMBARDE

VIA DI PORTA GIUSTIZIA

To
Palazzo Ravizza

PANTERA

SAN PIETRO

ONDA

Piazza
di Due Porte

VIA STALLOREGGI

PINACOTECA
NAZIONALE

0   200 yds
0   200 m

© MOON.COM

PASTICCERIA
BINI

VIA T. PENDOLA

To Orto Botanico
and Osteria Castelvecchio

14th century as a passageway for the many pilgrims on their way to or from Rome. The ceilings and walls are covered with frescos predating the Renaissance style that would later make Florence famous. Exhibitions are frequent and cover a wide variety of interests.

PINACOTECA NAZIONALE

Via San Pietro 29; tel. 05/7728-1161; www. pinacotecanazionale.siena.it; Tues.-Thurs. 1:15pm-6:45pm, Fri.-Sat. 8:15am-1:45pm, Sun. 9am-1pm; €8

Since the 1920s, Palazzo Buonsignori has housed the Pinacoteca Nazionale and a premier collection of Sienese artwork. Most of the paintings date from the 13th to 17th centuries, and the collection presents a clear picture of how art developed in the city over the years. There is an unrivaled quantity of gold-painted canvases, many of which were donated by local churches and convents. Works by Ambrogio and Pietro Lorenzetti, Sassetta, and Beccafumi are all on display. The sculpture room in the second-story loggia has an excellent view of the city.

TERZO DI CAMOLLIA

The Terzo di Camollia district is on the northern edge of the city; although it was rebuilt in recent centuries, many of its medieval monuments have been preserved. **Via di Camollia** runs through the center of the neighborhood and is the home of churches San Pietro and Santa Maria, completed in 1484. At the end of the road is Porta Camollia, one of the original medieval entrances to the city. Anyone who understands Latin will be able to read the inscription welcoming visitors to Siena.

BASILICA DI SAN DOMENICO

Piazza San Domenico 1; tel. 05/7728-6848; daily summer 7am-6:30pm and winter 8:30am-6pm

Saint Catherine is a pillar among the saints and admired by millions of devotees around the world. She was born into a humble Siena family and joined the church at a young age. She wrote hundreds of letters inspired by her visions inside Basilica di San Domenico where her relics are preserved. There are several portraits of Catherine inside this Gothic church that overlooks the Fontebranda Valley. Halfway along the nave on the right side is a chapel dedicated to the saint with a sculpture and frescoes by Sodoma recounting her brief, illuminated life. Mass is celebrated in Italian weekdays at 7:30am and 6pm and weekends at 7:30am, 9am, 10:30am, noon and 6pm.

TERZO DI SAN MARTINO

East of Piazza del Campo is Terzo di San Martino neighborhood. Via di Città is the main thoroughfare and is flanked by the city's finest palazzi. **Palazzo Piccolomini** is distinguished by immense blocks of ashlar Rossellino used to bring a little Florentine style to Siena. Almost directly opposite is the slightly curved **Palazzo Chigi-Saracini** that now houses a music academy. Farther down on the right is **Loggia dei Mercanti,** which marked a transition between Gothic and Renaissance architecture when it was added in the 16th century. The street also passes **Piazza Salimbeni,** enclosed on three sides by three buildings in three different styles. It's a good test for anyone who gets Gothic, Renaissance, and baroque confused.

ORTO BOTANICO

Via P. A. Mattioli 4; tel. 05/7723-2076; daily 10am-6pm; €5

Biagio Bartalini liked plants so much he founded the Orto Botanico in 1784. The 2.5-acre botanical garden situated in a small valley near Porta Tufi is divided into three sections. The first contains the most local Tuscan species you'll see in one spot. They include herbs, aromatics, and medicinal varieties that were used by Ospedale di Santa Maria in the 18th century. Aquatic plants, fruit trees, and cacti grow in the other areas and a tepidarium protects vulnerable leaves. The garden is a favorite destination of birds that serenade visitors with song. Serious horticulturists can reserve a tour of the grounds.

Food

Although it's less than 140 miles (230 kilometers) from Rome, Siena feels a lot farther away in gastronomic terms. Here the most popular pasta is *pici,* which resembles thick spaghetti; hearty vegetable *ribbolita* stews are served; and grilled meats are rarely missing from menus. The best places to try such dishes are the rustic *trattorie* scattered around the city. Don't worry if you have trouble choosing one; it's hard to go wrong. Wherever you eat, portions will be generous, and a complete meal rarely exceeds €20.

★ OSTERIA PERMALICO

Costa Largo 4; tel. 05/774-1105; Thurs.-Tues. noon-3:30pm and 7pm-10:30pm; €7-8

Italians are always on the hunt for *ottimo rapporto qualità/prezzo* (value for money). You'll find it here served by a young owner/chef who alters his menu nearly every day according to the availability of ingredients. First courses include homemade *pici* and *pappardelle* pasta covered in a variety of delicious stewed sauces. There's always a reliable special, a great house wine and an abundant tiramisu for dessert. The brick-walled interior is nice, but the simple tables outside on the terraced pedestrian street are even better.

HOSTERIA IL CARROCCIO

Via Casato di Sotto 32; tel. 05/774-1165; Thurs.-Tues. 12:15pm-2:45pm and 7:15pm-9:45pm; €8-10

Hosteria il Carroccio remains one of the most affordable options around Piazza del Campo. Service may be a little hurried but it's always efficient. Waitstaff dispense with menus in the evening and you may have to ask them to repeat the offerings. Antipasti includes *salumi* and there is generally some variation of wild boar pasta. Good salads are also served.

OSTERIA GRATTACIELO

Via dei Pontani 8; tel. 331/742-2835; daily 11:30am-3pm and 7:30pm-10pm, Mon. lunch only; €10

Cravings for cheese and cured meats can strike at any moment in Siena. When they do, *Grattacielo* (which means "skyscraper") has a cutting board ready. The *osteria* also prepares one locally inspired dish each night. But perhaps the best thing about this place is the feeling you get walking in the streets afterward realizing how little you paid for such good food.

OSTERIA CASTELVECCHIO

Via Castelvecchio 65; tel. 05/774-7093; daily noon-2:45pm and 7pm-10:45pm; €10-11

Mass tourism may have lowered the standards of some Siena restaurants, but Castelvecchio is not one of them. Simone Romi is attentive to the quality of food he serves and the service he provides both locals and visitors. The menu changes daily and the prix fixe (€25) is a good option if you want to get a wide sampling of Tuscan flavors. It comes with an antipasto, a choice from three different pastas, three seconds, and dessert.

GROTTA DI SANTA CATERINA DA BAGOGA

Via della Galluzza 26; tel. 05/7728-2208; Tues.-Sun. noon-3pm and 7pm-11pm, Sun. noon-3pm; €10-12

Getting to Grotta di Santa Caterina da Bagoga is half the fun. The labyrinth-like streets leading to the restaurant are some of the most suggestive in the city. The owner is a former *palio* rider and the tables outside provide a unique environment to have lunch or dinner. The cooking is strictly Sienese and offers a wide choice of seasonal dishes. Wine is mainly from the Rufina and local hillsides.

PASTICCERIA BINI

Via Stalloreggi 91; tel. 05/7728-0207; Tues.-Sun. 8am-8pm

Pasticceria Bini is a little outside the center but worthy of a pastry pilgrimage. They've been baking all the town's specialties, from *panforte margherita* to *cannoli alla mandorla,* since 1944. The selection is widest in the morning but there's still plenty to sample later in this elegant shop.

Festivals and Events

Lots of saints are celebrated in Siena but it's **Festa di San Giuseppe** on March 19 that's the most spirited. Via Dupre in the city center is lined with stalls displaying arts and crafts and selling toys and sweets. Around Piazza del Campo and the church of San Giuseppe the intoxicating smell of *frittelle* (fried rice) is hard to resist and outdoor stands remain open until late.

Twice a year Siena turns back the clock and transforms the Piazza del Campo into a racetrack where thousands cram to watch the **Palio delle Contrade.** For locals the main event is on July 2, while the second race on August 16 is nicknamed the "*palio* of the tourists." Both days begin with a parade around the outer perimeter of the *piazza*, which is covered in sand to prevent horses from slipping. It's best to arrive several hours before the midafternoon start. The best places to stand are on the outer edges to the left or right of the fountain from where nearly the entire course can be observed. The race consists of three laps and an anything-goes approach, with the winner carried back to his *contrade* for a victory dinner where the horse is the guest of honor.

Shopping

Via di Città is the main shopping street in Siena and contains clothing, book, food, and craft shops. Most days it's filled with tourists hunting for souvenirs. Don't let that stop you from taking a look and stopping by some of the more interesting addresses.

VETRATE ARTISTICHE TOSCANE

Via della Galluzza 5; tel. 05/774-8033; Mon.-Fri. 10am-1pm and 3pm-6pm

Stained glass may not be high on your souvenir list but the artists at Vetrate Artistiche Toscane may change your mind. Their secular and religious creations come in every size and shape and make a nice addition to nearly any wall. The store doubles as a workshop where craftsmen can often be observed. They also run glassblowing apprentice workshops during the summer.

ANTICA DROGHERIA MANGANELLI

Via di Città 71-73; tel. 05/7728-0002; daily 7:30am-7:30pm

Antica Drogheria Manganelli is what a supermarket looked like a hundred years ago. This one opened in 1879 and carries everything you need to faithfully recreate a Tuscan dinner when you get back home. The pasta is handmade by small producers in the area and some of the vinegar sold is over 80 years old.

Accommodations

★ ANTICA RESIDENZA CICOGNA

Via delle Terme 76; tel. 05/7728-5613; www.anticaresidenzacicogna.it; €85-100 s/d

The Cicogna family restored a medieval *palazzo* and turned it into an ideally located B&B minutes from Piazza del Campo and Duomo. Each of the five rooms at Antica Residenza Cicogna is decorated in a unique style and benefits from high frescoed ceilings. Breakfast is an opportunity to taste local biscuits and breads like *cavallucci, copate,* and *panforte.* Fresh fruit and yogurt are also served.

HOTEL ALMA DOMUS

Via Camporegio 37; tel. 05/774-4177; www.hotelalmadomus.it; €90-130 d

Hotel Alma Domus is located inside a former sanctuary and management clearly understands the relation between cleanliness and godliness. The modern rooms, however, have little to do with the past and are all equipped with comforts like air-conditioning and LED TVs. Many have balconies with great views of the city.

★ PALAZZO RAVIZZA

Pian dei Mantellini 34; tel. 05/7728-0462; www.palazzoravizza.it; €120-180 s/d

Palazzo Ravizza is a vintage 30-room *palazzo* that hasn't lost its Renaissance charm. The hotel dates from the 1920s and has been run by the same family in a peaceful *contrade* within walking distance of everything. Modern comforts have been added without sacrificing the building's character and the shaded garden provides a welcome summertime refuge. Parking is available and the international breakfast is a great way to start the day.

Information and Services

SIENA INFO POINT

Piazza del Campo 72; tel. 331/742-2646; www. sienainfopoint.com; daily 9:30am-7:30pm

The Siena Info Point is a good place to start a visit. Pick up a free map or sign up for their one-hour group tours (€15) led by authorized guides. It's an informative introduction to the city that leaves daily from their office at 11am with additional departures at 1pm and 6pm during the summer. If you prefer something private or gastronomic they offer dozens of interesting themed tours.

SIENA TOURIST OFFICE

Piazza del Duomo 1; tel. 05/7728-0551; www. terresiena.it; summer Mon.-Fri. 10am-7:30pm and Sat.-Sun. 10:30am-6:30pm, winter Mon.-Fri. 8:30am-1pm and 3pm-7pm

There's an official Siena Tourist Office facing the entrance to the Duomo. They offer free maps, basic information, and bathrooms (€0.50).

Getting There

FROM ROME

Trenitalia (www.trenitalia.it) offers dozens of daily train departures from Rome Termini to Siena between 6:03am and 8:05pm. Prices range €18-45 for a second-class seat, and the journey takes 3-4.5 hours, depending on the service you choose. All trains require a transfer at Grosseto or Chiusi. **Baltour** (www.baltour. it; tel. 0861/199-1900) operates 10 daily buses to Siena from Rome Tibutina station. The trip takes 2 hours 45 minutes and costs €15-32.

There are several ways to reach Siena from Rome by car. The fastest is the **A1** highway, and the 140 miles (230 kilometers) can be covered in 2.5 hours. The **A12** coastal highway is slightly more scenic but adds an additional hour to the journey. Tolls cost less on this route and drivers will need to exit onto the E78 near the town of Grosseto to reach Siena. The slowest and most picturesque alternative is the toll-free **SR2**, a one-lane state road that's backed up at times but passes through many beautiful small towns and villages in the Lazio and Tuscany regions.

FROM FLORENCE

Trenitalia (www.trenitalia.it) offers departures from Santa Maria Novella Station in Florence to Siena. The journey takes 90 minutes and tickets cost €9.50. **SITA** (Piazza Gramsci; tel. 05/7720-4246; www.trainspa. it) buses also leave from the train station and make a dozen stops along the way. A one-way ticket to Siena costs €8.80 and may be purchased at the SITA office in the *piazza* outside the station.

The 50-mile-long (78-kilometer-long) **Firenze-Siena highway** links Florence to Siena and takes one hour to drive. When arriving from the **A1** highway exit at Chiusi for a scenic drive along the N146 or take the following exit at Valdichiana to reach Siena faster.

Getting Around

The historic center of Siena has been pedestrian-friendly since the 1960s and there's no better way of exploring the narrow streets and alleys than on foot. Public buses run through the modern parts of town and there is extra-urban service to many of the surrounding communities that leaves from Piazza Gramsci.

Siena also runs a **SiPedala** (Via Federigo Tozzi 3; tel. 05/7722-8711; Mon.-Fri. 9am-1pm and 2pm-5pm) bike-sharing service with 18 pick-up points around the city including one outside the train station on Viale Vittorio Emanuele II. The accompanying **Bicincittà** app can be downloaded from Android or iPhone stores. It costs €10 for a 5-hour rental or €15 for a 10 hour rental.

Florence

Firenze, as locals call their city, has a justified
marble chip on its shoulder. After all, this was the cradle of the
Renaissance, where civilization was given a burst of creativity after
centuries of artistic stagnation.

Visiting Florence means exploring the neighborhoods that
Michelangelo, Leonardo da Vinci, Galileo Galilei, Dante Alighieri,
and many of history's most influential artists and thinkers called home.
Very little has changed. The Ponte Vecchio still spans the Arno River,
wine is still served in abundance, and the Uffizi remains the place to
go for art. On the other side of town, Michelangelo's *David* stands up
to all expectations, and Brunelleschi's brilliant dome looms majestically above the city.

Highlights

Look for ★ to find recommended sights, activities, dining, and lodging.

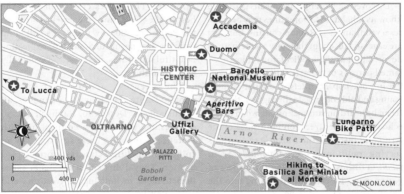

★ **Duomo:** This monumental icon of the Renaissance defied all the architectural odds and was nearly never built. Climb inside the dome to see how its unique structure defies gravity (page 175).

★ **Bargello National Museum:** One of the least crowded museums in Florence offers a look at Donatello's *David*, ancient military hardware, and the city's first police headquarters (page 182).

★ **Uffizi Gallery:** What started out as the private collection of the Medici family is now accessible to all. Discover how Florentine artists added a realistic dimension to art and transformed painting forever (page 185).

★ **Accademia:** It takes a special kind of genius to make marble come to life. Michelangelo's statue of *David* lives up to its global reputation and is even more impressive in person (page 186).

★ **Aperitivo Bars:** Never skip *aperitivo* time (happy hour). Order a local Negroni cocktail with light snacks and enjoy a relaxed transition from afternoon to evening (page 221).

★ **Hiking to Basilica San Miniato al Monte:** This church marks the highest point in Florence and provides dramatic views of the skyline. Take the quiet back route up the hillside to avoid the crowds (page 238).

★ **Lungarno Bike Path:** Get out of the city and head west on a bucolic bike path that runs next to the Arno River (page 239).

★ **Lucca:** Florence is just the beginning of Tuscany. Discover more of the region, starting with a day trip to this charming walled city less than an hour away (page 262).

Museums and basilicas aren't the only attractions. Florence seduces with its clean, well-ordered streets and pleasant yellow facades. Beauty is everywhere in this city. Old towers and lavish palaces as well as large portions of the medieval walls are still standing. There are secluded monasteries and tiny chapels to explore, where a little curiosity leads to unexpected discoveries. The city hasn't lost its creative touch either (although the Renaissance is a hard act to follow). Artisans pound away on the backstreets of the Oltrarno neighborhood, and the leather wallets sold along Via de' Tornabuoni make useful souvenirs.

Discovering Florence also means getting to know its inhabitants. Florentines may be more reserved than their Roman cousins, but they are eager to talk about their city and remain as devoted to it as the Medici family, Florence's famed patrons of the arts. Their pride is visible in workshops, markets, and squares where young and old congregate throughout the day. It can be heard on summer nights when music echoes down the streets on both sides of the Arno and tasted at the *trattorie* restaurants serving traditional *pappa al pomodoro* and *ribollita* dishes. Experiencing this aspect of Florence is a lot easier than getting into the Uffizi—and equally satisfying.

HISTORY

Florence's history is a long one and involves the usual suspects. There were Iron Age tribes who first occupied the area, Etruscans who founded a permanent settlement along the Arno River, and the unstoppable Romans who absorbed the town into their ever-expanding territory. Geography, as usual, played an essential role in Florence's growth. It was a natural funnel for travelers coming down from nearby mountains and headed north. The sea was also close, and the Mediterranean opened up markets for medieval wool merchants and other trades that brought wealth to the town. With wealth came leisure, and with leisure came art. The town's craftsmen were the best in the world, and fine jewelers still line the Ponte Vecchio. It was only a small jump from creating beautiful ornaments to creating beautiful sculptures, frescoes, and eventually entire buildings.

The greatest geniuses of Italy—Giotto, Dante, Machiavelli, Brunelleschi, Michelangelo, Donatello, Raphael, and so on—resided in or had a connection with Florence. Minds like these supported by an enlightened political class transformed civilization. They didn't call it the Renaissance then; to them, revitalizing the Western world was simply business as usual.

Orientation and Planning

ORIENTATION

Florence's **Historic Center,** or *centro storico,* is relatively small. Located north of the Arno River, it is split into four neighborhoods (Duomo, Santa Maria Novella, San Lorenzo, and Santa Croce). This is where the Romans originally founded the city, influential families like the Medici built imposing *palazzi,* and many Florentines still live and work today. The Duomo, visible from nearly every angle of the city, makes getting lost difficult. The Arno also facilitates navigation and creates a distinct divide.

The Historic Center of Florence is compact and flat, making walking or cycling the best way to get around. The only time you may want to consider hopping on a bus or hailing a taxi is on the climb to San Miniato al Monte or Fiesole, which is on the hillside overlooking the city. The Firenzecard+ (€7) is a

Previous: locks of love by the Arno River; the Duomo; path to Basilica San Miniato al Monte during fall

transportation card that provides single access to the city's bus and tram lines for 72 hours once activated. It also offers 10-15 percent discounts to selected restaurants, shops, and tourist services. Accompanied minors travel free of charge on Florence's public transportation network.

Tip: If arriving by rail, don't bother hunting for a **tourist information office** inside Santa Maria Novella station. It's across the street in Piazza Stazione 4 and helpful for finding last-minute accommodation or a map. A second tourist office is located on Via Cavour 1.

Duomo and Around

Most of Florence's major sights, including the **Uffizi** and **Palazzo Vecchio,** are located around the Duomo. There is a constant flow of visitors in this neighborhood at the heart of the Historic Center, which is lined with tall buildings with impressive stone facades. **Piazza della Repubblica,** with its cafés and merry-go-round, is the geographical center and the largest open space where the Roman Forum and later the Jewish Ghetto once stood. Much of the Duomo area is pedestrian-only, making it easy to browse the elegant shops and market stalls where leather belts, wallets, and bags are displayed and tourists rub the nose of a bronze boar for good luck. Many of the city's most expensive hotels are located here, and summer concerts are regularly scheduled in **Piazza della Signoria.**

Santa Maria Novella

Santa Maria Novella lies on the western side of the Historic Center and is the first neighborhood most visitors enter. The main train station, bus depot, and tram terminal are located here and it's busy throughout the day. The main attraction is the **Basilica di Santa Maria Novella** with its secluded monastery and smaller churches like **Chiesa di Ognissanti,** where Botticelli is buried and you can get a glimpse of a stunning *Last Supper* fresco. Buildings are less grand than those near the Duomo to the east, shops cater

to locals, and simple *trattorie* are likely to be filled with residents rather than tourists. Being near the train station means there are many hotels, hostels, and *pensione,* although these tend to fall into the lower price categories and offer few amenities other than a comfortable bed and a convenient location. Farther west along the banks of the Arno lies **Parco delle Cascine,** the city's largest park.

San Lorenzo and San Marco

San Lorenzo is south of San Marco and centered around the church of the same name that's surrounded by vibrant food and leather markets. **Mercato Centrale,** the city's largest covered market, is full of vegetable stands, gourmet shops, and historic eateries where tripe sandwiches and other local delicacies are prepared daily. The streets outside are lined with hundreds of leather kiosks. There are plenty of restaurants in the area, and the second floor of the market is a popular food court. It's not all chaos and commerce in San Marco or San Lorenzo: The farther north you walk, the more residential and quieter it gets.

San Marco forms a triangle north of the Duomo that was once delimitated on two sides by the old city walls and is now bordered by wide avenues built at the end of the 19th century when the city outgrew its medieval limits. This is where Florence's most famous family, the **Medici,** lived, prayed, and are buried. It's also where the statue of *David* was moved when the town's leaders decided it was too valuable to leave outside, and the streets around **Galleria dell'Accademia** are often jammed with visitors waiting to view Michelangelo's colossal masterpiece.

Santa Croce

Santa Croce is one of the liveliest and best-preserved sections of the city. It forms the eastern end of the Historic Center and is full of maze-like medieval alleys, bars attracting foreign drinkers, cheap eateries, and long pedestrian streets like **Borgo la Croce** where locals take their evening stroll. Life goes on here with little concern for the

Florence

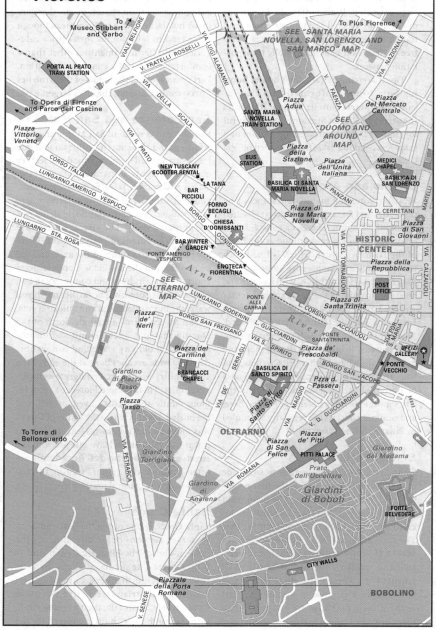

To Museo Stibbert and Garbo

VIALE BELFIORE

V. FRATELLI ROSSELLI

VIA LUIGI ALAMANNI

To Plus Florence

SEE "SANTA MARIA NOVELLA, SAN LORENZO, AND SAN MARCO" MAP

PORTA AL PRATO TRAIN STATION

VIA NAZIONALE

VIA DELLA SCALA

To Opera di Firenze and Parco delle Cascine

Piazza Vittorio Veneto

VIA IL PRATO

CORSO ITALIA

LUNGARNO AMERIGO VESPUCCI

LUNGARNO STA. ROSA

NEW TUSCANY SCOOTER RENTAL

LA TANA

BAR PICCIOLI

BORGO

FORNO BECAGLI

CHIESA D'OGNISSANTI

BAR WINTER GARDEN

PONTE AMERIGO VESPUCCI

ENOTECA FIORENTINA

Arno

OGNISSANTI

Piazza Adua

SANTA MARIA NOVELLA TRAIN STATION

V. FAENZA

Piazza del Mercato Centrale

SEE "DUOMO AND AROUND" MAP

Piazza della Stazione

BUS STATION

BASILICA DI SANTA MARIA NOVELLA

Piazza dell'Unità Italiana

V. PANZANI

MEDICI CHAPEL

BASILICA DI SAN LORENZO

MARTELLI

Piazza di Santa Maria Novella

VIA DEI TORNABUONI

Piazza di San Giovanni

HISTORIC CENTER

VIA CALZAIUOLI

Piazza della Repubblica

POST OFFICE

ACCIAIUOLI

River

L. CORSINI

PONTE ALLE CARRAIA

Piazza di Santa Trinità

PONTE SANTA TRINITA

VIA POR S. MARIA

UFFIZI GALLERY

SEE "OLTRARNO" MAP

Piazza de' Nerli

BORGO SAN FREDIANO

LUNGARNO SODERINI

L. GUICCIARDINI

VIA S. SPIRITO

Piazza de' Frescobaldi

BORGO SAN JACOPO

PONTE VECCHIO

Piazza del Carmine

BRANCACCI CHAPEL

SERRAGLI

VIA DE'

BASILICA DI SANTO SPIRITO

Piazza di Santo Spirito

Pza d. Passera

V. D. GUICCIARDINI

Piazza Tasso

To Torre di Bellosguardo

VIA PETRARCA

Giardino di Piazza Tasso

Giardino Torrigiani

OLTRARNO

VIA MAGGIO

Piazza di San Felice

Piazza de' Pitti

PITTI PALACE

Giardino del Madama

Giardino di Annalena

VIA ROMANA

Prato dell'Uccellare

Giardini di Boboli

FORTE BELVEDERE

CITY WALLS

Piazzale della Porta Romana

V. SENESE

BOBOLINO

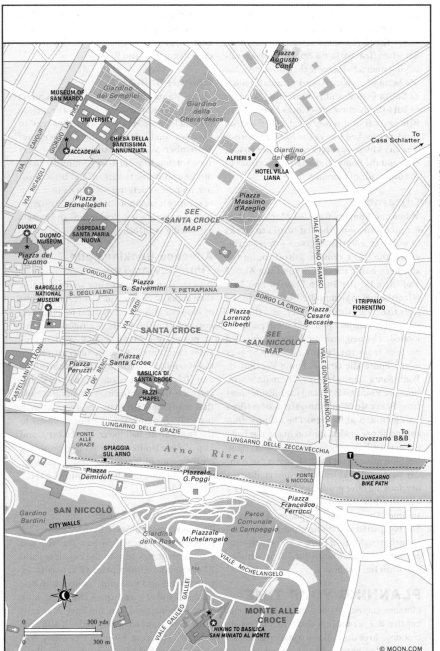

Piazza Augusto Conti

MUSEUM OF SAN MARCO

Giardino dei Semplici

Giardino della Gherardesca

UNIVERSITY

GIORGIO LA PIRA

ACCADEMIA

CHIESA DELLA SANTISSIMA ANNUNZIATA

ALFIERI 9

Giardino del Borgo

To Casa Schlatter

HOTEL VILLA LIANA

VIA CAVOUR

VIA RICASOLI

Piazza Brunelleschi

Piazza Massimo d'Azeglio

SEE "SANTA CROCE" MAP

DUOMO

DUOMO MUSEUM

Piazza del Duomo

OSPEDALE SANTA MARIA NUOVA

V. D. L'ORIUOLO

Piazza G. Salvemini

V. PIETRAPIANA

BORGO LA CROCE

Piazza Cesare Beccaria

I TRIPPAIO FIORENTINO

VIALE ANTONIO GRAMSCI

BARGELLO NATIONAL MUSEUM

B. DEGLI ALBIZI

VIA VERDI

SANTA CROCE

Piazza Lorenzo Ghiberti

SEE "SAN NICCOLÒ" MAP

CASTELLANI/VIA LEONI

Piazza Peruzzi

Piazza Santa Croce

VIA DE' BENCI

BASILICA DI SANTA CROCE

PAZZI CHAPEL

VIALE GIOVANNI AMENDOLA

LUNGARNO DELLE GRAZIE

LUNGARNO DELLE ZECCA VECCHIA

To Rovezzano B&B

PONTE ALLE GRAZIE

SPIAGGIA SUL ARNO

Arno River

LUNGARNO BIKE PATH

Piazza Demidoff

Piazzale G.Poggi

PONTE S NICCOLO

Gardino Bardini

SAN NICCOLÒ

CITY WALLS

Giardino delle Rose

Piazzale Michelangelo

Parco Comunale di Campeggio

Piazza Francesco Ferrucci

VIALE MICHELANGELO

VIALE GALILEO GALILEI

MONTE ALLE CROCE

HIKING TO BASILICA SAN MINIATO AL MONTE

0   300 yds
0   300 m

© MOON.COM

monuments only minutes away, and university students gather in the small squares or inside the city's second-largest covered market where **Trattoria da Rocco** has been satisfying stomachs for more than three decades. Michelangelo is buried nearby inside **Basilica di Santa Croce**, and you can visit the house he left to his nephew a few blocks away at **Casa Buonarroti** or discover what a Renaissance residence looked like at the **Museo Horne**. The city's historic soccer stadium lies farther east, and the Ponte alle Grazie bridge leads to the other side of Florence.

Oltrarno

When the Romans founded Florence, they set up camp along the flat northern banks of the river, and that decision forever influenced the city's growth. Oltrarno, on the southern bank, means "beyond the Arno," and includes the **Santo Spirito** and **San Niccolò** neighborhoods. Both developed later than the Historic Center, and thus are noticeably quieter areas that often get overlooked. The neighborhoods can be reached on foot from the Historic Center by way of the Ponte alle Grazie, Ponte Vecchio, or Ponte Santa Trinita bridges. The main attractions are **Palazzo Pitti** and the hillside views from **Piazzale Michelangelo** and **Basilica San Miniato al Monte.** The **village-like atmosphere** is ideal for seeking refuge from the masses, browsing for antiques, and enjoying Florentine street food. Here you can wander past medieval walls, up deserted paths overlooking olive groves, and through ornate gardens that remain pleasantly cool in the summer. Down below, in squares like **Piazza Santo Spirito** and the neighborhood's principle thoroughfare of **Borgo San Frediano,** are bars and restaurants that fill up with locals until the late hours.

PLANNING YOUR TIME

Florence may be 10 times smaller than Rome, but that doesn't mean it deserves any less attention. Three days allows you to visit all the memorable sights and have enough time to climb the hills overlooking the city, explore landscaped gardens, observe half-a-dozen *Last Suppers*, ride a bus out to Fiesole, and cycle along the Arno River.

Daily Reminders

Many sights (monasteries in particular) are only open mornings, while others close for lunch or on Mondays. Museums tend to have seasonal hours, closing a little earlier November-March. Check opening hours ahead of time to avoid disappointment. Ticket offices stop selling tickets an hour before closing, and metal detectors or some other form of security is common at entrances. Traveling light is advisable, but cloakrooms and lockers are usually available.

Advance Bookings and Time-Saving Tips

It's easy to spend more time waiting in line than actually visiting the iconic monuments of Florence. It's therefore vital to make reservations for the sights you intend to visit, or purchase a **Firenzecard**, which provides swift entry. Advance reservations for many sights, including the **Accademia** and **Uffizi,** can be made on the city's official website www.firenzeturismo.it. (Note that many sights require reservations during COVID outbreaks.) Visitor numbers to the **campanile** bell tower, **baptistery,** and **cupola** are limited to avoid overcrowding on the panoramic terraces, and access is by designated time slots booked online or at the ticket office.

Sightseeing Passes

The **Firenzecard** (www.firenzecard.it; €85) is the most comprehensive pass available and a convenient way to visit the city. It is valid 72 hours and allows priority access to 72 monuments and museums, major churches, gardens, towers, and the Uffizi. Just look for the Firenzecard sign and have your card ready to be scanned at each sight. It also provides Wi-Fi access. Even on a two-day visit it can be worth the investment, especially in summer when tourism is at its peak and lines are long. Children under 18 enter all sights for free when accompanied by parents who have the card.

Piazza del Duomo contains five of the city's most popular sights: the Cattedrale di Santa Maria del Fiore, Cupola di Brunelleschi, Campanile di Giotto, Battistero, and Museo dell'Opera, none of which are covered by the Firenzecard. All of the attractions are accessed with single tickets that can be re-serverved online well in advance. For the cupola, campanile, and baptistery you'll need to choose a day and time when you intend to visit. There is a **ticket office** (Piazza Duomo 14r; tel. 055/230-2885; www.museumflorence.com; daily 8:15am-6:30pm) near the bell tower, but if you wait to purchase your tickets there's a good chance all the time slots will be taken.

A **combined ticket** (www.uffizi.it/en/tickets; €38) is available for the Uffizi, Palazzo Pitti, and Boboli Gardens. It's valid three days and can be purchased online or directly at the Uffizi ticket office.

Pandemic Travel

During COVID outbreaks, locals and travelers in Florence are required to wear **masks** indoors and outdoors, large hotels may close, and restaurants provide digital menus available via QR code. Temperatures are checked at all museums, and personal information including name, address, email, and cell phone number is gathered at sit-down restaurants and hotels in order to facilitate contact tracing.

All major sights require reservations, including the **cupola, campanile, Battistero, Museo dell'Opera, Accademia, Uffizi, Palazzo Vecchio,** and **Palazzo Medici Riccardi.** Access each sight's website to select your slot and arrive on time or risk being refused entry. Bookings should be made a week or two in advance. **Sightseeing passes** and combined tickets remain valid during COVID outbreaks.

The **Italian Civil Protection Agency** (www.protezionecivile.gov.it) provides information in English on the latest pandemic alerts and regulations.

Itinerary Ideas

FLORENCE ON DAY 1

Spend your first day exploring Florence's Historic Center. Visit www.firenzeturismo.it to make reservations for the **Accademia** and **Uffizi** before arriving to the city.

1 Fortify with a coffee and breakfast pastry at **Ditta Artigianale,** located near the Uffizi.

2 Head to the **Accademia** before the crowds arrive to admire Michelangelo's larger-than-life *David.*

3 From the Accademia, it's a short stroll to the **Duomo.** Visit the inside of the church for free.

4 If you don't feel like trekking to the top of the cathedral, get an equally good view of the city a few blocks south at **Palazzo Vecchio,** where things are generally quieter. The inside of the city's most illustrious civic building also provides a vivid idea of how the Renaissance elite once lived.

5 Visit the **Mercato Centrale,** Florence's biggest and most animated neighborhood market where Florentines go for fresh produce and gossip. Order a tripe sandwich from Narbone or head upstairs to the second-floor food court.

Itinerary Ideas

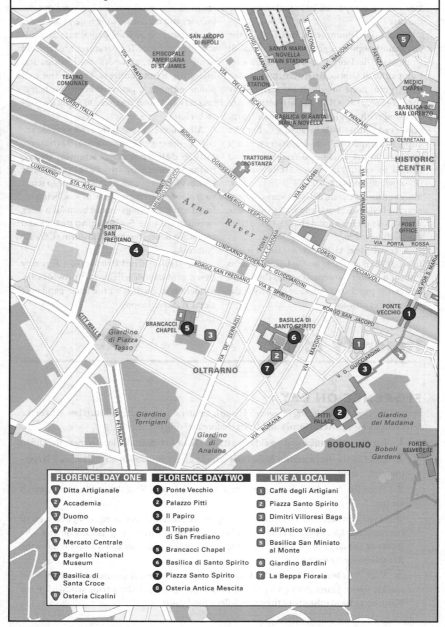

FLORENCE DAY ONE
1. Ditta Artigianale
2. Accademia
3. Duomo
4. Palazzo Vecchio
5. Mercato Centrale
6. Bargello National Museum
7. Basilica di Santa Croce
8. Osteria Cicalini

FLORENCE DAY TWO
1. Ponte Vecchio
2. Palazzo Pitti
3. Il Papiro
4. Il Trippaio di San Frediano
5. Brancacci Chapel
6. Basilica di Santo Spirito
7. Piazza Santo Spirito
8. Osteria Antica Mescita

LIKE A LOCAL
1. Caffè degli Artigiani
2. Piazza Santo Spirito
3. Dimitri Villoresi Bags
4. All'Antico Vinaio
5. Basilica San Miniato al Monte
6. Giardino Bardini
7. La Beppa Fioraia

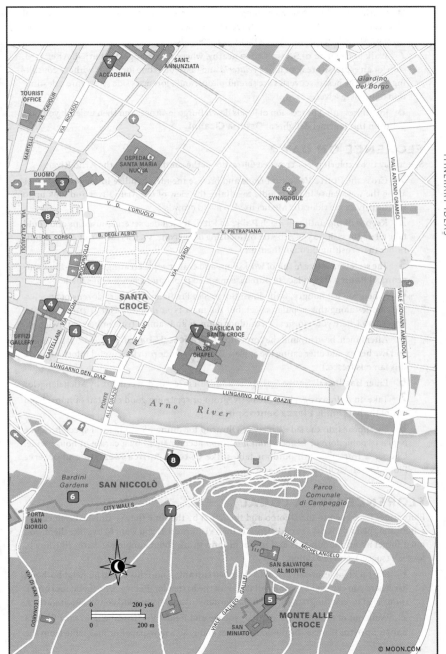

6 Getting into the Uffizi can be tough, even with reservations. The **Bargello National Museum** is a tranquil alternative. There are far fewer visitors, and you can admire sculptures by Michelangelo and Donatello in near solitude.

7 Walk to **Basilica di Santa Croce** nearby, where Michelangelo is buried. Afterward, stop for an espresso break or find a *gelateria* and take your cone for a tour without consulting a map. The best discoveries are serendipitous, and Florence's side streets are a destination unto themselves.

8 Join the evening procession of locals down Borgo la Croce, and then unleash your appetite on the gourmet delights at **Osteria Cicalini.**

FLORENCE ON DAY 2

Spend day two exploring less-crowded Oltrarno on the southern side of the Arno River.

1 Cross the **Ponte Vecchio** bridge and browse the merchandise in the jewelry shops along the way. Pause in the middle to admire the view of the Arno River and look up to see the private corridor the Medici used to avoid crowds.

2 Keep walking until you reach **Palazzo Pitti.** It includes several museums and could take all day to visit, so you're better off focusing on just one, such as the Royal Apartments, rather than rushing through them all.

3 The streets nearby are full of workshops and craftspeople creating one-of-a-kind souvenirs. **Il Papiro** is the place to purchase marbled paper and learn how it's made.

4 When you get hungry, walk down Borgo San Frediano. There are dozens of appetizing eateries along this popular street, but the most typical option is **Il Trippaio di San Frediano** where you can sit at an outdoor counter and sample tripe or beef sandwiches.

5 After lunch, head around the corner to the **Brancacci Chapel,** where you'll see Adam and Eve before and after eating the apple. (The audio guide provides useful information on this famous fresco.)

6 Enter **Basilica di Santo Spirito** to admire a rare wooden crucifix by Michelangelo.

7 Take an *al fresco aperitivo* break (Negroni or spritz are good cocktail options) from any of the bars lining **Piazza Santo Spirito.**

8 Disappear into the side streets of Oltrarno for dinner. Sample local specialties like *pappa al pomodoro* or *bistecca alla fiorentina* accompanied by a carafe of house wine. Choose a *trattoria* with outdoor tables like **Osteria Antica Mescita** and observe Florentine street life while you eat.

FLORENCE LIKE A LOCAL

Florentines have been to the Duomo and the Uffizi by the time they've finished elementary school and spend their days very differently than visitors do. If you want to live like them, you must forget about monuments and museums and think about simple pleasures like lunch, football (soccer), and relaxation.

1 Start with an espresso at **Caffè degli Artigiani,** a no-frills Oltrarno neighborhood bar where you can make some small talk with the bartender. *Buon giorno* (good morning), *tutto bene?* (everything okay?), and *bella giornata* (nice day) are good conversation starters.

2 Walk out of the small (triangular) square and follow Via Toscanella toward **Piazza Santo Spirito.** Browse the outdoor market and grab a newspaper or magazine from the newsstand on the corner. Sit down on a bench to read or watch the ongoing drama in the square.

3 Around the corner, shop for leather at **Dimitri Villoresi Bags.** This neighborhood boutique is perfect for watching designers in action and discovering unique styles.

4 When you're hungry, cross the Arno and head to **All'Antico Vinaio** (arrive before noon; otherwise you'll get stuck in a long line of tourists). Order one of their famous €5 *schiacciata* sandwiches and enjoy it wherever you like.

5 After lunch, cross back over the river and take the quiet scenic path up to **Basilica San Miniato al Monte** for a panoramic view of the city and to honor Pinocchio's creator.

6 Visit the *loggia* in the **Giardino Bardini** for an afternoon coffee, or get *aperitivo* hour started with a Negroni or spritz from the bar.

7 Have dinner *al fresco* at **La Beppa Fioraia.**

Sights

Generally speaking, Florence's three most popular sights (**Galleria dell'Accademia, Duomo,** and **Uffizi**) are nearly always inundated with visitors. To avoid long lines, make advance reservations, or consider a Firenzecard. There's a lot more to Florence, however, and many other wonderful museums, monuments, and gardens are surprisingly empty. Try to seek these out if you have the time and energy.

Museum staff all have passed rigorous state exams and are passionate and knowledgeable about where they work. Don't hesitate to ask questions, even if you don't speak Italian. You can also learn a lot from the audio and app guides available at many sights. These are inexpensive, easy to use, and informative, especially if you didn't attend (or don't remember) catechism and are unversed in the Old and New Testaments.

DUOMO AND AROUND

Piazza del Duomo is the religious heart of Florence and home to the Cattedrale di Santa Maria del Fiore, Cupola di Brunelleschi, Campanile di Giotto, Battistero, and Museo dell'Opera. Visiting requires patience and stamina. Those determined to do it all may want to start with the **Baptistery,** which opens the earliest and is the oldest of the bunch. You can then continue to the top of the dome before going inside the **Cattedrale** (also called the **Duomo**). The bell tower is open the latest. You can end a visit there or at the **Museo dell'Opera,** which was completely renovated in 2015 and is vital for understanding how Brunelleschi constructed the cupola. It also contains many works of art that have been removed from the other buildings for safekeeping such as the baptistery doors by Lorenzo Ghiberti. The **cupola** and **campanile** involve climbing hundreds of steps. If that sounds daunting, you may want to choose one or the other, as the views from the top are fairly similar.

The Firenzecard does not include the Duomo and related sights. Tickets to each of the sights in Piazza del Duomo are best purchased in advance online (www.duomo.firenze.it). (The Duomo itself is free.) Advance reservations are required for the cupola and baptistery.

★ Duomo
(Santa Maria del Fiore)

Piazza del Duomo; Mon.-Sat. 10am-5pm, Sun. 1:30pm-4:45pm; free
Florence was undergoing significant change

Duomo and Around

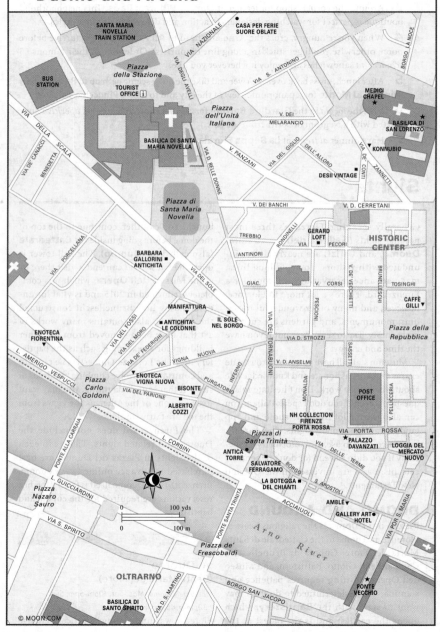

SANTA MARIA
NOVELLA
TRAIN STATION

CASA PER FERIE
SUORE OBLATE

VIA NAZIONALE

BUS
STATION

VIA DEGLI AVELLI

Piazza
della Stazione

TOURIST
OFFICE ℹ

VIA S. ANTONINO

BORGO LA NOCE

MEDICI
CHAPEL ★

Piazza
dell'Unità
Italiana

V. DEI
MELARANCIO

BASILICA DI
SAN LORENZO ★

BASILICA DI SANTA
MARIA NOVELLA

VIA D. BELLE DONNE

V. PANZANI

VIA DEL GIGLIO

DELL'ALLORO

VIA DE' CONTI

ZANNETTI

KONNUBIO

DESII VINTAGE

VIA DELLA SCALA

VIA DE CANACCI

BENEDETTA

Piazza di
Santa Maria
Novella

V. DEI BANCHI

V. D. CERRETANI

VIA PORCELLANA

BARBARA
GALLORINI
ANTICHITA

VIA DEL SOLE

TREBBIO

RONDINELLI

GERARD
LOFT

VIA
PECORI

HISTORIC
CENTER

ANTINORI

V. DE' VECCHIETTI

BRUNELLESCHI

TOSINGHI

GIAC.

V. CORSI

PESCIONI

CAFFÈ
GILLI

MANIFATTURA

ANTICHITA'
LE COLONNE

IL SOLE
NEL BORGO

VIA DEL FOSSI

VIA DEL MORO

VIA DE' FEDERIGHI

VIA DEL TORNABUONI

VIA D. STROZZI

Piazza della
Repubblica

ENOTECA
FIORENTINA

VIA VIGNA NUOVA

V. D. ANSELMI

SASSETTI

L. AMERIGO VESPUCCI

Piazza
Carlo
Goldoni

ENOTECA
VIGNA NUOVA

VIA DEL PARIONE

VIA

PURGATORIO

INFERNO

MONALDA

V. PELLICCERIA

BISONTE

ALBERTO
COZZI

POST
OFFICE

PONTE ALLA CARRAIA

L. CORSINI

Piazza di
Santa Trinita

NH COLLECTION
FIRENZE
PORTA ROSSA

VIA PORTA ROSSA

★ PALAZZO
DAVANZATI

LOGGIA DEL
MERCATO
NUOVO

ANTICA
TORRE

SALVATORE
FERRAGAMO

BORGO

VIA DELLE TERME

LA BOTEGA
DEL CHIANTI

S. APOSTOLI

Piazza
Nazaro
Sauro

L. GUICCIARDINI

VIA S. SPIRITO

PONTE SANTA TRINITA

ACCIAIUOLI

AMBLÈ

GALLERY ART
HOTEL

VIA POR S. MARIA

0   100 yds

0   100 m

Arno   River

Piazza de'
Frescobaldi

OLTRARNO

VIA D. S. MARTINO

BORGO SAN JACOPO

PONTE
VECCHIO ★

BASILICA DI
SANTO SPIRITO

© MOON.COM

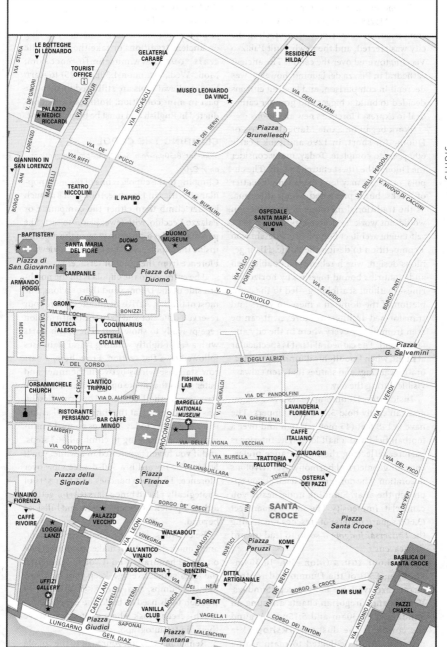

at the end of the 13th century. The churches of Santa Maria Novella and Santa Croce were completed, an outer ring wall protecting the city was erected, and the newly built Palazzo Vecchio towered over the center. The ancient cathedral in Piazza del Duomo, however, was decrepit in comparison, and leading citizens decided to build a bigger and grander cathedral to express Florence's new ambitions.

Work began on Santa Maria del Fiore, or Duomo for short, in 1296 and took nearly 600 years to complete. Today, many consider the Duomo the finest church in Italy. The cupola, or dome, may look like a simple matter of bricks, but it presented a huge dilemma, as the traditional methods of construction would not work for a dome its size. In 1417, self-taught architect Filippo Brunelleschi won a competition to design the dome. His ingenious design, which relied on a double shell and eight ribs bound together by horizontal rings—without scaffolding—led to the completion of the dome in a mere 16 years and transformed architecture forever. It can be seen from nearly everywhere in the city and far beyond. The cathedral itself is spectacular at night, when floodlights illuminate the decorative carvings and statues that aren't always visible during the day.

Inside, the Duomo appears even bigger and can easily hold 3,000 worshippers. The nave is 148 feet (45 meters) high and over a football field and a half long. The interior is austere, reflecting the Renaissance preference for geometrical harmony over frivolous decoration. The dome reveals itself as you approach the altar. Standing underneath, you can feel its immensity. The 38,750 square feet (3,600 square meters) of frescoes illustrating the *Universal Judgment* seem to lead toward the heavens.

One-hour **tours** (Mon.-Sat. 10:30am-11:30pm; €30) of the Duomo and rooftop terrace are available daily except Sundays. Vespers and Gregorian chants are sung on Sundays at 10:30am and 5:15pm. Around the corner is the dusty **workshop** (Via dello Studio 3) dedicated to maintaining the hundreds of carvings and sculptures inside and outside the church. You can have a glimpse of the modern stonemasons carrying on ancient traditions or take the 90-minute **craft tour** (www.museumflorence.com; Mon., Wed., Fri. noon-1:30pm; €25) to learn how medieval tools are still used to keep the past in mint condition. Both tours are conducted in English and must be booked online.

CLIMBING THE CUPOLA

Mon.-Sat. 8:30am-7pm, Sun. 1pm-4pm, reservations only; €20

Climbing to the cupola is one of the most popular activities in Florence, though it's a much harder climb than either the campanile or Palazzo Vecchio, with fewer places to rest. The payoff includes a close-up view of the mosaics inside the cupola, plus one of the best views of Florence from the outdoor terrace.

The entrance to the cupola is on the northern side of the Duomo and there's a long line most of the day. Arrive 10 minutes before your reserved time slot and have the confirmation receipt ready to show staff. The climb starts with a set of tightly winding spiral staircases followed by a flat section. From here, a narrow staircase winds between the inner and outer shells that make up the dome. This construction method, conceived by Brunelleschi, was revolutionary at the time and still astonishes engineers today. It takes about 12 minutes without stopping to climb all 463 steps, and if you haven't exercised in a while, you'll feel it. The reward is a 360-degree view over Florence. There are benches and four sets of strategically placed binoculars (€1) for getting a close-up view of the city below and hillsides beyond.

Be careful going down: Falls are frequent, and a quick descent can make you dizzy. Hold on to the handrails, and if you're taller than the Renaissance average, keep your head low to avoid bumps. Near the exit is a display of wooden tools used to build the cupola and a touch-screen kiosk where visitors can leave their digital autograph.

Remember to book your visit to the cupola

Campanile

Piazza del Duomo; daily 8:15am-7pm; €15

The campanile is one of the unique features of the Florentine skyline and arguably the most beautiful bell tower in Italy. It's also one of the only towers not directly connected to a church, which was partly due to the independent nature of Florence during the Renaissance. Getting to the top is easier than ascending the cupola, and there's often a line of tourists ready to climb its 414 steps.

The tower measures 279 feet (85 meters) in height and is only 50 feet (15 meters) wide. It's also called Giotto's Tower in reference to the artist who initiated work on it in 1337. He died three years later, and it was up to Andrea Pisano and Francesco Talenti to complete the job. They fitted the tower with its polychrome marble similar to the Duomo and added scores of sculptures illustrating the Old Testament and the *Redemption of Man*. Many pieces have been moved to the Museo dell'Opera to avoid damage by the elements. Completed in 1359, the campanile remains one of the finest examples of Gothic architecture in the city.

Your best chance of finding fewer visitors is arriving when it opens or an hour before closing. This is one of the most accessible climbs in Florence, and there are several intermediary platforms to rest and admire increasingly better views of the Duomo and city. Passageways are less hazardous than the cupola, but visitors going up and down must squeeze by each other, making the journey occasionally tricky. Protective fencing surrounds the upper terrace and there are two sets of binoculars (€1) for a close-up look at the city. The campanile is a working bell tower and rings hourly throughout the day.

Baptistery
(Battistero)

Piazza del Duomo; Mon.-Fri. 8:15am-10:15am and 11:15am-6:30pm, Sat. 8:15am-6:30pm, Sun. 8:15am-10:15am and 11:15am-7:30pm; €5 or €10 with Duomo Museum

The green-and-white marble Battistero was built around the 6th or 7th century. This is where citizens were baptized, and was one of the most revered buildings in Florence. Making it look good was a matter of civic as well as religious pride. The original wooden doors were eventually replaced with bronze doors that have been a major attraction ever since.

Andrea Pisano cast the first of the three sets of doors, which now face south, in 1336, and recount the life of John the Baptist. Lorenzo Ghiberti won the competition to design the next set of doors and spent 21 years working on them. The project would cost millions in today's currency. His doors are located on the north entrance of the baptistery and tell the life of Christ in 28 panels read from left to right starting at the bottom.

The city liked the result so much they commissioned Ghiberti to create a third set. This one took him 27 years to complete and became known as the *Porta del Paradiso,* or **Gates of Paradise,** a dazzling achievement that unofficially marked the beginning of the Renaissance. The *Gates of Paradise* were severely damaged during the great flood of 1966 and underwent restoration that was completed in 2012. During their absence, a replica—a great work in its own right—was created and has remained at the Battistero. The original set is now on display inside the **Museo dell'Opera.** If you're interested in understanding the significance behind each panel of the *Gates of Paradise,* download the app (€3) from the baptistery website.

The baptistery is the oldest of the five monuments and the one to start with if you like doing things chronologically. Inside, there's a lot to look at including the gold mosaic ceiling depicting the *Last Judgment* and hypnotically intricate floor tilings. Both are original and

were created at the dawn of the Renaissance when craftsmen began expanding the possibilities of art and architecture. You'll also find the only pope buried in Florence, John XXIII. Donatello and Michelozzo built the tomb, and the Latin epitaph ruffled a few feathers back in Rome. There are several rows of wooden benches on one side of the octagon-shaped building where mass is regularly performed, and visitors sit to admire the surroundings. Lines vary throughout the day from long to nearly none, and several sections have been recently restored.

Duomo Museum
(Museo dell'Opera)

Via della Canonica 1; tel. 055/230-2885; Mon.-Sat. 9am-7pm, Sun. 9am-1:30pm; €10 with baptistery

The Museo dell'Opera, located directly behind the Duomo, is essential for understanding how the cathedral was built and is an excellent place to start or finish a visit to the area. Throughout construction of the adjacent monuments it was used as a repository and workplace. It's where Brunelleschi confronted the day-to-day challenges of building the cupola, and it contains the large wooden model he used as a basis for construction. It's also where Michelangelo sculpted *David* and has a terrace with a great view of the Duomo.

Once the cathedral was completed, the building was transformed into a museum focused entirely on preservation and the safekeeping of over 750 works of art. It was renovated in 2015 and now covers 64,583 square feet (6,000 square meters) over three floors. Exhibits include many of the original relics and artwork from the baptistery, cathedral, crypt, and bell tower. The original *Gates of Paradise,* the famed doors Ghiberti created for the Battistero, are on display behind an immense glass case.

Once you've cleared security, follow the suggested itinerary projected on the floor or use the museum map. The first stop is an enormous hall housing the baptistery doors along with sculptures by Donatello and Arnolfo di Cambio. Many of these are set in their original positions on a faux cathedral facade built onto one side of the enormous space.

Around the corner stands one of Florence's greatest treasures: Michelangelo sculpted several versions of *La Pieta* over his lifetime, and although this one is not as famous as the work he created in Rome, it is noteworthy for the self-portrait contained in the scene, which was intended for his tombstone. Unfortunately, the marble was of poor quality, which explains why Jesus is missing a leg, and Michelangelo destroyed parts of the unfinished project in anger. The sculpture survived thanks to his devoted assistants and still ranks among Michelangelo's finest.

There are more interesting artifacts on the upper floors and a sunny roof terrace with benches from which to gaze up at the Duomo. It's a good angle to notice that sections of the octagonal drum supporting the dome remained unfinished. There are two explanations, both of which may be true. The first is that the elaborate balcony was too heavy to be completed, and the second that Michelangelo, who was not chosen for the job, ridiculed the work one day by comparing it to a cricket's cage (*gabbia di grillo*), which is what it has been called to this day.

Construction didn't always go well, and the circular **marble plaque** in the street outside marks the spot where the first gold ball crowning the Duomo fell. There's a nice gift shop on the ground floor with a variety of unique gifts, the majority of which are made in Italy, and a café at the museum entrance.

Orsanmichele Church
(Chiesa Orsanmichele)

Via dell'Arte della Lana; tel. 055/238-8606; daily 10am-5pm; €3

Chiesa Orsanmichele is a massive three-story church *palazzo* that looks more like a wealthy merchant's house than a place of worship. It began as a grain warehouse, and the ground

1: campanile **2:** Lorenzo Ghiberti's Baptistery doors **3:** Santa Maria del Fiore

floor was later transformed into a church after sightings of the Virgin Mary. The site was destroyed and rebuilt several times, and in 1336 the city decided to erect a building that would serve both religious and civic functions. The ground floor became a place to worship the Virgin Mary, while the upper floors were set aside for grain storage.

The government encouraged the guilds to decorate the exterior of the building, which occupied a place of special prominence between the Duomo and Palazzo Vecchio. Fourteen niches were created along the north and south sides. Over decades, these were filled with sculptures that led to an artistic evolution that fueled the Renaissance. No two niches are the same, and competition between the guilds meant that the most talented artists in the city were commissioned to contribute.

Donatello created two of the finest statues. The Guild of Armor and Sword Makers hired him to represent San Giorgio, while the linen workers opted for a portrait of San Marco. The resulting sculptures mark a rediscovery of classical forms of beauty. The statues have been replaced with copies that still have a powerful presence, while Donatello's San Giorgio now resides in Museo Bargello.

The church on the ground floor is devoted to the Virgin Mary and dominated by Andrea Orcagna's tabernacle. He spent 10 years perfecting his marble bas-relief of *The Death of the Virgin* and *Assumption*. On the opposite wall is Bernardo Daddi's *Virgin and Child,* in which baby Jesus tenderly touches his mother's cheek while angels look on. The **museum** (Mon. 10am-5pm) is accessed from here. Inside, you can view many of the original sculptures that once stood on the outside.

★ Bargello National Museum
(Museo Nazionale del Bargello)

Via del Proconsolo 4; tel. 055/238-8606; daily 8:15am-6pm; €8 or Firenzecard

While some of Florence's museums and monuments are besieged by tourists, the Bargello is often deserted. This is where you'll find Donatello's *David,* which preceded Michelangelo's version. Although it's overshadowed by the latter, Donatello's statue marks an important moment of the early Renaissance. Donatello accompanied Brunelleschi to Rome and played an essential role in the rediscovery of classical art. His sculpture was the first cast in bronze since the fall of the Rome Empire and inspired generations of artists.

The building itself is a holdover from the Middle Ages and was the first public office in the city. It was the headquarters of the chief of police (known as the *Bargello*) and was used as a prison for centuries. Torture and executions were conducted in the courtyard as punishment for offenses that would be classified as misdemeanors today. The death penalty was abolished, and the gallows destroyed in 1786, making Tuscany one of the first states to ban capital punishment.

The immense rooms overlooking the courtyard are nearly as interesting as the art within the museum. On the ground floor are a number of marble and bronze sculptures and several lesser-known works by Michelangelo. The great hall one flight up contains Donatello's *David* and the bronze door panels Ghiberti and Brunelleschi submitted for the baptistery competition. A little farther on is the chapel with faded frescoes where prisoners were given their last rites. On the upper floor is a fine collection of antique armor and weapons including swords, crossbows, lances, and early firearms.

Piazza della Signoria

Piazza della Signoria's asymmetrical shape has a lot to do with the buildings and towers that were torn down by the Guelphs in the mid-13th century to make sure their enemies never recovered. The resulting square became the administrative center of the city and is home to **Palazzo Vecchio, Loggia Lanzi,** and many fine statues and monuments. It's where Florentines gathered to defend the city, prisoners were executed, and public celebrations are still held today.

In the center of the *piazza* is the round

plaque marking the spot where Savonarola was hanged, then burned at the stake. Nearby, there's a bronze statue of Cosimo I on horseback and a marble Neptune that exalts the seafaring glories of the city. The *piazza* is one of the great urban spaces in Florence. It fills up with visitors during the day and is used to stage concerts during the summer.

Chiasso dei Baroncelli, adjacent to Loggia Lanzi, is closer to an alley than a street and the perfect escape from the crowds in the square. If you walk to the end, turn right, and continue through the intersection along Borgo Santi Apostoli, you'll arrive at **Piazza Santa Trinità** where street musicians perform throughout the day and night.

Palazzo Vecchio

Piazza della Signoria; tel. 055/276-8325; museum Oct.-Mar. Fri.-Wed. 9am-7pm, Thurs. 9am-2pm, Apr.-Sept. Fri.-Wed. 9am-11pm, Thurs. 9am-2pm, tower Oct.-Mar. Fri.-Wed. 10am-5pm, Thurs. 10am-2pm, Apr.-Sept. Fri.-Wed. 9am-9pm, Thurs. 9am-2pm; €12.50 for single sight, €15.50 combined ticket option or Firenzecard

The Duomo may get more attention, but the decision to build the cathedral and countless other matters that shaped the city were made inside Palazzo Vecchio. The *palazzo* served as the political and administrative hub where magistrates lived and nobles, dignitaries, and citizens gathered. The exterior looks impregnable, which is exactly what Arnolfo di Cambio intended when he began construction in 1298. Walls are made of rough-cut stone and rise high above the square. The 308-foot (94-meter) tower is even more impressive.

Palazzo Vecchio can be entered from the gateway next to the statue of David. The ticket office is located off the internal courtyard designed by Michelozzo and decorated with a graceful fountain. Even if you don't intend to visit the *palazzo*, it's worth a peek inside the courtyard and at the Roman remains underground, both of which are free. Take the stairs in the ticket office and follow the walkway overlooking the massive brickwork. The ancient ruins are the best example of Roman architecture in the city and provide a glimpse of what lies below street level.

The lower floors include residential quarters and reception halls that were the home of Cosimo I and other members of the Medici family when they rose to power. The grandest of these is the **Salone dei Cinquecento,** which has a high frescoed ceiling and two walls covered with gigantic paintings illustrating Florence's military successes. Michelangelo and Leonardo da Vinci were originally commissioned to decorate the room, but neither ever completed the task. Had they done so, the *salone* would be one of the unique artistic sights in Italy. Nonetheless it remains impressive, especially when viewed from the balcony on the third floor.

The route to the **tower** starts at the staircase near the front entrance. The number of visitors within the tower is limited, so there may be a short wait after a few flights. On the way up, you'll pass a small prison cell known ironically as the *alberghetto,* or little hotel, where Savonarola and other illustrious prisoners were detained. Farther along, you can circumnavigate two terraces that look down on the streets below. These are where soldiers once kept watch over the city. At the very top, views are obstructed by high ramparts except for a ledge where visitors take turns photographing the Duomo. Lookouts once observed the countryside from here and rang the bells that hung in the wooden structure above if they spotted enemies approaching. A friendly attendant is always present and happy to answer questions. The tower is closed whenever it rains and is off-limits to children under six.

There are evening **tours** (€4) of the tower during the summer and **tablet guides** (€5) to the *palazzo.* During COVID outbreaks, reservations are required and tours may be canceled.

Loggia Lanzi

24/7; free

The triple-arched Loggia Lanzi is the imposing structure next to Palazzo Vecchio on the southern side of Piazza della Signoria. A

loggia is an open-air building that was popular during the Renaissance and functioned as a market or meeting place. This one was completed in 1382 and was used to shelter government officials during ceremonies. When the Republic fell in 1530, artists were allowed to use the covered space as a workshop. Today it's a public gallery with statues from different periods; the only two placed in the *loggia* during the Renaissance were Giambologna's *Rape of the Sabine Woman* and Cellini's *Perseus*. The latter portrays the Greek hero holding Medusa's head and was an attempt to outdo Michelangelo's *David* standing nearby. It may not have succeeded, but the 12-foot (4-meter) bronze statue remains impressive. The number of visitors allowed to enter the *loggia* is limited, but turnaround time is quick, and sculptures are clearly visible from the *piazza*.

★ Uffizi Gallery
(Galleria degli Uffizi)

Piazzale degli Uffizi 6; tel. 055/294-883; www.uffizi. it; Tues.-Sun. 8:15am-6:50pm; €20, €38 combined ticket with Palazzo Pitti and Boboli Gardens or Firenzecard

Galleria degli Uffizi is the mother of all museums. What started out as a pastime for the Medici family ended up as one of the greatest art collections in the world. This grand 16th-century building stretches from Palazzo Vecchio to the Arno River. Inside are many of the world's finest paintings, from 13th-century religious frescoes to Renaissance masterpieces by the likes of Giotto, Beato Angelico, Botticelli, Mantegna, Leonardo, Raphael, Michelangelo, and Caravaggio. It's a match for any museum, and its relatively small dimensions make it possible to visit in a morning or afternoon.

You can pick up a map of the museum and an **audio guide** (€6 single/€10 double) which is essential for understanding the paintings to come, at the information desk. The gallery itself begins on the third floor, where 35

1: Palazzo Vecchio **2:** Donatello's bronze statue of *David* at the Bargello **3:** inside the Uffizi Gallery

rooms are organized around two enormous wings. Tourists huddle in front of the pearls of the collection, such as Botticelli's *Birth of Venus,* on display in room 10. The floor below contains a permanent collection as well as a number of temporary exhibition spaces. Dutch painters are housed in rooms 53 to 55, while works by Caravaggio hang in room 90.

Outside, artists and street vendors fill the long rectangular courtyard, while hundreds of visitors line up underneath the portico entrance. The shorter line is for reserved tickets (which can be picked up at the office on the opposite side) and Firenzecard holders. The longer one is for everyone else. If you take photos inside, turn the flash off. Selfie sticks are prohibited, as are umbrellas, large bags, and food. On the top floor is a **cafeteria** where you can have an espresso or light snack and sit on the spacious terrace with an up-close view of Piazza della Signoria.

The museum **gift shop** carries hundreds of books on art and history, including many titles in English. Several more rooms are filled with posters, gadgets, and clothing, and funnily enough, there's a small post office near the museum exit where travelers can send a postcard (€3) or purchase stamps.

The **Corridoio Vasariano** that connects the Uffizi with Palazzo Pitti is undergoing restoration and is scheduled to reopen in 2022. Cosimo I de Medici used this raised corridor to avoid the chaos of the Ponte Vecchio below. Once restored, the Corridoio Vasariano will allow visitors to follow in Medici footsteps and cross the Arno River in style. Special tickets will be required, and access to the corridor will be from an entrance on the ground floor of the museum.

During COVID outbreaks, reservations are required, and audio guides are not available.

Palazzo Davanzati

Via Porta Rossa 13; tel. 055/064-9460; Mon.-Fri. 8:15am-1:50pm and Sat.-Sun. 1:15pm-6:30pm; €6 or Firenzecard

Palazzo Davanzati provides an idea of how wealthy medieval Florentines lived. The

Davanzati were a family of lace merchants who ran their business on the first floor (where a small gift shop and ticket desk are now located) and lived on the upper floors. The difference between medieval and Renaissance-era *palazzi* is evident from the greater height of the building and its cramped courtyard and wooden staircase, which is humble by Medici standards. They did, however, have an internal well, decent plumbing, and en suite bathrooms that can be seen as you tour the well-preserved living quarters refurbished with period antiques. The third and fourth floors where the second banquet hall, kitchen, and medieval graffiti are located are accessible by tour only at 10am, 11am, and noon for a maximum of 25 visitors.

SANTA MARIA NOVELLA
Basilica di Santa Maria Novella

Piazza Santa Maria Novella 18; tel. 055/219-257; www.smn.it; Oct.-Mar. Mon.-Thurs. 9am-5:30pm, Fri. 11am-5:30pm, Sat. 9am-5:30pm, Sun. 1pm-5:30pm, Apr.-Sept. Mon.-Thurs. 9am-7pm, Fri. 11am-7pm, Sat. 9am-5:30pm, Sun. 1pm-5:30pm; €7.50 or Firenzecard

Basilica di Santa Maria Novella lies opposite the train station and is often ignored by travelers in a hurry to reach the city center. The basilica is called *novella* (new) because it was built over a smaller church by Dominican monks, who completed the structure in 1360. The recently remodeled *piazza* out front provides the best view of the green-and-white marble facade begun in the Middle Ages and completed in the Renaissance.

The basilica consists of a monumental church, a half-dozen chapels, and several cloisters. There's rarely a line to enter, and there's impressive artwork throughout. The most striking artifacts are the large wooden crucifix by Giotto hanging above the altar, a small fresco by Botticelli near the entrance, and *The Trinity* by Masaccio, one of the earliest examples of perspective in painting.

The **Chiostro Verde** (Green Cloister) is down a short flight of steps on the left side of the church. It's named after the green pigment used in the frescoes lining the walls that vividly recount stories of sinners and saints. Farther down is the **refectory** where monks ate meals and is now filled with restored artworks. Hanging on the wall is a painting of the Last Supper, and below are glass cases containing religious garments.

Mass is held daily in the **Capella della Pura** chapel at 7:30am and 7pm in July and August and 7:30am and 6pm the rest of the year. Sunday mass is at 10:30am and 7am during the former and 10:30am, noon, and 6pm during the latter. Services are in Italian and last 45 minutes.

Chiesa di Ognissanti

Borgo Ognissanti 42; tel. 055/239-8700; Mon.-Fri. 7:15am-noon and 4pm-8pm, Sat.-Sun. 9am-1pm and 4pm-8pm

Many religious orders were active in Florence, and Ognissanti was founded by the Umiliati in the 12th century and later used by the Franciscans, who were responsible for the baroque makeover of the facade. Being one of the most prestigious orders meant they could afford the best artists of the day, and Giotto, Botticelli, and Ghirlandaio all contributed to the interior. Many paintings were moved to the Uffizi, but what remains, such as Ghirlandaio's *Last Supper* in the adjacent monastery and Botticelli's *Saint Agostine*, are impressive. Botticelli is buried inside and it's common to find notes of admiration and flowers covering his tomb. The Vespucci family chapel is located along the right nave and is where famed navigator Amerigo once prayed.

SAN LORENZO AND SAN MARCO

TOP EXPERIENCE

★ Accademia
(Galleria dell'Accademia)

Via Ricasoli 58-60; tel. 055/098-7100; www.galleriaaccademiafirenze.beniculturali.it; Tues.-Sun. 9am-6pm; €8 or Firenzecard, €4 online reservation fee

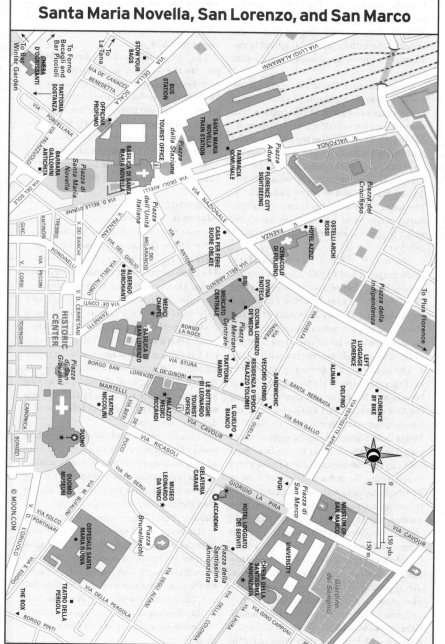

Santa Maria Novella, San Lorenzo, and San Marco

© MOON.COM

Michelangelo's *David,* the world's most famous statue, does not disappoint. He stands defiantly at the end of a long corridor on the pedestal the artist created, which adds additional height to an already monumental figure.

The portrayal of David's struggle against Goliath was a common theme among Renaissance artists, but Michelangelo's take was unique. In his version, David is not brandishing the severed head of the giant, nor is he celebrating his deed. Instead, Michelangelo's David sizes up his nemesis as he holds the stone he is about to sling. The tension is visible on his face and in his veined muscles. The statue is breathtaking from every angle. Fortunately, there is a wooden bench on which to pause and reflect on the mammoth creation.

The origin of the statue is legendary. Michelangelo liked to pick his own marble, often going to nearby quarries to get the best stone. But in this case, he chose a discarded hunk that had already been hacked at and abandoned by lesser artists. Michelangelo had the block hauled to his studio, where he began work on what would become his masterpiece.

The statue was not originally intended to be displayed indoors. Michelangelo was ambitious, and his statue was meant to rest on the Duomo itself. The difficulty of lifting the statue onto the church led it be placed in Piazza della Signoria (where a replica stands today) for centuries. After the unification of Italy, city officials began to worry the elements were harming the statue and decided to move it to the Accademia and create a special gallery to protect it. (Ironically, the toes of the statue were damaged by a disgruntled artist in 1991.)

The Accademia is the world's oldest art school and would be worth a visit even if it didn't contain Michelangelo's masterpiece, though the unique collection of medieval paintings, half-completed sculptures, Florentine art from the 12th-15th centuries, and some surprises are often overlooked. Other works by Michelangelo include four unfinished sculptures that were ordered for the

tomb of Pope Julius II but remained embedded in stone. The effect is eerie and inspired future generations of sculptors to adopt this *nonfinite* technique.

The line for unreserved ticket holders to get into the Galleria dell'Accademia often stretches around the corner, and the wait can be more than an hour during summer. The reserved ticket and Firenzecard line is shorter, but may still require patience. Only 600 visitors are allowed inside at any one time, so it's worth reserving a time slot in advance.

Reservations are required during COVID outbreaks and can be made online.

Museum of San Marco
(Museo di San Marco)

Piazza San Marco 3; tel. 055/088-2000; Mon.-Sat.
8:15am-1:50pm, open 2nd and 4th Sun. each month,
closed Mon. after Sun. openings; €6 or Firenzecard
The Dominican monastery that houses Museo di San Marco is a hidden gem just moments from the Galleria dell'Accademia but with only a fraction of the visitors. Inside you'll find frescoes by Beato Angelico, the city's first public library, and one and a half depictions of the Last Supper. This is also where the fanatical monk Girolamo Savonarola preached and resided. The completed *Cenacolo,* as the Last Supper is called in Italian, is by Ghiberti and notable for the vivid colors and the disciples' detailed expressions.

Upstairs, you'll find the 44 cells where monks lived. Each contains a fresco of Jesus in various states of crucifixion. San Domenico is also present and recognizable by the star above his head, while the order's first martyr (San Pietro di Verona) is usually depicted as bleeding. Beato Angelico oversaw the painting of the frescoes and worked on those closest to the entrance himself. Museum attendants on duty are happy to answer questions and share their insight with visitors. The library is on the same floor and where the monks studied. The delicately colonnaded space was built during the Renaissance and contains handdecorated manuscripts, some of which are on display.

Mission Michelangelo: Florence

Florence produced many geniuses during the late Middle Ages and Renaissance, but none acquired as much fame in life and death as Michelangelo. He left an unmistakable mark on the city that can still be seen today. Although some of his greatest works require standing in line, others are far more accessible and can be visited in a morning or afternoon.

- Casa Buonarroti houses Michelangelo's first serious attempts at sculpture, created when he was barely out of his teens. Some of the artist's architectural models and drawings are also on display (page 192).

- Michelangelo found refuge in Basilica di Santo Spirito after the death of his benefactor Lorenzo the Magnificent. The young artist was allowed to dissect cadavers in the church hospital, a task that played an instrumental part in his growth as an artist. He paid the monks back for their hospitality by sculpting a wooden crucifix in 1493 that still hangs in the basilica. It's a realistic and human portrayal of Christ that hints of the sculptures to come (page 195).

- After the Medici were exiled in 1494, Michelangelo journeyed to Rome, where he carved the *Pieta di San Pietro* and *Bacco*. These sculptures are the first signs of a mature artist at the height of his talents. They were eventually returned to Florence and now reside in the Bargello National Museum. The museum also contains other works from the same period, and comparing one with the other reveals a subtle evolution in style (page 182).

- Upon returning to Florence in 1501, Michelangelo created some of his most famous masterpieces including the statue of David. The Galleria dell'Accademia also contains his sensual uncompleted statues, in which rough chisel marks are visible and the figures appear trapped in stone (page 186).

- The Uffizi houses Michelangelo's first painting, *Tondo Doni,* on display in room 35. It's a colorful portrayal of the Holy Family and the only one of his paintings in Florence (page 185).

- Two members of the Medici family served as pope between 1515 and 1534, and during that time they commissioned Michelangelo to design and decorate the Medici Chapel. It's perhaps his most complete work, in which he demonstrated talent both as an architect and sculptor. He created two tombs on which muscular statues lounge and a symmetrical innovative interior that was very different from how chapels were designed at the time (page 190).

- Michelangelo's final sculpture was created in Rome and later moved to Florence, where it now resides inside Museo dell'Opera (page 181). The life-size figures are noteworthy for the expression of grief on their faces, and the self-portrait of the artist in the center. Michelangelo intended it for his tomb but didn't complete it in time, and the city commissioned another artist to decorate his final resting place inside Basilica di Santa Croce (page 192).

Downstairs, the fresco cycle along the cloister recounts the youth, conversion, and religious life of San Marco and begins diagonally from the entrance. It illustrates how Florence looked and locals dressed and acted during the 11th century. Beato Angelico painted the spaces above the doorways, all of which hint at the rooms beyond. The "Half Supper" is located in the refectory where monks had their meals. It isn't the highest quality but remains interesting for its realistic portrayal of the monks who inhabited the monastery.

The monk standing on the far left dressed entirely in white financed the work. Anyone who joined the brotherhood was required to give up their worldly wealth and apply any riches they had to the beautification and improvement of the monastery.

Basilica di San Lorenzo

Piazza di San Lorenzo 9; tel. 055/214-042; Mon. 10am-5:30pm, Tues.-Thurs. 10am-1pm, Fri.-Sat. 10am-5:30pm, Sun. 1:30pm-5:30; €7

Before the Duomo was completed, the Basilica

di San Lorenzo was the most important place of worship in Florence and the Medici family church. It's recognizable from the unfinished brick exterior and a simple gray interior designed by Brunelleschi, Michelozzo, Michelangelo, and Donatello. Visitors enter through the cloister, which was a common feature of many Florentine churches, and this one is characterized by a rare second-floor *loggia* with slender ionic columns. The adjacent underground museum is where Cosimo Medici is buried near his friend Donatello. Cosimo's offspring had a library built next door where 11,000 manuscripts are stored. The 16th-century **Biblioteca Medicea Laurenziana** (Mon.-Fri. 9:30am-1:30pm; €3) was the work of Michelangelo and the only structure he entirely built from scratch.

There are frequent exhibitions, but photography is not allowed and the church is closed to non-worshippers during mass. During COVID outbreaks, opening hours may be limited.

Medici Chapel
(Cappelle Medici)

Piazza di Madonna degli Aldobrandini 6; tel. 055/238-8602; Wed.-Fri. 2pm-6:30pm, Sat.-Mon. 8:45am-1:30pm; €9, audio guide €6 single, €10 double

Cappelle Medici is the final resting place of the members of the Medici dynasty. The chapel inside Basilica di San Lorenzo was the family's parish church and a short walk from their main residence on Via Cavour. The complex consists of an Old and New Sacristy built by Brunelleschi and Michelangelo. The latter is notable for its scale and the muscular statues lounging on the monumental tombs. The main octagonal chapel is covered in precious marble and rises to a towering 194 feet (59 meters). The family members are not actually resting inside the stone tombs; their remains are within the walls of the crypt at the entrance of the museum. Restoration of the chapel's interior and exterior are ongoing, and scaffolding is a common sight.

Palazzo Medici Riccardi

Via Camillo Cavour 3; tel. 055/276-0340; www. palazzomediciriccardi.it; Thurs.-Mon. 8:30am-7pm; €7 or Firenzecard

The Medici family combined wealth and political power in a way that was unprecedented and unequaled in Florence. Letting other families know their social status was not only a matter of pride, but it ensured their place in Florentine society. They wanted the biggest villa on the block and set a new standard in architecture by building it. Their massive 15th-century villa may look austere on the outside, but the inner courtyard and living quarters were full of Renaissance comforts. The most notable of these is the **Cappella dei Magi** chapel decorated with a fresco depicting different generations of the Medici dressed in their Sunday best. The house was later sold to the Riccardi clan, who made their own additions including the **Galleria degli Specchi,** or mirror gallery, where foreign dignitaries were entertained and lavish parties thrown. Outside in the small garden is a collection of Greek and Roman statues that Michelangelo and other local artists studied for inspiration. There are frequent exhibitions that vary in subject from Tutankhamun to Kurt Cobain.

Advance reservations are required during COVID outbreaks.

Chiesa della Santissima Annunziata

Piazza Santissima Annunziata; tel. 055/266-181; daily 7:30am-12:30pm and 4pm-7pm, Sunday mass 10am; free

It's easy to walk past Santissima Annunziata without a second look on your way to the Duomo but you'd be missing one of the most elaborate interiors of the city. Inside, the church is lined with over a dozen chapels on both sides of the central nave, which belonged to noble families responsible for their decoration. Competition and one-upmanship led

1: Basilica di Santa Croce **2:** frescoes inside Basilica di Santa Maria Novella **3:** Basilica di Santa Maria Novella

to some pretty extraordinary paintings, all of which show the evolution of Renaissance tastes. The small archway in the right corner was the private entrance of the Medici who preferred to enter unseen by ordinary citizens. The *piazza* outside is one of the most harmonious in Florence and hasn't changed since Brunelleschi designed the delicate porticoes that distinguish this quiet square.

Museo Leonardo Da Vinci

Via dei Servi 66/68R; tel. 055/282-966; www. mostredileonardo.com; daily 10am-6pm; €7

Inside this museum, you'll learn about the life of the multitalented artist and inventor and discover many of his creations. Dozens of wooden machines are on display in full or close-to-full scale. Best of all, most of the models are fully functional and meant to be touched. There are civil as well as military inventions, including the predecessor of the modern tank, da Vinci's famous flying machines, warships, and a section dedicated to the research and anatomy work he conducted with 3-D explanations. The museum is fun for kids, but the engineering ingenuity is also appealing for adults.

SANTA CROCE

Basilica di Santa Croce

Piazza Basilica di Santa Croce 16; tel. 055/246-6105; www.santacroceopera.it; Mon.-Sat. 9:30am-5pm, Sun. 2pm-5pm; €8 or Firenzecard

Basilica di Santa Croce lies on the eastern edge of the Historic Center in a working-class district (also called Santa Croce) that once housed tanneries and leather workshops. The Franciscan monastery was enlarged in the late 13th century and the facade was completed centuries later in 1863.

The basilica is designed in a Latin cross plan with three naves, a number of side chapels, and a vast wooden ceiling. The style is predominately Gothic with frescoes by Renaissance artists who set the early standards of Western art. None of these is more influential than Giotto, who decorated two chapels. His use of space and the positioning

of figures influenced generations of Florentine artists and significantly impacted the Renaissance painting that followed.

Santa Croce is the final resting place of Michelangelo, Machiavelli, and Galileo Galilei. Dante would be lying next to them had he not been banished from Florence; the city later made amends by installing a statue of the poet on the steps outside. Funerary monuments dedicated to the city's all-time greats are located along the walls. A passage, opposite the basilica entrance, leads to the peaceful 14th-century cloister and **Pazzi Chapel** designed by Brunelleschi. The architect died before work was completed, and the facade has remained unfinished.

The basilica is the city's most visited church after the Duomo, and lines form early. A free tour app is available for download, but you're better off asking the friendly volunteers who wait inside the church and organize impromptu free guided tours.

Worshippers can enter Monday-Saturday 7:30am-6:45pm from a separate entrance and are not required to wait in line or purchase tickets. Just inform attendants of your intentions and remain within the designated prayer areas on the left side of the nave. Mass is celebrated Monday-Saturday at 6pm and on Sunday at 11am, noon, and 6pm.

Casa Buonarroti

Via Ghibellina 70; tel. 055/241-752; www. casabuonarroti.it, Wed.-Mon. 10am-4:30pm; €8 or Firenzecard

Michelangelo's last name was Buonarroti but he didn't live in Casa Buonarroti, which was built by his nephew and transformed into a museum after the extinction of the family line. Today it houses Michelangelo's first serious attempts at sculpture, created when he was barely out of his teens. *Battaglia dei Centauri* and *Madonna della Scala* may not compete with his later work, but they do show clear signs of potential. In those early years Michelangelo used a bas-relief technique that requires chiseling away at a marble background and is best viewed from the

Santa Croce

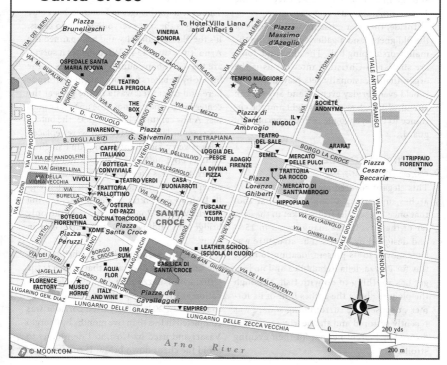

front. Some of the artist's architectural models and drawings are also on display along with personal belongings such as Michelangelo's shoes, which indicate he had small feet.

Museo Horne

Via dei Benci 6; tel. 055/244-661; www.museohorne. it; daily 10am-2pm; €7 or Firenzecard

This small villa, the former home of 19th-century English art critic Herbert Percy Horne, contains 14th-16th-century art that provides an idea of how upper-class Renaissance families once lived. The museum is off the radar and usually deserted, which means you're likely to be alone with the guardians who know the house intimately and are eager to show visitors around. Highlights include a painting by Giotto that Horne purchased for £9.

Tempio Maggiore

Via Luigi Carlo Farini 4; tel. 055/245-252; www. firenzebraica.it; Sun.-Thurs. 10am-10:30pm and Fri. 10am-5pm; €6.50 or Firenzecard

Unlike Rome and Venice, where the old Jewish ghettoes have remained standing, the neighborhood in Florence where Jews were once confined was demolished to make way for Piazza della Repubblica. You can still learn about the city's Jewish past and understand what the ghetto was like inside the Tempio Maggiore, or Great Synagogue. It's the second largest synagogue in Italy and the culmination of centuries of Jewish activity in Florence.

Construction began in 1871 a short way from the Historic Center, and the facade's pink-and-white stone is meant to recall those found in Jerusalem. The style is Arabesque and the inscriptions in Hebrew recount the Ten Commandments.

Inside, there's a museum with models of the old ghetto and a gallery overlooking the main worshipping hall. The altar and dome are similar to Christian interiors as is the organ that occasionally gets played. Service is held every Friday evening and anyone can attend, although security is tight and the entrance to the synagogue is under permanent guard.

Loggia del Pesce
Piazza dei Ciompi; 24/7; free

This elegant covered market consists of 20 arches supporting a long rectangular roof that once housed the fish market in the center of the city. It was inaugurated in 1568 and designed by Vasari. The structure was later moved to its present location to make way for Piazza della Rebubblica and no longer has anything to do with fish, although the plaques above the arches hint of its former purpose. The surrounding square was recently restored and the nearby streets are favored by Florentines out for their evening strolls.

OLTRARNO
Ponte Vecchio

There are many bridges in Florence, but Ponte Vecchio is the one everyone wants to cross. It's the oldest in the city and has spanned the Arno River since 1345. What makes it special are the workshops built on both sides of the bridge by butchers who once plied their trade here and discarded waste in the gaps at the center (where tourists now line up to take photos). A few centuries later, in 1593, the butchers were ordered to leave and were replaced with jewelry merchants who didn't smell as bad. Their boutiques can still be browsed today. Each has an elaborate wooden casing equipped with spyhole through which vigils kept an eye on the merchandise. During World War II, Ponte Vecchio was the only bridge left standing by the retreating German army.

Above the eastern side of the bridge runs the **Corridoio Vasariano** that connects the Uffizi with Palazzo Pitti. (It was under renovation at the time of writing and scheduled to reopen in 2022.) The raised corridor was completed in less than five months by Giorgio Vasari and used by Cosimo I de Medici to avoid the chaos down below. It runs straight

Loggia del Pesce

Oltrarno

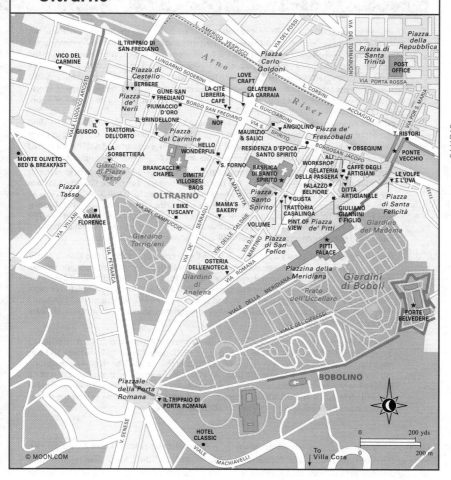

© MOON.COM

except for a section on the Oltrarno side where a family refused to sell their property.

Basilica di Santo Spirito

Piazza Santo Spirito 30; tel. 055/210-030; www. basilicasantospirito.it; Thurs.-Fri. 10am-12:30pm and 4pm-6pm; free

Basilica di Santo Spirito is one of only two basilicas in Oltrarno. From the outside it looks a little like the Alamo, with a plain

facade facing a modest tree-lined *piazza* that hosts a daily market in the morning and attracts a lively crowd at night. It was founded by Augustan monks in 1250, but a devastating fire led to the hiring of Brunelleschi to work on the reconstruction. Rebuilding and expanding the church was so costly that the monks were forced to give up one of their daily meals until work was completed. The famed architect died a few years after

Searching for Last Suppers

Over the centuries, artists have illustrated hundreds of episodes from the Bible—and one of the favorite images is the *Cenacolo* or *Last Supper*. Monasteries and convents frequently commissioned Middle Ages and Renaissance artists to paint this iconic scene. The basic scene is nearly always the same: Jesus sits in the center of a long table, with followers seated on either side. John is to the left and often hunched over in near sleep. Each figure sports a halo, except Judas, who is usually seated across the table from the other figures and portrayed with a dark beard. Everything else including the background, expressions, and the food itself were up to the artist, many of whom specialized in painting this single scene.

Florence counts over 50 versions of the Last Supper, and tracking a few down is a rewarding venture that costs next to nothing. Searching for *Last Suppers* requires a little planning, as many of the monasteries where they're located are only open mornings on certain days. The ones listed below are all within walking distance of one another and can be covered in a couple of hours:

- **Cenacolo di Ognissanti** (Borgo Ognissanti 42; tel. 055/286-700; Sat. 9am-1pm; free) stands near the Arno facing an elegant *piazza*. The *Last Supper*, completed by Domenico Ghirlandaio in 1488, covers the far wall in the refectory where monks gathered for meals. Ghirlandaio was an expert in the genre and completed several others around the city with the help of his brother and assistants. This one is notable for the detailed expressions and use of perspective. The artist sketched a rough draft that hangs on the side wall. Comparing the two makes for some interesting speculation about John. Botticelli is buried in the adjacent church.

- Head north toward the train station to reach the **Cenacolo di Fuligno** (Via Faenza 40; tel. 055/538-1123; Tues. and first Sun. every month 8:30am-1:30pm; free). Pietro Perugino worked three years on the fresco and completed the work in 1496. It was severely damaged during the great flood of 1966 and underwent a long period of restoration that was completed in 1990. The apostles in this portrayal are hungry, and all those to the left of Jesus are busy enjoying their food. The landscape above them is visible through the columns of an imaginary *palazzo* that adds depth to the scene.

- Walk up Via Nazionale and take a left on Via Ventisette Aprile to reach **Cenacolo di Sant'Apollonia** (Via XXVII Aprile 1; tel. 055/238-8607; daily 8:15am-1:50pm; free). This was once the biggest convent in the city, but there's a good chance you'll be the only one observing the painting Andrea del Castagno completed in 1450. He imagined the scene taking place inside a finely decorated room with a long table and many geometric patterns. Judas is notable for his dark features, and there's less interaction and more contemplation among the diners. Castagno painted each apostle's name (in Latin) near his feet.

construction started, but many of his plans were carried out, including the cupola and strict geometric proportions that give the interior an impressive harmony. Daily mass is held at 5:30pm.

Michelangelo spent time here with the Augustine monks and in gratitude sculpted a wooden crucifix that is accessible through an entrance along the eastern apse. It costs €2 to enter, and there's also access to the tranquil monastery where a handful of monks still reside and octogenarian volunteers sell handmade crocheted souvenirs most afternoons.

A small **museum** (Piazza Santo Spirito 29; tel. 055/287-043; Mon.-Sun. 10am-4pm; €4) to the left of the basilica was once part of the medieval convent and now contains a collection of religious artifacts and the remains of Andrea Orcagna's enormous *Last Supper* fresco. The apostles have disappeared, but Jesus remains high above on a crucifix surrounded by angels. The room itself is full of Gothic fittings and is a stark contrast to the Renaissance concepts employed inside the church. There are daily masses at 9am, 10:30am, 6pm, and 9pm, with confession in English on Thursdays 5pm-6pm.

Last Supper fresco inside Museo di San Marco

- Down the street inside **Museo di San Marco** (page 188) is another *Cenacolo* designed by Ghirlandaio and completed with the help of his brother in 1480. The background, tablecloth, and perspective are very similar to his earlier work; however, the colors are more vivid here and the artist took the liberty of adding a cat. Today the painting shares a room with a small bookshop.

- Seeing several *Last Suppers* in a single day requires getting up early, but if there's still time and you have the energy, walk east toward the city's second train station and **Cenacolo di Andrea del Sarto** (Via di S. Salvi 16; tel. 055/064-9489; Tues.-Sun. 8:15am-1:50pm; free). This one is the most recent of the bunch—it was completed in 1527—and is quite animated, with apostles on their feet in heated discussion. They haven't earned their halos yet, and John is wide awake while Judas on the far right of the fresco doesn't look so villainous. One of the figures above the main scene is said to be a self-portrait of the artist. Afterward you can walk back to the center along the Arno or search for your own supper in a neighborhood *trattoria*.

Brancacci Chapel
(Cappella Brancacci)

Piazza del Carmine 14; tel. 055/276-8224; Mon. and Wed.-Sat. 10am-5pm, Sun. 1pm-5pm; €8 or Firenzecard

Santa Maria del Carmine was founded by a group of Pisan monks in 1268. The inside was nearly completely destroyed by a fire in 1771, but the Cappella Brancacci survived. This chapel was commissioned by Felice Brancacci, a wealthy merchant and politician, and recounts the life of St. Peter. The frescoes were the result of three successive artists including Masaccio and Filippo Lippi, who completed the chapel in 1480. The interior is one of the few examples of Roman baroque in the city.

The most striking fresco depicts **Adam and Eve** before and after giving in to temptation, represented by a snake with a female head. Their body language and complexions are completely transformed. A keen observer may also notice the belly buttons on the first couple. Some speculate it was an oversight by the artist, as both Adam and Eve were created by God and would not have needed umbilical cords.

Only 30 people are allowed into the chapel

Ponte Vecchio at Sunset

For most of the day and night, Ponte Vecchio is filled with pedestrians admiring the storefronts and in no hurry to get to the other side. The bridge is best viewed from the streets running along the Arno and the neighboring bridges, which attract less attention. Locals and visitors gather on **Ponte Santa Trinità,** 150 yards downriver, to watch the setting sun gradually transform the pastel-colored shops on the bridge. **Ponte alle Grazie** on the opposite side is farther away and provides a better view in the morning. Both bridges lead to lesser-known parts of Oltrarno.

at a time, but lines are short, even in summer. The chapel is just beyond the bookshop on the far side of the cloister. If you're not well versed in the Bible, pick up the tablet (€3) at the shop. It's easy to use and makes sense of the fresco cycle one image at a time.

Pitti Palace
(Palazzo Pitti)

Piazza Pitti 1; tel. 055/294-883; Tues.-Sun. 8:30am-6:50pm; €16, €38 combo ticket or Firenzecard, audio guide €8 single, €13 double

Palazzo Pitti, the largest palace in Florence, can easily take a half day to fully explore. It was built in the 14th century for a wealthy banker (Luca Pitti) who wanted to show off his power and flattened a neighborhood to get his wish. His fortunes turned, and before the *palazzo* was completed it fell into the hands of his archrival, Cosimo I de Medici. Today, the palace contains two art galleries, several museums, a costume collection, the royal apartments, and an 11-acre (4-hectare) garden.

Galleria Palatina originated as the personal collection of the Medici and covers the entire first floor. Paintings hang as the last residents of the *palazzo* left them, with little concern for chronology. The haphazard display is refreshing, and the gallery labels read like a who's who of the art world. Works by Botticelli, Tiziano, Perugino, and Veronese fill 11 finely decorated salons. The entire collection owes its existence to Anna Maria Ludovica, who was the last Medici

heir and bequeathed her family's treasures to the city in 1737 on the condition they would never be divided, sold, or removed from the city.

The Royal Apartments provide further insight into the family's taste for luxury. The Dukes of Lorraine, who were later residents and lived in the *palazzo* until the 19th century, ordered the neoclassical redesign. They liked their décor ostentatious, and the climax is the plush throne room where visitors were received and tourists now gather. If you aren't suffering from artistic overload, visit the **Galleria d'Arte Moderna** (tel. 055/238-8616; Tues.-Sun. 8:15am-6:50pm) on the second floor. This gallery opened in 1924 and is dedicated to Italian painters between the late 18th century and World War I.

Museo degli Argenti, which the Medici used as their summer apartments, displays glassware and carpets, as well as fine jewelry cherished by the family. This part of the palace also includes the **Galleria dei Costume,** which is worth visiting if you're interested in 19th-century clothing and ancient fashions.

The palace also includes the elaborate **Giardini di Boboli** (daily Nov.-Feb. 8:15am-4:30pm, Mar. and Oct. 8:15am-5:30pm, Apr.-May and Sept. 8:15am-6:30, June-Aug. 8:15am-7:30pm, closed first and last Mon. every month; €10, €38 combo ticket or Firenzecard) gardens, which should not be skipped and come into full bloom in late spring. There are four entrances to the gardens, which are free on the first Sunday of

---

1: Ponte Vecchio **2:** Basilica San Miniato al Monte

San Niccolo

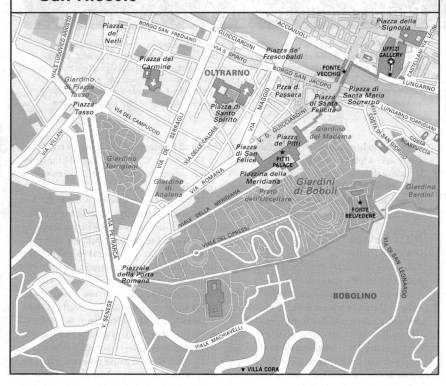

every month and provide a tranquil escape from the city.

Tickets to Palazzo Pitti are half-price if purchased before 8:59am and used prior to 9:25am.

Forte Belvedere

Via di San Leonardo 1; tel. 055/27681; Tues.-Sun. 10:30am-6:30pm; €3

Forte Belvedere lies on the hill above the Boboli Gardens and provides one of the best views of the city. This fortress is a little harder to reach than Piazzale Michelangelo, whose convenient parking makes it a mandatory stop for busloads of camera-happy tourists, but offers a closer look at the city. If you aren't planning on visiting Lucca or any of the other fortified towns in Tuscany, Belvedere's star-shaped ramparts are also an excellent primer in military architecture. The fortress was built at the end of the 16th century and served as insurance for the Medici, who were wary of attacks from outside the city and rebellions from within. It was also a reliable place to stash their treasure. Today you can walk around the upper and lower terraces, which often host summer art exhibitions.

The fort has two entrances. It can be reached directly from the northeastern exit of the Boboli Gardens or through the main entrance near the medieval walls, which also flank the nearby Giardino Bardini. Hours may vary according to the exhibitions taking place.

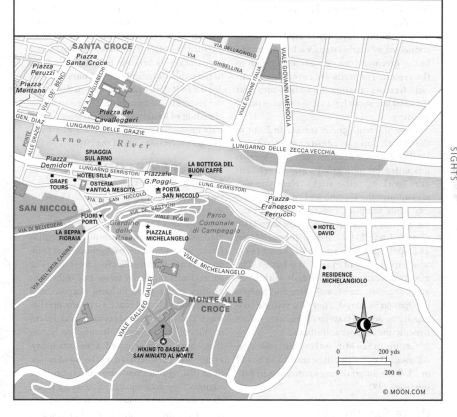

© MOON.COM

SAN NICCOLÒ
Piazzale Michelangelo

Piazzale Michelangelo is Florence's most famous observation point and a mandatory stop for many tourists. It was built during the city's brief stint as capital of Italy and sits on a hillside from where most of Florence is visible. You can arrive by car or bus (line 12) but most people climb up from the San Niccolò neighborhood. If you choose to walk you can take the pedestrian walkway past the rose garden or the winding monumental steps that begin from Piazza Giuseppe Poggi. In the center of the square stands a bronze copy of Michelangelo's *David*. There are several other copies of his work nearby. The elegant neoclassical *loggia* across the street was meant to

house a Michelangelo museum, but the project was never completed and has since become a restaurant and café serving local specialties.

The 1870s were a period of urban restructuring in Florence. Along with the *piazza*, tree-lined avenues leading to the square were created. Two of these, Viale Galileo and Michelangelo, wind through the countryside and offer further glimpses of the city.

Basilica San Miniato al Monte
Via delle Porte Sante 34; tel. 055/234-2731;
Mon.-Sat. 9:30am-1pm and 3pm-7pm and Sun.
8:15am-1pm and 3pm-7pm; free

The hilltop church of Basilica San Miniato al Monte is one of the oldest Romanesque churches in the city and was dedicated to the first Christian martyr of Florence. It's rarely crowded and the cool interior provides relief on hot summer days. There are three levels connected by marble steps; each is decorated in the green-and-white marble common to the region. The walls are covered with ancient frescoes of saints. An audio booth near the entrance sheds light on the origins of the building.

From the wide gravel terrace in front of the church you can admire the entire city. Unlike Piazzale Michelangelo, the view is unspoiled by tour groups and street vendors hawking selfie sticks. Here you can also admire the Duomo and rooftops of the city while sampling sweets prepared by the Benedictine monks in the adjacent **monastic shop** (tel. 055/234-2731; daily 10am-12:15pm and 4pm-6pm) or explore the **cemetery,** where the author of *Pinocchio* is buried. The monks celebrate Eucharist daily with Latin and Gregorian chants at 7:15am and 5:45pm (5:30pm on Sundays). They also provide hospitality to devout travelers who must follow Benedictine curfews and rituals.

Getting to San Miniato is a small endeavor. Although the church can be reached by bus 12 or 13, the most gratifying approach is by hiking (page 238).

Porta San Niccolò

Via dei Bastioni; tel. 055/276-8224; Jun.-Oct. daily 4pm-8pm; €6 or Firenzecard

If you're climbing back down from San Miniato, it's hard to miss Porta San Niccolò, a tower that overlooks the Arno and once guarded the city. It's the only surviving tower to maintain its original height and is open to the public July-September. Tours are conducted in Italian and English and depart on the hour. The 30-minute visit includes an explanation of Renaissance fortifications and a walk up the 160 steps to the terrace where you can get a riverside view of the city.

GREATER FLORENCE
Museo Stibbert

Via Federigo Stibbert 26; tel. 055/475-520; www. museostibbert.it; Fri.-Sun. 10am-6pm and Mon.-Wed. 10am-2pm; €6 or Firenzecard

Frederick Stibbert came from an Italo-English family with a military background and from an early age began collecting weapons. The collection is primarily formed of 16th-18th-century armor, hand-to-hand weapons, and firearms from Italy, France, Germany, and beyond. There are hundreds of items and dozens of suits of armor, many mounted on horses that were equally armored. Like cars today, armor was personalized as the owners saw fit to distinguish themselves and intimidate enemies. The collection is housed in a villa a short walk from the center. Otherwise, ride bus 4 from the train station through residential 19th-century neighborhoods and across the city's only canal.

Food

Tuscans have a reputation for some of the best cooking in Italy, and there is a myriad of rustic *osteria* to choose from. Food here is a tale of traditional rural recipes prepared generation after generation and new talents combining flavors in unexpected ways. Ingredients are simple and dictated by the seasons. The city offers a variety of unique dishes, many with humble origins that originated when food meant whatever was available. For the most

part, that was grains, legumes, vegetables, and every cut of meat imaginable from T-bone steaks to intestines. Those ingredients are still on menus and satisfying appetites today.

For centuries, Florentines have been heading to *trattorie* for hearty fare at next-to-nothing prices. Some of the oldest date back more than a hundred years and have been run by different generations of the same family in historically working-class neighborhoods.

They're not fancy and barely romantic, but they are full of charm and where *pappa al pomodoro* and *bistecca alla fiorentina* can be eaten side-by-side with locals. The city, however, doesn't lack culinary innovation, and if it's 21st-century flavors and décor you're after, you'll find them in Florence as well. There is something for every appetite, and tasting it is as thrilling as climbing the Duomo or gazing upon *David*.

DUOMO AND AROUND

There are hundreds of eateries in the *centro storico* in all categories and price ranges. The best and most authentic are nearly never located on major squares or thoroughfares that rely solely on the tourist trade. Good restaurants look as though they've been around for decades. Many have wonderful rustic interiors and good-natured staff who usually have time to share a word or a joke.

Tuscan
★ OSTERIA CICALINI

Via delle Oche 15r; tel. 055/205-2610; Tues.-Sat. 12:30pm-2:30pm and 7:30pm-10pm; €12-15, fixed-price €25-35

Cicalini is one of the newest gastronomic players in Florence and a serious contender for top eatery in town. They take wine seriously and pair it very deliberately. Food and drink go together for a reason: Each makes the other better, and that's the idea behind much of the menu. The fixed-priced options are refreshingly innovative and do away with the clichés of Italian cooking. Waiters are wonderfully attentive, and the décor is modern. The potato and ricotta gnocchi with creamed turnips, pecorino, and pistachios is a delicious option that you won't want to share.

Italian
GIANNINO IN SAN LORENZO

Via Borgo San Lorenzo 33-37r; tel. 055/239-9799; daily 11:30am-11:30pm; €12-20, pizza €7-9

Like many historic restaurants founded after World War II, Giannino in San Lorenzo has managed to survive thanks to a new generation of restaurateurs eager to keep old traditions alive. In this case Riccardo Bartoloni and his son are behind the renaissance. They serve great steaks, tripe in all its incarnations, and excellent pizza. There's something for everyone inside this venerable establishment where quality still matters.

KONNUBIO

Via dei Conti 8r; tel. 055/238-1189; daily 7:30am-11:30pm; €15-20

Konnubio is proof that Florentine dining isn't only about traditional dishes served within rustic interiors. This cosmopolitan restaurant around the corner from Basilica di San Lorenzo could easily be located in New York or Paris. The restaurant's four attractive rooms are decorated in contemporary style with wood-and-metallic furniture that is beyond cool. Tuscan, international, and vegan dishes are served nonstop from breakfast to dinner. Plate appearance matters as much as the ingredients used.

Seafood
FISHING LAB

Via del Proconsolo 16r; tel. 055/240-618; daily 11am-2:30pm and 7pm-11pm; €10-15

This lively restaurant in a vibrant frescoed location has great décor and a youthful staff who know their seafood. The menu includes raw, fried, and traditional options along with a street menu that can be ordered in half or full portions. Atmosphere is informal and service friendly and efficient.

International
RISTORANTE PERSIANO

Via dei Cerchi 25r; tel. 055/094-5695; daily 12:30pm-3:30pm and 7pm-11pm; €9-14

Dining possibilities have expanded exponentially in recent years thanks to places like Ristorante Persiano that has introduced new flavors to the city. The colorful eatery specializes in oriental flavors and the menu contains a mix of beef and chicken kebabs served with rice and yogurt, and exotic starters that provide a pleasant break from Italian food.

Best Food and Drink

★ **Osteria Cicalini:** Creativity and conviviality meet at this modern eatery where every ingredient matters (page 203).

★ **All'Antico Vinaio:** Tourists and locals line up for mammoth sandwiches stuffed with local cold cuts. Don't worry; the line moves fast (page 204)!

★ **Mercato Centrale:** Browse the ingredients at this animated market—the center of the Florentine food scene since 1872—before settling in at its second-floor food court (page 208).

★ **Vecchio Forno:** Tempting Tuscan bread and pastries are baked in the oven out back at this cute corner bakery (page 210).

★ **Trattoria da Rocco:** This modest eatery serves Florentine classics within a lively market (page 210).

★ **Il Nugolo:** Surprise your taste buds at this new entry on the Florentine dining scene (page 211).

★ **Gelateria della Passera:** Enjoy the creamiest gelato in the city on the lovely little square facing this tiny shop (page 219).

★ **Osteria Antica Mescita:** Enjoy down-to-earth dishes at affordable prices en route to admire the views from the hillside of San Miniato (page 220).

★ **La Bottega del Buon Caffè:** This Michelin-rated restaurant facing the Arno makes dishes that are close to art—at accessible prices (page 220).

Snacks and Street Food

The most reliable destination for thick sandwiches and generous platters of cold cuts and cheeses served with wine is **Via dei Neri.** It's one of the most mouthwatering streets in the city, with plenty of Florentine fast-food options to choose from.

★ ALL'ANTICO VINAIO

Via dei Neri 65r, 74r-76r; tel. 055/238-2723; daily 10:30am-10pm; €5

The secret to a great sandwich is fresh bread and quality fillings, and All'Antico Vinaio has nailed both—which explains why the line outside their shops (there are three located side-by-side) is 20-30 deep most days. What people are waiting for is enormous slices of focaccia filled with cold cuts, cheese, and vegetables, for just €5. The *Schacciatela,*

overflowing with prosciutto ham, is the most popular, but you can also pick from a tempting selection that includes a vegetarian option. To avoid the rush, arrive around 11am or 6pm. There are a few tables inside, but Florentines just sit on the curb of the pedestrian street outside.

L'ANTICO TRIPPAIO

Piazza de' Cimatori; tel 339/742-5692; daily 8:30am-8:30pm; €5

L'Antico Trippaio is a classic tripe kiosk specializing in one ingredient and one ingredient only. It's served in a bun and usually ordered for takeaway by Florentines in a hurry. Hours sometimes vary but the stand is generally open all day long.

1: Trattoria Sostanza **2:** the entrance to Trattoria Mario

VINAINO FIORENZA

Via Vaccherecccia 13r; tel. 055/264-482; Mon.-Fri.
10:30am-4pm, Sat. 10:30am-10:30pm, Sun.
10:30am-8pm; €4-6

At Vinaino Fiorenza you can choose between a dozen Italian sandwiches all made with regional ingredients. There's *mozzarella di bufala* from Campania, *porchetta* from Lazio, *'nduja* sausage from Calabria, and more. The glass case facing the street is filled with ready-made options that can be eaten at one of the stools inside the small shop or in Piazza della Signoria down the block.

LA PROSCIUTTERIA

Via dei Neri 54r; tel. 055/265-4472; daily
11:30am-11pm; €8-10

La Prosciutteria specializes in Chianti wine and locally produced cold cuts and cheeses served on long wooden cutting boards. It's a fun place where friends meet to share a meal in relaxed company that spills out onto the sidewalk.

BOTTEGA RENZINI

Via dei Neri 45r; tel. 055/010-6070; daily 10am-11pm;
€12

If the line at All'Antico Vinaio is too long, head down the street to Bottega Renzini. This welcome addition to the Florentine fast-food scene offers more than local specialties, and there's a little of nearly every Italian region inside. It's a gastronomic "best of" with an attractive interior and some gourmet options.

Gelato
GROM

Via del Campanile 2; tel. 055/216-158; daily
noon-11pm

Not all chains are necessarily bad, and Grom is the proof. This popular *gelateria* has made a global name for itself based on quality and original flavors. Prices are higher than average but for €4 you get an overflowing cone with creamy classics or fruity sorbets around the corner from the Duomo.

Coffee

Florence's historic cafés are elegant institutions that have been in business for decades. They continue to serve regulars and curious visitors inside little-changed interiors where artists and literati of previous eras spent their days in animated discussion.

BAR CAFFÈ MINGO

Piazza San Martino 1r; tel. 055/215-646; daily
8am-8:30pm; €1-3

Bar Caffè Mingo is stuck in time on a little square that has nothing very special about it except its refusal to change. Sit outside on the metal chairs away from the sun and watch the pedestrians pass. It doesn't feel like the center of Florence, but it's around the corner from everything and a good caffeine refuge.

DITTA ARTIGIANALE

Via dei Neri 32r; tel. 055/274-1541; daily
8:30am-7pm; €2-3

The key to great coffee is the bean. At Ditta Artigianale they choose theirs carefully and control every step in the blending process. The result is one of the best espressos in the city. You can also sip tea, have a light lunch, or enjoy a predinner cocktail inside this hip coffee hangout adorned with vintage furnishings.

CAFFÈ GILLI

Via Roma 1r; tel. 055/213-896; daily 7am-midnight;
€2-5

On the northeastern corner of Piazza della Repubblica lies Caffè Gilli, with its elegant chandeliers and closely spaced round tables. The location and Liberty-style décor have changed little since the 1920s and it's worth popping in for a quick espresso at the counter.

CAFFÈ RIVOIRE

Piazza della Signoria 4r; tel. 055/214-412; daily
7:30am-9pm; €2-5

Caffè Rivoire is diagonally opposite Palazzo Vecchio and has been in business since 1872. Initially they only served chocolate, but coffee, tea, and pastries were later added to the menu and attracted the cultural elite of the time. The shop still draws people who want to step into the past and enjoy a good view of the square. All that has changed are the topics of conversation and the prices—which are double or triple that of an average bar.

AMBLÉ

Piazzetta dei Del Bene 7a; tel. 055/268-528; Tues.-Sat. 10am-midnight and Sun. noon-midnight; €3-5

Nothing matches at Amblé, but that's part of the charm of this coffee and fruit bar moments from the Ponte Vecchio. The other part is the feeling of stumbling upon a place that can only be found by accident. Friends and couples relax outside on brightly colored deck chairs, benches, and stools all partially shaded by an ancient wall.

SANTA MARIA NOVELLA
Tuscan
LA TANA

Via Palazzuolo 156r; tel. 055/051-7127; Mon. 7pm-11pm and Tues.-Sat. noon-3pm and 7pm-11pm; €8-15

La Tana opened in 2019 and has been making a name for itself ever since by combining quality and value. There are two daily lunch specials, and €12 gets you a first, second, side, water, and wine. It's pretty much unbeatable—and tasty as well. The à la carte menu is also tempting and features Tuscan classics with twists of gorgonzola or sweet Tropea onions. Located near the train station, the *trattoria* makes a convenient first or last stop in the city.

TRATTORIA SOSTANZA

Via Porcellana 25r; tel. 055/212-691; Mon.-Sat. 12:30pm-2pm and 7:30pm-9:45pm; €10-14

Trattoria Sostanza began feeding Florentines in 1869 and the current décor dates from 1931. It has the character that comes from decades of preparing the same dishes a dozen times a day, and the seven marble tables are nearly always full. No attempt is made at reinventing traditional recipes and no one seems to care.

The daily handwritten menu includes pasta, soup, *Trippa alla fiorentina, bistecca alla fiorentina,* and side orders of beans.

Bakeries
FORNO BECAGLI

Borgo Ognissanti 92r; tel. 055/215-065; Mon.-Sat. 6:30am-8pm; €2-5

Florentine bakeries are often small, and Becagli is no exception. It is packed with loaves of saltless Tuscan bread, delicious cakes, traditional cookies, and holiday treats (every holiday has its dedicated treat in Florence). Point to what you'd like and say, "one of those" (*uno di quelli*). If you can't decide, try the *torta della nonna* (grandmother cake) or *pane al pescatore* (fisherman's cookies). The former is a cream-filled pie covered with pine nuts and a dusting of powdered sugar, while the latter is a sweetbread made with raisins and rosemary. Cold wine, water, and sodas are available from the fridge case.

Coffee
BAR PICCIOLI

Via Borgo Ognissant 118r; tel. 055/295-086; Mon.-Sat. 7am-9pm and Sun. 7am-2pm; €1-3

This versatile local bar attracts few tourists. Grab a quick espresso or cappuccino at the counter or wait to be served at the tables outside. There's a good selection of homemade sweats to accompany the caffeine, a variety of sandwiches at lunch, and spritzes throughout the day.

SAN LORENZO AND SAN MARCO
Tuscan
TRATTORIA MARIO

Via Rosina 2r; tel. 055/218-550; Mon.-Sat. 12:30pm-3:30pm; €10-12, cash only

The word has been out about Mario since 1957, and this compact *trattoria* is nearly always busy with young and old seated close together eating whatever the daily handwritten menu has on offer. It's always delicious, and the compact, tiled dining room is

Florentine Cuisine

In a country known for food, Tuscany is recognized by Italians as one of the best regions in which to eat. Meals don't have to be formal, and simple dishes are often the best. Besides traditional *trattorie* where you can sample local cuisine, the city has a long tradition of street food. Here are some tips for tasting Florence's most authentic dishes:

AT THE *TRATTORIA*

Nearly every Florentine *trattoria* has *ribollita* and *pappa al pomodoro* stews on their menu. Both are vegetarian friendly and highly filling. Fortunately, you can order a half portion *(mezza porzione)* of either and sample both.

- *Antipasti:* Appetizers, a delicious way to begin any meal. Choices include *crostini* along with local cold cuts and cheeses, often served in wine bars on wooden platters and accompanied by honey and olives. Central Italy is a major producer of prosciutto and other hams. The local variety is slightly spicy.

- *Crostini:* A lighter version of *bruschetta* that consists of grilled unsalted bread topped with oil, chopped tomatoes, or *fegato* (ground chicken liver similar to pâté).

- *Ribollita:* An authentic vegetarian stew, often made in winter when the black cabbage in the recipe is in season, though it can also be found throughout the year with substitute vegetables.

- *Pappa al pomodoro:* A vegetarian, tomato-based stew that's perfect in summer. It's reminiscent of gazpacho, although the bread used gives it a thicker texture.

- *Bistecca alla fiorentina:* A thick T-bone steak that is the most popular main course in Florence. It's cut from *Chianina* beef, a local cattle breed raised along the Tuscan coast and prized for its flavor. It's priced by weight and usually comes to €40-50 per kilogram. A kilo is usually enough for two, but you can order the exact amount you want to eat. Don't bother asking for medium or well done: *Fiorentina* steaks are grilled for three minutes on either side and served alone on a plate close to rare. *Contorni* (sides) are ordered separately and generally consist of green beans *(fagioli)*, broccoli, zucchini, and roast potatoes *(patate arrosto)*.

- *Vino:* Wine! Tuscany is home to some of the finest vineyards in Italy. Chianti and Barolo are world-renowned. If you're not an expert, the *vino della casa* (house wine) of any decent restaurant is always drinkable. Order it by the glass, quarter, half, or full carafe. Cold *vino bianco* (white wine) is popular in summer, while *vino rosso* (red wine) accompanies meat and cheese dishes.

nearly always full. Mario and Romeo prepare a steady stream of *ribollita* and tripe dishes in the open view kitchen while their wives and children keep the food coming. It's a good place to try *bistecca alla fiorentina* that's always tender and served rare. Reservations aren't accepted, but they'll take your name and seat you on a wooden stool as soon as a space opens up.

★ MERCATO CENTRALE
Piazza del Mercato Centrale; tel. 055/239-9798; daily 10am-10pm; €12-14

If you can't decide between pizza, pasta, or a T-bone steak, the food emporium on the second floor of the recently restored Mercato Centrale is the solution. It contains over 20 quality eateries that can satisfy multiple cravings. It's a popular lunch and dinner spot

pappa al pomodoro

STREET EATS

The favorite fast-food ingredient in Florence is tripe (*trippa*), made from the inside of a cow's four stomachs (not intestines). This traditional ingredient is a holdover from the Middle Ages, when peasants wasted nothing. Tripe in fact has great gastronomic possibilities and has generated a variety of dishes. Locals can point the way to the best historic stands that still serve the ingredient in various forms. Favorites depend on tenderness of the meat, concentration of spices, and personality of the vendors.

- *Lampredotto:* Tripe simmered for hours with tomatoes, onions, and parsley. It's eaten as a stew accompanied by a green herb sauce or in a sandwich. Find it at mobile kiosks around the city and inside Mercato Centrale.

- *Trippa alla fiorentina:* Tripe sautéed with vegetables, tomatoes, and Parmesan, then simmered until the liquid slowly evaporates. It's on many menus and a good introduction to tripe.

- *Schiacciata:* The Florentine version of *focaccia,* served at bakeries to make sandwiches or enjoyed straight up. It's a speedy and delicious snack that's thick and doughy, and often topped with grilled vegetables or stuffed with local cold cuts.

where diners bring whatever they like back to the central eating areas or sit and watch dishes being prepared at the counters. Beer and wine have their own dedicated sections and local soccer fans gather to watch games on Sundays.

Snacks and Street Food
SANDWICHIC

Via San Gallo 3r; tel. 055/281-157; Mon.-Thurs. 10am-11pm and Fri.-Sun. 10am-midnight; €5

Sandwichic is housed inside a former haberdashery. Panini have replaced textiles and sewing machines, but thread and buttons are still on display. The three street chefs aren't trying to revolutionize the sandwich—they're just obsessed with using the best bread and local hams to make them. Wine is self-served for €1 a cup. Daily specials are written on the blackboard or fresh ingredients can be chosen to create the sandwich of your dreams.

Bakeries

★ VECCHIO FORNO

*Via Guelfa 32; tel. 055/265-4069; Mon.-Sat.
7:30am-8pm; €3-5*

Florentine bread lacks salt. According to legend this was due to a Pisan blockade and the inability to import the mineral for several years. The taste for unsalted loaves stuck and dozens of *forni* (bakeries) in the center bake it every morning. Vecchio Forno is a small shop on a corner where locals come for typical *pan di ramerino,* sweet bread made with raisins and rosemary. Glass cases display tempting sandwiches, cakes, and tarts, and shelves are filled with an assortment of Tuscan breads. You can order to go or sit at one of the half-dozen stools and listen to local chatter.

GARBO

*Via Dino del Garbo 2r; tel. 055/437-8740; Mon.-Fri.
7am-8pm and Sat. 7:30am-2:30pm; €3-5*

People obsessed with bread won't mind the long walk to Garbo, a neighborhood bakery run by Carlo Scorpio and his wife, Silvia. They can spend hours talking about flour and yeast. Everything here is made by hand using local ingredients and a grindstone Carlo claims is the secret to great bread. You'll notice the difference from the smell wafting from the ovens and the perfectly stacked loaves behind the counter. Every day is dedicated to a different flavor: If you arrive on a Saturday you can sample the *paillasse* (Florentine baguette) and dried fruit buns. They also create pastries and serve a lunch menu that can be eaten on-site or taken away.

PUGI

*Piazza San Marco 9b; tel. 055/280-981; Mon.-Sat.
7:45am-3pm; €5*

If you haven't tried *schiacciata all'olio* (Tuscan focaccia), grab a number and get in line at Pugi. The *schiacciata* comes dabbed with olive oil and topped with zucchini, sliced potatoes, and red peppers, or stuffed with prosciutto ham. When it's your turn just point and gesture to the friendly uniformed ladies behind the counter. They also have great desserts and seasonal specialties at Carnevale, Easter, and Christmas. There are several other locations around the city in case you develop a habit.

Gelato

Gelato prices start at around €3 for two scoops in a cup or cone. Each additional scoop is €1. Whipped cream (*panna*) is free but you may have to ask for it.

LE BOTTEGHE DI LEONARDO

*Via de'Ginori 21r; tel. 388/345-0986; daily
12:30pm-9pm; €3-5*

Le Botteghe di Leonardo makes a great dark chocolate, but if you ask Francesco what he suggests combining it with, he won't give you a straight answer. Fortunately, he'll let you sample any flavor you like on the menu board. The gelato is kept in metal containers and out of sight. Once you've made a decision you can enjoy it on the chairs facing a *fresco.* This *gelateria* is part of a cooperative and there are several others around the city.

GELATERIA CARABÈ

*Via Ricasoli 60r; tel. 055/289-476; Mon.-Sat.
10am-midnight and Sun. 10am-9pm; €3-5*

Gelateria Carabè takes the Sicilian approach to gelato, which explains the *granite* and *cannoli* that are also available. Watch the gelato being made and enjoy it on one of the benches inside or out. Every flavor uses fresh ingredients, including almonds, hazelnuts, and pistachios imported from Sicily. There's even an olive oil and several gluten-free flavors. (Gelato is often gluten-free, but some shops use flour as a thickener, and flavors like tiramisu may contain wheat.)

SANTA CROCE

Tuscan

★ TRATTORIA DA ROCCO

*Piazza Ghiberti; tel. 339/838-4555; daily
11am-3:30pm; €5-6*

Locals have been coming to Trattoria da Rocco for more than 35 years for honest portions, Florentine specialties, and low prices.

Firsts are €6, non-fish seconds €7, and sides of vegetables €4. Rocco still does a lot of the cooking and serving and keeps regulars entertained with his good humor and jokes. The house wine, stored in straw-covered bottles, is priced by how much you drink, and desserts are all homemade. Booths at this small diner-like institution can be hard to come by and are often shared between hungry strangers. Service is fast and always cheery.

OSTERIA DEI PAZZI

Via dei Lavatoi 1r; tel. 055/234-4880; Tues.-Sun. 12:30pm-2:30pm and 7:30pm-10:45pm; €7-10

Osteria Dei Pazzi is an unassuming restaurant around the corner from Piazza Santa Croce. The sign above the entrance is vintage 1960s and little on the inside has changed since then. The food is typical Tuscan, and Italians occupy most of the tables under ceiling fans that keep the large dining room cool.

TRATTORIA PALLOTTINO

Via Isola delle Stinche 1r; tel. 055/260-8887; Tues.-Sun. 12:30pm-2:30pm and 7:30pm-10:30pm; €8-10

Trattoria Pallottino has been serving local Tuscan dishes since 1911. They make an excellent *pappa al pomodoro* and *ribollita*. The narrow dining room is paved with cobblestones and lined with wooden tables and chairs that have been used by generations of diners. There's outdoor seating along the pedestrian street near Santa Croce. Daily specials are written on a blackboard near the entrance.

ADAGIO FIRENZE

Via de' Macci 79r; tel. 055/051-7094; Mon.-Sat. 12:30pm-2:30pm and 7:30pm-11pm, Sat. dinner only; €10-12

The culinary concept behind this trendy bistro is to highlight a different Italian region every month and, depending when you arrive, you could enjoy *pesto* from Liguria or *polenta* from Alto Adige. They also feature a permanent menu of local favorites and delicious chocolate desserts.

★ IL NUGOLO

Via della Mattonaia 27r; tel. 055/094-4712; Tues.-Sat. 7:30pm-10:30pm; €10-14

Nugolo opened in 2020. So far, it seems to have survived that challenging year, and the young chefs have been rewarded for their gamble. This cozy eatery is unlike anything else in the city and gives diners a chance to sample innovative flavors from a kitchen that combines creativity with seasonal ingredients harvested from the owner's garden just outside the city. Tomatoes in dozens of varieties are the main attraction, and plating is so good it's almost a shame to eat.

Seafood

VIVO

Largo Annigoni 9 a/b; tel. 333/182-4183; Tues.-Sun. 12:30pm-2:45pm and 7:30-10:30pm; €12-15

Vivo is the latest restaurant in an up-and-coming *piazza* lined with tempting eateries. The open-plan dining room and contemporary atmosphere are a break from rustic interiors. Fish is the main attraction, and the fact that the menu changes based on the daily catch is a healthy sign.

Pizza

Pizza isn't native to Florence. It was introduced by Neapolitan immigrants and is thicker than the Roman version. Few restaurants are entirely devoted to pizza but it does appear on many menus.

LA DIVINA PIZZA

Via Borgo Allegri 50r; tel. 055/234-7498; Mon. 6:30pm-midnight, Tues.-Sat. 11:30am-3:30pm and 6:30pm-midnight; €6-8

Pizza enthusiasts who aren't interested in décor should visit La Divina Pizza. It's a *pizza al taglio* shop run by an enthusiastic father-and-son team. They pull out mouthwatering tins of pizza and *focaccia* all day long and serve it by the cut to a steady stream of clients. Choose three or four kinds and eat them inside on a little wooden tray or ask for takeaway (*per portare via*) and enjoy your pizza in Piazza Santa Croce or along the river.

CAFFÈ ITALIANO

Via dell'Isola delle Stinche 11/13r; tel. 055/289-368;
daily 12:30pm-3pm and 7pm-11pm; €8

The owner of Caffè Italiano has a wood-burning oven and is obsessed with using fresh ingredients in traditional ways. That's probably why they only serve three types of pizza: Margherita, Napoli, and Marinara. The lack of variety hasn't stopped Vincenzo D'Anetra from building a loyal following that can make finding a table inside this brick and wood-paneled *osteria* difficult.

BOTTEGA CONVIVIALE

Via Ghibellina 134r; tel. 055/246-6318; Tues-Sun.
noon-2:30pm and 7pm-11:30pm; €8-13

If you like Neapolitan-style pizza this is the place to go. There aren't that many varieties but all you really need is a good Margherita, sausage and broccoli, or four cheese, and they've got those covered. Thinner oval shaped pinsa (a mix of pizza and focaccia) are also served along with a handful of pasta dishes that are only €7 at lunch. Waiters are friendly and frequently serve complimentary drinks to locals and tourists.

CUCINA TORCICODA

Via Torta 5r; tel. 055/265-4329; daily 7pm-10:30pm;
€10-14

In recent years Cucina Torcicoda has distinguished itself with its versatility: it's a restaurant, *osteria,* and pizzeria all in one. San Marzano tomatoes, Campania mozzarella, and Tuscan oil find their way into the daily pizza special and great *calzone.* All the ingredients from the menu can be purchased at the little gourmet shop in the back.

International

The influx of Japanese and Chinese tourists as well as a steady stream of North African and East Asian immigrants has led to the diversification of dining options in Florence over the last decade. Today it's easy to find sushi and noodles in the center, and kebab shops and Indian takeaway along the streets north of Mercato Centrale where many newcomers have settled.

ARARAT

Borgo La Croce 32r; tel. 375/572-1739; daily
12:30pm-2:30pm and 7:30pm-11:30pm; €9-12

Ararat may be your only chance to taste Armenian/Georgian food in Italy, so take it. Arman and Vartan will initiate you into their culinary world and guide you through a menu of spicy skewered meats, spicy salads, and stuffed flat breads. The atmosphere is soothing and the closest you can get to Tbilisi without stepping on a plane.

DIM SUM

Via Magliabechi 9r; tel. 055/284-331; Tues.-Sun.
noon-3pm and 7pm-11pm; €14-16

Dim Sum is a small, modern restaurant with a bright interior and an open kitchen where chefs prepare southern Chinese specialties. Diners are greeted with a cup of green tea (which is continually refilled) and a menu that includes steamed appetizers, dumplings, pot stickers, noodles, and rice dishes. It fills up fast on weekends and reservations can be useful.

KOME

Via dei Benci 41; tel. 055/200-8009; Mon.-Sat.
noon-3pm and 7pm-11pm; bento box lunch special
€15, tasting menu €36

There are quite a few sushi restaurants in Florence, and Kome is one of the largest. Choose between the *kaitan* belt (€25-40) on the ground floor where experienced chefs keep the sushi, sashimi, and tempura plates coming, or head to the grill-it-yourself tables for Japanese barbecue (€40-60 for two). It's a lot of fun, but if all you're after is a shot of *sake,* the downstairs lounge has a regular Wednesday happy hour that includes appetizers.

Snacks and Street Food

The area around the Mercato di Sant'Ambrogio market is a haven for street food and several long-standing *trippaio* or **mobile tripe stands,** including **I Trippaio Fiorentino,** still operate near here.

HIPPOPIADA

Via Santa Verdiana 6r; tel. 055/246-9013; Mon.-Sat. noon-3pm and 7pm-midnight, Sun. 7pm-midnight; €4-6

Piadina wraps—flatbread stuffed with cold cuts—are an Italian fast-food favorite, and although they did not originate in Tuscany, you'll find a delicious variety at Hippopiada. The list of fillings is long and there's no English translation. Basically, it boils down to the kind of cold cut you fancy. There's baked ham, turkey, cured ham, speck, sausage, salami, and bresaola to choose from, plus which vegetables, cheese, and sauces are added. If you can't decide, pick a number from 1 to 63 and surprise your taste buds. Tuna, salmon, and vegetarian options also available.

GAUDAGNI

Via Isola delle Stinche 20; tel. 055/239-8642; Mon.-Sat. 9am-7pm; €5-8

Alimentari are small deli-like shops most visitors never enter. They carry food and drink supplies as well as freshly prepared sandwiches, pasta salads, and occasionally pizza. Gaudagni is a neighborhood stalwart around the corner from Santa Croce run by husband and wife Stefano and Stefania. They've seen the neighborhood change dramatically in the last 30 years and greet local customers like old friends. It's the perfect place to improvise a picnic or enjoy a cold beer outside in the little square. Drinks are reasonably priced and can be drunk openly—though Stefania does suggest moderation.

I TRIPPAIO FIORENTINO

Via Vincenzo Gioberto 133r; tel. 335/821-6680; Mon.-Sat. 9am-8pm; €6

Long before there were food trucks, there were food carts like this one just outside the old city walls serving tripe, better known as *lampredotto.* This working-class lunchtime meal remains popular and is prepared in a sandwich with different sauces or straight up with salt and pepper like the locals eat it. Get past any preconceptions you may have regarding organ meat and give it a try. Once you do, you'll likely be coming back for more. Beer and refreshments also served.

SEMEL

Piazza Lorenzo Ghiberti 44r; no tel., Mon.-Sat. 11:30am-2:30pm; €6-8

Locals love this cozy snack spot and gather for lunch to drink wine and feast on gourmet sandwiches filled with anchovies, fennel, and other original ingredients enjoyed on a narrow wooden counter inside or on the sidewalk outside.

Gelato

VIVOLI

Via dell'Isola delle Stinche 7r; tel. 055/292-334; Tues.-Sun. 9:30am-11pm; €3-5

Vivoli has maintained its quality since the 1930s. This is the old-school approach, with classic cream and fruit flavors and little concern about innovating or improving their English skills. Hazelnut, coffee, pear, and lemon are among the dozens of flavors available in a cone or cup at prices that may keep you coming back for more.

RIVARENO

Borgo degli Albizi 46r; tel. 055/011-8039; daily noon-midnight

If you need a benchmark to understand what great gelato should taste like, visit Rivareno. They only serve the naturally creamy good stuff that's all made on-site. Flavors include *nocciola, stracciatella,* coffee, and seasonal fruit sorbets. If you want to really indulge, have some scoops served on a crepe or waffle and kiss your dietary inhibitions goodbye.

OLTRARNO

There are fewer restaurants across the Arno River. Most are small, rustic places serving traditional Tuscan food at affordable prices. There are some notable exceptions where Michelin-starred chefs create culinary

Gelato

Gelato is just milk, sugar, and natural fruit and cacao flavors, but when those ingredients are fresh and combined with care something special happens. Here are a few basic guidelines for finding the best:

- **Avoid unnatural colors and showy displays.** Overly bright colors and gravity-defying mounds are often a sign of artificial flavoring and preservatives.

- **Sample the classics.** Start with fundamental flavors like chocolate (*cioccolato*), cream (*crema*), and hazelnut (*nocciola*).

- **Taste test.** Clerks readily provide small samples on miniature plastic spoons. Just ask: *posso provare?* (may I try?)

- **Go cone-less.** *Gelaterias* always offer a choice between cone or cup. Purists advocate the latter on the grounds of taste.

- **Get the scoop(s).** Gelato is ordered in several different sizes that usually translate into two, three, and four scoops. Each scoop can be a different flavor. There's only one size of cone, while cups come in multiple dimensions.

- **Say *sì* to whipped cream.** At the end of every order the clerk will ask an important one-word question: *panna?* Whipped cream and gelato go wonderfully together, so say *sì*! It's also free. The best *gelateria* prepare fresh *panna* daily.

One final tip: Unless you exert some authority inside a crowded *gelateria*, you may never place an order. Determine who is the last person in line when you walk in and make sure you are served after them. *Scusi, ero primo* (excuse me, I was ahead) can be very useful.

TOP *GELATERIE* IN FLORENCE

- **Rivareno:** Further proof that gelato can have an instant impact on mood. One lick and it's impossible not to smile (page 213).

---

masterpieces and *al fresco* dining includes views of olive trees and medieval walls. **Borgo San Frediano** near the river is particularly rich in gastronomic options and is lined with dozens of inviting eateries. Neighborhood squares like **Piazza Santo Spirito** are also reliable destinations for those in search of authentic flavors. Here coffee, pasta, cocktails, and gelato can all be had within a short radius. Snack bars and restaurants near the Ponte Vecchio and Palazzo Pitti often cater exclusively to tourists and are best avoided.

Tuscan
IL BRINDELLONE
Piazza Piattellina 10; tel. 055/217-879; Tues.-Sun. noon-2pm and 7:30pm-10pm; €7-10

If décor isn't essential and all you're after is Florentine classics, Il Brindellone is ideal for lunch or dinner. This *trattoria* is popular with locals, and there's jovial banter between the owner and regulars who come for the T-bones. They also prepare a very tasty *ribollita* and *pappa al pomodoro* that can easily feed two. Don't worry about reservations or dressing up.

OSTERIA DELL'ENOTECA
Via Romana 70r; tel. 055/228-618; Thurs.-Sun. 12:30pm-2:30pm and 7:30pm-11pm; €10-12

This modern rustic restaurant with a romantic brick vibe serves freshly pressed pasta and flamed grilled T-bone steaks. The lunchtime tasting menu (€40) includes a starter, steak, side, dessert, wine, water, and coffee. It's more

Gelato comes in dozens of flavors.

- **Le Botteghe di Leonardo:** The secret here is the freshness: Milk comes from Trentino, the eggs are delivered daily, and all of the fruit is seasonal (page 210).

- **Vivoli:** Classic flavors from the oldest *gelateria* in Florence. They know what they're doing and have been doing it longer than anyone else (page 213).

- **Gelateria della Passera:** Not only can you get a great scoop here, but the small triangular piazza opposite is the perfect spot to enjoy it (page 219).

than satisfying and may leave you needing a nap.

IL GUSCIO

Via dell'Orto 49a; tel. 055/224-421; Mon.-Fri. 12:30pm-2pm and 7:30pm-11pm, Sat. dinner only; €12-15

Il Guscio is a friendly, informal restaurant where first courses arrive before you can begin nibbling on the bread, and seconds include *bistecca alla fiorentina* and seared tuna. Portions are enviable and prices honest. The wine cellar includes over 400 Tuscan vintages and you can order Chianti by the glass or carafe.

TRATTORIA CASALINGA

Via Michelozzi 9r; tel. 055/218-624; daily 12:30pm-2:30pm and 7pm-10pm, Sun. lunch only; €13-15

Casalinga has been serving lunch and dinner to Oltrarno residents since 1963. Nello and Oliviero have retired now, but their three children maintain the tradition inside this simple *trattoria* where waitstaff in red aprons dash from table to table delivering local favorites. The menu is quite dense and there are dozens of possibilities for creating a memorable meal. One tasty option is the mixed *crostini* plate, followed by minestrone soup and *bollito misto*. Ask about daily specials and leave room for the *torta della nonna* dessert. If you can't arrive around opening time, make a reservation.

GUNE SAN FREDIANO

Via del Drago d'Oro 1r; tel. 055/493-9902; Tues.-Sun. 6pm-11pm; €14-16

Gune is fine dining without the pretension but all the dedication. Service is impeccable, the atmosphere is stylishly blue, and leaving is difficult. That's why it's best to show up early and have Veronica prepare you a house cocktail before sitting down to a dining experience you will remember. If you want to discover what heaven tastes like, order the radicchio risotto with tuna tartar and raspberry sauce.

Italian
TRATTORIA DELL'ORTO

Via dell'Orto 35a; tel. 055/224-148; Wed.-Mon. noon-3pm and 7:30pm-11:30pm; €8-12

Owner-chef Arturo Caminatti spends his mornings selecting ingredients from local meat and vegetable suppliers and the rest of the time in his kitchen at Trattoria dell'Orto. The result is mouthwatering plates of *crostini*, cold cuts, and chargrilled steaks that look as good as they taste. The bottles lining the movie set-like interior aren't only for show, and there's more in the vaulted cellar down below. The garden is a lovely place to eat during the summer.

ANGIOLINO

Via di Santo Spirito 36r; tel. 055/239-8976; daily 12:30pm-3pm and 7pm-10:30pm; €10-14

Angiolino is a historic *trattoria* run by three jubilant brothers, where Florentine families come for long Sunday lunches. Their menu includes handmade pasta, grilled meats, and specialty sandwiches such as lobster roll and roast beef club. Wine can be ordered by the bottle or glass, and the dark wood interior is perfect for escaping the heat outside.

Pizza

Florence doesn't have the same pizza-making tradition as Rome, but there are still plenty of places where it can be found. Most common is the thick, soft-crust Neapolitan variety. You'll also find *pizza al taglio* shops offering freshly baked trays of pizza with various toppings. These are sold by the kilo *(taglio)* and you can choose whatever dimensions you like.

VICO DEL CARMINE

Via Pisana 40r; tel. 055/233-6862; daily 7pm-midnight; €6-9

Vico del Carmine is a traditional Neapolitan pizzeria with a wood-fired oven that has satisfied several generations of stomachs. The family who runs the place also prepares southern Italian specialties, fried *antipasti,* and homemade desserts. The rustic interior is decorated like a small shrine to Naples. Getting there is a pleasant walk through the old city gates and down Borgo S. Frediano.

GUSTA

Via Maggio 46r; tel. 055/285-068; Tues.-Sun. noon-3:30pm and 7pm-11pm; €6-10

Gusta is one of the most popular pizzerias in the neighborhood, with a mix of university students, locals, and visitors vying for tables inside or outside this small and unpretentious establishment. Service is fast but friendly. Arrive early to avoid the rush or ask for takeaway and eat on the steps of Santo Spirito just a minute away.

BERBERE

Piazza de'Nerli 1; tel. 055/238-2946; Mon.-Thurs. 7pm-midnight, Fri.-Sun. 12:30pm-2:30pm and 7pm-midnight; €6-12.50

Berbere is a slightly frenetic pizzeria where you can grab a stool at the marble counter and watch pizza being made or sit down in the back room for a little more intimacy. There's a choice of dough, original toppings, and thick crust that always gets sliced before being served to diners. The selection of regionally produced craft beer is worth sampling and the

---

1: panini to go **2:** Gusta **3:** the ever-popular All'Antico Vinaio **4:** outdoor dining at La Beppa Fioraia

Focacce € 4,00

GUSTA

ll'antico Vinaio

Un Caffè, Per Favore...

Coffee is a daily ritual for thousands of Florentines who crowd into bars for their morning fix and often end their lunches with a cup. Most locals drink at the counter where there's hardly ever a wait. It's one of the cheapest pleasures in the city and rarely exceeds a euro, unless you sit down at a table or find yourself in front of Piazza della Signoria where the views increase the cost.

WHAT TO ORDER

- **Caffè:** Espresso served black. This is the most popular way of drinking coffee in Italy. Espresso has become so popular that when you order a *caffè* (coffee) you automatically receive an espresso. The espresso is served in a ceramic cup, unless *al vetro* is requested—in which case it will be poured into a shot glass.

- **Caffè Corto:** An espresso served short (*corto*), making it slightly stronger.

- **Caffè Lungo:** An espresso served long (*lungo*), making it slightly weaker.

- **Caffè Macchiato:** Espresso with a dash of steamed milk. (*Macchiato* means stained; the milk "stains" the espresso.)

- **Latte Macchiato:** The opposite of caffè macchiato—a glass of milk stained with a little coffee.

- **Cappuccino:** One of Italy's greatest exports. In Florence it's almost always ordered in the morning and often accompanied by a pastry. A cappuccino is served in a larger cup and is creamier than a caffè macchiato.

- **Marocchino:** A cross between a caffè macchiato and miniature cappuccino topped with cacao and served in a glass or ceramic cup.

- **Caffè Freddo:** Italians don't stop drinking coffee in summer, but they often order iced espresso when temperatures rise. It's served black, with milk, or topped with whipped cream.

- **Shakerato:** An espresso blended with crushed ice and served in a glass. It occasionally comes presweetened and presented in a martini glass.

- **Spremuta d'Arancia:** Tired of coffee? Order a fresh-squeezed orange juice. Most bars have sophisticated juicers and oranges are in season nearly all year long.

FLORENCE'S BEST COFFEE SHOPS

- **Amblé:** The perfect caffeine break, located near Ponte Vecchio but remote enough to feel out of the way (page 207).

- **Ditta Artigianale:** Coffee connoisseurs with locations on both sides of the Arno. This is where locals like to chill (page 206).

- **La Cité Libreria Café:** A cozy coffee hangout with comfy sofas and lots of books to browse (page 220).

piazza outside becomes a popular post-pizza hangout during the summer.

Snacks and Street Food
IL TRIPPAIO DI SAN FREDIANO
Piazza dei Nerli; no tel., Mon.-Sat. 10:30am-8:30pm; €5

Tripe has a long history in Florence and is served at market stalls and kiosks around the city. Il Trippaio di San Frediano is one of the oldest and a good place to begin a tripe tour. The menu includes the classic sandwich (€4) and gets progressively more intricate as vegetables, beans, and other meats are added. There's a row of stools facing the outdoor counter and takeaway option, which can get messy if you're not careful.

IL TRIPPAIO DI PORTA ROMANA
Piazzale di Porta Romana; no tel.; Mon.-Sat. 9am-3pm; €5

Skipping Il Trippaio di Porta Romana is like missing out on the Duomo. Mario and Manola Albergucci set up their mobile kiosk just outside the medieval walls and have been serving tripe sandwiches here for decades. He's a former butcher and prepares *lampredotto* with passion while she dishes out sides of beans, artichokes, and whatever else is in season. Diners eat at portable counters set up underneath the trees. When you're done, take a stroll through the Boboli Gardens or explore Viale Machiavelli.

Bakeries
S. FORNO
Via Santa Monaca 3r; tel. 055/239-8580; www. ilsantobevitore.com; daily 7:30am-7:30pm; €4

S. Forno is more than a bakery. At breakfast they offer a vast assortment of breads, muffins, scones, and tarts. At lunch, soups, salads, and freshly made sandwiches are accompanied by fruit juice, wine, or beer. Pull up a stool and eat underneath the barrel vaulting or head to Piazza Santo Spirito to enjoy an *al fresco* picnic. If you have a canine buddy inquire about their homemade dog biscuits.

MAMA'S BAKERY
Via della Chiesa 34r; tel. 055/219-214; Mon.-Fri. 8am-5pm, Wed.-Sun. 9am-4pm; €5

Homesick? Make a beeline for Mama's Bakery, where Matt Reinecke and his wife, Christina, prepare bagels, American-inspired cookies, cupcakes, pies, and brownies that can cure any gastronomic nostalgia. Matt can also inspire anyone contemplating a full-time move to Italy. The California native launched the bakery in 2008 and has rarely been out of the kitchen since. Mama's is popular with expats and locals who have developed a taste for American flavors made with Italian ingredients.

Gelato
★ GELATERIA DELLA PASSERA
Via Toscanella 15r; tel. 055/291-882; Tues.-Sun. noon-11pm; €2-5

Gelateria della Passera is a tiny shop facing a lovely little square. Flavors are made on the premises with fresh natural ingredients. A short line is always possible, as there's little space inside and some important decisions to make. Enjoy the flavors on one of the nearby benches where locals often gather.

LA SORBETTIERA
Piazza Torquato Tasso 11r; tel. 055/512-0336; daily 12:30pm-midnight; €2-5

Over in Piazza Tasso, children play and grandparents keep an eye them. The only *gelateria* on the square is La Sorbettiera, where people have been getting gelato since 1934. There's less variety but what they do have is top-notch. A little counter faces the street and clients order from outside. Enjoy the gelato on a stool facing a neat line of parked mopeds or in the park.

GELATERIA LA CARRAIA
Piazza Nazario Sauro 25r; tel. 055/280-695; daily 11am-midnight; €3-5

People come to Gelateria La Carraia for the chocolate and come back for all the other flavors. The cones here are nearly as tasty as the gelato and come in different colors, shapes, and varieties. This inviting parlor is located on a corner facing the two Arno bridges west of the Ponte Vecchio.

Coffee

There are coffee bars in most squares and a choice of three or four in Piazza Santo Spirito that all come with views of the church; the outdoor tables at **Caffè Ricchi** (daily 7am-11pm) are nice for sipping coffee or cocktails. Over in the triangular *piazzetta* where Via dello Sprone meets Via Toscanella, **Caffè degli Artigiani** (Via Dello Sprone 16r; tel. 055/291-882; daily 8am-1am) serves coffee out of an intimate little bar that barely seats one. Fortunately, the espresso is good and there's outdoor seating around the corner.

There are several bars in Piazza Pitti facing the palace. Street traffic and the flow of tourists along the sidewalk make these less inviting regardless of the view. For a more relaxed and authentic afternoon coffee stick to the lesser-known streets and squares of the neighborhood.

DITTA ARTIGIANALE
Via dello Sprone 5r; tel. 055/045-7163; daily 8:30am-7pm; €2-3
If you start to crave coffee and a place to hang out, head to Ditta Artigianale. The mini caffeine chain has two locations in Florence. This one is the quieter option, populated with locals sipping cappuccino on stools and comfortable armchairs or having light lunches at the tables set on two levels or out back. Baristas are friendly and there's a good chance of meeting expat bloggers like Georgette Jupe (aka Girl in Florence) who's a regular here.

LA CITÉ LIBRERIA CAFÉ
Borgo San Frediano 20r; tel. 055/210-387; daily 10am-midnight; €3-5
La Cité Libreria Café is part coffee shop, part bookshop, and both parts are bohemian. The relaxed space close to the Arno is a cultural lounge that mixes good coffee with literature, music, and theater. Rest here for as long as you

like browsing the books, using the free Wi-Fi, and discussing politics with staff.

SAN NICCOLÒ
Tuscan
★ OSTERIA ANTICA MESCITA
Via di S. Niccolò 60r; tel. 055/234-2836; daily noon-12:30am; €8-12
A number of restaurants and bars line the street leading toward Piazzale Michelangelo and San Miniato. Osteria Antica Mescita is one of the simplest. The outdoor tables are an excellent place to seek Tuscan nourishment before or after walking up the hillside. The menu consists of a half-dozen firsts and seconds, none of which exceeds €10 or has been translated into English (which is usually a good sign). If you're hungry, you can have a two-course meal for a very reasonable €12, which includes water. The house wine is more than satisfactory and served by the glass or carafe.

Italian
LA BEPPA FIORAIA
Via dell'Erta Canina 6r; tel. 055/234-7681; daily 12:30pm-2:30pm and 7:30pm-11pm; €10-13
Make the second right just beyond the medieval gates and you'll stumble onto La Beppa Fioraia. This large restaurant with indoor and outdoor seating is popular with locals for the convenient parking and happy-go-lucky atmosphere. It's perfect for families; the large lawn facing an olive grove allows children to play while parents relax in the shade. The menu includes a variety of *tagliere*-tasting platters with different combinations of cheese, cold cuts, honeys, and fruits. Vegetarians are catered for and fresh bread is served with every meal by an enthusiastic staff.

★ LA BOTTEGA DEL BUON CAFFÈ
Lungarno Benvenuto Cellini 69r; tel. 055/553-5677; Mon. 7:30pm-10:30pm, Tues.-Sat. 12:30pm-3pm and 7:30pm-10:30pm; €38, tasting menus €80-130
There are five Michelin-starred restaurants in Florence, but the elegant La Bottega del Buon Caffè is the only one facing the Arno.

Here a team of young chefs diligently prepares dishes that look like they belong in a modern art museum. What each plate lacks in quantity it makes up for in flavor and creativity. The kitchen garden supplies vegetables while other ingredients, like venison, lamb, and pigeon are all locally sourced. The interior is simple but refined, with vaulted brick ceilings and comfortable chairs, and waitstaff who anticipate every need. There are several memorable six-course tasting menus with wine pairings. Reservations recommended.

Nightlife and Entertainment

In Florence, nightlife doesn't start at night. It begins in the lazy part of the afternoon when locals stop thinking about work, and officially commences once *aperitivo* is ordered. That leads to dinner and the opportunity to dine *al fresco*. Florence is a small and dynamic city, and you're bound to stumble upon music, dancing, or a lively, crowded square. Market workers dismantling their stalls along with the shutting of doors and the opening of others are all clues to the onset of nightlife. Most of the city's nightlife options are located around the Duomo, with a few in Oltrarno and some outside the Historic Center. At bars and clubs, expect to pay €5-10 for a drink.

If you prefer a good night's rest, you won't be alone. Most Florentines turn in early, and the city doesn't have a reputation for nightlife like Rome. Still, there are enough young professionals, artists, *bon vivants,* university students, and curious travelers to provide a pleasant, relaxed energy at night.

Much of the time that energy isn't organized—it's just dozens of people watching the Ponte Vecchio at sunset or hanging out in a square. Any search for nightlife should include both sides of the Arno. **Piazza Santo Spirito** is a good destination whatever the time, and the bars and restaurants along **Borgo San Friediano** in Oltrarno are bustling from dinner until after midnight. Other likely sources of nightlife are villas and parks where stages with live music pop up during the summer. It can also be generated by a single bar or kiosk where people crowd onto sidewalks and steps, transforming a street into an outdoor lounge.

★ *APERITIVO* BARS

Locals flock to *aperitivo* bars in the late afternoon to sip on cocktails and socialize with friends. Many have outdoor seating and the coziest are located in lovely pedestrian squares like Piazza Santo Spirito where conversation flows easily and there's never any rush to get up and go. Spritz and Negroni are the most popular drinks, but Florentine barkeepers can mix more than that.

Duomo and Around
★ MANIFATTURA
Piazza di San Pancrazio 1; tel. 055/239-6367; Wed., Thurs., Sun. 5pm-midnight, Sat.-Sun. 6pm-2am

Come to this quirky cocktail bar for an excellent selection of Negronis prepared by skilled barmen who take their liquor seriously. Fresh juice extractions are served with a wide selection of gin, vodka, and vermouth. The menu is in Italian only, but staff speak many languages and are happy to advise. The indoor and outdoor seating is usually populated with groups of joyful locals. There's a great vintage playlist and finger food.

VANILLA CLUB
Via dei Saponai 14r; tel. 055/088-3708; daily 10pm-4pm

The password at this speakeasy is *over the teeth and through the gums look out stomach here it comes.* Once you've said that and filled out the €5 membership card, you're invited to enter an intimate 1930s era living room where vintage-clad bartenders serve cocktails of all kinds. The menu is hidden between the pages of old books, and complimentary snacks are served during happy hour. Dress the prohibition part and avoid wearing shorts, sneakers, and T-shirts if possible.

Santa Maria Novella
★ BAR WINTER GARDEN
Piazza Ognissanti 1; tel. 055/2716-3770; daily 11am-1am

The Winter Garden recently earned its first Michelin star and deserves it on the decoration alone; come to this hotel along the Arno for drinks, and its great hall will provide an eyeful of architecture and elegance. The meticulous bar and buffet are well stocked, and cozy living room-like niches await. A Bloody Mary prepared with the addition of *Grappa di Brunello* is the house cocktail.

Santa Croce
THE BOX
Borgo Pinti 5r; tel. 328/463-0072; daily 6pm-2am

The secret to a great bar is the welcome, and here strangers are greeted like old friends and making new ones is easy. The artsy bric-a-brac décor attracts a steady crowd of university students and flaneurs enjoying beer, wine, and cocktails in plastic cups. Prices are economical, which means the small interior fills up fast and patrons often spill out onto the sidewalk in summer.

EMPIREO
Lungarno della Zecca Vecchia 38; tel. 055/26236; daily 7:30pm-midnight

Lots of hotel bars have great views, and Plaza Luchese is no exception—but the Empireo bar on the top floor of this hotel also boasts a spectacular riverside terrace and swimming pool. From Monday to Thursday the *aperitivo* includes a meticulously prepared buffet with live music for a modest €14. On weekends there's an à la carte menu.

Oltrarno
VOLUME
Piazza Santo Spirito 5r; tel. 055/238-1460; daily 8am-1am

Don't bother asking them to turn down the music at Volume. They like things loud at this workshop-turned-bar where carpentry tools are still on display and none of the armchairs match. Bands often perform inside, though conversation is possible on the outdoor patio overlooking the square.

★ PINT OF VIEW
Borgo Tegolaio 17r; tel. 055/288-944; Sun.-Thurs. 4pm-midnight, Fri.-Sat. 4pm-1am

At Pint of View, the name is deceiving: Although they do have a quality selection of craft beer on tap, it's their original cocktails and Korean food that makes this gastropub stand out. They've created 10 unique cocktails with names like Please Don't Shoot the Zombie (Sailor Jerry Rum, pineapple and basil shrub, lime, Doppio Carvi, Caribbean syrup) and My Gun Is Only Bubbles (Beefeater 24, *prosecco*, pink grapefruit, hibiscus syrup, yuzu marmalade, egg white) that combine ingredients in surprisingly delicious ways. Happy hour is 6pm-7pm daily and includes an affordable menu of mini *bao* snacks. Staying put for dinner is a wise decision.

NOF
Borgo San Frediano 17-19r; tel. 333/614-5376; www. nofclub.it; Wed.-Mon. 7:30pm-2am

It's hard to walk past NoF and not notice musicians playing in the front window. Inside this dark, intimate bar stripped back to the essentials, Lapo, the bartender, serves pints of Heineken in plastic cups (€5) to a young-to-middle-age crowd. Dancing isn't allowed but there's lots of listening and the music gets loud. Monday is dedicated to jazz, Wednesday indie, Thursday tribute bands, and weekends feature rockers singing in Italian or English.

LOVE CRAFT
Borgo San Frediano 24r; tel. 055/269-2968; daily 6pm-2am

Whiskeyphiles will be impressed with the wall of bottles behind the bar of Love Craft. The black-clad tenders know their mash and can mix it any way you like or straight up.

Aperitivo Hour

aperitivo hour in Piazza Santo Spirito

Florentines are social, so they love to sit down for an *aperitivo* (pre-dinner drink) with friends. The city even has its own cocktail invented nearly a century ago by Count Camillo Negroni. The drink, called a Negroni, consists of Campari, vermouth, and gin. Today, cocktails are served with complimentary light snacks from 5pm onward at bars throughout Florence. There's an abundance of venues to choose from, but these are some of the best:

- **Bar Winter Garden:** Sophisticated hotel bar with plenty of plush seating and old-world décor (page 222).

- **Manifattura:** Stylish good-time bar that takes cocktails to the next level (page 221).

- **Pint of View:** Unique mix of cocktails and Korean food (page 222).

- **Coquinarius:** Shrine to Tuscan wines made even better with plates of local cheeses and cured hams (page 224).

- **Le Volpe e L'Uva:** Out-of-the-way *enoteca* with a tremendous selection of Italian vintages available by the glass or bottle (page 225).

Purists can enjoy whiskey tasters that include three varieties inside this fun-loving bar.

VILLA CORA

Viale Machiavelli 18; tel. 055/228-790; daily 7pm-midnight

Viale Machiavelli is an elegant tree-lined avenue that begins in Piazzale di Porta Romana and snakes its way up the Oltrarno hillside. There are many villas along the way, but Villa Cora is where Napoleon III's wife and conductor Claude Debussy chose to reside. You'll understand why once you get there. There are several bars and restaurants inside this refined five-star hotel including a pool bar, bistro, and roof terrace. Evenings are devoted to cocktails, tapas, and live jazz on weekends. It's a 20-minute walk or short taxi ride from Palazzo Pitti.

WINE BARS

Tuscany produces some of Italy's best wines and you can discover just how good it is at restaurants and bars around the city. But if you're really serious about wine, visit an *enoteca*. These shops are entirely dedicated to grapes and are stocked with thousands of bottles waiting to be uncorked. The varieties most commonly grown on the hillsides overlooking Florence are Sangiovese, Canaiolo, and Trebbiano. These are pressed to create Chianti, which is the world's favorite wine and tastes good with everything. If your palate craves something more sophisticated, you're ready for Brunello.

If you can't decide, that's not a problem. *Enoteche* are run by people who are passionate about wine and love sharing their knowledge. Drink rarely goes without food in Italy, and *enoteche* are great for understanding how each vintage tastes when paired with meats, cheeses, and other staples of the Tuscan larder.

Duomo and Around
★ COQUINARIUS

Via delle Oche 11r; tel. 055/230-2153; daily 12:30pm-3pm and 5:30pm-10:30pm

You'll find a mix of loyal regulars and satisfied visitors underneath the arched ceilings of Coquinarius. Every wine has a tale and you're likely to hear a few by the end of the night. This jovial *enoteca* with bare wood tables and chairs is just around the corner from the Duomo. It's full of character and serves deliciously simple dishes. Come even if you aren't hungry to enjoy a glass and read a book within a timeless setting. They also have a second location just outside Fiesole (Via Mantellini 2b; bus 7).

ENOTECA ALESSI

Via delle Oche 27r; tel. 055/214-966; shop Mon.-Sat. 9:30am-7pm, wine bar Mon.-Sat. 11:30am-7pm

When Florentines want wine, they head to this historic shop. There are over 2,500 different labels in the cellar and Tuscan wines rightfully get the majority of shelf space. Tastings are organized upstairs with themes like Tuscan Classics (€18), Great Wines of Italy (€25), Italian Whites (€15), and North to South (€29), all of which can be accompanied with plates of cured meats and cheeses. Wine purchases can be shipped back home.

ENOTECA VIGNA NUOVA

Via dei Federighi 3r; tel. 055/280-778; daily noon-midnight

This modern wine bar has a vast selection of Tuscan wines by the glass or bottle. Prices are honest, and there's plenty of tempting cheese and cold cut boards to sample along with the wine. The friendly, knowledgeable staff can answer most questions about vintages and terroir and offer plenty of advice.

Santa Maria Novella
ENOTECA BRUNI

Borgo Ognissanti 25r; tel. 055/388-0177; daily 12:30pm-2:30pm and 7:30pm-10:30pm

They know a lot about wine at Enoteca Bruni and are continually learning more about their favorite subject. They take pleasure in the infinite possibilities and have a preference for biological vineyards in Tuscany. Jonathal can advise you on single or mixed varietals and accompany them with original appetizers.

San Lorenzo and San Marco
DIVINA ENOTECA

Via Panicale 19r; tel. 055/292-723; Tues.-Sun. 10:30am-8:30pm

As you read this, Brunello, Chianti, and Montalcino are aging in the cellar below Divina Enoteca opposite the San Lorenzo market. What started as a deli serving fried cod has become a reliable address for sampling classic Tuscan vintages. To accompany a glass, choose from a *bruschetta*, panini, or mixed plates of cured meat served with bread. It's all eaten on a marble table where strangers frequently become friends.

Santa Croce
VINERIA SONORA

Via degli Alfani 39r; tel. 055/386-0191; Tues.-Sun. 5pm-1am

Vineria Sonora translates to Sound Winery,

Renaissance Wine Windows

Small holes built near the entryways of many Renaissance palaces allowed 16th-century wine merchants to carry on doing business during the plagues that periodically devastated the city. Clients would slip their flasks through the miniature windows to be filled. Contact during payment was avoided by placing coins on metal pallets that were disinfected with vinegar.

Today, nearly 180 of these *buchette del vino* (wine windows) are still visible around the city, and several found new life after the coronavirus pandemic hit in 2020. You can use a wine window to order wine, spritz, or ice-cream at **Osteria delle Brache** (Santa Croce, Piazza dei Peruzzi 5r; Tues.-Sun. 11am-4pm and 6pm-midnight), **Babae** (Oltrarno, Via Santo Spirito 21r; Tues.-Thurs. 6pm-midnight, Fri. 6pm-2am, Sat. noon-2am), and **Vivoli** (Santa Croce, Via Isola delle Stinche 7r; Tues.-Sat. 7:30am-midnight; Sun. 9am-midnight).

The **Buchette del Vino Cultural Association** (https://buchettedelvino.org) provides a map that simplifies finding the windows around town.

Wine is served through Renaissance-era windows scattered around Florence.

and the idea here is to combine good music with great wine. It works, and every week musicians or DJs liven up this small, all-white locale. Natural organic wines without additives feature heavily on the list, and owners Andrea and Laura personally select all their labels. Reservations are accepted and useful if you want to ensure a seat.

Oltrarno
★ LE VOLPE E L'UVA

Piazza dei Rossi 1r; tel. 055/239-8132; daily 11am-3pm and 6pm-9pm

Minutes from the Ponte Vecchio, Le Volpe e L'Uva has been serving some of the city's hardest-to-find Italian and French wines for over 20 years. They do it unpretentiously and with a passion that is contagious. The *stuzzichini* (appetizers) are simple but satisfying. Cheese plates served with honey and mustard and *crostone* topped with Asiago are set tantalizingly on a circular counter where wine is the favorite topic of conversation. Reservations are useful for getting a table outside.

OBSEQIUM

Borgo San Jacopo 17; tel. 055/216-849; Tues.-Thurs. 11am-8pm and Fri.-Sun. 11am-10pm

A reliable place for sampling local Tuscan vintages. Choose a bottle or a glass and accompany it with *taglieri* (plates) of regional cured hams, cheese, and fresh Tuscan bread. The owners are happy to advise inside this bright two-room rustic shop lined with bottles. It's perfect for making conversation and educating one's palate.

San Niccolò
FUORI PORTI

Via del Monte alle Croci 10r; tel. 055/234-2483; daily noon-11:30pm

The San Niccolò area of Oltrarno has a wonderful bohemian feel that remains unspoiled by tourism. It's a great place to drink wine, and the fact that Fuori Porti has wine glasses set on the tables is a good sign. In summer, you can sit outside and choose from over 500 labels the owners have selected from the region's smaller wineries. The *crostini* and *carpaccio* make wonderful appetizers and there's plenty on the menu if you develop an appetite.

PERFORMING ARTS
Concerts

Music isn't hidden away in Florence. It's out in the open and you'll hear violinists performing on street corners and singers belting out *arias* in neighborhood squares. Street musicians are common and a variety of instruments from accordions to flutes serenade pedestrians. Melodies reverberate off the stone walls in summer, and finding music only requires following your ears. Organized concerts are held in the larger squares like Piazza della Signoria where orchestras perform from the Loggia Lanzi. Summer events are also staged in parks and historic villas around the city. There are musical festivals from May to September and many bars regularly feature live music nights or DJ sets. Florence is also an occasional stop for international acts, and megaconcerts are held in the soccer stadium or Nelson Mandela Forum.

Squares, villas, and churches have concerts scheduled throughout the summer. The city's youth orchestra performs several times a week in Piazza della Signoria. They usually start in the late afternoon and impromptu audiences sit wherever they can.

Theater and Opera
TEATRO VERDI

Via Ghibellina 99; tel. 055/212-320; www. teatroverdionline.it; box office Mon.-Sat. 10am-1pm and 4pm-7pm; €15 and up

Teatro Verdi near Santa Croce is one of the longest-operating theaters in the city. It has a classic red-velvet interior and six tiers of seating that soar above the stage. There's room for over 1,000 spectators who come for the Tuscan regional orchestra, which performs a varied repertoire from October until May. Throughout the year the theater also hosts concerts, musicals, ballet, and plays.

TEATRO DELLA PERGOLA

Via della Pergola 12-32; tel. 055/076-3333; www. teatrodellapergola.com; box office Mon.-Sat. 9:30am-6:30pm; €18 and up

Teatro della Pergola was one of the first theaters to introduce box seats in Italy. These were owned by wealthy families and some say the divisions were built to prevent bickering between rival clans. Only one is still privately held and they all provide great views of the ornate chandeliered ceiling and gilded wooden interior, which looks like a wedding cake. Plays are the mainstay of the theater and some of the finest Italian actors regularly appear on the illustrious stage. If you can't make a show, come for a drink at the Caffè (Tues.-Sun. 10am-late) inside the grand entrance hall or enjoy the buffet *aperitivo* on performance nights 7pm-9pm.

TEATRO NICCOLINI

Via Ricasoli 3-5; tel. 055/094-6404; www. teatroniccolini.com

Located near the Duomo, Florence's oldest theater is the third largest in the city and recent renovation has restored all its 17th-century charm. Acoustics are great, sight lines perfect, and performances of the highest standards. There's a nice café inside and tickets to cozy box seats located along the four tiers are surprisingly reasonable. The season includes a mix of orchestra and theatrical works.

OPERA DI FIRENZE

Piazza Vittorio Gui 1; tel. 055/200-1278; www. operadifirenze.it; box office Mon.-Sat. 10am-6pm

The Opera di Firenze provides a stark architectural contrast to the rest of the city. The modern interior is split into several levels with comfortable seating and fantastic sound. Classics like *Madame Butterfly* and *The Barber of Seville* are seasonal mainstays. Ticket prices range from €10 for the upper gallery to €80 for front-row seats. The opera house is located west of the center near Parco delle Cascine and can be reached by tram or on foot in less than 20 minutes from the train station.

TEATRO DEL SALE

Via dei Macci 111r; tel. 055/200-1492; www.
teatrodelsale.com; Tues.-Sat. 9am-10:30pm and Sun.
9am-2:30pm

Perhaps the most original theater in Florence is Teatro del Sale, located in a 14th-century convent. It's a dinner theater operated in association with the Cibreo restaurant and serving dazzling dishes created by Fabio Picchi. The curtain rises in the early evening and performances range from classical, jazz, and blues to poetry readings and one-act plays. To enter this versatile locale, you'll need to become a member; it's a formality practiced by many clubs in the city and in this case only costs €5. Reservations recommended.

FESTIVALS AND EVENTS

Florence has a rich and varied cultural calendar, but the most dramatic annual events are those related to religious holidays and feast days. Many involve re-creations with hundreds of participants in historical costume. It may appear like playacting for the sake of tourists, but these celebrations have ancient origins and are ingrained into Florentine consciousness. Although religious fervor has declined, thousands of locals are still passionate about these unique events and participate with pride.

Like many cities Florence has its own changing of the guard ceremony that dates back to 1529 when the city was under siege by Carlo V. The threat of attack is long gone but local members of the Corteo Storico (historic parade) keep the tradition alive on the first Sunday of every month in front of Palazzo Vecchio. Guards are accompanied by a contingent of musicians all dressed in detailed Renaissance costumes. The exchange of arms occurs at 9am, 10am, 11am, noon, and 1pm, and lasts around 15 minutes. It is cancelled in the event of rain.

Spring

Easter isn't a formality in Florence; it's a highlight. Even if you aren't a fan of organized religion you can taste the treats and watch festivities like the Scoppo del Carro (Blowing Up of the Cart) on Easter morning. The tradition dates back to the Crusades when a local knight brought back three stones from Christ's tomb. The rocks were later used to light sparks that symbolized the renewal of life and brought fire to the hearths of the city's families. It was a big deal then and still fills Piazza del Duomo with thousands of onlookers. Festivities start with a historical parade at 10am that weaves through the center and arrives at the Duomo at 11am, where the archbishop lights an enormous cart piled high with fireworks.

Summer

The Feast of San Giovanni (June 24) celebrates one of the city's most loved heroes. Giovanni Battista was known for his teachings as well as his courageous and determined spirit. He was made patron saint of Florence in the 11th century, and June 24 has been his day ever since. Events are held throughout the day. At 8am, you can attend mass in the baptistery or watch the long parade that sets off a half hour later from Via Folco Portinari. Participants in Renaissance-era dress parade slowly through streets until arriving in Piazza del Duomo. Honors are bestowed upon the deserving at Palazzo Vecchio in the afternoon and the Calcio Storico final is played at 5pm in Piazza Croce. The day ends with fireworks over the Arno (best viewed from the bridges and the Oltrarno hillside) at 10pm.

Many Florentines leave the city during the summer, but there are still enough around to celebrate the popular saint and protector San Lorenzo on August 10. At 10am a parade of citizens in Renaissance regalia heads from Palazzo di Parte Guelfa near Ponte Vecchio to Palazzo Vecchio; there the city banner is collected and brought to Basilica di San Lorenzo. Festivities continue from 9:30pm onward in Piazza San Lorenzo with a traditional feast of *pasta al pomodoro* and free watermelon. There's music and dancing, too.

Fall

Festa della Rificolona (Sept. 7) is a popular feast connected to harvest season, when farmers would make the journey to Florence to sell their goods and celebrate the birth of Mary. They carried lanterns held aloft on long sticks that remain an integral part of the celebration. You can find them at the traditional folk and food market held for the occasion in Piazza Santissima Annunziata behind Galleria dell'Accademia. At night floating lanterns are lit in the San Niccolò neighborhood and placed in the Arno to slowly drift downstream.

Every guild has its day, and for winemakers it's the last Saturday of September. Since the 13th century this has been the time to bring new wine into town to be blessed. The wine in question was Valdisieve, and today the **Carro Matto** (Crazy Cart) re-creates the winemakers' ingenious way of transporting 2,800 flasks on a single carriage. The event begins with an afternoon procession from Piazza del Duomo through the surrounding streets. It's a colorful parade of heralds, flag wavers, and trumpeters performing traditional pageantry. Later the cart is drawn to Piazza della Signoria where festivities continue and wine flows freely for all to enjoy.

Winter

La Cavalcata dei Re Magi is held on Epiphany (Jan. 6) and is celebrated with an elaborate parade. It begins at 2:15pm and is led by the wise men, who walk from Palazzo Pitti over Ponte Vecchio and through Piazza della Signoria to Piazza del Duomo. The most spectacular part is the 500 participants representing all walks of Renaissance society. There are soldiers, monks, farmers, aristocrats, and maidens bearing flags, playing drums, pulling carts, and doing everything the way they were done in 1417 when the tradition started.

You can tell **Carnevale** season has begun when calorie-intensive desserts begin appearing in pastry shop windows. Festivities last from late January until *martedi grasso* (Mardi Gras or Fat Tuesday). It was the traditional day of excess when peasants filled up on the foods they would give up for Lent (meat, eggs, and milk) and occurs 47 days before Easter. The favorite temptation is *Schiacciata Fiorentina,* a two-level sponge cake with a cream filling topped with powdered sugar and a pinch of cacao. But eating isn't the only festivity: The masked fun begins on the Thursday prior to Mardi Gras. The highlight is the parade on the following Tuesday when floats leave Piazza Ognissanti and weave their way around the city until they reach Piazza della Signoria. There's always an international element, with participants from Brazil, China, Mexico, or the United States. At the end a prize is awarded to the best costumes and a local children's choir performs. There are many other events around the city and younger travelers can wear their disguises to the **Carnevale dei Bambini** (Sat.-Sun. 2pm-6pm) in Piazza Ognissanti.

Shopping

Shopping in Florence ranges from international boutiques housed in Renaissance-era buildings to simple open-air street markets. The city offers plenty of fashion products. After all, this is where Guccio Gucci was born, and where stylists like Ferragamo and Cavalli began their illustrious careers. The Historic Center is lined with luxury boutiques that attract the brand-conscious. For everyone else, there are outdoor leather markets lined with scores of stalls where bags, wallets, and belts come in countless variations. Clothes, antiques, leather, stationery, and ceramics can all be found in the city at prices that are lower than in Rome or Venice.

Although many traditional shops have

closed or moved outside the city, handmade products can still be found in Florence. To find them just stroll through the backstreets. These often lead to dusty workshops where craftspeople are busy chiseling stone, sanding wood, painting canvas, welding metal, and performing ancient skills that have been preserved for generations. For curious travelers, these shops are the most interesting and where you can actually see how things are made.

Most of the city's commercial activity occurs in the Historic Center, so it's a good place to begin a shopping spree. Besides the megastores, the largest streets and covered markets are located here and provide a lively experience that may require some bargaining. When negotiating, remember that if the asking price seems high it probably is and it never hurts to ask for a discount. Italians do it all the time. There's also a good chance you may be approached on the street. Itinerant peddlers are less aggressive than in Rome; however, they usually offer the same selfie sticks, fake bags, trinkets, and other gadgets of dubious quality. Unless you absolutely need a glow-in-the-dark rubber bracelet, save your money for something that's made in Florence.

DUOMO AND AROUND
Leather
BISONTE
Via del Parione 31-33r; tel. 055/215-722; Mon.-Sat. 10:30am-7pm
Everything is meticulously handmade at the Bisonte, where new collections are presented every year and exported all over the world. Great bags, wallets, belts, and accessories for men and women.

Stationery
IL PAPIRO
Piazza del Duomo 24r; tel. 055/281-628; daily 10am-7pm
Florence's primary sustainer of the art of paper production is Il Papiro, which operates six shops in the Historic Center and one over the river in Oltrarno (Via Guicciardini

47r; tel. 055/277-6351). These are like small temples devoted to stationery and the art of writing. If you still enjoy using a pen and sending letters or postcards, this is a mandatory stop. Three of the shops provide demonstrations of how marbled paper is made. These occur spontaneously when stores aren't busy and shop assistants have the 15-20 minutes it takes to make a sheet of marbled paper. You can search for a colorful book cover, notepad, or card while you wait for your piece of craftsmanship to finish. Prices range, but there's stationery for every budget.

ALBERTO COZZI
Via del Parione 35r; tel. 055/294-968; Tues.-Sat. 9am-1pm and 2:30pm-7pm
The smell of paper is strong at Alberto Cozzi. It's all made by Alberto and his siblings in a small workshop dedicated to rebinding and restoring worn-out editions of old books along with creating new stationery of all kinds and colors. There's a second location over the river on Via Sant'Agostino 21.

Clothing and Accessories
The area around Piazza della Repubblica is the fashion heart of Florence. Gucci, Prada, and many other designer labels are all located here. Luxury is concentrated around Via de' Tornabuoni and Via della Vigna Nuova and many flagship stores are housed within *pallazi* that would make any museum envious. The big names can be slightly intimidating but entering does not necessarily lead to buying—and walking through the elegant interiors is a pleasure in itself. There are also many appealing lesser-known boutiques that are usually a great deal less expensive. If you happen to arrive in August or January, you'll also be in time to enjoy the sale season when merchandise is significantly discounted.

SALVATORE FERRAGAMO
Piazza di Santa Trinita 5r; tel. 055/356-2846; daily 11:30am-7pm
Salvatore Ferragamo began making shoes in Hollywood before returning to Florence and

setting up shop in **Palazzo Spini Feroni**. It's one of the largest buildings in the city and the ground floor is still used to display the fashion house's latest creations. The architecture is as interesting as the shoes, but if you have a fetish **Museo Ferragamo** (€8, free first Sun. of every month) contains hundreds of pairs from different eras. An audio guide is available along with guided tours in English on the first Saturday of every month at 10am and 11am upon reservation (tel. 055/356-2466).

DESII VINTAGE

Via de Conti 17-21r; tel. 055/230-2817; Mon.-Sat. 10:30am-7:30pm

On a side street off Via de' Tornabuoni, somewhat less glamorous shops like Desii Vintage wait to be discovered. Desii is an original vision of menswear that combines old and new, hip and classic, into one wearable look. It's difficult to resist buying at least one shirt or sweater and making the rest of your wardrobe jealous.

GERARD LOFT

Via dei Pecori 36r; tel. 055/282-491; Mon. noon-7:30pm, Tues.-Sat. 10am-7:30pm, Sun. 2:30pm-7:30pm

Gerard Loft sells cool. The shop stocks men's, women's, and children's brands that are a couple of seasons ahead of fashion. Labels include Munich Vintage 55, Swear, N.D.C., and limited-edition lines. The store feels like a gallery where the clothes are the art. Prices are high but there are discounted items on the second floor.

Antiques
ANTICHITA' LE COLONNE

Via del Moro 38; tel. 055/283-690; Mon.-Fri. 10am-7pm, Sat. 9am-6pm

Antichita' Le Colonne is a large shop filled with furniture and curiosities. Merchandise is randomly displayed between stone columns and not always easy to reach. The owners can date items and explain the use of some devices that haven't been operated for decades.

Souvenirs
LA BOTEGGA DEL CHIANTI

Borgo Santi Apostoli 41r; tel. 055/283-410; Mon.-Fri. 8am-7pm, Sat. 9am-7pm

La Botegga del Chianti hasn't changed much since it opened in 1934. You'll find the same wooden spoons, olive oil, copper tins, and ceramics they've always sold. It may be a little dusty and crammed with an eclectic mix of Tuscan products, but you're bound to find an interesting gift.

Markets
LOGGIA DEL MERCATO NUOVO

Piazza del Mercato Nuovo, intersection of Via Calimala and Via Porta Rossa

Loggia del Mercato Nuovo is one of the prettiest covered markets in the city and has been used for different commercial activities since it was completed in 1551. Where silk and straw hats were once sold, leather is now the trade of choice and a dozen or so kiosks set up shop every day 9am-6:30pm. Visit the *loggia* after the market has closed and see the *pietra dello scandalo,* a circular stone embedded in the center of the market where debtors were chained and beaten during the Renaissance. Also within the market is the **Fontana del Porcellino** (bronze boar fountain) whose shiny nose is rubbed for good luck by tourists and locals alike.

Ceramics

In Italy, pottery is a little like pasta—every region produces its own particular style. Historically, the town of Montelupo a short distance down the Arno supplied ceramics to Florence and became famous for its colorful style depicting floral and abstract patterns. Today, decorative and everyday pottery is still produced and sold.

IL SOLE NEL BORGO

Via della Spada 30r; tel. 055/246-6495; Mon.-Fri. 11am-1pm and 4:30pm-6pm, Sat. 11:30am-5pm

The pottery inside Il Sole Nel Borgo is less traditional in design and has a vibrant country feel that can brighten a meal. Colorful jugs, plates, and platters are hand-painted by the two sisters running the shop, which doubles as a bistro where you can try drinking from the ceramics before buying.

ARMANDO POGGI

Via dei Calzaiuoli 103; tel. 055/211-719; Mon.-Sat. 10am-7:30pm, Sun. 11am-7pm

Armando Poggi has been selling ceramics since the 1930s. The store has an array of elegant objects as well as platters, trays, vases, and pitchers for everyday purposes. They're used to dealing with international customers and ship everywhere in the world.

SANTA MARIA NOVELLA
Antiques

Tuscany has always been a good source of antiques, and there's been a thriving trade in relics, artwork, furniture, and bric-a-brac since the Renaissance. Dozens of stores can be found along **Via dei Fossi** and **Via del Moro**. These vary from galleries with a limited number of fine pieces to small shops cluttered with collectibles.

BARBARA GALLORINI ANTICHITA

Piazza degli Ottaviani 9r; tel. 055/230-2608; daily 10am-7pm

Barbara Gallorini Antichita is crowded with interesting items. The owner believes that anything can become a collectible, and it shows in her shop, which is filled with jewelry, candelabra, frames, books, and sculptures from different centuries. Although prices are marked, don't hesitate to ask for a discount *(un sconto)* when wavering to purchase or not.

Perfume
OFFICINA PROFUMO

Via della Scala 16; daily 9am-8pm; tel. 055/436-8315; daily 10:30am-7pm

Officina Profumo is Florence's oldest pharmacy, dating back to when pharmacies sold mixed herbs and medicine was in its infancy. Locals don't understand what all the fuss is about but the cavernous rooms attract a steady stream of visitors who come to sniff the neatly arranged essences, perfumes, and soaps. Many of the aromatic scents are created using centuries-old formulas. Helpful multilingual assistants can guide you through the vast assortment of cosmetic and holistic products.

SAN LORENZO AND SAN MARCO
Leather

A good place to start searching for leather is the **San Lorenzo street market** that runs along Via dell'Ariento adjacent to the central market. It is open from early morning to early evening 365 days a year. The street is lined with stands selling every type of leather product. Behind these are narrow shop fronts with even more leather to be examined.

There are many shops beyond the market that transform leather into stylish designer goods. If you're after shoes, Via dei Cerretani and Via Pellicceria near the Duomo are good streets to browse.

BIBI

Via dell'Ariento 12r; tel. 055/230-2400; daily 9am-7pm

Maurizio arrived in Florence in 1970 from Iran to become an architect but ended up in the leather trade instead. He opened BiBi several decades ago and has been a fixture of the San Lorenzo street market ever since. Outside his stall is lined with handbags, wallets, book covers, and key chains of every type. Inside his narrow store next door you'll find jackets, belts, and larger accessories on the walls.

Books

Bibliophiles and librarians will appreciate the amount of shelf space in Florence. Anyone looking for secondhand editions and out-of-date manuscripts should examine the bookshops on **Via dei Servi** (Bartolini at 72) and around the **Biblioteca Nazionale** (Piazza dei Cavallegeri 1; Mon.-Fri. 8:15am-7pm and Sat. 8:15am-1:30pm). A large **Feltrinelli** (Piazza della Stazione 14; Mon.-Sat. 7am-8pm and Sun. 8am-8pm) with a bar is located inside the train station and is a good place to

pick up reading material before departing for Rome or Venice. A second, less hectic location is located in Piazza della Repubblica 26-29 (Mon.-Sat. 9am-8pm and Sun. 10am-8pm).

Markets
MERCATO CENTRALE

Piazza del Mercato Centrale/Via dell'Ariento; tel. 055/239-9798; daily 8am-midnight

Mercato Centrale is the largest covered food market in Florence and attracts as many local shoppers as curious visitors. Florentines huddle around the fruit, vegetable, meat, and fish stands while tourists take pictures and browse the cheese and wine shops. There are dozens of stalls selling dried as well as fresh foods, making it a good place to purchase ingredients for a picnic. Mornings are busy with greengrocers entertaining clients and sharing gossip. At one end of the ground floor are a number of stalls selling specialty dishes that can be eaten at tables and counters that fill up fast at lunchtime. Head to **Narbone,** part of the market since it opened in 1872, where Stefano has been preparing beef and tripe sandwiches over half his life. Salt and pepper are the traditional condiments, and if there's room at the marble tables you can sit and watch the stream of visitors who come to this historic eatery. The food court on the second floor of the market is open daily 10am-midnight.

SAN LORENZO STREET MARKET

Piazza San Lorenzo and Via dell'Ariento; daily 8am-8pm

The San Lorenzo Street Market is a busy open-air market on the pedestrian streets immediately surrounding Mercato Centrale. There are hundreds of regulated stalls selling T-shirts, jewelry, notebooks, and, most of all, leather. It's a browser's paradise and the multicultural vendors aren't too pushy. Many operate stand-alone stores behind their stalls where you can find higher-quality products.

Prices are pretty standardized throughout the market and relatively cheap, but haggling is not uncommon and feigning disinterest can save you money. It's open 365 days a year from early morning to late afternoon.

SANTA CROCE
Leather
BOTEGGA FIORENTINA

Borgo dei Greci 5; tel. 055/295-411; Mon.-Sat. 10am-7pm

Botegga Fiorentina near Piazza Santa Croce is a good destination for bags. They pay close attention to stitching which can make a big difference in how a bag looks and how long it can resist daily wear and tear. Several other stores nearby offer original leather creations.

LEATHER SCHOOL (SCUOLA DI CUOIO)

Via S. Giuseppe 5r; tel. 055/244-533; www. scuoladelcuoio.com; daily 10am-6pm, closed Sun. in autumn and winter

Many *bottegas* were once located in the streets around Santa Croce, and the area remains a good place to hunt for leather goods. You can even visit the Scuola di Cuoio or Leather School to discover how leather is transformed. Prices are slightly higher and products are on the classic side, but it doesn't get more authentic than this. They also provide 1-hour tours (10:30am and 2:30pm; €16) that recount the history of the school and demonstrate the production process. Anyone obsessed with leather can sign up for one of their courses or intensive workshops (Mon.-Fri.; €110-220, prices vary according to participants) where you'll learn how to make book covers, belts, or pouches from leather masters. Tours and workshops must be reserved in advance.

Arts and Crafts
FLORENCE FACTORY

Via dei Neri 6-8r; tel. 055/205-2952; Tues.-Sat. 11:30am-7:30pm

This neat contemporary shop carries handmade clothing and decorative objects produced by creative local artisans. There's a

---

1: San Lorenzo street market **2:** traditional antique market in Piazza Santo Spirito **3:** Viviana at work inside Hello Wonderful **4:** La Botegga del Chianti

stylish mix of jewelry, hats, shoes, and household items that make far superior souvenirs than any of the cheap plastic stuff sold around the Duomo. Stock is constantly replenished, and dedicated staff are happy to recount the story behind every item. Great prices considering the quality.

Clothing and Accessories
SOCIÉTÉ ANONYME
Via Giovan Battista Niccolini 3f; tel. 055/386-0084; Mon. 3:30pm-7:30pm and Tues.-Sat. 11am-7:30pm
Browse this chic minimal womenswear boutique to discover next season's trends. They carry a variety of cool brands and have many sizes in stock. The young staff are friendly and aren't in a rush to sell anything. There is a great shoe section with prices you'd expect for top labels.

Perfume
Perfume isn't often associated with Florence, but it should be. During the Renaissance, the art of making perfume prospered in Florence. The city might still be associated with perfume if Caterina de Medici hadn't embarked to Paris with her personal perfumer, who shared his *savoir faire* with an eager audience of noblemen and women. They enthusiastically adopted the habit of dousing themselves in scent and helped make France the new center of perfume production.

AQUA FLOR
Borgo Santa Croce 6; tel. 055/234-3471; daily 10am-1pm and 2pm-6pm
They haven't forgotten how to make perfume in Florence, and a visit to Aqua Flor will dazzle the nose. Inside this elegant shop you can sniff hundreds of essences and choose one of the unique blends contained in beautiful bottles on which your initials can be engraved. If you're really serious, spend an afternoon with the house perfumer who will analyze the pH level of your skin and help create a personalized scent. It's expensive and the session must be reserved in advance, but there's nothing like *eau de you*. Ready-to-wear scents start

from €50 and a one-of-a-kind perfume costs €500.

Markets
MERCATO DI SANT'AMBROGIO
Piazza Lorenzo Ghiberti; tel. 055/248-0778; Mon.-Sat. 7am-2pm
Mercato di Sant'Ambrogio is a lively food market a few minutes north of Piazza Santa Croce. It hasn't been gentrified for tourists, and locals make up the majority of shoppers. Outside it's a bazaar with a little of everything on display including seasonal fruit and vegetables. Inside is entirely dedicated to gastronomy, with stalls covering all food groups. If you're not looking for ingredients but just want to sit down and eat, **Trattoria da Rocca** (daily 11am-3pm) is the neighborhood institution. Arrive as close to noon as possible as the booths fill up fast. The menu is as simple as the décor but soup and pasta dishes are substantial and priced to please.

MERCATO DELLE PULCI
Largo Pietro Annignoni; Mon.-Sat. 9am-7:30pm
The flea market is located across the street from Mercato di Sant'Ambrogio in a new covered building. The neatly arranged shops sell an odd mix of antique toys, watches, vintage clothes, plates, 19th-century postcards, and used doorknobs. If you're hunting for vinyl records or first-edition books, there's a good chance of finding them here.

OLTRARNO
In Oltrarno shopping takes on more intimate dimensions. Few if any fashion labels are located here and the area is home to smaller shops and studios devoted to objects of art, antiques, craft, and one-of-a-kind items.

Leather
Production of leather goods in Florence has decreased dramatically over the last few decades and the workshops that were once common are getting harder to find. Those that do remain operate on a very small scale and produce everything on-site.

Made in Florence

LEATHER

Leather has a long history in Florence, where the transformation of hide into articles of clothing, bags, and other items goes back centuries. Most leather is still made near Florence but production has moved to large industrial sites outside the city. That doesn't mean leather is cheap. Both the raw material and the skilled labor are costly.

Today there are countless shops selling goods and not all quality is the same. There are a couple things every leather shopper should consider:

- **Label:** If the label is sewn on, it's a good sign. If it's glued on or the stitching is faulty, walk away.

- **Location:** Outdoor stalls and markets meet the demands of millions of tourists looking for low-priced souvenirs, but the best leather products aren't found on the street. If you're serious about leather, you need to shop indoors, where the finest handcrafted items are displayed.

- **Price:** A nice wallet should run around €20, a handbag €50, and a medium-sized carrying bag €100. Prices vary, and browsing is the best way to find a compromise between quality and cost. Whatever sounds too cheap probably is. The saying around here is: *è meglio pagare di più una volta che di meno molte volte* (it's better to pay more once than less many times). It's a convincing argument.

MARBLED PAPER

Paper production has a long history in Florence, though the marble variety for which the city is famous didn't originate here. Turks had been using the technique long before the Florentines, who did have the good sense to begin creating their own. The skill was widely diffused throughout Europe; however, today only Florence continues to produce significant quantities.

The process is fairly simple. First, colors are added to a rectangular glass basin containing a little water. Next, they're delicately brushed into the characteristic marble pattern. Finally, a sheet of stock paper is placed on top. The paper absorbs the color and is removed and hung to dry. At that point it's only a matter of minutes before the piece is finished.

Il Papiro has a near monopoly on marbled paper, and there are a handful of shops around the city where you can purchase stationery and watch how it's made. The branch at Via de'Tavolini 13r periodically demonstrates the process and allows customers to make their own colorful sheets (page 229). **Giuliano Giannini e Figlio** on the other side of the Arno has no intention of becoming a chain store—and that's a good thing for anyone who stops in and learns from the father-and-son team who are keeping the art of stationery-making alive (page 236).

ALI WORKSHOP

Via Toscanella 9r; tel. 055/217-025; Mon.-Sat. 11am-5pm

At Ali Firenze Laboratorio, Alicia and Ivana cut and sew leather into handbags, key chains, and other interesting accessories. Prices are reasonable and you can watch them at work inside their one-room studio.

DIMITRI VILLORESI BAGS

Via D'Ardiglione 22; tel. 366/453-4867; Mon.-Sat. 9:30am-1pm and 3:30pm-8pm

At Dimitri Villoresi Bags you're guaranteed to find one-of-a-kind leather accessories. Owner and artisan Dimitri Villoresi does all the designing and stitching himself. He's been advocating the importance of craftsmanship for over a decade and after a few minutes in his workshop you'll know exactly what "made in Florence" means. Prices are higher than the leather markets on the other side of the river, but items are guaranteed to last decades and get better with age.

Stationery
GIULIANO GIANNINI E FIGLIO
*Piazza Pitti 37r; tel. 055/212-621; Mon.-Sat.
10am-7:30pm and Sun. 11am-7pm*

Giuliano Giannini e Figlio is one of the oldest shops in Florence and has been selling stationery since 1856. There's a pleasant smell of paper and ink inside this unlikely shop near Palazzo Pitti. The inside is lined with shelves full of temptations for office or home, and workshops are organized by the fifth generation of the same family. Basic demonstrations last 30-40 minutes, but if you want to learn how to bind a book you should count on a couple of hours. Reservations are required and prices vary depending on the number of participants.

Antiques
There are a number of antique stores in Oltrarno. **Via Maggio** is the main thoroughfare for serious antique hunters.

MAURIZIO & SALICI
*Via Santo Spirito 32r; tel. 328/716-7049; Mon.-Sat.
9am-7pm*

Maurizio of Maurizio & Salici sells items you don't need but would like to own anyway. Don't call it shabby chic, or he'll remind you everything is antique down to the 1920s office plaques and late-19th-century gilded mirrors. Generally speaking, nothing here is more than 200 years old. It all looks good on a coffee table, shelf, or mantle. Prices are not listed and there's some room for negotiation, but like every good dealer, Maurizio knows the value of everything he sells.

PIUMACCIO D'ORO
*Borgo San Frediano 65r; tel. 055/239-8952;
Mon.-Fri. 8:30am-1pm and 2:30pm-7:30pm, Sat.
9:30am-12:30pm and 3:30pm-7:30pm*

The Malenotti family has operated Piumaccio d'Oro for over 70 years. That's a lifetime of antique restoration and creation. The techniques practiced in the small workshop and displayed in the store result in one-of-a-kind tables, chests, chairs, and smaller objects found nowhere else.

Clothing and Accessories
HELLO WONDERFUL
Via Santa Monaca 2; no tel.; daily 10:15am-7:30pm

Hello Wonderful was made possible thanks to a city initiative encouraging artisans to repopulate Florence. Viviana and Livia won the craft competition and have been designing, making, and selling women's clothing ever since, inside their small studio boutique. It's an original-yet-wearable style made from rolls of local fabric discarded by the large fashion houses and sewn into attractive blouses, skirts, and dresses. Everything is handmade and they've got the sewing machines in the back to prove it.

Jewelry
Jewelry means one thing in Florence: **Ponte Vecchio.** The bridge is lined with dozens of stores selling rings, necklaces, bracelets, pendants, and earrings of all sorts. The downside of shopping here is that the bridge is jammed with visitors most of the day and browsing can become a claustrophobic endeavor. Avoid the crowds by arriving early or late and enter the boutiques in order to examine gold, silver, diamonds, and gems undisturbed. If you don't like the look of merchandise at one shop, simply say *grazie* and pop into the next.

T. RISTORI
*Ponte Vecchio 1-3r; tel. 055/215-507; Tues.-Sat.
9:30am-7:30pm*

T. Ristori is an elegant and tasteful place to start shopping on Ponte Vecchio and carries well-known jewelry brands as well as their own handcrafted line. It's also a good opportunity to see the inside of a *bottega* and catch a glimpse of the Arno without being crushed by the people outside. The red staircase in the corner of the shop was built for Francesco I de' Medici and is the only direct access to the corridor above to the bridge.

Markets

There are fewer markets on this side of the river. Those that do exist don't thrive off tourists, but attract locals who buy their fruits and vegetables and browse racks of cheap clothing, shoes, and household gadgets. The busiest is in **Piazza Santo Spirito** and held Monday-Saturday 8am-2pm. It has a handful of stands hawking cheap women's wear, shoes of every kind, undergarments, and vegetables. The **Arti e Mestieri D'Oltrarno** arts and crafts market also takes place 7am-7pm in the square on the second Sunday of every month except July and August.

Activities and Recreation

PARKS AND GARDENS

There are few parks in Florence's dense Historic Center, but the southern side of the Arno is another story. Here, wealthy families created splendid gardens for themselves. Most of these, like the Giardini di Boboli, are now museums or privately run and charge admission. The Giardino delle Rose is an exception and offers panoramic views of the city. Parco delle Cascine, the city's biggest public park, is outside the center and great for a cycle or stroll.

GIARDINI DI BOBOLI

Piazza Pitti 1; daily 8:45am-6:30pm summer and until 4:30pm winter; €10, €38 combo ticket or Firenzecard
It's easy to overdose on art in Florence. Fortunately, there are gardens like Giardini di Boboli where you can relax and give your eyes a rest. The garden was created by the Medici family and blends an initial perfectly manicured section with a wilder natural park opened to the public in 1766. Even here art isn't entirely absent, and there are grottoes, fountains, and statues lining many of the alleys. Boboli Gardens are off-limits to cyclists and pickup soccer games. Visitors must keep off the grass, remain on the footpaths, and refrain from climbing trees. You can, however, bring food and drink into the garden and eat on the benches as long as you clean up after yourself. Free 10-minute visits of the Buontalento Grotto depart hourly 11am-6pm in summer.

Giardini di Boboli

The gardens are big and visitors usually skip large swathes, but if you have the time to see it all, enter from the Porta Romana entrance at the opposite end of the palace or from Via del Forte di S. Giorgio underneath the Forte Belvedere castle. This way you can explore it all. Otherwise, if your clock is ticking, stick with the formal gardens near Palazzo Pitti.

GIARDINO BARDINI

*Costa San Giorgio 2 or Via dei Bardi 1r;
tel. 055/2006-6206; www.villabardini.it; daily
8:45am-7:30pm summer, daily 10am-6pm winter; €10*

Giardino Bardini is a fraction of the size of the Boboli Gardens and only a short distance away near Forte Belvedere. The advantage of this park is not only its manageable dimensions (divided into three distinctive areas), but also the wonderful gravel terrace overlooking the city. The villa at the entrance of the property was built in 1641 and opened to the public in 1965. It contains two small museums and an exhibition space. Guided tours of the elaborate gardens can be reserved, and the coffee house within the *loggia* has a great view of the garden and city below.

GIARDINO DELLE ROSE

*Viale Giuseppe Poggi 2; tel. 055/234-2426; daily
9am-7pm; free*

Giardino delle Rose is located off the stairs leading up to Piazzale Michelangelo and is a fragrant stop in late spring and early summer when more than 400 varieties of roses bloom. Interspersed among the plants are metal sculptures, small fountains, and wooden benches offering wonderful views.

PARCO DELLE CASCINE

*Piazzale delle Cascine; tel. 055/365-707; www.
parcodellecascine.comune.fi.it; 24/7; free*

Parco delle Cascine is Florence's largest park. It's located just west of the Historic Center along the Arno River and can be easily reached by foot, tram, or bike. The latter is the best option for exploring the long paths that run through the park and lead past meadows, woods, and sporting complexes. On summer weekends it can be quite animated. It's a park where few tourists tread and locals come to cycle, run, or just stroll along the banks of the Arno. There's a pedestrian bridge over the Arno you can cross to explore the residential neighborhood of low-rise apartment blocks immersed in green, or ride along dirt paths overlooking the river. In summer, the former racetrack and amphitheater within the park are used for concerts and exhibitions.

HIKING

TOP EXPERIENCE

★ HIKING TO BASILICA SAN MINIATO AL MONTE

Distance: *2 miles (3.5 kilometers) round-trip*
Duration: *1 hour round-trip*
Effort level: *moderate*
Starting point: *Ponte Vecchio*

The most memorable way to approach Basilica San Miniato al Monte, an uncrowded respite with lovely views, is by hiking up along **Via San Niccolò** and through the old medieval gate. Take the second right onto **Via dell'Erta Canina** and continue a short way to the path on the left that leads uphill. It's also called **Erta Canina,** but you'll know you're on the right track if there's grass growing in between the rough paving stones and no one's in sight.

As you climb, you'll pass olive groves and cottages that appear more suited to a village than the city behind you. At the end of the narrow road you can turn left onto **Viale Galileo** or cross the avenue and continue up the improvised steps through a glade of pines until you come to the fortifications hastily constructed by Michelangelo during a siege of the city. The dirt path eventually disappears; follow the walls in either direction and you'll eventually reach the basilica.

CYCLING

Cycling is a safe and convenient way to explore Florence. Most of the city is flat and traffic is respectful of cyclists. There are bike racks in nearly every *piazza* and dedicated lanes along both sides of the Arno and many streets. Rental prices for an hour or an entire day are reasonable, and many bike shops also offer tours.

If you're serious about cycling, head for the hills surrounding the city and discover the Tuscan countryside on two wheels. Travelers can rent a bike and board any regional train with a bike symbol. There are special bike compartments for up to 15 bikes that must be loaded and unloaded by the cyclists themselves. Tickets for transporting bikes are €4 one-way and valid 24 hours.

Bike Paths

The long paths in **Parco delle Cascine** are excellent for exploring by bicycle. **Viale Galileo** and **Michelangelo** near Piazzale Michelangelo both wind through lovely countryside and have bike lanes that fill up with local cyclists on weekends.

★ LUNGARNO BIKE PATH

Distance: *7 miles (12 kilometers) round-trip*
Duration: *60-75 minutes round-trip*
Effort level: *easy*
Starting point: *Ponte Vecchio*

Both sides of the Arno River are equipped with bike paths, but the one on the northern bank west of the city is the longest and most panoramic. Once you reach the end of the Parco delle Cascine, ride west under the modern red bridge and out of the city. The dirt path is flat and popular with cyclists and joggers. If you pedal all the way, you'll reach **Parco dei Renai** (daily 9am-12:30am) where you can go for a swim in the park lake, get a bite to eat at the park café, or play mini golf. On the way back, enjoy an outdoor *aperitivo* at the **Palazzina Indiano** (Piazzale dell'Indiano 1; tel. 055/088-0600; May-Oct. Tues.-Sat. 9am-1pm and 4:30pm-10pm, Sun. 9am-10pm, Nov.-Apr. Wed.-Sun. 9am-5:30pm) café and cultural center, located at the northwestern tip of Parco delle Cascine near the bike path.

Rental Companies

In addition to the rental companies listed below, there is also a bike-sharing service in the city. Visitors can sign up online and download the app that allows you to find a bike and use it for however long or little you need. **Mobikes** (www.mobike.com) are orange and gray, and cost €0.50 every 30 minutes.

FLORENCE BY BIKE

Via S. Zanobi 54r; tel. 055/488-992; www. florencebybike.it; Mon.-Sat. 9am-1pm and 3:30pm-7:30pm

Florence By Bike is close to the train station and provides city, mountain, touring, and road bikes that can be rented for an hour, half day, full day, or multiple days. Prices depend on the model and a half day with a good Dutch-style city bike is €9 while a mountain bike is double that. All sizes are available and accessories like baskets and child seats are an additional €3. Helmets and locks are included in the rental price. They also offer tours in and around Florence. **Tuscany Cycle** (Via Ghibellina, 133; tel. 055/289-681; www. tuscanycycle.com; daily 9am-7pm), also near the train station, is a similar option.

FLORENT

Via Della Mosca 10r; tel. 055/019-6770; www. noleggiobiciclettefirenze.it; daily 10am-7pm

Florent provides well-maintained city, 6-7 speed, electric, and hybrid bikes for four hours (€9-29) or the entire day (€12-39). Staff are super friendly and provide loads of advice and maps especially for riders who want to discover what's beyond the city center. Locks and helmets are included. Children's bikes and child seats are available.

MOPEDS

If you've never ridden a moped, Florence is a good place to start and is significantly safer than Rome. Drivers don't go very fast and there are fewer cars overall. Mopeds are perfect if you have a little experience and want to get outside the city. The best direction is south along the **SR222** state road, which winds its way through Chianti and plenty of picturesque countryside. Helmets are mandatory for drivers and passengers.

NEW TUSCANY SCOOTER RENTAL

Via Il Prato 50r; tel. 055/538-5045; www. vesparental.eu; Mar.-Nov. daily 9am-6pm

New Tuscany Scooter Rental has a small fleet of colorful Vespas (€60 per day) that are fun to ride. All you need is a regular license, and you'll be set. They provide helmets, maps, and full insurance if you're anxious about scrapes or dents.

ALINARI

Via San Zanobi 40; tel. 055/280-500; www. alinarirental.com; Mon.-Sat. 9am-7pm and Sun. 9:30am-6:30pm

Alinari rents classic Dutch bikes and Honda SH 125 mopeds for €15 an hour or €55 the entire day. Credit card and ID are required.

BEACHES

SPIAGGIA SUL ARNO

Piazza Giuseppe Poggi; www.easylivingfirenze.it; May-Sept. daily 10am-1:30am

Florence is only 55 miles (90 kilometers) from the sea and many residents spend their weekends and holidays on the Tuscan coast—but if you can't make it to the beach, the beach can make it to you. Every summer the city organizes an informal riverside beach along the sandy southern bank of the Arno River east of Ponte alle Grazie bridge. Spiaggia sul Arno attracts families and hipsters looking to relax. During the day you can sip drinks at the kiosk bar, rent lounge chairs, or practice beach yoga; after the sun goes down on weekends, musicians and DJs alternate rhythms.

SPECTATOR SPORTS

Calcio Storico

According to popular belief the English invented soccer, but Florentines know that *Calcio Storico*, an early form of the game, originated here in the 16th century—which may explain why Italy has won four World Cups and England only one. It's a bruising game

that combines elements of soccer and rugby and in which head butting, punching, and elbows are allowed. A competition is held every year between teams representing the four historic neighborhoods of the city and takes place in Piazza Santa Croce during the second and third weeks of June. Matches last 50 minutes and enthusiastic crowds fill the bleachers around the square. The final is played on June 24, the feast day of Florence's patron saint, and the winning team gets bragging rights and a free dinner. Tickets (www.boxol.it) are priced €21-52 and go on sale in May.

Football

Fiorentina is the local soccer (*calcio*) team. They regularly finish in the top half of the Italian Serie A championship, although they haven't won a title in over four decades. They play at the **Artemio Franchi** (Viale Manfredo Fanti 4; tel. 055/503-011) stadium, which opened in 1931 and was remodeled to host matches during the 1990 World Cup. Capacity is 47,000 but games are rarely sold out unless one of the league's top teams are in town. Matches are usually played on Sunday afternoons. Tickets can be purchased directly at the stadium gates or the team shop on the second floor of **Mercato Centrale** (Piazza del Central Mercato; daily 10am-6pm). Seating is relatively close to the action, and unlike in Rome there's no running track around the field. The side tribunes provide the best views, while the curves offer more atmosphere and are where you're likely to hear fans chanting insults at the opposition. The stadium is 1.5 miles (a couple kilometers) northeast of the center and can be easily reached from Stazione Santa Maria Novella or Piazza San Marco via buses 7, 17, or 20.

During COVID outbreaks, games are played without spectators.

TOURS AND LOCAL GUIDES

There are more than 2,000 registered guides in Florence and dozens of agencies offering tours of the city and Tuscan region. These range from walking and cycling tours to Segway and Vespa outings. The following tours are all led by English speakers.

Walking Tours
ELISA ACCIAI
tel. 339/626-2031; elisaacciai@libero.it
Elisa Acciai always dreamed of being a tour guide in her native city, and she's been doing it professionally for over a decade. Her interest began on school trips when monotone guides put her classmates to sleep with a dull monologue of names and dates. She decided to take the opposite approach and brings her city to life with facts and insights that will transform your perspective on Florence. You can customize tours based on your interests (monuments, neighborhoods, markets, food, etc.) or let her surprise you. Tours are €65 per hour for groups of up to six, and travelers packing a Moon guide get a €10 discount.

Cycling Tours
FLORENCE BY BIKE
Via S. Zanobi 54r; tel. 055/488-992; www. florencebybike.it
Florence By Bike offers guided tours of various lengths inside and outside Florence. The four-hour tour (€39 including rental) along the Arno and through Parco delle Cascine leaves at 3:30pm on weekdays and 9am on weekends. If you want to pedal even farther they organize 40-60 mile (60-100 kilometer) trips to Chianti, Siena, and other Tuscan destinations.

I BIKE TUSCANY
Via del Campuccio 88; tel. 342/935-2395; www. ibiketuscany.com; daily 9am-7pm; €145
I Bike Tuscany specializes in single-day and multiday rides outside the city. Destinations include Siena, Chianti, and San Gimignano. Groups leave every morning and follow scenic routes through the Tuscan countryside past olive groves, vineyards, and villages where riders stop for lunch and gelato. Tours include 27-speed hybrid bikes, transfer to starting points, tastings, helmets, and water.

Bus Tours
FLORENCE CITY SIGHTSEEING
Piazza Santa Maria Novella; tel. 055/290-451; www. firenze.city-sightseeing.it
Several companies offer bus tours. Florence City Sightseeing operates red double-decker buses with open tops along two different routes. You can ride them for 24 (€23), 48 (€28), or 72 (€33) hours. The starting point is Santa Maria Novella train station and a complete circuit lasts one or two hours with numerous stops where passengers are free to get on and off. Tickets can be purchased online or on board and include audio commentary in English and seven other languages. They also provide group-walking tours of the Uffizi and other monuments and discounted family rates.

Horse-and-Buggy Tours
Horse-and-buggy teams line the *piazza* around the Duomo waiting to pick up fares for a trot around the center. It can be a lovely way to discover Florence; just avoid the 5pm rush hour and negotiate the price prior to departure. A 30-minute ride usually costs around €80 and a buggy can seat up to four adults.

Wine-Tasting Tour
GRAPE TOURS
Via dei Renai 19-23r; tel. 333/722-9716; www. tuscan-wine-tours.com; €25-110 pp for groups of 3-8
Wine tours can seem expensive, but the best provide a memorable day of discovery that's hard to replicate on your own. Grape Tours organize half- and full-day visits to local wineries that include a light lunch and vineyard visits. At each stop you'll meet vineyard owners and learn about what makes their vintage special. The quality of the soil, the amount of rain, and the type of containers used for storage all influence flavor. You'll get to sample a number of bottles at each stop, and with the help of passionate guides you'll begin to distinguish the subtle differences between Chianti and other Tuscan wines. The more people on a tour the less it costs.

Vespa Tours

The Vespa is Italy's most famous scooter brand and a synonym for mobility. It's easy to ride even if you have little or no motoring experience and is a delightful way of exploring the countryside around Florence. All agencies require a valid driver's license and include some form of insurance in the price. To avoid any surprises, make sure to check what any eventual damages will cost should the worst happen.

TUSCANY VESPA TOURS

Via Ghibellina 34r; tel. 055/386-0253; www.tuscany-vespatours.com; Mar.-Nov.

Tuscany Vespa Tours run extended in-depth tours that explore the region. These depart at 10am and head south into Chianti for seven-hour visits of the area. Along the way there's a stop at a 12th-century castle with a wine cellar and olive oil-producing facilities. Once you've climbed the tower and enjoyed the view, it's back on the moped along winding country roads to a family-run *trattoria* where a traditional lunch is served. Total distance is 21 miles (35 kilometers) completed at a leisurely pace. Drivers pay €120 and passengers €90.

Vespas are a great way to discover the Tuscan countryside.

WALKABOUT

Via Vinegia 23r; tel. 055/264-5746; www.walkaboutflorence.com

Walkabout uses restored vintage Vespas to take small groups on four-hour tours outside the city. There are several stops along the way to admire the views and explore narrow roads past castles and villas. Lunch is eaten *al fresco* and includes prosciutto, cheese, and Chianti. Tours depart at 9am and 2:30pm all year long and cost €110 for a single rider and €170 for two. Helmets with two-way radios are provided by the English-speaking guides. As the name suggests, they also provide walking tours.

ITALY AND WINE

Corso dei Tintori 13; www.italyandwine.net; Mon.-Fri. 9am-6pm

Italy and Wine offers dozens of one-day private and group tours of the region. A typical day out includes a tasting at two wineries and a light lunch at an authentic *trattoria* along the way. Participants are picked up at their hotel and accompanied by a sommelier who can help all levels of drinkers distinguish between grape varieties and understand the intricacies of wine production. The big advantage Vittorio and his team have are the relationships they've cultivated with vineyards over the years. Participants get more than a generic tour and tasting; they get an intimate, behind-the-scenes look at what it means to live and breathe wine every day. There are a number of itineraries to choose from and shared tours start from €140 per person; the cost of private tours varies according to the number of participants, which never exceeds eight.

CLASSES
Cooking
MAMA FLORENCE

Viale Petrarca 12; tel. 055/220-101; www. mamaflorence.it; €110 and up

Mama Florence is a cooking school geared toward visitors who already know how to handle a knife. Classes are run by an all-star lineup of mostly female chefs, including Beatrice Segoni from the Convivium restaurant, who balance theory with practice inside a state-of-the-art kitchen. Once you've finished cooking you get to enjoy your effort with a good bottle of wine and the company of other gastronomic enthusiasts. Classes cover the classics like making homemade pasta and pizza and last around four hours, including time spent eating your creations.

CUCINA LORENZO DE'MEDICI

Piazza del Mercato Centrale; tel. 334/304-0551; www.cucinaldm.com

Cucina Lorenzo de'Medici is located on the second floor of Mercato Centrale and has been spreading Italian culture for the last 40 years. The cooking school is equipped with 16 single workstations and all the utensils needed to complete any recipe, as well as tablets for following chefs who are filmed as they cook. Lessons start from €65 while lunch or dinner with a chef is €38 and up. Classes last two hours and are based around menus of pizza, pasta, and desserts. All ingredients are top quality and positive feedback is provided from beginning to end.

Accommodations

Florence has a range of accommodation options including hostels, *pensiones*, residences, B&Bs, apartments, hotels, and monasteries. There are many low-star hotels and residences clustered near Stazione Santa Maria Novella where tour groups tend to stay. That isn't always bad, especially on short visits, but the city is small enough to make getting to and from most accommodations easy. If arriving by car, check the availability of hotel parking and ask for the necessary permits in order to enter the ZTL (limited traffic zone).

The proximity of the Tuscan countryside makes *agriturismo* (farmhouse accommodation) feasible. This is especially pleasant during the summer on extended stays when you can spend the morning visiting the city and hot afternoons relaxing by a pool. *Residenza d'epoca* (period residences) are another interesting option. This category of accommodation is based on meticulous attention to historical detail as well as comfort.

There are generally two seasonal rates in Florence: High season extends throughout late spring, summer, and on major holidays, and low season comprises the rest of the year. Overall, hotel prices are lower than in Rome or Venice, and this is the place to spend a little extra in order to get a lot more. All accommodation types charge a daily city tax that's not included in the list price; it ranges from €2-6 based on the category of accommodation.

Most hotels are located in the Historic Center but very few have over 100 rooms. Residences and lower-end hotels are concentrated around Stazione Santa Maria Novella, especially on Via Nazionale. Large buildings are often shared between several establishments. Higher-end hotels are located close to major monuments and along the Arno where prices grow incrementally. Many of these are located within historic *palazzo* where only the furnishings have changed and guests can get an idea of how the Florentine elite once lived.

DUOMO AND AROUND
€100-200
RESIDENCE HILDA

Via dei Servi 40; tel. 055/288-021; www. residencehilda.com; €150-175 d

A stay at Residence Hilda gives you an idea of what it's like to live in Florence. The suites are all decorated in light tones with simple, modern furniture. Each is equipped with a small kitchen and there's a food delivery service if you don't feel like choosing your own tomatoes. Robiglio downstairs is the perfect coffee bar to start the day. From here, all major sights are within walking distance.

Family-Friendly Florence

the carousel in Piazza della Repubblica

Florence has little traffic and plenty of churches, gardens, streets, parks, and gelato shops to explore. Children under 18 get free entry to all sights covered by the Firenzecard when accompanied by parents who have the card, making it an excellent purchase for families.

· The city offers free Family Tours for ages 6-13 that include a bag, dedicated app, and materials for discovering museums the fun way. There are several itineraries starting from Museo di Palazzo Vecchio (Piazza della Signoria; Oct.-Mar. daily 9am-6pm and Apr.-Sept. Fri.-Wed. 9am-11pm, Thurs. 9am-2pm; €10, kids under 18 free), Istituto degli Innocenti (Piazza SS Annunziata 12; Mon.-Sat. 7am-8pm), Museo Novecento, and the Archeological Museum in Fiesole. These treasure hunt-like activities are a journey for the hands, eyes, and imagination that bring the city to life. Museum entry is not included but most provide discounts or don't charge children.

· Toddlers can chase pigeons in the city's *piazze* or explore elaborate gardens like Giardini di Boboli (Piazza Pitti 1; €10 adults, €5 kids) where they can race Mom or Dad to the next fountain.

· Younger children can ride the old-fashioned merry-go-round (€2) in Piazza della Repubblica or board a horse and buggy.

· Older kids and teens may enjoy getting on bikes and pedaling around the city or to Parco delle Cascine (Piazzale delle Cascine; free) where local families cool off in the Olympic-size pool.

· Markets are enjoyable for all ages and a good place to spend holiday allowance money.

· There's also nothing like gelato to bring a family together. Consider a cup rather than a cone to keep toddlers clean.

· Temper tantrum? Head to the nearest newsstand. Most kiosks have several racks filled with small toys, collectibles, playing cards, and gadgets that offer instant distraction.

· Give older teenagers the freedom to spend a couple of hours on their own. Florence is one of the safest cities in Italy and exploring it alone is an experience they'll never forget.

€200-300

NH COLLECTION FIRENZE PORTA ROSSA

Via Porta Rossa 19; tel. 055/271-0911; www.nh-hotels. it; €200-250 d

Although part of a chain, the NH Collection Firenze Porta Rossa has plenty of character and all the quality you'd expect from a four-star hotel. Rooms range from standard to presidential and mix modern furnishings with original vaulted ceilings and 13th-century detailing. The multilingual personnel are friendly and an extensive buffet breakfast is served in an elegant dining hall.

★ ANTICA TORRE

Via Tornabuoni 1; tel. 055/265-8161; www. tornabuoni1.com; €210-260 d

A night at Antica Torre provides is like a sleepover with the Medici. This medieval tower house in the center of Florence was restored with comfort and authenticity in mind. All rooms and suites have original antique furnishings and are equipped with a minibar, air-conditioning, and Wi-Fi. The best reason to stay here, however, are the stunning views from two rooftop terraces where breakfast is served and guests spend summer evenings sipping Chianti.

GALLERY ART HOTEL

Vicolo dell'Oro 5; tel. 055/27263; www. lungarnocollection.com; €240-300 d

If after a day of gazing upon the past you crave something trendy and modern, Gallery Art Hotel is the place to stay. From the sculptures attached to the facade to the dark and cozy hotel bar, nothing is farther from the Renaissance than this luxury hotel around the corner from the Ponte Vecchio. Fashion designer Ferragamo recently redesigned the well-proportioned interiors and offset the whiteness of the walls with elegant brown furnishings. Rooms on the upper floors have private terraces with spectacular views. The Fusion restaurant downstairs provides a delicious alternative to traditional Tuscan flavors.

SANTA MARIA NOVELLA

Under €100

OSTELLI ARCHI ROSSI

Via Faenza 94r; tel. 055/290-804; www. hostelarchirossi.com; €60-90 d, €28 for bed in shared room

Ostelli Archi Rossi is a laid-back hostel around the corner from the train station that's popular with students, families, and solo travelers. There are simple private rooms with en suite baths as well as dorm-style rooms with bunk beds and lockers that sleep up to nine. Guests eat downstairs at the convivial shared tables where a cafeteria-style breakfast (7am-9:30am) with eggs and bacon is served. Dinner and bar service are also available, along with €8 walking tours that leave the hostel at 10am.

CASA PER FERIE SUORE OBLATE

Via Nazionale 8; tel. 055/239-8202; www. oblatespiritosantofirenze.it; €60 d, summer only

Once you enter the thick wooden doors of Casa Per Ferie Suore Oblate the noise of the city disappears. This accommodation run by Catholic nuns houses university students during the academic year and visitors during the summer. Rooms are simple, large, and clean. Doubles consist of two single beds and a private bathroom. Several of the nuns speak fluent English. An 11pm curfew is enforced, but that may seem reasonable after a day walking the streets of Florence.

€100-200

HOTEL AZZIZI

Via Faenza 56; tel. 055/213-806; www.hotelazzi.com; €70-110 d

Many hotels near the train station survive on location rather than quality, but Hotel Azzizi benefits from both. This friendly three-star establishment on the edge of the Historic Center offers a handful of bright, recently renovated rooms with modern bathrooms. They all come with air-conditioning, Wi-Fi, and an abundant buffet breakfast served in the comfortable common area where guests can relax on the sunny balcony.

Best Accommodations

★ **Antica Torre:** Live like a Medici at this medieval tower house with rooftop terraces and stunning views (page 245).

★ **Hotel Loggiato Dei Serviti:** Travel back in time at this former monastery, located on one of Florence's most beautiful squares (page 246).

★ **Il Guelfo Bianco:** Soak in the genuine Tuscan hospitality at the best three-star option in Florence (page 246).

★ **Alfieri9:** Cozy boutique hotel on the eastern edge of the Historic Center with comfortable classic, superior, and junior suite rooms (page 247).

★ **Monte Oliveto Bed & Breakfast:** Enjoy a warm welcome at this B&B tucked away in a charming neighborhood that most tourists never see (page 247).

★ **Torre di Bellosguardo:** This *agriturismo* is a virtual Eden on the outskirts of Florence (page 250).

ALBERGO BURCHIANTI
Via del Giglio 8; tel. 055/212-796; www.
hotelburchianti.it; €90-130 d

This cozy hotel halfway between the train station and the Duomo provides a perfect welcome to the city. Rooms are refined with plenty of style and all the amenities needed for a comfortable stay. Some have 18th-century frescos and all are equipped with antique furnishings, safes, and minibars. Room service is available 24/7 and breakfast is served in a lovely dining hall.

SAN LORENZO AND SAN MARCO
Under €100
PLUS FLORENCE
Via Santa Caterina d'Alessandria 15;
tel. 055/628-6347; www.plushostels.com; €60 d,
€16-20 shared

The hippest hostel in town is Plus Florence, which attracts a young and international crowd who often forget about sightseeing and remain frolicking by the pool or panoramic terrace and drinking sex-inspired cocktails (€6). Private and shared, mixed, and female-only rooms are clean and minimal in design. An all-you-can-eat breakfast is served in the restaurant lounge, which transforms into a disco at night.

€100-200
★ HOTEL LOGGIATO DEI SERVITI
Piazza della Santissima Annunziata 3;
tel. 055/289-592; www.loggiatodeiservitihotel.it;
€110-180 d

Hotel Loggiato Dei Serviti is the quickest way to travel back in time. Located inside a former monastery, this historic residence is in one of the most beautiful squares of the city and underneath an ancient portico that monks once called home. The inside has changed very little and there's an antique atmosphere that history buffs and anyone fascinated by the past will love. About the only concession to modernity is the Wi-Fi access and armchairs scattered around the cozy sitting rooms.

€200-300
★ IL GUELFO BIANCO
Via Cavour 29; tel. 055/288-330; www.
ilguelfobianco.it; €150-225 d

Why Il Guelfo Bianco only has three stars is a mystery. The colorful hotel, located moments from Galleria dell'Accademia, provides instant hominess and effortless charm that more luxurious accommodations struggle to match. All the rooms, from singles to suites, have been tastefully restored to their Renaissance best with the addition of antique furnishings, modern art, minibars, and air-conditioning. A sweet and savory breakfast is served inside a bright dining area or outside in the private courtyard where staff are on the lookout for coffee cups to refill. The front desk is on duty 24 hours a day and can make reservations to museums or the adjacent hotel restaurant (daily noon-10pm).

RESIDENZA D'EPOCA PALAZZO TOLOMEI

Via de' Ginori 19; tel. 055/292-887; www. palazzotolomei.it; €180-230 d

Staying at Residenza d'Epoca Palazzo Tolomei is a little like staying inside a museum and would satisfy members of the Medici family: Rooms are spacious; ceilings high and frescoed; floors covered in terra-cotta, marble, and wood; and mirrors gilded. Waking up here is the perfect beginning to a day in Florence. An Italian breakfast can be enjoyed in your room or at a nearby bar.

SANTA CROCE
€100-200
HOTEL VILLA LIANA

Via Vittorio Alfieri 18; tel. 055/245-303; www. hotelliana.com; €110-150 s/d

Hotel Liana is a short walk from the Duomo in an elegant residential neighborhood near the botanical gardens. The 18th-century *palazzo* once housed the English consulate and has maintained an old-world atmosphere uncorrupted by bad taste. Each of the 24 rooms contains refined yet comfortable furnishings.

★ ALFIERI9

Via Vittorio Alfieri 9; tel. 055/263-8121; www.alfieri9. it; €110-160 d

Alfieri9 occupies the first floor of a residential building 15 minutes from the Duomo and makes a convenient base for anyone wanting to escape from tourists and experience

another side of Florence. Rooms are stylish, clean, and comfortable. Each comes with LED TVs, air-conditioning, safe, and well-stocked minibars (water, soda, juice, beer, and *prosecco*). Breakfast is a highlight served with a myriad of homemade sweet and savory options that provide all the calories you need to climb the *campanile*. The nearby park is perfect for taking a break from art and history.

OLTRARNO

There are considerably fewer accommodations on this quiet side of the river, but waking up here provides an opportunity to observe the everyday habits of residents as they go about their morning routines. Several luxury hotels cluster around the Ponte Vecchio but for the most part accommodations consist of comfortable B&Bs, residences, and low-star hotels.

€100-200
RESIDENZA D'EPOCA SANTO SPIRITO

Via Santo Spirito 6; tel. 331/669-8881; www. viasantospirito6.it; €90-140 d

Residenza d'Epoca Santo Spirito is a historic residence with 10 lovely rooms named after famous women. All are elegantly furnished and conveniently equipped with kitchenettes, Wi-Fi, and air-conditioning. It's a tranquil place where guests relax in the courtyard garden or second-floor lounge with sofas and a fireplace. The residence is on one of the neighborhood's nicest streets minutes from the Ponte Vecchio, Palazzo Pitti, and the unexplored sights of Oltrarno.

★ MONTE OLIVETO BED & BREAKFAST

Via Domenico Burchiello 67; tel. 055/231-3484; www. bebmonteoliveto.it; €80-150 d

Monte Oliveto is a slightly off-the-beaten-track B&B near neighborhood restaurants and shops most tourists never see. Donatella provides a warm welcome along with a hearty homemade breakfast that can be served in her private garden or the comfortable common area. The four guest rooms are bright and airy with views of the hillside or the quiet street out front.

HOTEL CLASSIC
Viale Machiavelli 25; tel. 055/229-351; www.
classichotel.it; €140-170 s/d

It's easy to forget you're in a city once you enter Hotel Classic. Nature is all around this delightful villa. A continental breakfast is served in the vaulted dining room, garden, or in your room. Parking is available and the Ponte Vecchio is just 12 minutes away on foot.

€200-300
PALAZZO BELFIORE
Via dei Velluti 8; tel. 055/264-415; www.
palazzobelfiore.it; €170-230 d

The team at Palazzo Belfiore like sharing their city with travelers. They do that by welcoming guests to their 14th-century residence with real gusto and making loads of suggestions. Saying they care is an understatement, and if you don't already have a friend in Florence it will feel like you do the moment you arrive. The eight cozy apartments have terra-cotta floors, wood beams, plush sofas, and antique furnishings that can be used rather than admired. They all come with small cooking corners and reliable Wi-Fi connections.

SAN NICCOLÒ
€100-200
RESIDENCE MICHELANGIOLO
Viale Michelangiolo 21; tel. 055/681-1748; https://
residencemichelangiolo.it; €90-120 d

Residence Michelangelo is situated along an elegant tree-lined avenue close to the Arno and a short walk from the center. The attractive three-story villa is surrounded by a garden with outdoor seating and free parking. Rooms are bright and spacious with compact kitchenettes and real king-size beds that aren't just two twins pushed together. Reception staff are attentive and can reserve museum tickets or restaurants should the need arise.

HOTEL DAVID
Viale Michelangelo 1; tel. 055/681-1695; www.
davidhotel.it; €110-125 s/d

Antique furniture, wrought-iron beds, and parquet flooring are the hallmarks of Hotel David where all rooms are soundproof and equipped with shower and bath. Drinks from the minibar, international phone calls, and daily happy hour (6:30pm-8pm) are free at this jovial hotel 25 minutes from the train station. Breakfast is served in a pleasant garden retreat where guests gather on summer evenings to exchange impressions of Florence while enjoying Chianti.

€200-300
HOTEL SILLA
Via dei Renai 5; tel. 055/234-2888; www.hotelsilla.
it; €180-220 d

The Silla isn't the most modern hotel in Florence but it is one of the friendliest. Everyone from the front desk to the kitchen staff go out of their way to help guests. If you need an electrical adaptor, want to make restaurant reservations, or have any dietary concerns they'll resolve the matter quickly. Rooms are pleasantly decorated and those in the front have a view of the Arno River. The streets nearby are filled with good restaurants and the center is only a short walk away.

GREATER FLORENCE
Under €100
ROVEZZANO B&B
Via Aretina 417; tel. 055/690-0023; www.rovezzano.
com; €70-90 s/d

Bed & Breakfast Rovezzano is located in a residential area a 10-minute walk from the center. There's free parking and a swimming pool. Rooms are rustic, with thick shutters that block all light. Breakfast is served in a large common living area where fellow travelers gather in the evening.

€100-200
CASA SCHLATTER
Viale dei Mille 14; tel. 347/118-0215; www.
casaschlatter-Florence.com; €85-105 d

Casa Schlatter was the home of a 19th-century Swiss painter. His ancestors have transformed the house into an elegant B&B. There are three rooms with large en suite bathrooms and modern fittings. Alessandra, the great-granddaughter of the artist, is an excellent host and serves breakfast in the small garden or the bright communal area where guests can relax.

Information and Services

VISITOR INFORMATION
Tourist Information Centers

There are two official **tourist offices** in the center and another at the airport. The office opposite the train station (Piazza Stazione 4; tel. 055/212-245; Mon.-Sat. 9am-7pm and Sun. 9am-2pm) is the largest and busiest but lines move fast and the multilingual staff are extremely helpful. You'll find more friendly staff at the office on Via Camillo Cavour 1r (tel. 055/290-832; Mon.-Fri. 9am-1pm). Both provide maps, event calendars, and sell the **Firenzecard** pass.

TRAVELER SERVICES
Luggage Storage
KI POINT

Santa Maria Novella Train Station; daily 8am-9pm
Ki Point is located midway along track 16 and identifiable by a blue *Depositi Bagagli* (Left Luggae) sign. Lines can be long and staff disinterested, but it is convenient. It's €6 for the first 5 hours and €1 every hour after that. Retrieve luggage at least 30 minutes before your train departs.

STOW YOUR BAGS

Via dell'Albero 22; tel. 055/398-5288; www. stowyourbags.com; daily 7am-11pm
Stow Your Bags is a safe, fully automated luggage storage service just outside the train station with multiple-size lockers that can be reserved online in advance or in person. They also have a second location near Santa Croce (Via dell'Anguillara 58). A small locker for 1 hour is €1.50 and goes up to €13 for the entire day.

LEFT LUGGAGE FLORENCE

Via Ventisette Aprile 39r; tel. 055/045-0705; www. leftluggageinflorence.com; daily 8am-8pm
This conveniently located left luggage service is perfect for taking advantage of extra hours in Florence. It's operated by friendly staff who tag and load bags onto shelves the old-fashioned way. Storage fees are €1 per hour per bag for the first 5 hours and €5 for the entire day. That includes a bottle of water, map, and as much advice as you can handle.

Laundry
DELFINO

Via Santa Reparata 10; tel. 334/875-3460; daily 7:30am-11pm
There are a handful of laundromats in the city center, and this is one of the nicest. The owner is usually on hand to help, and detergent is available from a vending machine. Loads are priced according to the size (8 kg/€4 and 16 kg/€7) and drying is €1 per 12 minutes. There's plenty of clean counter space for folding, free Wi-Fi, and a selection of books to read while you wait.

LAVANDERIA FLORENTIA

Via Matteo Palmieri 5r; tel. 055/234-5215; Mon.-Fri. 8am-7pm, Sat. 8am-1pm
Florentia provides same-day wash, dry, and fold service. They also provide dry-cleaning and hemming in case any newly purchased clothes need adjusting. Shirts and pants can be dry-cleaned and ironed for €5 per item or an entire wardrobe can be washed and dried for €4 per kilo.

Agriturismi Near Florence

Agriturismi are working farms that also provide accommodations and encourage guests to take part in rural activities. There are hundreds throughout Tuscany that produce everything from artichokes to wine and provide urbanites with an opportunity to relax and understand where the food chain originates.

★ TORRE DI BELLOSGUARDO

Via Roti Michelozzi 2; tel. 055/229-8145; www.torrebellosguardo.com; €285-330 d
You don't have to travel far from Florence to leave the crowds behind and immerse yourself in green fields, olive groves, and vineyards. Torre di Bellosguardo is barely 10 minutes from the center by car yet a world away. This grand historic residence surrounded by lush gardens seems trapped in time and occupies a quintessential corner of Tuscany. The inside of the palatial estate is fit for a Medici and every antique-clad room hints of other eras and the city's fabulous past. On the grounds is a bountiful vegetable patch that supplies the kitchen, and owner Ana Franchetti can show guests how to transform seasonal ingredients into traditional local dishes. There are donkeys, ducks, and rabbits that are an instant hit with children, who can fill their days exploring the garden paths and diving into the pool overlooking the city.

CASALE GIUNCARELLI

Via di Baccano 4; tel. 392/798-0419; www.casalegiuncarelli.com; €140 d
Casale Giuncarelli is on a hillside about a 10-minute walk from Fiesole. The rustic farmhouse contains five self-catering flats of different sizes, all with private entrances and access to a large shared garden with barbecue area and pool. Furnishings are in style with the house and are perfect for travelers who don't feel the need to sightsee in the city all day. Car is the most convenient way of reaching the bumpy dirt road leading to the property, which can be a little hard to find; you can also take a taxi. Daniela provides a warm welcome and the location is great for anyone with the time to explore Tuscan hill towns and countryside.

FATTORIA MONTIGNANA

Via Montignana 4, San Casciano, Val di Pesa; tel. 055/807-0135; www.montignana.com; €90-160 s/d, 2-night minimum stay
There's no possibility of running out of wine at Fattoria Montignana. This family-owned winery 20 minutes south of Florence has been producing Chianti Classico for generations, and the vines are right outside their door. During a stay you can visit the ancient cellars and sample as much of the latest vintages as you like. Accommodation is in one of 11 authentically restored apartments that accommodate from two to six guests. Outside there's a pool and plenty of open road to explore on foot or by bike.

Public Restrooms

There are a half-dozen public toilets in the Historic Center and a couple in Oltrarno. There's one near Palazzo Vecchio on Via Filippina 6r, another on Borgo Santa Croce 29r and one in Piazza Santo Spirito 24n. They cost €1 and are generally open daily 10am-6pm. The alternative is walking into any bar and using the restrooms for free. Bars will also provide a glass of tap water to anyone in need of hydration in a hurry.

Lost and Found

If you lose something in Florence, you have a good chance of recovering it. Head to the **Ufficio Oggetti Smarriti** (Via Francesco Veracini 5; tel. 055/334-802; Mon., Wed., Fri. 9am-12:30pm and Tues., Thurs. 2:30pm-4pm) 20 minutes northwest of SMN station. They receive thousands of objects every year and it's worth checking with them before giving up all hope. It's better to go in person, as they may have difficulty understanding your English over the phone.

Foreign Consulates

The **U.S. Consulate** (Lungarno A. Vespucci 38; tel. 055/266-951) is open weekdays 9am-12:30pm and can assist travelers in a jam. Canadians in trouble should head to the **Canadian Consulate in Rome** (Via Zara 30, Rome; tel. 06/854-441; Mon.-Fri. 8:30am-noon and 2pm-4pm) or the **Canadian Consulate in Milan** (Piazza Cavour 3, Milan; tel. 02/6269-4238; Mon.-Fri. 9am-1pm). **Australia** (Via Antonio Bosio 5, Rome; tel. 06/852-721; Mon.-Fri. 9am-2:30pm), **New Zealand** (Via Clitunno 44, Rome; tel. 06/853-7501; www.nzembassy.com; Mon.-Thurs. 1:30pm-5pm), and **South Africa** (Via Tanaro 14, Rome; tel. 06/852-541; www.lnx.sudafrica.it; Mon.-Fri. 9:30am-12:30pm) have consulates in Rome.

HEALTH AND SAFETY

Emergency Numbers

For medical emergencies, dial **118** which will connect you with a nurse or doctor who can have an ambulance dispatched within minutes.

Police

Florence is a safe city and there's less chance of being targeted by pickpockets than in Rome. There are a number of state and municipal police stations in the center. The most centrally located is the **Polizia Municipale Zona Centrale** (Via delle Terme 2; tel. 055/328-3333). This is where to go to report a theft or any criminal activity.

Hospitals and Pharmacies

There are dozens of pharmacies on both sides of the river. Locals can usually direct you to the nearest one.

OSPEDALE SANTA MARIA NUOVA

Piazza Santa Maria Nuova 1; tel. 055/69381; www. uslcentro.toscana.it; 24/7

Ospedale Santa Maria Nuova is a hospital located in the Historic Center just east of the Duomo. If you can't walk, call a taxi or take bus 1, 7, 11, 17, or 23. If you're staying in a hotel, notify the front desk; many accommodations are prepared to handle any medical issues that may arise. For general health questions call 05/527-581.

HOSPITAL PEDIATRICO MEYER

Viale Gaetano Pieraccini 24; tel. 055/56621; www. meyer.it; 24/7

Hospital Pediatrico Meyer is a couple of miles (a few kilometers) north of Florence and one of the most modern children's hospitals in Italy.

FARMACIA COMUNALE

SMN Station, Piazza della Stazione 1; tel. 055/216-761

Farmacia Comunale inside the main train station is open 24 hours a day. You can also call 800/420-707 to find the nearest open pharmacy.

COMMUNICATIONS

Wi-Fi

The city of Florence has created more than 450 free indoor and outdoor Wi-Fi hotspots (info-wifi@comune.fi.it). Most of the center is now covered, along with public libraries and the tram lines. However, there is a 2-hour/300-megabyte limit, registration is required, and the network can be difficult to access without a European smartphone account. You can ensure coverage for 72 hours by purchasing the Firenzecard, or visit any of the many bars and restaurants that offer free Wi-Fi. Most accommodations provide unlimited access to Internet, as do high-speed trains to and from the city.

Newspapers

Newspaper stands are getting harder to find in Florence but still operate in the larger squares like Piazza Santo Spirito and Piazza Pitti. They sell a variety of local, national, and international papers as well as **Firenze Spettacolo** (www.firenzespettacolo.it; €2), a monthly event guide to the city with a dedicated English section. The influx of foreign visitors means that many European dailies are available at the **Feltrinelli** bookstore (Piazza della Stazione; Mon.-Sat. 7am-8pm and Sun. 8am-8pm) inside the train station.

Transportation

GETTING THERE

Air

AEROPORTO AMERIGO VESPUCCI

FLR, Via del Termine 11; tel. 055/30615; www. aeroporto.firenze.it

Amerigo Vespucci Airport is located 3 miles (5 kilometers) west of Florence. There are daily flights to and from major European and Italian cities including Rome's Fiumicino Airport and Venice. Most **Alitalia** (www. alitalia.com) flights land in Pisa. Total travel time to Rome is 50 minutes and one-way economy light tickets start from €75. Flights to Venice usually require a lengthy stopover in Rome.

Between Rome, Florence, and Venice's airports, Amerigo Vespucci Airport is the smallest, with no direct flights to North America, Australia, New Zealand, or South Africa. There are regularly scheduled flights to and from London, Birmingham, Edinburgh, and other UK destinations with British Airways (www.britishairways.com), City Jet (www. cityjet.com), and Vueling (www.vueling. com). The airport suffers from a high percentage of cancellations due to fog and wind, and even minor inclement conditions can cause delays.

Ataf/SITA (800/424-500; www.ataf.net) operates **Volainbus** (€6) shuttle buses that depart every 30 minutes from outside the arrivals terminal 5am-10:30pm and drop visitors off at Santa Maria Novella train station. A taxi ride to or from the center takes 15 minutes and costs €15-20. The **T2 Tram** (€1.50) departs every 10 minutes and reaches SMN station in under 30 minutes.

AEROPORTO INTERNAZIONALE GALILEO GALILEI

Piazzale d'Ascanio 1; tel. 050/849-111; www. pisa-airport.com

Tuscany's busiest airport is Pisa Galileo Galilei, an hour from Florence by bus, train, or car. **Sky Bus Lines Caronna** (tel. 366/126-0651; www.caronnatour.com; €13) buses depart from outside the arrivals terminal six times a day between 9:30am and 11:50pm (Sun. 9:15am-11:50pm) and drop passengers off at Stazione Santa Maria Novella in Florence. The slightly longer option is to ride the **PisaMover** (www.pisa-mover.com; daily 6am-midnight; €5) light metro that departs every 8 minutes from the airport to Pisa Centrale train station, and from there board a regional train (€8.70) to Florence SMN station. Combined tickets (€12) are available from the Information Office inside the arrivals hall. There are few direct flights from North America, and none from Australia, New Zealand, or South Africa to Pisa but many connecting flights via major European cities. Ryanair (www.ryanair.com), Easyjet (www.easyjet.com), and British Airways (www.britishairways.com) operate daily direct flights from London.

Train

The easiest, most convenient way of getting to Florence is high-speed train to **Stazione Santa Maria Novella,** near the city center. Rail tickets can be purchased online through **Italo** (www.italo.it) or **Trenitalia** (www. trenitalia.it) or directly from train stations in Rome and Venice. Both operators provide frequent daily service and multiple levels of comfort that make rail a convenient and comfortable option.

From Rome: Trains are direct and arrive in 90 minutes from Termini and Tiburtina stations. One-way standard fares start from €35.90 with over 50 daily departures between 5:35am and 10:35pm. Slower, cheaper fares are also available on regional trains. Passengers have access to Wi-Fi and outlets for charging electronic devices.

From Venice: The high-speed journey from Venezia Santa Lucia station takes a little over two hours. Standard fares start from €41.25, with dozens of departures throughout the day. Transfers in Padova are occasionally required depending on the service.

Car

Florence is roughly halfway between Rome and Venice. Driving is a viable option, although the cost of tolls and fuel as well as the challenge of finding parking in the city center can offset any benefits.

If you prefer taking a car but don't want to drive, there are a number of ride-sharing services available. The most popular is **BlaBlaCar** (www.blablacar.it), which costs around €15 per passenger. There are plenty of daily offers for the Rome-Florence route by drivers who are rated and insured. It's a memorable way to cut costs and get to know a stranger at the same time.

From Rome: The journey north from Rome along the **A1** highway is direct and the 143 miles (230 kilometers) can be covered in two hours. You'll need to get onto the **Grande Raccordo Annulare** ring road and take exit 10 toward Florence (*Firenze* on all signage). There's a toll (€18.40) that's paid when you leave the highway and 10 rest stops along the way. The speed limit on Italian highways is 130 kmp (80 mph) and there are a half-dozen speed cameras that are kindly indicated in advance. The single-lane **Cassia state road** (SS2) is the scenic alternative. It won't get you to Florence quickly, but it does cross some remarkable Tuscan countryside and is free to drive. Once you've left Lazio and entered Tuscany, there are opportunities for panoramic lunch stops and interesting detours in Viterbo, Siena, or smaller hill towns along the way.

From Venice: Florence is 162 miles (260 kilometers; €19.70 toll) from Venice and the drive can be covered in under three hours. It's not as direct as the trip from Rome: You'll have to take the **A57, A13,** and **A1** highways.

Stazione Santa Maria Novella

Cycling from Rome to Florence

Cycling may seem like an extreme option for traveling between Rome and Florence, but it's probably the most memorable. It requires time, a good bike, and traveling light. Intermediate and advanced riders can cover the 186 miles (300 kilometers) from Rome in three days along the **Via Cassia**. The road is sparsely trafficked, and although there are many hills, the climbs and descents are manageable. Along the way you'll pedal past vineyards, lakes, Roman amphitheaters, and tiny hill towns. Rome to Bolsena, Bolsena to Siena, and Siena to Florence are convenient stages, but there are many possible itineraries for travelers on two wheels.

Anyone considering this mode of transportation would probably prefer to bring their own trusted bike from home, but there are several long-term bicycle rental companies in Rome. **Top Bike Rental** (Via Labicana 49; tel. 06/488-2893; www.topbikerental.com; daily 10am-7pm) has one of the largest selections of sturdy mountain, trekking, and electric bikes. You'll need a good carbon frame and needle bearing forks to offset the ruts along the way. Cannondales, Haibikes, and KTMs don't come cheap, and a three-day rental ranges from €60-120 depending on the model. Subsequent days are cheaper and cost €12-35. Rentals include helmets and locks, but you need to contact the shop in advance if you want to attach a luggage rack.

You can continue pedaling from Florence to Venice but that requires crossing steep, rugged terrain. It's more convenient to bypass the Apennine Mountains on board the regional trains that permit bikes and get off in Bologna. The rest of the journey is flat and can be covered in two or three days.

Fortunately, signage is clear and *Firenze* (Florence) is well indicated. The final 20 miles (32 kilometers) of the route crosses the Apennine Mountains and there are many tunnels, curves, and speed traps.

Bus

Bus is the cheapest and slowest way of getting to Florence. It's only an option if you enjoy cramped seating, dodgy toilets, and the din of strangers speaking on cell phones, and it doesn't provide significant savings. A number of companies operate the Rome-Florence and Venice-Florence routes, and depart from the train stations in those cities.

From Rome: Tickets start from €7 and the trip takes over three hours. There are several companies that operate the route and nearly all depart from Tiburtina station. **Flixbus** (tel. 02/9475-9208; www.flixbus.it; daily 7am-10pm) is a low-cost operator with a modern fleet of buses. There are 15 daily departures (€21.99-34.99) on weekdays between 7:25am and 10:45pm and slightly more on weekends. The **InterFlix** option provides 5 journeys for €99 each of which must be reserved 2 days before departure. Onboard amenities include Wi-Fi, restrooms, electric plugs, and snacks. It's not a bad option, but it's still a bus.

From Venice: Flixbus provides daily service from the Tronchetto bus terminal in Venice to Santa Maria Novella station in Florence. Journey time varies between 4-5 hours depending on the number of stops in between. One-way tickets start from €20.99.

GETTING AROUND

Addresses in Italy consist of street names followed by numbers. The system in Florence, however, is slightly different and distinguishes between residential and commercial properties. Black numbers are used for houses and red ones for shops and businesses. Most restaurants, therefore, will have an "r" (*rosso* means red) and may sometimes be out of chronological order. Via Garibaldi 50r, for instance, is not necessarily next to Via Garibaldi 48 and can be several doors or blocks away. If you can't find the address you're looking for, don't assume they've gone out of business. Just keep searching.

Much of the center is pedestrianized and

distances between monuments are short. If your accommodation is located in the Historic Center or Oltrarno you won't need public transportation unless you want to visit Fiesole or Parco delle Cascine. That said, getting on a bus or tram from the train station and riding it to the end of the line is always fun. Florence has many lovely residential suburbs where tourists rarely tread and you can get a different perspective on the city.

Bus and Tram

Florence ATAF (www.ataf.net) operates a transit network that consists primarily of buses. The **C**1, **C**2, **C**3, and **D** buses crisscross the Historic Center and can be boarded at **Stazione Santa Maria Novella** (Piazza della Stazione; tel. 055/89-2021; daily 4:15am-1:30am), which is practically in the center of the city and is a major transportation hub. Scenic lines include the **Bus 7** between Stazione Santa Maria Novella, San Domenico, and Fiesole, and **Bus 12** or **13** from Stazione Santa Maria Novella to Piazzale Michelangelo. Two modern tram lines stop at the train station and connect the Historic Center with the southwestern outskirts (T1) of the city and the airport (T2). The T1 is fun to ride and provides an entirely different view of Florence. A third line (T3) is scheduled to open in 2020.

The second train station is **Stazione Campo di Marte** (Via Mannelli; daily 6:20am-9pm) northeast of Basilica di Santa Croce. It is accessible on the 12, 13, and 33 bus lines.

Single tickets (€1.50) are valid 90 minutes on buses or trams. Tickets can be purchased at the **Ataf Point** (www.ataf.net; Mon.-Sat. 6:45am-8pm), located at windows 8 and 9 inside Santa Maria Novella train station, and at many newsstands or tobacco shops around the city. They can also be purchased for €2.50 on board buses. Tickets are available in discounted **Carta Agile** packs of 10 (€14). Tickets must always be validated in the designated machines on board at the beginning of every journey.

Bicycle

Bikes are everywhere in Florence, and most of the Historic Center is flat and easy to pedal around. Most rental agencies offer one-hour or five-hour periods on standard city bikes. If you want a more challenging ride you can rent a mountain bike and head over the river to the hillsides above Oltrarno or make an entire day of it and climb up to Fiesole. There are bike paths stretching along both sides of the Arno but the center is often a free-for-all. Locals ride fast and the sound of bells warning distracted tourists to get out of the way is common.

Taxi

Taxis aren't that useful in a city this small, but they are available from stands in Piazza Santa Maria Novella, Piazza della Repubblica, Piazza Ognissanti, and other large squares. They can also be summoned by calling **Taxi Firenze** (4390 or 4242) and are useful at night or if you want to reach Fiesole quickly without taking a bus. On weekdays fares start at €3.30 and increase €0.85 per kilometer. Weekends start from €5.30 and at night (10pm-6am) the initial charge is €6.60. There's also a €1 supplement for luggage and a fourth passenger. A ride from the train station to Palazzo Pitti costs around €12.

Car

If entering Florence by car, keep in mind the city operates a **ZTL** (Limited Traffic Zone) in the Historic Center that's active weekdays 7:30am-8pm and Saturdays 7:30am-4pm (hours may vary during the summer). The zone is clearly indicated and a map of the boundary is available from **SAS** (tel. 055/40401; www.serviziallastrada.it). The best thing to do if your hotel is located within the zone is contact them and obtain a waiver or park at one of the lots on the edge of the ZTL. Vehicles rented in Florence are not subject to ZTL restrictions.

Street parking in the Historic Center of Florence is hard to find, and you can avoid searching for a spot by using one of 15 lots

Firenze Parcheggi (tel. 055/5030-2209; www.firenzeparcheggi.it) manages around the city. Rates range between €1-3 per hour or €15-20 per day at their Stazione SMN, Mercato Centrale, and Sant'Ambrogio garages. There are a number of private garages on both sides of the Arno and some hotels provide complimentary parking. During the summer many Florentines leave town and there are more free spots especially south of the Arno River around Piazzale di Porta Romana. Spaces are usually available along Via Pietro Metastasio and from there it's only a 20-minute walk to Palazzo Pitti.

Most major rental companies have locations at the airport and on Via Borgo Ognissanti minutes from the train station. Avis (Borgo Ognissanti 128; tel. 05/213-629; www.avisautonoleggio.it; Mon.-Fri. 8am-6pm, Sat. 8am-4:30pm, Sun. 8am-1pm), Hertz (Via Borgo Ognissanti 137r; tel. 055/239-8205;

www.hertz.it; daily 8am-7pm), and Europcar (Via Borgognissanti 153r; tel. 055/238-1147; www.europcar.it; Mon.-Fri. 8am-7pm, Sat. 8am-4pm, Sun. 8:30am-12:30pm) are all located here.

Enjoy (www.enjoy.eni.com) car sharing provides 75 red Fiat 500s around Florence. They're permitted to enter the ZTL, exempt from street-parking fees, and can be used for however long or little you like. Costs are reasonable and based on a formula of time and mileage (€0.10 per minute/€0.25 per km). An entire day is €50 and you don't have to pay for gas. Registration is simple and done online. All you need is a passport, driver's license, international driving permit (available from AAA branch offices for $20; www.aaa. com/vacation/idpf.html), and credit card. It's a good alternative to traditional rentals and a convenient way to set off on day trips with zero hassle.

Day Trips

Tuscany is one of the most scenic regions in Italy, and the countryside around Florence is dotted with hill towns, castles, wineries, and villas waiting to be explored. This is the place to take a day trip. Unlike Rome or Venice, getting out of Florence is quick and easy by rail, road, bike, or even on foot.

FIESOLE

Florence owes a lot to Fiesole. The ancient hill town was founded by Etruscans on the hillside overlooking the Arno Valley in 7th-8th century BC and was the first major town in the area. It was later expanded by Romans who used it as a base from which to settle Florence. If you've been to the top of the Duomo or climbed the slopes of Oltrarno, you've probably already spotted Fiesole in the distance. Today the roles have been reversed and it's a sleepy little town where Florentines spend summer evenings, and visitors come to escape

the heat, visit ancient ruins, and enjoy incredible views.

Piazza Mino is the center of Fiesole and where you'll likely start your exploration of town. It's close to all the major sights and trails, and has a tourist office that is open on weekends. Most of the town's eateries border this triangle-shaped square featuring a double equestrian statue of Garibaldi and Italy's first king. Outdoor tables set up throughout the year make for a pleasant lunch or dinner.

Sights
THE DUOMO
Piazzetta della Cattedrale 1; tel. 055/59242; daily 7:30am-6pm; free
The Duomo stands in the center of town in the space once occupied by the Roman Forum. It was completed in 1208 and contains frescoes by Cosimo Rosselli and a triptych above the altar by Bicci di Lorenzo. The bell tower looks

more defensive than spiritual and is nearly 160 feet (50 meters) tall.

ARCHEOLOGICAL MUSEUM

Via Portigiani 1; tel. 055/596-1293; www. museidifiesole.it; Mar.-Oct. daily 9am-7pm, Nov.-Feb daily 10am-3pm; archeological area €7, archeological area plus museum €10, archeological area, museum and Museo Bandini €12, or Firenzecard

Behind the Duomo is the Archeological Museum and Archeological Area that are in much better shape than the Roman remains in Florence. There's a well-preserved **amphitheater** with seating for 3,000 and thermal baths dating from Emperor Adriano's reign. Close examination sheds light on how the Romans heated their saunas, and an informative multimedia guide is included with the entry fee. **Etruscan ruins** are also visible in the shape of a massive stone wall and the foundations of a temple excavated in the 19th century. Relics from successive digs are on display inside the museum. Guided tours (tel. 055/596-1293; info. musei@comune.fiesole.fi.it) of the museum and archeological site are available for €5. There's also a nice café and souvenir shop inside.

MUSEO BANDINI

Via Dupre 1; tel. 055/59118; www.museidifiesole. it; summer Fri.-Sun. 9am-7pm, winter Fri.-Sun. 10am-3pm; €5, €12 combo ticket or Firenzecard

Museo Bandini, the little museum across from the Roman ruins, contains a small collection of 12th-century religious icons and Della Robia ceramics. There's a small, unkept garden and nice views.

Hiking

If you like breaking a sweat, lovely views, narrow lanes, and steep climbs, you'll love Fiesole. The town has three **walking routes** past nature, history, and art. They all start in **Piazza Mino,** and you can download a **map** (www.fiesoleforyou.it) or get a hard copy from the **tourist office** (Via Portigiani 3). Each route takes under an hour to complete,

follows mostly paved roads, and passes numerous points of interest.

To find your way, look for the brown *passeggiata panoramica* (panoramic route) signs in Piazza Mino and around town. Unfortunately, they aren't always in the most visible places and are easy to miss. The best thing to do if you've lost your way is to ask local residents who have grown accustomed to pointing travelers in the right direction.

PIAZZA MINO TO CONVENTO DI SAN FRANCESCO

Distance: *1 mile (1.5 kilometers) round-trip*
Duration: *30-40 minutes round-trip*
Effort level: *easy-moderate*
Starting point: *Piazza Mino*

This panoramic walk starts in the northwestern corner of the square and follows a steep stone road to the convent of San Francesco. Views get progressively better, and there are two benches at the top where you can sit and look out over Florence. When you're done gazing over the city, continue along the forest path opposite the convent (which is often open) and down toward the old Etruscan walls along Via delle Mura Etrusche, and then back through town to the starting point.

PIAZZA MINO TO CONVENTO SAN DOMENICO

Distance: *0.8 miles (1.2 kilometers) one-way*
Duration: *20-30 minutes one-way*
Effort level: *easy*
Starting point: *Piazza Mino*

This leisurely downhill stroll passes three fabulous villas, including Villa Medici, on the road that was once the only way into town. The walk ends at Convento San Domenico, which has a checkerboard interior and several frescoes painted by Beato Angelico. You can ride bus 7 back to Florence from here or continue along Via S. Domenico all the way to Florence.

PIAZZA MINO TO MONTE CECERI

Distance: *1.7 miles (3 kilometers) round-trip*
Duration: *60 minutes round-trip*

Effort level: *moderate*
Starting point: *Piazza Mino*
The third option is an intermediate level up and down quiet lanes to the Parco Monte Ceceri (450 meters above sea level) park and the town's ancient quarries. The most secluded section is along a well-marked trail through a pine forest. Comfortable shoes, long socks to protect from stinging nettles, plenty of water, and determination will get you up to Piazzale Leonardo at the summit, where da Leonardo da Vinci is said to have tested his flying machines for the first time. You can take the same path back or continue and follow Via Corsica and Via Poeti back into Fiesole.

Food

A number of small bars and restaurants line Piazza Mino and Via Antonio Gramsci. Most of these have outdoor seating and several include views of Florence.

PERSEUS
Piazza Mino da Fiesole 9r; tel. 055/59143; Mon.-Sat. 12:30pm-2:30pm and 7:30pm-10:30pm; €8-12
Perseus is famous for homemade cooking without any pretensions. Start with a plate of their mixed Tuscan *antipasto* and continue with a homemade pasta dish. Choose from ravioli, *pici* (thick, spaghetti-length pasta), or *tagliolini* (long, ribbonlike pasta). Brightly colored tables and chairs are set outside from early spring to late autumn. The *gelateria* next door is a reliable place for dessert.

LA REGGIA DEGLI ETRUSCHI
Via San Francesco 18; tel. 055/59385; daily 12:30pm-2pm and 7pm-10pm; €12-14
For an excellent meal with an amazing view, reserve a table at La Reggia degli Etruschi on the outskirts of town near the Franciscan convent. Food, service, and wine are all top notch and the walk up hill to the restaurant is worth the effort.

ALCEDO
Via Antonio Gramsci 39; tel. 055/59349; Tues.-Sun. 7am-8pm
After an excursion around town, stop into this pastry shop and bar for great coffee and delicious homemade sweets.

Shopping

There isn't much in the way of shopping in Fiesole unless you happen to arrive on market Sunday when the main square fills up with kiosks selling antiques and arts and crafts. Otherwise, you can pick up handmade ceramics at **Cobalto** (Via Portigiani 4; tel. 055/599-241; Mon., Wed.-Fri. 10am-1pm and 4pm-7pm, Sat.-Sun. 10am-6pm) opposite the tourist office. This association exhibits a number of skilled potters creating all sorts of functional and decorative pieces. It's also possible to join a class and create a souvenir for yourself.

Festivals and Events
ESTATE FIESOLANA
Via Portigiani 3; tel. 055/596-1293; www. estatefiesolana.it; ticket office daily 9am-6:30pm
Estate Fiesolana is a music, dance, and theater festival held annually throughout June and July. Events are staged in an ancient Roman amphitheater and performers from around the world demonstrate their takes on classical, jazz, pop, rock, and many other genres. The **box office** is near the Archeological Area and performances usually take place in the evening.

Information and Services

The **tourist office** (Via Portigiana 3; tel. 055/596-1311; Fri.-Sun. 10am-1pm and 4pm-6pm) has limited days and hours, but if it is open, speak with Sara to get the latest news on what's happening in town. She'll set you up with maps and pamphlets and provide all the local information you need.

Getting There

Fiesole is 15 minutes from Florence by car or taxi along the panoramic **Via San Domenico** that snakes its way up to town. The trip is slightly longer by bus from Stazione SMN on the **number 7 bus**. Make sure to validate your ticket on board as checks are frequent and unvalidated tickets result in fines of €50. It's a pleasant ride that ends in Piazza Mino da Fiesole.

City Sightseeing (tel. 055/265-6764; www.city-sightseeing.com) Linea B (red) tour buses makes hourly stops in Fiesole during the summer.

The area around town is steep and anyone contemplating cycling from Florence should bring plenty of water and extra energy. You can also rent a mountain or e-bike once you arrive in Fiesole from **Fiesolebike** (Piazza Mino; tel. 345/335-0926; www.fiesolebike. it) and join one of their two-hour tours (€25) or countryside treks (€110 half day, €200 full day). Giovanni and his team will also let you explore on your own and return bikes in Florence at their **Ciclo City** (Via G. Orsini 4a) location. All bikes and tours must be reserved in advance.

MEDIEVAL VILLAS

The hills to the north and south of Florence are dotted with medieval villas where the town's elite once retreated during the hot summer months. A visit offers great views of the city as well as walks through some of Italy's most delightful gardens.

La Petraia Villa

Castello, Via della Petraia 40; tel. 055/452-691; summer daily 8:15am-7:30pm, winter daily 8:30am-3:30pm, closed second and third Mon.; free

La Petraia Villa was constructed in the 13th and 14th centuries and changed hands several times before becoming property of the Medici. Additions to the house and garden were frequent and Ferdinando I hired Bernardo Buontalenti to rebuild it from scratch.

The Italian-style garden that surrounds the villa on three sides was laid out to complement the building. It contains a variety of geometric designs around a central fountain. There's also a long rectangular pool on the second terrace where fish were once stocked. The views of the city are magnificent. Free tours of the villa are organized hourly from 8:30am until closing. La Petraia is 20 minutes from Florence by car. Head northeast toward Sesto Fiorentino and follow the signs for the villa. Or take bus 2 or 28 from SMN train station in Florence.

Villa Gamberaia

Via del Rossellino 72; tel. 055/697-205; www. villagamberaia.com; daily 9am-6pm; €15 garden, €10 villa

Villa Gamberaia is just outside the small village of Settignano and has attracted sculptors and painters for centuries. The building was badly damaged during World War II and painstakingly restored. Today, it's an expensive luxury hotel, but the gardens are open to all visitors and the elegant interior can be toured Tuesday-Saturday 9am-noon by reservation only.

Anyone who has ever planted a bush or seeded a lawn will appreciate the gardens divided into a succession of unique environments. The most interesting part is on the south side of the building, where two local gardeners divided the area into four rectangular pools of water, bordered by box hedges and arch-shaped cypress trees. Nearby there's a long lawn adorned with statues and a gate that leads to a smaller garden bordered by hydrangeas. The grotto at the end was built out of sandstone and contains terra-cotta statues. The view from the shaded terrace is worth a long pause.

The villa is 3 miles (6 kilometers) from the center and can be easily reached with the number 6 bus from SMN train station or Piazza San Marco. Get off at the end of the line in Settignano and walk the rest of the way.

GREVE IN CHIANTI

Greve is the first sizable town on the road from Florence to Siena and considered the gateway to Chianti. It's an ancient market town notable for its architecture and gastronomy. The arcades that run along the sides of

Piazza Matteotti are filled with traditional shops and restaurants. The statue in the middle is Giovanni da Verrazzano, who was born nearby in Castello di Verrazzano and made several journeys to the New World.

If the trademark rolling hills of Chianti don't excite you, the wine will. Wineries, which are located a short distance from town, are the real reason to visit the area. Each has its own personality and produces a different variety of Chianti Classico. The first mention of grapes in the region dates from the 12th century and an export business began soon after that. By the 18th century cultivation was firmly established, and early European travelers were taking note.

Sights

Santa Croce (Piazza Santa Croce; free) lies at the pinnacle of the *piazza* on the site where a medieval chapel once stood. It's not as old as it looks: It was completed in 1835 by Luigi de Cambray-Digny in a neo-Renaissance style. Inside the works of art include a triptych of the *Madonna and Child* by Bicci di Lorenzo.

Shopping

The market spirit has not faded in Greve, and the *piazza* regularly fills up with farmers and merchants selling locally produced goods. On the last Sunday of each month **Il Pagliaio** (Piazza Matteotti) is the occasion to sample handmade olive oils and cheeses. Producers are happy to explain the process involved to curious visitors discovering new flavors. Between May and September on the third Thursday of each month late-night snacks are served in the square. **Stelle e Mercanti** (Piazza Matteotti) is a nocturnal market that starts at 6pm and runs until 11pm.

Festivals and Events

Cantina Aperta (Open Cantina) is the best time for a wine lover to be in Tuscany. It's when wineries open up their doors and allow visitors to sample the latest wines. Not every vineyard in the region takes part but there's a high level of participation in Greve. The event

is scheduled every year on the last Sunday in May.

Food and Nightlife
★ ANTICA MACELLERIA FALORNI
Piazza Matteotti 66; tel. 055/853-029; Mon.-Tues. 11am-7pm, Sat.-Sun. 11am-9pm; €5-6

Falorni is what you get when you combine butcher shop and self-service bistro. Take a number, then pick your meat. There are lots of cold cuts on cutting boards, sandwiches with truffle sauce, and tartare with different seasonings. Grab a seat outside in the square and wait for your feast to arrive. Don't forget a glass of the house red (€4) to wash it all down.

MANGIANDO
Piazza Matteotti 80; tel. 055/854-6372; Tues.-Sun. noon-3pm and 7pm-11pm; €8-11

Underneath the porticos is a small restaurant where Mirna serves her husband's dishes. Mangiando doesn't stray very far from tradition, and the *crostini* are a classic Tuscan appetizer. There are a half-dozen pastas, but if you've had your fill of carbohydrates the steaks are an excellent protein alternative. Chianti is the prevalent wine.

ENOTECA FALORNI
Piazza delle Cantine 6; tel. 055/854-6404; Thurs.-Mon. 10am-7pm

For wine, visit Le Cantine di Greve. This well-stocked *enoteca* carries 1,000 types of wines, over 100 of which can be sampled by the glass. Chianti Classico gets the majority of shelf-space but other parts of Tuscany are also represented. There's also a small museum inside this wonderful brick vaulted grape mecca.

Wine-Tasting

You can learn a lot about wine in Florence, but there's something raw and earthy about drinking it at the source. There are two ways to do that: either you join a wine tour and follow a preordained path or you set out on your

---

1: panoramic view of Lucca **2:** the view from Fiesole **3:** Greve in Chianti

own. The latter is the adventurous option and only requires reaching Chianti. Almost as soon as you leave the city limits, you'll see signs pointing to **Castello di Verrazzano** wineries. Dozens are clustered around the SR222 and it's impossible not to stumble on great wine.

Most vineyards around Greve in Chianti have their own shops where tours and tastings are organized. Vineyard tours often need to be reserved but tastings are spontaneous and nearly always available. They usually involve several different vintages and may include light snacks or lunch. Whenever something strikes your palate, buy a bottle or have a case shipped directly home. The interesting thing about vineyard hopping is discovering how much difference a few kilometers can have on the same grape.

VILLA CALCINAIA
Via Citille 84; tel. 055/853-715; www.villacalcinaia.it; Mon.-Fri. 9am-6pm

Villa Calcinaia is located on an elegant estate 1.2 miles (2 kilometers) north of town. They produce red, white, and rosé from a number of different grape varieties. Visits can be booked with Vincenzo, who will show you around the vineyard and explain the production process. Tours last one hour and start on weekdays at 11am and 2:30pm. Afterward you'll sample four recent vintages with cheese and cured meats (€30 per person). Lunch and dinner can also be organized for a minimum of six people and accommodation in rustic apartments is available in case you want to extend your stay.

CASTELLO DI VERRAZZANO
Via Citille 32a; tel. 055/854-243; www.verrazzano. com; Mon.-Fri. 10am-5pm and Sat.-Sun. 11am-3pm

On a hilltop five minutes away lies Castello di Verrazzano, where grapes and olives have been grown since 1150. The estate belonged to the Verrazzano family and is the birthplace of the famous explorer. There's a lot of history here and plenty of great stories waiting to be told. Guided visits reveal vineyards, gardens, and cellars where wine ages in oak casks.

The **Wine Tour Classico** (Mon.-Sat. 10am and 3pm; €21) lasts 90 minutes and includes three glasses of Chianti Classico and a sampling of the family's olive oil, goat cheese, and balsamic vinegar. If you plan on being hungry, book the **Wine and Food Experience** (Mon.-Fri. noon; €58) and have a three-hour visit of the winery and lunch you'll never forget.

Information and Services
The **tourist office** (Piazza Giacomo Matteotti 10; tel. 055/854-6299; Nov.-Mar. Mon.-Fri. 10am-1pm and 3pm-6pm, Sat. 10am-5pm, Sun. 10am-1pm, Apr.-Oct. daily 10am-7pm) can help find last-minute accommodations and provides a list of monthly events. **KM Zero Tours** (Via Luciana 18, Val di Pesa; tel. 349/352-9601; www.kmzerotours. com) is a source for gastronomic itineraries and one-day trip in the area.

Getting There and Around
Greve is 18 miles (30 kilometers) south of Florence on the **SS222.** SITA buses from **Stazione SMN** are available daily and take 45 minutes to reach town. There's a taxi stand in the central *piazza* where scooter and car rentals are also available.

You can pay someone to take you on a wine tour or you can set off on your own vineyard journey to discover grapes firsthand. A **car** is necessary; you can rent one or use the car-sharing option available in Florence. Once you've decided who the designated driver will be, head south along the SR222 that starts on the outskirts of Florence.

★ LUCCA
Few Italian towns are as thoroughly well-preserved as Lucca, where winding alleys, bell towers, and squares have changed little over the centuries. The street pattern is a remnant of ancient Roman engineering, and they built their designs atop Ligurian and Etruscan foundations. A thriving silk trade and shrewd banking led to steady growth during the late Middle Ages and Renaissance.

There were periods of friction and war with larger cities including Pisa and Florence, but Lucca's independence was never extinguished due in large part to the massive walls surrounding the town. Accessible by train from Florence, Lucca is an easy day trip to organize and a great opportunity to see the Tuscan countryside.

Sights

The **ramparts** of Lucca are the symbol of the city and probably have had a lot to do with preserving the beauty inside. They're actually the fourth set of walls; they were transformed into a park during the 20th century before being rediscovered as one of the great attractions of the town. A walk or bike ride around the 2.5-mile (4-kilometer), tree-lined perimeter provides wonderful views of Lucca and the surrounding countryside. The walls include 10 heart-shaped bulwarks that stick out from the wall and were built to resist attacks. The ramparts can be reached from any of the six gates or by way of numerous streets within the town.

SAN MICHELE IN FORO

Piazza San Michele; tel. 058/358-3150; Mon.-Sat. 7:40am-noon and 3pm-5:30pm; free

San Michele in Foro may not be as large as the churches in Florence, but size doesn't matter when the details are this good. Each column in the triple-tiered facade is different and the inlaid marble fits to perfection. Religious iconography is absent from the exterior except for the winged figure of St. Michael above the pediment. The inside is unusually bare, which makes it good for meditation.

CASA DI PUCCINI

Corte San Lorenzo 9; tel. 058/358-4028; www. puccinimuseum.org; May-Sept. Wed.-Mon. 10am-7pm, Oct.-Apr. daily 10am-6pm; €9

Down the block from the cathedral is the home where the fabled opera composer Giacomo Puccini was born in 1858 and spent most of his youth. The museum was recently restored, and each of the rooms returned to

their 19th-century best. Even if you don't like opera the house provides insight into Victorian-era tastes and standards of living. A small **gift shop** (daily 9:30am-6:30pm) is located nearby in Piazza Cittadella 5.

TORRE DELLE ORE

Via Fillungo 20; tel. 058/348-090; Apr.-Sept. daily 9:30am-6:30pm, Mar. and Oct. 9:30am-5:30pm, closed Nov.-Feb.; €5 or €12 combo ticket with Torre Guinge and Orto Botanico

Several of the towers that once dotted Lucca's skyline are still standing. Legend has it that the devil was once spotted on Torre delle Ore along Via Fillungo, the main thoroughfare of the city. It's the city's highest tower and so named for the clock that was installed in 1754. If you climb the 207 wooden steps to the top, you'll pass the clock mechanics that require daily winding.

During COVID outbreaks, the number of visitors may be restricted.

TORRE GUINIGI

Via S. Andrea 45; tel. 058/348-090; Apr.-Sept. daily 9:30am-6:30pm, Mar. and Oct. 9:30am-5:30pm, Nov.-Feb. 9:30am-4:30pm; €5 or €12 combo ticket with Torre delle Ore and Orto Botanico

You can get an equally great view from Torre Guinigi. The tower was built in the 14th century and distinguishes itself by the holm oaks growing on top. On clear days there are good views of the Apuan Alps north of town.

During COVID outbreaks, the number of visitors may be restricted.

PIAZZA DEL MERCATO

Piazza del Mercato has a strange shape to it. The reason lies in the **Roman amphitheater** that once stood here. In the Middle Ages the stone from the amphitheater was used to build houses, but in 1830 the Bourbons cleared the central area to preserve the original elliptical form. Remains of the two rows of 54 ancient arches can still be seen. Even though it's called Market Square, the stalls once set up here were transferred to the nearby Mercato del Carmine in the 19th century.

Lucca

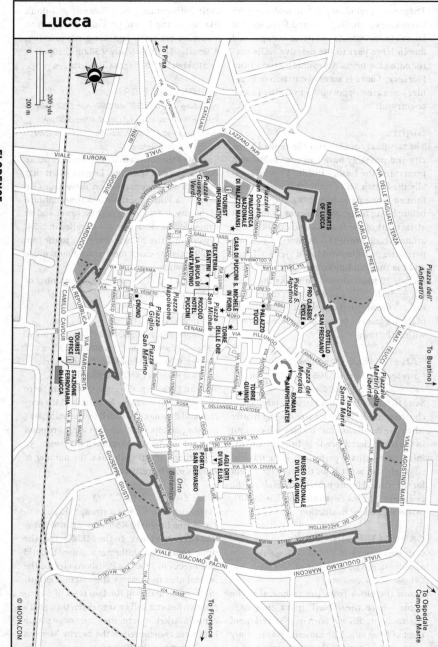

To Pisa

VIALE EUROPA

VIA LAZZARO PAPI

RAMPARTS OF LUCCA

Piazzale Giuseppe Verdi

TOURIST INFORMATION

San Donato

PINACOTECA NAZIONALE DI PALAZZO MANSI

CASA DI PUCCINI

GELATERIA SANTINI

LA BUCA DI SANT'ANTONIO

PICCOLO HOTEL PUCCINI

Piazza Napoleone

Piazza d. Giglio

CRONO

Piazza San Martino

Piazza San Michele

S. MICHELE IN FORO

TORRE DELLE ORE

PALAZZO TUCCI

Piazza S. Agostino

PRO CLASSIC CYCLE

SAN FREDIANO

OSTELLO

Piazza dell' Anfiteatro

Piazzale Martiri della Libertà

To Buatino

Piazza del Mercato

ROMAN AMPHITHEATER

TORRE GUINIGI

Piazza Santa Maria

TOURIST OFFICE

STAZIONE FERROVIARIA DI LUCCA

PORTA SAN GERVASIO

Orto Botanico

AGLI ORTI DI VIA ELISA

MUSEO NAZIONALE DI VILLA GUINIGI

VIALE GIUSEPPE GUSTI

VIALE GIACOMO PACINI

VIALE GUGLIELMO MARCONI

To Florence

To Ospedale
Campo di Marte

VIALE AGOSTINO MARTI

To Florence

0   200 yds
0   200 m

© MOON.COM

MUSEO NAZIONALE DI VILLA GUINIGI

Via della Quarquonia 4; tel. 058/349-6033; www. luccamuseinazionali.it; Tues.-Sat. noon-7:30pm; €4 or €6.50 combo with Palazzo Mansi

Museo Nazionale di Villa Guinigi displays cultural artifacts and paintings across three floors of an elegant villa. The archeological section on the ground floor contains many fragments from the past and examples of ancient funerary monuments. The shield once worn by a medieval Lombard warrior is impressive, as are paintings by Fra Bartolomeo and his Renaissance contemporaries.

PINACOTECA NAZIONALE DI PALAZZO MANSI

Via Galli Tassi 43; tel. 058/355-570; Tues.-Sat. noon-7:30pm; €4 or €6.50 combo with Villa Guinigi

Pinacoteca Nazionale di Palazzo Mansi was the home of a 16th-century nobleman and has since been transformed into a museum. The luxurious interior includes a hall of mirrors and hall lined with intricate tapestries. The museum has a varied collection donated by Leopold II in 1847. Venetian, Lombard, Roman, and Flemish artists are all present. Tuscan paintings include work by Bronzino, Andrea del Sarto, and Pontormo's Portrait of a Young Man.

ORTO BOTANICO (Botanic Garden)

Via del Giardino Botanico 14; tel. 058/395-0596; www.lemuradilucca.it; Apr.-Oct. daily 10am-6pm, Nov.-Mar. upon reservation only; €5 or €12 combo ticket with Torre Guingi and Torre delle Ore

For a complete change of scenery without having to leave the Historic Center, stroll the Orto Botanico, which was built along the walls and contains hundreds of rare species. It's a quiet place to take a stroll under shaded trees and flowering plants that reach full bloom in late spring. The 18th-century formal gardens and baroque statues of **Palazzo Pfanner** (Via degli Asili 33; tel. 058/395-4029; www.palazzopfanner.it; Apr.-Nov. daily 10am-6pm;

€5 garden, €6 garden and residence) offer a similar experience.

Food

GELATERIA SANTINI

Piazza Cittadella 1; tel. 058/355-295; summer daily 9am-midnight, winter Tues.-Sun. 9am-9pm; €3-4

Gelateria Santini has been open since 1916 and they've learned a lot about gelato in that time. Besides a dozen homemade flavors they prepare delicious zuccotti and semifreddi desserts.

AGLI ORTI DI VIA ELISA

Via Elisa 17; tel. 058/349-1241; Thurs.-Tues. noon-2:30pm and 7:30pm-11pm, Thurs. dinner only; €8-12

Agli Orti di Via Elisa is operated with gusto by an enthusiastic team of chefs. The two large dining rooms offer traditional gastronomy and oven-baked pizzas within an elegant interior.

BUATINO

Borgo Giannotti 508; tel. 058/334-3207; Mon.-Sat. noon-3pm and 6pm-10:30pm; €10-14

Lunchtime service at Buatino can be hectic—everyone's eager to get their forks into the specials. Dinner is more relaxed and the atmosphere often includes live music. The tagliatelle al piccione (pasta with pigeon) makes a good first course and seconds include bollito misto in salsa verde (mixed meat stew with green sauce). The wine menu lists over 150 bottles from Tuscany and other Italian regions.

★ LA BUCA DI SANT'ANTONIO

Via della Cervia 3; tel. 058/355-881; Tues.-Sat. noon-3pm and 7:30pm-10pm, lunch Sun.; €14-16

What started out as an inn where weary travelers could rest their horses and feed themselves hasn't changed much. Although the horses are gone, the hearty soups at La Buca di Sant'Antonio are pretty much the same. Puccini and Pound were known to dine here, and the candles and white tablecloths make it popular with couples.

Shopping

Lucca's shopping district is concentrated along **Via Fullungo**. The town's many **markets** provide pleasant atmospheres and original gifts. **Mercato dell'Antiquariato** is the second-largest antiques and ethnic market in all of Italy, and it fills half a dozen squares in the center with hundreds of stalls. Treasure hunters will find furniture and collectibles of every style, period, and type. The popular event is held on the third weekend of every month and closes much of the center to traffic.

Bike Routes

Bike lovers have come to the right town! Depending on how much time you have, you can pedal around Lucca's paved ramparts for an hour or head out on longer treks. Terrain is flat and surfaces are mostly hardened dirt that can be walked as well as biked. The city's old aqueduct to the south is among the most popular riding areas, and you won't be alone if you do decide to explore it. Much of the center is off-limits to traffic, and streets like **Via del Fosso,** with its canal, are interesting to explore.

RAMPARTS

Distance: *2.5 miles (4 kilometers; total circumference)*
Duration: *20-30 minutes at medium speed*
Effort level: *easy*
Starting points: *any of the six gates and numerous ramps within town*

The ramparts of Lucca are the symbol of the city and have had a lot to do with preserving the beauty inside. They're the fourth set of walls and were transformed into a park in the 20th century. A walk or bicycle ride around the 2.5-mi (4-km) tree-lined perimeter provides wonderful views of Lucca and the surrounding countryside. The walls include 10 heart-shaped bulwarks that stick out from the wall and were built to resist attacks. Several cafés along the way make good pitstops for thirsty riders.

PARCO DEL NOTTOLINI

Distance: *2.5 miles (4 kilometers) one-way*
Duration: *30-35 minutes one-way*
Effort level: *easy*
Starting point: *Behind the train station, across Via Civitali footbridge*

To the south, Parco del Nottolini is an easy ride that starts behind the train station and over the Via Civitali footbridge. The path extends straight 2.5 miles (4 kilometers) on Via degli Aquedotti toward the Pisani Mountains next to a 39-foot-high (12-meter-high) aqueduct completed by Lorenzo Nottolini in 1851. The 459 arches lead to a spring in San Quirico di Guamo. The narrow dirt trail crosses several roads, and there are a couple of drinking fountains along the way. Once you get to the end of the aqueduct, you can keep going up the hill to the source where locals often picnic.

Bike Rentals

There is no shortage of rental shops, prices are fairly standardized, and bike quality is excellent.

TOURIST CENTER LUCCA

Piazzale B. Ricasoli 203; www.touristcenterlucca. com; daily 9:30am-7pm

You can rent bicycles from Tourist Center Lucca, near the train station. They provide basic city bikes (€8 for 3 hours or €12 per day) with a front basket and lock, and sturdier all-terrain mountain bikes (€30 per day). It's possible to leave luggage (€3 for 3 hours/€5 per day) behind while you cycle.

CRONO

Corso Garibaldi 93; tel. 058/349-0591; www. chronobikes.com

Crono rents bikes and arranges personalized cycling tours. Olympia hybrid bikes rent for €25 a day, while ultra-light Nytro Pinarello e-bikes with click pedals are €50. These are perfect for any of the longer excursions outside of Lucca. Tandems, quads, and rickshaws are also available for slow rides around town.

PRO CLASSIC CYCLE

Via Cesare Battisti 60; tel. 058/346-4657; www.
proclassiccycle.com; Mon.-Sat. 9am-12:30pm and
2:30pm-7pm

If quality matters and you know the difference between a cog set and crank set, head to Pro Classic Cycle. Bicycles are in mint condition, and Cesere makes sure every bike he rents matches the journey riders want to take. Prices (€20-35 per day) vary depending on make and model. City bikes are also available by the hour (€4).

Accommodations

Lucca is the perfect day trip from Florence, but if you decide to spend the night there are plenty of inexpensive accommodations. Be careful where you stay, however, as parts of the city—especially the southern part of town near Porta San Pietro—can get very loud during the summer when bars remain open late and dance music fills the streets until the early hours. Quieter nights can be assured in residential areas or outside the city walls where accommodation is generally cheaper and only a short walk away. Prices increase substantially during the Lucca Comics festival in late October and throughout the Summer Festival.

OSTELLO SAN FREDIANO

Via della Cavallerizza 12; tel. 058/344-2817; https://
ostello-san-frediano.business.site; €30 pp or €70 d

Ostello San Frediano challenges many of the stereotypes surrounding hostels. First, it's not a large dormitory for backpackers, and second, it's not located far from the city center. Instead rooms are many different sizes and the location between Piazza San Frediano and Piazza Antifiteatro is enviable. What remains true, however, is affordability. A buffet breakfast is included in the price and the €20 all-inclusive lunch and dinner served in the large dining room is one of the best deals in Lucca. Guests do need to register for an AIG hostel card, but that can be done on-site at the front desk.

PICCOLO HOTEL PUCCINI

Via di Poggio 9; tel. 058/355-421; www.hotelpuccini.
com; €75-100 s/d

It doesn't get more central than Piccolo Hotel Puccini. All of the town's monuments are around one corner or the other of this comfortable hotel. Breakfast is an extra €4 that will seem wisely spent. These are simple, clean accommodations that may not be glamorous but leave a good impression. Windows are double-plated and keep noise from the street below out.

PALAZZO TUCCI

Via C. Battisti 13; tel. 058/346-4279; www.
palazzotucci.com; €150-190 d

The entrance is the first clue Palazzo Tucci is not the average B&B. This historic residence provides an idea of how 19th-century nobles once lived. The high frescoed ceilings and six spacious rooms and suites ornately decorated in period furnishings are authentic down to the bedposts. Satellite TV, Wi-Fi, and air-conditioning are the only concessions to modernity of this peaceful accommodation that will satisfy even the lightest of sleepers.

Information and Services

Lucca goes a long way to welcome visitors. The main tourist office or **Centro di Accoglienza Turistica** (Vecchia Porta San Donato 15; tel. 058/358-3150; www. luccaturismo.it; summer daily 9:30am-6:30pm, winter 9:30am-4:30pm) is located near Porta San Donato along the eastern walls of the city. You can deposit bags, grab a free map, and purchase tickets to museums and concerts here. They'll also help you find a hotel in your price range at no charge if you decide to spend the night in Lucca. A second **tourist office** (Piazza Curtatone; tel. 058/344-2213; Wed., Fri., Sat. 9am-1:30pm, Tues., Thurs. 9am-1:30pm and 2:30pm-5:30pm) with similar services but fewer opening hours is located a couple blocks from the train station which makes it a good first stop before exploring the city.

Both offices organize **group tours** of the city on Wednesday and Saturday mornings at 11am and every afternoon at 2pm. These cost €13, last two hours, and can be purchased at the office or with the guide, who alternates between Italian and English, waiting near the church in Piazzale San Michele.

Lucca has two combination ticket offers. The Pinacoteca Nazionale and Museo Nazionale ticket are €6.50 while two towers and the botanical garden can be visited for €12. Both offers are good for two days and can be purchased from any of the participating sights.

Ospedale Campo di Marte (Via Ospedale 1; tel. 058/39701; www.uslnordovest.toscana.it) is just outside the walls near Porta San Jacopi. Consultations can be made over the phone and there are several pharmacies in the center for resolving minor mishaps. If you can't find the right words just mime the injury or ailment. **Farmacia Comunale** (Piazza Curtatone 7; tel. 058/349-1398) is open 24 hours and located in front of the train station. Most *tabacchi* carry stamps, but you can also pick them up at any of the three **post offices** within the city walls. The main office is on Via Vallisneri 2 and there are smaller branches at Via S. Gregorio 8 and on Viale Regina Margherita. Make sure to grab a ticket to ensure your place in line.

Getting There and Around

The easiest way to reach Lucca from Florence is by train. There are frequent departures and the regional service (€7.90-10.10) takes under two hours. A transfer in Pisa or Pistoia is required. Trains depart from Stazione Santa Maria Novella and arrive in **Stazione Ferroviaria di Lucca** (Viale Camillo Benso Cavour 15; www.trenitalia.it) just outside the city walls and within walking distance of Lucca's Historic Center. The last train back to Florence departs at 10:40pm. Tickets can be purchased from automated machines in SMN or the ticket booths inside the station. Trains are rarely crowded and there's plenty of scenic countryside to enjoy along the way.

There's a taxi stand outside the train station as well as in Piazza Santa Maria, Piazzale Verdi, and Piazza Napoleone. To order a cab, call **Radio Taxi** (tel. 05/8333-3434) or **Taxi Lucca** (tel. 05/8395-5200). Lucca is located off the A11 highway that links the A1 near Florence with the A12 near Pisa. Drivers can choose from 10 paying parking lots (€1.50 per hour) within the walls or park for free in the neighborhood streets outside and walk the rest of the way.

Between Florence and Venice

BOLOGNA

Bologna is home to the world's oldest university, founded in 1088, miles of arcades and some of the best food in Italy. The city is relaxed about its scholarly reputation, and there's a pleasant collegial atmosphere throughout the city's Historic Center. It's a great place to meet students from all over Europe at the many bars and cafés along Via Zamboni and its offshoots, where famous regional dishes are served.

Bologna is surrounded by fertile lands and has a strong gastronomic tradition. It's particularly famous for *tortellini* (ring-shaped pasta filled with meat or cheese) and *mortadella*, cured ham that tastes remotely like bologna (but much, much better).

Rain or shine, Bologna feels like a medieval and slightly dark town, owing to its 654 **arcades**—roughly 24 miles (39 kilometers) long—that were constructed during the Middle Ages. The arcades have spawned a life of their own, particularly throughout the Historic Center and university area, where students and everyone else can be seen engaged in lively conversation under the stately cover of the arcades.

Sights

The **Bologna Welcome Card** (www.bolognawelcome.com) includes entry to all the city's museums, the two towers, church terrace, a two-hour guided walking tour, open bus tour, map, and discounts to local spas and restaurants. It comes in two varieties, valid 48 (€25) or 72 (€40) hours and available online or from the **tourist office** in Piazza Maggiore. The card is free for children under 12 accompanied by an adult.

SAN PETRONIO BASILICA

Piazza Galvani 5; www.basilicadisanpetronio.org; daily 8:30am-12:30pm and 3pm-6pm; free, €3 Capella dei Magi

Bologna's central **Piazza Maggiore** is majestic, lively, and lived-in at the same time. The centerpiece is San Petronio Basilica, which is flanked by the Notaries' Palace, City Hall, and the Governor's Palace, all of them elegant without being ostentatious. You can see it all here: Large-screen movies every night of the week during the summer, businesspeople bustling to work, and students crooning Italy's beloved resistance song, *Bella Ciao*, on the church steps in the wee hours of the morning. The basilica is the world's fifth-largest church and a stunning example of Gothic architecture. Work on it was started in 1390, initially with the intention of making it larger than St. Peter's in Rome (that ambition was blocked by the Vatican). The immense, austere, and unfinished facade is well guarded by volunteers who make sure you turn off your mobile phone before entering. The simple but magnificent interior bodes well for symphonic concerts at Christmas and other major Roman Catholic holidays.

There's a great panoramic view of the city from the **San Petronio Basilica terrace** (daily 10am-1pm and 3pm-6pm; €5) 177 feet (54 meters) up. It's a fairly easy climb that benefits from an elevator part of the way.

LE DUE TORRI

Piazza di Porta Ravegnana; www.duetorribologna.com; summer daily 10am-6pm; €5

Le Due Torri (two towers) are fraternal, rather than identical, towers in the center of the city. The **Garisenda Tower** leans more and is about half as tall as the **Asinelli Tower,** which is the tallest leaning medieval tower in the world and a must-climb. They're named for the families believed responsible for their construction in 1109-1119. Visitors can climb to the top of the Asinelli Tower, which is 318.8 feet (97.2 meters)/498 steps/1.3 degree lean for the best view of the city.

During COVID outbreaks, the number of visitors may be restricted.

Food

With its colder climes, Bologna does not follow the Mediterranean diet, and winter is the best time to get a taste of why the city is known for its food. The entire country has embraced Bologna's staple dish, *tortellini* with broth, as a Christmas Eve dinner tradition. The ring-shaped pasta comes stuffed with meat, ricotta cheese, or pumpkin.

DA BERTINO

Via Lame 55; tel. 051/522-230; Mon.-Sat. 12:15pm-2:30pm and 7:15pm-10:30pm; €10-12

If you like meat, Da Bertino is the place to eat. Brave travelers should try the *bollito,* boiled parts of animals most people have never tasted—such as beef tongue and veal brisket. More traditional dishes such as roast lamb and pork can satisfy carnivorous appetites, while cold meats like mortadella and prosciutto serve as tasty appetizers. Fresh pasta is also made daily.

ANTICA TRATTORIA DELLA GIGINA

Via Stendhal 1b; tel. 051/322-300; daily 12:15pm-3pm and 7:30pm-10:30pm; €8-14

Known as the temple of *tagliatelle* pasta, Antica Trattoria della Gigina has developed a solid reputation over 50 years for some of the best handmade pasta in the city: lasagna, *tortelli,* and *tortellini* served with classic Bolognese meat sauce (which the rest of the world calls *ragù*) or butter and sage. Try the *zuppa inglese* to finish it off. It's close to the town racetrack just outside of the city center.

CESARINA

Via Santo Stefano 19b; tel. 051/232-037; Tues.-Sun. 12:30pm-2:30pm and 7:30pm-10:30pm, closed Tues. lunch; €12-15

Try *tortellini* with broth in the elegant Cesarina, a legendary restaurant in a 14th-century palazzo beneath the arcades in the city center. Also worth sampling are the lasagna, ravioli, and gnocchi, followed by oven-roasted rabbit or goat seasoned with truffles and herbs. In winter they serve *zampone,* pork sausage stuffed inside *zampa* (pig's foot). Italians all over the country eat it with lentils on New Year's Eve for good luck.

Getting There and Around

Bologna is easy to reach by car from Florence. The drive takes less than 90 minutes along the **A1** highway. It's only slightly longer from Venice by way of the A57 and A13. Getting to Bologna does not require a detour for those traveling between Florence and Venice. Bologna is also on the same high-speed train line that connects Rome, Florence, and Venice, so it makes a convenient stop if you're curious about *tortellini*. **Bologna Centrale** station is a 15-minute walk from the center on Via dell'Independenza and bags can be deposited (€6) inside 7am-9pm. **Guglielmo Marconi International Airport** (tel. 051/647-9615; www.bologna-airport.it) is located 4.3 miles (7 kilometers) northwest of the city and serves domestic and European destinations.

Although Bologna is small enough to traverse on foot, buses operate in the Historic Center and stop at Piazza Nettuno and Piazza Maggiore. Tickets are available at newspaper stands and *tabacchi* shops. Single tickets costs €1.50 and are good for one hour; for €6 you can get a 24-hour pass. Validate your ticket as soon as you get on board to avoid being fined.

RAVENNA

Ravenna is an often-overlooked small city that hosts relatively few tourists. That means there's little wait to view the town's main attraction, a collection of early Christian and Byzantine mosaics. Ravenna is also the final resting place of the great Florentine poet Dante Alighieri, who nearly singlehandedly codified the Italian language. His tomb is in the center of town, as are many ancient churches that can be visited in a couple of hours.

Sights

The **Mosaic Ticket** (€12.50) is good for seven days and allows entry to Basilica di Sant'Apollinare Nuovo, Battistero Neoniano, Basilica di San Vitale, Mausoleo di Galla Placidia, and Cappella Arcivescovile. Buy it at the first monument you visit, and then see the others. Single tickets are not sold.

BASILICA DI SAN VITALE

Via San Vitale 17; tel. 05/4454-1688; www. ravennamosaici.it; Mar.-Oct. daily 9am-7pm, Nov.-Feb. 10am-5pm; €12.50 combo ticket

Basilica di San Vitale is one of Ravenna's eight UNESCO World Heritage Sites. The octagonal church, begun in AD 527, has the largest and best-preserved Byzantine mosaics outside Constantinople. Ceilings and walls are covered with golden portraits of Emperor Justinian, Empress Theodora, and images of the Old Testament. Tickets allow entry to a half-dozen sites nearby.

MAUSOLEO DI GALLA PLACIDIA

Via San Vitale 17; Mar.-Oct. daily 9am-7pm, Nov.-Feb. 10am-5pm; €12.50 combo ticket

The city's oldest mosaics are housed in the Mausoleo di Galla Placidia, built by Emperor Teodorico for his daughter Galla Placidia. The mausoleum contains many powerful images, particularly *The Good Shepherd,* which utilizes blue and yellow tiles rarely seen anywhere else.

1: Basilica di San Vitale in Ravenna **2:** Piazza Maggiore in Bologna

DANTE ALIGHIERI'S TOMB

Via Alighieri Dante 9; Mon.-Fri. 10am-6pm and Sat.-Sun. 10am-7pm; free

You can feel the silence of reverence as you approach Dante Alighieri's tomb, in part because of a city ordinance and in part because Italians have great respect for their premier poet. Ravenna was the last place he lived, and where he wrote the final verses of *Il Paradiso*, part of his masterpiece trilogy *The Divine Comedy*, before his death in 1321. A votive lamp filled with oil from Florence hangs above his tombstone. The tomb was undergoing restoration in 2020 and scheduled to reopen in early 2021.

CHIESA DI SAN FRANCESCO

Piazza San Francesco 3; summer daily 7am-7:30pm, winter daily 7am-noon and 3pm-7pm; free

The austere-looking Chiesa di San Francesco, near Dante's tomb, is where the poet's funeral is believed to have been held. Hold your breath before you visit the stunning 10th-century mosaics beneath the flooded crypt. It's best to visit early or late as the church is closed to tourists during mass.

Food

PASTICCERIA VENEZIANA

Via Salaria 15; tel. 054/212-171; Mon., Thurs., Sun. 6:30am-1pm, Tues., Wed., Fri., Sat. 6:30am-1pm and 3pm-7pm; €3-5

To sample Ravenna's famous *brioche* pastries (Italian-style croissants) and other sweet temptations visit Pasticceria Veneziana. The modern bar/bakery also serves light sandwiches, fresh juices, and coffee indoors or at a handful of tables on a quiet street near the center.

ANTICA TRATTORIA AL GALLO

Via Maggiore 87; tel. 054/421-3775; Wed.-Sat. 11:30pm-2pm and 7pm-11pm, Sun. 11:30pm-2pm; €8-12

The family-run Antica Trattoria al Gallo has been cooking pasta right for nearly a century. The largely vegetarian menu owes nothing to trends; they simply use Italy's best products, and never stray from seasonal ingredients.

★ CA' DE VEN

Via Corrado Ricci 24; tel. 054/430-163; Tues.-Sun. 11:30am-2:30pm and 6:30pm-11pm; €12-13

Ca' De Ven is a cavernous winery and restaurant in the center of town that serves traditional meat-and-potato-style dishes. Even the basic *pasta e fagioli* (pasta with beans) is done exceptionally well, not to mention the *cappelletti* and *tortelloni*. The house red wine is excellent, and *ravioli con marmalade* makes for a sumptuous dessert.

Getting There and Around

Ravenna is 117 miles (188 kilometers) from Florence on the Adriatic coast. By car, head north on the **A1** until you reach Bologna and then take the **E45** and **A14** highways to the city, which is clearly indicated. The town is 90 miles (144 kilometers) from Venice. To get there, drive south from Venice on the scenic **SS309,** a one-lane state road that skirts the coast. The journey by train from either Florence or Venice takes around three hours and requires a transfer in Bologna. One-way tickets cost between €20-40 depending on the service.

FERRARA

Ferrara is roughly halfway between Florence and Venice and easily reached by car or train. It's a beautiful small city that makes a nice extended lunch stop.

Great minds worked hard to make Ferrara spectacular. There was a sharp increase in building activity during the Renaissance and the city paved the way for modern urban planning. The center is easily visited on foot or bike and was added to UNESCO's heritage protection list in 1995. A couple of hours are all you need to admire the architecture and explore the streets that are ideal for pedestrians and cyclists.

Sights

PALAZZO DEL DIAMANTE

Corso Ercole I d'Este 21; tel. 053/224-4949; www.palazzodiamanti.it; daily 11am-9pm; €10

Palazzo del Diamante was named for its

stunning facade made from white diamond-shaped stones. It was the residence of the Estes family, who were the local equivalent of the Medici in Florence, and is used for exhibitions and to house the city's art gallery. Guided tours (€6) lasting an hour and 15 minutes are available Saturdays at 5pm and Sundays at noon. Reservations are required and can be made by emailing visitamostraferrara@gmail.com or calling 333/158-1942 (Mon.-Fri. 2pm-6pm). **Pinacoteca Nazionale** (Corso Ercole I d'Este 21; tel. 053/220-5844; Tues.-Sat. 10am-5:30pm, Sun. 10am-6pm; €6) is located on the second floor and displays a permanent collection of regional masters.

CASTELLO ESTENSE

Largo Castello 1; tel. 053/229-9233; www.castelloestense.it; daily 9:30am-1:30pm and 3:30pm-7:30pm, closed Tues. morning; €12, guided tours €4, tower €2

In the center of town Castello Estense is the epitome of a castle and even has a shallow moat. It was built to defend the Estes family against tax rebellions at the end of the 14th century. It's said that inside the invincible walls is where one of the Estes nobles discovered that his wife and son were lovers. Visit the underground prison where he tortured them before having them beheaded. Today the government occupies most of the *castello* but a few rooms replete with original frescoes are open to the public along with a café and bookshop.

DUOMO

Piazza della Cattedrale; tel. 053/220-7449; Mon.-Sat. 7:30am-noon and 3:30pm-6:30pm, Sun. and holidays 7:30am-12:30pm and 3:30pm-7:30pm; free

Ferrara's Duomo combines beauty and substance. Its three-tiered marble facade attracts and holds the gaze. Inside, Sebastiano Filippi's fresco of *The Last Judgment* inspired Michelangelo's version in the Sistine Chapel. Along the church's right-hand side are 15th-century artisans' shops known as the *Loggia dei Merciai* that re-create Ferrara during the Renaissance.

Food

The best reason to visit Ferrara is the food. The Emilia Romagna region has a strong gastronomic reputation, with local dishes to savor.

AL BRINDISI

Via Adelardi 11; tel. 053/247-1225; daily 11am-midnight; €10-12

At Al Brindisi they claim to have fed Renaissance greats Titian and Benvenuto Cellini. The restaurant opened in 1435 and has had plenty of time to hone the marriage of good regional cooking and fine wine. The menu changes with the seasons but usually includes the town's famous *tagliatelle* and *cappellacci* pasta dishes. There are also six satisfying fixed-price menus ranging €15-50.

LA PROVVIDENZA

Corso Ercole d'Este 92; tel. 053/220-5187; Tues.-Sun. noon-2:30pm and 8pm-10:30pm; €10-14

If you develop an appetite during a visit to the Certosa Monastery, La Provvidenza is just around the corner. Try the fresh pasta with porcini mushrooms and truffles or stuffed ravioli. The restaurant is proud of its many illustrious visitors that included Andy Warhol, Federico Fellini, and dozens of Italian politicians.

QUEL FANTASTICO GIOVEDÌ

Via Castelnuovo 9; tel. 053/276-0570; daily 12:30pm-3:30pm and 7:30pm-midnight, closed Aug.; €11-14

Quel Fantastico Giovedì is a favorite with locals who come for eclectic dishes that include duck liver. If you're not feeling adventurous, they also prepare less intimidating handmade pasta. Meals are often accompanied by live jazz and improvised singing. Service is friendly and the atmosphere relaxed.

Information and Services

The **tourist office** (Largo Castello 1; tel. 053/229-9303; www.ferrarainfo.com; daily 9am-6pm) is located inside Castello Estense and provides free maps and sight information. They sell the **MyFe Card** (€15/2 days) that provides entry to all the major monuments in town.

Getting There

Ferrara is a two-hour drive from Florence in the direction of Venice. Take the **A1** and then follow the **A13** after Bologna. There are two exits for Ferrara; the second gets you to the center slightly quicker. Paid **parking** is

available on Viale Cavour and the side streets near Piazza Castello.

Ferrera is 70 miles (114 kilometers) from Venice, which can be reached in a little over an hour by rejoining the A13 highway or **SS16** state road in double that time.

Train service to Ferrara is high speed or regional and usually requires one or two transfers. Tickets start from €15 and there are hourly daily departures from Florence and Venice.

Venice

Venice is unlike any city in the world, an improbable spot founded on islets in a flood-prone lagoon.

Historically, commerce was king, and individual freedoms existed like nowhere else. At one time, Venice was the most populated city in the world, and everyone who was anyone did business or indulged here. Germans, Jews, Spaniards, Turks, French, and Arabs were all welcome. Nationality mattered less than money, and even the Vatican didn't have much sway in the lagoon.

Venice's economy relied on the sea and on trade with Europe, Asia, and the Middle East. Along with the goods that came in and out of its ports, Venice was exposed to new ideas, architecture, flavors, and culture. That East-meets-West crossroads atmosphere is still alive today,

Highlights

Look for ★ to find recommended sights, activities, dining, and lodging.

© MOON.COM

★ **St. Mark's Basilica:** Thousands of golden mosaics line the ceilings of this stunning cathedral (page 289).

★ **Doge's Palace:** No building in Venice has more history than this one. Step inside to discover what made Venice great over the centuries—and what happened to anyone who broke the law (page 293).

★ **Rialto Bridge:** This iconic bridge is the center of Venetian commerce, with markets, food stalls, and shops of all kinds on and around it (page 296).

★ **Guggenheim Foundation:** Leave historic Venice behind and fast-forward a few centuries at this unique gallery filled with 20th-century masterpieces (page 299).

★ *Vaporetto* **Ferries:** Navigate canals with a single or multiday pass to experience the aquatic side of the city and lagoon islands. These public ferries are more functional than gondolas—and can be just as romantic (page 313).

★ *Cicchetti* **Appetizers:** Enter a traditional *bacaro* bar to feast on a remarkable selection of Venetian finger food, accompanied by sparkling *prosecco* wine (page 324).

★ **Kayaking Venice's Canals:** Paddle your way through a maze of canals and get an alternative take on the city (page 353).

★ **Glassmaking Workshops on Murano:** Venice and nearby Murano island are famous for glassmaking. Visit a workshop to view a glassmaking demonstration, shop for one-of-a-kind pieces, or take a class to learn to blow glass yourself (page 371).

★ **Burano:** Take a break from Venice on a remote island filled with colorful houses and picturesque fishing boats (page 374).

from the Arabesque shape of windows overlooking the Grand Canal to the spices used in local kitchens.

The greatest sight in Venice is not a museum or a monument but the city itself. Buildings may be slowly decaying, but Venice has lost none of its golden-age flair, and hundreds of artisans, shopkeepers, fishermen, and chefs preserve the Venetian way of life. Gondolas still glide along canals, bells still toll the daylight hours, and glass is still blown into fabulous shapes. The absence of cars and the extraordinary presence of boats make everything about the city even more magical. The best way to experience Venice is to stow away your map, resist the urge to photograph every beauty, and lose yourself in the city. Whichever byway, bridge, or canal you follow, it's impossible to stray from the enchanting labyrinth that is Venice. Regardless of how many tourists surround you there is always an alley or *sotoportego* leading to an intimate, deserted corner of the city. Let Venice lead you in unexpected directions, and when you get thirsty or require sustenance, do as the locals do and enter a *bacaro* bar for a glass of *prosecco* and delicious Venetian appetizers.

Warning: There is a high probability of falling in love with Venice, and once you do you will spend the rest of your life dreaming of the city and longing to return.

HISTORY

Like all cities, Venice is a result of coincidence. It just so happened that the Roman Empire was in decline, Germanic tribes were invading the Italian peninsula, and local people needed a place to survive. In Tuscany and most of Italy they built walls, but in Venice the sea was the wall. The small fishing villages on the mainland were no longer safe and the best refuge from Vandals were the maze of small islets scattered around the Venetian Lagoon.

Many islands were settled, but Venice is the one that eventually emerged thanks to its position and geography. Soggy land was gradually urbanized over the centuries and trade with Adriatic port cities and exotic Eastern empires allowed it to flourish. The city was organized into a semidemocratic republic ruled by *doges*, who were king-like figures with great power and privilege; they were guided by a council of advisers and supported by influential Venetian families. There were 120 *doges* in all and their portraits decorate the Doge's Palace from where they reigned.

After the body of St. Mark was smuggled to the city in an attempt to gain prestige and religious clout, pilgrims from across Europe began traveling to Venice. Visitors have been welcomed ever since, and along with trade were fundamental in the city's rise. Goods, language, and ideas from Asia Minor left a unique cultural impression that still permeates the city today. New palaces were built, basilicas consecrated, canals dug, and sailing ships launched. At its height Venice had a population of 160,000 and controlled large stretches of the Mediterranean from Crete to Lebanon. Vast wealth was accumulated and invested in art and architecture.

It wasn't all good times, though, and frequent plagues led to the decimation of the population and the formation of charitable associations known as the Scuole Grande that cared for the sick and opened the city's first hospitals. They built grand meeting halls like the Scuole Grande di San Rocco and commissioned the decoration of interiors by Renaissance artists such as Titian and Tintoretto, who developed a unique Venetian style and were capable of remarkable feats of painting.

A thousand years of independence came to an end in 1797 when Napoleon captured the city, and the Venetian Republic—already past its heyday and slowly degenerating—went out with a whimper. But a city like Venice could

Previous: Grand Canal; dome of St. Mark's Basilica; *vaporetto* ferry

Venice

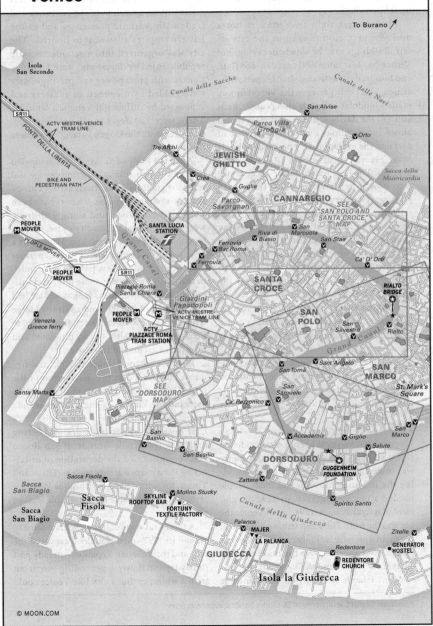

To Burano

Isola
San Secondo

Canale delle Sacche

Canale delle Navi

San Alvise

Parco Villa
Groggia

Orto

SR11

ACTV MESTRE-VENICE
TRAM LINE

PONTE DELLA LIBERTÀ

Tre Archi

JEWISH
GHETTO

Sacca della
Misericordia

BIKE AND
PEDESTRIAN PATH

Crea

Guglie

CANNAREGIO

SEE
"SAN POLO AND
SANTA CROCE"
MAP

PEOPLE
MOVER

Parco
Savorgnan

PEOPLE MOVER

SANTA LUCIA
STATION

Riva di
Biasio

San
Marcuola

San Stae

Ferrovia
Bar Roma

PEOPLE
MOVER

SR11

Ferrovia

Ca' D' Oro

Venezia
Greece ferry

Piazzale Roma
Santa Chiara

SANTA
CROCE

RIALTO
BRIDGE

PEOPLE
MOVER

Giardini
Papadopoli

ACTV MESTRE-
VENICE TRAM LINE

SAN
POLO

Rialto

ACTV
PIAZZALE ROMA
TRAM STATION

San
Silvestro

Grand Canal

San Tomà

Sant'Angelo

SAN
MARCO

Santa Marta

SEE
"DORSODURO"
MAP

Ca' Rezzonico

San
Samuele

St. Mark's
Square

San
Basilio

Accademia

Giglio

San
Marco

San Basilio

Salute

DORSODURO

GUGGENHEIM
FOUNDATION

Zattere

Spirito Santo

Sacca
San Biagio

Sacca Fisola

SKYLINE
ROOFTOP BAR

Molino Stucky

Canale della Giudecca

Zitelle

Sacca
Fisola

FORTUNY
TEXTILE FACTORY

Palanca

MAJER

LA PALANCA

Redentore

GENERATOR
HOSTEL

Sacca
San Biagio

GIUDECCA

REDENTORE
CHURCH

Isola la Giudecca

© MOON.COM

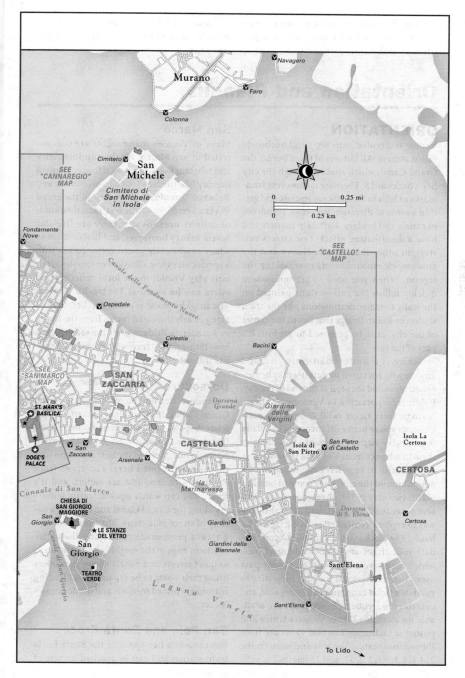

Murano

Navagero

Faro

Colonna

Cimitero

San
Michele

Cimitero di
San Michele
in Isola

SEE
"CANNAREGIO"
MAP

Fondamente
Nove

SEE
"CASTELLO"
MAP

Canale delle Fondamento Nuove

Ospedale

Celestia

Bacini

SEE
SAN MARCO
MAP

SAN
ZACCARIA

Darsena
Grande

Giardino
delle
Vergini

ST. MARK'S
BASILICA

CASTELLO

Isola di
San Pietro

San Pietro
di Castello

Isola La
Certosa

DOGE'S
PALACE

San
Zaccaria

Arsenale

la
Marinaressa

CERTOSA

Canale di San Marco

Darsena
di S. Elena

Certosa

CHIESA DI
SAN GIORGIO
MAGGIORE

San
Giorgio

LE STANZE
DEL VETRO

Giardini

San
Giorgio

Giardini della
Biennale

Sant'Elena

TEATRO
VERDE

Canale di San Giorgio

L a g u n a

Sant'Elena

V e n e t a

To Lido →

0   0.25 mi

0   0.25 km

never decline for long, and it was only a matter of time before it was rediscovered and glorified by 19th-century intellectuals, writers, and musicians. Soon the entire world knew about Venice and has been trying to get there ever since.

Orientation and Planning

ORIENTATION

Venice is divided into six neighborhoods called *sestiere*. All but one of these border the Grand Canal, which snakes through the city like a backward *S*. There are no towering landmarks or hills to facilitate navigation, and getting a sense of direction isn't easy. Hundreds of canals and bridges don't help matters and have a disorienting effect. Few streets run straight other than Strada Nuova and the *fondamente* embankments overlooking the lagoon. When you need to get somewhere quickly follow the yellow signs painted on the walls to major destinations like the train station or Rialto Bridge that lies in the center of the city. Still, be prepared to get lost: It's part of the fun.

Venice is a **pedestrian-only** city, and anyone who isn't used to walking may be surprised how tired they feel at the end of the day. Public transportation in Venice isn't cheap. A single ferry ticket valid 75 minutes costs €7.50, so you're better off investing in a daily or multiday *vaporetto* **pass.** You can buy them in advance from **Venezia Unica** (www.veneziaunica.it) or at ferry stations and sales points around the city. They come in one-day (€20), two-day (€30), three-day (€40), and seven-day (€60) versions, and are a thrilling way to explore Venice and outlying lagoon islands. The clock starts ticking once you validate your ticket at the dockside machines, which means you can use the 24-hour pass over a two-day period if you like. Forgetting to validate a ticket can result in a heavy fine, and controls are frequent. Route maps are available for download from Venezia Unica and posted at each stop. The best views are from the outdoor seats at the bow and stern on the 2, 4.1, 4.2, 5.1, 5.2, 12, and 13 ferries.

San Marco

Many of Venice's major sights are concentrated in San Marco. It's the administrative and religious hub where you'll find symbols of the city like the **Basilica di San Marco** and **Palazzo Ducale,** both located in the grand **Piazza San Marco,** which attracts thousands of daily visitors. Nearby there are five-star hotels, luxury boutiques, and **historic cafés** where exorbitantly priced coffee comes with a spectacular view. Classical ensembles regularly play Vivaldi in the local churches and opera can be heard at **Teatro La Fenice.** The neighborhood is easily reached on foot along clearly indicated routes from the Rialto or Accademia Bridges, or by the sea, which is how 18th-century travelers arrived (and purists still do).

Dorsoduro

Dorsoduro lies on the western side of the Grand Canal. It's a residential *sestiere* with fewer shops and a large university community that gathers in **Campo Santa Margherita** on weekends. Some of the best museums and galleries are located here. The views from **Punta della Dogana** are superb and it's where you can watch aquatic traffic motoring along the Grand Canal and listen to a variety of street musicians. The **Fondamenta Zattere** promenade runs along the entire southern edge of the neighborhood and leads to quiet streets and canals where gondoliers bring their boats to be repaired, and finding reasonably priced *trattorie* and outdoor cafés is easy.

San Polo and Santa Croce

Santa Croce lies opposite the Santa Lucia train station and can be reached by way of the **Ponte degli Scalzi** and **Costituzione** bridges to the left and right of the train station. It's the smallest of the six *sestiere* and remains underexplored by visitors intent on reaching San Marco. Stray from the main thoroughfare to discover backstreets, empty churches, and ancient palaces facing the Grand Canal. **Ca' Pesaro** is one of the finest of these and houses the city's museum of modern art.

San Polo is the commercial center of Venice; it was one of the first areas settled due to its relatively elevated terrain. Shakespeare refers to it in *The Merchant of Venice,* and there are lively **markets** where Venetians buy fish, vegetables, and fruit and tourists shop for glass and lace. The *sestiere* was named after the church of San Polo in the *campo* of the same name. The closer you get to the **Rialto** the busier things get. Crossing the city's most famous bridge can be agonizingly slow in summer, while the district's religious and artistic sights—**Santa Maria Gloriosa dei Frari** and **Scuola Grande di San Rocco**—are often deserted. It's also home to a large concentration of *bacari* bars and a small but active nightlife.

Cannaregio

Cannaregio is home to the **Santa Lucia train station** and the first *sestiere* most travelers experience. The gateway to the area is **Rio Terra Lista di Spagna,** which is lined with souvenir shops and leads to **Strada Nuova,** one of the widest thoroughfares in the city packed with visitors on their way to the Rialto. Most of the neighborhood, however, is quiet and it's the place to learn how to row a Venetian boat, set off on a kayak tour, or go stand-up paddling. Ferries depart from **Fondamente Nuove** to the islands of Murano and Burano throughout the day and the bars lining **Fondamenta della Misericordia** are filled with locals and visitors at night.

Castello

Streets become narrower the closer you get to Castello and regularly intersect with tiny squares where locals congregate. The neighborhood is one of the largest and least-visited *sestieres* in the city—except during the **Venice Biennale,** when art lovers converge here. It's also where Venetian galleons were built in the **Arsenale** shipyards, and antique vessels can be admired inside the **Museo Storico Navale.** There are several lovely churches and some of the best **workshops** in the city where masks are still patiently made by hand. At the southern edge of Castello is the grand **Riva degli Schiavone** embankment lined with ferry boats, souvenir stands, and outdoor cafés with expansive views of the lagoon.

Giudecca

Although the island of Giudecca is technically part of Dorsoduro, it has its own distinct atmosphere. That's because it's the only part of Venice that can't be reached on foot and thus attracts fewer visitors. There aren't many blockbuster monuments besides the **Chiesa del Redentore** and a long embankment overlooking the Giudecca Canal. Nevertheless, in recent decades this traditionally blue-collar neighborhood of laborers and fishermen has been gentrified. Abandoned factories have been transformed into luxury lofts and **five-star hotels.** The **Palanca** ferry station is a good place to disembark and explore the mix of modern and 19th-century architecture. At the eastern end lies the island of **San Giorgio,** which has a bell tower worth ascending.

PLANNING YOUR TIME

While many visitors spend as little as one day in Venice, it really shouldn't be rushed. Each *sestiere* (neighborhood) has its own character, and exploring these is the most enjoyable activity of all. Three or four days will allow you to discover the secrets of the Doge's Palace and stroll through remote parts of the city where tour groups rarely tread. It will also provide sufficient time to explore the lagoon islands of Burano and Murano or the Lido and follow any path you choose without checking your watch.

Plans are often affected by weather in Venice. The city is hot during the summer and it rains considerably more than in Rome or Florence. Flooding is a possibility throughout the year and is common in autumn and spring. Water usually recedes in a day or two but not all parts of the city are soaked. San Marco is usually the first place to flood, as it's built at sea level. The city is accustomed to coping with the inconvenience and has developed a warning system for residents and visitors. If you hear a siren followed by a series of high-pitched tones, get your boots on. The higher and longer the tone, the higher the water. Raised wooden walkways are installed along flooded streets and make getting around possible in adverse conditions. Flooding may be a nuisance for residents but can be a memorable adventure for everyone else. It could, however, be a thing of the past as the city recently completed construction of mobile floodgates that will protect the lagoon from rising tides. The pharaonic project took decades to build and cost billions but will keep Venice dry when fully operational at the end of 2021.

Daily Reminders

Some sights in Venice, like the Doge's Palace, are open daily. Others, including the Guggenheim Foundation and Galleria dell'Accademia, are closed or close early on Mondays. Museums shut on January 1, May 1, and December 25. Opening hours are usually extended from March to October and reduced during winter. Most museums stop selling tickets one hour before closing and are less crowded very early or late. Outdoor markets operate in the morning and are closed on weekends. The Burano island market is open Monday, Wednesday, and Saturday mornings.

Advance Bookings and Time-Saving Tips

Mornings are best for visiting major monuments, and the lines to the bell tower and Basilica di San Marco are still reasonably short

Rise and Shine to Beat the Crowds

The best time to experience Venice is in the morning, when locals still outnumber tourists, cruise ships have yet to dock, high-speed trains haven't arrived, and thousands of visitors inside and outside the city are still sleeping. If you're up and about by 7am or 8am, you'll see the whirlwind of activity that only happens in the morning: university students on their way to classes, parents accompanying children to school, bakers carting loaves to clients, fruit vendors laying out their stands, retirees walking dogs, musicians on the way to the conservatory, ladies dragging trolleys to the butcher, laborers hammering at streets, and swallows flying in the sky above.

You can catch the show at any large *campo* (square) like Santa Margherita or San Polo. When you've had your fill, head to a *bacaro* or bar for a late breakfast.

at 9am before they open to the public. Other than the monuments in Piazza San Marco and the pedestrian jam over Rialto Bridge, museums, galleries, and historic buildings are not especially crowded. If you don't plan on entering more than a couple of sights, you can rely on single-entry tickets; otherwise, invest in a sightseeing pass.

Sightseeing Passes

There are a lot of things to see in Venice, and sightseeing passes can save you time and money. **Venezia Unica** (www.veneziaunica. it) is the official tourism website and offers several different passes:

San Marco City Pass (€33.90): Covers Doge's Palace, three civic museums in Piazza San Marco, plus entry to three churches of your choice. Good basic card for a multiday visit. The **Junior Pass** (€21.90) is a slight misnomer and provides the same benefits for 6- to 29-year-olds.

San Marco City Pass + Transport (€73.90): Includes all of the above plus unlimited three-day *vaporetto* ferry boat access.

Rules of Venice

Venice attracts millions of visitors each year and is at serious risk of becoming a victim of its own success. For that reason, it's essential to treat Venice with special care and ensure future generations have the opportunity to experience the city. Following the rules is a good way to start. Some are courtesy and others are the law and will result in fines if broken. It's a privilege to visit Venice, and preserving it should be a priority for everyone.

- **Walk on the right and avoid causing jams.** This is especially pertinent when stopping to browse shop windows or examine restaurant menus on crowded streets leading to the main tourist attractions.

- **Make way for two-wheeled trolleys.** These are used to transport food, merchandise, waste, and luggage around the city. It's especially true on mornings when deliveries are made, and zigzagging heavy loads through tourists makes work even harder.

- **Do not sit on bridge steps.** Doing so creates unnecessary and annoying obstructions. At night or in quiet areas where few people pass, the rule can be overlooked.

- **Respect places of worship.** Tourists may outnumber parishioners, but that doesn't mean "anything goes" inside churches. Dress accordingly, keep voices low, leave food and drink outside, and do not use a flash or tripod when taking pictures.

- **Avoid sunbathing.** It may be tempting to remove clothing and sit or lie on the stones of Venice, but it's considered disrespectful (bare-chested men can be fined!). You're better off hopping on a ferry and enjoying sand and sea on the beaches of the Lido.

- **Do not drag luggage over bridges.** Lift suitcases and trolleys to avoid damaging steps. If you're traveling with a heavy load, hire one of the porters waiting outside the train station (prices start at €10 per bag).

- **Remove backpacks on *vaporetti*.** Carry them in your hands. This is less a matter of pickpockets (rare in Venice) than to maximize space and avoid disturbing fellow passengers.

- **Never discard waste in streets or canals.** This includes cigarette butts, unwanted food, and everything else. There aren't many trash cans in Venice, but you can always walk into a bar and use their bin.

- **Do not feed the pigeons.** It's forbidden and isn't a joking matter. Not only can pigeon droppings come back to haunt you, but over time their corrosiveness damages buildings. Any offers of birdseed from peddlers in St. Mark's Square should be politely declined.

- **Do not swim in canals.** Local newspapers regularly report tourists diving into canals. It may be funny to some, but it's illegal and there are better ways to explore the city's waterways. Also, canals aren't that clean and leave an odor that can take days to wash away.

VENICE
ORIENTATION AND PLANNING

The **Junior City Pass + Transport** (€49.90) is valid for under 29-year-olds.

St. Mark's Square Pass (€25, €13 for under 26-year-olds): Allows access to the Doge's Palace and three museums within Piazza San Marco. Single tickets are not sold. The pass is valid three months and does not include the clock tower or *campanile*.

Museum Pass (€35): Covers Venice's 11 civic museums, including the Doge's Palace, Museo Correr, and Glass Museum in Murano. It's available at all participating museums and valid six months. The **Family** version (€19) is good for two adults and any number of children over 14.

Island Pass (€13): Glass Museum in Murano and Lace Museum in Burano.

Chorus Card (www.chorusvenezia.org; €12): Provides entry to 14 churches, including Chiesa del Redentore in Giudecca and Basilica di Santa Maria Gloriosa dei Frari. Entry to St. Mark's Basilica is free. Most member churches are open Monday to Saturday 10am-4:30pm and the card can be purchased from any of the churches or online. Church entry without the card is €3. **Chorus Pass Family** (€24): Valid for two adults and unlimited children under 18. Children under 11 free.

Beware: purchasing too comprehensive a pass over too short a period can add unnecessary pressure to see it all. When choosing, consider your tolerance for museums as well as length of stay. You can purchase passes online and print them out at home or buy them at the main tourist office in Piazzale Roma, automated ticketing machines outside the train station, and authorized shops around the city.

Children under 5 and visitors with documented handicaps can enter sights for free while 6- to 29-year-olds and over 65s receive discounts to most museums and monuments in Venice. Private institutions like the Guggenheim and Palazzo Grassi have slightly different discount policies and it's always worth asking at ticket offices before buying. **Rolling Venice Card** (www.veneziaunica.it; €6) provides discounted *vaporetto* travel for 6- to 29-year-olds. Under 6s always travel free and don't need a card.

Pandemic Travel

Venice is a dense city whose narrow streets and passageways make it difficult to maintain social distancing. During COVID outbreaks, busy pedestrian streets near Piazza San Marco become one-directional in order to reduce contact. **Masks** are required inside and outside with local police issuing heavy fines to anyone flouting the rules.

Unlike some Italian cities, most **museums** in Venice do not require advance bookings; however, they will reduce their opening hours, limit visitor numbers, and suspend tours and audio guides. (The **Guggenheim Foundation** is the one notable exception and requires advance bookings during outbreaks, which can be made a week or so before arrival.) All **sightseeing passes** listed above remain valid during COVID outbreaks. All major monuments are equipped with thermoscanners and personnel who ensure that visitors sanitize their hands before entry.

Venice offers plenty of opportunities for outdoor **drinking and dining,** from the elegant cafés of Piazza San Marco to the gritty canal-side bars of Cannaregio, and during the summer you're more likely to find locals outside than in.

For the latest information during an outbreak, consult www.veneziaunica.it.

Itinerary Ideas

Millions of visitors spend less than 24 hours in Venice every year, but to really discover the city and appreciate its particularities you'll need at least a couple of days.

VENICE ON DAY 1

Spend your first day in Venice exploring San Marco followed by a ferry ride to Isola di San Giorgio for lagoon views from the city's second tallest bell tower.

1 Sightseeing starts as soon as you step out of Santa Lucia train station. Hop on the number 1 or 2 *vaporetto* at the landing outside the station and sail down the **Grand Canal.**

2 Disembark at **Piazza San Marco** and walk around the square. Enter Basilica di San Marco and take the secret tour of the Doge's Palace next door to learn how the Bridge of Sighs got its name.

3 Ride the 2 *vaporetto* to **Isola di San Giorgio.** Climb the bell tower for a view as stunning as the one from the *campanile,* but without the lines.

4 Continue to Giudecca and the panoramic promenade that stretches along the entire northern side of this quiet island. Take a caffeine break at **Majer,** near the Palanca ferry station.

5 Ride the 2 *vaporetto* over to Dorsoduro and stop at **Al Bottegon** for *prosecco* in a plastic cup and an assortment of *cicchetti* snacks while watching gondolas being repaired in the dry dock opposite.

6 Continue to the **Galleria dell'Accademia** to brush up on Venetian Renaissance masterpieces or check out modern art at the Guggenheim Foundation.

7 Browse for souvenirs at the workshops and galleries along **Calle del Bastion,** then walk to the tip of the Dorsoduro neighborhood to watch boats entering the Grand Canal.

8 Ride a *vaporetto* or navigate your way on foot to **Campo Santo Stefano** and enjoy the rest of the evening eating and drinking in this animated square.

VENICE ON DAY 2

Explore the maze of streets around the Rialto Bridge, along with the San Polo and Cannaregio neighborhoods on your second day in Venice.

1 Get up early and observe the city coming to life. Order coffee at the counter of **Pasticceria Rizzardini** accompanied by *pan del doge* or *Mori di Venezia* pastries.

2 Head to the **fish market** to watch the mongers in action and stroll among foreign and local shoppers.

3 Cross the **Rialto Bridge** before it gets overwhelmed with tourists.

4 Browse *trattoria* menus north of the bridge and choose one like **Cantina Do Mori** where locals gather regularly for lunch.

5 Discover the enormous canvases Tintoretto painted inside the **Scuola Grande di San Rocco.**

6 Cross the Grand Canal on a gondola ferry (€2) from the dock near the markets and stroll along **Strada Nuova** accompanied by a gelato.

7 Join an hour-long stand-up paddle tour of Cannaregio with **SUP in Venice** and discover the canals from a unique perspective.

8 Zigzag your way to **Fondamenta della Misericordia.** Order a beer, spritz, or *prosecco* from any of the bars lining the canal and get an outdoor table at one of the *trattorie* nearby for dinner.

VENICE LIKE A LOCAL

Venetians are outnumbered dozens to one by tourists who flood the city every day. Although natives are rare, what they lack in numbers they make up for in style and charisma. Today you'll explore parts of Dorsoduro and Cannaregio, ending with dinner in Castello—one of Venice's most residential neighborhoods.

1 Do not delay getting up. Grab a front-row seat to Venice on one of the red benches in **Campo Santa Margherita.** Watch early-morning commuters passing through the square and the drama of the city gradually coming to life.

2 Exit the *campo* north along Rio Terà de la Scoazzera and cross the bridges into San

Itinerary Ideas

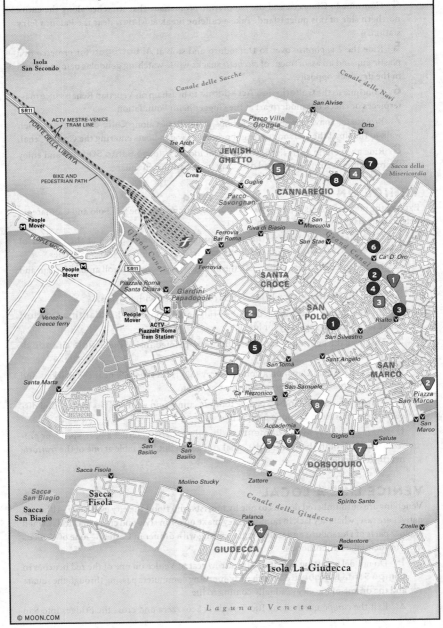

© MOON.COM

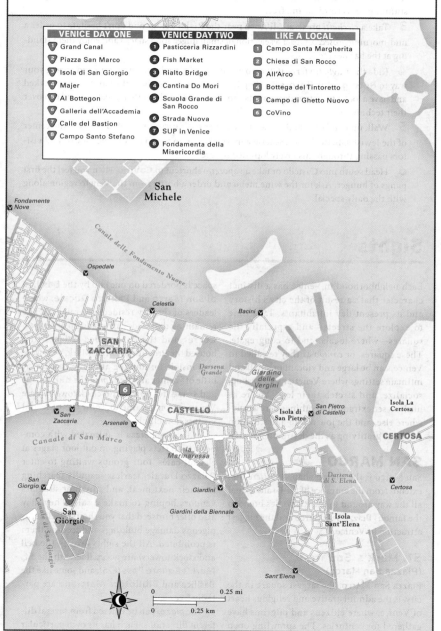

VENICE DAY ONE
1. Grand Canal
2. Piazza San Marco
3. Isola di San Giorgio
4. Majer
5. Al Bottegon
6. Galleria dell'Accademia
7. Calle del Bastion
8. Campo Santo Stefano

VENICE DAY TWO
1. Pasticceria Rizzardini
2. Fish Market
3. Rialto Bridge
4. Cantina Do Mori
5. Scuola Grande di San Rocco
6. Strada Nuova
7. SUP in Venice
8. Fondamenta della Misericordia

LIKE A LOCAL
1. Campo Santa Margherita
2. Chiesa di San Rocco
3. All'Arco
4. Bottega del Tintoretto
5. Campo di Ghetto Nuovo
6. CoVino

San Michele

Fondamente Nove

Canale delle Fondamento Nuove

Ospedale

Celestia

Bacini

SAN ZACCARIA

Darsena Grande

Giardino delle Vergini

Isola di San Pietro

San Pietro di Castello

Isola La Certosa

San Zaccaria

Arsenale

CASTELLO

CERTOSA

Canale di San Marco

la Marinaressa

Darsena di S. Elena

Certosa

San Giorgio

San Giorgio

Giardini

Giardini della Biennale

Isola Sant'Elena

Sant'Elena

0   0.25 mi

0   0.25 km

Polo to pay homage to Tintoretto, one of the city's most beloved painters, in the **Chiesa di San Rocco.** The church is located next to Scuola Grande di San Rocco, but is equally stunning, less crowded, and free.

3 Take a *cicchetti* break at **All'Arco** near the Rialto Bridge and don't hesitate to order a mid-morning *prosecco*. Order a selection of small finger-food snacks and enjoy them standing at the bar next to locals.

4 Ride the *traghetto* ferry (€2) across the Grand Canal to Cannaregio and zigzag your way to **Bottega del Tintoretto.** Pop into the workshop where the painter once worked and have a look at what modern artists can do. Ask them about their creations and discover their techniques.

5 Walk up Fondamenta de la Sensa and over to **Campo di Ghetto Nuovo,** the center of the Jewish Ghetto. Take a seat on a marble bench in the shade to watch locals and visitors passing through this lovely lopsided square.

6 Head south into Castello or take a *vaporetto* shortcut to **CoVino** when you feel the first pangs of hunger. Ask for the wine menu and order a bottle from the Veneto region along with the daily special.

Sights

Each neighborhood in Venice has a distinct character that's a result of the city's history and its present-day inhabitants. Take time to explore the streets—and especially the squares—where locals tend to congregate. These squares, or *campo* as they're called in Venice, can be large and vibrant or small and intimate settings where Venetians go to shop, socialize, and stretch their legs. You're as likely to see extraordinary things here as anywhere else, and the journey to a destination can be as gratifying as the destination itself.

SAN MARCO

San Marco is the thumb-shaped *sestiere* that extends from the entrance of the Grand Canal all the way around to the Rialto. It's home to the famous Piazza San Marco and the biggest attraction in Venice.

St. Mark's Square
(Piazza San Marco)

Piazza San Marco, the largest square in the city, is the administrative and religious heart of Venice, where citizens and pilgrims have gathered for centuries. The sprawling open space is bordered on one end by the **Basilica di San Marco** and **Palazzo Ducale,** where leaders of the city resided and reigned. The remaining three sides are made up of **Museo Correr** and the colonnaded palaces that housed the Procurators of St. Mark, who were responsible for looking after the basilica. A little off-center are the *campanile* **bell tower** and **Torre dell'Orologio** clock tower, where Venetians once came to know the time and visitors now climb.

Today, the *piazza* is animated with competing quartets playing on outdoor stages at elegant cafés, tour groups waiting to enter Palazzo Ducale, fearless seagulls searching for their next meal, and itinerant sunglass vendors hoping to make a sale. They may also offer birdseed that you should decline, as pigeons damage buildings and feeding them is prohibited. All the sights (except the bell and clock towers) are accessible with the **St. Mark's Square Pass** (€25), and some like the Basilica and **Biblioteca Marciana** are partially free.

The *piazza* can be entered from several different directions. Each has its own particular charm. You can take the direct route from the Rialto through the clock tower archway or approach from the Ponte dell'Accademia bridge along the winding streets leading to Museo Correr. The most dramatic approach, however, is by boat, which was the most common way of reaching the *piazza* before the train station was built.

★ St. Mark's Basilica
(Basilica di San Marco)

Piazza San Marco 328; tel. 041/270-8311; www. basilicasanmarco.it; Mon.-Sat. 9:30am-5pm, Sun. 2pm-4:30pm; free

Basilica di San Marco, founded in 832, was built to house the remains of St. Mark, which were smuggled from Egypt in a pork-laden basket (to deter Muslim customs officials) by two enterprising merchants who wanted Mark to be the patron saint of their city. The basilica was influenced by Greek, Byzantine, and Islamic art and architecture. The five domes are reminiscent of a mosque, and the floor plan is a Greek cross. Mosaics above the entrance recount the saint's arrival to the city, and a team of four bronze horses plundered from Constantinople stand triumphantly above the central portal.

Inside, golden mosaics embellish over 40,000 square feet (3,716 square meters) of the cavernous church. The uneven marble floor is also decorated in exotic patterns, and it's clear how much the ground has shifted over the centuries. Biblical tales like the *Descent of the Holy Ghost* are beautifully illustrated on the dome interiors. Just behind the altar is the *Pala d'Oro*, or Golden Ball, which was created by the city's goldsmiths and adorned with hundreds of precious gems. The chapel is connected to the church and although a velvet rope separates it from the rest of the basilica, you can get a good look at the interior in relative peace. Over the centuries the basilica was decorated with columns, marble, sculptures, gold, and precious spoils of war brought back by the city's merchants after

the sack of Constantinople and other military victories.

Also inside the Basilica is the **Museo di San Marco** (Basilica di San Marco; tel. 041/270-8311; daily 10am-6pm; €5), dedicated to mosaics, textiles, and ancient relics such as the original *quadriga* statue of four bronze horses. A detour here provides access to the second-story balcony overlooking Piazza San Marco. This is where *doges* and dignitaries greeted crowds on special occasions and visitors now gather for a great view of the square below. If you watched the final episode of *The Young Pope* (season 1) it will already be familiar. The basilica's **Treasury** (daily 9:35am-5pm; €3) and **Pala d'Oro** (daily 9:35am-5pm; €2), a stunning gold and gem-encrusted altarpiece begun in the 10th century by Byzantine jewelers, can also be visited.

There's no better time to experience the basilica than during **mass** (weekdays 8:30am, 10am, 6:45pm, Sun. 8:30am, noon, 6:45pm), when lights are switched on and thousands of mosaics are fully illuminated. The ceremony isn't intended for tourists, so if you aren't religious, be prepared to sit through a 45-minute sermon conducted in Latin and Italian. Masses are held every morning, but only the Sunday evening service includes spotlights.

When visiting the basilica, remember to dress appropriately (no bare shoulders or knees) and keep quiet, and no photos or filming are allowed. Free one-hour **tours** (tel. 041/241-3817; Mon.-Fri. 11am, 2:30pm, 4pm) are organized on a month-by-month basis in English by the Pastoral and Pilgrimage Office of Venice. They start in the basilica atrium and reservations are not necessary, although you may want to call and ensure there will be one that day, as the schedule fluctuates throughout the year.

If the line at the main entrance is too long, try entering the church through the prayer door on the side of the church in Campo Leoni. The facade and other parts of the basilica are often undergoing restoration and may be partially covered or closed.

During COVID outbreaks the basilica may

San Marco

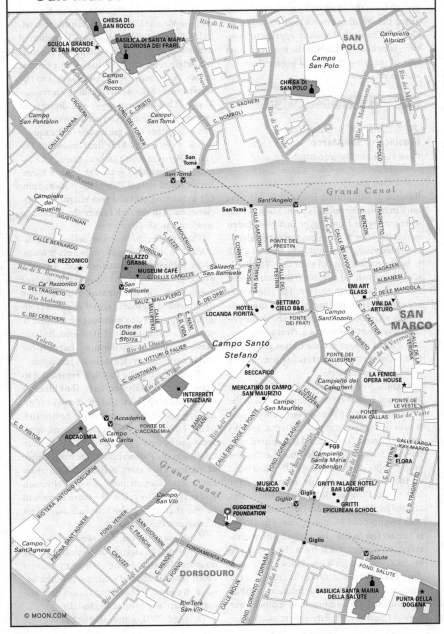

© MOON.COM

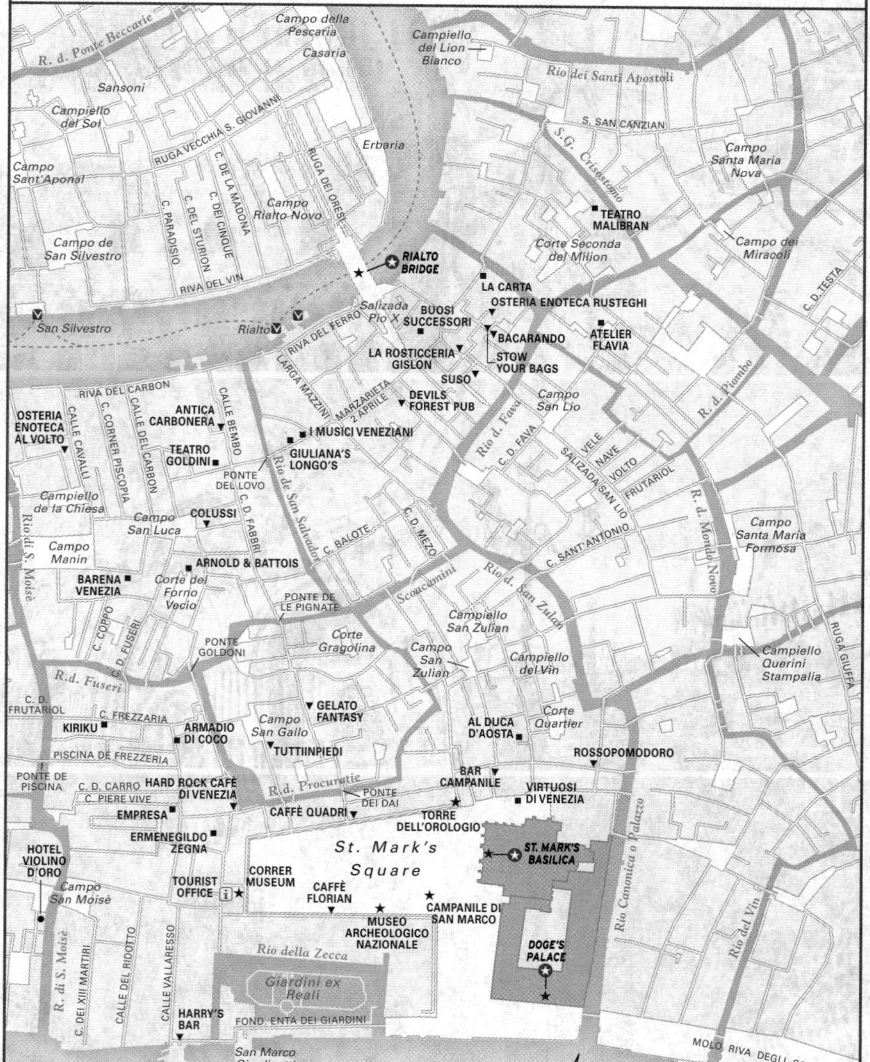
Campo della Pescaria
Casaria
Campiello del Lion Bianco
R. d. Ponte Beccarie
Rio dei Santi Apostoli
Sansoni
Campiello del Sol
RUGA VECCHIA S. GIOVANNI
Erbaria
S. SAN CANZIAN
S.G. Crisostomo
Campo Santa Maria Nova
Campo Sant'Aponal
C. DE LA MADONA
C. DEI CINQUE
C. DEL STURION
C. PARADISIO
RUGA DEI ORESI
Campo Rialto Novo
TEATRO MALIBRAN
Campo de San Silvestro
Corte Seconda del Milion
Campo dei Miracoli
RIALTO BRIDGE
LA CARTA
RIVA DEL VIN
OSTERIA ENOTECA RUSTEGHI
C. D. TESTA
Salizada Pio X
BUOSI SUCCESSORI
San Silvestro
Rialto
RIVA DEL FERRO
BACARANDO
ATELIER FLAVIA
LA ROSTICCERIA GISLON
STOW YOUR BAGS
SUSO
LARGA MAZZINI
R. d. Piombo
RIVA DEL CARBON
MARZARIETA 2 APRILE
DEVILS FOREST PUB
Campo San Lio
OSTERIA ENOTECA AL VOLTO
CALLE CAVALLI
C. CORNER PISCOPIA
CALLE DEL CARBON
CALLE BEMBO
ANTICA CARBONERA
I MUSICI VENEZIANI
Rio d. Fava
C. D. FAVA
VELE
NAVE
VOLTO
FRUTARIOL
SALIZADA SAN LIO
TEATRO GOLDINI
GIULIANA'S LONGO'S
PONTE DEL LOVO
Rio de San Salvador
Campiello de la Chiesa
R. d. Mondo Novo
Campo Santa Maria Formosa
COLUSSI
Campo San Luca
C. D. FABBRI
C. BALOTE
C. D. MEZO
C. SANT'ANTONIO
Rio di S. Moisè
Campo Manin
ARNOLD & BATTOIS
BARENA VENEZIA
Corte del Forno Vecio
Scoacamini
Rio d. San Zulian
PONTE DE LE PIGNATE
Campiello San Zulian
C. CORPO
C. D. FUSERI
PONTE GOLDONI
Corte Gragolina
Campo San Zulian
Campiello del Vin
Campiello Querini Stampalia
RUGA GIUFFA
R.d. Fuseri
C. D. FRUTARIOL
C. FREZZARIA
GELATO FANTASY
Campo San Gallo
Corte Quartier
KIRIKU
ARMADIO DI COCO
AL DUCA D'AOSTA
TUTTIINPIEDI
PISCINA DE FREZZERIA
ROSSOPOMODORO
PONTE DE PISCINA
C. D. CARRO
C. PIERE VIVE
HARD ROCK CAFÈ DI VENEZIA
R.d. Procuratie
PONTE DEI DAI
BAR CAMPANILE
VIRTUOSI DI VENEZIA
EMPRESA
CAFFÈ QUADRI
TORRE DELL'OROLOGIO
ERMENEGILDO ZEGNA
St. Mark's Square
ST. MARK'S BASILICA
HOTEL VIOLINO D'ORO
Campo San Moisè
CORRER MUSEUM
TOURIST OFFICE
CAFFÈ FLORIAN
CAMPANILE DI SAN MARCO
MUSEO ARCHEOLOGICO NAZIONALE
Rio Canonica o Palazzo
Rio del Vin
DOGE'S PALACE
R. di S. Moisè
C. DEI XIII MARTIRI
CALLE DEL RIDOTTO
CALLE VALLARESSO
Rio della Zecca
Giardini ex Reali
HARRY'S BAR
FOND. ENTA DEI GIARDINI
MOLO RIVA DEGLI SCHIAVONI
San Marco Vallaresso
San Marco Giardinetti
San Zaccaria
F
F
San Zaccaria
D
C
Canaale di San Marco
0
250 ft
0
100 m

★ Doge's Palace
(Palazzo Ducale)

Piazza San Marco 1; tel. 041/271-5911; www. palazzoducale.visitmuve.it; Apr.-Oct. 8:30am-7pm, Nov.-Mar. 8:30am-5:30pm; St. Mark's Square Pass €25 or Museum Pass €35, audio guide €5

Understanding Venice requires visiting Palazzo Ducale. This imposing palace on the southeastern corner of Piazza San Marco is where the *doge* resided and the Venetian senate met to make decisions that maintained the city's power throughout the Mediterranean. It's a White House and Capitol Hill rolled into one, where dignitaries were received, powerful men slept, and prisoners were kept.

The palace is an immense U-shaped complex with stunning facades and sumptuous interiors. The exterior is wrapped in a columned arcade that supports an intricate *loggia*. The upper stories are covered in smooth brick decorated in a diamond pattern. *Doges* addressed the citizens gathered below from the ornate balconies. Inside, there's a vast courtyard, grand reception rooms, a chapel, luxurious sleeping quarters, prison cells, and a museum. This is where you'll find several of the world's largest oil paintings by the likes of Tintoretto, Titian, and Veronese.

The fixed itinerary leads visitors through grand chambers where the city counselors gathered, and an extensive armory stocked with swords and early firearms used by the *doge's* guards and auxiliary troops. *Sala dei Consigli*, the next stop, is one of the largest rooms in Europe. It's where *doges* were elected, and up to 2,000 counselors met every Sunday to express their grievances. Paintings depicting Venice's greatest triumphs and the portraits of 76 *doges* cover the ceiling and walls. The hall is lined with wooden benches and no matter how crowded the palace gets there's always room to sit and admire the grand space.

Sala dei Consigli is exited through a small doorway that leads to the cramped *Palazzo dei Prigioni* prisons. The narrow stone passageway crosses the **Bridge of Sighs,** where prisoners were once led to the gallows and through a long series of cells and chambers that make it clear how the Republic deterred anyone from breaking the law. This is where Casanova was briefly detained and less fortunate prisoners met their end. The itinerary ends in a bookshop and café near the main courtyard.

The Doge's Palace is the most visited monument in Venice. Lines form early, but if you arrive at 9am the efficient ticket office is nearly empty. If you want a behind-the-scenes look at the palace, reserve the **Secret Itineraries** (daily 10:10am, 12:10pm, 1:30pm and 2:10pm; €28 or €15 for holders of the Rolling Venice card) tour. This 75-minute guided walk through lesser-known parts of the *palazzo* is conducted in English and is a great option if you aren't planning on visiting the other sights in Piazza San Marco. Afterward you are free to explore the rest of the palace. Reservations are required and can be made online (www.palazzoducale.visitmuve.it) or by phone (tel. +39 0414/273-0892 outside of Italy or 848/082-000 inside).

Visitors entering the palace must pass through a metal detector and have their bags checked. Leave large backpacks at your hotel; otherwise, they'll have to be checked in at the cloakroom on the right side of the courtyard.

During COVID outbreaks, audio guides and some tours may not be available.

Campanile di San Marco

Piazza San Marco; www.basilicasanmarco.it; daily Apr. 16-Oct. 10:30am-9:20pm, Nov.-Apr. 15 9:30am-5:30pm; €10

The Campanile di San Marco, or bell tower, is nearly 328 feet (100 meters) high and would be the oldest in the city if it hadn't collapsed in 1902. Fortunately, it was entirely rebuilt to 12th-century specs and an

1: view of St. Mark's Basilica and Doge's Palace 2: Doge's Palace 3: mosaic outside St. Mark's Basilica 4: Piazza San Marco

What's a *Doge?*

Doge is a title that derives from the Latin *dux,* or commander (duke in English). It was used in Venice from AD 697 until the fall of the Republic in 1797. During those thousand years, the position evolved from primitive military leader to something close to a king and eventually a mere figurehead.

ELECTION AND RESPONSIBILITIES

Becoming a *doge* was nearly as complicated as becoming pope. The elaborate and complicated rules of the election system were intended to dissuade any overeager aristocrats from taking shortcuts to power. Each *doge* was, however, required to pay for his furnishings and expenses, which meant only the richest Venetians could aspire to the position. In the city's 15th-century heyday the *doge's* primary responsibility was representing Venice during public ceremonies and overseeing diplomatic relations with other states. He (there were no female *doges*) could recommend foreign policy, but his advice was not always taken and he wasn't allowed to meet with ambassadors without the presence of his counselors.

Eventually the election of *doges* became the responsibility of a council of aristocrats, and the independence of *doges* was severely limited. They could not marry foreign princesses, abdicate, write or receive letters without the presence of a witness, conduct business, own land outside the palace, or leave the city without special permission. Toward the end of the Republic the position was diminished to presiding over the government without any real power, and by then a *doge* was simply a fancy magistrate whose gondola was no nicer than those of the other nobles. The biggest benefit was residing in the most prestigious palace in town. The only title that was never stripped was commander in chief of the navy in times of war.

DOGES IN PALAZZO DUCALE

Doges can be seen in many paintings inside Palazzo Ducale and are often portrayed wearing scarlet robes with a fur collar and an oddly shaped hat. Power was gradually siphoned away from the *doge* by an emerging merchant class who distrusted too much power concentrated in one office. The sculpture of a *doge* bowing in submission to a lion (above the palace entrance nearest the basilica) is the expression of that distrust and a visible reminder of who was serving who.

elevator was added to make reaching the top easy. Only one of the original five bells survived the crash but they were all eventually replaced. Each has a name and had a specific function. *Marangona*, the main bell, signaled the start and end of the working day, while the *Trottiera* called patricians to the Doge's Palace and *Renghiera*, the smallest bell, announced executions. They still ring out today but only to tell time and celebrate holidays. Galileo demonstrated his first telescope here in 1609, and the lightning conductor fitted on the roof a century and half later was the first of its kind.

From the upper terrace there's an unobstructed view of the city and lagoon islands. The elevator has a capacity of 16 passengers, and the terrace accommodates 20-25 visitors at a time. There are coin-operated binoculars at the top and you can remain as long as you like. Tickets are available inside the bell tower, which may be closed in the event of high winds, flooding, or adverse weather.

Lines to enter the bell tower can be long and if you don't feel like waiting, ride the number 2 *vaporetto* across the mouth of the Grand Canal to **Isola di San Giorgio.** There's another bell tower that's less crowded and provides equally great views of the city.

During COVID outbreaks, the number of travelers allowed to ride the elevator to the top is reduced.

Torre dell'Orologio

Piazza San Marco; tel. 848/082-000 or
tel. 041/4273-0892 from abroad; www.torreorologio.it

In the 15th century, knowing the time meant looking at the sun or listening to church bells. The Torre dell'Orologio clock tower in the northeastern corner of Piazza San Marco changed all that with Renaissance high-tech ingenuity.

The blue facade of the enormous astronomical clock contains rotating panels that tell the hour, day, lunar phase, and zodiac sign. It was a great innovation, even without a minute hand, and provided essential information for sailors, senators, and merchants, all of whom came to rely on the clock and checked it regularly. Visitors gather hourly in front of the tower to see the bronze sculptures on top strike a large bell. The statue on the left strikes two minutes before the hour to represent time that has passed, while the statue on the right hammers two minutes after the hour to signify the time to come.

You can observe the clock tower for free from the square or reserve a tour of the inside and discover what keeps it ticking. Reservations must be made in advance or on the same day at the Correr Museum ticket office, from where the 50-minute visit departs. English-speaking tours are held Monday-Wednesday at 10am and 11am and Thursday-Sunday at 2pm and 3pm. Tour groups do not exceed 12 visitors.

During COVID outbreaks the clock tower may be closed to the public.

Correr Museum
(Museo Correr)

Piazza San Marco 52; tel. 041/240-5211; www.correr. visitmuve.it; daily Apr.-Oct. 10am-7pm, Nov.-Mar. 10am-5pm; St. Mark's Square Pass or Museum Pass

Museo Correr is a behemoth of a museum on the western edge of Piazza San Marco. The 17th-century palace contains over 70 rooms. Most people head straight to the ones filled with Venetian Gothic art, but you could also discover where an Austrian princess resided, admire 19th-century sculpture, or learn Venetian history.

The Quadreria picture gallery located on the second floor is filled with religious effigies, portraits of aristocrats, and scenes documenting everyday Venetians like the *Two Ladies of Venice* in room 15. The neoclassical rooms on the same floor display the marble sculptures by Antonio Canova, a skilled artist-diplomat who managed to bring back much of the art shipped off to Paris after Napoleon captured the city.

Before Museo Correr became a museum, it was a royal residence and hosted Empress Sissi of Austria during her mid-18th-century visit to Venice. The Imperial Apartments are a miniature Versailles and include a throne room, dining area, audience hall, study, bedroom, and boudoir complete with period furnishings. The Civiltà di Venezia rooms downstairs provide insight into how the city once operated and are organized by themes including the *doge,* military, maritime trade, and daily life. Most rooms contain explanation panels in English. Private tours (€100/1-4 people) are available.

The museum cafeteria is one of the least expensive places to have a coffee or light snack in Piazza San Marco. The views are great and the drink-sandwich combo only costs €10. The Biblioteca Marciana (Piazzetta San Marco 7; Mon.-Thurs. 8:20am-7pm, Fri.-Sat. 8:20pm-1:30pm; free) can be entered through the museum. The library contains a monumental reading room decorated by Tiziano, Tintoretto, and Veronese. Tours (tel. 041/240-7238; St. Mark's Square Pass or Museum Pass) in Italian last 50 minutes and can be arranged in advance.

During COVID outbreaks, parts of the museum may be closed to the public.

Museo Archeologico Nazionale

Piazza San Marco 17; tel. 041/522-5978; Apr.-Oct. 10am-7pm, Nov.-Mar. 10am-5pm; St. Mark's Square Pass or Museum Pass

Museo Archeologico Nazionale is the smallest museum on the square and the least visited. The collection of Greek and Roman sculptures, ceramics, coins, and stones dates back to the 1st century BC and was amassed by wealthy Venetian families who eventually donated the antiquities to the state. It can be visited in under an hour and skipped entirely if you've already seen ancient sculptures in Rome. Access is through the Napoleonic wing of the Correr Museum.

During COVID outbreaks, advance reservations are required for the Egyptian room, which only two visitors can access at a time.

La Fenice Opera House
(Teatro La Fenice)

Campo San Fantin; tel. 041/786-672; www.festfenice. com; daily 9:30am-6pm; €11 with audio guide

Opera is an Italian invention, and the ornate theaters where Rossini, Verdi, and other great composers premiered their works are legendary. Teatro La Fenice is among the most prestigious in the world and has staged thousands of hours of melodies since it was opened in 1792. It has seen more than its share of drama and twice burned down only to be rebuilt, most recently in 1996. The simple neoclassical exterior gives little hint of the opulent five-tiered seating inside. Unless you attend a performance, the best way to visit the theater is with the self-guided **audio tour** in English that lasts 45 minutes and includes a permanent exhibit dedicated to Maria Callas. Music lovers can go backstage, see contemporary sets, sit in the royal box, and learn about the tenors and sopranos who sang here. Venetian audiences have extremely high standards and even the greatest performers have been booed on this stage.

Campo Santo Stefano

The largest *campo* in San Marco is a vibrant intersection where visitors pause on their way to and from Piazza San Marco and local children run free. It was once used for bullfights, masked balls, and processions during *Carnevale* and is lined with modest *palazzi* and outdoor cafés. The statue in the center honors Niccolò Tommaseo, one of the city's hometown writers, and the steps at the base are usually occupied with people-watchers.

The Gothic church of Santo Stefano has a simple brick facade and a ceiling shaped like a ship's keel. There's a small **museum** (tel. 041/522-2362; Mon.-Sat. 10am-5pm; €3 or Chorus Card) in the adjacent cloister with a *Last Supper* by Tintoretto. On the other side of the *campo* is the Chiesa di San Vidale, where classical concerts are held every evening. The repertoire nearly always includes Vivaldi.

Palazzo Grassi

Campo San Samuele 3231; tel. 041/200-1057; www. palazzograssi.it; Fri.-Mon. 10am-7pm; €15 with Punta della Dogana

Palazzo Grassi was purchased by French billionaire and art collector Francois Pinault in 2005. It was the last palace built before the end of the Republic and he hired Japanese architect Tadao Ando to transform the dilapidated interior into a minimalist shrine to contemporary art. Exhibitions alternate every six months and include pieces from the philanthropist's personal collection along with retrospectives of established artists like Damien Hirst and Cindy Sherman. The building itself is great, especially the second floor with its large airy rooms, ornate ceilings, and views of the canal. There are free lockers downstairs, an exceptionally good **museum café,** and plenty of knowledgeable staff ready to answer questions.

There are free **guided tours** in Italian every Saturday at 3pm; group tours are available the rest of the week by reservation (tel. 041/2719031; visite@palazzograssi.it; €85, €160 for Palazzo Grassi and Punta della Dogana). The ticket includes entry to Pinault's second contemporary art emporium across the Grand Canal at **Punta della Dogana.** A handy map available from the box office makes getting from one to the other easy. It's a 15-minute walk along some of the most scenic streets in the city.

★ Rialto Bridge

There are four bridges spanning the Grand Canal, but the Rialto is the grandest, and the one everyone wants to cross. It's divided

Lingering in *Campi*

Venice would be a dark and dreary place without its *campi*. These oddly shaped squares provide light and space for locals to commune, children to play, and pigeons to gather. They come in all sizes and are recognizable by the wellheads, flagpoles, and red benches that characterize them. Tourists walk quickly through, but these aren't just stone paving between destinations—they are destinations in themselves, where you can observe local rituals, fill up a bottle of water, and enjoy a spritz at an outdoor café.

There are dozens of *campi* in each neighborhood and they are hard to miss. Some are large and busy at all hours like **Campo Santo Stefano** (Dorsoduro), which is lined with eateries and popular with students from the nearby universities; others are semideserted and lacking in commerce such as **Campo S. Agnese** (Dorsoduro), where the biggest attraction is the shade from the trees and street musicians playing violins and accordions.

On the other side of the Grand Canal **Campo Santo Stefano** (San Marco) is a mix of the two types. It's flanked on either end by churches and sees a constant stream of visitors on their way to and from Piazza San Marco. At its outdoor tables you can enjoy a drink in the sun and try to distinguish Venetians from tourists (hint: Venetians walk a little faster, are dressed more elegantly, and know where they're going).

Some *campi* overlook canals like **Santa Maria Formosa** and **Campo San Lorenzo** (Castello), where gondoliers wait patiently for fares and lines form outside small gelato shops. They are natural pit stops for enjoying ice cream or browsing vegetable stalls in search of fresh fruit. **Campo San Polo** (San Polo) is one of the biggest and nearly empty most of the year—except during the Venice Film Festival when a giant outdoor screen is erected and spectators watch the latest international releases and enjoy pints of beer at the pizzeria on the corner.

There's a *campo* for everyone, whether you prefer a boisterous or desolate atmosphere, and whichever you choose you'll be able to admire the beauty of the city from a unique urban setting.

VENICE SIGHTS

into three lanes, the outermost of which provides good views of the canal. Like the Ponte Vecchio in Florence it's flanked with shops and is a magnet for commercial activity. The bridge is crowded throughout the day and can be difficult to cross, let alone enjoy. Early mornings and late evenings are the best time to appreciate the harmonious stonework and twin archways in the middle without being bumped. The Rialto can also be viewed from the embankments on both sides of the Grand Canal and looks better than ever after a renovation project was completed in 2018.

There's been a succession of bridges on the same spot since the 13th century and each increased in size as the city grew in power and wealth. The current version of the Rialto was the result of a competition held in 1524 to replace a wooden bridge. Although Palladio and Michelangelo were among the participants, a little-known local architect named Antonio da Ponte (*ponte* coincidentally means bridge

in Italian) got the job. He completed the project in less than three years using stone and a single 157-foot (48-meter) arch to span the canal. Critics at the time predicted the audacious design would collapse, but the Rialto continues to pass the test of time.

DORSODURO
Accademia
(Galleria dell'Accademia)

Campo della Carità 1050; tel. 800/150-666; www.gallerieaccademia.it; Mon. 8:15am-2pm, Tues.-Sun. 8:15am-7:15pm; €12, audio guide €6

Galleria dell'Accademia contains the greatest collection of Venetian art in the world and traces the evolution of the city's changing tastes from the Middle Ages to the 18th century. Paintings by Mantegna, Titian, Tintoretto, and Veronese can all be found inside the former church that opened to the public in 1817.

The collection spans five centuries and is

Dorsoduro

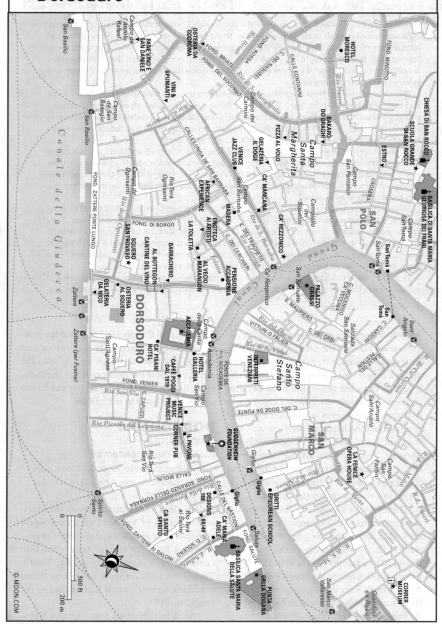

arranged chronologically. There is no better place to gaze upon Venetian masters, which explains why the museum is the third most visited attraction in the city. Even the lesser-known works demonstrate brilliance and the Venetian love of vibrant colors and light. One of the most interesting pieces is Veronese's *Last Supper* that includes dogs, midgets, and drunkards. It was deemed too racy for the time and nearly got the artist locked up. He eventually passed the censors by changing the title of the work to *Feast in the House of Levi* (room 10).

Bags must be checked (€1) and fire regulations limit the number of visitors allowed into the museum at any one time. That often causes 30-45-minute queues in summer that can be reduced by reserving tickets in advance on the museum website for a small fee. The audio guide (€6) reveals the story behind every canvas.

During COVID outbreaks, paper maps and exhibition pamphlets are removed and made available online.

★ Guggenheim Foundation

Fondamenta Venier 704 or 701; tel. 041/240-5411; www.guggenheim-venice.it; Fri.-Mon. 10am-6pm; €15
America's savviest art patron, Peggy Guggenheim, moved to Venice in 1949 and assembled a vast collection of modern art in Palazzo Venier. The Guggenheim Foundation is her legacy and a lasting gift to art lovers. It's located along the Grand Canal in a modest 18th-century *palazzo* where she lived and encouraged artists to ignore boundaries until her death in 1979. The all-star cast of painters includes Chagall, Dalí, Duchamp, Miró, and other giants of 20th-century art.

The museum is entered through narrow stone archway that can be easily missed and leads to a peaceful sculpture garden. The villa is smaller than you might expect and filled with eager visitors getting close-up views of Pollocks and Picassos. A historic photograph in each room shows how things looked in Peggy's day. Most of the furniture is gone but the artwork remains. If you have

any questions about the art or the heiress, ask the multilingual interns stationed around the foundation. You can also enjoy the view of the canal from the terrace at the front of the building.

Visitors can pick up an audio guide (€7) or join free 10-minute **Art Talks** (daily 11am and 5pm) that focus on a single painting. Brief explanations about the life and times of Peggy Guggenheim (daily 12:30pm and 4pm) in Italian and English are given every day. Hour-long in-depth tours (tel. 041/240-5440; €85) can also be reserved. The café is bright but slightly overpriced and the foundation **gift shop** (Thurs.-Mon. 10am-6pm) is around the corner on Fondamenta Venier dai Leon.

During COVID outbreaks, advance online reservations are required, and a maximum of 70 visitors are allowed to enter the foundation at a time.

Basilica Santa Maria Della Salute

Campo della Salute 1; www.basilicasalutevenezia.it; daily 9:30am-noon and 3pm-5:30pm; free
Basilica Santa Maria della Salute dominates the entrance to the Grand Canal and has dazzled visitors with its white baroque facade since it was completed in the 17th century. The basilica was commissioned by the Venetian senate in gratitude for ending a plague that devastated the city and consists of an octagonal plan topped by an enormous dome that can be seen throughout the lagoon. The monumental steps are a wonderful place to sit and watch boats traveling up and down the canal.

Inside are works by Titian and Tintoretto as well as a small gallery museum (€4) in the sacristy to the left of the altar. There are free afternoon concerts that start at 3:30pm when the church organist, Paolo Talamini, plays the massive instrument alone or accompanied by a chorus. Venetians are still thankful to the Virgin Mary for ending the plague and every year on November 21 they show their respect. A pontoon bridge is assembled from

San Marco and locals come to light votive candles and gondoliers have their oars blessed.

Punta della Dogana

Campo della Salute 2; tel. 041/200-1057; www. palazzograssi.it; Wed.-Mon. 10am-7pm; €15 with Palazzo Grassi

The Punta della Dogana was in disrepair until Francois Pinault purchased this iconic building and transformed it into the second piece of his contemporary art empire. The triangle-shaped former customhouse and warehouse was an important entry point for commercial vessels, and salt can still be seen encrusted on the brick walls inside. Tadao Ando gave the interior a zen makeover and today his trademark gray prevails throughout the immense gallery. There are a dozen spacious rooms exhibiting photography, installations, video, and sculpture on a rotating basis. Much of the art leaves an impression and challenges the senses. At the end of the complex are a bar, museum shop, and stairs leading to the lookout tower where spotters once scanned the lagoon for incoming ships. There are guided tours (free) in Italian every Saturday at 3pm; group tours are available the rest of the week by reservation (tel. 041/271-9031; €85, €160 for Palazzo Grassi and Punta della Dogana).

The **Fondamenta Salute** embankment leads to the easternmost tip of Dorsoduro and one of the best views of the city. It's a great place to stop and admire Venice. Afterward, avoid backtracking and follow **Fondamenta Zattere** along the wide promenade facing Giudecca.

Squero San Trovaso

Fondamenta Bonlini 1097; tel. 041/522-9146

Although the number of gondoliers is in steady decline, new boats are still built and old ones are always in need of repair, a paint job, and maintenance. Squero San Trovaso

is one of four remaining gondola shipyards where that highly specialized work gets done.

The best view of the small alpine-like huts and teams of workers hammering, sawing, and painting away is from Fondamenta Nani, which links the Grand Canal with the Giudecca Canal. There are usually several gondolas in dry dock being cared for by a team of workers. It can take up to a year to complete a new gondola, and each artisan has his own specialty handed down from generation to generation. Although there are occasional tours, they prefer if you watch from afar unless you're interested in buying a boat. **Osteria Al Squero** is perfectly positioned for observing the shipyard and is popular with visitors and locals who gather to watch the action and enjoy a drink.

Ca' Rezzonico

Fondamenta Rezzonico 3136; tel. 041/241-0100; Wed.-Mon. 10am-6pm; €10 or Museum Pass, audio guide €4

Like most palatial estates lining the Grand Canal, Ca' Rezzonico had a series of illustrious owners who wanted to demonstrate their power through art and architecture. Some of them went bankrupt in the process, and the palace changed hands many times before becoming the temporary home of Robert Browning and later Cole Porter. It was purchased by the city in 1935 and transformed into a house museum where you can discover how Venetian nobility lived.

The **audio guide** is useful for deciphering the 18th-century paintings, furnishings, and the Murano chandeliers decorating all three floors of the pristine *palazzo*. There are great views of the Grand Canal upstairs and a cozy shaded garden out back. Ca' Rezzonico is delightfully uncrowded and has its very own water stop, which makes it an easy destination to reach.

Campo Santa Margherita

Campo Santa Margherita is a relief from history. There are no major monuments, no earth-shattering churches, and no reason not

---

1: Campanile di San Marco **2:** Basilica Santa Maria Della Salute **3:** Campo Santo Stefano

to relax in this square. It's simply a popular university hangout lined with pretty houses and neighborhood shops where regulars eat at affordable *trattoria*. Most mornings there's an animated fish and vegetable market, and there's always plenty of space on the red benches that dot the large rectangular square. The oddly positioned building at the southern end of the *campo* is the *scuola piccola* (confraternity) where local tanners once met.

SAN POLO AND SANTA CROCE

Museum of Natural History
(Museo di Storia Naturale)

Santa Croce, Salita Fontego 1730; tel. 041/270-0370; www.msn.visitmuve.it; Jun.-Oct. Tues.-Sun. 10am-6pm, Nov.-May Tues.-Fri. 9am-5pm, Sat.-Sun. 10am-6pm; €8 or Museum Pass, audiopen €3.50

Venice's natural history museum isn't just for kids interested in dinosaurs (although there are plenty of those)—it's also the best place to learn about lagoon fauna and biodiversity. Many exhibits are interactive and several rooms contain artifacts dating from the Iron Age.

The museum is housed in the former **Fondaco dei Turchi,** a warehouse once used by Turkish merchants. Foreign traders operating in the city often built their own designated warehouses. This allowed city officials to keep an eye on their movements and confiscate money and weapons upon arrival. No Christian women or children were allowed to enter the area, which was originally equipped with a bathhouse and Turkish eateries. The Fondaco was used for trade until 1838 and eventually transformed into a natural history museum after extensive restoration.

Palazzo Mocenigo

Santa Croce, Salizzada di San Stae 1992; tel. 041/721-798; www.mocenigo.visitmuve.it; Apr.-Oct. Tues.-Sun. 10am-5pm, Nov.-Mar. Tues.-Sun. 10am-4pm; €8 or Museum Pass

Palazzo Mocenigo provides a glimpse of Venetian aristocrat life. Part of this modest museum is dedicated to perfumes (first floor) and the rest to textiles and costumes. In the 18th century, Venice was continually importing new scents from the Orient and combining them into new creations for the city's well-to-do. Visitors can smell the most popular of these and visit a laboratory where this ancient craft was conducted. Upstairs is filled with fashionable Venetian clothing from yesteryear. The collection includes period ball gowns, waistcoats, hats, and shoes.

You can learn more about perfume making by joining one of the museum's olfactory workshops (two hours, includes tour of museum). Participants discover the basic concepts and classifications of fragrance and create their own personal scent. Workshops must be reserved at least four days in advance and are usually held weekdays 10am-noon. The cost ranges €80-100 per person depending on the number of participants, which never exceeds 12.

The wealthy Mocenigo family who inhabited the *palazzo* included a number of *doges* and financed the building of the **San Stae** church down the street from their residence. The grand classical facade is anything but modest and opens out on the Grand Canal where people wait on the watery steps for the next *vaporetto* to arrive.

Rialto Fish and Produce Markets

There are markets in squares around the city where everyday Venetian life goes on as it always has, but the Rialto markets are the original center of commerce. The area even has its own *vaporetto* stop. If you disembark at *Rialto Mercato* any morning you'll discover the chaotic covered **fish market** (daily 7am-2pm). It doesn't get any fresher than this and a stroll beneath the shaded colonnades reveals chefs, housewives, and old-timers bantering with vivacious fishmongers hawking the merits of their catch. There are more kinds of fish and crustaceans here than at any supermarket, and having a look is the perfect

---

1: the Guggenheim Foundation 2: Rialto Bridge

San Polo and San Croce

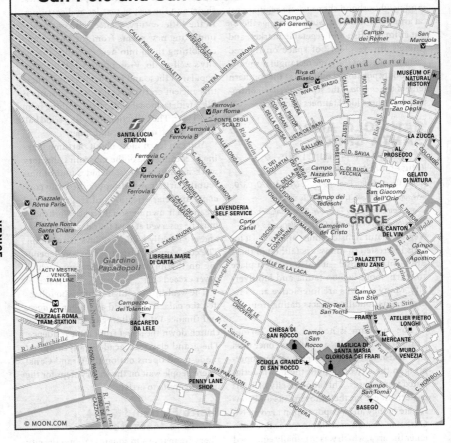

preview for lunch or dinner. Adjacent to the fish market are the green stalls of the **fruit and vegetable market** (daily 7am-8pm) selling the latest harvest from the Veneto region and beyond.

You can make a quick getaway to and from the markets on board the *traghetto* ferry that shuttles locals and visitors across the Grand Canal in a modified gondola. It departs every 10 minutes or whenever filled, from the northeastern corner of the fish market. This is one of the best rides in Venice and only costs €2.

Basilica di Santa Maria Gloriosa dei Frari

San Polo, Campo dei Frari 3072; www.basilicadeifrari. it; tel. 041/272-8611; Mon.-Sat. 9am-6pm, Sun. 1pm-6pm; €3 or Chorus Pass, audio guide €2

The Basilica di San Marco may be Venice's most famous church, but Basilica di Santa Maria Gloriosa dei Frari is the biggest—and that's not the only thing it has going for it. Inside the plain brick facade favored by Franciscan monks are works by Venetian masters including Vivarini, Bellini, and Titian, who died of the plague and is buried

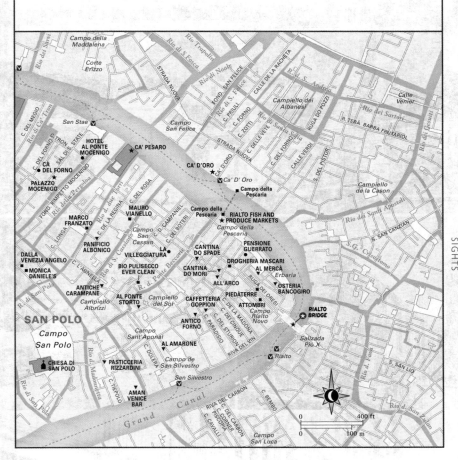

here along with several *doges*. A monument dedicated to him stands near the entrance on the right while the enormous *Annunciation* he painted hangs over the altar. It's not just paintings that stand out—it's the overall craftsmanship visible in the choir stalls, tombs, murals, and wooden sculptures. The 15th-century choir in the center of the church is a masterpiece of carpentry, with 50 carved panels illustrating everyday life in Venice.

Scuola Grande di San Rocco

San Polo, Campo di San Rocco 3052;

tel. 041/523-4864; www.scuolagrandesanrocco.org; daily 10am-5:30pm; €10, audio guide €5

Scuola Grande di San Rocco was the last confraternity founded and the best preserved in Venice. The interior avoided looting during Napoleon's sojourn in the city in 1797 and is filled with 73 paintings by Tintoretto. The ambitious artist won the competition to paint his first canvas inside by famously installing a completed work rather than the sketch judges were expecting. He avoided a prison sentence by donating the painting and later became a member of the *scuola* where he spent the next

23 years decorating the walls and ceilings of the institution.

Enormous paintings fill the rectangular *Sala Terrena* on the ground floor that was open to the public and where religious ceremonies were held, and upstairs in the *Sala dell'Albergo* where members still gather. Tintoretto began work on the *Sala Capitolare* next door in 1574. Most of the paintings are religious in nature and recount stories from the New Testament, including the *Fall of Man* and the *Sacrifice of Isaac,* and New Testament themes like the *Last Supper.* The *Sala dell'Albergo* contains Tintoretto's competition-winning entry *St. Roch in Glory* and a stunning *Crucifixion.* An explanation of the paintings is available in English at the entrance.

Chiesa di San Rocco

Campo San Rocco; daily 9:30am-1pm and 3pm-5:30pm, Sun. mass 11am; free

The Tintoretto tour can continue at the Chiesa di San Rocco opposite the Scuola Grande. The church is owned by the confraternity and contains several paintings that predate the artist's work in the main building. The first of these is *San Rocco che Visita gli Appestati* and depicts the life of St. Roch assisting victims of the plague. The church and school were both named after the saint and the brotherhood was very active in plague relief.

The church is a great place to escape summer heat and observe masterpieces. Canvases are dark yet vivid, and to the right of the altar the future saint is portrayed in a squalid prison cell tending to victims. It's a crowded scene populated by suffering men and women, a dog in the foreground, and a corpse who didn't make it. There is another immense canvas on the opposite side and several more undergoing restoration. The guardian might be convinced to let you have a peek at these if you demonstrate interest and discretion.

Another notable aspect of the church is

the *cantoria.* These baroque structures were added to many churches during the 18th century as a stage for organs and singers. This one was removed and lost for nearly a century until it was accidently discovered in a school gym. The *scuola* spent years and millions of euros (it was *lire* at the time) restoring it with the help of local apprentices. If you look at the two-story construction from the altar it blends in perfectly and the columns at the entrance appear as solid as the walls behind them. Once you touch them it's clear they're hollow and made of wood. The restored *cantoria* is often used and there are frequent free concerts.

Campo San Polo

Campo San Polo became the largest square in the *sestiere* when a canal was filled up and paved over. The parallel lines of white stone on the curved end of the square indicate where the waterway once ran. Venetians have used the square for horse racing, bullfights, and masked *Carnevale* parties for centuries. Today it's a playground for children and a peaceful retreat for residents who sit on the red benches in the shade of a half-dozen trees. There's a newsstand at one end near the flagpole that gets used on special occasions. From July to September the *campo* is transformed into an open-air cinema (www.culturavenezia.it; free) and throughout the Venice Film Festival movies are projected after their Lido premieres.

CHIESA DI SAN POLO

Salita San Polo; Mon.-Sat. 10:30am-4:30pm; €3 or Chorus Pass

Chiesa di San Polo, located in the *campo*, is even older than the square and was founded by Doge Pietro Gradonico in AD 737 with significant modifications in the 14th and 15th centuries. The church doesn't face the square and visitors must walk around the corner to reach the entrance and see the **bell tower** with the two stone lions carved into its base that represent the city.

1: Isola di San Giorgio **2:** Basilica di Santa Maria Gloriosa dei Frari **3:** Jewish Ghetto **4:** Ca' d'Oro overlooking the Grand Canal

Schools of Venice

Scuole or schools were (and in some cases, still are) important institutions in Venice. The word shouldn't be confused with its modern definition; it takes the Greek meaning of *association* or *confraternity*. Historically, *doges* and ruling nobles of Venetian society were more interested in politics, trade, and war than they were in their citizens' well-being. The first *scuola* were founded in the 11th century in reaction to this, as a way to assist the poor and provide plague relief to citizens and foreigners residing in the city.

Scuole are secular organizations. There were six great schools, or *scuole grande,* and hundreds of little schools, or *scuole piccole.* The latter represented the interests of the various trades active in the city and acted a little like modern unions. They also settled disputes between members, regulated trade standards, and oversaw apprenticeship. The *scuole grande* were concerned with charitable activities and ensured the city survived plagues and natural disasters that regularly befell Venice.

The *scuole grande* grew from small, meager groups into wealthy bastions, each with its own meeting house and church or chapel. The desire to impress and outdo one another meant a lot of time and money was invested into the embellishment of facades and interiors where the public and members met. Leading artists were commissioned, and no expense was spared. Napoleon closed most of the schools during his occupation of the city in 1797 and sent a lot of art back to the Louvre museum in Paris. The only exception was Scuola Grande di San Rocco, which the French general allowed to go on assisting the devasted population.

Today, San Rocco continues its charitable mission and carries on many traditions that were initiated centuries ago. New members must still be presented by an existing member and receive a majority of votes to be accepted. During the annual ceremony, a golden ball is used to ensure brothers don't leave the meeting early. Everyone is given a numbered ticket, and at the end members are called one by one to pick from an urn filled with hundreds of bronze metal balls and a single golden ball. If the *palla d'oro* is not selected (due to absentee members) the gold is donated to charity.

Ca' Pesaro

Santa Croce, Fondamenta de Ca' Pesaro 2076; tel. 041/721-127; www.capesaro.visitmuve.it; Tues.-Sun. 10am-6pm; €14 or Museum Pass

Ca' Pesaro isn't just a pretty facade along the Grand Canal. It's home to two remarkable museums in one stunning 17th-century *palazzo.* The first two floors are occupied by the **Galleria Internazionale d'Arte Moderna** with works by Chagall, Kandinsky, Klee, Matisse, and Moore. Paintings from early editions of the Venice Art Biennale also ended up hanging here. Highlights include *Giudetta II* by Klimt and a version of *The Thinker* by Rodin. Guided two-hour tours (education@fmcvenezia.it; €100/1-4 people) of the collection explore the artistic trends and innovations of the 20th century.

Upstairs, the **Museo d'Arte Orientale** displays more than 30,000 artworks and artifacts Prince Enrico di Borbone gathered during his grand tour of Asia. It's the largest collection of Edo-era objects outside of Japan and a drastic departure from Venetian culture. There are kimonos, lacquer furnishings, porcelain, paintings, shadow puppets, weaponry, and everyday personal items. The dark wood-paneled rooms also contain jade-and-gold-painted shells from China. A short video in Italian and English explains the origins of the collection.

A single ticket provides entry to both museums. There's a small cafeteria on the ground floor and a cloakroom and bookshop near the main entrance.

CANNAREGIO
Grand Canal
(Canal Grande)

The Grand Canal is the busiest and most

Cannaregio

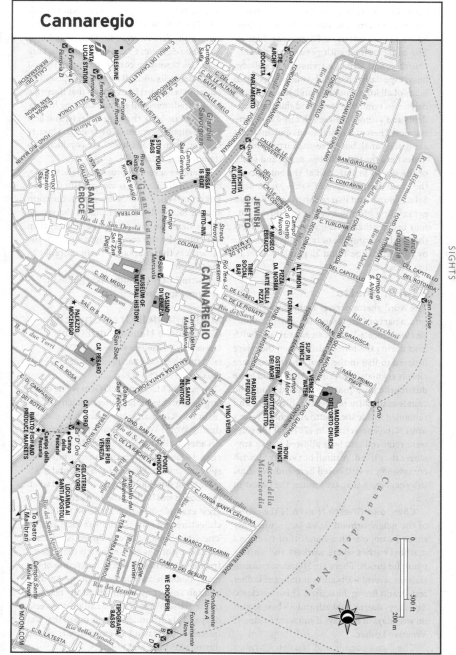

@MOON.COM

important waterway in Venice. It snakes through the center of the city from Stazione Santa Lucia station to Piazza San Marco. The canal is lined with prestigious *palazzi,* churches, and former warehouses. It's always busy, especially on weekday mornings when boats of all kinds move up and down making deliveries, removing trash, and shuttling residents and visitors between floating *vaporetto* stations. There is no continuous embankment along the canal, but there are partial promenades near the train station, north and south of the Rialto Bridge, and at the entrance to the canal itself in front of Santa Maria della Salute church and Piazza San Marco. You can get inviting glimpses of the canal from the four bridges that cross it or the many streets that lead to it, but the only way to see it all is by *vaporetto* (line 1 and 2), gondola, or renting a boat.

Jewish Ghetto

The word *ghetto* derives from the Venetian *geto,* a part of Cannaregio where iron foundries were located. It became associated with Jews during the 14th century when they were ordered to live in the area. Their lives were closely regulated: Although they could leave during the day, guards stationed along the canals made sure residents returned to and remained inside the ghetto at night. It wasn't until Napoleon arrived in 1797 that the gates were removed and Jews allowed to live anywhere they liked. A small but vibrant Jewish community is still based here and worships in synagogues that are among the oldest in Italy.

Campo di Ghetto Nuovo is the center of the neighborhood. It's a large, unevenly shaped *campo* with a handful of trees and marble benches where workers and visitors pause for lunch. There are Holocaust memorials on several walls and a number of kosher restaurants lining the square. These are closed Saturdays during Sabbath and it's best to visit on weekdays or Sundays if you want to sample Venetian kosher.

The **Synagogue** and **Museo Ebraico** (Cannaregio, Campo Ghetto Nuovo; tel. 041/715-359; www.museoebraico.it; Jun.-Sept. Sun.-Fri. 10am-7pm, Oct.-May Sun.-Fri. 10am-5:30pm; €12 or Museum Pass) are in the southwestern corner in front of the old rainwater wells and tall wooden flagpole. The museum is divided in two parts that illustrate Jewish traditions and recount the long history of Venetian Jews through objects, images, and firsthand accounts. **Tours** depart hourly starting from 10:30am and are conducted in Italian and English.

There are several approaches to the Ghetto, but the historic route is along **Calle Ghetto Vecchio.** When approaching from the train station follow Rio Terra Lista all the way to Ponte delle Guglie. Cross the bridge, turn left, and take the second right through the underpass that marks the main entrance to the Ghetto.

During COVID outbreaks, guided tours may be suspended.

Madonna dell'Orto Church
(Chiesa della Madonna dell'Orto)

Cannaregio, Fondamenta Madonna dell'Orto; tel. 041/719-933; Mon.-Sat. 10am-5pm, Sun. noon-5pm; €3 or Chorus Pass

Chiesa della Madonna dell'Orto is one of the largest churches in the *sestiere,* which may explain why German troops used it as a stable during World War II. It was in bad shape for decades until an Englishman (buried in the chapel near the altar) bequeathed funds to restore the church. The elegant façade and modest interior now look as good as they did when the church was built in the 14th century. It's a great example of Venice's take on Gothic architecture and was Tintoretto's local parish. The artist donated over a dozen large-scale biblical paintings to the church that draw a trickle of tourists. If you're lucky, one of the many dedicated volunteers will be on duty and can answer questions about the building or the artist. **Mass** is held daily at 9am weekdays and 11am Sunday, but the organ that was intended for Teatro La Fenice is only played during weddings and funerals.

Tintoretto is buried inside the church, and there are often flowers lying on the marble plaque marking his tomb. The artist lived and worked just over the bridge facing the church on Fondamenta dei Mori.

Bottega del Tintoretto

Cannaregio, Fondamenta dei Mori 3400; tel. 041/722-081; www.tintorettovenezia.it; daily 10am-7pm; free

There's no museum or trace of the painter but it's still worth stopping by Bottega del Tintoretto to watch the artisans, sculptors, printers, and lithographers who now occupy the building. If you're interested in ink, bookbinding, and printing, Roberto and other members of his craft association will gladly explain their techniques.

Ca' d'Oro

Cannaregio, Calle Ca' d'Oro 3932; tel. 041/520-0345; www.cadoro.org; Tues.-Sun. 10am-6pm; €10, audio guide €4

Venice never fully embraced Renaissance architecture, and instead maintained the Gothic status quo long after the movement had gone out of fashion in other cities. That explains the intricate facades lining the Grand Canal. If you're going to enter any of these ornate family residences the Ca' d'Oro is a good choice. The home dates from the 15th century but it's the later restoration that is visible today; it was donated to the city in 1916 along with an extensive collection of sculpture, tapestries, paintings, and pottery that's on display.

The ground floor contains a small courtyard with the original well and early 20th-century mosaic paving that leads to a private dock. Temporary exhibitions of modern artists are staged in the former reception halls upstairs while the smaller rooms are lined with religious paintings, including Mantegna's *St. Sebastian*. The best feature of the building is the terrace that overlooks the waterway and allows visitors to observe the comings and goings along the Grand Canal.

CASTELLO

Scuola Grande di San Marco

Fondamenta Mendicante 6776; tel. 041/529-4323; www.scuolagrandesanmarco.it; Tues.-Sat. and first Sun. every month 9:30am-5:30pm; €8

With its ornate entrance and statue of St. Mark, it's easy to mistake Scuola Grande di San Marco for a church, but the refined *palazzo* facing Campo Giovanni e Paolo isn't a religious building. Scuola Grande is a *scuola,* the Venetian version of the Lion's Club, founded by do-gooders in the 13th century and used as a fancy clubhouse until Napoleon abolished fraternal organizations in the city.

The *scuola* was reopened in 2013 and the facade is an eyeful. There are interesting uses of perspective, elaborate stonework that distinguishes Venetian Renaissance architecture from Florentine and Roman designs, and plenty of lions. The grand entrance on the left leads to a reception hall while the relatively modest doorway on the right provides access to the *albergo* and is usually closed. The interior was stripped of artwork after the brotherhood disbanded but the two main rooms upstairs regained their former opulence during a lengthy restoration. *Sala Capitolare* contains a collection of medical artifacts and several paintings by Tintoretto recounting the life of St. Mark. The walls in *Sala dell'Albergo* next door are also dedicated to the saint. Both rooms have massive engraved ceilings.

The square out front is one of the nicest in Castello and a lovely place to linger. Café tables line the southern side underneath a bronze equestrian statue of a local mercenary and gelato is available nearby.

Basilica Santi Giovanni e Paolo

Fondamento Dandolo; tel. 041/523-5913; Mon.-Sat. 9am-6pm, Sun. noon-6pm; €3.50

The cavernous Basilica Santi Giovanni e Paolo is the final resting place of many illustrious Venetians, with enormous stained-glass windows created in Murano that are best viewed

Cruising Venice's Canals

Venice is a city at one with the sea, and if you don't step on board a gondola, *vaporetto*, or water taxi, you're missing out on the best part. The views from a boat help make sense of the city and seduce the eyes in a way walking cannot. For a more active option, explore the canals by kayak (page 353).

GONDOLA

Gondolas are so closely linked with Venice that it's hard to imagine one without the other, and a ride will live up to expectations. If you decide to hire a gondola, it's important to choose a good point of departure. There are eleven gondola stations as well as vessels docked in ones or twos around the city. Some, like those near San Marco, are so busy shuttling passengers under the Bridge of Sighs that it feels like being on a merry-go-round. You'll also share the experience with hundreds of eager onlookers and end up as the backdrop in countless photographs. It's more romantic to depart from quieter *sestiere*, like Dorsoduro or Castello, where canals are uncluttered and you can glide past one of the last *squero* (gondola workshops) in Venice.

The profession is highly regulated, and prices are fixed at €80 for a 40-minute ride during the day and €100 after 7pm on a gondola that seats up to six passengers. The gondoliers themselves are romantic figures dressed in red- or blue-striped shirts and conscious of the historical role they play. Some will point out landmarks along the way while others will keep to themselves, silently navigating the canals. None are required to sing, although a couple do. The profession is often handed down from generation to generation and it's not uncommon for multiple members of the same family to practice this ancient trade. Today there are 453 gondoliers left and they are nearly all men, although several women have obtained licenses in recent years. Getting one from the city council is a time-consuming and strenuous affair that can take up to 10 years.

TRAGHETTO

Anyone who doesn't want to invest time or money in a full-fledged gondola excursion can get the condensed experience at the *traghetti* (gondola ferry) stations along the Grand Canal. There are three landings still in activity: Santa Sofia (weekdays 7:30am-7pm, weekends 8:45am-7pm), San Tomà (weekdays 7:30am-8pm, weekends 8:30am-7:30pm), and Santa Maria del Giglio (weekdays 7am-6pm, weekends 9am-7pm), where two-man teams shuttle residents and adventurous travelers across the Grand Canal in refitted gondolas. One of the ferry points is located in Cannaregio near the Ca d'Oro and connects the neighborhood with the fish market in San Polo close to the Rialto. The other two are near Piazza San Marco. Santa Maria del Giglio is especially convenient for reaching the Punta della Dogana lookout point in Dorsoduro. A single ride (€2) lasts less than five minutes and is the most thrilling way of crossing Venice's busiest canal.

from the inside. Mass is held at 8am and 6:30pm on weekdays and 9am, 11am, and 6:30pm on weekends.

San Giorgio Church
(Chiesa di San Giorgio dei Greci)

Calle dei Greci; tel. 041/523-9569; Mon.-Sat. 9am-12:30pm and 2:30pm-4:30pm, Sun. 9am-1pm; free

Greeks have a long history in Venice. They were attracted to the city for its commercial ties to the Orient and tended to settle in Castello where their numbers grew even larger after the Turks captured Constantinople in 1453. Eventually the Orthodox community wanted a church of its own. Permission to build the Chiesa di San Giorgio was granted in 1498. The single-nave structure was

aquatic traffic along the Grand Canal

★ *VAPORETTO*

Vaporetti, the aquatic equivalent of buses, are typical Venetian ferries that carry up to 210 passengers and form the backbone of the city's public transportation network. They've been serving the city since the late 19th century and make getting around easy. They regularly serve water stops along the Grand Canal, around the city's circumference, and in outlying islands throughout the lagoon. *Vaporetti* can be crowded and finding a seat on deck is often difficult, but standing along the open railing provides an equally great view and is quite romantic, especially at night when there are far fewer passengers and the distant lights of the city take on mysterious tones. You can buy a single ticket (€7.50), but the best option is a 24-hour (€20) or 48-hour (€30) pass that allows unlimited travel. *Vaporetti* operate day and night and make it fun to discover secluded parts of the city like Giudecca, Isola di San Giorgio, and the Biennale Gardens, all of which are impossible or difficult to reach on foot.

The number 1 or 2 *vaporetto* from Santa Lucia train station provide a dramatic introduction to the city. They make 15 stops along the Grand Canal all the way to Piazza San Marco in 30-40 minutes. There are 21 lines in all and maps can be downloaded from ACTV (www.actv.avmspa. it) or studied at individual stops. There is a dedicated night service (N) and several seasonal lines that only operate during the summer.

completed a century later in one of the most tranquil parts of the city. The imposing bell tower cannot be visited, but a small museum can and contains a collection of colorful Byzantine icons.

Arsenale

Campo del Arsenale; tel. 041/521-8711; Mon.-Fri. 9am-6pm; free

Venice wouldn't have been possible without an imposing fleet of ships that controlled the Eastern Mediterranean and the islands of Crete and Cyprus. Those vessels were built in the Arsenale, the world's first large-scale shipyard. The Arsenale was active for seven centuries, employing over 2,000 workers at its peak, and takes up 15 percent of the city's land mass.

Castello

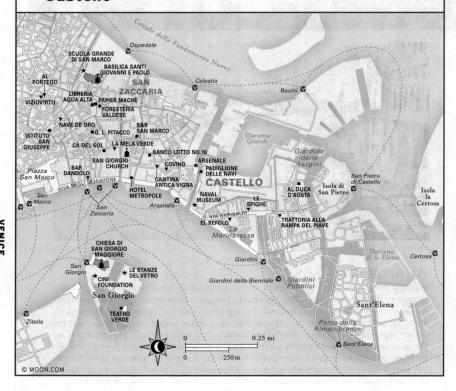

© MOON.COM

Today, it's used by the Italian Navy and as an exhibition space during the **Venice Biennale.** The best view of the complex is from the wooden bridge at the end of Fondamenta dell'Arsenale. Four immense stone lions guard the imposing twin-tower entrance and demonstrate just how important the site was to the city. Although there are plans to transform the Arsenale into a cultural center, most of the area is closed to the public and open during special exhibitions. What can be visited is entered near either of the two *vaporetto* stops (Celestia or Bacini Arsenale). Arriving on the 4.1 or 5.1 ferries not only makes a dramatic entrance but can save you walking to one of the most distant parts of the city.

Naval Museum
(Museo Storico Navale)

Riva S. Bagio 2148; tel. 041/244-1399; daily 10am-6pm; €10 with Padiglione delle Navi

To get an even better idea of Venice's seafaring past head to Museo Storico Navale, located near the Arsenale. This museum covers five floors and several centuries of history. The first two are the most relevant and document how Venice created and retained its naval superiority. There are extensive collections of navigational instruments, uniforms, and models of vessels used for trade and warfare.

Padiglione Delle Navi

Rio della Tana Castello 2162/C; tel. 041/2424; daily 8:45am-5pm; €10 with Naval Museum

Tintoretto: The Little Tanner

The name Jacopo Robusti (1519-1594) doesn't ring a lot of bells, but you may have heard of Tintoretto. It means *little tanner*, a nickname the artist earned as a child working in his father's tannery. The boy was always ambitious and grew up to be one of the most remarkable painters of his age. His reputation was greatly enhanced by the writings of John Ruskin (1819-1900), who was a great admirer and marveled at the size and visual depth of the canvases.

Unlike Rome and Florence, Venice's damp climate was unsuited for fresco painting and wood or canvas were preferred by artists. This was advantageous to painters like Tintoretto who could work in his studio located along the Fondamenta dei Mori, saving him the kind of grueling backaches Michelangelo endured working on the Sistine Chapel. That didn't mean Tintoretto's paintings were any smaller than his Renaissance contemporaries. He mastered the ability to cover colossal spaces with scores of dramatic figures in epic scenes.

Unlike many artists who traveled around Italy painting for patrons, Tintoretto remained in Venice his entire life, which may explain why he isn't the most famous Renaissance painter. Even in his hometown he generated contrasting opinions but worked steadily throughout his life and left behind an enormous artistic inheritance that can be seen in churches, palaces, *scuole,* and museums throughout Venice. He was buried in the Madonna dell'Orto Church and it's not uncommon to find fresh flowers on his tomb, presumably laid by one of his modern-day fans.

WHERE TO SEE TINTORETTO'S ART

The best places to appreciate Tintoretto's canvases are Chiesa della Madonna dell'Orto (page 310) and the Scuola Grande di San Rocco (page 305) where the painter audaciously won a competition by installing a completed work rather than submitting a sketch. The *scuola* contains 73 works from the painter in the immense ground- and first-floor halls where Venetians met. Subjects are religious in nature and cover both the Old and New Testaments. At a time of widespread illiteracy these were vital ways to illustrate the Bible and remind citizens of the power of man and god. The first painting he completed for the *scuola* is across the square in the Chiesa di San Rocco (page 307).

VENICE
SIGHTS

Historic merchant ships, warships, and gondolas can be seen up close a short walk away inside the Padiglione Delle Navi (Boat Pavilion). Dozens of boats are on display and a single ticket allows entry to both the pavilion and the Naval Museum.

Riva degli Schiavone

Venice has a split personality, one that's depressingly crowded and another that's refreshingly tranquil. Sometimes the two can be experienced in a single location, and depending on the hour you may love or hate Riva degli Schiavone. In the early morning and evening, this wide promenade stretching from Piazza San Marco to the Biennale Gardens is nearly deserted and the dramatic views of the lagoon can be enjoyed in relative peace. In between those times the embankment is lined with pleasure boats, souvenir stands, and itinerant salespeople selling cheap gadgets to tourists and cruise ship passengers. Choose your moment wisely, and remember that the farther you get from Piazza San Marco the quieter things become until you eventually reach the solitude of Sant'Elena Island at the southeastern tip of Venice.

Sant'Elena Island
(Isola Sant'Elena)

There's little to see in the touristic sense on Sant'Elena Island—and that's what makes it worth visiting. It's out of the way by Venetian standards and can take ages to reach on foot. It's easier to ride the *vaporetto* and get off at the Sant'Elena stop. The island is wrapped in a tree-lined park and most of the residential housing in the center was built in the 1920s. There are few businesses and only a couple of simple eateries serving unadulterated classics.

On the westernmost point is the modest Chiesa di Sant'Elena, where the remains of Emperor Constantine's mother are preserved. Nearby are two marinas filled with private yachts and a rickety stadium where Venice's lower-league soccer team plays.

GIUDECCA

There's another side to Venice, and it's called Giudecca. It may be less beautiful and house fewer monuments than its more illustrious neighbors, but it's also blissfully less crowded. Although part of Venice, Giudecca can only be reached by *vaporetto,* which keeps tour groups and day-trippers away. Here you get a real sense of what it feels like to live on an island and watch locals going about their business as though they didn't live in the world's most beautiful city.

The long **embankment** that runs along the northern edge of Giudecca is the main artery and provides great views of Dorsoduro. Most bars and restaurants are clustered along here, and the **Palanca** *vaporetto* stop is the liveliest bit. If you've made it this far you should explore the backstreets of the island (actually 13 islets in one) where you'll stumble on churches, public housing, hostels, stray cats, a women's prison, a luxury rooftop bar, and some surprises in between.

The biggest surprise and the only time of year Giudecca attracts thousands of visitors is during the **Festa del Redentore** when the city celebrates the end of a medieval plague and a temporary pontoon bridge is built across the Giudecca Canal.

Redentore Church
(Chiesa del Redentore)
Campo del SS. Redentore 195; tel. 041/275-0462; Mon.-Sat. 10:30am-1:30pm and 2:30pm-5pm, Sun. 10am-6:30pm; €3 or Chorus Pass

Plagues were an everyday reality in 16th-century Venice, and when they hit they decimated the city's population. After nearly 50,000 people died from a plague in the early 1570s, it was natural to commemorate the end of the epidemic by building a church. Palladio

was commissioned and Chiesa del Redentore was completed in 1580. The exquisitely proportioned façade looks out over the waterfront and is topped with a distinct white dome flanked by twin spires.

The church was decorated by Bassano and Tintoretto but it's the overall harmony of the space inside that makes it stunning. This is where the city's most popular festival takes place on the third Sunday in July, during which a footbridge is erected over the Giudecca Canal that attracts thousands of fervent Venetians.

San Giorgio Island
(Isola di San Giorgio)

San Giorgio is a small island in front of Piazza San Marco and next to Giudecca that can only be reached by *vaporetto.* It's worth making a detour here to climb the bell tower and visit a superb glass gallery. Isola di San Giorgio has one ferry station that can be reached with the number 2 *vaporetto.* It's one stop from Zattere in Giudecca or S. Zaccaria (F) near Piazza San Marco.

CHIESA DI SAN GIORGIO MAGGIORE
Isola di San Giorgio Maggiore; daily 7am-6pm; free

Travelers who make the effort to reach San Giorgio Island can visit the Chiesa di San Giorgio Maggiore and adjacent Benedictine monastery where Cosimo de Medici stayed while banished from Florence. The church is enormous and if the architect's intention was to make parishioners feel small, he succeeded. Supporting columns are massive and the unadorned ceilings nose-bleedingly high. There are several paintings by Tintoretto and few visitors most mornings.

The main attraction is the view from the *campanile* (**bell tower;** €6) that lies opposite the entrance. On your way to the ticket office take a look at the choir behind the main altar with its intricately carved seating and Q*bert-like marble floor patterns. The *campanile* is slightly smaller than its San Marco counterpart but was also rebuilt after an unexpected collapse. Lines are shorter here and

The Smallest Street in Venice

Venice has dozens of streets that are so narrow you can touch both walls at the same time. In these remote, dimly lit passages, silence reigns, and the city seems suddenly distant. Many are difficult to find and some are so small they don't appear on maps—let alone Google Street View. Most travelers avoid these secret routes and choose more inviting directions, but the miniature streets of Venice are a remarkable and exciting part of the city's extraordinary urban landscape.

There's debate on which *calle* is the tiniest, but most locals agree **Calletta Varisco** (Cannaregio, near Campo Widman) holds the title. At its narrowest point the alley measures 21 inches (53 centimeters) across and turns two-way pedestrian traffic into a game of Twister. Fortunately, there are few people around, and once you pass the Doric column time stands still. The *calle* dramatically ends in a canal and one might wonder why it was built in the first place. Dead ends, however, are an essential part of the city's transportation network. Where paving stops, water always begins.

Across the Grand Canal in San Polo, **Calle Stretta,** 26 inches (66 centimeters) connects Campiello Albrizzi with the Furatola underpass. To the north in Santa Croce near the Riva de Biasio ferry station is **Calle di Ca' Zusto,** barely 27 inches (68 centimeters) wide. **Calesela dell'Occhio Grosso** near Campo dell Gorne underneath the walls of the Arsenale is a mere 23 inches (58 centimeters) wide.

the stairs are out of order with little hope of being restored, making an elevator the only way up. The panorama at the top is sweeping with Venice, the Lido, Murano, and a distant Burano all in view. This is a great place to observe the busy maritime traffic and occasional cruise ship being tugged into the city. It can get very windy and you may be startled when the largest of the nine working bells rings out the hour or half hour.

The church and bell tower can be combined with a visit of the **Cini Foundation** (Isola di San Giorgio Maggiore; tel. 041/271-0217; www.cini.it; daily 10am-5pm; €13), which includes paintings, sculpture, and furniture. The foundation is located inside a former Benedictine monastery attached to Chiesa di San Giorgio Maggiore and has played an instrumental part in redeveloping the island and supporting local culture. To see the cloisters, garden, *Last Supper,* library, and labyrinth

visitors must join one of the guided audio tours that last 45 minutes and departs every hour on the hour.

LE STANZE DEL VETRO
Isola di San Giorgio Maggiore 1; tel. 041/522-9138; Thurs.-Mon. 10am-7pm; free

At Le Stanze del Vetro you can discover how ancient and modern craftspeople manipulate glass, which is an incredibly versatile material. The gallery is located behind the church of San Giorgio and run by an association that organizes two exhibitions per year. Spring and early summer are dedicated to contemporary artists from around the world, while the rest of the year celebrates the city's own glassmaking tradition. Exhibitions are free and shown in a bright, modern gallery that's a pleasure to visit. Documentary videos explain the creative process and a small gift shop sells Fabriano stationery and a few select pieces of glass.

Food

Venetian culinary traditions have a lot to do with geography and history. Unlike the landlocked cities of Rome and Florence, Venice has easy access to the sea. The fisheries you may have noticed as your train approached the city raise sea bass, sole, and sardines that are available at the central fish market, which also sells shrimp, crab, and other crustaceans that end up on plates around the city.

Venice's status as a seafaring power meant that exotic flavors and spices like pepper, clove, and cinnamon were imported from around the Mediterranean and adapted to local dishes. Long voyages meant food was prepared and preserved in creative ways. Large communities of Jews, Greeks, and Turks also contributed a multicultural element that is still present in dishes today.

Each *sestiere* is divided into smaller neighborhoods with their own church and, equally important, bakery where residents come for bread and local pastries. These are wonderful shops with large gas or electric ovens where dough is baked daily for residents.

Dining Tips

Take care when choosing a restaurant in Venice. Many eateries near the train station and along busy routes to the Rialto and Piazza San Marco rely entirely on one-time tourist trade, and no Venetian with an appetite would ever eat there. Also, remember that fish is often priced by the 100 grams, which can result in an astronomical bill if you're not careful.

Expect the price of eating out in Venice to be higher than Rome or Florence. This is due to added transportation costs, a limited number of venues, and high demand. Fish is pricier than meat, and it's hard to find a first course under €10 or a second under €15. Fortunately there are many wonderful places to dine or snack and it's difficult not to be satisfied after an authentic Venetian meal.

A final note: All establishments are legally obliged to provide customers with a receipt. If they forget, remind them by asking for *il scontrino, per favore* (Ill scon-TREE-no Pear fah-VOR-ay). By doing so, you're ensuring they pay taxes and doing all Italians a favor.

SAN MARCO
Venetian
LA ROSTICCERIA GISLON
Calle della Bissa 5424a; tel. 041/522-3569; daily 9am-9:30pm; €8-12
La Rosticceria Gislon is the Venetian version of a cafeteria. You can sit at a table or the counter next to locals vying for sandwiches and roast fish and meat dishes served from large tins behind the counter. This is where the postman goes for lunch. Most tourists are intimidated by the confusion inside, but it's hard to find a more affordable lunch spot so close to the Rialto. If the downstairs area is too crowded, head upstairs.

VINI DA ARTURO
Calle Degli Assassini 3656; tel. 041/528-6974; Mon.-Sat. noon-2:30pm and 7pm-10:30pm, closed Aug.; €15, cash only
With 20 seats, one waiter, and a chef, Ernesto Ballarin's small restaurant is a wonderful place to take a breather just north of Teatro La Fenice. While many Venetian restaurants focus on fish, meat and vegetables are the stars here. There are tender filets of beef, breaded pork chops (*maiale alla veneziana*), distinctive salads, and plenty of pasta (*spaghetti alla gorgonzola*). Framed photos of satisfied celebrities hang on the wood-paneled walls. If you're curious to see all the famous faces Ernesto has fed, ask to see the photo albums.

★ MUSEUM CAFÉ
Palazzo Grassi, Campo San Samuele 3231; Wed.-Mon. 10am-7pm; €16-20

Best Food and Drink

★ **Museum Café:** Delicious proof that great food can be combined with great art (page 318).

★ **Al Bottegon:** Enjoy authentic Venetian flavors inside this wonderfully gritty *enoteche* or outside along a canal (page 325).

★ **Gelateria Da Nico:** The historic shop where hazelnut and cacao-flavored *giandiotto* gelato was invented. Its terrace has scenic canal views (page 326).

★ **Antiche Carampane:** The best fish in the city served in a simple but elegant atmosphere (page 327).

★ **Cantina Do Mori:** Fresh fish, delivered daily, is transformed into delicious creamed cod and fried calamari, accompanied by *prosecco* (page 327).

★ **Vino Vero:** This hole-in-the-wall is packed with grape enthusiasts enjoying tempting *cicchetti* appetizers (page 329).

★ **Aman Venice Bar:** An elegant second-story bar at the Aman Venice Resort Hotel overlooking the Grand Canal (page 337).

VENICE FOOD

The Museum Café is as stylish as the rest of Palazzo Grassi in which it's located, and an original lunch option. Several tables look out over the Grand Canal and the menu includes a vegetarian burger. Chef Marta Munerato, who trained under Gordon Ramsey and legendary Italian chef Gualtiero Marchesi, conjures up a daily special from scratch every morning. Expect stellar dishes at reasonable prices. Entry to the café requires a ticket to Palazzo Grassi but combining lunch with a visit of the modern art gallery stimulates all the senses.

Seafood

BECCAFICO

Campo Santo Stefano 2801; tel. 041/527-4879; daily noon-3pm and 7pm-11pm; €15-20

Campo Santo Stefano is one of the most vivacious squares in Venice, and dining on the outdoor terrace of upscale Beccafico is a treat. The restaurant provides a Sicilian twist on local specialties. The fresh fish and crustaceans are the best reason to come. First courses like pasta with sardines and

zuppa di cozze (mussel soup) are abundant and flavorful. The delicate seconds include grilled bream with citrus, stuffed swordfish, and large plates of fried fish and vegetables. Sicilian-style pizza is also served at lunch and the kitchen closes later than most Venetian restaurants.

ANTICA CARBONERA

Calle Bembo 4648; tel. 041/522-5479; Thurs.-Sun. 11:30am-11pm; €14-30

Antica Carbonera has been maintaining Venetian gastronomic traditions since 1894. Portions are generous and served in copper skillets by an attentive staff. There are several dining rooms and the ground floor is decorated in salvaged nautical furnishings. It's cozy, especially if you sit in one of the booths lining the wall. Upstairs is a modern dining area and small terrace. The menu is all about fish, and *Crudité di Giornata* (daily raw fish plate) includes fresh salmon, sea bream, bass, tuna, shrimp, and oysters. Pasta and desserts are all handmade daily at this historic *trattoria*.

Venetian Cuisine

Venice offers flavors unlike any others in Italy, and a world away from Rome or Florence. The results will surprise taste buds and make you rethink your definition of Italian food.

APPETIZERS *(ANTIPASTI)*

- *Sarde in saor:* Fried sardines served with caramelized onions cooked in vinegar sauce.

- *Baccalà mantecato:* Boiled and whipped cod spread on thin slices of fresh bread. Also available as a second.

- *Insalata di mare:* Cuttlefish, shrimp, and celery salad dressed in lemon juice and olive oil.

FIRST COURSES *(PRIMI)*

- *Risotto:* Rice plays a major role in local diets and is usually served with *risi bisi* (peas) or *sparasi* (asparagus) in early spring and summer.

- *Spaghetti con le vongole:* Spaghetti and clams, available year-round.

- *Spaghetti al nero di seppia:* Pasta with cuttlefish ink seasoned with parsley, wine, and garlic.

- Other first courses include *zuppa di pesce* (fish soup), *pasta e fagiole* (pasta and beans), and *bigoli in salsa* (a thicker version of spaghetti) served with a sardine-and-onion sauce.

SECOND COURSES *(SECONDI)*

Fish is the king of second courses, and restaurants use a multitude of varieties to prepare a vast array of dishes. It comes fried, grilled, baked, sautéed, creamed, or marinated, and is usually always fresh. To get an idea of what your stomach can expect, take a stroll through the fish market near the Rialto that supplies many of the city's restaurants. *Bisato su l'ara* (eel), cuttlefish, *sardelle* (sardines), lagoon clams, soft-shell crab, sea bass, gray mullet, monkfish, calamari, and octopus are transformed into original dishes that are difficult to find anywhere else.

- *Fritto misto:* A heaping plate of fried shrimp, calamari, sardines, and squid. Served in restaurants and *bacari*, where it can be ordered to go.

- *Bacalà con polenta:* Cod that's creamed or slowly stewed in tomato sauce and served with polenta.

- *Branzino al forno:* Sea bass baked with onions and tomatoes, topped with lemon.

- *Fegato alla veneziana:* Pork or veal liver with white onions. Often accompanied by polenta.

SIDES *(CONTORNI)*

Second courses are usually served unaccompanied by vegetables, so if you want a little variety, you'll need to order a *contorno*.

- *Carciofi impanati:* Breaded artichokes.

- *Patate alla veneziana:* Beans, onions, and potatoes stewed in vegetable broth.

- *Melanzane alla Giudea:* Jewish-style fried eggplant dish.

- *Polenta:* Polenta is common in northern Italy, but in Venice it's made from white corn flour and has a smoother consistency than the yellow variety.

WINE *(VINO)* AND OTHER DRINKS

There are dozens of local appellations to choose from in the Veneto region. White grape varieties tend to do better due to the colder climate, but there are exceptions. House wine is generally a safe bet.

Aperol spritz and *antipasti*

- Bardolino: Dry red wine from the hills around Verona with a hint of bitterness and delicate aftertaste. Goes well with meat.

- Soave: Popular white wine produced from garganega or trebbiano grapes. Perfect as an appetizer or with pasta and fish.

- Prosecco: Widely produced sparkling white wine that's a valid alternative to Champagne. Can be drunk as an aperitif, a nightcap, or with a meal.

- Spritz: A mix of *prosecco*, Aperol or Campari bitters, and seltzer.

DESSERT *(DOLCI)*

Venetian desserts have Jewish, Austrian, and Middle Eastern roots and rely on cacao and nuts for sweetness and crunch. During the run-up to *Carnevale*, fried *(frittole)* pastries stuffed with cream, raisins, or pine nuts appear in bakery windows, and each holiday is celebrated with a particular dessert. Fortunately, most sweets are available year-round.

- *Pan di doge:* Almond-covered biscuits baked in honor of the *doge.*

- *Moro di venezia:* A large brownie-like cookie, made from chocolate and hazelnuts, available in most bakeries.

- *Pinza veneziana:* Rustic cake made with dried raisins and topped with pine nuts.

- *Burranei:* Unevenly shaped butter cookies coated with powdered sugar and found in bakeries and pastry shops.

Cicchetti

BACARANDO

*Calle dell'Orso 5495; tel. 041/523-8280; daily
10:30am-11:30pm; €7-10*

Bacarando is one of the newer *bacaro* bars in the city. It's spread out on two floors and features live music on Wednesday nights. There's seating outside in a pleasant courtyard where a range of *cicchetti* (€1-3) can be enjoyed with inexpensive wine.

OSTERIA ENOTECA AL VOLTO

*Calle Cavalli 4081; tel. 041/522-8945; daily
10am-4pm and 6pm-10pm; €10*

Located on a quiet street near the Grand Canal, Osteria Enoteca al Volto can satisfy any *cicchetti* craving. There isn't much room inside the wood-paneled interior, and most visitors stand at the bar sipping glasses of wine and wondering whether to order the creamed cod or fried calamari on a stick. If you're lucky, one of the tables outside will be free and you can go back for frequent refills of the €3 house *prosecco*.

Pizza

Venetian pizza is thick and closer to *focaccia* than the thin kind served in Rome. *Pizzerie* and by-the-cut shops are not very common and those that do exist can be found along busy streets catering to tourists.

ROSSOPOMODORO

*Calle Larga Rosa 404; tel. 041/243-8949; daily
noon-3:30pm and 7pm-11pm; €10-12*

Not all chain restaurants should necessarily be avoided. If you feel like having a Neapolitan pizza in Venice, Rossopomodoro can satisfy a *Margherita* craving. You won't wait long at this large, modern restaurant, which has indoor and outdoor seating and a wood-burning oven in one corner where you can watch pizza being prepared. Toppings are fresh and prices reasonable given the proximity to Piazza San Marco.

Snacks and Street Food

TUTTIINPIEDI

*Calle Cavalletto 1099/A; tel. 041/241-0279; daily
noon-4pm and 6pm-9:30pm; €6-8*

Tuttiinpiedi literally means *everybody standing*, and that's what you'll be doing inside this tiny eatery serving freshly cooked pasta. It's all done on the fly by a jovial owner-chef who treats everyone like a friend. One of the cheapest, most satisfying places to eat in Venice. Arrive early and come back often.

Bakeries

COLUSSI

*Campo San Luca 4579; tel. 041/522-2659; Mon.-Sat.
8am-2pm and 4:30pm-7:30pm; €3-5*

The Colussi family has produced six generations of bakers and know what they're doing when it comes to bread. Inside their marble-clad shop you'll find an array of fresh loaves and Venetian cookies including *Zaletti, Pan del Pescatore*, and *Buranelli*. Many are pre-packed and make delicious gifts.

Gelato

GELATO FANTASY

*Calle dei Fabbri 929; tel. 041/522-5993; daily
10am-11:30pm; €3-5*

For a generous scoop from a takeout-only *gelateria*, try Gelato Fantasy. Nutella is the house specialty but they also make great dark chocolate and strawberry. If you're undecided let the friendly, English-speaking staff guide you or choose at random. It's impossible to go wrong.

SUSO

*Calle della Bissa 5453; tel. 348/564-6545; daily
10am-midnight; €4-6*

Suso is a small *gelateria* amid the busy streets around the Rialto and can be difficult to find. Flavors change according to the season and they're one of the only shops in the city that offer edible cups and cacao-flavored cones. *Moro di Venezia* and chocolate are the local favorites.

Coffee

The cafés of San Marco are nearly as famous as the square itself and have shared in the history of the city. They're extremely elegant, with chandeliered interiors, plush furnishings, and uniformed waitstaff who have spent lifetimes serving visitors. Each café provides outdoor seating from where you can admire the monuments and listen to musicians playing classical music on small stages facing the square.

Location and history come with a price tag. Do not expect to pay the same for an espresso or *prosecco* in Piazza San Marco as in other squares. A cup of coffee that usually sells for €2 can cost €7 or more. If you add a couple of drinks, some snacks, and a dessert, you could be looking at a three-digit bill. Either you don't care and count it as a once-in-a-lifetime experience or go inside and drink at the bar where there's as much atmosphere at a fraction of the cost. Prices vary at these institutions where Arturo Toscanini, Charlie Chaplin, and Orson Welles all hung out.

CAFFÈ QUADRI

Piazza San Marco 121; tel. 041/522-2105; daily 10:30am-midnight; €5 inside

Caffè Quadri doesn't disappoint with its mirrored walls, high ceilings, and gold-leaf moldings. At the counter you'll find a limited selection of high-quality *cicchetti* (€2 each) that can be accompanied by a glass of *prosecco* or spritz (€4). The coffee is excellent and affordable unless you choose to be served at an outdoor table.

CAFFÈ FLORIAN

Piazza San Marco 57; tel. 041/520-5641; daily 9am-midnight; €5-10 inside

Caffè Florian has been in business since getting to the New World meant a long journey on a wooden ship. The café once attracted Venice's nobles, politicians, and intellectuals. Today, the plush furnishings and uniformed staff provide an aura of elegance. The view of Piazza San Marco from the tables is wonderful, while the interior provides more intimacy.

Inside there are distinctly themed rooms (Chinese, Oriental, Senate, and Illustrious) decorated in 18th-century style. This is where local patriots plotted independence from Austria and artists hatched the idea of a Venice Biennale.

DORSODURO
Venetian
OSTERIA DA CODROMA

Fondamenta Briati 2540; tel. 041/524-6789; Tues.-Sat. noon-2:30pm and 7pm-10pm; €8-12

One of the places local Venetians can still be found enjoying traditional recipes and tapas is Osteria da Codroma. Under soft lighting and white wooden beams you'll receive a warm welcome and are likely to be the only tourist in sight. Silver-haired septuagenarians and students from the nearby university occupy most of the dark rustic tables, enjoying *sardee in saor* (sardines with onions), marinated fish, spaghetti with cuttlefish ink, and other Venetian delicacies. The kitchen is actually located across the street, but that doesn't seem to bother waiters.

AL VECIO MARANGON

Calle della Toletta; tel. 041/277-8554; daily noon-10pm; €13-15

Al Vecio Marangon has a lot going for it including a quiet side street, handwritten menu, working fireplace, rustic wooden interior, soft jazz, large portions, and low-priced Venetian fare. It's a small one-room *trattoria* and if you don't like rubbing shoulders with other diners you probably won't like it here, but there are tables on the street outside.

ENOTECA AI ARTISTI

Fondamenta della Toletta 1169a; tel. 041/523-8944; Tues.-Sat. 12:45pm-2:45pm and 7pm-9:30pm; €14-16

Cozy Enoteca Ai Artisti is a little out of the way but worth finding. It's open from breakfast to dinner and serves creative *cicchetti* throughout the day. Fish is from the Rialto market and transformed into Venetian classics with an edge. The wine cellar is stocked with labels from small Italian vineyards and

☆ Sampling *Cicchetti*

A gastronomic highlight of any Venetian vacation is sampling the delicious assortment of finger food known as *cicchetti*. Reminiscent of tapas, *cicchetti* consist of sliced bread topped with creamed fish, sautéed vegetables, cheese, and many other enticing ingredients. Chefs take advantage of the abundance of fresh calamari and octopus and often serve them raw or dipped in light batter and fried.

Cicchetti are served at *bacari,* traditional Venetian bars that also sell wine by the glass or pitcher. Most *bacari* are delightfully unglamorous institutions that have been around for generations. They're small and darkly lit with rustic interiors where patrons stand around socializing while they eat and drink. Staff can be charmingly brusque, and most *bacari* open and close early. A crowded sidewalk near a *bacaro* is always a good sign.

To order, get the proprietor's attention and point to the *cicchetti* you want to taste. They'll be served on a small tray or plastic plate and ready to eat immediately. Individual portions cost €1-2 and are an inexpensive way to sample a variety of local flavors. Be sure to order a glass of *prosecco,* Venetian sparkling white wine, to savor with your snacks.

Every neighborhood has a handful of *bacari,* though they are particularly plentiful in San Polo, where workers from the nearby markets take their breaks. You'll find many hidden along the narrow streets north of the Rialto. Once you've tried one, it's hard to resist a *bacari* binge. Start near the fish market and continue sampling *cicchetti* along the **Fondamenta della Misericordia** in Cannaregio, **Fondamenta Nani** in Dorsoduro, and lively squares like **Campo Santa Margherita.**

Here are some good destinations for *cicchetti* hopping:

- **Cantina Do Mori:** Legendary *bacaro* reputed to be where Casanova liked to start his evening escapades (page 327).

- **Al Timon:** A local hangout serving cold and hot *cicchetti* for €1 a shot indoors or outside overlooking a canal (page 330).

- **Vino Vero:** An addictive little bar serving gourmet cheese and meat platters that can easily substitute for dinner (page 329).

the menu changes daily. Tables are limited inside, so if you don't want to be left standing at the bar arrive early or make reservations for one of two dinnertime slots (7pm or 9pm). Afterward you can browse the shelves at **La Toletta,** one of the city's oldest bookshops down the street.

PANE VINO E SAN DANIELE

Campo dell'Angelo Raffaele 1722; tel. 041/523-7456; Thurs.-Tues. noon-3pm and 7pm-10:30pm; €14-18

There is an entire menu of reasons to eat at Pane Vino e San Daniele. Devoted out-of-towners come for the grilled seasonal vegetables. Cured meat and steaks are some of the best but vegetarians have nothing to fear. The flowered terrace on a hidden square is the icing on the *tiramisu*. There is no English menu but waiters are patient and happy to explain any dishes you may be curious about. Wine is a bit expensive but there's a good selection and several by-the-glass options.

Cicchetti

Three of the neighborhood's best *cicchetti* bars are all located along the Rio de S. Trovaso canal. They are often crowded, but if one is too busy just move on to the next, and if you can try them all you won't regret it.

Venetian finger food

- **Al Bottegon:** Once you enter you may never want to leave this friendly *bacaro* with wines priced to drink (page 325).

- **Osteria Al Squero:** It may be crowded, but it's the only place to nibble on *cicchetti* while watching gondolas being repaired (page 326).

- **Bacareto da Lele:** Lele's is the quintessential *bacaro*: simple food, simple surroundings, and lots of smiling faces (page 327).

BARRACHERO

Fondamenta Bonlini 1078; Mon.-Sat. 10am-11pm; €5-8

When nearby snack bars are full to the gills, head down the *fondamenta* and over the bridge to Barrachero. The name means "the drunk" in Cuban slang and the mother, son, and aunt team who run the place are happy to get travelers tipsy inside their little shop selling wine from a tap, mini sandwiches (€2), and fried specialties (€2-3). Order a glass and sit inside or out next to the canal, but be wary of aggressive seagulls that occasionally swoop down to steal food from distracted diners.

★ AL BOTTEGON

Fondamenta Nani 992; tel. 041/523-0034; Mon.-Sat. 8:30am-8:30pm; €6-10

You can tell from the aging sign above Al Bottegon that this *bacaro* has been around for a while. Inside, three generations of the Gastaldi family keep the institution running on good wine and addictive *cicchetti*. The grape selection is written on a chalkboard and features over 30 varieties that can be ordered by the cup or carafe. This is one of the best *enoteche* in the city and the perfect place to enjoy red, white, or *prosecco* in the wonderfully worn interior or outside along the canal.

OSTERIA AL SQUERO

Fondamenta Nani 943; tel. 041/296-0479; Mon.-Sat.
10am-2pm and 5:30pm-9pm; €6-10

There's a reason Osteria Al Squero is always crowded. The *cicchetti* are good, the wine is cheap, and you can enjoy both on a canal overlooking the San Trovaso workshop where gondolas are repaired. Service is fast but you'll need to get in line and move toward the counter with determination. Once it's your turn don't hesitate. Choose a plateful of appetizers (4-5 make a good snack) and two glasses of *prosecco* to avoid a return trip. It's all quickly served on plastic plates and cups, so have your money ready and enjoy.

Pizza
PIZZA AL VOLO

Campo Santa Margherita 2944; tel. 041/522-5430;
daily 11am-1pm; €5-8

Order a slice or an entire pie at Pizza al Volo, a takeaway pizzeria with an oven in view and plenty of toppings to choose from. It's a favorite with university students and travelers who appreciate the large portions at low prices. You can satisfy an appetite here for around €5 without sacrificing quality—and enjoy the action in the square as you eat.

International
AFRICAN EXPERIENCE

Calle Lunga S. Barnaba 2722; tel. 041/476-7865;
Tues.-Sat. noon-3pm and 6pm-midnight, Sun.
noon-3pm and 6pm-9pm; €12-16

Culinary diversity has declined since Venice ruled the waves but there are still some interesting places to eat for anyone looking to surprise their palate. This Ethiopian restaurant serves exotic plates of skewered meats, spicy vegetables, savory sauces, and stuffed breads. It's prepared by a young expatriate staff who now call Venice home and have introduced new flavors to their adopted city.

Snacks and Street Food
60/40

Rio Terà dei Catecumeno 129a; tel. 041/476-4997;
Mon.-Sat. 8am-6pm; €6

There aren't that many eateries around the eastern end of Dorsoduro near Punta della Dogana, but fortunately there is 60/40. This takeaway deli is ideal for stocking up on sandwiches that can enjoyed on the nearby embankments or church steps. Just choose your bread and fillings and it's all made to order by the smiling staff. There are also fresh juices, coffee, pastries, and a small counter looking out on the street.

Gelato
GELATERIA IL DOGE

Rio Terà Canal 3058a; daily 9am-noon; €2-6

Just off Campo Santa Margherita, Gelateria il Doge quenches sweet cravings. They scoop great gelato and refreshing fruit flavored Sicilian *granite* ices into cones or cups inside or from a street-front window. All-star flavors include coffee, hazelnut, *tiramisu,* and the house specialty, *Gianduiotto del Doge*. The first scoop is €1.50 and every scoop after that is a euro. No seating but there are benches and steps to sit on in the adjacent square.

★ GELATERIA DA NICO

Fondamenta Zattere al Ponte Lungo 922;
tel. 041/522-5293; Fri.-Wed. 6:30am-10pm; €4-8

Da Nico is famous for the hazelnut and cacao-flavored *giandiotto* gelato (€6) that was invented in Venice and has been served here for over 80 years. Besides the elegant interior there's a sunny terrace facing Canale della Giudecca where gelato connoisseurs gather to enjoy the 25 flavors on offer. The San Basilio ferry station is nearby, making this a sweet stop before or after a visit to Giudecca on board the number 2 *vaporetto*.

Coffee

The best thing about Venetian coffee bars is that they nearly always serve delicious pastries to accompany a cappuccino or espresso.

CAFFÈ POGGI DAL 1919

Calle Nuova Sant Agnese; tel. 041/520-6466;
Tues.-Sun. 8am-7pm; €3-5

Coffee can get pretty expensive in Venice but

Poggi has reasonable prices, wonderful pastries, and a clientele of locals who go about their business as though Venice weren't the most beautiful city in the world.

SAN POLO AND SANTA CROCE
Venetian
★ ANTICHE CARAMPANE
San Polo, Rio Terà Rampani 1911; tel. 041/524-0165; Tues.-Sat. 12:30pm-2:30pm and 7:30pm-11pm; €12-15

Being hard to find keeps Antiche Carampane real. There's no pizza, no tourist menu, and no watered-down traditions here—just fresh fish served in a simple but elegant atmosphere. If you haven't had a three-course meal in Italy yet this is the place to have it. The fried calamari, spider crab (*grancevola*), and turbot fillet (*rombo*) are stalwarts of a menu that changes according to what's available at the fish market. Expect superb desserts you won't want to share and a small, carefully selected wine list. Getting a table here can be difficult, especially during the Venice Film Festival when stars like Uma Thurman and Audrey Tautou show up.

AL PONTE STORTO
San Polo, Calle Bianca Cappello 1278; tel. 041/528-2144; Tues.-Sun. noon-3pm and 6pm-10pm; €14-16

Al Ponte Storto is cozy without being quaint. Alberto is a jovial host who welcomes guests and runs the restaurant with his brother, who mans the kitchen. Mom fills in on weekends when necessary and entertains guests with her lovely broken English and stories of her glass workshop on Murano. The menu changes four or five times a year depending on what's in season and there's always a fixed option (€35) that includes an appetizer, first course, dessert, carafe of wine, water, and coffee. Dishes combine tradition with a few flights of fancy and portions are neither too big nor too small. Aperitivo starts at 6pm and includes an inviting array of Venetian finger food accompanied by wine or beer that can be enjoyed on the romantic little square overlooking

the uneven bridge after which the *osteria* is named.

Cicchetti
BACARETO DA LELE
Santa Croce, Fondamenta dei Tolentini 183; tel. 347/846-9728; Mon.-Fri. 6am-8pm, Sat. 6am-2pm; €5

Bacareto da Lele is one institution that lives up to its reputation and is hard not to love. There's a crowd inside and out of this tiny *bacaro* that churns out over 2,000 mini sandwiches a day. Lele prepares them in the back while his son works the counter and keeps a stream of regulars, university students, and tourists satisfied. There are 6-7 sandwiches (€1 each) to choose from with different fillings and if you're undecided, sample one of everything. Red and white wine is listed on a blackboard and ordering a double glass (€2) will save you from waiting in line again. People eat standing along the canal or on the steps facing the little square. Lele opens and closes early but if you're searching for a late-night bite **Arcicchetti Bakaro** (daily 11am-11pm) next door serves tasty open-faced *cicchetti* (€1 each) until 10pm. Both are only 10 minutes from the train station, which makes them a great gastronomic introduction or farewell to Venice.

AL MERCÀ
San Polo, Campo Bella Vienna 213; tel. 346/834-0660; daily noon-2:30pm and 6:45pm-9:30pm; €5-8

Al Mercà is in the adjacent *campo* and one of the smallest *bacaro* in the city. There's hardly room to enter and consider which of the miniature panini sandwiches to order. Most cost €3 and are filled with *prosciutto*, meatballs, salami, or creamed cod. There's a classic assortment of red and white wines, local beers, and spritz. Diners stand outside holding plates or reclining on the nearby steps.

★ CANTINA DO MORI
San Polo, Calle do Mori 429; tel. 041/522-5401; Mon.-Sat. 8am-7:30pm; €7-10

The shelves at Cantina Do Mori are lined with large vats of red and white wine on tap. The long wooden counter fills up fast during *aperitivo* with clients jostling to order triangular *tramezzini* sandwiches stuffed with crab, shrimp, and other lagoon delicacies. Legend has it Casanova was a regular at this historic *bacaro*, where you can forget about itineraries and just enjoy being in Venice.

ALL'ARCO
San Polo, Calle Arco 436; tel. 041/520-5666; Mon.-Sat. 8am-3pm; €8-10

A popular spot with street-side seating and a rustic interior. The friendly staff is always busy making plates of tempting appetizers that often include their famous boiled-beef sandwich. Most of the *cicchetti* come from the nearby fish market and the owner will happily explain any mystery ingredients. The only drawbacks are the lines and early closing time.

OSTERIA BANCOGIRO
San Polo, Campo San Giacometto 122; tel. 041/523-2061; Tues.-Sun. 9am-midnight; €8-12

There are several *bacari* in the squares adjacent to the Rialto. One, Osteria Bancogiro, is under the portico where wealthy Venetians sent their servants to pay and collect outstanding debts. You can sample the miniature surprises chef Jacopo Scarso creates at the small bar or sit down for something more substantial and equally delicious with a view of the Grand Canal.

CANTINA DO SPADE
San Polo, Calle do Spade 859; tel. 041/521-0583; daily 10am-10pm; €12-15

Cantina do Spade has a dark wood interior with a glass case filled with *cicchetti* that include fried calamari, stuffed zucchini flowers, creamed cod, and liver pâté. It's one of the few old-style *bacari,* with inside seating and plenty of red and white wine along with regional beer such as Pedavena lager.

Pizza
ANTICO FORNO
San Polo, Ruga Rialto 973; tel. 041/520-4110; daily 11:30am-9:30pm; €5-8

Antico Forno specializes in reasonably priced takeaway pizza. Toppings aren't overly elaborate and the best sellers are the *marinara* and *margherita*. The pizza is thick and doughy with a focaccia-like taste and appearance. There's no seating inside but you can enjoy a slice in the tranquility of Campo di San Silvestro a couple of minutes away.

Vegetarian
Venice has more vegetarian restaurants per capita than Florence or Rome, and going meatless here is easy.

LA ZUCCA
Santa Croce, Calle dello Specier 1762; tel. 041/524-1570; Mon.-Sat. 12:30pm-2:30pm and 7pm-10:30pm; €14

La Zucca is a cozy *osteria* with a soothing wood-paneled interior and street-side seating. The kitchen prepares imaginative pasta dishes like *tagliatelle con carciofi e pecorino* and *lasagna con zucchine e mandorle*. Waiters are happy to list ingredients, and there are several fish and duck options for carnivores. Reservations are useful in high season.

International
FRARY'S
San Polo, Fondamenta dei Frari 259; tel. 041/720-050; daily 11:30am-3pm and 6pm-11pm; €14-18

Middle Eastern eateries were once quite common in Venice, but today if you get a craving for tajine, hummus, falafel, or flat bread Frary's is the only place to go. The menu includes dishes from Greece to Iraq.

Bakeries
PANIFICIO ALBONICO
Santa Croce, Calle della Regina 2268b; tel. 041/524-1102; Mon.-Sat. 7:30am-7:30pm; €4-6

Panificio Albonico is on a narrow thoroughfare where walking sometimes gets difficult. This homey, wood-paneled bakery provides instant relief from the crowds and during *Carnevale* season they prepare all sorts of fried *frittelle* treats. The rest of the year you'll find olive buns, mini pizzas, and *pincia,* a traditional sweet bread that comes in many varieties, all of which the owners are happy to explain.

Gelato
GELATO DI NATURA
Santa Croce, Campo San Giacomo dall'Orio 1628; tel. 041/302-7435; daily 10:30am-11:30pm; €4
Before you proclaim your favorite *gelateria* in Venice visit Gelato di Natura, where Pierangelo has been churning out organic gelato since 1982. All the flavors are made fresh daily using top ingredients, including hazelnuts from Piedmont and Sicilian pistachios that are mixed with organic milk, eggs, and mascarpone. There's something for every palate inside this attractive shop with bilingual labels next to every vat. They also create mint, lemon, and pear sorbets on sticks as well as vegan and lactose-free options that don't sacrifice flavor.

Coffee
PASTICCERIA RIZZARDINI
San Polo, Campiello Meloni 1415; tel. 041/522-3835, Wed.-Mon. 7am-8pm; €3-5
The pastry selection at Pasticceria Rizzardini is extensive, and once you've picked a *crostata* or *canolo* pastry you can order a coffee at the metal counter. It's standing room only inside this classic bar with few signs of modernity and plenty of local drama.

CAFFETTERIA GOPPION
San Polo, Ruga Rialto 644; tel. 041/523-7031; daily 7am-8pm; €3-5
Caffetteria Goppion combines years of experience with quality coffee. The cheerful staff busily grind beans and serve cups to locals and visitors waiting anxiously at the long counter. There are sweet and salty snacks throughout the day at this pleasant bar with large plate-glass windows through which you can observe the flow of daily Venetian life.

Venetian
OSTERIA DEI MORI
Campo dei Mori 3386; tel. 041/524-3677; Thurs.-Mon. 7pm-11pm, Sat.-Sun. 12:30-2:30pm and 7pm-11pm; €16-18
Tucked between Chiesa della Madonna dell'Orto and Fondamenta della Misericordia, Osteria dei Mori is usually filled with locals. The menu provides a good mix of meat and fish to which the Sicilian chef adds a dash of southern Italian flavor. Notable dishes include the fried fish and vegetable plate along with a memorable *baccalà mantecato* (creamed cod). Rubbing the steel nose of the statue outside is said to bring good luck.

Seafood
FRITO-INN
Cannaregio, Campo San Leonardo 1587; tel. 041/564-7451; Mon.-Fri. 11am-8pm, Sat.-Sun. 10am-10pm; €8-10
Venetians like their fish fried, and the mother/daughter team at Frito-Inn are happy to oblige. This tiny joint around the corner from a busy street can be smelled before it's seen. They fry a range of fish and vegetables but the house specialty is the calamari and shrimp rolled in flour, fried in sunflower oil, and served in paper cones perfect for carrying away or eating on the chairs facing the small square.

Cicchetti
★ VINO VERO
Fondamenta della Misericordia 2497; tel. 041/275-0044; Tues.-Sun. noon-midnight, Mon. 6pm-midnight; €6-10
Vino Vero is packed with a young crowd of grape enthusiasts. The wine list covers an entire wall and the *cicchetti* are temptingly lined up behind a glass case at the counter where clients jostle to be served. It's a small, modern space, but there are some stools outside and they serve *crostini* on ingenious wooden trays with glass holders that make it easy to eat and drink while standing.

AL TIMON

Fondamenta dei Ormesini 2754; tel. 041/524-6066; daily 6pm-1am; €10

Al Timon is a small *osteria* just north of the Ghetto that caters to snackers and diners. The best *cicchetti* in the neighborhood can be ordered at the counter while the restaurant prepares Venetian-Tuscan dishes. If you missed out on *bistecca alla fiorentina* in Florence this is the place to go. There's a row of canvas-backed chairs and tables facing the canal but the best seats are on the boat moored out front where musicians occasionally perform and large groups of friends gather.

Pizza

Pizza isn't that common in Venice, but in addition to Tre Archi (a sit-down pizza restaurant), there are also two great takeaway pizza options in the neighborhood: Pizza da Norma and Arte Delle Pizza.

ARTE DELLA PIZZA

Calle de l'Aseo 1861a; tel. 041/524-6520; Tues.-Sun. 5pm-9pm; €5-7

Arte Della Pizza has an original selection of toppings and several rectangular tins and round doughy mini pizzas on display behind a glass counter waiting to be wrapped up to go.

TRE ARCHI

Fondamenta Savorgnan 552; tel. 041/716-438; daily noon-3pm and 6:30pm-11pm; €12

Most pizzeria also serve traditional dishes. Ai Tre Archi is an exception and prepares over 50 kinds of pizza, with original toppings that will take a while to choose. Staff is friendly and there are shaded tables overlooking the Cannaregio Canal.

PIZZA DA NORMA

Fondamenta dei Ormesini 2712; tel. 041/524-2915; daily 11am-3pm and 5pm-11pm; €5-15

Pizza da Norma offers Neapolitan style slices (€2) or normal and maxi pies that come in 39 variations. The menu is on the wall and translated into English. An order takes around 10 minutes and customers devour their slices outside along the canal.

Snacks and Street Food

Fondamenta della Misericordia is a great destination day and night for street food and drink. The canal-side promenade is lined with restaurants, bars, and *bacari* where locals and visitors huddle outdoors enjoying good food and wine. Don't be intimidated by the chaotic lines—just jump right in and persevere until you're served. Go back and forth between these informal establishments and find your favorite.

COCAETA

Fondamenta San Giobbe 549; Fri.-Tues. 12:30pm-3:30pm and 6:30pm-10:30; €5-12

Savory or sweet crepes stuffed with original fillings like salmon, goat cheese, and pesto or Nutella and fresh raspberries are the mainstay of Cocaeta. Prices are reasonable but the one-man operation can be a little slow, which makes arriving early or late a good idea.

PARADISO PERDUTO

Fondamenta della Misericordia 2540; tel. 041/720-581; Thurs.-Mon. 11am-midnight; €14-19

At Paradiso Perduto there are usually people waiting to choose from the counter filled with plates of fried fish dishes. When it's your turn, point to as many delicacies as you can handle. Most of the internal seating fills up fast but you can sit along the canal and enjoy a cup or carafe of house wine. There's a regular calendar of musical events on the small stage inside.

Bakeries

EL FORNARETO

Calle del Forno 2668; tel. 041/522-5426; Mon.-Sat. 6am-1:30pm and 4:30pm-7:30pm; €4-7

El Fornareto is one of Venice's oldest bakeries and even has a street named after it. The historic premise is equipped with a 19th-century oven that's still used. If you're interested, Silvia or her sister will open it up and reveal the scorching interior where loaves of bread, focaccia, panettone, and bussolà cookies are baked. Mornings are the best time to visit—the bread is still warm and pastries haven't sold out yet.

Gelato
GELATERIA CA' D'ORO
Strada Nuova 4273b; Mon.-Wed. 3pm-10pm, Thurs.-Sat. 11:30am-11:30pm, Sun. 11am-8:30pm; €3-6
There are fewer *gelateria* in Venice than in Rome or Florence, but the gelato is just as good and prepared with care and attention to ingredients. The local flavor is *Crema del Doge* (vanilla cream), which is available at Gelateria Ca' d'Oro alongside some of the shop's own unique creations. Cones and cups come in four sizes and can be enjoyed in the adjacent square off the main street.

CASTELLO
Venetian
LE SPIGHE
Via Garibaldi 1341; tel. 041/523-8173; Mon.-Sat. 10:30am-2:30pm and 5:30pm-7:30pm; €10-12
At this casual vegan eatery, Doriana sells organic dishes by the kilo and serves them at a convivial communal table. There are lots of couscous-based dishes with grilled vegetable toppings and East Asian influenced stir fries.

TRATTORIA ALLA RAMPA DEL PIAVE
Via Giuseppe Garibaldi 1135; tel. 041/528-5365; Mon.-Sat. 6am-4pm and 7:30pm-10pm; €8-14
Castello is one of the less-visited parts of the city, which also makes it one of the least expensive. Trattoria alla Rampa del Piave is a case in point. The *trattoria* is located at the end of Via Garibaldi in front of a red flagpole and floating fruit and vegetable market. The décor is nothing special but the simple interior is often packed with local workers taking advantage of the fixed-price lunch menu (€14). It's a good place to try *risi e bisi*, *polenta e baccala* (cod), and *spaghetti al nero*.

AL PORTEGO
Calle della Malvasia 6014; tel. 041/522-9038; daily 10:30am-2:30pm and 5:30pm-10:30pm; €12-15

If you want to find a table at Al Portego you need to reserve in advance or arrive early. This small *osteria* five minutes from the Rialto is popular and fills up quickly. Fortunately, you can sample their fish *cicchetti* while you wait. Once you sit down it can be difficult to get a waiter's attention, but service is friendly and prices are reasonable. It's a good place to try Venetian classics like *baccalà mantecato* and *bigoli* pasta prepared the old-fashioned way.

COVINO
Calle Pestrin 3829a; tel. 041/241-2705; Thurs.-Sun. 1pm-3pm and 7pm-10:30pm; €15, cash only
Put expectations aside and make a reservation at CoVino. This wonderfully intimate restaurant with a festive host provides a multitude of flavors that blend tradition with creativity. A fixed-price menu (€30 2-course or €40 3-course) includes a choice of starter, second, and dessert. Depending on the season this could include tartare, sardines, baked cod, veal sausage, tiramisu, and chocolate cake. Tables are close together and the restaurant gets loud—but that's because everyone is having a good time.

Chocolate
VIZIOVIRTU
Calle Forner 5988; tel. 041/275-0149; daily 10am-7pm; €5
VizioVirtu is a sweet hideaway on a busy corner with trisecting streets. Once you've passed through the well-worn wooden doors of this chocolate boutique, the world disappears. Virtuous Vice is an appropriate name, since this is where cacao gets transformed into tempting pralines waiting to be devoured. There's a large assortment of desserts, including exotic bonbons, gelatin candies, and homemade gelato. Just point and let Maria Angela place your treats in a small plastic sachet for takeaway.

Gelato
LA MELA VERDE
Fondamenta de l'Osmarin 4977a; tel. 349/195-7924; daily 11am-11pm; €4-6

La Mela Verde is located on a pleasant canal near the Greek Orthodox church. The gelato and sorbet are made on site by a friendly staff who take the time to explain the flavor of the day and allow customers to sample before choosing between pistachio, *torroncino, limone,* and many others. They've also recently started serving chocolate-filled crepes.

GIUDECCA

Fewer tourists venture to Giudecca than other parts of Venice and as a consequence it has fewer places to eat. Most of these are located near the Palanca ferry station and have outdoor seating with great views of the city.

Italian
LA PALANCA
Fondamenta Sant'Eufemia 448; tel. 041/528-7719; Mon.-Sat. 7am-9pm; €12-15

There's a good chance you'll be greeted by the jovial Andrea Barina and seated outdoors at one of the tables along the water. The menu has five or six pasta dishes with or without fish and a dozen seconds including grilled calamari, *seppie con polenta,* creamed cod, and a daily fish special.

MAJER
Fondamenta Sant'Eufemia 461; tel. 041/521-1162; daily 9am-11pm; €13-20
Majer is a reliable breakfast, lunch, or dinner eatery with seven locations around the city. The Giudecca branch is the latest and has been decked out in pleasant earth tones. They do their own baking and serve a great almond croissant and cappuccino that can be slowly sipped at the long wooden sharing table as you look out onto the canal and wait for the next *vaporetto* to arrive.

Nightlife and Entertainment

When the sun goes down, Venice is transformed. An exodus of tourists and workers drains swiftly out of the city, reducing a daytime population of 100,000 to less than half that number. The result is invigorating for anyone who stays behind to explore the city at night. Take a starlit stroll and enjoy the silence.

If you want human contact you can find it, although anyone with images of Casanova-style decadence will be disappointed. You won't find discos or dancing, though there's no shortage of canal-side bars, lively squares, and rustic *enoteche* where wine flows until late. After-dinner diversions include listening to classical music, gambling at the casino, and sipping cocktails inside seven-star hotels. The drink of choice is a white sparkling wine called *prosecco* that's produced in the Veneto region and could be mistaken for Champagne. It's poured everywhere across the city and accompanied with delicious finger food known as *cicchetti*. Also omnipresent is the spritz,

a cocktail consisting of *prosecco,* Aperol or Campari bitters, and seltzer. A spritz or glass of *prosecco* may be all the nightlife you need. You'll pay €6-12 for a drink in Venice.

One of the most popular nighttime areas with Venetians and visitors is **Campo Santa Margherita** in Dorsoduro. The large rectangular square is dotted with bars that are filled from happy hour to the early hours. **Campo Erberia** overlooking the Ponte di Rialto in San Polo is also reliably animated. Sure signs of nightlife can always be found along Cannaregio's **Fondamenta della Misericordia,** lined with *bacari,* restaurants, and wine bars.

SAN MARCO
Bars and Pubs
HARRY'S BAR
Calle Vallaresso 1323; tel. 041/528-5777; daily 10:30am-11pm
Harry's Bar opened in 1931 and attracted illustrious regulars like Hemingway, Charlie

Chaplin, and Alfred Hitchcock. Today the regulars are mostly tourists soaking up the atmosphere at this landmark institution where you can sip Bellini cocktails (€16) from wooden tables or at the counter. Food is available too, but it's equally pricey and nothing to write home about.

BAR CAMPANILE

Piazza S. Marco 310; tel. 041/522-1491; daily 8am-1am

Bar Campanile is just north of Piazza San Marco and has a different personality depending on the time of day. In the morning it's dedicated to coffee, at lunch it's *tramezzini* sandwiches, and at night it's all about cocktails. Staff is friendly and spritz can be ordered any time, but if the Cuban bartender is around order the mojito. Prices are cheaper if you stand at the bar, where drinks are served with light snacks, although there's not much room after dark and it remains crowded with Venetians and visitors until closing. There are DJ sets on Saturdays.

HARD ROCK CAFE DI VENEZIA

Bacino Orseolo 1192; tel. 041/522-9665; daily 11:30am-12:30am

The Hard Rock Cafe di Venezia is different. You can tell from the red Murano chandelier hanging from the ceiling and the Venetian tiles on the floor. The music is good (DJs start at 9pm), the drinks are strong, and the views *do* rock. The café is located near Piazza San Marco in an historic *palazzo* overlooking a gondolier station. It's the smallest Hard Rock in Europe which can lead to lines forming outside on weekends.

DEVILS FOREST PUB

Calle dei Stagneri O de la Fava 5185; tel. 041/520-0623; daily 11am-midnight

The Devils Forest Pub is a favorite with American and English visitors who become remarkably agitated whenever soccer or rugby is playing on the large TVs. It can be fun to partake in the joy and pain of supporters even if you don't know the offside rule or how to

score a *try*. Regardless of the results everyone enjoys the beer at this authentic-looking pub with Strongbow, Guinness, and Harp on tap and wooden booths in the back.

Wine Bars

OSTERIA ENOTECA RUSTEGHI

Corte del Tentor 5513; tel. 338/760-6034; daily 11:30am-3pm and 6:30pm-1am

Wine rarely goes without food in Italy and you can choose either at Osteria Enoteca Rusteghi. This wine bar hidden away in a tiny courtyard near the Rialto lies just beyond the tourist masses, where Giovanni D'Este keeps the art of Venetian hospitality alive. He's usually stationed behind the counter pouring difficult-to-find wines to clients who eagerly listen to his gastronomic tales. Most glasses are €6-8 and can be accompanied by *bruschetta*, cheese plates, and other appetizers. It's best after dark when locals take back their city.

Hotel Bars

BAR LONGHI

Gritti Palace Hotel, Campo Santa Maria del Giglio 2467; tel. 041/794-611; daily 11am-1am

Inside the expensive Gritti Palace Hotel is Bar Longhi where you can order the cocktail of the same name and sit back amid the opulence of mirrored walls, 18th-century paintings, and antique settees. Hemingway called this the best hotel in the city and never passed up an opportunity to drink here. Today Cristiano Luciano does the mixing dressed in black-tie attire. The bar serves light fare along with Champagne and oysters on weekends. The house cocktail contains Campari, dry vermouth, China Martini, and orange. If you prefer to drink outdoors, try the **Riva Lounge** on the terrace facing the Grand Canal.

Opera and Concerts

There are few large concert halls in Venice. Historically, most nobles had music played to them inside their homes, and today associations of musicians perform in churches and historic *palazzi*. These are informal performances in splendid settings that are accessible to all and a great way to begin or end an evening. Repertoires nearly always feature local hometown favorite Antonio Vivaldi, but baroque and opera classics are also performed. *The Four Seasons* is at the top of the hit list and played nearly every evening at different venues. Tickets are reasonably priced given the quality of the music and the surroundings.

LA FENICE OPERA HOUSE (TEATRO LA FENICE)

Campo San Fantin 1965; tel. 041/786-654; www. teatrolafenice.it; €39-180

Teatro La Fenice is one of the meccas of lyrical music, and if you enjoy opera—or even if you're just curious—this is the place to see and hear it. The season runs from September to mid-July and nearly always includes crowd pleasers like *La Traviata* and *Madame Butterfly*, which are subtitled in Italian and English. Tickets aren't cheap and the most affordable seats in the upper galleries sell out fast. Most performances begin at 7pm and can last up to three hours with several intermissions. Jacket and tie are expected on opening nights, but semi-elegant will do after that; any unnecessary items must be checked into the cloakrooms. The theater also presents a varied symphonic program performed by its own philharmonic (www.filarmonica-fenice. it) and many illustrious guest conductors.

TEATRO GOLDINI

Calle del Teatro 4650b; tel. 041/240-2011; www. teatrostabileveneto.it; €8-35

La Fenice may be the most famous theater in Venice but Teatro Goldini is the oldest still in existence and may have the best acoustics in town. The theater has a capacity of over 1,000 and an intimate four-tiered interior where drama takes center stage. Sundays are reserved for families and shows that everyone can enjoy.

INTERPRETI VENEZIANI

Campo San Vidal; tel. 041/277-0561; www. interpretiveneziani.com; showtime 8:30pm, €30, €25 for under 25-year-olds

The Interpreti Veneziani are one of the oldest chamber groups in the city and have recorded dozens of albums and toured extensively. The ensemble consists entirely of string players and performs in **Chiesa San Vidal** (Campo San Vidal/Santo Stefano) across from the Ponte dell'Accademia. Concerts are held daily during the summer and there's a high probability of listening to Vivaldi's *Four Seasons* as well as lesser-known compositions by the Venetian native. Tickets can be purchased directly at the church and performances begin at 9pm.

I MUSICI VENEZIANI

Scuola Grande di San Teodoro, Campo San Salvador 4810; tel. 041/521-0294; www.imusiciveneziani.com; 8:30pm; €25-40

I Musici Veneziani are big fans of Vivaldi, whose works they regularly perform, but they're also passionate about baroque and opera. They play the greatest hits by Verdi, Puccini, Rossini, and many others inside a *palazzo* with exceptional acoustics. All the musicians and singers dress in 17th-century regalia, which adds instant drama to every performance.

VIRTUOSI DI VENEZIA

Ateneo di San Basso, Piazza San Marco; tel. 041/528-2825; www.virtuosidivenezia.com; 8:30pm; €29

Vivaldi sounds better in Venice and the Virtuosi di Venezia is one of the reasons why. This small chamber orchestra regularly pays tribute to the composer and performs *The Four Seasons* along with opera medleys. The arias feature a talented tenor and mezzosoprano who sing in the Ateneo di San Basso overlooking Piazza San Marco.

MUSICA PALAZZO

Palazzo Barbarigo Minotto, Fondamenta Duodo or Barbarigo 2504; tel. 340/971-7272; www. musicapalazzo.com; 8:30pm; €85

If you want to experience opera up close, to be inches from sopranos and listen to the classics in an intimate setting, then Musica Palazzo is the ticket. This talented ensemble leads audiences through itinerant performances set in the stunning rooms of a meticulously preserved villa facing the Grand Canal. Doors open at 8pm and shows last two hours. Smart casual dress is encouraged and tickets may be booked online.

TEATRO MALIBRAN

Campiello del Teatro 5873; tel. 041/272-2699; box office open Mon.-Sat. 9am-3:30pm; €10-100

Teatro Malibran may not be as grand as La Fenice but it has an equally glorious past. It's the site of over a hundred operatic debuts since being inaugurated in 1678 and is now used as the second stage for La Fenice productions and music recitals. These are newer works for the most part and an opportunity for audiences to discover contemporary operas and up-and-coming musicians. Ticket prices are more affordable than La Fenice and start at €10 for seats with partially blocked views.

DORSODURO
Bars and Pubs
BAKARÒ DO DRAGHI

Calle della Chiesa 3665; tel. 041/712-4080; daily 10am-2am

There are lots of bars in Campo Santa Margherita, but Bakarò Do Draghi is around the corner on the edge of the square. That doesn't mean it's not crowded—it is, and like many bars in Venice patrons often spill out onto the street. That's what happens in a city without cars, and it's an especially good thing at this colorful bar where it's impossible to go over budget ordering spritz served in large glasses and snacks that keep university students and young travelers merry. Wine is even cheaper and starts at €1 a glass.

CORNER PUB

Calle della Chiesa 684; tel. 349/457-6739; daily 8:30am-midnight

This scenic watering hole features well-worn tables, wood-beam ceilings, and the requisite Guinness poster hanging on the wall. The good food and better beer attract a mix of expats, tourists, and locals. One pint can easily lead to the start of a festive evening.

Wine Bars
ESTRO

Calle Crosera 3778; tel. 041/476-4914; Wed.-Mon. noon-3pm and 6pm-10:30pm

There are many reasons to love Estro, the relaxed atmosphere, delicious food, and two enterprising brothers from Murano make drinking here enjoyable. The wine list includes over a hundred labels (20 of which are available by the glass) the pair have personally selected from small producers they never tire of touting. You can drink at the bar and select from a myriad of *tramezzino* sandwiches stuffed with boiled meat, creamed fish, and vegetables, or chose from a full menu featuring the fish of the day, vegetarian lasagna, and soups served in a rustic décor near Campo Santa Margherita.

★ CANTINE DEL VINO

Fondamento Nani 992; tel. 041/523-0034; Mon.-Sat. 8:30am-8:30pm

You don't need much to be happy in Venice, and what you do need is available here. No matter how busy it gets inside this wine mecca there's always room along the canal outside to drink delightful regional vintages and tasty *cicchetti* appetizers that never exceed €1.50. They come in an assortment of delicious varieties that are best ordered by the plateful and enjoyed with a cup of cold *prosecco*.

Opera and Concerts
VENICE MUSIC PROJECT

Chiesa Anglicana di San Giorgio, Campo San Vio 729a; tel. 345/791-1948; www.venicemusicproject. it; €30-50

Venice Music Project was launched a decade ago by an ensemble of local musicians with a

Wine to Go

Some traditions only exist in Venice. One of those is the *cantina* or wine shop (sometimes also called *vinerie*), which has nothing to do with fancy labels or rows of expensive bottles. Inside these historic locales you'll find large vats from which plastic takeaway bottles are filled. Most of the wine is from the Veneto region and hauled to the city by boat. There's always a good selection of young red, white, and bubbly *prosecco* that's extremely drinkable and quite refreshing on hot summer days. Prices are unbeatable and most of the customers are locals. There are about a dozen *cantina* scattered around the city, and you'll find at least one in every *sestiere*. Most have been in business for decades and have a dusty appearance that keeps tourists at bay. Don't let that put you off. Owners usually take long lunch breaks, shut by 8pm, and are closed on Sundays, so arrive early and enjoy one of Venice's enduring traditions.

These shops deal exclusively in the sale of wine. It can't be consumed on the premises; instead it must be taken away and free bottles are provided.

- **Nave de Oro** (Cannaregio, Rio Terà S. Leonardo 1370; tel. 041/719-615; Mon.-Sat. 9am-1pm and 5pm-7:45pm) provides an opportunity to sample local wines fresh from the cask. The husband-and-wife owners have been providing *rosso, biancho,* and *frizzanti* to faithful customers and curious travelers since 1984.

- Locals and adventurous visitors fill up bottles of wine from the half-dozen vats at **Al Canton del Vin** (Santa Croce, Calle del Tentor 1562a; tel. 329/166-6648; Mon.-Sat. 9am-1pm and 4pm-7:30). They'll provide you with plastic bottles if you arrive empty-handed and tempt you with soave or cabernet. It's cheap, extremely drinkable, and close to several pleasant squares where you can drink outdoors in peace.

- **Vini & Spumanti** (Dorsoduro, Calle de l'Avogaria 1614; tel. 041/522-6396; Mon.-Sat. 9am-1pm and 4pm-7pm) is a common name among *cantine,* and Danilo has been running his shop for decades. There are over 20 red, white, and bubbly varieties on tap that he happily fills in half-liter or liter-and-a-half plastic bottles. All varieties are produced in the Veneto region and very affordable.

- Dorsoduro has one of the highest concentrations of *cantine,* and you'll find another at the western entrance of **Campo Santa Margherita.** Like most it doesn't have any signage outside and there's little hint of what goes on inside. That doesn't stop it from doing a very busy trade. New vats come in every morning and are usually empty by closing time. Clients run the gamut, but the vicinity of the university makes it popular with students who gather in the square and get progressively louder as the evening wears on.

passion for baroque and musical archeology. They hunt for forgotten manuscripts and perform long-lost compositions that haven't been played in hundreds of years using period instruments. It sounds great and helps maintain an important local tradition. The season runs from March-June with Saturday and Sunday concerts that usually start at 5pm or 7pm. Bach, Vivaldi, Mozart, and Haydn are stalwarts of their repertoire along with many lesser-known artists who sound just as good. The church where they play is small with good acoustics and comfortable wooden pews.

VENICE JAZZ CLUB

Ponte dei Pugni 3102; tel. 340/150-4985; daily except Thurs. and Sun. 7pm-11pm, closed Dec.-Feb. and Aug.; €20 weekdays, €25 Fri.-Sat.

If you're searching for jazz (recorded or live) with a sense of history, check out the Venice Jazz Club. Nights are dedicated to standards, Latin, and Bossa Nova, the cocktails are strong, and the wine is priced to uncork. The house quartet performs regularly and entry to live shows includes a drink. Bands take to the small stage at 9pm. Expect to listen rather than dance as space is limited.

SAN POLO AND SANTA CROCE

Bars and Pubs

IL MERCANTE

San Polo, Fondamente Frari 2564; tel. 347/829-3158;
Mon.-Sat. 7pm-2am

Il Mercante is an anomaly in a city filled with rustic bars happy to stick with tradition. Things are different here and the cocktail menu alone makes it worth a visit. It's filled with creative concoctions and international influences that will satisfy serious drinkers and novices alike. The laid-back vibe, soul soundtrack, and cool interior make this a great place to end an evening.

Wine Bars

MURO VENEZIA

San Polo, Rio Terà Cazza 2604b/c; tel. 041/524-5310;
Mon.-Fri. noon-3pm and 6pm-10:30pm, Sat.-Sun.
noon-10:30pm

There are a lot of reasons to stop by Muro Venezia but probably the best is that it's one of the liveliest places in the city after dark. Inside the intimate restaurant-bar someone is usually playing guitar and dozens of people are drinking outside in the little square close to the Rialto. During the day it makes a good happy-hour pit stop, and on Saturdays at noon they start serving fried fish and chardonnay outdoors for an unbeatable €8.

AL AMARONE

San Polo, Calle Sbianchesini 1131; tel. 041/523-1184;
Thurs.-Tues. 10am-11pm

Al Amarone is an excellent place to learn about local Veneto wines. They serve over 30 red, white, and sparkling vintages by the regular and double glass in a spacious, contemporary setting. There are also a number of interesting tasting offers (five glasses each) with different themes meant to educate palates. Wine can be accompanied with reasonably priced finger food, cheese, and cured meat platters or a selection of hearty pasta dishes.

BASEGÒ

San Polo, Campo S. Tomà 2863; tel. 041/850-0299;
Wed.-Mon. 11am-10:30pm

Chardonnay, chianti, pinot nero, merlot. They've got it all at Basegò and most of it is served by the glass at this small modern bar. Spritz is only €3 and can be enjoyed in the quiet square opposite.

AL PROSECCO

Santa Croce, Campo San Giacomo de l'Orio;
tel. 041/524-0222; Mon.-Sat. 9am-9pm

Any enoteca named Al Prosecco should leave no doubt what to order. You can discover different varieties of Venetian bubbly along with organic wines while seated in a lively square. Food isn't an afterthought and abundant plates of cheese, grilled vegetables, and gourmet sandwiches are served.

Hotel Bars

★ AMAN VENICE BAR

San Polo, Calle Tiepolo Baiamonte 1364;
tel. 041/270-7333; daily noon-12:30am

The Aman Venice Resort Hotel, around the bend from the Rialto, is the only seven-star hotel in Venice. Its Venice Bar consists of grand chandeliered rooms on the *piano nobile* (second or noble floor). It's a little like Versailles with modern furniture and an elegant backdrop that's perfect for a proposal of any kind. Signature drinks pay homage to Lord Byron and gin aficionados will find a collection of juniper distilled in rare variations.

Opera and Concerts

PALAZETTO BRU ZANE

San Polo, Corte del Calderer 2368; tel. 041/30376;
www.bru-zane.com; box office Mon.-Fri.
2:30pm-5:30pm; €15, €5 for under 28-year-olds

Palazetto Bru Zane aims to keep 18th-century classical music alive and presents 30-40 concerts per season (Sept.-June) in a refurbished villa. Concerts are small-scale (the hall seats 100) and feature emerging international ensembles playing chamber, symphonic, and choral works. Free guided tours of the elaborately decorated building are available in English on Thursday afternoons at 3:30pm.

CANNAREGIO
Bars and Pubs
AL SANTO BEVITORE
Fondamenta de Ca' Vendramin 2393a; tel. 328/672-0828; daily 4pm-2am
For a pint in a no-nonsense Italian pub, pull up a stool at Al Santo Bevitore. The attraction isn't the décor but the long row of taps behind the bar. They're all connected to thirst-quenching kegs of stout, bitter, and ale. You can try local brews made from fermenting Japanese and New Zealand hops together, sip Belgian strong ales like La Chouffe (8 percent) and Kwak (8.4 percent), or cross the Channel for a pint of Punks Do It Better (4.3 percent). A small courtyard overlooks a canal and musicians occasionally give impromptu concerts on Monday nights.

AL PARLAMENTO
Fondamenta Savorgnan 511; tel. 041/244-0214; daily 7:30am-1:30am
Don't come to Venice expecting bars like the ones back home. In Venice a bar can be more than a place to drink. Al Parlamento is a good example of that: Although you can come to take advantage of their €5 happy hour from 6pm to 9pm you can also order seafood *risotto* and a couple of other dishes that will help you avoid a spritz hangover. The space has been refurbished with attention to design but hasn't lost its charm, and still has scenic outdoor tables overlooking the city's second-widest canal.

IRISH PUB VENEZIA
Corte dei Pali 3847; tel. 041/639-6692; daily 10am-2am
There's no shame in going to a pub in Venice, especially if you carry your pint outside. At the originally named Irish Pub Venezia you can do just that with a glass of Kilkenny or

Bitburger in a little courtyard away from the crowds of Strada Nuova. Inside you're likely to find the television tuned to rugby or *calcio* (soccer).

TIME SOCIAL BAR
Rio Terà Farstti 1414; tel. 338/363-6951; daily 6pm-2am
A speakeasy-like bar without the hassle of passwords or secret passages. Instead, you get perfectly mixed drinks by attentive bartenders who stylishly prepare an original selection of cocktails. The music is good and the metal stools are filled by friends and couples.

Casinos
CASINO DI VENEZIA
Ca Vendramin Calergi 2040; tel. 041/529-7111; www.casinovenezia.it; daily 11am-2:45am, tables open at 4pm
Anyone who wants to try their luck in Venice can bet inside the oldest gambling house in the world. Casino di Venezia opened in 1638 and moved to Ca' Vendramin Calergi along the Grand Canal in the 1950s. If you don't know the rules to *Chemin de Fer, Punto Banco,* or *Midi Trenta* you can stick with roulette, blackjack, or the slot machines. Tables are spread over three floors. When you're ready to spend your earnings (or tire of losing), hit the sophisticated restaurant (Fri.-Sun. 7:30pm-11:30pm; €25-35), modern pizzeria (daily noon-3:30pm and 7pm-11:30pm; €15-20), or lounge bar with nighttime views of the Grand Canal. A jacket is required to enter the upstairs parlors but can be borrowed for free at the door. ID is also required and the €10 entry fee includes a chip, cloakroom service, and shuttle from the train station to the casino's private dock.

CASTELLO
Bars and Pubs
EL REFOLO
Via Giuseppe Garibaldi 1580; Tues.-Thurs. 5:30pm-midnight, Fri.-Sun. noon-midnight
Castello is not the most happening

neighborhood after dark, but El Refolo may be the most happening bar in Castello. You'll find people drinking most of the day and the reason is cheap spritz, wine, and beer. The other magnet are the tasty mini sandwiches filled with cheese and cold cuts. One is never enough, and after a few you can forget about lunch or dinner plans.

Wine Bars
CANTINA ANTICA VIGNA
Calle Crosera 3818; tel. 041/523-1318; Mon.-Sat. 8am-8pm and Sun. 9am-1:30pm
If you like your wine bars small and simple, Cantina Antica Vigna is the perfect spot. Nothing about this standing-room-only enoteca is fancy and that's what makes it special. That and owner Ferdinando Benettelli, who has a lot of stories to tell and isn't thrifty when it comes to pouring the local wine he's been serving for decades. Try either of the two white wines on tap at the wooden counter with a stuffed *tramezzino* sandwich—if there are any left.

Hotel Bars
BAR DANDOLO
Hotel Danieli, Riva degli Schiavoni 4196; tel. 041/522-6480; daily 9:30am-1am
Hotel Danieli is located in a 14th-century *palazzo* overlooking the Grand Canal. The narrow front entrance leads to a lavish four-story lobby that has changed little in the last six centuries. Bar Dandolo is located on the ground floor, and managed by Roberto Naccari who is an expert at mixing Vesper martinis along with his own creations. Try the After Eight, a drink consisting of Ombra digestif, mint syrup, and double cream. There are comfortable armchairs and velvet love-seats in the intimate bar that's perfect for exchanging confidences. The dress code is smart casual and afternoon tea is served at 4pm sharp. The Danieli also has a rooftop bar with views of the lagoon. It's open from May until September and *aperitivo* is served 3pm-6:30pm.

GIUDECCA
Hotel Bars
SKYLINE ROOFTOP BAR
Fondamenta S. Biagio 810; tel. 041/272-3311; daily 7pm-midnight
The Skyline Rooftop Bar sounds cool because it is cool. This lounge bar on top of the Hilton hotel occupies a unique location, and the view from the converted factory is one of the best in the city and compensates for the commute. The bar shakes and stirs original drinks at reasonable prices given the surroundings and is perfect for a sunset *aperitivo* or nightcap.

GENERATOR
Generator Hostel, Fondamenta Zitelle 86; tel. 041/877-8288; daily 5:30pm-2am
Along the embankment in the opposite direction you'll find Generator. The hostel bar may not be as fancy as the Hilton but it's a whole lot hipper and nearly always filled with twentysomething travelers from all over the world. It's the liveliest place to drink in Giudecca, where newly made friends hang out on sofas and play pool.

Opera and Concerts
TEATRO VERDE
Isola di San Giorgio; tel. 366/909-9241; €30-70
Venice isn't just about classical music and if you're into musicians outside the pop mainstream like Kings of Convenience, Melody Gardot, or Patti Smith, Teatro Verde is the place to go. The outdoor amphitheater on the island of San Giorgio is worth the *vaporetto* trip. Concerts are staged throughout the summer and start at 9:15pm. Tickets can be purchased on-site or at any tourist office. Prices vary, but the cheapest seats come with the best views of the canal. Doors open at 7:30pm and there's a temporary restaurant and bar.

FESTIVALS AND EVENTS
Spring
Festa della Sensa, one of Venice's oldest celebrations, began around AD 1000 as a way

of marking the city's maritime rise to dominance and conquest of the Adriatic. The *doge's* ship would lead boats out of the lagoon into the open sea where prayers were recited to San Nicolo, the patron saint of sailors. The dropping of a precious ring by the *doge* was later added as a symbolic marriage of the city with the sea. The ritual is reenacted on the last Sunday in May with great pomp. Today, the mayor leads the procession, which is best viewed from the northern shore of the Lido.

Summer

One of the most popular celebrations in Venice is **La Festa del Redentore** (third Sun. in July). It originated in 1576 when locals vowed to build a church if the plague that was devastating the city ended. The disease miraculously relented and Venetians have shown their gratitude ever since. During the day they walk over a pontoon bridge to the Chiesa del Redentore in Giudecca—which was built as promised—and at night thousands watch fireworks that illuminate the sky from 11pm onward. Riva degli Schiavone in Castello and Fondamenta Zattere in Dorsoduro offer the best views but provide little elbow room, especially if you arrive late. After the pyrotechnics, younger Venetians continue the celebrations on the beaches of the Lido. The day after a special morning mass is held in the church and the temporary bridge remains in place for several days, offering a rare opportunity to cross the Giudecca Canal on foot.

During late August and early September it's not uncommon to spot international film stars zipping around Venice on motorboats. They're here for the **Venice Film Festival** (tel. 041/521-8711; www.labiennale.org) that's been held on the Lido since 1932 and is one of the oldest festivals of its kind. In Venice the best film is awarded a golden lion and stars walk the red carpet at the art deco Palazzo del Cinema (Lido, Lungomare Guglielmo Marconi) facing the Adriatic. The theater has a 1,100-seat screening room where entries are projected day and night. Tickets are available once the program is announced and many showings are open to the general public. It's an opportunity to see great films in an exceptional environment and possibly glimpse a famous face. Exhibitions and collateral events are organized throughout the city during the 10-day festival, including an outdoor cinema in Campo San Polo.

Fall

Gondoliers have been competing with one another for centuries, and the **Regata Storica** (first Sun. in Sept.) fills both sides of the Grand Canal with thousands of spectators. The regatta is divided into four categories according to the type of vessel and number of oars used. A lucky few watch from *palazzi* balconies while everyone else maneuvers for space on the bridges or along the *fondamente*. The event begins at 4pm with a parade of boats manned by sailors in colorful 15th-century attire and led by someone dressed as a *doge*. Boats depart from the Giardini Publici (Castello) and row up the Grand Canal to the train station and back to the finish line opposite Palazzo Ca' Foscari. The climax of the event features gondolas oared by teams of two. Each heat has 9 or 10 competitors. The first four to place are awarded cash prizes and a red, white, green, or blue standard depending on how they finished. Winning is a big deal, but the most prestigious honor is the *Re del Remo* (King of the Oar) title that is achieved by winning five consecutive regattas. Only seven gondoliers have won it in the history of the race.

Venice Glass Week (www.theveniceglassweek.com; second week of Sept.) was founded in 2017 to celebrate and support local glassmaking. Exhibitions, demonstrations, and events are organized in dozens of venues around the city. Each year there is a different theme and tours are conducted to help visitors discover this ancient art.

Venice may look old on the outside but it's often brand-new on the inside. That's the

---

1: handmade stationery **2:** SUP in Venice **3:** a group of *Carnevale* goers

contrast mayor Riccardo Selvatico wanted to create when he founded the **Venice Biennale** (Castello, Giardini Publici and Arsenale; tel. 041/521-8711; www.labiennale.org; Tues.-Sun. 10am-6pm, May-Nov. in odd years) in 1895. Initially dedicated to sculpture and painting, the event has evolved into the premier showcase for contemporary art and architecture. Today the event remains on the cutting edge and introduces leading artists from over 90 countries to a global audience of critics, enthusiasts, and collectors. The event has also expanded to include music, dance, theater, and cinema. Each edition has a curator responsible for choosing a theme and selecting participants.

The Biennale is centered on a cluster of pavilions in the **Giardini Publici** and **Arsenal** warehouses on the eastern tip of the Castello neighborhood. The Giardini Publici at the southeastern corner of the *sestiere* is the original exhibition space where countries built a handful of small pavilions in the gardens over the decades. Arsenal, five minutes north, was added later and provides large industrial spaces where conceptual artists let their imaginations run wild. The art isn't restricted, however, only to Castello—there are installations in galleries and museums around the city. If you like art, it's a great time to visit. If you aren't a fan, Venice goes on as usual.

The Biennale offers several ticket options including a **Regular Ticket** (€25) for one-day and **Plus Ticket** (€35) for three-days. Both allow entry to multiple locations and are available from the box offices located at **Giardini Publici** (Viale dei Giardini Publici) and **Arsenale** (Campo della Tana). If you want to have the art explained there are daily **group tours** (€7 per venue) that don't require advance reservations and are conducted in Italian and English at 11am (Giardini) and 2pm (Arsenale). **Private tours** (tel. 041/5218-828; Mon.-Sat. 10am-5:30pm; €90) can also be arranged. An architectural version of the Biennale was launched in 1980 and is held in even years. It's nearly impossible, therefore, to miss out on cutting-edge art or architecture as the two alternate years and find ways to outdo each other every edition.

Winter

Epiphany usually lands on January 6. It's a holiday throughout Italy but in Venice they celebrate *la Befana* a little differently. A huge stocking is hung from the Rialto and the **Regatta delle Befane** race is held. Participants are dressed as the legendary witch who gives children candy or coal depending on how they've behaved. The procession departs from the San Tomà dock at 11am and heads up the Grand Canal toward the Rialto. It's a short race that lasts less than 15 minutes. Afterward there's plenty of steaming *vin brulé* wine and an opportunity to meet *Babbo Natale* (Father Christmas).

Carnevale began in 11th-century Venice as a gluttonous celebration before the arrival of Lent and its period of abstinence. By its 18th-century licentious peak, beautiful, sophisticated, outlandish, and amusing characters all joined the party. Celebrants disguised their identities behind masks and costumes that temporarily eliminated social distinctions. Its later decadence brought about a 19th-century decline and eventual disappearance until it was revived in the 1970s. Travelers shouldn't come to Venice during *Carnevale* unless they want to take part. Streets are choked with spectators and orchestrated costume parades while most Venetians are either out of town or at private parties. Piazza San Marco is the center of the action but all the larger squares organize music and dancing. You can watch the gaiety, or better yet, dress up and join the fun. If you haven't packed a costume there are plenty of rental shops, but a simple mask and a little creativity is all you need to join the mayhem.

Carnevale season starts on the ninth Sunday before Easter and climaxes two weeks later on *martedi grasso* (Mardi Gras or Fat Tuesday). The exact dates vary each year according to when Easter falls but it generally takes place in February.

Shopping

Shakespeare never imagined writing a play called the *Merchant of Paris* or *London*. He wrote the *Merchant of Venice* because that's where the shops were. In the 16th century the streets, markets, and docks around the Rialto were jammed with traders. Merchants came from all over Europe to Venice—the most active port in the Mediterranean—to trade with their Ottoman, Indian, and Chinese counterparts. Pigments, leather, textiles, spices, perfumes, precious wood, and foodstuffs were exchanged for gold, silver, and armaments. Local workshops transformed these materials into valuable objects that brought the city wealth and fame.

Many trades have survived, making shopping in Venice an adventure. The most celebrated of these create glass, lace, and papier-mâché. Although the number of craftspeople has declined, they can still be found plying their skills across the city. Historic workshops are common in Dorsoduro, where both **Calle del Bastion** and **Calle della Chiesa** are dotted with one-room galleries where artisans work in the back and display textiles, prints, and jewelry in the front. You can find glass and lace in showroom boutiques and souvenir shops around San Marco, but if you want to go to the source you'll need to board a *vaporetto* and head out to the furnaces of Murano or the backstreets of Burano where lacemaking refuses to die. Always ask permission before taking photos.

Venice only has one megastore, but many designer boutiques. Major brands cluster along the most trafficked areas, such as the streets north and west of **Piazza San Marco** or in the **Strada Nuova** in Cannaregio, which stretches from the train station all the way to the Rialto. Both sides of the Rialto Bridge are heavily commercialized, and the arcades and market stalls on the San Polo side are a good place to search for T-shirts, jewelry, and masks. **Rio Terra Lista di Spagna,** the

gateway to Cannaregio, is lined with shops, but it's very touristy and best avoided.

Smaller Venetian shops are generally open 9am-1pm and 3pm-7pm, though many sacrifice the traditional lunch break, especially during summer. Most shops close on Sundays and many remain closed on Monday mornings.

SAN MARCO

San Marco is one of the most commercial *sestiere* in Venice, but you don't have to scour the entire neighborhood when you can find it all in **Calle Frezzaria.** This narrow street just west of Piazza San Marco provides a mix of new and old boutiques where nothing is off the assembly line and quality, selection, and fun still matter. It's a pleasant walk with stores that are close to each other on a street that isn't overly crowded and is shaded most of the day. Elite fashion brands like Gucci and Prada can be admired nearby in Calle Larga XXII Marzo, while Merceria II Aprile leading to the Rialto is lined with affordable shops selling clothes, shoes, and accessories. The newly restored Fontego dei Tedeschi is a grand food hall and fashion mecca that attracts lots of tourists searching for luxury labels.

Glass

The majority of glass shops are located in the busy commercial streets north and west of Piazza San Marco. Lower-end outlets sell fairly anonymous sculptures, jewelry, and trinkets; if you can't make it to Murano, they make decent souvenirs. If you want something larger and more impressive, you'll also find dozens of higher-end boutiques in the area.

FGB

S. Maria del Giglio 2514; tel. 041/523-6556; daily 10am-6:30pm

It's hard to imagine a more inviting location than FGB. This glass workshop is housed

Made in Venice

Venice is famous for glass, lace, and papier-mâché masks, but that doesn't mean all the glass, lace, and paper masks you'll find in Venice were made in Venice. Local supply simply can't keep up with demand and has led many shop owners to import their wares from other parts of the world. Venetian merchants have been doing that for centuries, but if you've come all this way you may as well get the real deal. That will almost always cost more, but handmade has advantages like craftsmanship and originality that are worth paying extra.

GLASS

Glass production is centered in Murano but many furnaces supply boutiques in San Marco and offer one-of-a-kind glassware that's difficult to imitate. Genuine glass usually comes with certification (Vetro Artistico Murano; www.muranoglass.com) and large pieces are often signed. There's something for all budgets, from glazed jewelry to colorful vases and immense chandeliers. Many workshops are equipped with ovens where artisans create and sell what they make. That's always a good sign and an opportunity to observe and ask questions about the glassmaking process.

LACE

Lace or *merletti* hasn't resisted globalization as well as glass; by some estimates over 90 percent of the merchandise in Venice is made outside the city. The school that once taught lacemaking on the island of Burano closed years ago and most practitioners are in their 50s or older—but don't let that discourage you. Authentic Venetian hand-stitched lace can be hard to find, but it's still out there and recognizable by its imperfections and price tag.

MASKS

You'll spot masks being sold as soon as you step out of the train station, but most of these are cheap plastic lacking in personality. A papier-mâché mask takes time and, most of all, imagination to shape and hand-paint. It's an art that has dwindled down to a small circle of dedicated practitioners. The few remaining shops are crammed floor to ceiling with sensational characters that stop window shoppers in their tracks and can provide a fantastic reminder of your journey to Venice.

within an ancient tower of which only the base has remained. Inside, a couple uses the lume technique to create jewelry and decorations. They heat colored glass rods up to 500 degrees and shape them into beads of different dimensions that are then used to make colorful earrings, bracelets, and necklaces. You can find a nice gift here for under €20.

EMI ART GLASS

Calle della Mandola 3803; tel. 041/523-1326; Mon.-Sat. 9am-7:30pm

To help consumers distinguish between Murano-made and everything else, the glassmaker's association created a special *Vetro Artistico Murano* label that only shops selling authentic local glass can display. You'll find it at EMI Art Glass, which sells blown vases,

marine sculptures, and solid-glass objects that would look good on a mantle or shelf. Pieces are as expensive as they are heavy and shipping can be arranged.

Once you begin shopping for glass it may be hard to stop—but the more time you spend examining the goods, the better you'll become at distinguishing made in China from made in Murano.

Masks and Costumes
ATELIER FLAVIA

Corte Spechiera 6010; tel. 041/528-7429; www. veniceatelier.com; Mon.-Sat. 10am-6pm

The historically accurate costumes, papiermâché masks, tuxedos, wigs, capes, hats, and shoes at Atelier Flavia could transform anyone. It's the ideal place to come before

Carnevale for an *Eyes Wide Shut* (or any other) look. Costumes are available for rental or purchase. If you miss the festivities you can still rent a costume for an hour (€50 women/€80 men) and take as many pictures as you want in the adjacent streets or have a professional photographer (€320) immortalize you dressed as a Venetian.

Clothing and Accessories

AL DUCA D'AOSTA

Piazza San Marco 284; tel. 041/520-4079; daily 10am-7pm

Anyone with the instinct of a dandy will enjoy a trip to Al Duca d'Aosta Venezia 1902. This venerated gentleman's brand combines traditional British style with elegant Italian tailoring. It's where princes came for fashion that never fades and modern gentlemen come for wool jackets, cashmere sweaters, and cotton shirts that cross seasonal divides.

GIULIANA'S LONGO'S

Calle del Lovo 4813; tel. 041/522-6454; Mon.-Sat. 10am-7pm

Items at Giuliana's Longo's hat shop are made right here in Venice. In fact, Giuliana herself makes the hats she stocks. Inside her shop Panama, gondolier, *Carnevale*, felt, and straw hats are haphazardly arranged in armoires and on antique hat stands. This little corner of hat history is about as far as you can get from mass production. Giuliana is usually working away at her little desk on one-of-a-kind pieces that all have their own personality. Try one on and see if the hat fits.

BARENA VENEZIA

Calle Minelli 4260b; tel. 041/523-8457; Mon.-Sat. 10am-1pm and 4pm-7:30pm

If you want to dress like a Venetian, visit Barena Venezia. This men's and women's shop has been creating versatile and functional clothing since 1961. Coats, jackets, and sweaters are made using local textiles and are inspired by 20th-century lagoon style. Everything is comfortable and easy to wear.

ERMENEGILDO ZEGNA

Bocca di Piazza San Marco 1241; tel. 041/522-1204; daily 10am-7pm

Gentlemen ready for an Italian makeover can head to Ermenegildo Zegna. Customers are coddled by expert staff who also offer made-to-measure clothing, which can be delivered overseas.

BUOSI SUCCESSORI

San Bortolomio 5382; tel. 041/520-8567; daily 10am-7:30pm

Buosi has kept Venetian men looking good since 1897. They sew shirts, jackets, trousers, and suits to measure and have a selection of ready-to-wear pieces including ties any man would want to receive.

KIRIKU

Calle Frezzaria 1729; tel. 041/296-0619; Mon.-Fri. 9am-8pm, Sat.-Sun. 10am-8pm

If you need an evening cocktail dress, skirt, or blouse—or even if you don't—Kiriku boutique is worth browsing. The wall racks are filled with emerging designers that have a retro-chic style that looks and feels good. A small selection of bags, shoes, and accessories are in the back next to the white revolving armchair where patient partners recline and express their approval.

EMPRESA

Calle Frezzeria 1586; tel. 041/241-2687; Mon.-Fri. 10am-8pm

Leather and other materials for both men and women await at Empresa. You'll find great jackets and accessories in this finely decorated store, which is run by five friendly brothers who aren't in a rush to sell anything. Their original pieces can add personality to any outfit.

ARNOLD & BATTOIS

Calle Fuseri 4271; tel. 348/412-3797; daily 10am-1pm and 3:30pm-7:30pm

Arnold & Battois creates handbags in unique shapes that turn heads and fashionable women adore. Seasonal collections are inspired by and

Shopping for Masks

Throughout the 18th century, Venetians used masks to enjoy stigma-free decadence. Nobles wore masks to visit brothels, youth to escape from parents, the poor to frequent the rich, the rich to frequent the poor, aristocratic ladies to enter dark alleys, clergy to temporarily break vows, and so on. Famous Venetian Giacomo Casanova wore a mask as he went to meet his lovers at the Cantina Do Mori, where he was a regular.

Masks are still used today and are one of the most common sights at street-side stalls and gift shops around the city, where cheap versions can be had for €5-10. These have little to do with the papier-mâché originals carefully made in a dozen or so ateliers around the city. These versions sell for €30 to €300 and are based on classic molds that have been used for centuries. The most common is the white *Bauta* mask that allows the wearer to eat and drink while remaining hidden from view. It is worn by both men and women and often paired with a black *tabarro* cape. Another popular mask is the *Medico della Peste,* recognizable by the long nose that resembles a bird's beak. It was invented by a doctor in the 17th century who wanted to protect himself from patients dying from the plague and was later adopted by *Carnevale* goers. The *Colombina* is a half mask that covers eyes and cheeks. It continues to be favored by Venetian ladies and often comes painted in silver or gold and adorned with feathers and beads.

These and many other historical masks along with newer creations are available at workshops around the city where you can learn more about the origins of your disguise. Castello is a good neighborhood to start shopping for masks. Below are some shops to check out:

- **Cà del Sol:** The place to play 12th-century dress-up with a patient owner who explains the traditions behind the different costumes on display (page 350).

- **Papier Maché:** Authentic handmade masks created to order or purchased off the shelf. Prices are higher here but worth it (page 350).

- **Ca' Mancana:** Friendly, unpushy staff with a wide selection of masks for varying budgets (page 347).

entirely made in Venice. Leather is the material of choice and the designs are a result of experience and slow production.

ARMADIO DI COCO

Calle Frezzeria 1797; tel. 041/476-7340; Tues.-Sun. 10:30am-1:30pm and 3pm-7:30pm

Armadio di Coco is an elegant vintage shop that would make an ideal walk-in closet. Dior, Chanel, Fendi, Valentino, and other designer labels are there, along with bags, belts, shoes, and hats all neatly arranged on secondhand racks and shelves. The clothes may be used but it's nearly impossible to tell. Many have been given new hems and necklines by the young designer/owner, who wields thread and needles in her backroom workshop.

Stationery
LA CARTA

San Marco 5547a; tel. 041/520-2325; daily 9:30am-7:30pm

In front of the post office, La Carta sells handmade paper and specializes in marbleized sheets, calendars, and agendas. If you forgot your diary at home this is the perfect place to buy a new one and start jotting down your impressions of Venice. There's also a decent selection of pens and pencils.

Markets
MERCATINO DI CAMPO
SAN MAURIZIO

Campo San Maurizio; Fri.-Sun. 9am-7pm

Mercatino di Campo San Maurizio, a seasonal

antiques market, is perfect for aimless meandering. Dealers from across Italy show a trove of collectibles and curiosities from the 17th to the 20th centuries and all decades in between. A variety of Murano glass is on display along with silver dinnerware, military regalia from both World Wars, textiles, phonographs, vintage clothing, and more. Browsing the covered wooden stalls is fun whether you're a collector or just interested in history. If you spot something you like, inquire about date and origin before asking the price, which can often be negotiated down. The market is generally held the weekend before Easter and the second weekends of September, October, and December but dates vary slightly every year.

DORSODURO

There are fewer shops in Dorsoduro than other *sestiere* but the ones you will find are often owned by craftspeople who split their time making glass or paper creations and assisting costumers. If you haven't found the right souvenir yet, Calle del Bastion, the narrow street connecting the Guggenheim to Punta della Dogana, is a good place to start looking. It's lined with small art galleries, jewelry workshops, and a great stationery store.

While you're browsing, keep an eye out for Bence; the lute-playing Hungarian expat can be found in Campiello Barbaro or in the nearby passageway leading to Punta della Dogana. Compositions are his own and sound like a baroque version of *Stairway to Heaven*. He makes his living from donations and sales of his CD (€10). Over the canal, another street musician is usually playing classical music using wine glasses filled with water. Vivaldi sounds surprisingly good played this way and crowds tend to gather in the little square facing a church. CDs are also available here.

Glass
DESIGNS 188

Calle del Bastion 188; tel. 041/523-9426; Mon.-Sat. 11am-7pm

The secret to Giorgio and Trina's 30-year marriage is having separate workshops where they create distinctive glass jewelry. Granted the shops are on the same street and Giorgio is often working the flame in his wife's studio, but that doesn't seem to effect marital longevity. Earrings, bracelets, and necklaces inside Designs 188 are all beautifully intricate and colorful, which makes choosing hard. Prices are reasonable and if you want to contrast and compare head to Giorgio's shop (Calle del Bastion 167) down the street on the corner. In between are a number of modern galleries featuring paintings and other ingenious objects by local artists.

Masks and Costumes
CA' MANCANA

Calle de le Botteghe 3172; tel. 041/520-3229; daily 10am-8pm

Masks are everywhere in Venice but few shops sell their own handmade models. Ca' Mancana is one of the finest and uses traditional papier-mâché techniques to create both classic *Carnevale* and fantasy characters. Anyone can hide their identity for as little as €30. This is where Stanley Kubrick came when he wanted masks for *Eyes Wide Shut*. If you want to learn how masks are made or are traveling with kids, ask about the maskmaking workshops that last a couple of hours and keep young and old entertained.

Books
LA TOLETTA

Sacca della Toletta 1214; tel. 041/523-2034; Mon.-Sat. 9am-7:30pm, Sun. 11am-1pm and 2pm-7pm

You can never have too many books, and even if you don't read Italian you can judge by the covers at La Toletta and choose a novel or nonfiction work for your bookcase back home. There are different sections to browse in this shop, which opened in 1933 and has retained a vintage 1970s look. Talks and lectures are regularly scheduled on weekends.

Stationery
IL PAVONE

Calle Venier dei Leoni 721; tel. 041/523-4517; daily 10am-5:30pm

Fabio Pelosin has worked for over 30 years inside Stamperia il Pavone hand-decorating paper he uses to cover notebooks, photo albums, bookmarks, pencils, frames, and boxes. The process can be observed through the little window that divides the small showroom from the workshop where Fabio or his assistant can be found working on new creations. He begins by drawing a motif, which he then carves into a wooden block. The stamp is then covered with paint and applied to paper. The unique results make colorful souvenirs you won't find anywhere else.

Housewares
MADERA

Campo San Barnaba 2762; tel. 041/522-4181; Mon.-Sat. 10am-1pm and 3:30pm-7:30pm

Madera offers a contemporary range of dining and cooking ware. Local designers produce most of the dishes, utensils, and cutting boards and the owner makes many of the wooden items herself. The style is more Nordic than Venetian, but every piece would be a valuable addition to a kitchen. Nearby is a second store that sells jewelry and accessories with the same artisanal mantra.

SAN POLO AND SANTA CROCE
Glass
MARCO FRANZATO

Santa Croce, Corte Piossi 2176; tel. 041/524-0770; daily 10am-6pm

Marco Franzato is a master glassmaker who has restored the windows of many ancient *palazzi* including Palazzo Ducale. He opened his workshop in 1993. Inside he creates rose glass displays, lampshades, and collectibles. The jewelry is the most accessible in price and ease of transport, although direct shipping can be arranged. Marco uses a number of techniques to create one-of-a-kind earrings, necklaces, and rings that take shape in the lab at the back of the shop.

Masks and Costumes
ATELIER PIETRO LONGHI

San Polo, Campo S. Polo 2608; tel. 041/714-478; Mon.-Sat. 10am-7pm

Atelier Pietro Longhi rents (€160) and sells (€1,500) period costumes. They also tailor original disguises to measure from paintings, photos, comic books, or dreams. It usually takes about a week before you can wear it. Mask also available to buy or rent.

Books
LIBRERIA MARE DI CARTA

Santa Croce, Fondamenta dei Tolentini 222; tel. 041/716-304; Tues.-Sat. 9am-1pm and 3:30pm-7:30pm

Venice is the perfect location for a bookshop dedicated to the sea, and Libreria Mare di Carta is lined with nonfiction and fictional tales in which waves are the protagonist. Cristina Giussani is both an accomplished sailor and bookseller who can point you to the right shelf. Most of the literature is in Italian but there's also a great quantity of maps, model boats, prints, and comics that are easily understood.

Woodworking
DALLA VENEZIA ANGELO

San Polo, Calle del Scaleter 2204; tel. 041/721-659; Mon.-Sat. 8am-1pm and 4pm-8pm

It's easy to pass Dalla Venezia Angelo without a second thought, but if you're interested in how wood gets transformed into miniature objects step inside and let Angelo show you around. He's been keeping the tradition of woodworking alive since 1959 and will gladly explain the dusty workshop where he carves and sands planks of Swiss pine and Tuscan olive into rings and pyramids using a vintage wood-spinning machine that allows him to transform wood into apples and pears. This isn't mass production and prices aren't cheap, but everything is unique and represents a lifetime of dedication.

Clothing and Accessories
MONICA DANIELE'S
San Polo, Calle del Scaleter 2235; tel. 041/524-6242; Mon.-Sat. 9am-6pm

Monica Daniele's shop is where adults play dress up. Monica nearly singlehandedly rescued 18th-century Venetian accessories from fashion oblivion. One item in particular she saved from fashion extinction is the *tabarro*, a wool cloak once commonly spotted on wintery Venetian streets. It comes in blue, black, or gray and goes well with the extensive range of felt hats on display in the window and around this informal shop.

PIEDÀTERRE
San Polo, Ruga dei Oresi 60; tel. 041/528-5513; daily 10am-7:30pm

Shoes aren't complicated at Piedàterre. The colorful boutique under the arcades of the Rialto has refashioned traditional footwear for the 21st century. The shoes in question are slipper-like and inspired by those once worn by gondoliers and peasants. Today, velvet has been added and recycled tires are used for the soles. They come in all colors for children and adults and make a comfortable summertime walking shoe.

PENNY LANE SHOP
Santa Croce, Salizada San Pantalon 39; tel. 041/524-4134; Tues.-Sat. 9am-1pm and 4pm-6pm

The high student population may explain the number of funky and vintage clothing shops in the neighborhood, but these small boutiques are for anyone who values retro style and enjoys hunting for new and slightly used hats, bags, and clothing. One of the oldest is the Penny Lane Shop, which stocks colorful northern European brands made from a range of materials. Try on jewelry accessories in the side room dedicated to *haut vintage*.

Jewelry
ATTOMBRI
San Polo, Sottoportico degli Orefici 65; tel. 041/521-2524; Mon. 3:30pm-7:30pm, Tues.-Sat. 10am-1pm and 3:30pm-7:30pm

The arcades leading to the Rialto are the traditional domain of goldsmiths, and many jewelers still work along this busy thoroughfare. The brothers who run Attombri combine traditional metals with contemporary design. They create necklaces, bracelets, and earrings in silver, copper, and glass that are elegant and wearable.

Spices
DROGHERIA MASCARI
San Polo, Ruga dei Spezieri 381; tel. 041/522-9762; Mon.-Sat. 8am-1pm and 4pm-7:30pm

There are strict rules about the food travelers can bring home, but fortunately the gastronomic goods on offer at Drogheria Mascari will pass customs. This wonderful-smelling shop is full of tempting ingredients like dried porcini mushrooms, sweet paprika, saffron, candied fruits, and mysterious spices. The well-stocked gourmet section also carries truffle-inspired condiments and *mostarda veneta* (Venetian mustard) that elevates meat and cheese.

Rialto Markets
The Rialto is the commercial heart of Venice, and both sides of the bridge have been crammed with activity since the 15th century. The area on and around the bridge feels like one continuous market, with arcades and squares filled with all sorts of businesses that attract locals and tourists alike. The San Polo side is the busier of the two and where the city's main markets are located. **Ruga dei Oresi,** on the northern side of the bridge, was once the domain of jewelers who worked in the small shops lining the arcades, but most have been replaced with boutiques and stalls selling glass, masks, clothing, and souvenirs of varying quality. You can escape the crush of visitors by exploring the alcoves parallel to the main street or by heading north to the nearby **Campo Cesare.** There's a little more breathing room and dozens of kiosks (daily 8:30am-6pm) selling Venetian logoed T-shirts, sweatshirts, and hats in adult

and child sizes. **Nicolo** (recognized by his shaved head and good-natured cynicism), like most of the merchants here, offers a discount on multiple purchases. Farther along and facing the Grand Canal are the **fish market** and **produce market.**

CANNAREGIO

Antiques

ANTICHITÀ AL GHETTO

Calle Ghetto Vecchio 1133/1134; tel. 041/524-4592; Tues.-Sun. 9:30am-1pm

You'll find antique lace, purses, pillows, ceramics, and furniture at Antichità al Ghetto. Elisabetta and Giuliano opened their shop in 2006 and have been trading in history ever since. The friendly couple is knowledgeable about the goods they sell and will happily explain the origin and use of any item.

Stationery

MOLESKINE

Stazione Santa Lucia, Fondamenta Santa Lucia 20; tel. 041/740-913; daily 9am-7pm

Want to follow in the literary footsteps of Bruce Chatwin or Ernest Hemingway? Stop in at the local Moleskine branch. The modern shop inside the train station sells more than the famed black diary that made the company famous. You'll also find bags, wallets, e-reader cases, and pens and writing implements with the same unmistakable style.

TIPOGRAFIA BASSO

Calle del Fumo 5306; tel. 041/523-4681; Mon-Sat. 9am-1pm and 2:30pm-6pm; cash only

The smell of ink and paper is the sign you've arrived at Tipografia Basso. Inside the small atelier, Gianni works away on letterpress, lithographic, and offset printers but can always find the time to explain the different printing processes and demonstrate why the old-fashioned way is sometimes the best way. You can buy small prints of Pinocchio and other classic images or order a set of personalized hand-printed business cards.

Markets

MERCATINO DEI MIRACOLI

Campo Santa Maria Nova; tel. 041/271-0022; Mar.-Dec. Sat.-Sun. all day

Venetian flea markets are never shabby and always offer an opportunity to find unique (often antique) Murano glass, lace, silverware, and mixed oddities with loads of historical charm. If you're in Venice on the right weekend that's what you'll find at Mercatino dei Miracoli. Passionate hobbyists and collectors organize this small open-air market in a lovely *campo* where objects of all kinds can be discovered on the second weekend of the month.

CASTELLO

Masks and Costumes

CÀ DEL SOL

Fondamenta dell'Osmarin 4964; tel. 041/528-5549; daily 10am-8pm

The walls of Cà del Sol are covered in masks. All the classics are here, including *bauta, columbine,* harlequin, plague, and scores of one-off creations handmade using papier-mâché, leather, ceramic, and iron. The shop has been around since 1986 and helped revitalize the art of maskmaking in the city. It's run by a collective of artisans who patiently answer questions and aren't uptight about allowing customers to try on masks. They organize maskmaking demonstrations and five-day courses, and rent elaborate costumes during *Carnevale.*

PAPIER MACHÉ

Calle Lunga Santa Maria Formosa 5174; tel. 041/522-9995; Mon.-Sat. 9am-7:30pm

It takes a while to distinguish between the different mask types, but the quality of the structure and painted detailing is immediately evident at Papier Maché. Four decades of maskmaking experience is on display in the windows of this boutique, which has a large selection of ornate masks with designs you won't see anywhere else. Prices are a little high, but this is the real deal—and perhaps the finest way to keep your identity a secret.

Books
LIBRERIA AQUA ALTA
Calle Longa Santa Maria Formosa 5176b;
tel. 041/296-0841; daily 9am-8pm
Books are haphazardly stacked at Libreria Aqua Alta in bathtubs and boats along narrow aisles that would have driven Melvil Dewey crazy. Yet it's hard not to like this bookshop and be absorbed by titles that range in subject and language from architecture to Swahili. Outside near the sleeping literary cats are a collection of vintage postcards, prints, and other paper materials that make unusual gifts.

Clothing and Accessories
BANCO LOTTO NO.10
Salizada Sant'Antonin 3478; tel. 041/522-1439;
Mon.-Sat. 9:30am-7:30pm
Prison and fashion may seem incompatible, but over the last decade the woman's penitentiary in Giudecca has collaborated with local dressmakers to help inmates learn a useful trade. The result is affordable and stylish women's clothing stocked in Banco Lotto no.10 in eastern Castello. You can also find original accessories like bags made from discarded coffee sacks sold for as little as €10.

Stationery
G. L. PITACCO
Ruga Giuffa 4758; tel. 041/520-8687; Mon.-Sat.
3pm-8pm
Bookbinder G. L. Pitacco specializes in traditional and modern bindings. The little shop stocks diaries, photo albums, and address books of all dimensions. You can also have books

bound or repaired. They hand-make sheets of marbleized paper that are different from the Florentine variety; their sheets can also be found at **Domino Arte** (Via Giuseppe Garibaldi 1649; tel. 041/277-1325; Fri.-Wed. 1:30pm-7:30pm).

Markets
MERCATINO DELLE ROBE DA MAR
Via Garibaldi
Venice's most popular market is held several times a year on the first or last Sunday of the month. Mercatino delle Robe da Mar translates to "stuff of the sea market" but that doesn't mean it's only nautical in nature—you'll find everything from antique stamps to used vinyl LPs. It's also a chance to visit one of the lesser-tread parts of the city and discover the eastern tip of Venice.

GIUDECCA
Textiles
FORTUNY TEXTILE FACTORY
Fondamenta S. Biagio 805; tel. 041/825-7651;
Mon.-Fri. 10am-1pm and 2pm-6pm
Giudecca is a long way to go for a shopping spree, and there aren't that many shops to begin with. Yet Venice's longest island does have some industrial gems like the Fortuny textile factory. The long brick building overlooking the canal next to the Stucky wheat mill began producing bolts of cloth in 1921 and still operates today. Though the factory doesn't allow visitors, the showroom does, and it's filled with textiles from the company's past and present. There's also a lovely garden next door that can be visited by appointment.

Activities and Recreation

PARKS AND GARDENS
Grass is rare in Venice and there are few green open spaces. The parks and gardens that do exist are small and simple. They're usually quiet places where tourists have no time to tread and Venetians retreat to push grandchildren around in strollers and read the newspaper.

GIARDINO PAPADOPOLI
Santa Croce, Fondamenta Papadopoli; daily
7am-8:30pm
Giardino Papadopoli is located on an island opposite the train station. It's interspersed with gravel paths that circle a surprising variety of trees and bushes. There's a good

playground for little climbers, benches, and a small lawn where you can lie down and forget where you are.

GIARDINI SAVORGNAN

Cannaregio, entrances at Fondamenta Venier, Calle Pesaro, and Calle Vergola; daily 8am-8:30pm

On the other side of the Grand Canal, Giardini Savorgnan provides even greater tranquility and a space for street musicians to relax after lunch and toddlers to swing and slide. Like most parks in Venice it doesn't impress in scale or design but it is clean and provides a bucolic break from canals and streets.

PARCO DELLA RIMEMBRANZE

Castello, Viale IV Novembre; 24/7; Sant'Elena vaporetto station

The largest park in Venice is Parco della Rimembranze on Sant'Elena Island at the southern tip of Castello. This is as far from the train station as you can get and well off the tourist radar. It's an everyday park that's well maintained and comes with lagoon views, playgrounds, and shaded walkways. What's also nice is the adjacent neighborhood where residents go about their business seemingly unaware of the rest of the city. There are wide *calle*, several greengrocers, and unadorned bars with tables immersed in green.

GIARDINI PUBBLICI

Castello, Viale Giardini Pubblici; 24/7; Giardini vaporetto station

The Giardini Pubblici, or public gardens, are nearby over a bridge. These gardens attract art lovers who come to visit the Art Biennale held here on odd-numbered years. The playground has seen better days, but the **Paradiso Café** near the dock is a nice place to rest a few minutes and has its own little art gallery.

GIARDINI EX REALI

San Marco, Riva degli chiavone; 24/7

Closer to the center and just around the corner from Piazza San Marco the Giardini ex Reali provides a tiny refuge from the tourists wandering along the promenade out front.

The beech trees and goldfish-inhabited fountains inside this gated garden were part of Napoleon's royal palace and laid out in the late 1800s. There are plenty of empty benches (red seems to be the favorite color for benches in Venice) and the nearby **tourist office** makes it a strategic spot to plan your next move or spend a few minutes doing nothing.

ROWING

ROW VENICE

Cannaregio, Sacca Misericordia Marina, Fondamenta Gasparo Contarini 5540; tel. 347/725-0637; www. rowvenice.org; daily 8:30am-4pm; 1-2 people €85, 3/€120, 4/€140

Boats are different in Venice. Shallow canals means most are flat bottomed and rowed standing up to gain maximum visibility. This characteristic led to a particular rowing style, which is practiced in few places outside the city and can be experienced at Row Venice. An Australian expat and her association of 20 female instructors run 90-minute lessons that cost the same as a gondola ride and are twice as fun. Participants learn the basics of navigating a locally made *batellina* vessel, which was once ubiquitous along the canals and looks like a gondola without the regalia. Lessons are conducted in English and start with a demonstration of basic strokes and a briefing on the rules of Venetian waterways. The group operates off a quiet canal and participants take turns paddling and steering. Wannabe sailors should wear loose-fitting clothes and comfortable shoes.

BOATING

Why sweat on a rowboat when you can relax in a motorboat? It is a somewhat riskier option and some boating experience is preferable, but Venetian maritime laws are surprisingly lenient when it comes to rentals.

BRUSSA IS BOAT

Cannaregio, Fondamenta Labia 331; tel. 041/715-787; www.brussaisboat.it; Mon.-Fri. 7:30am-6pm, Apr.-Oct. Sat.-Sun. 8:30am-7pm

No license is required to navigate the small motorboats available from Brussa Is Boat. All you need is a credit card, valid ID, and a desire for adventure.

Daniele or one of his colleagues will familiarize you with the 23-foot pleasure craft and the essentials of Venetian navigation. The *topetta* (traditional flat-bottomed boat) seats six and the 15hp outboard engine is steered from the tiller. The key is to go slow, stay on the right, and avoid busy or narrow canals. This isn't a free-for-all expedition and you can't go anywhere you like. There are seven preestablished itineraries around the lagoon that cover the islands of the Lido (red), Burano (green and purple), and Venice (yellow). That still leaves plenty of exploring to do for an hour (€35 first hour and €25 each additional hour plus tax) or an entire day (€160 plus tax). Fuel is included and reservations should be made in advance during high season. If your nautical skills aren't up to Venetian waterways you can hire someone to do the sailing for you.

★ KAYAKING

Vaporetto and gondola aren't the only ways of getting around Venice. Adventurous travelers can do their own paddling and discover the city's waterways.

VENICE KAYAK

Certosa Marina, Certosa Island; tel. 041/523-6720; www.venicekayak.com; daily 8am-8pm; half day €110, full day €160; vaporetto 4.1 or 4.2

Venice Kayak offers a variety of guided tours for both novices and experienced kayakers. Daily half-day excursions for 2-6 people depart mornings (9:15am-1pm) or afternoons (2:15pm-6pm) from the island of Certosa and crisscross the *sestiere* of Castello and San Marco. Expect about 6 miles (10 kilometers) of paddling in single or double kayaks at a relaxed pace. Full-day tours of Venice and the lagoon islands are also available. Dress with the expectation of getting wet and don't bring a camera unless it's waterproof.

VENICE BY WATER

Cannaregio, Calle Brazzo 3346; tel. 389/985-1866; www.venicebywater.com; daily 9am-9pm

Venice by Water provides short day and night kayak tours that last 30 (€35), 60 (€50), or 120 (€90) minutes. Several combine paddling with breaks for food and drink. All tours are guided and explore lesser-trafficked canals around Cannaregio, Arsenale, and Murano. Kayaks seat two people and are equipped with foot pedals in case you tire.

STAND-UP PADDLING

SUP IN VENICE

Cannaregio, Calle Brazzo 3347; tel. 389/985-1866; www.supinvenice.com; €70 per 100 minutes

There are many ways to explore Venetian canals, but stand-up paddle is the most fun. If you're an experienced paddler or have decent balance and want to give it a try head to SUP in Venice. Eliana Argine discovered the sport on a trip to California in 2009 and founded her company nearly as soon as she got back to Venice. She's been enthusiastically leading tours and navigating the city ever since. Routes vary depending on number of participants (max four), weather, tide, and traffic and take one or two hours to complete. Excursions are organized from March to November and comfortable attire is required (no bare chests or bikinis).

TOURS

Walking Tours

It's inevitable to have questions in Venice, and spending an hour or two with someone who knows the answers is essential if you're serious about getting to know the city. There are many guides to choose from now that the certification process has been simplified and guides are allowed to work anywhere in Italy. That means it's more important than ever to check qualifications and ensure your guide is an expert on Venice. If the guide is a native that's even better, and if they can combine facts with passion to make the city come alive that's the best.

There are over 400 licensed guides in

Family-Friendly Venice

Venice is a dream city for kids. It may not have a children's museum or amusement park but it has water, boats, and bridges. Parents can relax knowing there are no cars to look out for and give kids full reign to run around the squares chasing pigeons and playing ball with local youth. There are no limits to the imagination in Venice, and the city delights and stimulates children in ways they will never forget. Unfortunately, parents with babies and young walkers may suffer, as carrying a stroller up and down the city's many bridges is an arduous task. It's easier to use a hiking carrier or stick to the *fondamente* promenades. Although bicycles and other wheeled objects are prohibited in Venice, strollers are allowed.

- To generate a little fun, just buy a **mask.** Parents can find cheap plastic versions (€2) at souvenir stands and shops around the city. Let children pick their own and walk masqueraded through the streets. Note: Inexpensive doesn't always mean made in China. Low-priced plastic and rough papier-mâché masks are also fabricated in Italy. They come in many varieties and may be tricky to tie.

- There are several **playgrounds** (Giardino Papadopoli, Giardini Savorgnan, Giardini Publici) equipped with traditional swings, slides, and wooden climbing castles. Toddlers to 10-year-olds will love them.

- All ages will love riding the *vaporetto* **boats** that magically eliminate whining—and are free for all passengers under six.

- Hungry kids? That's not a problem in Venice! The mini portions served mornings and afternoons at *bacari* **bars** make delicious snacks and may convince fussy eaters to try something new.

- Kid-friendly museums include the **Museo Storico Navale** with its collection of ancient sailing vessels and the **secret dungeons** in Palazzo Ducale.

- **Glassblowing** demonstrations on the island of Murano, along with **bell towers** (Piazza

Venice and passing the certification exam is not a formality. It takes a combination of historical, artistic, and cultural knowledge as well as excellent language skills. Visitors can choose from group tours organized by the city, private tour companies, and independent guides. While the former costs less, the latter are usually smaller and allow for greater personalization. Whatever you choose, it's a good idea to have a tour early in your stay so you can become familiar with the city as soon as possible. It will help you appreciate and spot red flagpoles, winged lion, and a thousand other things you could easily overlook. Taking a walking tour is also a unique opportunity to let yourself be led by someone who doesn't need a map and rarely gets lost.

Private certified guides charge a standard €70-80 hourly fee and two-hour tours are recommended. Prices are the same whether two or eight people participate. **Group tours** are cheaper but less personal and can include up to 30 visitors. They start from €30 per person for a 90-minute visit. There are fewer itineraries and most generally focus on the San Marco area. If you're interested in food, modern art, or anything off the beaten track you're better off with a private guide.

PRIVATE GUIDES

Venice native **Luisella Romeo** (tel. 349/084-8303; www.seevenice.it) got her tour-guide license back when the exam was nearly impossible to pass and included a written and oral test. She was one of 27 guides selected from 800 applicants and it's clear why the moment

kids watching glass being made

San Marco, Isola di San Giorgio Maggiore, or Torcello), will captivate even the shortest attention spans.

- With a little planning you can also organize papermaking workshops and classical concerts for artistically minded adolescents.

- Consider booking a hotel room at kid-friendly Flora in San Marco, where strollers, highchairs, and cots are all available at no extra cost, or La Villeggiatura in San Polo, where children under nine sleep for free.

she starts telling the story of the city. Not only does she know her art and history, but she also knows how to make it interesting and absorb visitors with her enthusiasm. Today she runs **See Venice Tours** and provides many different ways to experience the city. Visits cost €75 per hour regardless of group size, and two hours with Luisella provides a perfect introduction to Venice.

Sara Grinzato (tel. 345/850-1309; www. guidedvenice.com) is another local who knows her city well and loves sharing her knowledge with visitors. After a couple of hours together you'll see Venice differently and things that made no sense will seem normal. She can customize visits according to your interest in art, food, or shopping, but tours often start with an overview of classic destinations like Piazza San Marco and the

Rialto. You can arrange to meet both guides at your accommodation and organize fun treasure hunts for young children and teens.

FREE TOURS

Venice Free Walking Tour (www. venicefreewalkingtour.com) sounds too good to be true—but isn't. This nonprofit initiative leads 2.5-hour morning and afternoon tours that cover the foundation of the city, traditions, gastronomy, and plenty of facts and figures. Tours start from the old wellhead in Campo Santi Apostoli (Cannaregio) and proceed over a historic 2-mile (3-kilometer) route. Guides are passionate local volunteers who get a kick out of helping curious visitors uncover their city. All tours are conducted in English.

Once you've fallen in love with Venice,

you may want to help preserve it, and there are many organizations dedicated to just that. **Save Venice Inc.** (Dorsoduro, Palazzo Contarini Polignac 870; tel. 041/528-5247; www.savevenice.org; Mon.-Fri. 9am-5pm) helps repair and restore the city one painting, sculpture, and *palazzo* at a time. You can go to their office and speak with Leslie or Holly about the organization's activities, visit their library, and follow one of their **self-guided tours** dedicated to art and architecture. Each lasts about 90 minutes and the suggested donation of €20 that goes to funding future restoration projects is appreciated.

Boat Tours

Several companies including **City Sightseeing** operate boat tours around Venice. Travelers can compare the options along the **Riva degli Schiavoni** waterfront from where they regularly depart. Journey times and itineraries vary and the biggest advantage compared to public transportation is the assurance of getting a seat. The convenience and widespread availability of *vaporetto,* however, make boat tours nearly superfluous.

IL BURCHIELLO

Padova, Via Porciglia 34; tel. 049/876-0233; www. ilburchiello.it; Mon.-Fri. 9am-6pm; €60 half day, €99 full day

Il Burchiello operates expeditions up the Brenta Canal that connects Venice to Oriago and Padova. Boats depart at 9am from the Pietà ferry station (Riva degli Schiavoni) near Piazza San Marco on Tuesdays, Thursdays, and Saturdays. The *bateau mouche*-like vessels have air-conditioned interiors, but the best seats are upstairs on the roof deck. It's a slow ride through pretty countryside, with numerous stops to visit palatial estates along the way. Lunch is €22-29 extra and the tour is one-way only. Getting back to Venice from Oriago (half day) by bus or Padova (full day) by train is easy and a good excuse to discover another beautiful city.

CLASSES

Cooking

GRITTI EPICUREAN SCHOOL

San Marco, Gritti Palace Hotel, Campo Santa Maria del Giglio 2467; tel. 041/794-611; www. thegrittiepicureanschool.com; Mon.-Fri. 9:30am-8:30pm; €245-290

Learn the secrets of Venetian cuisine at the Gritti Epicurean School where a half-day class begins by choosing seasonal ingredients at the Rialto market with chef Daniele Turco. There's time for a *bacaro* break before heading back to the professionally equipped kitchen to prepare a Venetian lunch. It's a practical slicing-and-dicing introduction to local specialties that often includes fish. The class ends with a well-deserved three-course meal. Participants range from two to eight and courses are held twice a month or by request. All ingredients and wine are included in the price.

Glassmaking

MAURO VIANELLO

Santa Croce 2251; tel. 351/837-8466; www. glasshandmade.it; Mon.-Sat. 10:30am-1:30pm and 2pm-6pm.

Mauro Vianello has been working glass for 30 years and sharing his love for the material for nearly as long. When he's not giving demonstrations he's behind the flame in his small classroom workshop spreading the gospel of glass. Students learn how to manipulate the tools of the lume rod technique and should be comfortable around fire. Experience welding or operating torches is useful but beginners are welcome, too. Classes run one hour per day for a week (€450 plus VAT) or one day (€200 plus VAT) 10am-5pm with a lunch break. By the end of either option you'll be manipulating glass into brightly colored fish, glass candy, and anything else you can imagine. If you don't have time for a course, Mauro also provides 40-minute demonstrations for €30 or for free if you purchase a piece. (Glass seashells are €120 each.) Courses and demonstrations can be reserved by email in advance.

Accommodations

There's nothing like waking up in Venice, though finding a hotel room can be challenging and more expensive than either Florence or Rome. The influx of visitors combined with limited space means low season only lasts from November to January, when rain and falling temperatures dissuade travelers. Italians migrate to beaches and second homes in July and August and hotels often charge midseason rates. Occupancy and prices are high the rest of the year. Advance reservations are essential at peak times like *Carnevale* in February, the Venice Film Festival in September, and major holidays.

Fortunately, hotels aren't the only option. B&Bs and self-catering apartments provide convenient alternatives for travelers who enjoy staying with locals or prefer the independent approach. Many religious institutions also offer accommodation at relatively affordable prices. Rooms are clean and simple, but expect a curfew and little charm. The city's hostels (several of which are located on the island of Giudecca) aren't just for youthful backpackers and often include cool décor and convenient services at significantly lower prices.

Whatever option you choose, it will likely be small. Space comes at a premium in a city where most buildings are several hundred years old. There are five-star exceptions, but these are costly and not always stylish. Many rooms around the city suffer from flamboyant furnishings, gilded headboards, and ugly wallpaper. On the bright side, romantic views of canals, rooftop terraces, and secluded courtyards make up for inconveniences like the absence of elevators (rare except in large establishments) or weak Wi-Fi. If stairs are a problem, check what floor you're on before booking.

San Marco has the largest concentration of hotels but can be a hassle to reach with luggage. It's also the busiest *sestiere,* which

means that you may prefer staying in more intimate neighborhoods like **Dorsoduro** or **Cannaregio.** Of course, you can always pay a porter to cart your bags up and down the bridges or ride a water taxi to wherever you need to go. Just make sure you settle on a price before setting off and ask reception to organize the return journey. If you have difficulty finding accommodation in Venice the nearby towns of Mestre and Marghera or farther-away cities like Padova or Vicenza are easy commutes by bus, tram, or train.

SAN MARCO
Under €100
★ HOTEL LOCANDA FIORITA
Campiello Novo 3457a; tel. 041/523-4754; www. locandafiorita.com; €90-105 d
The flowered facade of Hotel Locanda Fiorita looks out onto a miniature square around the corner from the bustle of Campo Santo Stefano. It's a delightful oasis to come home to and hosts Alessandra and Paolo make it even more enjoyable. Rooms have the right amount of baroque along with dark wooden floors, exposed beams, and earth-toned furnishings that soothe the eye. Rooms 1 and 10 each have their own shaded terrace.

SETTIMO CIELO B&B
Campiello Santo Stefano 3470; tel. 342/636-2581; www.settimocielo-venice.com; €100 d
Settimo Cielo B&B does have flamboyant Venetian style and ornate furniture, but they just seem to work here. This eclectically styled B&B on the edge of Campo Santo Stefano is secluded enough to guarantee a good night's sleep and central enough to reach any *sestiere* in the city in less than 15 minutes. The complimentary breakfast is closer to a banquet than a buffet. The only inconvenience is the stairs for anyone staying on the third floor.

Best Accommodations

★ **Hotel Locanda Fiorita:** Five-star service and comfort at a one-star hotel in the heart of San Marco (page 357).

★ **Hotel Galleria:** This affordable option has helpful hosts, antique furnishings, and views of the Grand Canal (page 359).

★ **Pensione Accademia:** An affordable, hospitable option in a 17th-century *palazzo* that retains all its charm and boasts a peaceful garden (page 359).

★ **Cà del Forno:** Waking up inside a real Venetian home has its advantages, especially if that home is in a 15th-century *palazzo* and belongs to part-time chef Maria Grazie (page 360).

★ **Hotel Metropole:** No two rooms are alike at this stylish hotel, which has a canal-side entrance and a Michelin-starred restaurant (page 361).

★ **Generator Hostel:** The coolest hostel in Venice is located in a former granary complete with canal views and free walking tours (page 361).

€100-200
FLORA

Calle dei Bergamaschi 2283a; tel. 041/520-5844; www.hotelflora.it; €170 d

None of the 40 rooms at Flora are the same. Each has custom furniture, tapestries, and Murano glass fittings. The hotel gives off a worldly atmosphere and has been run by the same family for over half a century. Children are particularly welcome and strollers, high chairs, and cots are all available at no extra charge. The highlight of the hotel is the lovely garden where breakfast is served and guests relax in bucolic tranquility.

HOTEL VIOLINO D'ORO

Campiello Barbozzi 2091; tel. 041/277-0841; www.violinodoro.com; €180 d

Prices can range widely depending on your view at Hotel Violino d'Oro. If you come during the low season, ask for a room overlooking the *Campiello* or San Marco Canal. You can sometimes find real bargains at this hotel, which is classically furnished in tones of gold, ivory, and blue.

Over €300
GRITTI PALACE HOTEL

Campo Santa Maria del Giglio 2467; tel. 041/794-611; www.thegrittipalace.com; €615 d

The Gritti Palace Hotel is no ordinary hotel. It's *the* hotel. This is the only 15th-century *palazzo* Churchill, Hemingway, Garbo, Stravinsky, and a long list of 20th-century legends would consider when in Venice. Yes, there are five-star rivals, but the Gritti does luxury without trying. The €36 million restoration in 2013 has only made things better, and staying here on the edge of the Grand Canal could become the highlight of your entire trip. It's like entering the home of a Venetian aristocrat with plush old-world furnishings in every room and a well-mannered staff who know what you want before you do. It's not a bargain but you get everything you pay for and a lot more.

DORSODURO
Under €100
CA SANTO SPIRITO

Rio Terra Saloni 94; tel. 393/852-6854; www.casasantospirito.it; €90-100 d

This intimate hotel has five tastefully decorated rooms that feel a lot like home. Alessandro and Veronica provide a warm welcome and make sure travelers have everything they need to enjoy the city. Air-conditioning and a full continental breakfast are included. The hotel is near the secluded tip of Dorsoduro, which guarantees a quiet night's sleep.

€100-200
★ HOTEL GALLERIA

Rio Terrà Foscarini 878; tel. 041/523-2489; www. hotelgalleria.it; €100-130 d

Affordable accommodation overlooking the Grand Canal is hard to come by, but views that won't break the bank are available at Hotel Galleria. Six of the nine rooms in the hotel face the water and all are decorated with functional antique furnishings. Breakfast in bed can be arranged with Luciano and Stefano, who will happily recommend bars or restaurants and gladly recount the history of their city.

★ PENSIONE ACCADEMIA

Fondamenta Bollani 1058; tel. 041/521-0188; www. pensioneaccademia.it; €130-170 d

Pensione Accademia feels like a five-star hotel at a fraction of the price. It's run by the Salmaso family, who live and breathe hospitality and have been welcoming guests for decades. The 17th-century *palazzo* has retained all its appeal and what rooms lack in size they make up for in charm. The communal hall and garden are great for recovering from a day on the streets and the front desk can assist with dinner reservations and theater tickets, as well as arrange for chilled *prosecco* and roses to be waiting upon arrival.

€200-300
HOTEL MORESCO

Fondamenta del Passamonte 3499; tel. 041/244-0202; www.hotelmorescovenice.com; €190-220 d

They understand the importance of first impressions at the Hotel Moresco, where the staff is welcoming and prepared to go the extra kilometer for guests. The hotel is a short distance from the train station and can easily be reached on foot or by water taxi. Each of the 23 elegantly furnished rooms have oak flooring, soundproofed windows, and modern bathrooms. The garden and study are pleasant places to relax after a day exploring the city.

CA' PISANI HOTEL

Rio Terrà Foscarini 979a; tel. 041/240-1411; www. capisanihotel.it; €200-240 d

Ca' Pisani Hotel mixes modern with art deco design two minutes from the Ponte dell'Accademia. All 29 rooms are decorated with original 1930s furnishings and come in a number of sizes including family rooms and junior suites. The small restaurant and wine bar offer the perfect end to a long day of sightseeing.

Over €300
CA' MARIA ADELE

Rio Terrà Catecumeno 111; tel. 041/520-3078; www. camariaadele.it; €330 d

Ca' Maria Adele offers a variety of styles and prices. These include ornate deluxe rooms fit for an opera singer and five themed rooms, like the *Doge's* Room (for anyone who likes red) and the Marco Polo Oriental Room.

SAN POLO AND SANTA CROCE
Under €100
HOTEL AL PONTE MOCENIGO

Santa Croce, Fondamenta Mocenigo 2063; tel. 041/524-4797; www.alpontemocenigo.com; €95 d

It's not the number of stars that matters, but the experience, and Hotel Al Ponte Mocenigo delivers in that respect. The décor reflects the fact you're in Venice without going over the top, and the little courtyard where breakfast is served is a great spot to start the day. The Grand Canal is a short walk away and there are dozens of good, reasonably priced restaurants nearby.

€100-200

PENSIONE GUERRATO

San Polo, Calle Drio La Scimia 240a;
tel. 041/522-7131; www.hotelguerrato.com; €110 d

Pensione Guerrato is a one-star hotel with personality. Most of the furniture in this 20-room *pensione* is secondhand, making the 13th-century *palazzo* feel like home. There's a *vaporetto* station five minutes away and plenty of action in the surrounding streets, so it can get loud during the summer when local bars stay open late. Rooms are on the third floor and several overlook the Grand Canal. There's no elevator and Wi-Fi only works in the lobby, but proud owner Roberto Zammattio and his warm and genuine staff make up for any minor drawbacks.

★ CÀ DEL FORNO

San Polo, Calle del Forno 1421a; tel. 041/523-7024; €120 d

If you're Italian you might recognize Maria Grazie Calò from her former appearances on popular cooking shows; if you're not you'll just be happy she prepares breakfast at Cà del Forno. The B&B she runs on the second floor of a 15th-century *palazzo* near the Rialto is a classic Venetian home with high ceilings, antique furnishings, and oil paintings on every wall. There are three double rooms, two of which can be converted into triples or quads, with private baths and pleasant views. The price is excellent for Venice and the warm welcome is just what you need after a day meandering through the city.

LA VILLEGGIATURA

San Polo, Calle dei Botteri 1569; tel. 041/524-4673; www.lavilleggiatura.it; €140-160 d

At La Villeggiatura, B&B rooms are as large as hotel rooms. There may not be a great view and the outside of the *palazzo* could use a paint job, but the inside is immaculate and the six rooms on the third floor are spacious (especially Casanova and *Doge*), well decorated, and all come with king-size beds. Rates vary according to the season but children under nine stay for free all year long.

CANNAREGIO

Under €100

WE CROCIFERI

Campo dei Gesuiti 4878; tel. 041/528-6103; www. we-gastameco.com; €80 d

We Crociferi provides student housing inside a former monastery throughout the year and welcomes everyone from July 15 to August 15. It's comfortable, clean, includes breakfast at the adjacent bar and restaurant, and is located on a lovely square. Rooms and apartments have en suite bathrooms with showers, or you can book a bed in a shared room (€40). There's a major *vaporetto* station less than two minutes away that connects the city with the islands of Murano and Burano.

€100-200

LOCANDA AI SANTI APOSTOLI

Campo Santi Apostoli 4391a; tel. 041/241-1652; www. locandasantiapostoli.com, €120 d

Locanda ai Santi Apostoli is a reliable three-star hotel overlooking the Grand Canal. The 11 rooms are located on the third floor of a historic *palazzo* on the main street in Cannaregio that makes finding the hotel and reaching other parts of the city easy. Rooms are large and nicely decorated.

PONTE CHIODO

Calle de la Racheta 3749; tel. 041/241-3935; www. pontechiodo.it; €125 d

Ponte Chiodo overlooks a canal minutes away from the best *bacari* and nightlife in the neighborhood. The guesthouse provides Wi-Fi, air-conditioning, and breakfast pastries supplied by a local bakery. There's a delightful garden out back, a railless bridge out front, and an owner inside always willing to talk Venice.

CASTELLO

Under €100

ISTITUTO SAN GIUSEPPE

Calle al Ponte della Guerra 5402; tel. 041/522-5352; www.sangiuseppecaburlotto.it; €80 d

Istituto San Giuseppe is simple, clean, and guarantees a good night's sleep. This comfortable religious residence with 14 rooms has an early curfew and if you're not back by 10pm you'll have some explaining to do to the monks.

B&B SAN MARCO

Fondamenta San Giorgio Schiavoni 3385;
tel. 041/522-7589; www.realvenice.it; €90 d
The best thing about B&B San Marco are the hosts, Marco and Alice, who go out of their way to welcome guests. The three rooms of this intimate B&B are large and well decorated and have views of rooftops and canals. Only one has an en suite bath, so book ahead if you don't like sharing. Breakfast is served in the kitchen and consists of Nutella, fresh bread, coffee, fruit juice, and homemade surprises.

€100-200
FORESTERIA VALDESE

Calle della Madoneta 5170; tel. 041/528-6797; www.
foresteriavenezia.it; €120 d, dormitory €35
Foresteria Valdese, one of Venice's religious accommodations, is run by Italian Methodists who converted an 18th-century *palazzo* into a 14-room guesthouse. Rooms range from private doubles with en suite bathrooms and canal views to beds in one of two ground-floor dormitories. These are often filled with schoolchildren and youth groups who are quiet at night but vivacious during the day. There's no curfew, complimentary breakfast is served 8am-9:15am, and multiple-night stays are discounted.

€200-300
★ HOTEL METROPOLE

Riva degli Schiavone 4149; tel. 041/520-5044; www.
hotelmetropole.com; €250 d
Hotel Metropole is a stylish hotel a short walk from Piazza San Marco. No two rooms are the same at this hotel, which looks out on the lagoon and has a canal entrance for making dramatic entries. Doubles, suites, and deluxe rooms are decorated with elegant period furnishings, velvet curtains, rare books, and chandeliers. It's all done tastefully and provides a wonderfully romantic atmosphere. The concierge can handle nearly any request including currency exchange, daily newspaper delivery, babysitting, breakfast in bed, and dry-cleaning. The Michelin-starred restaurant inside the hotel serves a modern mix of fusion dishes that confound the eye and surprise the stomach. Tea is served in the bar every afternoon and live music played every evening.

GIUDECCA
Under €100
★ GENERATOR HOSTEL

Fondamenta Zitelle 86; tel. 041/877-8288; www.
generatorhostels.com; €20 per bed in shared room,
€80 d
Generator is cool. The interior of this former granary feels more like a club, and the bar and lounge areas are perfect for recounting Venetian adventures with travelers from all over the world. There are mixed and female-only rooms of different dimensions with modern and comfortable furnishings. Several cozy double rooms are also located in the attic and look out onto the Canale della Giudecca. The hostel offers complimentary Wi-Fi, 24-hour reception, a restaurant, and free daily walking tours of the neighborhood. The buffet breakfast is served 7am-10am but isn't particularly appetizing. You're better off with a cappuccino and pastry from **Majer** (Fondamenta Sant'Eufemia 4611 tel. 041/521-1162; daily 9am-11pm) down the Fondamenta Zitelle near the Palanca *vaporetto* stop.

Getting to Giudecca requires a ferry and the 2, 4.1, 4.2, and N serve the island's five stations. A single ticket is €7.50 but you're better off opting for a daily (€20) or multiday pass. Once you ride one *vaporetto* you'll want to ride others and staying on the island won't seem like such a big inconvenience.

Information and Services

VISITOR INFORMATION

Venezia Unica (www.veneziaunica.it; tel. 041/2424; daily 9am-6pm for live operators and 24/7 for recorded info) is the city's tourist official department and provides information about transportation, cultural events, and Venezia Unica Cards. You can purchase tickets to many events online, by phone or at one of several tourist offices around the city. The **Info Point** (daily 7am-9pm) outside Santa Lucia train station sells museum and transport passes; if the office is too crowded you can use the automated machines near the Grand Canal. A second **Info Point** (daily 9am-7pm) is located inside Museo Correr in Piazza San Marco.

There are additional offices in **Piazzale Roma** (daily 9:30am-3:30pm) and inside the arrivals hall at **Marco Polo Airport** (daily 9am-8pm). During the summer an info point also operates on the **Lido** (Gran Viale 6a; daily 9am-noon and 3pm-6pm).

TRAVELER SERVICES

Luggage Storage

There are a dozen luggage storage facilities around Venice. There's one inside the **train station** (www.grandistazioni.it; daily 6am-11pm) near platform 1 on the right as you enter the station. The first five hours is €6; it's €0.90 for the 6th-12th hour and €0.40 each additional hour after that.

Trasbagagli (tel. 041/523-1107; www.trasbagagli.it; daily 7:30am-7:30pm) has several locations including one in Piazzale Roma that charges €5 per item for 3 hours and €7 the entire day. They also deliver luggage to and from the airport if necessary.

Stow Your Bags (Cannaregio, Calle dello Spenzer 193 and San Marco, Calle de l'Orso 5512a; www.stowyourbags.com; daily 7am-11pm) provides reliable automated service that can be reserved online in advance. Most hotels will hold bags before check-in and after checkout.

Laundry

There are fewer laundromats in Venice than Rome or Florence and doing a load here is more expensive.

LAVENDERIA SELF SERVICE

Santa Croce, Calle Sechera 665a; tel. 346/972-5446; daily 7am-11pm

Lavenderia Self Service is located near the train station. Machines have several programs (hot, warm, cold, delicate), and a wash cycle is €8 with detergent available for €2 a pack. Drying is another €8 and an automated cash point manages everything. You can wait inside or at the bar next door.

BIO PULISECCO EVER CLEAN

San Polo, Calle Drio Le Carampane 1535; tel. 041/718-414

Bio Pulisecco Ever Clean can remedy any dry-cleaning emergencies and provides professional, same-day service.

Lost and Found

There's always hope if you've lost something in Venice. Objects forgotten on ferries are stored for seven days inside the **ACTV lost and found office** (Santa Croce; tel. 041/272-2179; daily 7:30am-7:30pm) in Piazzale Roma on the ground floor of the city parking garage. After that items are transferred to the **central office** (tel. 041/274-8225; www.comune.venezia.it; weekdays 9am-1pm). The city issues a monthly online list of objects with the date and location they were found. You can also try the **airport lost and found** (tel. 041/260-6436) in the arrivals terminal and the **Vigili Urbani** (Piazzale Roma; tel. 041/522-4576). Found items that aren't retrieved are eventually sold at auction.

Foreign Consulates

Report lost or stolen passports to the **U.S. Consulate** in Milan (tel. 02/290-351;

Mon.-Fri. 9:30am-12:30pm). They can also help with any emergencies you may encounter.

HEALTH AND SAFETY
Emergency Numbers
For medical emergencies dial the **118** hotline or the **Guardia Medica Turistica** (Ca' Savio; tel. 041/530-0874), which is dedicated entirely to diagnosing the ailments of visitors. For emergencies requiring police assistance call **112**.

Police
Report crimes at the **Police Headquarters** (Ponte della Liberta; tel. 041/271-5511) in Santa Croce near the train station or any of the smaller **precincts** like the one in Castello (Fondamenta San Lorenzo 5053) opposite Campo San Lorenzo. The police emergency number is **113**. Violent crime is low in Venice, and pickpockets are surprisingly rare for a city that attracts so many tourists.

Hospitals and Pharmacies
If you need a hospital, go to **Ospedale Fatebenefratalli** (Cannaregio, Fondamenta Madonna dell'Orto 3458; tel. 041/783-111; www.fatebenefratelli.it; 24/7) or **Hospital SS Giovanni e Paolo** (Castello 6777; tel. 041/529-4111; www.aulss3.veneto.it). The latter has an emergency room. Make sure to bring your passport and if you or anyone you're traveling with suffers serious injury inform the consulate as soon as possible.

There are plenty of pharmacies around Venice and you'll find one in each of the *sestiere* neighborhoods including **Farmacia Santa Lucia** (Cannaregio, Lista di Spagna 122; tel. 041/716-332; Mon.-Sat. 8:30am-8pm and Sun. 9am-1pm) near the train station and **Farmacia San Polo** (San Polo, Campo San Polo; tel. 041/522-3527; Mon.-Fri. 9am-1pm and 3:30pm-7:30pm, Sat. 9am-12:45pm). Most are located on busy streets and squares, and recognizable by their green neon cross. Take a ticket at the entrance and wait until your number is called.

COMMUNICATIONS
Wi-Fi
Venice (www.cittadinanzadigitale.it) has installed wireless infrastructure around the city, Lido, and lagoon islands. Most large squares and major monuments are now covered by over 200 hotspots that provide limited free access. You can supplement this with the **Venezia Unica Card** (www.veneziaunica.it) and 24 hours of connectivity for €5. Many hotels, restaurants, and bars also offer free Wi-Fi access, but if you're feeling nostalgic for a copy shop with Internet access or want some digital photos printed visit **E Copie da Toni** (Castello, Calle del Pistor 5645; tel. 041/522-5100; Mon.-Fri. 9:30am-1pm and 3pm-6pm).

Transportation

GETTING THERE
Air
UK travelers can choose daily departures with EasyJet (www.easyjet.com) and Ryan Air (www.ryanair.com) that often land at **Treviso Airport** (TSF) 30 minutes by car and an hour on public transport from Venice.

AEROPORTO DI VENEZIA
VCE; Viale Galileo Galilei 30; tel. 041/260-6111; www. veniceairport.it

Aeroporto di Venezia is a medium-sized airport with runways overlooking the lagoon that guarantee dramatic takeoffs and landings. There are few direct flights from North America and none from Australia, New Zealand, or South Africa, but many connecting flights from across Europe. The newly renovated interior is easy to navigate and lines move quickly. The well-organized arrivals hall provides passengers with clear indications for reaching Venice by bus, taxi, or boat. There's also a **tourist office** where travel cards and maps are available. Wi-Fi access is limited and requires registration. There are few scheduled flights from Rome and none from Florence.

The cheapest connection to Venice from the airport is by **bus.** The **ATVO booth** in the arrivals hall sells **Airport Shuttle** (tel. 042/159-4671; www.atvo.it; €8 one-way, €15 round-trip) tickets and the ride takes 20 minutes. Clearly marked buses are waiting outside and operate daily 5:20am-12:20am. Passengers are dropped off in Piazzale Roma from where you can walk or catch a *vaporetto* ferry.

The most exciting way to reach Venice from the airport is by water, and you can buy tickets from the same ATVO booth. **Alilaguna** (tel. 041/240-1701; www.alilaguna.it) operates four **ferry** lines (blue, orange, red, and green) with convenient daily service to stops around the city including San Marco, Rialto, Murano, and Burano. One-way tickets are €15 (€27 round-trip) and allow for one suitcase and one carry-on item with a €3 surcharge for extra bags. Ferries operate daily 7:45am-12:20am and there are several departures per hour.

The fastest and most dramatic aquatic entry to the city is by **water taxi,** of which there are a number of private companies to choose from. **Consorzio Motoscalfi** (tel. 041/522-2303; www.motoscafivenezia.it) is a consortium of water taxis that operate 24 hours a day and can drop you off anywhere you like. A ride for up to 10 passengers and 10 bags to the Santa Lucia train station is €115. To take either a public ferry or private taxi follow the signs for **water transport** and walk to the ferry terminal five minutes from the arrivals hall.

Call **RadioTaxi** (tel. 041/5964; www.radiotaxivenezia.com) or head to their office in the arrivals hall if you prefer arriving by land. Fares from the airport to Venice are fixed at €40. Taxis do not operate within the city; they'll drop you off in Piazzale di Roma near the train station.

Train

Getting to Venice from Rome or Florence is a pleasant journey on board high-speed trains that depart regularly from both cities. **Italo** (www.italo.it) and **Trenitalia** (www.trenitalia.it) provide affordable and comfortable service to Venice.

Trains terminate at **Santa Lucia** station, from where the city is accessible on foot. Exiting Santa Lucia train station and seeing the Grand Canal for the first time is one of the most dramatic entrances you can make in a city. Along the canal front are automated machines and ticket offices selling *vaporetto* passes for travelers wishing to make an immediate aquatic getaway. Otherwise there are three choices: You can turn right toward Piazzale Roma and Dorsoduro, turn left toward Cannaregio, or cross the Ponte degli Scalzi and enter the Santa Croce neighborhood.

From Rome: Italo (www.italo.it) and **Trenitalia** (www.trenitalia.it) high-speed trains from Rome Termini and Tiburtina stations to Venice take less than four hours and cost as little as €69 if reserved in advance. There are dozens of daily departures. Slower regional service costs half as much but takes twice as long.

From Florence: Trains from Florence Stazione Santa Maria Novella station to Venice take less than two hours and cost as little as €39. All high-speed trains headed to Venice from Rome stop in Florence. Frequent special offers are publicized to email subscribers and on the websites of both rail operators.

Car

The drive to Venice from Rome or Florence is straightforward and can be undertaken on two-lane modern highways. Driving does take longer than train and comes with the added expense of tolls, fuel, and the occasional frustration of traffic jams. The journey ends once you've crossed the Ponte della Libertà, where cars must be parked in one of several easily accessed indoor garages or outdoor lots. Prices at the **Tronchetto Parking Lot** (Isola Novo di Tronchetto 33m; tel. 041/520-7555; www. tronchettoparking.it; 24/7) are €21 per day and prices are higher at the garages around Piazzale Roma. A **People Mover** (daily 7am-11pm, €1.50) shuttles visitors from Tronchetto to Piazzale Roma where the city really begins.

Parking can be difficult during special events like *Carnevale* or the Venice Film Festival. A thrifty alternative is to park in the nearby town of **Mestre** on the mainland where rates are about half the price and travelers can reach Venice by bus or train in 15 minutes. If you want to save on rental fees, leave the driving to someone else, and make some new acquaintances try Italian **car sharing** (www.blablacar.it).

From Rome: The route from Rome to Venice is clearly indicated and consists mostly of two-lane highways with a speed limit of 80mph (130kph). Follow signs for Firenze (Florence) along the **A1** highway. The journey to Florence is 234 miles (377 kilometers) and takes a little over three hours. Once you reach the city follow the directions below.

From Florence: If you're parked in Florence's historic center, cross the Arno and continue west along the river. You'll eventually see signs for the **A1** highway and should follow indications to Bologna. Once you reach

that city take the **A13** all the way to Padua and complete the journey along the **A57** that runs directly to Venice. The entire journey is 162 miles (260 kilometers), a distance that can be driven in 2.5 hours.

Part of the journey crosses the Apennine Mountains that run up and down the Italian peninsula and there are many tunnels, curves, and inclines. Be prepared for occasional roadwork and possible traffic jams during the summer. There are several alternative routes in case you prefer a longer and slower drive.

Bus

Passengers arriving by bus are deposited at the **Tronchetto Bus Terminal,** a man-made island on the western edge of the city. Fortunately, the efficient **People Mover** (tel. 041/272-7211; www.peoplemover.avmspa.it; daily 7am-11pm; €1.50) shuttles passengers into and out of the city in minutes and there are continuous departures.

From Rome: The bus journey from Tiburtina station in Rome to Venice can last over eight hours, but tickets are cheap (from €26). You can compare fares on the **Omio** (www.omio.com) travel planner. There are frequent departures for Venice.

From Florence: Flixbus and Eurolines

Santa Lucia train station

operate from Piazzale Montelungo near Santa Maria Novella station. Journey time is around four hours and one-way tickets start at €16. Flixbus also carries bikes for €9. Buses depart a dozen times per day.

Boat

You'd think a city surrounded by water is best reached by water, but that isn't always practical. It's true that cruise ships arrive every day and disgorge thousands of passengers, but none of these stop in Rome or Florence. The only other alternative would be hiring a vessel, which is costly and time-consuming. It's best therefore to save the boats for once you arrive in Venice.

GETTING AROUND

The two most common ways of exploring Venice are by foot or *vaporetto*. Although it's small, you're likely to walk more in Venice than Rome or Florence. When you tire, board a boat and discover the city from a different angle. The canals are full of different types of boats loading and unloading goods and passengers throughout the day. There are three principle modes of water transportation in Venice: *vaporetto, traghetto,* and water taxi.

Vaporetto

Public transportation is unique, necessary, and rewarding in Venice. It comprises 24 **ACTV** (tel. 041/2424; actv.avmspa.it) ferry lines that are served by *vaporetti* (ferry boats). Each neighborhood has a handful of *vaporetto* stations and digital signs indicate how long commuters must wait for the next boat. *Vaporetti* on the main routes arrive every 20 minutes, so waiting time is minimal. Service is efficient and makes getting around Venice fast and fun. Stations have color-coded maps that can also be downloaded from the ACTV website. Tickets are expensive for tourists (locals pay a different rate) because boats are harder to maintain than buses. They also require a skilled captain to steer and a crew member to help passengers on and off. *Vaporetti* are the most common way of

getting around Venice. These omnipresent ferries run up and down the Grand Canal, circumnavigate the city, and connect it with outlying islands in the lagoon. Boats come in varying sizes and several seasonal routes are added during the summer. All have indoor seating and the 2, 4.1, 4.2, 5.1, 5.2, 12, and 13 lines have outdoor seats, which you should try to grab.

Always validate tickets upon first usage, enter water stops through the designated entrance, and allow passengers to disembark before boarding. It can get chilly riding *vaporetti* in early spring and late autumn or even at night during the summer, so have a scarf and hat handy.

Tickets can be purchased at larger stations such as Piazzale di Roma just over the Ponte della Costituzione bridge, or outside the train station. There are many booths, as well as automated vending machines, so lines are short. Some newsstands also sell tickets. You can choose from **single tickets** (€8/75 minutes), **24-hour** (€20), **48-hour** (€30), **72-hour** (€40), and **7-day** (€60) passes. These must be validated at the machines outside each station and passengers may be asked to show their passes by controllers who issue on-the-spot fines of up to €100. Once validated for the first time, you have unlimited travel possibilities until your time limit runs out. Passes do not cover the ferries that operate to and from the airport, which must be purchased separately. Children under 6 travel for free and there are discounts for 6- to 29-year-olds with the Rolling Venice Card.

Vaporetti are great fun and riding them without a destination is always a pleasure. If you want to get a good look at Venice, the **4.1, 4.2, 5.1,** and **5.2** lines circumnavigate the city and terminate in **Fondamente Nuove** where you can transfer onto larger ferries heading to Murano, Burano, and Torcello. Lines **1** and **2** go up and down the Grand Canal and you can ride either from Piazzale Roma to San Marco or vice versa in under 30 minutes.

Vaporetti are usually crowded in summer and have a capacity of up to 250 depending on

Venetian Vocabulary

Geography combined with foreign linguistic influences have formed a unique dialect in Venice that's used to describe the city's unusual urban landscape. The faster you absorb this vocabulary the easier it will be to identify different aspects of the Venetian cityscape and appreciate the beauty of Venice.

- *Calle, calleta:* Street, alley, or thoroughfare that can vary substantially in length and width. The former are wider than the latter.

- *Campo, campielo:* Unevenly shaped square of varying proportions. *Campo* means *field*, and these spaces were originally grassy meadows where food was grown and animals grazed. Most have been paved over and today provide visual and physical relief from the narrow *calle*. A *campielo* is a smaller version of a *campo*.

- *Fondamenta:* Any *calle* located next to a canal or *rio*. *Fondazione* means *foundation*, and these streets helped reinforce the islands and allow for urbanization. They can feature stone or iron railings—or none at all—and have stairs for making getting on and off boats easier. *Fondamente* (plural) are often lined with shops, bars, and restaurants.

- *Ca':* Short for *casa* (house) and used to indicate important residences like the Ca' d'Oro or Ca' Rezzonico. The word is usually followed by a family name indicating the original residents.

- *Corte:* A small dead-end courtyard surrounded by residential buildings. They're generally reached through a *sotoportego* or *calleta* and are the center of micro-neighborhoods where Venetians once spent their days washing, sewing, preparing meals, and socializing.

- *Pietra d'Istria:* Dense, impermeable limestone quarried from the Istria peninsula and an essential material in the construction of Venice. Used to build and decorate *calle*, bridges, canals, churches, homes, and palaces.

- *Rio:* Small canal. There are hundreds throughout the city that function both to enhance communication and permit the tides to flow freely through the city and prevent stagnation.

- *Rio Terrà:* Any canal that's been filled in and transformed into a street.

- *Riva:* Wide walkway bordering the Grand Canal or San Marco Canal.

- *Sestiere:* Historic neighborhood or district. There are six in Venice and they are symbolically represented by the six metal strips decorating the prow of every gondola.

- *Sotoportego:* Underpass connecting *calle, campi,* or *fondamente*. These were usually created by removing the ground floor of houses and often contain small shrines or sacred images of the Virgin Mary and other popular saints.

the boat. Each line has different hours but service usually starts around 6am and continues until midnight. There's also a night service (N) that runs 11:30pm-5am and serves Grand Canal and Lido stations.

Water Taxi

Water taxis are the quicker, more expensive way of getting around Venice. These slick motorboats zip passengers along the canals in style. Pickup can be arranged in advance or simply by going to the nearest water taxi station. There are several at Piazzale Roma, Piazza San Marco, and other locations around the city.

Prices depend on distance, time, and operator. A one-hour tour for four passengers ranges from €150-250. You can decide any itinerary you like with your driver and should ask to explore quieter canals. A ride from Santa Lucia station to Piazza San Marco is €65 for 1-4 passengers, while a trip to the airport is €70-115. Additional passengers are charged €6 each.

The boats are extremely comfortable and resemble miniature floating limousines, with leather seats, wood paneling, and sunroofs that can be slid open or closed depending on the weather. Water taxis are much smaller than *vaporetti* and are susceptible to waves, especially when going down the Grand Canal or out into the open lagoon. Some drivers will point out interesting sights but most are happy to leave passengers to themselves and periodically check their smartphones.

Boats can be reserved from **Water Taxi Venice** (tel. 342/106-8412; www.consorziovezeniafutura.it) or **Acqua Taxi Venezia** (tel. 351/2026881; www.taxiserviceh24.com), which is slightly cheaper.

You can always recognize licensed water taxis by their yellow stripe and clearly marked license number. Avoid unlicensed operators posing as official drivers who charge significantly higher rates. Also, remember tipping is not required.

Traghetto

Private gondola rides, which can seat up to six passengers, are expensive (the rate is fixed at €80 for a 40-minute ride), but you can save money by taking advantage of the *traghetti* (gondola ferries; Mon.-Sat. 7:30am-7pm and Sun. 9am-7pm; €2) that operate on the Grand Canal. A ride lasts five minutes and is a fun and practical way to get from one neighborhood to another. Dozens of these ferry points once operated, but today there are only three left—and it's worth riding them all. They can be boarded at the docks near Santa Maria del Giglio opposite the Guggenheim, San Tomà halfway between Ponte dell'Accademia and the Rialto, and next to the covered fish market near the Rialto. Locals usually stand during the crossing, but you can also sit on the side railing and watch as two gondoliers skillfully oar their way from one bank to the other.

Bus and Tram

The only place you'll see buses or trams (€1.50 or €3 on board) in Venice is Piazzale Roma, just over the Ponte della Costituzione bridge from the train station. They are primarily used by locals commuting from the mainland town of Mestre and tourists taking the airport shuttle (€15) but are not for getting around Venice itself. **Tickets** are available from automated machines near the modern awning in the center of the *piazza* as well as newsstands and *tabacchi* shops.

Day Trips

There are dozens of islands and countless islets in the Venice Lagoon, but Murano, Burano, and Torcello are the most popular destinations. Each has its own distinct personality and all three can be visited in a day by *vaporetto*. **Murano** is the closest, largest, and most populated. It's famous for glass and could be mistaken for Venice's younger brother. The other two islands are farther away and smaller. **Burano,** known for lace production, is a feast for the eyes and stomach. It's covered with brightly painted houses where fishermen and knitting ladies still reside. **Torcello** is the greenest and least visited, and retains traces of Middle Age glory and American literary greatness.

Murano, Burano, and Torcello are usually visited in that order, but you can reverse it, or limit yourself to one or two islands. Torcello often gets skipped. If you visit all three, it's hard not to pick a favorite. You can also continue exploring other directions of the lagoon toward the beaches of the **Lido,** where the Venice Film Festival is held and where bike riding is permitted.

As with most sights in Venice, sights in this section do not require advance reservations, even during COVID outbreaks.

Venice's Lagoon Area

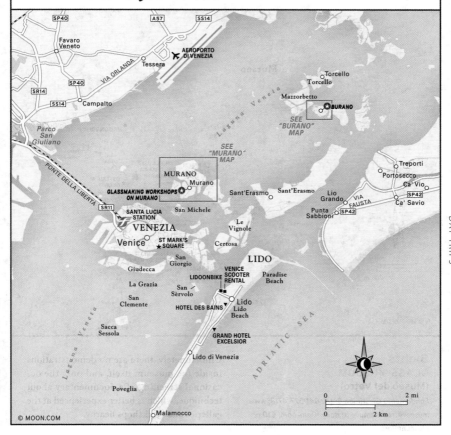

© MOON.COM

MURANO

Murano, synonymous with glassmaking, resembles a miniature Venice. It's a quarter of the size and consists of six separate islands interconnected by canals and bridges. The Canal Grande di Murano splits the town in two and can be crossed at the Ponte Vivarini iron bridge. On the northern side you'll find the Glass Museum and Santa Marta e Donato church. Glass boutiques and souvenir shops line most of the *fondamente* and the farther you walk from these the closer you get to the bucolic residential reality of low-rise housing, pretty pedestrian streets, and vegetable gardens.

The first *vaporetto* stop in Murano is the busiest and where most visitors usually disembark to browse the storefronts and discover how glass is blown. From Colonna station you can walk up Fondamenta dei Vetrai through the center of town and visit lovely little squares where lunch awaits. If you remain on board until the Venier stop you can discover the island from the inside out, get a good look at all the canals, and rub shoulders with locals in Campo San Bernardo.

Murano

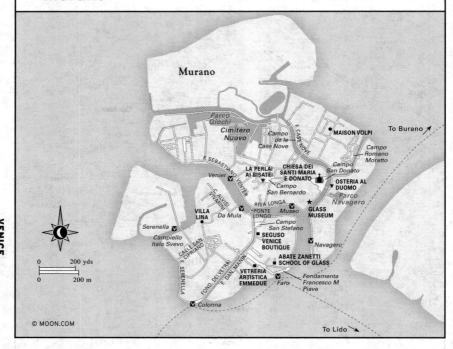

Murano

Parco Giochi
Cimitero Nuovo
Campo de le Case Nove
MAISON VOLPI
To Burano
Campo Romano Moratto
F SEBASTIANO VENIER
F CASE NOVE
Venier
LA PERLA AI BISATEL
CHIESA DEI SANTI MARIA E DONATO
Campo San Donato
OSTERIA AL DUOMO
Campo San Bernardo
Parco Navagero
C. ALVISE VIVARINI
RIVA LONGA
Museo
GLASS MUSEUM
VILLA LINA
Da Mula
PONTE LONGO
Campo San Stefano
Serenella
Campiello Italo Svevo
SEGUSO VENICE BOUTIQUE
Navagero
CALLE SAN CIPRIANO
ABATE ZANETTI SCHOOL OF GLASS
F. SERENELLA
FOND. DE VETRAI
F. DAN MANIN
VETRERIA ARTISTICA EMMEDUE
Faro
Fondamenta Francesco M Piave
Colonna

0   200 yds
0   200 m

© MOON.COM

To Lido

Sights

GLASS MUSEUM

(Museo del Vetro)

*Fondamenta Giustinian 8; tel. 041/527-4718; www.
museovetro.visitmuve.it; daily 10am-6pm; €10 or
Museum Pass*

The Museo del Vetro glass museum is organized chronologically, starting with ancient
Roman glassware. The pieces on display
show how 700 years of Murano glassmaking tradition evolved from the 13th century
to the present. There are frequent exhibitions
of contemporary artists who use glass in creative ways. The collection is located inside one
of Murano's oldest *palazzi* and takes less than
an hour to visit.

Guided tours of the Glass Museum on
Tuesdays and Thursdays at 2:30pm are followed by a live demonstration (€18) at a local
glass school nearby; arrange in advance.

Unfortunately, there are no demonstrations
inside the museum itself, and only the occasional screening of a documentary about
technique, which is better experienced at the
galleries and workshops nearby.

CHIESA DEI SANTI
MARIA E DONATO

*Campo San Donato 11; tel. 041/739-056; Mon.-Sat.
9am-6pm, Sun. 12:30pm-6pm; free*

Unlike most churches in Venice, you can
walk nearly all the way around the exterior
of Chiesa dei Santi Maria e Donato. It feels
like each side is different, and progressive
makeovers since 1141 are probably the cause.
The Gothic facade is imposing but plain and
the only decoration is a relief sculpture of St.
Donatus above the entrance. The side right
is more impressive and lined with windows
set within lovely brick arches that could be

mistaken for 20th-century design. The back of the church, or apse, provides the biggest eyeful, and the double tiers supported by twin arches and intricate brickwork deserve closer inspection.

Inside is nearly as interesting. Besides the remains of a saint you'll find a 12th-century mosaic of the Virgin Mary, a Roman sarcophagus, and an incredible floor that looks too nice to walk on. Mass is held on Monday, Wednesday, and Friday at 6pm and Sunday at 11:15am and 6pm.

TOP EXPERIENCE

★ Glassmaking Shops and Workshops

Glass is an active export trade and not just for the tourists drawn to Murano. The island once housed thousands of glassmakers and there are still hundreds earning their livelihoods from this ancient craft. The Murano version became renowned for its clarity and color thanks to a unique combination of ingredients and the skills of its artisans.

Of the three options below, the first is a working shop where you can see demonstrations as well as purchase glass; the second is purely a shop; and the third is a studio where you can learn to blow glass yourself. Prices for handmade glass pieces vary widely. Please note that most shops do not allow photos.

VETRERIA ARTISTICA EMMEDUE

Calle Miotti 12A; tel. 041/739-503; daily 9am-4:30pm
Murano furnaces combine glass selling with glassmaking demonstrations, allowing visitors to witness the magic moment of glass creation. Vetreria Artistica Emmedue puts on demonstrations nearly continuously for groups who arrive by the boatload. Walk through the narrow entrance to the shop and head straight to the back, where bleacher seating has been set up around the furnaces and you can get a close-up look as glass takes shape. Expert artisans all over the island tend to make miniature horses for audiences, and things are no different here. There's usually a brief explanation in several languages, and once the free demonstration is over visitors are encouraged to ask questions, get a closer look at the tools of the trade, and browse the shop.

SEGUSO VENICE BOUTIQUE

Fondamenta Manin 77; tel. 041/527-5333; daily 9am-1:30pm and 2:30pm-5:30pm
The Seguso family has been blowing glass

VENICE
DAY TRIPS

Canal Grande di Murano

Murano Glass

Glassmaking has existed in the Venice region since antiquity and was largely influenced by the Middle East, where the craft originated. Murano officially became the center of production when the Venetian Republic prohibited glassmaking in Venice in 1291 to avoid fires. It was a lucrative business, and artisans were obliged to live on the island and forbidden to leave without permission for fear they would reveal their secrets to rival cities.

THE MURANO TECHNIQUE

In the 14th century, Murano glassmakers developed new techniques and designs that found receptive overseas markets. The island produced the highest quality in the world by grinding local quartz with soda ash from the eastern Mediterranean. The formula allowed artisans to create a product that could be tinted by adding ground-up coloring agents that were melted into the glass.

GLASSMAKING DEMONSTRATIONS

These days, many of the remaining active furnaces on Murano offer demonstrations that are repeated throughout the day. Many of these are free and some involve a small fee. There's usually a brief explanation of the glassmaking process followed by an artisan skillfully creating a small statuette. Demonstrations last 10-15 minutes, after which visitors are encouraged to visit the adjacent galleries. Prices range widely; it's worth shopping around until you find something you like.

Many demonstrations have a zoo-like atmosphere in which the *maestro* is on display; still, it's interesting to see glass heated to 1,000 degrees and scooped out of an oven like molten honey, then shaped by the hands of a master. If you can't make it to Murano, Lumeart in Burano (page 376) and FGB in Venice (page 343) are also among the best.

for 23 generations and keeping their techniques secret since 1397. Inside their Seguso Venice Boutique are vases, glasses, lampshades, and jewels that mix traditions of the past with a desire to innovate and push the boundaries of glassmaking. The showroom (Fondamenta Venier 29) regularly organizes visits to their nearby factory and other glass-related events.

ABATE ZANETTI
SCHOOL OF GLASS

Calle Briati 8b; tel. 041/273-7711; www.
lascuoladelvetro.it; Mon.-Fri. 9am-1pm and 2pm-6pm
Once you've seen sand heated to a thousand degrees and transformed into glass you may want to try making some yourself. What looks simple, however, isn't—and most glass-blowers have been practicing their craft for decades. To understand what's involved in the process you'll need to go to school, and the best place to do that is the Abate Zanetti School of Glass. Students learn how a furnace

functions and the basics of shaping raw material through marbling and blowing techniques. Most courses are for beginners and last 20 hours over several days, but there are also weekend courses in lampworking (€400) and glassworking (€480) for groups of 4-10 people. Single-day private lessons (€120) are also available and participants get to keep their creations.

Food

Most restaurants in Murano are located along the busy canals, and Fondamenta Manin and Venier are good places to start reading menus.

LA PERLAI AI BISATEI

Campo S. Bernardo 6; tel. 041/739-528; Mon.-Sat.
10am-3pm; €5-10
If you venture down the residential back streets of Murano you'll eventually stumble onto La Perlai ai Bisatei. This neighborhood *osteria* on a quiet square is popular with locals who come for *cicchetti* and conversation.

a glassmaking demonstration

The menu isn't extensive but includes essentials like *spaghetti alle vongole* (spaghetti with clams) and grilled fish. It's a jovial, family-friendly place where glassworkers come for lunch and a half liter of house wine costs €4.

OSTERIA AL DUOMO

Fondamenta Maschio 21; tel. 041/527-4303; daily 11am-10pm; €12-15

Osteria Al Duomo, across the bridge from Maria e Donato church, is a pleasant refuge from the heat. The neat white facade hides a large shaded garden where diners enjoy fish, meat, or pizza prepared in a wood-burning oven.

Accommodations

Murano is the perfect place to retreat to after a busy day of visiting Venice. It's relaxing and quiet and well connected to the city by *vaporetto* ferries. There are several hotels on the island but the majority are of the flowery wallpaper-and-gold-plated-headboard type in need of a makeover. The best option are the B&Bs and residences, which offer just as much service for double the charm.

MAISON VOLPI

Calle Volpi 39; tel. 333/456-7561; www.maisonvolpi. it; €150 d

Maison Volpi is a good self-catering option. This single-family home is tucked away in the heart of a residential neighborhood where few tourists wander. The spacious house covers two floors and the bright rooms are decorated with an abundance of antiques. The luminous kitchen is a cozy place to come home to and looks out on a little garden. The minimum stay is three nights, although the owner will occasionally make exceptions.

VILLA LINA

Calle Dietro gli Orti 12; tel. 041/739-036; www. villalinavenezia.com; €140-200 d

Villa Lina is five minutes from the Colonna *vaporetto* station directly on a canal. The three comfortable rooms inside the pretty pink villa are filled with modern furnishings and each equipped with air-conditioning, Wi-Fi, mini-bar, safe, and a surprisingly small TV. It's a B&B that feels like an intimate hotel. Guests have their own keys and can enjoy the enchanting garden after exploring the town. Breakfast is served on the terrace with a distant view of Venice.

Getting There and Around

Murano can be reached from Venice on the 3, 4.1, 4.2, 7, 12, 13, or N *vaporetto* lines. The **3** (daily 6:15am-7:15pm) departs from Piazzale Roma and stops at the train station before heading directly to Murano. The **4.1** and **4.2** (daily 6:10am-11:22pm) circumnavigate Venice and stop in Fondamente Nuove, from where they set off to Murano. All three lines stop at the seven *vaporetto* stations on Murano and take less than 15 minutes to make the crossing.

★ BURANO

Burano, known for its lace production, is a magical island and pleasant escape from Venice. The photogenic canals and streets are lined with brightly colored houses and shops selling linen, lace, and glass jewelry. Most visitors proceed straight from the ferry dock up Viale Marcello past a concentration of boutiques. The quieter route is to the left along the lagoon to the first canal that splits the island nearly in half.

There are two other canals to stroll along and many lovely streets to explore, complete with drying laundry and stray cats. A bell tower leans perilously next to the church on Piazza Baldassarre Galuppo where the Lace Museum is located. Fishing still plays an important role here in both the economy and the gastronomy. There are hundreds of small fishing boats docked along the canals and three small ports. Burano can be circumnavigated in less than an hour, but it's an island that's hard to leave.

Sights

LACE MUSEUM
(Museo del Merletto)

Piazza Galuppi 187; tel. 041/730-034; Tues.-Sun. 10am-6pm; €5 or Museum Pass

Burano is really about walking and letting your eyes enjoy the scenery, but if you're passionate about lace, visit the Museo del Merletto. The museum explains the tradition, evolution, and commercial importance of lace with a 40-minute documentary and more than 200 intricate patterns. The highlight is watching the little group of skilled ladies working away on new designs and demonstrating an art that is slowly fading.

GIUSEPPE TOSELLI'S HOUSE

Corte del Pistor 275

All the houses on Burano are colorful but Giuseppe Toselli's house stands out. Giuseppe Toselli, or *Bepi* to the islanders, was a former handyman and candy vendor who spent his spare time painting geometric patterns and shapes on his house. The result is something original in an already original town. Although Giuseppe passed away over a decade ago he hasn't been forgotten, and his much-loved facade was recently restored. It's not possible to enter the privately-owned home, but it's the exterior that's worthwhile anyway.

FONDAMENTA CAO MOLECA

The easternmost canal along Fondamenta Cao Moleca has few shops or restaurants but is a good place to soak in the colorful homes Burano is known for. Locals tell different stories about why the houses are brightly painted, but the most common answer has to do with helping returning fishermen locate their homes through morning fog.

Food

It may be impossible to choose a bad restaurant in Burano. They're all more or less good and specialize in fish, which is the most

Burano

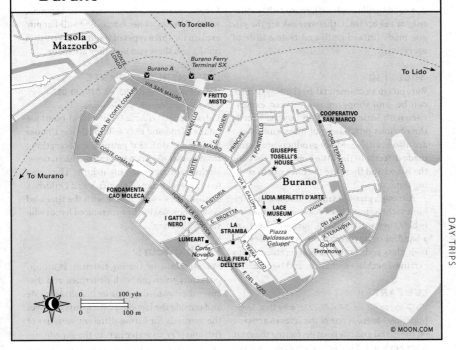

abundant ingredient on the island. Fishermen work hard in Burano and go out five days a week in search of mullet, bream, crustaceans, mollusks, and more. Traditional methods of line and net fishing are still used to supply the island and all of Venice with varieties that you may never have tasted before.

FRITTO MISTO

Fondamenta dei Squeri 312; tel. 041/735-198; daily 9:30am-8:30pm; €12

Fritto Misto is an informal outdoor eatery opposite the ferry landing. Given its location, you'd be right to avoid it out of principle—but that would be unfortunate for your taste buds. The delicately fried shrimp, calamari, and sardines served over fries on an edible plate made of bread are delicious and go great with a cold beer. The menu option includes a drink and a generous plate of lagoon fish for €17. Wait for your order at the counter and then choose a wooden stool in the shade and enjoy the lagoon views.

I GATTO NERO

Via Giudecca 88; tel. 041/730-120; Tues.-Sat. 12:30pm-3pm and 7:30pm-9pm, Sun. 12:30pm-3pm; €14-26

A handful of *trattorie* are concentrated on Via Baldassarre Galuppo that leads to the only *piazza,* but if you ask locals where to eat most will mention I Gatto Nero. It's always busy and the tables overlooking the canal will be occupied unless you arrive early or reserve. Nearly every dish includes fish or crustaceans and the house appetizer is a wonderful way to start a meal. Firsts are a tempting toss-up between *bigoli in salsa* (thick spaghetti-length pasta in sardine sauce) or the rice specialty, *risotto alla Buranella*. Anyone hungry for more can order grilled sole, eel, monkfish, cuttlefish, or sea bream. Otherwise ask for the *griglia mista* (mixed grill) and taste a little of everything.

Shopping

Burano isn't commercial in the way Venice can be, and shopping is a relaxed experience with little pressure on buyers. Lace is the obvious purchase, but glass and masks are also available. Many products are handmade directly in the little boutiques that dot the island and these are the ones worth seeking out.

Although glassblowing is more famous, the lume technique of small-scale jewelry making is how they work glass in Burano. There are a handful of tiny workshops where maestros melt glass rods (at lower temperatures) into earrings, necklaces, charms, and figurines.

LUMEART

Via Giudecca 40; tel. 041/527-2278; daily 11am-5pm
Massimo Mauro is one of the veteran artisans on the island and has been perfecting the craft since boyhood. The compact corner studio of Lumeart is where his wife sells his creations. It's filled with delicate objects born from his imagination and the tools of his trade. Like many expert craftspeople in Venice, Mauro uses the lume technique, which involves melting long, thin rods of colored glass into small objects or jewelry. It requires lower temperatures and less space to undertake than traditional glass blowing.

ALLA FIERA DELL'EST

Rio Terrà del Pizzo 166; tel. 041/527-2234; daily 10am-6:30pm
Alice dei Rossi couldn't decide between glass, felt, papier-mâché, or terra-cotta, so she decided to use them all. She transforms the materials into jewelry and clothes inside Alla Fiera dell'Est, which is painted electric blue on the outside.

LA STRAMBA

Calle della Providenza 270; daily 9:30am-6pm
Fabiola creates masks and lace at La Stramba, which doubles as her home. She will happily explain the three types of traditional Venetian masks and show you how they are made.

LIDIA MERLETTI D'ARTE

Via Baldassarre Galuppi 215; tel. 041/730-052; www. dallalidia.com; daily 9:30am-6:30pm
Lidia Merletti d'Arte is the oldest boutique on the island and only sells local lace. Choose from many different patterns on everything from household linen to handkerchiefs, tablecloths, bedcovers, and nightshirts. They even have several racks of women's and children's clothing. Prices are in line with the time and effort employed by the experienced hands who supply the shop.

Fishing Tours

Pescaturismo, or fishing tourism, is an opportunity to go out with fishermen and discover the day-to-day realities of fishing inside and outside the lagoon. Participants discover the methods for luring different varieties of fish and play an active part in the expedition. Once back on shore you learn how the fish you've caught are prepared and cooked before tasting the results of your labor.

COOPERATIVO SAN MARCO

Via Terranova 215; tel. 041/730-076; www. pescaturismoburano.com
Igor at the Cooperativo San Marco can arrange an excursion. These usually last 2-3 hours and leave daily at 10am. Boats are open and 26-32 feet (8-10 meters) long during the summer and slightly larger and covered in winter. This initiative, started in 2012 by the cooperative, shares the fishing traditions of the island with visitors. Although it is primarily aimed at larger groups, Igor will happily give you a quote on smaller groups. A fishing tour for four is around €300. For an extra

---

1: colorful Burano **2:** Ponte del Diavolo in Torcello
3: Chiesa dei Santi Maria e Donato in Murano
4: Lido Beach

€25pp you can also enjoy a lunch of freshly caught fish.

Getting There and Around

There are daily scheduled *vaporetto* departures from Fondamente Nuove station in Cannaregio to Burano on the 12 line. Ferries operate 4:20am-11:20pm and leave every 20-30 minutes. Journey time is 40-50 minutes and there's only one stop in Burano. You can also arrive by **water taxi** from anywhere in Venice. The cost for up to four passengers is €120-130. The entire island is pedestrianized and can be circled in less than an hour.

You can reach other lagoon islands from Burano by foot (Mazzorbo), *vaporetto* (Torcello, Murano), or water taxi to wherever you choose. **Water taxis** can be found at the main dock or near the Carabinieri station behind Piazza Baldassarre Galuppi. They can also be reserved by phone (tel. 041/522-2303).

If you want to take a little detour and arrive in Burano on foot without any tourists, disembark one stop early on the island of **Mazzorbo.** Turn left from the dock and follow the *fondamenta* along the water until you reach the wooden bridge that connects the two islands.

TORCELLO

Torcello was the first inhabited island in the lagoon and was thriving when Venice was still a backwater. The tide did turn, and today there are only 14 permanent residents, a couple of farms, plenty of flamingoes, and a few remaining churches and towers that hint at the island's past. The main canal, lined with a smattering of bars and restaurants, is next to the ferry dock and splits the island in half. There's far less frenzy here than in Venice or on most other islands in the lagoon. Torcello is a good place to escape back to nature for a couple of hours, have lunch in a historic restaurant, and reflect on the fragility of civilization.

Sights

Torcello has a single brick road (**Strada della Rosina**) that runs along a canal and leads to the island's ancient remains. Along the way there are several possibilities for getting sidetracked into the rural scenery. The first is 200 yards (180 meters) from the dock on the left near the first house. It's a dirt path that leads through grasslands to **Casa Museo Andrich** (tel. 041/735-542; www.museoandrich.com; daily 1-hour tours at 11:30am and 2:30pm; €15), an informal house museum created by two local artists to display their lagoon-inspired paintings and sculptures. Tours of the house should be reserved in advance.

Continue along the canal (you'll see the *campanile* in the distance) to reach a bridge known as **Ponte del Diavolo** (Devil's Bridge) because it lacks any protective railing. If you want to give tourists the slip, cross the bridge and follow the gravel path to a second wooden bridge. Cross that one and walk left along another canal. You can take the next bridge back to the main route or continue straight toward the bell tower. You may need to make your own path and cross a wooden plank at some point, but you will eventually arrive at a final bridge leading to the historic monuments of the island. All detours are short and take less than 25 minutes to complete.

The historic center of Torcello lies at the end of Strada della Rosina where the canal takes a sharp turn and a dirt path commences. The town once boasted over a dozen churches but the only ones standing today are the Basilicas of Santa Maria Assunta and Santa Fosca.

SANTA MARIA ASSUNTA

Fondamenta dei Borgognoni 24; tel. 041/730-119; daily 10:30am-5:30pm; €6 or €9 with campanile bell tower and audio guide

Santa Maria Assunta is one of the oldest structures in the lagoon and was part of a religious complex that included a baptistery, of which the circular foundations are still visible. The Gothic facade consists of 12 receded arches punctuated by a half-dozen windows. It dates from AD 639 but the present building was more or less completed in the first millennium. The entrance is on the right near the ticket office and reveals a simple interior that shows its age. The back wall is entirely covered in Venetian byzantine mosaics of the *Universal Judgment.*

The *campanile* (Tues.-Sun. 10:30am-5pm; €6 or €9 with basilica) is behind the basilica and worth climbing for a view of the island as well as Burano and Venice in the distance. It's the only tower in the city (open to visitors) without an elevator and is a fun climb. It gets windy at the top and there's not much room along the narrow corridors along the upper terrace.

Tickets are available from the basilica office. Adjacent to the basilica is the church of **Santa Fosca** (free), begun in the 12th century. It's vaguely reminiscent of the Basilica di San Marco and is a rare example of a Greek Orthodox plan with Byzantine influences.

Underneath the tree in the grassy yard opposite the churches are several well caps and the marble **throne** on which Attila the Hun is alleged to have sat. The seat more likely served local officials, but it remains a popular photo opportunity nonetheless.

MUSEO PROVINCIALE
Piazza Torcello; tel. 041/730-761; Tues.-Sun. 10:30am-5:30pm; €4

Archeologists still conduct digs on the island and their finds are stored in the Museo Provinciale opposite Santa Fosca. This small museum houses Greek and Roman antiquities, Etruscan and Paleo-Veneto finds from the estuary, ancient documents, and church treasures.

Food and Accommodations
TAVERNA TIPICA
Fondamenta dei Borgognoni 5; tel. 041/099-6428; daily 9:30am-7pm; €13-18

Taverna Tipica is a down-to-earth option and the first eatery along Strada della Rosina. It's a casual *osteria* with outdoor dining on wooden tables and benches next to a large grassy field where children play and parents rest. Rice and

fish dishes are the mainstays of the menu that includes *Risotto alla Buranella* and *Bis di Saòr,* both of which can be accompanied with a carafe of great wine.

★ LOCANDA CIPRIANI
Piazza Santa Fosca 29; tel. 041/730-150; Wed.-Thurs. and Sun.-Mon. noon-3pm, Fri.-Sat. noon-3pm and 7pm-9pm; €26-28

There are several *trattorie* along the main canal, but Locanda Cipriani is the institution. It was opened in the 1930s by the legendary restaurateur who had already turned Harry's Bar and the Cipriani Hotel into international success stories. The Locanda was more low-key but still attracted postwar VIPs including Queen Elizabeth, Charlie Chaplin, and Ernest Hemingway (who became friends with Cipriani and spent a good deal of time on Torcello, where he hunted ducks and wrote *Across the River and Into the Trees*). During the summer you can dine outside on the terrace or garden of this elegant hideaway, whose experienced kitchen turns out carpaccio classics and reinterpretations of Venetian favorites.

Eventually, Cipriani added accommodations, with five rooms (two suites and three singles; closed Jan. and Feb.; €140 pp) where Hemingway stayed at various times and guests can enjoy a good night's sleep today. Rooms are spacious and classically furnished with hardwood floors, large beds, and pleasant views. The surroundings are romantic and often used for wedding receptions, and you can always stop at the bar to savor the past.

Getting There and Around
Torcello can be reached on board the number 9 *vaporetto* from Burano and by the N night service. Journey time from Burano is 7 minutes and ferries depart every 30 minutes. The schedule is posted at the dock and is worth memorizing to avoid a wait. The island is best explored on foot, but if you do decide to get off the main walkway make sure to wear proper footwear—especially if it's been raining.

THE LIDO

The Lido di Venezia is a thin stretch of land that separates Venice from the Adriatic and made the lagoon possible. The island's original beach bums were Romantic writers like Goethe, Byron, and Shelley who were seduced by their surroundings in the late 19th century. Their books and poems boosted popularity of the Lido, which became the world's largest beach resort. It still attracts crowds in the summer and provides a nice break from Venice. There's a stylish, laid-back nostalgia about the place and plenty of five-star elegance. Things get really glamorous during the **Venice Film Festival** when Hollywood and the rest of the film world relocate to the Lido for 10 days in September.

Most of the island's 17,000 inhabitants live in the northern half of the island closest to Venice and the main *vaporetto* station. The two smaller localities of **Malamocco** and **Alberoni** in the south are quieter and attract fewer visitors. You can reach both by bus or bike and exploring the Lido is the perfect antidote for tired feet and ochlophobia (fear of crowds).

It's a pleasant place to pedal, lie on the beach, or take a scenic seaside stroll. You can pick up a map of the island along with the summer event calendar at the tourist **Info Point** (Gran Viale 6a; daily 9am-noon and 3pm-6pm, summer only).

Unlike Venice, cars are allowed on the Lido, so be careful when crossing streets and intersections.

Beaches
LIDO BEACH

Sunbathers will enjoy the long stretch of yellowish sand that lines the entire eastern side of the island. The sand owes its unique hue to the Piave River, which carries sediment from the Dolomite Mountains that contains quartz and magnetic iron. Erosion has become a problem in recent years and the beach narrows considerably the farther away you get from town. In all parts the sea remains shallow for some distance, which makes it a tranquil spot for children and swimmers of all levels. Stroll along the beach to pick your favorite *stabilimento* (beach club), where you can rent an umbrella and *lettini* (lounge chairs).

PARADISE BEACH
Via Klinger; tel. 041/526-1560; www. spiaggiaparadiso.it; Apr.-Sept.

Lido beaches get crowded in summer and Venetians tend to favor the *stabilimente* farthest from the Hotel des Bains where tourists congregate. Paradise Beach is at the tip of the island and can be reached on the A bus line. It's favored by families and couples who rent cabins and spend much of their summer enjoying the sun here. It's open to everyone though and a *lettino* and umbrella is €10 for a half day and €15 for the entire day. A front row view of the sea costs slightly more and sells out by 10am. Wi-Fi is free, a lifeguard is on duty 9am-6pm, and there's a restaurant that's open from breakfast to dinner.

For even more privacy head to the **Alberoni Dunes** at the southern tip of the Lido. This part of the island is a WWF sanctuary and far less populated, with only a couple of beach establishments.

BAGNI ALBERONI
Strada Nuova dei Bagni 26; tel. 041/731-029; www. bagnialberoni.com; May-Sept. daily 8:30am-midnight

You can set up a towel wherever you like or rent a lounge chair (€8) and umbrella (€8) from Bagni Alberoni. It's a colorful, laid-back beach club with a simple bar and restaurant where you can order spaghetti with clams or a cocktail. Locals rent the blue cabins for the season or the day (€40-90) and the cost depends on how close you are to the sea. The A bus stops directly out front and there's a good chance of listening to live music on summer evenings.

Bike Routes

Bicycles aren't allowed in Venice, but cycling is popular on the Lido. The island is flat and great for pedaling. Lido residents do own cars, but islanders drive slowly. The Lido's population triples in size during the summer but most Venetian holidaymakers stick to the beaches, and biking is a great way to explore the island. Bike paths run on both sides of the Lungomare Guglielmo Marconi road on the eastern edge of the island.

SEAFRONT PATH TO SAN NICOLÒ LIGHTHOUSE

Distance: *7.5 miles (12 kilometers) round-trip*
Duration: *1 hour*
Effort level: *easy*
Starting point: *Lido vaporetto station*

Once you've rented your wheels, head north to the San Nicolò lighthouse at the isolated tip of a long causeway. It's a flat ride on good surfaces with some twists and turns along the way. There's a wide public beach halfway to the lighthouse that's rarely crowded and perfect for picnics.

SEAFRONT PATH: SOUTHERN ROUTE

Distance: *12 miles (22 kilometers) round-trip*
Duration: *2-3 hours*
Effort level: *easy-moderate*
Starting point: *Lido vaporetto station*

The southern route is longer than the path to the lighthouse, and you have to continue on the **Via Malamocco path,** which leads to the remote southern end of the Lido. The ride takes in nearly the entire island and covers some lovely rural landscapes.

Along the way you can stop in the pleasant hamlet of **Malamocco** and have lunch or grab some picnic supplies. The road skirts the lagoon the rest of the way and becomes surprisingly verdant the closer you get to the Venice Golf Club and Alberoni ferry station. You'll have to cycle the same route back unless you hop on the 11 *vaporetto* to Santa Maria del Mare. This island is nearly as long as the Lido but twice as narrow and entirely tourist-free.

Bicycle and Scooter Rentals
LIDOONBIKE

Gran Viale Santa Maria Elisabetta 21b; tel. 041/526-8019; www.lidoonbike.it; Mar.-Sept. daily 9am-7pm, closed Oct.-Feb.

There are a handful of bike rental shops near the main Lido ferry station and you can rent Dutch-style city bikes, tandems, quadricycles, and fun family bikes at Lidoonbike. Ninety minutes on a standard bike is €5 and comes with a lock. Deposit and ID are required; make sure to read the rules carefully before setting off. **Venice Bike** (Gran Viale Santa Maria Elisabetta 79a; tel. 041/526-1490; https://venicebikerental.business.site; Mar.-Oct. daily 9:30am-7pm) just down the block offers similar rates as Lidoonbike for similar bikes.

VENICE SCOOTER RENTAL

Via Perasto 6b; tel. 388/8888-842; www.scooterrentvenice.com; daily 10am-7pm

Venice Scooter Rental rents scooters and electric bikes both by the hour (€20) or day (€35). No experience is necessary, although you will need a driver's license and can carry up to one passenger on the light, easy-to-ride 50cc scooters. Hybrid, fat bikes, and e-bikes are also available.

Helicopter Tours
HELIAIR

Aeroporto G. Nicelli; tel. 347/786-0653; www.heliair.it

Venice lacks the hillsides of Rome or Florence, and even climbing the *campanile* in San Marco doesn't provide a full bird's-eye view of the city. The only way to get that is by helicopter, and Heliair, based on the small airstrip at the northern tip of the Lido, can give you instant perspective on the city. The 10-minute tour of the northern lagoon and Venice, which includes a mid-air pause above Piazza San Marco, is €130 per person. Longer excursions are also possible on board Robinson R44 helicopters that seat a maximum of three passengers. The airport can be reached on bus A or take the 17 *vaporetto* and get off at the Lido San Nicolò stop. It's only a five-minute walk from there.

Golf
CIRCOLO GOLF VENEZIA

Strada Vecchia 1; tel. 041/731-333; www.circologolfvenezia.it; Tues.-Sun. 8am-8pm; 18-hole green fee €80 weekdays, €95 weekends

According to legend, when Henry Ford visited Venice in 1928 he asked his aristocratic host where he could play golf. At that time there was no course in the area, but not wanting to disappoint future guests Count Giuseppe Volpi had a 9-hole course built on the Lido. Circolo Golf Venezia was one of the earliest clubs in Italy and later enlarged to an 18-hole par-72 course near a wild beach where Goethe came to watch the waves. It's not particularly challenging except on windy days, but it's fun to play and native flora and fauna can be observed along the fairways. Clubs and cart can be rented for €30 from the pro shop and tee times should be reserved in advance.

Nightlife and Entertainment

The first beach platforms went up in 1857, followed in 1888 by wooden *capanne* (family beach huts) and luxury hotels not long after. Stop in for a cocktail at **Hotel Des Bains** (Lungomare Guglielmo Marconi 17; tel. 041/260-2309) or the **Grand Hotel Excelsior** (Lungomare Guglielmo Marconi 41; tel. 041/526-0201) down the boardwalk to enjoy the posh early-20th-century atmosphere that established the Lido as one of the world's most luxurious beach resorts. There's drinking inside the iconic **Blue Bar** (daily 10am-midnight) or **Pool Bar** facing the sea.

Getting There and Around

The Lido lies 10 minutes from Piazza San Marco or 50 minutes from the train station by *vaporetto*. The main ferry terminal can be reached on the 1, 2, 5.1, 5.2, 6, 10, 14, and N lines. Two smaller stations are located to the north and served by the 17, 8, and 18 of which the latter two only operate during high season. Another two serve the southern half in summer. The island extends 7.5 miles (12 kilometers) from north to south and buses A, B, C, N, V, and 11 connect the center with the southern tip near the golf course along two routes.

Background

History

ETRUSCANS AND GREEKS
(9TH CENTURY BC-4TH CENTURY BC)

The **Etruscans** were the first major civilization to settle in modern-day Italy. Recent DNA tests indicate they emigrated from the Near East and possibly originated in Turkey. They began to spread throughout the center of the peninsula in the 9th century BC and established towns in Lazio, Tuscany, and Umbria. Although their language remains a mystery, archeologists have learned a lot from the thousands of tufa rock tombs they left behind. At one point in the 6th century

BC, Etruscan kings ruled over Rome, and although the city eventually ousted their occupiers, Etruscan culture had a lasting influence on Roman traditions. The best place to experience Etruscan culture is in the small town of Fiesole overlooking Florence, Cerveteri with its ancient tombs and fortifications, or the National Etruscan Museum in Rome that contains the largest collection of Etruscan artifacts in Italy.

Simultaneously, Greek colonists were busy settling the coasts farther south. They were especially active in Puglia, Calabria, and Sicily, where they founded dozens of societies. Syracuse and Akragas dominated central Mediterranean trade routes and became wealthy in the process. Temples at Agrigento and Paestum are nearly as impressive as anything built in Athens and have remained in much better shape. Power struggles between individual cities and the rise of the Romans led to a slow decline, but like the Etruscans (who were occasional rivals and frequent trading partners) a great deal of Greek art, religion, and philosophy formed the foundation of Roman culture. Romans also borrowed Greek architectural expertise rather than invent their own, and temples such as Hercules and Portunus are examples of that imitation. Artistic similarities between the two civilizations can be observed at the Vatican Museums and Palazzo Massimo in Rome.

ANCIENT ROME
(8TH CENTURY BC-5TH CENTURY AD)

No one predicted Rome would become an eternal city. At its legendary founding in 753 BC, it was little more than a backwater on the banks of the Tiber River. Yet over the centuries that followed, the village on Palatine Hill expanded into a city that dominated the Mediterranean.

There are three distinct periods in Rome's ancient history: Kingdom, Republic, and Empire. The first was the shortest and the only time the city was subjugated. Etruscan kings were overthrown in 509 BC and a republic was established that over centuries conquered and consolidated the entire Italian peninsula. Roman customs, language, and law were imposed on native peoples who were integrated into the new society. It wasn't until the turn of the millennium that social tensions provided Julius Caesar the opportunity to take absolute power and do away with the old checks and balances. Although he was assassinated in the process, he changed the course of history and paved the way for the emperors to come.

Rise

After the Etruscans were expelled, Rome spent 100 years at war with the nearby cities of Etruria and subjugating neighboring tribes. Most tribes were allowed to remain independent as long as they accepted Roman hegemony. New colonies were set up in strategic locations so that conquered lands had no choice but remain loyal to Rome. Attention was then turned to the only power left in Italy: the Samnites, who were defeated along with their Etruscan and Celtic allies. By 283 BC, nearly the entire peninsula was in Roman hands.

Once Rome had domesticated the peninsula, leading families of the city began contemplating overseas conquests. Carthage was another rising power at the time and the Mediterranean wasn't big enough for two ancient superpowers. They faced off in three epic wars. In the First Punic War (264-241 BC) Rome secured Sardinia, Corsica, and parts of Sicily. The defeat did not go down well with the Carthaginians, who broke the peace accords and sent their legendary general, along with elephants, over the Alps to destroy the Romans once and for all.

Hannibal (247-183 BC) was one of the greatest military strategists in history and

---

Previous: statue at Palazzo Vecchio in Florence

nearly succeeded in crushing Rome during the **Second Punic War** (219-202 BC). He inflicted the bloodiest defeat the Roman army ever experienced at **Cannae,** and had he received proper reinforcements tourists might be visiting Carthage (modern-day Tunis) today rather than Rome. As it turns out, the Romans recovered from the devastating loss and Scipio's legions made a dramatic comeback at the Battle of Zama in what is now Tunisia. Hannibal ended up in voluntary exile and became the ultimate mercenary, advising Eastern rulers until he was betrayed and committed suicide. Decades of heavy reparations crippled Carthage, and the **Third Punic War** (149-146 BC) was the final act and foregone conclusion. Rome annihilated its historic enemy and became master of the Mediterranean.

Empire

Until **Caesar** (100-44 BC) came along, the Republic was governed by two consuls elected to one-year terms by the Senate. Although new territories meant wealth for a few, many Romans were having a tough time surviving. Cheap grain imports from Egypt put farmers out of business, and land was becoming scarce. Famines were frequent, and the ruling class was deaf to the calls of reform. Populist statesmen who did advocate change often met with violent ends.

These were volatile times, and slave revolts like the one **Spartacus** (111-71 BC) led in 73-71 BC were common. On the other hand, new conquests gave more power to Roman generals who could count on the loyalty of their troops who were rewarded with land and loot. Caesar was the most successful of these. After he prevailed over the **Gauls** in modern-day France he crossed the Rubicon and returned to Rome in 49 BC to assume total power. His assassination four years later marked the end of Republic and began an era in which the Senate was reduced to rubberstamping the wisdom and whims of emperors.

The first of these emperors was **Augustus** (63 BC-AD 14), the adopted son of Caesar, who ushered in a long period of stability and had the **Ara Pacis** built to remind Romans of his accomplishments. The empire eventually stretched from the Red Sea to Great Britain. Although some emperors like Nero succumbed to debauchery, the wisdom of Trajan, Hadrian, and Marcus Aurelius in the 2nd century AD led to higher standards of living for all. Slaves performed much of the heavy work, wheat was free, and entertainment was only as far as the amphitheaters and baths present in every Roman town. Most monuments visible today, such as the **Colosseum** and **Pantheon,** were built during the Imperial era, and many cities were founded during this period, including **Florence,** which Caesar established in 59 BC as a settlement for his veteran soldiers.

Decline and Fall

Over the centuries, the Roman legions lost their edge and had to rely on an influx of foreign recruits who were no longer the cream of the crop. Equipment became obsolete and tactics were superseded by those used by Germanic forces who threatened the empire from the north.

Constantine (AD 272-337) moved the capital to Constantinople (modern-day Istanbul) in AD 312, which led to the split of the Empire. While the eastern half survived for another thousand years in the guise of the **Byzantine Empire,** the west could not hold back the Vandals, Franks, and Visigoths pouring over the Alps. The last emperors kept their courts in army headquarters in Mediolanum (Milan) and then in Ravenna on the Adriatic Sea. During this time, **Christianity** grew and became an officially recognized religion; the first Christian temples were built and these later formed the foundations (literally) on which the Vatican, Duomo, and many other churches were built.

Alaric (AD 370-410) and his Visigoth army finally sacked Rome in AD 410. Soon afterward Saint Augustine announced the end of the world and **Attila the Hun** obliged him with years of chaos when it was hard to distinguish Roman from barbarian. The **Dark Ages** had begun, and Italy would have to wait a thousand years for the next golden age. It was around this time that fishermen in northern Italy escaping the violent newcomers formed the earliest island settlements in the Venetian lagoon, which would eventually become **Venice.**

MIDDLE AGES
(6TH CENTURY-13TH CENTURY)

After the fall of the Western Empire, foreign invasion became the rule in Italy. **Lombards** arrived and founded their capital in Pavia, only to be replaced by the **Franks** and **Charlemagne** (742-814), who was crowned Holy Roman Emperor. In the south, **Saracen** pirates landed in Sicily, followed by **Normans** who went on to build some of their most impressive fortifications in Puglia.

In the fray of the early middle ages, many cities managed to break free of feudal lords and slowly form independent Republics. **Venice** was one of the most successful of these and grew rich by importing silk and spice from the Orient and shipping crusaders off to the Holy Land. In 1271, **Marco Polo** (1254-1324) set off with his father on his famous journey to China and returned 25 years later with stories from the court of Kublai Khan that were later transformed into the world's first travelogue. Genoa and Pisa also rose to prominence and were great maritime republics on the Tyrrhenian Sea.

Inland Milan and **Florence** took advantage of conflict between the **Papal States** and Holy Roman Empire to flex their growing muscle. Bands of mercenaries were paid by towns to conquer their rivals. Competition was not just about winning on the battlefield: Perugia wanted to outdo Siena in architecture. Florentine rulers wanted grander cathedral doors than Pisa and they commissioned a dome that would come to dominate the city and all of Tuscany. Most of the squares and churches visible today were begun during this period. A sense of civic pride developed, along with a skilled class of tradespeople who paved the way for the Renaissance that was to come.

While many Italian cities were experiencing growth and stability, **Rome** remained a backwater for centuries after the fall of the empire. A population that had reached over one million at its ancient peak was down to a mere 30,000 and past glories were all but forgotten. Monuments fell into disrepair and only the church provided some semblance of order. There was no Vatican at this time and Popes had total authority over the entire city. That hegemony slowly spread to other parts of Italy as alliances were formed with powerful allies such as the Franks, who gained religious prestige in exchange for protecting papal interests.

RENAISSANCE
(14TH CENTURY-17TH CENTURY)

Although the term **Renaissance** wasn't used until centuries later, people at the time knew they were living during a special period. Great churches were slowly rising toward the heavens and overshadowing low medieval skylines, and art was taking on new extraordinary forms. Business was good, and much of it handled by newly founded Italian banks. Coins were minted in large quantities and Venetian *ducats* and Florentine *florins* were happily accepted throughout Europe. Economic expansion required investment, which in turn encouraged greater productivity. Usury, however, was considered a sin and the task of early money lending fell upon Jews who were confined to specific neighborhoods in Rome, Florence, and Venice. The practice of charging interest gradually became an accepted part of doing business and fueled further growth. A check was used for the first time in Pisa in the 14th century and was commonplace by the middle of the 15th. Early capitalism spread fast, and once money was available the wealthy and ruling classes needed something to spend it on.

Nobles and merchants who vied for control of their respective domains began to take interest in the arts. The **Medici** in Florence, popes in Rome, and Sforza in Milan wanted to make a statement with their *palazzi,* and interior decoration became important. Art and culture mattered again, as it had under the Romans. Antiquity was rediscovered and an incredible generation of artists was born in the right place at the right time.

Leonardo da Vinci, Michelangelo, Donatello, Raphael, and Titian all managed to make the transition from craftsman to artist. Painting and sculpture became vital to city life. Competitions were held for important commissions and Brunelleschi's scale model of Florence's cathedral dome is still on display in the Duomo museum. Signs of the Renaissance are everywhere in Italy. Although Florence was the epicenter of the movement, Rome and Venice were also transformed during this incredibly productive period that produced thousands of buildings, paintings, statues, and frescoes including the **Sistine Chapel** and **statue of** *David.*

Of course, not everything was rosy. Throughout the Middle Ages and Renaissance plagues routinely decimated Italian cities. Populations had little means of protecting themselves, and in 1631 alone one-third of Venice was decimated. The resulting loss of life had a significant effect on culture, religion, and politics.

UNIFICATION
(18TH CENTURY-19TH CENTURY)

Modern Italy began in the 1750s with the birth of a Republican movement determined to unite a fragmented peninsula. The **Risorgimento** (resurgence) was a challenging endeavor. One of the great leaders of the period was the charismatic **Giuseppe Garibaldi** (1807-1882). He was a George Washington-like figure and the father of the country who's dedication and perseverance never waned. There's a statue, square, or street dedicated to him in nearly every village, town, and city in Italy.

The first hurdle of reunification was Austria, which after the Treaty of Vienna in 1815 occupied northeastern Italy from Lombardy to Friuli. Garibaldi fought three wars against the Austrians. He lost two, but was on the verge of winning the third when the Austrians surrendered to Prussia, thus avoiding any territorial losses. To this day one of the worst names you can call someone in Northern Italy is a *Croato,* a reference to the Croatian soldiers conscripted to fight for the Austrians.

Garibaldi's other problem was farther south: the **Kingdom of the Two Sicilies,** overseen by Bourbon monarchs who ruled over southern Italy from their capital in Naples. In 1860, Garibaldi set off from Genoa with 1,000 volunteers equipped with hand-me-down weapons and red shirts for uniforms. What they lacked in training and material, however, they made up for in spirit. After landing in Marsala, they captured Palermo and the rest of Sicily with little bloodshed. The going got tougher in Campania but the Bourbons eventually surrendered Naples and withdrew to France.

Italy was a little closer to unification, but there was still the matter of the Papal State that controlled Rome and much of central Italy. The real problem was Napoleon III, who supported the Vatican and had sent troops to guard the city. Later that decade, however, the Prussians defeated the French, who were forced to pull out of Rome—thus clearing the way for Garibaldi's red shirts. The Aurelian wall was pierced at Porta Pia and a statue later erected on the historic spot. Resistance was light and the Swiss Guard didn't put up much of a fight. An accord was drawn between the nascent state and the Church that recognized the new Republic.

WORLD WAR I
(1914-1919)

Italy entered the 20th century united under a single king but still in search of itself. The country was not threatened, yet politicians and intellectuals alike succumbed to the fervor of war as the events rocking other European capitals spread to Rome. Which side Italy joined wasn't settled until the last days when the Allies made a better offer and promised to expand Italy's borders and regain lands from Austrian control. It wasn't until the end of **World War I**, when Austria ceded Trentino and Trieste, that Italy reached its current territorial state.

The country entered the war with little preparation and forethought for what everyone predicted would be a short conflict. The army eagerly set off, badly equipped and ill commanded, toward the Alps. Reality set in after the **Battle of Caporetto** in 1917 when Italian forces suffered a major defeat and nearly buckled under a combined German and Austro-Hungarian offensive. A long, hard-fought campaign ensued that saw very little progress. By 1919 over 650,000 Italians had died and a million had been wounded in fighting of little strategic significance.

FASCISM
(1920-1945)

Postwar Italy was greatly deprived, and it was during this period that many peasants packed their bags and headed for the United States, Argentina, and Australia. Many of those who remained survived on a meager diet, and the feeling of disappointment was rife throughout society. The promises of war had not been fulfilled and territorial gains were a small compensation compared to everyday suffering. The economy was weak and a revolution in Russia gave workers something to contemplate. Extremes began to form and both sides were convinced that the liberal policies of the government were outdated.

One proponent of change was **Benito Mussolini** (1883-1945). Before the war, Mussolini had been an editor of the Socialist Party newspaper and had displayed a talent for increasing circulation. His idea of **Fascism** evolved slowly and remained heavy on propaganda and light on philosophy. Economic hardship made recruiting easy, and a private security force known as the **Blackshirts** was established to protect landowners, fight communists, and beat Slavs. In October 1922 Mussolini announced he would march on

Rome. King Emmanuel III refused to sign a decree of martial law that might have stopped the Fascists, and instead promoted Mussolini to prime minister.

Order was quickly restored, trains began arriving on time, and opponents of the party could still show their faces. Things changed after the elections of 1924 and the assassination of Giacomo Matteotti, a socialist politician who spoke out against corruption and dictatorship. Over the next few years Fascists used parliamentary means to convert Italy into a virtual dictatorship and inspired other European dictators to do the same. Mussolini started giving his famous speeches from the balcony in Piazza Venezia in Rome and a love affair with the Italian people began in earnest. He used large-scale infrastructure projects to keep workers employed and the new mediums of cinema and radio to glorify his achievements and reinforce his hold on Italy. The Roman neighborhood of **EUR** was begun at this time and many archeological excavations were conducted in an effort to link Roman greatness of the past with the Fascist present.

WORLD WAR II
(1939-1945)

One of Mussolini's favorite slogans was *whoever stops is lost*. He didn't stop, and Italians lacked the democratic means to stop him. He invaded Ethiopia and joined the Spanish Civil War on the side of Franco in 1936. This endeavor forged an alliance with Hitler that would eventually be fatal. Once again Italy was led unprepared into a world conflict, except this time they chose to fight on the wrong side. The military and civilian casualties were greater than during World War I, and even the magic of propaganda could not sugarcoat defeats in North Africa and the Balkans.

U.S. and British troops commanded by Generals Patton and Montgomery reached Sicilian shores in July 1943, by which time it was clear the tide had turned against Mussolini and his Axis allies. An **armistice** was hastily drafted and signed in Brindisi, but that didn't end the conflict. German divisions were sent to defend Italy and made the Allies pay a heavy price for every mile they advanced up the peninsula. The **Battle of Monte Cassino** in 1944 was one of the bloodiest five months of the war and a throwback to the futility of trench warfare. Throughout the **Italian Campaign** a network of Italian resistance fighters, organized behind the enemy lines, aided the Allies. The **Partisans** hampered German movement and managed to liberate many parts of northern Italy before Allied tanks rolled into the region toward the end of the war.

Mussolini was caught trying to escape to Switzerland in April 1945. He and his mistress were shot and their tortured bodies were publicly displayed in Milan. He remains popular with a small segment of the population and his granddaughter was elected to parliament several times.

POST WAR
(1946-TODAY)

A **referendum** was held in 1946 to choose between monarchy and democracy. Italians voted for the latter. A new constitution was adopted and the **Italian Republic** was born. There were still many years of rationing and hunger until the country fully recovered from the war, but by the late 1950s and 1960s Italy began a spectacular period of growth that transformed cities and saw new neighborhoods and infrastructure emerge from the ruble.

Rome was at the forefront of the revival. Italian style and cinema caught the attention of the world. Rossellini, De Sica, and Fellini portrayed the gritty realism of Italy as the economy rebounded. Factories in the north began to increase production and Fiats rolled off the assembly lines in Turin at unprecedented speed. Highways were built, the Vespa moped became a national success story, and Italians regained their optimism. Inequality still existed but poverty was concentrated primarily in the south.

As a founding member of the European Union, Italy was instrumental in allowing free movement, eliminating tariffs, and establishing a single currency among EU nations. The oil crisis of the 1970s and the steady rise of globalization, however, had a significant impact on the economy and led to job losses and social unrest. Prominent politicians and judges were assassinated and acts of domestic terrorism by extremist groups and organized criminals were an everyday reality in the late 1970s and early 1980s. Then, in the 1990s, a series of political scandals provided an opportunity for media tycoon Silvio Berlusconi to rise to power. His unique charisma and television empire ushered in a new era that altered Italian popular culture and has influenced several generations of Italians. Berlusconi was first elected prime minister of Italy 1994 and served three further terms in 2001, 2005, and 2008. Italy's current prime minister, Giuseppe Conte, is a law professor and jurist who was plucked from anonymity by ruling parties. Although he had never held political office before, he has maintained a high approval rating among Italians.

In 2020, Italy became one of the first countries to suffer the consequences of the global coronavirus pandemic. On March 10, the Italian government decreed a total lockdown that lasted 31 days. Only essential services, such as hospitals and supermarkets, were allowed to open, and anyone outside their home was required to carry documentation stating their motive and destination. The nightly news was devoted entirely to tragedy and a macabre body count that kept rising for weeks. To slow the spread of the virus, Italians quickly adopted new measures of social distancing, hand-washing, mask-wearing, and confinement. They did it for the most part in unison and without hesitation, demonstrating solidarity and discipline unlike any period since World War II.

Art and Architecture

If you could put a price tag on all the frescoes, paintings, sculptures, churches, castles, and palaces in Italy, you'd be close to infinity. The Borghese Gallery alone is stuffed with more beauty than most cities. A stroll in any town is a walk through a patchwork of styles, from classical to baroque to modern.

ARCHITECTURAL STYLES

Classical

The first architects in Italy were Greek, and the temples they erected inspired Romans to lay foundations that are still visible. The most distinguished feature of these buildings is the column, which is often the last thing standing. Columns come in three orders: **Doric** (flat), **Ionic** (curved), and **Corinthian** (flowery). All three orders can be spotted on the Colosseum and were recycled by Renaissance designers hundreds of years later. Structures that remain from antiquity include amphitheaters, triumphal arches, and public baths. Advances in the casting of concrete and the use of the arch allowed Roman builders to think bigger than ever before. The dome was perfected, exteriors adorned with marble, and interiors decorated with elaborate mosaics and frescoes that have survived in **Ostia Antica,** outside of Rome, and many other ancient towns.

Romanesque

Churches are the great architectural legacy of the Middle Ages. The first paleo-Christian places of worship were small and appeared toward the end of the empire. There was a boom in **baptisteries** around AD 1000 and each region had its own take on the style. Buildings in this era had simple facades and small windows, which were later enlarged once glass became widely available. It was common to make alterations throughout the centuries as architectural trends and tastes changed, and few buildings from the period escaped without

some form of external or internal renovation. Increased wealth and civic power gave rise to more ambitious building programs. A black-and-white style was developed in **Siena** and **Florence** and competition between these two cities and many others throughout Italy spurred creativity and construction.

Romanesque layouts were generally in the form of a crucifix and consisted of single **nave.** Interiors weren't fancy and nothing was meant to distract worshippers from salvation. Many basilicas were decorated with **frescoes** recounting stories from the Bible, and **mosaics** were especially popular in Venice. Santa Maria in Trastevere and Santa Cecilia in Rome, along with San Miniato al Monte in Florence and Santi Maria e Donato in Murano, are especially well-preserved examples of Romanesque style.

Gothic

Architecture eventually developed beyond the confines of rigid shapes and traditional forms. Gothic emerged in the 12th-16th centuries and seeped down the peninsula from the north. Groups of masons, like the Campionese masters, built cathedrals and basilicas from Milan to Assisi. In Venice the style was combined with Asian influences, giving the city a unique look of its own. Ornament was added to churches and archways pointed the way to heaven. Cathedrals rose higher than ever before, supported by rib vaulting. This meant that walls could be thinner, which allowed for the introduction of stained glass and rose windows imported from France. In Rome, many Gothic buildings were given a baroque makeover, though they reveal their true identity in the mosaics and paintings that were spared. Florence's Basilica di Santa Croce and

1: Giotto's *Ognissanti Madonna,* considered a landmark in Renaissance painting **2:** ancient plaques in Rome **3:** the Roman Forum

Duomo exemplify late-Gothic architecture, which also inspired public buildings such as the Doge's Palace in Venice and many private residences along the Grand Canal.

Renaissance

Renaissance architecture was less spectacular than the art that emerged from the period. There were certainly outstanding achievements—like **Brunelleschi's dome** in Florence and **Michelangelo's cupola** for St. Peter's—but it was also a time of confusion and aesthetics that failed to take off the way sculpture and painting did. Antiquity was greatly admired and provided a convenient model for architects. Practitioners like Bramante and Codussi left behind marvelous palaces financed by a growing upper class eager to outdo their neighbors. Bramante's **Tempietto** and Michelangelo's **Campidoglio** are two of the most famous examples of a period that left behind thousands of sculptures and paintings now on view inside the Vatican and Uffizi museums.

Baroque

Baroque is easier to identify than Renaissance architecture. A baroque building catches the eye with elaborate lines and decorative flare. It's a love-it-or-hate-it style that grew out of the ideals of the Counter-Reformation in the 17th and 18th centuries. Many church interiors were remodeled, which explains why you can't always judge a cathedral by its facade. It wasn't just churches that were being transformed by the movement—so were public monuments, and perhaps the best-known example of baroque is the ornate **Trevi Fountain** in Rome.

Rome led the way in the movement, thanks to the genius of **Bernini** (1598-1680) and **Borromini** (1599-1667). Popes indulged themselves on irreverent designs that were not universally adopted. Florence and Venice mostly passed on the artistic trend and the southern Italian incarnation took the studied excess in a new direction. **Italian gardens** also sprang up in this era, exemplified by those at Tivoli, and matched the splendor of the palaces they were meant to accentuate.

Neoclassicism

Italy lost her supremacy on the art and architecture scene during the 18th century. Neoclassicism dusted off Roman designs and gave them an updated look. Symmetry and the use of architectural standards of the past are its notable characteristics. Grand **opera houses** sprang up in major cities, along with enclosed **shopping galleries.** Public buildings became extravagant. Much of the Vatican Museums, along with Piazza del Popolo and Villa Borghese park in Rome, were significantly transformed during this period, while the **Colosseum** was restored and many ancient monuments began to be recognized and appreciated for their historic value.

Toward the early 19th century, the movement evolved into **Umbertine,** best expressed in the massive Vittorio Emanuele II monument in Rome, which Caesar would have loved but is merely accepted by modern residents. Harder to find and on a much smaller scale are examples of **art nouveau,** which spread from France; although short-lived, it marked the beginning of modern architecture. The best examples of this distinctive style are often linked to the burgeoning tourist industry and the luxurious hotels, spas, and casinos that were built along the Italian Riviera and **Venice Lido.**

Modern

Modern architecture evolved late in Italy, and steel and glass never replaced reinforced concrete as the material of choice. With the rise of Fascism, a stark, monumental style was promoted that's visible in **EUR** and many southern Italian cities, several of which were built from scratch. **Train stations** also benefited from new ideas in architecture, and old stations in Rome, Florence, and Venice were all torn down to make way for sleek marble versions. After World War II, trends mixed and postmodernism slowly snuck into a few skylines. **Pier Luigi Nervi** (1891-1979) was one of the first 20th-century Italian architects to combat dreariness with skyscrapers.

Architecture Today

Getting a building permit in Italy is difficult, and even homegrown architectural stars like Massimiliano Fuksas and Renzo Piano have trouble realizing their visions. Today's buildings often look obsolete as soon as they are completed. There was no shortage of controversy when Richard Meier inaugurated his **Ara Pacis Museum** in Rome and Santiago Calatrava installed the **Ponte della Costituzione** footbridge in Venice. New is often shunned in favor of conventional and downright ugly. Hundreds of buildings could do with a little dynamite and the rationalist mistakes of the 1960s eradicated for good. In spite of bad taste and bureaucratic hurdles, good contemporary architecture does exist in Italy and can be seen in Rome, where structures like **Parco della Musica, MAXXI Museum,** and **Tiburtina train station** stand in stark contrast from the buildings that surround them.

VISUAL ARTS
Medieval

When the Roman Empire fell, creativity wasn't extinguished. It flourished in all three cities and especially in Venice, where contact with the outside world brought new ideas and skills. The **mosaics** inside St. Mark's Basilica were created during this period, along with many of the sculptures and carvings on church facades in Rome and Florence. Craftsmen organized themselves into **guilds** and specialized in everything from jewelry making to glassware. Most large-scale painting and sculpture were intended for religious purposes and inspired by the Old and New Testaments. Stone remained the preeminent material but metal, glass, leather, wood, and textiles were also used to create highly refined objects.

Renaissance

The Renaissance was a time of artistic leaps and bounds. **Tuscany** was the cradle of this golden age and Da Vinci, Raphael, and Michelangelo led the creative way. Rather than simply copy ancient works, they expanded upon medieval traditions and explored new possibilities of expression. Many artists began as apprentices under veteran craftsmen before leapfrogging their masters. Florentine style was exported beyond the region by its purveyors, who spread their ideas and techniques throughout Italy. Painting and sculpture lost its stiffness and began to look lifelike. Space on canvas and walls was redefined and the world reflected like never before.

Giotto helped redefine perspective and used it in his wooden cross inside Santa Maria Novella and buildings like the *campanile* in Florence. Artists traveled up and down the peninsula painting church interiors, and the greatest were given commissions in Rome. Michelangelo was among these; he spent over a decade at work on the Sistine Chapel, using colors in ways no one had imagined before. Around the same time Sandro Botticelli was busy painting his *Birth of Venus* (Uffizi) and Raphael was at work on the *School of Athens* in the Vatican. Many lesser-known artists were busy decorating monasteries, and Florence in particular has an incredible number of frescoes depicting the Last Supper and other Biblical scenes.

Mannerism

Mannerism developed in the mid-16th century in response to the High Renaissance and new political realities. Rome was sacked, freedom restrained, and religion was splitting at the seams. Artists became less interested in the observation of nature and more interested in the style or manner in which they painted. Compositions were unordered and focal points disappeared. Proportions were exaggerated and figures elongated or twisted into graceful postures. Colors often clashed and instability was favored over the balance depicted by previous generations of artists. Tiziano was one of the most productive proponents of the style; his paintings can

Historical Timeline

- **753 BC:** Rome founded by legendary twin brothers Romulus and Remus.
- **509 BC:** Roman Republic established after Etruscan rulers expelled from the city.
- **146 BC:** Rome defeats Carthage in Third Punic War and gains hegemony over the Mediterranean.
- **44 BC:** Julius Caesar assassinated, putting a definitive end to the Republic.
- **27 BC:** Augustus becomes first Roman emperor, and Pantheon built in Rome.
- **AD 80:** Roman Colosseum opens, with festivities lasting 100 days.
- **312:** Constantine becomes first emperor to convert to Christianity.
- **410:** Visigoths led by King Alaric sack Rome and mark the decline of the Empire.
- **421:** Venice is founded by settlers seeking refuge from invading barbarians.
- **828:** Relics of Saint Mark smuggled to Venice and construction of St. Mark's cathedral begins.
- **1201:** Fourth Crusade results in Venetian territorial growth and domination of the spice and silk trade.
- **1320:** Dante completes the *Divine Comedy,* which spreads Tuscan Italian and standardizes language around the peninsula.
- **1397:** Medicis open a bank in Florence, eventually becoming the largest and most powerful in Europe.
- **1401:** Ghiberti and Brunelleschi compete to build baptistery doors in Florence, marking unofficial start of the Renaissance.
- **1436:** Duomo in Florence is completed.

be found inside Basilica di Santa Maria della Salute and hanging throughout the Galleria dell'Accademia in Venice. Many Venetian interiors favored the style, and the ceilings of the **Scuole Grande** brotherhoods throughout the city contain remarkable examples of the style.

Baroque

The Council of Trent (1545-1563) did more than reform Catholic dogma. It started a reevaluation of art, of which the church was a major benefactor, and began a return to spirituality and tradition. Art was no longer just for the well-to-do but was intended to stir every soul. Inspiration came from the saints, the Virgin Mary, and the Old Testament. Rome was the center of the movement and

Caravaggio and the Carracci brothers took turns innovating church interiors, fountains, and grand living rooms around the city. Drama is the common denominator. Bernini emerged as the greatest exponent of the period. His battling baroque *David* stands in stark contrast to Michelangelo's contemplative version. Viewers could not help being moved and monuments like the Trevi Fountain were designed to deliver a strong visual impact. Sculpture gained multiple viewing angles and resembled actors on a stage. There was a return to group figures and props were used to add to the drama.

Futurism

Futurism was the last great Italian contribution to the art world. It was a response to

- **1504:** Michelangelo unveils statue of *David*.

- **1571:** Venetian navy defeats Ottomans at Battle of Lepanto and halt Turkish expansion into Europe.

- **1637:** World's first opera house opens in Venice.

- **1797:** Napoleon conquers Venice and ends over 1,300 years of independent rule.

- **1861:** Italian city-states and regions unify into a single nation governed by a constitutional monarchy.

- **1884:** Espresso machine invented in Turin.

- **1922:** Mussolini marches on Rome and takes political control of Italy.

- **1944:** American and Allied troops liberate Rome from German forces.

- **1946:** Italians vote to become a republic in national referendum.

- **1955:** Fiat manufactures the model 600 car and postwar economic recovery accelerates.

- **1960:** Federico Fellini releases *La Dolce Vita*.

- **1982:** Italy wins World Cup.

- **1994:** Berlusconi elected Prime Minister.

- **2006:** Italy wins fourth World Cup in overtime shootout against France.

- **2018:** 5 Star anti-establishment movement gains parliamentary majority.

- **2020:** Italy is one of the first countries affected by the coronavirus pandemic.

Cubism and reflected three principal elements: speed, technology, and modernity. The movement was born in the early 20th century with Filippo Marinetti's avant-garde manifesto calling for the burning of libraries. Artists gradually followed in his intellectual footsteps and began portraying sensations and capturing the essence of objects. Canvases and sculpture moved just as fast as the world on the verge of war. Factories and machines were idealized and artists unknowingly paved the way toward Fascism. The movement merged with others around Europe and shared many traits with Russian Constructivism. Good examples of the genre are hanging in Rome's Galleria Nazionale d'Arte Moderna e Contemporanea.

Also attracting international attention during the 20th century were the mysterious, metaphysical works of De Chirico and the oddly thin sculptures of Giacometti. The **Venice Biennale** was founded and became a hub for contemporary artists around the world to gather and share their work. It continues to set artistic trends and is held every two years.

The Landscape

From your window seat on the high-speed train connecting Rome, Florence, and Venice you'll see vineyards, olive groves, hilltop villages, and the mountain ranges that are a defining feature of the country's geography. You'll also go through many tunnels, which explains why Italy wasn't easy to unify and why such a relatively small country feels so big. It's a land that has fostered genius and civilization, and a landscape that is as memorable as the food, art, or people you'll meet.

GEOGRAPHY

Italy is roughly the size of Colorado but has enough geologic diversity to fill a continent. The long, boot-shaped peninsula was formed millions of years ago in the Cenozoic Era when tectonic plates underneath Europe and Africa slowly collided and transformed the earth's surface. Over the last million years alternating warm and glacial periods shaped the terrain and formed mountain ranges, valleys, lakes, and rivers. A journey down the length of the country reveals Alpine peaks, active volcanoes, hot springs, and desert-like settings.

It's a mountainous and hilly land, and less than a quarter of its total surface is perfectly flat. The **Alps** lie imposingly to the north and form a natural border with France, Switzerland, Austria, and Slovenia. The **Po River** starts on the northwestern peaks and winds its way east along wide plains that form the country's breadbasket. The **Apennine** mountain range runs southward down the peninsula. They're rarely out of sight in central Italy, and have helped and hindered human activity. Today it's still faster to travel north to south than east to west.

The sea is never far away in Italy. Before tunnels were blasted through mountains and highways were built, goods were moved by water. The **Mediterranean** surrounds most of the country and provides its characteristic shape. There are 4,722 miles (7,600 kilometers) of coastline that vary from Dover-like cliffs to long stretches of sandy beaches where Italians like to spend their summers. Sicily and Sardinia are the two largest Italian islands

umbrella pines in Villa Borghese, Rome

but there are hundreds more dotted around the coast, and some of the most famous lie in the lagoon surrounding Venice.

CLIMATE

Weather follows a fairly predictable pattern in Italy and seasons are relatively well defined. Temperatures, however, vary considerably from north to south, and it can easily be 10 or more degrees warmer in Rome than in Venice. The latter's position in a lagoon makes it susceptible to humidity, fog, and flooding, especially during early spring and late autumn. Snow is common in Venice but remains rare in Florence and Rome, although flurries did fall in 2018 and schoolchildren enjoyed the novelty of a snow day.

The fact that most **Romans** hang their clothes out to dry and don't own dryers says a lot about the city's climate. Summers are hot and dry and skies remain mostly blue throughout the year. Winters are mild except for January and February. Heavy rains arrive in November when torrential storms can disrupt traffic and lead to street and subway closures.

Florence has a similar Mediterranean climate, but its position farther inland makes it slightly cooler and wetter. Over the last hundred years the Arno River has flooded dozens of times, most dramatically in 1966 when water reached the Duomo walls and devastated much of the historic center. **Venice** is naturally flood prone, and Piazza San Marco is regularly covered in water in early spring and late autumn. Sirens warn residents and visitors of inclement weather and

shops start selling disposable rainwear. The city is prepared and elevated walkways are erected along major thoroughfares whenever necessary.

From December through February, the average temperature in Rome is around 48°F (9°C). Florence is slightly cooler, and Venice hovers around 39°F (4°C). July is the hottest month, with an average temperature of around 79°F (26°C) in Rome and Florence and 73°F (23°C) in Venice.

ENVIRONMENTAL ISSUES

Italy's environmental concerns range from poor building practices in earthquake-prone areas to air pollution. Rome suffers from smog, and city hall closes the center to cars whenever air quality deteriorates below acceptable levels. Over the last decade seasons have begun to stray from their clockwork patterns and people have started to recognize the greater variability, which has led to some regional climate disasters. Summers aren't just hot, they can be excruciating, and local TV broadcasts regularly advise viewers throughout July and August how to avoid sunstroke and heat exhaustion.

Italy also suffers from environmental criminals who think dumping toxic waste into rivers and fields is the business of the future. Unfortunately, the practice is profitable and difficult to stop. Many acres of productive agricultural land have been tarnished in southern Italy, and it's not uncommon for Italians living in affected areas to wonder if local food is safe to eat.

Government and Economy

Italian government can appear ramshackle and enigmatic to outsiders. Even Italians have trouble understanding their election laws, which are often changed and appear designed to ensure no party gains a significant majority. Over 60 governments have been formed since the end of World War II and it's rare for politicians to finish their mandate. Elections often end in stalemate and the 2018 vote exemplifies the problem. The two winning parties spent months negotiating the political future of the country with very little progress and recently set the record for the longest period of time Italy has operated without a government in place. New elections may be held to solve the turmoil of the last ones, which explains why many Italians have lost confidence in politicians and voter turnout is in decline.

Below politicians are the bureaucrats and government agencies that keep Italy in business. It's a big organization that has had a difficult time slimming down or adapting to new realities. Italians pay more for their government than citizens of other western democracies, and most wouldn't say they are getting their money's worth. The system does supply TV talk shows with plenty of content and allows new parties to periodically emerge with promises of reform. Yet change remains elusive, and passing meaningful legislation can be an excruciatingly long process.

ORGANIZATION

The Italian parliament consists of a **Chamber of Deputies** and a **Senate.** According to the Constitution of 1948, both have the same rights and powers. They are independent of each other and joint sessions are rare. The main business is the enactment of laws. For a text to become law it must receive a majority in both houses. A bill is discussed in one house, and is then amended and approved or rejected. If approved, it is sent to the other house, which can amend, approve, or reject.

If everything runs smoothly, the text is proclaimed law by the President of the Republic and enacted.

The **president**, however, is more of a figurehead than a leader. That job is reserved for the **prime minister,** who nominates key ministers and is susceptible to losing power if the majority is lost. It's also not uncommon for members of parliament to switch parties. A vote of confidence can be called at any time, and should a government fail to pass such a test it must resign and make way for new elections. That means fixed terms aren't guaranteed and stability can be difficult to attain.

The Italian **justice system** has its own problems and is in regular conflict with politicians who seek to reduce its power and openly criticize its judgments. The **Constitutional Court** is Italy's version of a Supreme Court. It's composed of 15 judges. One-third are appointed by the president, one-third elected by parliament, and the remainder are elected by lesser courts. They have their work cut out for them, and there is a tremendous backlog of cases throughout the system. Both civil and criminal judgments can take years to obtain and the wheels of justice turn very slowly.

POLITICAL PARTIES

Italy is as far as you can get from a two-party system. There are dozens of officially organized groups that run the gamut from hardcore communist to right-wing separatist. In between are small and medium-sized groups, none of whom are large enough to govern on their own. The political landscape is divided into right, left, center, and radical. Obtaining a majority can be hard, which explains why the country has experienced so many governments since the end of World War II. In Italy governments don't last for a designated amount of time; they can be toppled whenever the ruling party loses its majority in parliament. The result is instability and grid-lock that hampers the country's legislative needs.

The rise of Berlusconi in the early 1990s and his *Forza Italia* party led to political consolidation. Since the turn of the 21st century there has been a trend toward three or four large political forces vying for power. These include the centrist *Partito Democratico*, which lost significant parts of its electorate in the 2018 election and right-leaning *Lega*, which currently has significant influence over policy making and is the second most popular party in the country.

One of the newest political players is the *Movimento 5 Stelle* (5 Star Movement) that was founded in 2009 and has capitalized on discontent with politicians. Their founder, Beppe Grillo, is a comedian with a sharp tongue and popular blog who helped nurture a new generation of leaders. They have gradually gained seats at local and national levels including the mayoral seats of Rome and Turin. This is currently the most popular party, which is why they're often labeled as populist or anti-establishment and feared by old-school politicians. Things can change quickly in Italian politics, however, and often do.

ELECTIONS

The **Chamber of Deputies** is located in Palazzo Montecitorio in Rome and has 630 members elected by Italian citizens over the age of 18. Deputies are elected for five-year terms unless the president dissolves parliament. Reforms in 2005 significantly complicated matters. The electoral system combines proportional representation with priority for the coalition securing the largest number of votes so a ruling government can achieve a majority. That hasn't been the case in recent elections and there's regular talk of further electoral reform.

The **Senate** is located in Palazzo Madama and has 315 members, elected for five-year terms by Italian citizens over the age of 25. Members are elected by proportional representation based on party lists from each of Italy's 20 regions. Six Senators represent Italians living abroad and seven are granted senatorship for life. Italy has more representatives than most countries double or triple its size, which leads to inefficiencies and a large government payroll. It came as no surprise that Italians passed a referendum to reduce their parliamentarians in 2020.

Italians don't elect their national leaders directly. They vote for parties and those parties determine who represents the people. It's like buying a car without specifying the model, and guarantees the same old faces. Turnout is generally high and hovers around 80 percent. Participation has declined as of late as electors lose faith in a system, which is renowned for mayhem and corruption. The electoral system is subject to intense debate and regularly modified. Politicians, however, are uniquely unqualified to fix the problem and are more interested in avoiding term limits and guaranteeing perennial power than resolving matters.

ECONOMY

Italy is the eighth-largest economy in the world with a GDP of $2 trillion and an average income per capita of over $40,500. The introduction of the euro, however, has taken its toll on disposable income and salaries have not increased as fast as prices. Growth is beneath the European average and has suffered from stagnation since the recession of 2008 and was further aggravated by the coronavirus pandemic of 2020. In addition, there's a striking economic divide between regions in the north and those in the south. The country's main trading partners are Germany, France, Switzerland, and the United States. Unemployment hovers around 9 percent and is particularly high among young adults.

Many advanced industries operate in Italy; however, a decline in research-and-development investment has led thousands of recent university graduates and researchers to search for opportunities abroad. Reversing this trend is one of the political challenges of the future.

Fiscal pressures are high in Italy and tax evasion is common. The Italian tax agency estimates tens of billions of euros go unpaid every year and their collection would have a significant impact on GDP. For this reason, the government has passed legislation encouraging a transition toward a cashless society, and you can pay for nearly everything using a debit or credit card.

Industry

Italy has a long history of innovation. Today, agriculture, aerospace, automobiles, light industry, textiles, tourism, and creative services make up the main economic activities. From 1951 to 1963, the economy grew by more than 6 percent per year. Fiat led the economic postwar recovery and its cars still make up the largest slice of the domestic auto market. Other goods include precision machinery, pharmaceuticals, home appliances, luxury goods, textiles, clothing, and ceramics.

The country lacks deposits of iron, coal, or oil. Most raw materials and much of the country's energy sources must be imported. One of Italy's strengths is small and medium-size businesses. Over 90 percent of all companies employ fewer than 10 people. These firms take pride in their work and manage to maintain high levels of craftsmanship.

The Minister of Finance has one of the toughest jobs in Italy. The country must balance a rising trade deficit, high labor costs, and substantial national debt. *Reform* is a dirty word and taxes couldn't be any higher. Italian companies are at a disadvantage compared to their European rivals and competition from Asia is driving many manufacturers out of business. Nevertheless, Made in Italy still matters to consumers around the world, and there are plenty of success stories.

Tourism

Italy is the fifth most visited country in the world and attracted over 64 million visitors in 2019. Germans (12 million), Americans (5.6 million), and French (4.7 million) are the tourists you're most likely to meet, although the country is also a favorite with Chinese and British travelers. The most popular destinations are Rome, Milan, Naples, Venice, and Florence. Considering the number of monuments in Italy and the potential for expanding the industry, investment is still lacking. Funding from private companies is often required to restore sites, including the Spanish Steps (Bulgari) and Rialto Bridge (Diesel), both of which reopened in 2017. Overall, tourism is well organized and nearly every large town and city has a tourist center and visitor cards that simplify sightseeing.

Tourism can be a double-edged sword and some cities like Venice are suffering from a mass influx of tourism. Plans to cope with the demands of tourists include expanding airports in Rome and Florence, as well as additional high-speed train links between Italy and France. There are also cultural initiatives like slow tourism that encourage travelers to spend longer and get a deeper understanding of the places they visit. The coronavirus significantly disrupted the country's tourism industry in 2020 and it's yet to be seen how hotels, resorts, restaurants, and other destinations that rely on international visitors will recover.

People and Culture

DEMOGRAPHY

Italy is one of the most densely populated countries in Europe, with over 60 million inhabitants. Rome is the largest city, with a population of 4.3 million, followed by Milan (3.2 million) and Naples (3.1 million). The average life expectancy is 85 years for females and 81 for males. There are also plenty of people pushing 100 and the country has a median age of 45.5 (It's 38.1 in the United States). That's the third highest in the world, which is explained by low birth rates and the high life expectancy. Immigration, however, prevents the population from declining.

IMMIGRATION

Immigration is a relatively new phenomenon in Italy. Up until 1989 more people left the country than arrived. Today, the official number of foreign-born residents is over five million, and represents 8.7 percent of the total population.

The largest immigrant communities are from Romania, Albania, Poland, Morocco, and China. Most are male and attracted to Rome and cities in northern Italy where the chances of finding a job are good. Many work as day laborers, builders, cleaners, dishwashers, and caretakers. The second generation of this immigration wave is now emerging into Italian society and it's not uncommon to see Italo-Bangladeshi chefs preparing pizza, Italo-Nigerian children on their way to school, or Italo-Chinese contestants on TV quiz shows.

Ongoing conflict in Syria and sub-Saharan Africa has greatly increased immigration to Europe overall. The issue has reached crisis proportions over the last decade, with some nations unable or unwilling to deal with the influx. Several Eastern European countries have built fences, but that only diverts refugees to other destinations. Italy is not a primary haven for Middle Eastern migrants, who usually travel through Turkey and into Greece on their way to Germany and Nordic countries. Most immigrants/refugees to Italy cross the Mediterranean from Africa, and smugglers regularly pack boats with people desperate to start a new life abroad. You'll see some of them selling bags and other trinkets to tourists in the center of Rome and other large cities.

Italians generally favor legal immigration and recognize their own emigrant past, but immigration is one of the hot political topics, with several parties making it a pillar of their platform.

RELIGION

The vast majority of Italians are **Catholic**, although the number of those who regularly attend church is on the decline. The Lateran Agreement of 1929 officially formalized the relationship between the Italian State and the Vatican, which continues to benefit from substantial tax breaks. Although church and state are divided in the constitution it's not uncommon to see crucifixes in police stations, hospitals, and schools. Every town has a patron saint that is still celebrated with feasts and festivals.

Islam, Buddhism, and **Orthodox Christianity** are the fastest-growing religions in Italy. Many Muslims face Mecca inside improvised mosques, as some Italian cities have been reluctant to provide building permits for new mosques. Jews have been present in Italy since the reign of Julius Caesar and the oldest synagogue in Europe can be found in Ostia Antica, outside of Rome. Their treatment varied through the centuries, and Rome, Florence, and Venice all contained ghettos where Jews were once forced to live.

LANGUAGE

Modern Italian derives from Latin and owes a great debt to **Dante Alighieri** (1265-1321),

Breaking the Language Barrier

Learning a new language takes time, dedication, and practice. If you want to experience a fundamental aspect of Italian culture put aside any reservations you may have and just start. Set aside 20 minutes per day for undistracted study at least two weeks prior to arrival.

Download an Italian learning app (**Duolingo** or **Babbel**), invest in a book, or enroll in a course. Listen to Italian music on your way to work, and browse the headlines of Italian newspapers online. Stimulating your eyes and ears with as many sources of Italian as possible will make it easier to understand and use Italian once you arrive. Discover Italian singers (Jovanotti, Giorgia, Ligabue, Subsonica, etc.) you like and add them to your playlist, watch short films or cartoons, and, if you have the benefit of a friend or traveling partner, try out new grammar and vocabulary as often as possible. Imagine situations you're likely to encounter (restaurant, ticket office, bar, etc.) and role-play interactions until you're comfortable ordering a cappuccino and asking for a bottle of house wine.

It's impossible to master a new language in a month but you can absorb enough grammar and vocabulary to adapt to the linguistic surroundings and break through the language barrier. The more effort you put in at home, the more gratifying the journey will be.

who was the first to codify and utilize the dialects spoken on the Renaissance streets of Florence in his tales of heaven, purgatory, and hell. Not all Italian sounds the same and a trained ear can detect the differences between Roman, Florentine, and Venetian **accents.** Besides regional differences, there are minority languages such as Sardo, spoken by over

a million people in Sardinia, and Friulano, widely used in Friuli. Ladino is confined to an alpine valley in Alto Adige and Catalan is spoken on the northwestern coast of Sardinia. Both are remnants of foreign occupation, and their gradual mixture with Italian has led to colorful words and expressions that aren't found in dictionaries.

Essentials

Transportation

AIR

Airports

Rome's **Aeroporto di Roma-Fiumicino** (FCO; Via dell' Aeroporto 320; tel. 06/65951; www.adr.it), aka **Leonardo Da Vinci Airport,** is a hub for intercontinental routes. It has four terminals and scheduled nonstop flights to dozens of North American cities. The airport is 18 miles (30 kilometers) southwest of Rome and there are convenient bus and train connections to Termini train station in the center. **Ciampino** (CIA; Via Appia Nuova 1651; tel. 06/65951; www.adr.it) is Rome's

second airport. It's mainly used by charter and low-cost airlines flying to Italian and European destinations. The airport is small and often overcrowded but it's close to the city and there are bus connections to the center.

Venice's **Aeroporto di Venezia** (VCE; Via Galileo Galilei 30; tel. 041/260-6111; www.veniceairport.it) is a medium-sized airport with a handful of direct flights to North America and many connections to cities throughout Europe. From the airport, travelers can reach Venice by train, bus, ferry, or water taxi.

Florence's **Aeroporto di Firenze-Peretola** (FLR; Via del Termine 11; tel. 055/30615; www.aeroporto.firenze.it) is the smallest option, with no direct flights to the United States (although planned renovations may open the airport to intercontinental routes in the future). Delays and cancellations due to inclement weather are common. Tuscany's busiest airport, **Aeroporto di Pisa-San Giusto** (Piazzale D'Ascanio 1; tel. 050/849-111; www.pisa-airport.com) in Pisa, is less than an hour and a half away from Florence by bus, train, or car. There are direct flights from JFK to Pisa during the summer.

Airlines
FLYING FROM NORTH AMERICA
There are over 50 daily nonstop flights from the United States to Italy, and most land in **Rome**. **Alitalia** (www.alitalia.com) operates many of these and flies Boeing B777s and Airbus A330s to the capital from Boston, New York, Miami, and Toronto. **Delta** (www.delta.com), **American** (www.aa.com), **United** (www.united.com), and **Air Canada** (www.aircanada.com) also serve Rome from major cities in North America. There are a handful of direct flights to **Venice** with Alitalia, American, or Delta; all depart from New York or Philadelphia. There are no direct flights to Florence and only one seasonal flight to Pisa.

FLYING FROM EUROPE
There are hundreds of connecting flights from London, Paris, and Amsterdam with **Air France** (www.airfrance.com), **BA** (www.britishairways.com), or **KLM** (www.klm.com). Low-cost airlines like **Vueling** (www.vueling.com), **Ryanair** (www.ryanair.com), and **EasyJet** (www.easyjet.com) also fly to Rome, Florence, and Venice from many European capitals. **Aer Lingus** (www.aerlingus.com) operates flights from Dublin airport, which is equipped with a U.S. immigration office. Passengers are screened in Ireland and bypass customs when returning to the United States.

Alitalia operates most domestic flights, with three daily departures between Rome and Florence and five to Venice. Flight time is around an hour and tickets are inexpensive when purchased in advance. There are no direct flights between Venice and Florence, and a stopover in Rome is required. Other European airlines such as **Swiss** (www.swiss.com), **BA,** and **Air France** cover the routes but require layovers outside of Italy that significantly lengthen travel time.

FLYING FROM AUSTRALIA AND NEW ZEALAND
Getting to Italy from down under is a long journey and there are no direct flights to Rome or Venice. **Quantas** (www.qantas.com), **Emirates** (www.emirates.com), and **Etihad** (www.etihad.com) operate daily departures from Sydney, Melbourne, and Perth. Most flights require a transfer in Dubai or Abu Dhabi and total travel time is around 22 hours. **China Southern** (www.csair.com) is often the cheapest option but requires one or two stops in China and can take up to 40 hours. Travelers from Auckland can transfer in Australia with the above airlines or fly **Qatar** (www.qatarairways.com), **Korean Air** (www.koreanair.com), and Emirates on single-stop flights with transfers in Hamad, Seoul, or Dubai.

FLYING FROM SOUTH AFRICA

Travelers from Durban, Cape Town, and Johannesburg can reach Rome or Venice with **Ethiopian Airlines, Qatar, Emirates,** and **Turkish Airlines,** each of which requires a transfer in its respective hub. **Alitalia** offers direct flights (10 hours) between Johannesburg and Rome.

TRAIN

European train networks are well integrated but getting between countries by rail can still take a long time. There are daily departures from Paris to Rome, Florence, or Venice on board the **Thello** (www.thello.com) overnight service that leaves the French capital in the early evening and arrives the next morning. If you want to avoid a neckache it's worth purchasing a berth in one of the sleeping cabins (*couchettes*). There are also many trains from northern European cities to Venice. Single tickets can be purchased through www.trenitalia.it; if you are on a European vacation and plan on visiting many countries, purchase a rail pass from **Eurail** (www.eurail.com) or **Rail Europe** (www.raileurope.com).

Over the last decade successive Italian governments have invested billions in an expanding network of high-speed tracks that have drastically reduced journey times between Italian cities. Today, traveling between Rome, Florence, and Venice is fast, easy, and convenient. There are two operators. The state-owned **Trenitalia** (www.trenitalia.com) and private **Italo** (www.italo.it) both provide frequent daily departures between all three cities. The Trenitalia **Frecciarossa** (red arrow) service is slightly more expensive and operates more trains, making it popular with business travelers; tourists generally prefer Italo. Both companies share the same track and same stations located in city centers. Journey time between Rome and Florence is 90 minutes, Florence to Venice is 2 hours, and Venice to Rome 3.5 hours.

Italian high-speed trains are modern, clean, and equipped with Wi-Fi, electrical outlets, leather upholstery, snack machines, and bar cars. Tickets can be purchased online or at train stations from automated machines or service booths. The Italo website is easier to navigate and if you sign up for their newsletter you'll receive discount codes every month. There are several levels of comfort on board but even standard seating is adequate.

Trenitalia also operates local, regional and intercity trains throughout Italy. These are slower and make more stops. Tickets are inexpensive, and train interiors have a romantic wear and tear about them. The **Regional Veloce** from Rome takes nearly four hours to reach Florence and leaves five times a day. Only high-speed service is available between Florence and Venice.

Passengers with COVID symptoms should avoid traveling by train. Trains are regularly sanitized, and masks must be worn throughout the journey. Tickets are reimbursable in the case of COVID-related disruptions, and both Italo and Trenitalia provide the latest pandemic guidelines on their websites.

BUS

Buses are an inexpensive alternative to trains or cars. Several companies operate between Rome, Florence, and Venice. **Eurolines** (www.eurolines.com) and **Flixbus** (www.flixbus.com) provide similar service on buses that seat around 40 passengers. One-way tickets rarely exceed €20 and depots are located near train stations. Most intercity buses leave from **Termini** or **Tiburtina** station in Rome, **Stazione Santa Maria Novella** in Florence, and **Santa Lucia** in Venice. All are equipped with restrooms and baggage storage. There are stops along the way, and travel is two or three times longer than train service.

During COVID outbreaks the temperature of all passengers will be checked upon boarding. Anyone with a temperature above 99.5°F (37.5°C) will not be allowed to travel. Passengers must also fill out a form autocertifying their state of health. Masks must be worn throughout the journey and buses will be sanitized after every journey.

Rail Connections

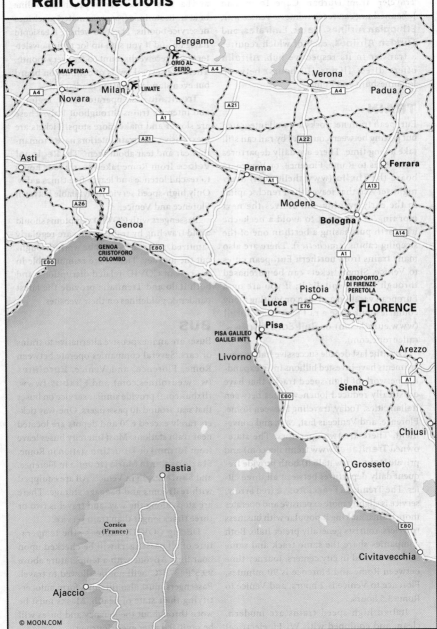

© MOON.COM

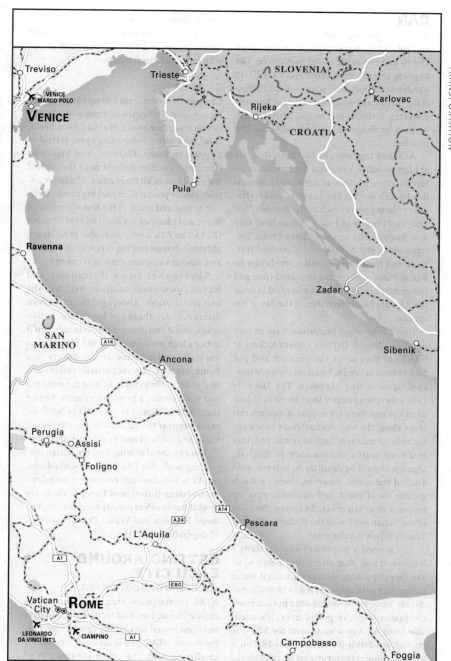

CAR

The **Schengen Agreement** removed border controls between members of the European Union and has made travel hassle-free. The ongoing immigration crisis and COVID-19 pandemic has led some governments to reinstate checks and temporarily close borders. Entering Italy from France, Switzerland, Austria, or Slovenia, however, isn't usually a problem.

As many highways in northern Italy are at high altitudes, snow and fog in winter can lead to delays. Millions of northern Europeans head south during the summer and traffic near crossing points such as the Brenner Pass and Ventimiglia is heavy throughout July and August. The recent Genova bridge collapse along the A7 highway disrupted traffic to and from France until a new bridge by Renzo Piano was erected in record time and inaugurated in 2020. Smaller roads that cross the Alps are best driven during the day at low speeds.

Italy's **highways** (*autostrade*) are in very good condition. Drivers collect tickets at booths as they enter the network and pay tolls in cash or credit, based on distance traveled, upon exiting highways. The 310-mile (500-kilometer) journey from Rome to Venice costs €39 and there are dozens of modern rest stops along the way. **Autostrade** (www.autostrade.it) manages highways and provides real-time traffic information in English. Signage should be familiar to drivers from around the world; however, there's a much greater use of **yield**, and **roundabouts** are frequent in urban areas. To review the rules of the Italian road, visit the **Italian Office of Tourism** (www.italia.com).

You'll need a **passport** and a **driver's license** if you plan on renting a moped or car. (Specify automatic transmission if you're unfamiliar with manual.) An **international driver's permit** is not required but can avoid confusion if you're pulled over. It's available from **AAA** (www.aaa.com) for $20. The **minimum driving age** in Italy is 18. Police and Carabinieri frequently set up road blocks

and randomly stop cars. The **blood alcohol limit** in Italy is 0.5, which is lower than in the United States and UK (both 0.8) but on par with most European nations.

CAR RENTALS

Cars can be rented from **Europcar** (www.europcar.com), **Sixt** (www.sixt.com), **Maggiore** (www.maggiore.com), **Hertz** (www.hertz.com), and other companies upon arrival at airports in Rome, Florence, and Venice or from rental offices located near the central train stations in all three cities. The latter option is more practical, as parking can be difficult to find and much of the historic center in Rome and Florence is a **limited traffic zone** (ZTL). The ZTL is only accessible to residents, although drivers renting cars within the zone and anyone using car-sharing is exempt.

Skyscanner (www.skyscanner) and **Kayak** (www.kayak.com) can help find the best rental prices. Always get the maximum insurance. Anything can happen on Italian roads, and if you observe cars carefully you'll notice a high percentage of dents. Florence has less traffic and more considerate drivers than Rome. Many streets are partially pedestrianized and it's easy to find a spot on the outskirts and walk or ride a bus to the center. Venice is entirely off-limits to cars except for dedicated lots near the entrance to the city, which are linked to the center by a light-rail system.

You can avoid renting and try Italian carpooling with **Bla Bla Car** (www.blablacar.co.uk), which connects passengers with drivers traveling throughout Europe. There are several dozen offers per day for rides between Rome, Florence, and Venice. Prices range €15-30 depending on distance.

GETTING AROUND EACH CITY

Public Transportation

ATAC Rome (www.atac.roma.it) operates subway, tram, bus, and train service to destinations in and around the city. In Florence, **Florence ATAF** (www.ataf.net) operates a smaller network that consists primarily of buses and two tram lines (one is currently under construction). Public transit in Venice is made up of over 20 **ACTV** (actv.avmspa.it) ferry lines (*vaporetti*) that circumnavigate the city and connect it to islands around the lagoon.

Tickets and travel passes in all three cities must be **validated** upon first use inside subway stations, on board buses or trams, or at validating machines on ferry stations. Controllers do occasionally check passengers and will fine anyone without a ticket. Daily and multiday travel cards are available in all three cities and are more convenient and cheaper than repeatedly purchasing single tickets.

Bicycle

Rome may have 150 miles (240 kilometers) of bike paths, but it still doesn't qualify as bike friendly. Cyclists in the eternal city face innumerable obstacles—from cobblestones to distracted tourists to haphazardly parked cars. **Florence** is another story, and the rows of bikes locked outside Santa Maria Novella train station are a sign of the city's fondness for two-wheeled transport. Roads are well paved and there is little automotive traffic. Much of the center is pedestrianized and cyclists are common.

Rome and Florence both have bike-sharing schemes, which are simple to use and inexpensive. **Obike** (www.o.bike) is the most widespread, but new companies are entering the market all the time and prices average €0.50 per 30 minutes. It's perfect for getting around and allows more freedom than the classic rental. Bikes are easy to find and may be left (safely parked) anywhere. They may be taken on board Rome's subway system weekdays before 7am, between 10am-noon, and from 8pm until closing. Saturdays and Sundays there are no limitations and the first carriage is dedicated to cyclists.

Bicycles and mopeds are banned from **Venice** and wouldn't be very useful even if they weren't. The city's hundreds of bridges and stairs make these forms of transport

impractical. You can, however, rent bikes on the **Lido** and cycle along the Adriatic Sea.

Car

CAR SHARING

Enjoy (www.enjoy.eni.com) and **Share Now** (www.share-now.com) are the two largest car-sharing services in Italy. They are easy to use and provide access to hundreds of vehicles in Rome and Florence. Registration is online and requires a passport, driver's license, and international permit. Once the app is downloaded you can locate and use cars for as little or as long as you like. You're also exempt from parking fees and don't pay for gas. It's a practical way of getting around and costs less than a taxi. Share Now operates a fleet of white two- and four-seat Smart cars while Enjoy uses red Fiat 500s that seat four.

The cost of Enjoy is €0.25 per minute up to a maximum of €50 per day while Share Now is €0.19 per minute and €59 per day. Cars can leave the zones in each city where they are found but must be returned to these zones once you're finished driving them. Both services also have dedicated parking areas at Rome's two airports. Trunk space, however, is limited and travelers arriving late are likely to find empty lots.

The ever-increasing number of car, moped, and bike-sharing services has led to the creation of aggregation applications that provide access to all transport from a single platform. **Urbi** (www.en.urbi.co) is one of the latest. Once you're registered you can choose from thousands of vehicles in Rome, Florence, and beyond.

PARKING

Parking garages are convenient but expensive, and there's a good chance of being fined if street parking goes unpaid. White lines mean spaces are free of charge, blue is €1.50 per hour, and yellow is off-limits. Automated payment stations are located at regular intervals on most streets and can be ignored on Sundays. In **Rome** (and, to a lesser extent, Florence) unofficial parking attendants appear after sundown to wave drivers into free spots. They expect a euro or two for their effort, but if you want to dissuade them just ignore or act like you're from a country where such practices don't exist.

Taxi and Ride-Hailing Apps

Cabs are stationed at or near large squares and train stations day and night. Vehicles are privately owned and range from small to reasonably sized. All are white and topped with signage that indicates if cars are available or in service. Spontaneously hailing taxis is possible but rarely done by locals, and it's easier to reserve one by phone. Response time is fast and travelers rarely wait more than 10 minutes. Just dial **3570** in Rome or **4390** in Florence. Taxis operate 24 hours a day and vehicles for special-needs passengers are available.

Taxi fares are relatively high and calculated according to time and distance. Weekend and night rates are extra. Drivers don't expect tips but fares can be rounded up to the nearest euro. If you use **Uber** (www.uber.com) at home you can keep doing so in Italy, although fees are often higher than standard taxis. A ride from Fiumicino airport to Piazza Navona via Uber Black will set you back €70 compared to €48 by taxi.

Visas and Officialdom

PASSPORTS AND VISAS

UNITED STATES AND CANADA

Travelers from the United States and Canada do not need a visa to enter Italy for visits of 90 days or less. All that's required is a passport valid at least three months after your intended departure from the European Union (EU).

UNITED KINGDOM

Now that Brexit is a done deal, the United Kingdom is officially no longer a member of the European Union (EU). That means UK citizens have lost many of their EU privileges. You don't need a visa for stays of under 90 days, but you will need to pack your **Global Health Insurance Card** (www.gov. uk), ask your mobile operator about roaming charges, and stand in separate queues at airports. Should a new wave of COVID strike, you could also be restricted from entering Italy and other EU countries. On a positive note, your **drivers license** is still valid.

EUROPEAN UNION/SCHENGEN

Citizens from all 27 countries belonging to the European Union can travel visa-free within the European Union.

AUSTRALIA AND NEW ZEALAND

Visas are not required for Australian or New Zealand citizens visiting Italy for 90 days or less within any 180-day period in the Schengen Area (European Union). New Zealanders between 18-30 can apply for a special working holiday visa at the Italian Embassy in Wellington.

SOUTH AFRICA

Visas are required to visit Italy and can be obtained through **Capago** (tel. 087/231-0313; www.capago.eu). The application process begins online and requires stopping into one of the visa application centers located in Cape Town, Durban, Sandton, and Pretoria. Getting a visa takes two weeks and there is a fee.

EMBASSIES AND CONSULATES

Lost or stolen passports can be replaced at the **United States Embassy** (Via Veneto 119a/121; tel. 06/46741; www.italy.usembassy. gov; Mon.-Fri. 8:30am-noon) in Rome or the **consulate** (Lungarno A. Vespucci 38; tel. 055/266-951; Mon.-Fri. 9am-12:30pm) in Florence. Proof of citizenship and a photo ID are required. Replacements are issued on the spot and cost €135. In addition to assisting with missing passports, the U.S. Embassy in Rome can help travelers deal with medical or legal emergencies. There's also a **consular agency** (Marco Polo Airport; tel. 041/541-5944) in Venice. Citizens with after-hours problems can contact the embassy at any time by calling 055/266-951. The embassy and consulates are closed during Italian and U.S. holidays. For bureaucratic questions before arriving to Italy call the **U.S. Department of State** (tel. 1-888/407-4747 from the United States or 1-202/501-4444 from any other country; Mon.-Fri. 8am-8pm EST).

The **British Embassy** (Via XX Settembre 80a; tel. 06/4220-0001; www.gov.uk) in Rome provides consular services by appointment only. Emergency assistance, however, is available by phone 24/7. The **British Consulate** (Via S. Paolo 7; tel. 02/723-001) in Milan can assist travelers throughout Northern Italy.

The **Canadian Embassy** (Via Zara 30; tel. 800/2326-6831; Mon.-Fri. 8:30am-noon) handles all citizen services and is located northwest of the historic center in Rome. The **Australian** (Via Antonio Bosio 5; tel. 06/852-721), **New Zealand** (Via Clitunno 44; tel. 06/853-7501; www.nzembassy.com), and

South African (Via Tanaro 14; tel. 06/852-541; www.lnx.sudafrica.it) embassies are also located in Rome. None of these countries have offices in Florence or Venice.

Consulate hours and days of operation may be reduced during COVID outbreaks.

CUSTOMS

Travelers entering Italy are expected to declare any cash over €6,000 and are prohibited from importing animal-based food products into the country. Duty-free imports for passengers from outside the European Union are limited to one liter of alcohol, two liters of wine, 200 cigarettes, 50 cigars, and 50 milliliters of perfume.

Bags are more likely to be heavier upon leaving Italy, and U.S. citizens are limited to $800 worth of goods deemed for personal use. Anything over that amount must be declared and will be taxed. Fresh fruit and vegetables, cheese, and animal-based products are not allowed into the United States. Further details regarding what can and cannot be imported into the country are available from the **U.S. Department of State** (www.state.gov).

Canadian regulations are fairly lenient and allow cheese, herbs, condiments, dried fruits, baked goods, and candies; for a complete list, visit the **Canadian Border Services Agency** (www.cbsa-asfc.gc.ca). Australian regulations are particularly stringent and customs officers go to great lengths to avoid contamination. All fruit, vegetables, ham, salami, and meat products are forbidden. Fake designer goods will also be confiscated and may lead to a fine. If you're in doubt consult the **Australian Department of Immigration and Border Protection** (www.border.gov.au).

Food

There are all sorts of places to eat in Italy, and travelers should attempt to experience as many of these as possible. When choosing where to eat, avoid restaurants where staff actively encourages you to enter and menus are displayed in more than three languages. Authentic establishments attract Italians and are not located next to major monuments. Generally, however, it's hard to have a bad meal in Italy, and if it looks good it usually tastes even better.

ITALIAN EATERIES
Restaurants

The most common sit-down eateries are *trattorie, osteria,* and *ristorante.* The first two have humble origins and are cheaper than *ristorante.* The typical *trattoria* serves local dishes within rustic surroundings. The best have been in business for generations and have a devoted local following. Service can be ad hoc and waiters are not overly concerned with formality. *Osteria* are similar, but have fewer items on their menus and rarely stray from tradition. *Ristorante* are more expensive and more elegant. They may have uniformed waiters, an extensive wine cellar along with a sommelier, and fine table settings. Menus often diverge from tradition and combine flavors in novel ways. *Trattorie, osteria,* and *ristorante* are open lunch and dinner, and continuous service throughout the day is rare.

Rome is the best place outside of Naples to order pizza. Although it's available in Florence and Venice, those cities lack pizza pedigree. Traditional round pies and sit-down service are available at Roman *pizzeria,* which also serve a variety of fried starters such as *suppli* (rice balls stuffed with mozzarella) and *fiore di zucca* (zucchini flowers with anchovies). Pizza is also a staple of many restaurant menus and easy to find. Quality is generally good and it's hard to pay more than €8 for a pie. The Roman version is thin and toppings tend to be simple.

Rome is an international city with international flavors. Chinese and Japanese restaurants are common but it's also easy to find Middle Eastern, Indian, African, and South American eateries. Kosher restaurants are concentrated around the Roman and Venetian ghettos and closed during Sabbath. New restaurants open all the time and recent trends have introduced steak houses, burger joints, vegan-bio, express pasta shops, and sandwich bars to all three cities.

Street Food

The most popular street food in Italy is pizza, which is available on demand at *pizza al taglio* (pizza by the cut) shops from midmorning onward. The pizza inside these standing-room-only shops with little or no seating is baked in large rectangular tins. There are a dozen varieties waiting to be cut, and customers randomly line up to order whatever they like. Slices are weighed and reheated if necessary, and they can be eaten immediately or wrapped up for future consumption. Payment is usually made at a dedicated cashier.

Markets are another good destination for tasty fast food from morning to early afternoon. Stalls in the Testaccio Market in Rome and Mercato Centrale in Florence have been serving the same flavors for generations and you can sample beef or tripe sandwiches, drink inexpensive local wine, and buy seasonal fruits.

Bakeries and *Pasticceria*

Fornaio (bakeries) open before dawn and remain busy until midafternoon. There's one in every neighborhood and they supply locals with all types of bread, buns, and sweets. You'll also find cakes, cookies, tarts, pastries, white or red pizza, and unique treats served during holidays. Most items are priced by the kilo and purchased for takeaway. *Fornaio* can

Dine Like a Local

Italians have their own way of doing things—especially when it comes to food. Here's how to blend in with locals:

- **Embrace a light breakfast.** Forget eggs and bacon: Sidle up to locals at the nearest bar and order a cappuccino and *cornetto* pastry.

- **Learn the coffee culture.** Italians drink coffee at specific times. Cappuccinos are rarely ordered after noon or in restaurants, and should never accompany or immediately precede a meal. Espressos are ordered at the end of lunch and/or dinner, and during midday or midafternoon breaks.

- **Skip extra salt and olive oil.** You won't find salt, olive oil, or Parmesan on tables so don't search for them. Food is meant to be eaten the way it's served.

- **Forget eating on the go.** Italians eat standing at bars and sitting in restaurants, but you'll rarely see them eating while they walk. The only exception is gelato, which makes strolling through historic streets even sweeter.

- **Dine later.** Restaurants in Italy don't open until 7pm or 7:30pm. If you're accustomed to early dinners, a late afternoon snack will help you reach local mealtime and ensure you're not dining alone.

- **Be patient.** Service may be slower than you're used to. It might be hard to get the waiter's attention, or the second bottle of wine may take a while to arrive—just remember the sun is probably shining and you are in Italy. A little patience along with good-natured persistence will ensure a pleasant time. Frustration won't.

be crowded in the morning, and some use numbered ticketing systems to avoid confusion. There's a big difference between what's baked in Rome, Florence, and Venice. Each city has its own specialties that vary in form and substance.

Pasticceria shops are entirely dedicated to sweets and keep roughly the same hours as bakeries. They prepare cookies, tarts, and cakes along with an array of smaller finger-sized pastries Italians serve as midafternoon snacks (*merenda*) or offer to visiting friends. Some *pasticceria* serve coffee and prepare one or two items for which they are famous. There's a tremendous variety, and the pastries in Rome and Florence taste and look different from the ones prepared in Venice.

Coffee Bars

Coffee bars and cafés open nearly as early as bakeries and provide different services throughout the day. In the morning they supply locals with espressos or cappuccinos and

cornetti (breakfast pastries), which are either plain or filled with cream, jelly, or chocolate. *Cornetti* rarely exceed €1 and are a cheap and tasty way to start the day. Most bars are supplied by bakeries, but some have their own ovens.

By midmorning, coffee bars trade sweets for triangular *tramezzino* and **panini** sandwiches stacked behind glass counters. These cost €2-4 and can be eaten at the counter, table, or taken away. Larger bars provide *tavola calda* (lunchtime buffets) with a selection of first- and second-course dishes. It's hard to spend more than €15 for a complete meal with water and coffee.

Bars usually operate on a "consume now, pay later" policy with a dedicated cashier off to one side who calculates checks. Counter service is slightly cheaper, always faster, and where most locals do their eating and drinking. There's a big difference between neighborhood bars and those overlooking heavily touristed squares like Piazza Navona or Piazza

San Marco. **Cafés** in those squares are far more elegant and some have been around for centuries. Prices are higher although the food is more or less the same. The biggest advantage is the view, and the tables outside are usually filled with tourists.

Venice is different from other Italian cities in many ways. Although you can find bars similar to those in Rome and Florence, the city has developed its own particular eatery. Venetian *bacari* serve bite-size slices of bread topped with vegetables, meat, or fish called *cicchetti*. These creative and inexpensive appetizers are accompanied by wine or beer from late morning until early evening. *Bacari* interiors are rustic, seating is limited, and service is friendly.

Gelateria

Gelateria are nearly as common as bars in Italy and are open late during the summer. They specialize in gelato and sorbet, which come in countless flavors. The best are made on the spot with seasonal ingredients, while less dedicated owners cut corners by using preservatives and compressed air to give gelato bright colors and gravity-defying forms. Gelato is priced by the scoop and served in cone or cups. Clerks always ask if you want *panna* (whipped cream) at no extra cost.

MENUS

Italian menus are divided into courses with an established order. *Antipasti* (starters) are the first thing you'll see and can be as simple as *bruschette* (toasted bread topped with tomatoes) or *fiori di zucchini* (fried zucchini flowers stuffed with anchovies). The point of *antipasti* is to relieve hunger and prepare stomachs for the meal to come. House starters *(antipasto della casa)* are a safe culinary bet and plates of local cold cuts and cheeses are meant to be shared.

The *primo* (first course) can be pasta, *risotto,* or soup. There are hundreds of traditional pasta shapes, all of which are combined with particular sauces that include vegetables, meat, or fish. This is a chance to get adventurous. Romans tend to serve simple white or red sauces flavored with thick cuts of bacon (*amatriciana*), pepper and goat cheese (*cacio e pepe*), or clams (*pasta alle vongole*). Soups are popular in Florence and fortified with pasta, beans, and barley. Rice is as common as pasta in Venice and usually served with fish or crustaceans.

Many people surrender after the first course, and that's a shame for stomachs. If you need help getting through a three-course meal, order a *mezzo porzione* (half portion) and leave room for the **secondo** (second course). It consists of meat or fish and is the gastronomic main event. Let waiters know if you want meat rare *(al sangue),* medium rare *(cotta),* or well done *(ben cotta).* Unless you order a **contorno** (side) your steak will be lonely. These generally consist of grilled vegetables or roasted potatoes and are listed at the end of the menu along with desserts and drinks.

Restaurants often have a separate wine menu and daily specials that waiters will translate when possible. Food is relatively inexpensive in Italy and a satisfying three-course lunch or dinner with dessert and coffee runs around €25-40 per person.

DRINKS

Italy has hundreds of natural springs and Italians drink more **mineral water** per capita than any other country in the world. The first question waiters often ask is the type of **acqua** (water) you want. You can choose between **frizzante** (sparkling) or **naturale** (still). A liter costs around €3 and sometimes there's a choice of brands. *Acqua di Nepi* is one of the oldest Roman waters and reputed to aid digestion. That's not to say **acqua del rubinetto** (tap water) is bad. It's regularly tested by authorities and safe to drink.

It's difficult to find a restaurant that doesn't have a decent **wine** list. Many eateries have a separate wine menu that includes local, regional, and international bottles. House wine is also available and generally very drinkable. It can be ordered by the glass or in different-sized carafes. **Tuscany** is the epicenter of Italian oenology and the place to uncork legendary Chianti and Super Tuscans. Geography and a cooler climate make Veneto suitable for growing white grapes, and the region is renowned for its sparkling *prosecco*. The Lazio region (Rome) isn't famous for wine production but still turns out respectable vintages and quality has improved in recent years. A glass of house wine is €3-4, a half carafe €4-6, and a full carafe €8-10. Prices are nearly always indicated on menus, but if they're not—or if a waiter brings you a bottle—ask the price before indulging.

Most Italians end lunches with an *espresso* and occasionally conclude dinners with a *digestivo* (digestif). The latter are high-grade alcoholic spirits and reputed to help digestion. The most famous of these is *grappa*, which is served in a small glass and sipped. **Soft drinks** are available but not very common on restaurant tables.

SEASONAL SPECIALTIES

Locals can tell the date by what's on display inside bakeries and *pasticcerie*. Most seasonal specialties revolve around sweets, which are prepared during major holidays.

The weeks preceding Christmas transform grocery and supermarket shelves, with entire aisles devoted to chocolate, nuts, dried fruit, and, especially, *pandoro* cakes made from flour, eggs, butter, and sugar. During *Carnivale*, fried pastries are the gastronomic excess of choice. The most popular are the doughnut-like *castagnole alla romana* and fried dough *frappe* covered with powdered sugar and available in bars and bakeries. Easter wouldn't be the same for Italians without *colomba* (dove) cakes topped with almonds and granulated sugar. All are available in bakeries and supermarkets.

New Year's meals nearly always include lentils, which are eaten for good luck, along with *cotechino* (pig's foot). Christmas lunches involve fish while roast lamb is a feature of Easter menus. Season influences what you'll find on tables the rest of the year. Soups are a mainstay of Florentine menus throughout the winter, while spring is the time to try artichokes prepared *alla romana* or *alla giudea* in Rome. Italian diets are regulated by the harvest and the produce available at outdoor markets varies considerably throughout the year.

HOURS

Restaurants are typically open 12:30pm-2:30pm for lunch and 7:30pm-10pm for dinner. Most close one day a week and many take an extended break in August or January. Reservations aren't usually necessary, but to guarantee a seat at popular eateries it's wise to arrive early or late. Bakeries open before sunrise and close in the midafternoon, while coffee bars remain open all day long and *pizzeria* and *gelateria* stay open late. Italians tend to eat later in summer when they wait for the sun to set and temperatures to fall.

TIPPING

Tipping is neither required nor expected in Italy. Most restaurants include a €1-3 surcharge *(coperto)* for bread, utensils, and service per customer. Waiters earn a decent living but no one refuses money, and leaving €3-5 behind after a good meal is one way to show appreciation. The other way to express gastronomic gratitude is with words. Italians are proud of their cuisine and compliments are always welcome. Customers at coffee bars often leave a low-denomination coin on the counter.

Produce Calendar

Italians eat according to the seasons, which means you won't find cherries in winter or kiwis in summer. What you will find is fresh and grown locally. To get an idea of what's in season visit an open-air market like Campo di Fiori in Rome or Campo della Pescheria in Venice. Consult the list below to make sure what you're ordering is ripe:

Spring	Summer	Fall	Winter	Year-Round
artichokes	eggplant	pumpkin	pumpkin	carrots
asparagus	zucchini	white and black truffles	artichoke	endive
green beans	turnips	cabbage	cauliflower	dried beans
fava beans	radishes	mushrooms	broccoli	lettuce
new potatoes	peas	cauliflower	winter melons	leeks
cauliflower	cucumbers	broccoli	Brussels sprouts	celery
broccoli	fava beans	Roman broccoli	radicchio	spinach
cabbage	green beans	chestnuts	oranges	potatoes
zucchini	peppers	grapes	mandarins	chicory
tomatoes	mushrooms	figs	clementines	apples
kiwi	cherries	oranges	grapefruit	pears
strawberries	prunes	mandarins	kiwi	lemons
medlars	peaches	clementines		
peaches	apricots	grapefruit		
	figs			
	melons			
	wild berries			

Shopping

The majority of family-owned shops are dedicated to one thing and one thing only. This can be a single product like shoes, hats, books, clothing, or furniture, or materials like leather, ceramics, paper, or glass.

Most businesses are small and have few employees. Department and flagship stores exist in the center of Rome and Florence but attract as many tourists as locals, who prefer to shop in malls and outlets on the outskirts of cities. Luxury boutiques are concentrated around major monuments like Piazza di Spagna and Piazza San Marco. Although you're unlikely to find a discarded Giacometti in Roman or Florentine flea markets, collectors with patience will be rewarded. There's a great variety to rummage through and antique markets have something for everyone.

SHOPPING ETIQUETTE

Italians entering a shop (or bar) greet assistants with *buongiorno* or *buonasera* (good morning/good afternoon). Most shop owners and employees are not overbearing and welcome browsing. They're happy to leave shoppers alone; however, they are professional and helpful once you demonstrate interest in an item and will happily find your size or explain how something is made. When leaving a store say *grazie* (thank you) or *arrivederci* (goodbye) regardless of whether you've made a purchase or not.

Bargaining

Shopping in Italy is a chance to practice your negotiating skills and discover the thrill of haggling. Price can be theoretical at souvenir stands, flea markets, antique stalls, and even smaller shops, where no one will be offended if you ask for a *sconto* (discount). If a price sounds too high, it probably is—and can likely be lowered.

SHIPPING ITEMS HOME

Don't worry if something that's larger than your suitcase catches your eye. Stores, especially Venetian ones selling glass, are accustomed to tourists and can arrange for shipment directly to your door. Expect to pay up to 10 percent of the purchase price for home delivery.

SALES

January and September are the best times to shop in Italy. All stores begin the official sale season in unison during these months and windows are plastered with discounts. Every price tag should contain the original and sale price. Check items carefully before buying and don't hesitate to try clothes on, as Italian sizes generally run smaller and fit slightly differently. The sale season lasts four weeks, but most of the good stuff and sought-after sizes disappear after 10 days.

HOURS

Italy has its own unique rhythm, and nowhere is that more evident than in shops. Family-owned stores and smaller businesses nearly always close between 1pm and 3pm. Many also close on Sundays and Monday mornings. Larger stores and those located in heavily trafficked streets have continuous hours. Businesses in the Roman and Venetian Jewish ghettoes observe Sabbath and shut down from sunset Friday until sunset on Saturday.

Accommodations

HOTELS

Italian hotels are graded on a system of stars that ranges from one to five. How many stars an establishment has depends on infrastructure and services. Criteria varies from region to region but most three-star hotels are quite comfortable. Reservations can be made online and most hotels have multilingual websites. A passport or ID card is required when checking in and early arrivals can usually leave luggage at the front desk. Many smaller hotels operate a "leave the key" policy in which keys must be left and retrieved whenever entering or leaving the accommodation.

Large international chains like Hilton (www3.hilton.com), Sheraton (www.starwoodhotels.com), and Best Western (www.

bestwestern.com) all operate in Italy, along with budget accommodations like Ibis (www.ibis.com) and Mercure (www.mercure.com). Service may be better and rooms slightly larger in these hotels, but they often lack character and could be located anywhere in the world. Many travelers will find themselves better off staying in smaller boutique or family-operated hotels that have managed to retain their charm.

Valuables are best carried or deposited in a hotel safe if available. In addition to the room rate, expect to be charged a city hotel tax of €1-5 per guest/per day depending on the number of stars and accommodation type. It's a small price to pay for waking up in Rome, Florence, and Venice.

HOSTELS AND *PENSIONI*

Hostels (*ostelli*) aren't just for young travelers: there's no age limit to staying in them. They provide clean, affordable accommodation and many are less sparse than you might imagine. Most include single, double, and quad options in addition to classic dormitory-style rooms. A bed costs around €20 per person and may include breakfast. The best thing about hostels, however, is the ambience. They're filled with travelers from all over at various stages of round-the-world adventures. Bathrooms are often shared although many also have private rooms with en suite baths. Italian hostels are overseen by the **Associazione Italiana Alberghi per la Gioventù** (tel. 06/487-1152; www.aighostels.it).

Pensioni are small, lower-grade accommodations that are usually family-run. Rooms are clean and functional, although you may be required to share a bathroom. They're often located near train stations or city centers in large buildings that may not have elevators. Some enforce curfews and it's best to check at the front desk (if there is one) before heading out for the night.

AGRITURISMI AND CAMPING

Agriturismi are a wonderful Italian invention that combine B&B-type accommodations with rural living. Most of these are located in converted farmhouses on land used to grow crops and raise animals. Decor is rustic and the number of rooms is limited. Half- and full-board options are available and meals consist of local ingredients. Owners are happy to show you around and the proximity to countryside provides a relaxing break from the city. Many are located on the hillsides surrounding Rome and Florence and have swimming pools. **Agriturismo** (www.agriturismo.it) lists thousands of such accommodations throughout Italy.

All three cities also have **campsites** that remain open from April to September. Facilities usually include a bar or restaurant, showers, and telephones. Some locations are better than others and there are several grounds in Florence that are within walking distance of the historic center. Camping in Rome and Venice requires a slightly longer commute. Equipment can be rented if you've forgotten your tent, and bungalows options are available. For a full list of sites visit the **Italian Campsite Federation** (tel. 05/588-2391; www.federcampeggio.it).

B&BS AND APARTMENTS

Italy has experienced a **B&B** boom over the last decade and the country now offers thousands of options. It allows you to stay with local residents and gain an insider's perspective.

To really do as the Romans do, rent an **apartment** and get an instant native feel. Short-term rental is especially convenient for families and groups of traveling friends. Not only are prices lower than many hotels, but staying in an apartment allows you to call the mealtime shots and relax in a home away from home. **Airbnb** (www.airbnb.com) and **VRBO** (www.vrbo.com) are good places to start apartment hunting. **Hometogo** (www.hometogo.com) searches over 250 international and local rental sites.

Conduct and Customs

LOCAL HABITS

Italians are attached to their habits and especially those related to food. Mealtimes are fairly strict and most eating is done sitting down at precise hours. Locals generally have a light breakfast and save themselves for lunch and dinner, which are served at 1pm and 8pm. You won't see many Italians snacking on the subway or bus or walking while they eat. Meals are usually divided *alla Romana* (Dutch) between friends but no one will take offense if you offer to pay. Rounds of drinks are not offered as they are in the United States; groups of colleagues each buy their own. Drinking in general is done over a meal rather than with any intention of getting drunk, and displays of public drunkenness are rare.

Most of the things considered rude in North America are also considered rude in Italy. One exception is cutting in line, which is a frequent offense. Italian lines are undisciplined and can feel like a fumble recovery. If you don't defend your place by saying *scusi* or coughing loudly you may be waiting all day for a cappuccino or slice of pizza. Fortunately, number dispensers are used in post offices, pharmacies, and deli counters. Personal space in general is smaller than in Anglo-Saxon countries, and Italians tend to use their hands as well as words to emphasize ideas.

GREETINGS

Italians are exceptionally sociable and have developed highly ritualized forms of interaction. Daily exchanges with friends and acquaintances often involve physical contact, and kisses on both cheeks are common. Bars and squares are the urban settings for unhurried conversation, which is a normal part of everyday Italian life.

Kissing is how Italians demonstrate respect, friendship, and love. The practice is as Italian as pizza. The most common form is the double cheek kiss. It can be uncomfortable for the uninitiated but no one will impose it on you, and a handshake is equally acceptable. If you observe carefully you'll see women kissing women, women kissing men, men kissing women, men kissing men, and everyone kissing children.

Kisses are exchanged at the beginning and end of most social encounters. An Italian man introduced to an Italian woman (or vice versa) will exchange kisses. Men will shake hands with each other and women may kiss or shake hands. Non-Italians can greet however they like. While citizens of other countries tend to exchange good-byes quickly, Italians love to linger. The time between verbal indication of departure and actual physical departure can be surprisingly long and is generally spent discussing the next day and making preliminary plans for a future meeting.

Coronavirus and social distancing have had an enormous effect on the physical contact demonstrated by Italians who are now constrained to fist- and elbow-bumping. It isn't quite the same and hopefully it will soon be safe for kisses and hugs to be exchanged between family and friends once again.

ALCOHOL AND SMOKING

Legislation regarding alcohol consumption is more relaxed than in North America. Alcohol can be purchased in supermarkets, grocery stores, and specialty shops all week long by anyone over 18 and consumed in public. That's a major draw for North American exchange students who can be spotted staggering down Roman and Florentine streets on weekends. Most locals are not prone to excessive drinking, and public drunkenness is rare.

Smoking has been banned in bars, restaurants, and public spaces since 2005, and if you want to take a puff you'll need to step outside or request an outdoor table. Although there is a high percentage of smokers in Italy that

Italian Survival Phrases

- *Ciao* [ch-OW] This world-famous word is an informal greeting that means both hello and good-bye. It's used between friends or once you have gotten acquainted with someone.

- *Buongiorno* [bwon-JUR-no] / *Buonasera* [bwo-na-SEH-ra] The first means hello (or literally, good day) and the latter good afternoon. These are formal variations of *ciao* and the first words to say when entering a restaurant or shop.

- *Scusi* [SKU-zee] is an invaluable word that sounds very much like its English counterpart: excuse me. It can be used whenever you want to get someone's attention, ask for something, or need to excuse yourself.

- *Per Favore* [PEAR fa-VOR-eh] / *Grazie* [GRA-zee-eh] are pillars of Italian politeness. *Per favore* is useful when ordering at a bar or restaurant and can go at the beginning or end of a sentence (*un café per favore* or *per favore un caffè*). Once you've been served something it's always polite to say *grazie*.

- *Dov'è...?* [doe-VAY...?] The Italian phrase for *where* can save you from getting lost. Just add the location to the end and do your best to comprehend the answer. *Scusi, dov'e la Fontana di Trevi?*

- *Parli inglese?* [par-LEE in-GLAY-zay?] should only be used as a last resort, but if you must it's more polite than launching directly into English.

number is falling steadily, and laws regarding nonsmoking areas are respected. Cigarettes are sold at specialized *tabacchi* shops for around €5 a pack. Venice is particularly serious about keeping the city clean, and smokers can be fined for throwing cigarette butts into canals or streets.

DRUGS

Italy's position in the center of the Mediterranean, coupled with the country's 4,971-mile (8,000-kilometer) coastline, makes drug smuggling difficult to eradicate. There are major markets for heroin, cocaine, hashish, and synthetic drugs imported by sea from South America, North Africa, the Balkans, and Afghanistan. That said, it's very rare to be offered drugs in Italy during the day and the hardest drug you're likely to be offered at night is hashish (a substance derived from cannabis and mixed with tobacco). Most dealers aren't threatening and will take no for an answer. Discos and nightclubs are more likely to be the scene of cocaine or amphetamines, which kill their share of Italian teenagers every year. Marijuana and hashish

are classified as light drugs and are illegal but have been decriminalized since 1990. Personal use in public will not lead to arrest but may bring about a fine or warning. It's not worth the risk, and there's enough perfectly legal wine to go around. Harder drugs such as cocaine, heroin, ecstasy, LSD, and so on are all illegal.

DRESS

Italians like to look good. Even if the standards of formality have fallen in recent years locals of all ages remain well-groomed and careful about appearance. It's not just the clothes that are different but the way Italians wear clothes and the overall homogeneity that exists on city streets. Women are elegant, men well-fitted, and even retirees look like they're wearing their Sunday best. It's easy to differentiate locals from tourists, who are blissfully unaware of the fashion *faux pas* they are committing. Tourists can usually be spotted a kilometer away: They're the ones wearing baseball caps, white socks with sandals, and khaki shorts. Fitting in means paying a little more attention to how you look and may require some shopping to acquire Italian style.

At Places of Worship

Most churches have a dress code, which is often posted outside. Revealing too much flesh may result in being denied entry. Lower legs, shoulders, and midriffs should be covered. Do not expect to enter St. Peter's or St. Mark's wearing flip-flops, miniskirts, above-the-knee shorts, or cut-off T-shirts. The same rules also apply to some museums and monuments.

Entry may be restricted during mass and a certain amount of decorum (maintaining silence, refraining from eating and drinking, and acting in a respectful manner) should be observed at all times. Photography is usually allowed but rules vary. Flash photography is not permitted inside some churches and museums where light can damage delicate frescoes.

Health and Safety

EMERGENCY NUMBERS

In case of a medical emergency, dial 118. Operators are multilingual and will provide immediate assistance. The U.S. Embassy (tel. 06/46741) and British Embassy (tel. 06/4220-0001) offer their citizens phone access any time for matters regarding illness or victimization of any sort. Carabinieri (112), police (113), and the fire department (115) also operate around-the-clock emergency numbers.

CRIME AND THEFT

Italian cities are safe and muggings and violent crime are rare. Still, it's best to travel in pairs late at night and be aware of pickpockets at all times. They're especially common in Rome and operate in fewer numbers in Florence and Venice. Most petty criminals work in teams and can be quite young. Roma (nomadic itinerants) often beg for change at traffic intersections or on church steps and supplement that income by playing music on subways, recycling scrap metal, and dumpster diving.

Crowded train stations and subways are ideal places for petty thieves. It's best to keep wallets and other valuables in a front pocket or locked in a hotel safe. Leave jewelry, smartphones, and cameras out of sight and always count your change before leaving a store. Make a photocopy of your passport and other vital documents and call your credit card company immediately if your wallet is stolen. If you are the victim of a pickpocket or have a bag snatched, report it within 24 hours to the nearest police station. You'll need a copy of the police report (*denuncia*) in order to make an insurance claim.

MEDICAL SERVICES

Italian medical and emergency services are relatively modern and ranked second in the world by the World Health Organization. First aid can be performed by all public hospitals and urgent treatment is entirely free of charge. A symbolic copayment is often required for non-life-threatening treatment but does not exceed €30. The emergency medical service number is 118. If you can't wait, go directly to the *pronto soccorso* (emergency room) located in most hospitals.

Vaccines are not required for entering Italy, but a flu shot can prevent unnecessary time in bed if you're visiting in winter.

PHARMACIES

Pharmacies are recognizable by their green neon signs and very common in city centers. Many operate nonstop hours and remain open during lunch. If a pharmacy is closed, you can always find a list of the closest open ones posted in the window. Pharmacists can be very helpful in Italy and provide advice and

Italy and the Coronavirus

Italy was one of the first countries hit by the coronavirus pandemic in 2020. By the end of summer in 2020, more than 287,000 Italians had been infected with COVID-19, and 35,000 had died. During the second wave in late 2020, the government issued new guidelines to prevent the spread of the virus. Passengers' and visitors' **temperatures** are measured at airports, museums, and major monuments, and **masks** are required both indoors and outdoors. **Social distancing** is mandatory inside public transportation, shops, and restaurants. **Hand sanitizer** is ubiquitous wherever people gather, and **washing your hands** is often a prerequisite for entry nearly everywhere. Many **sporting and cultural events** such as the European Soccer Championships, Venice Film Festival, Carnival Festivities, and Christmas markets were canceled in 2020 and are not certain to be held in 2021.

How long these guidelines remain in effect is impossible to predict. Until the virus is eradicated or a vaccine is discovered, traveling will be a different experience. On the positive side, it's likely you'll have a much calmer experience of Italy than travelers in the past. Tourists have evaporated from St. Mark's Square, there are no lines at the Uffizi, and seeing the Pope is easy.

Now more than ever, Moon encourages its readers to be courteous and ethical in their travel. We ask travelers to be respectful to residents, and mindful of the evolving situation in their chosen destination when planning their trip.

BEFORE YOU GO

- Check local websites (listed below) for **local restrictions** and the **overall health status** of the destination and your point of origin. If you're traveling to or from an area that is currently a COVID-19 hot spot, you may want to reconsider your trip.

- If possible, take a **coronavirus test** with enough time to receive your results before your departure. Some destinations may require a negative test result before arrival, along with other tests and potentially a self-quarantine period, once you've arrived. Check local requirements and factor these into your plans.

- If you plan to fly, check with your airline and the destination's health authority for updated **travel requirements.** Some airlines may be taking more steps than others to help you travel safely, such as limited occupancy; check their websites for more information before

nonprescription medicine for treating minor ailments. You'll also find practical items such as toothbrushes, sunscreen, and baby food along with automated prophylactic vending machines out front. Pharmacies are also the best place to go for masks and hand sanitizer.

SECURITY

Security in Italy has tightened considerably since the 2015 Paris attacks and there is a greater police and military presence at airports, train stations, and around major monuments. The new measures are most evident in Rome, where churches, museums, and other popular destinations have adopted new entry procedures involving metal detectors and the

depositing of backpacks and oversize bags in cloakrooms. Security around French and U.S. embassies, schools, and cultural associations has also been bolstered and will remain so for the foreseeable future.

There haven't been any terrorist attacks in Italy since the 1980s, and the country has kept a low profile compared to other allies that have actively intervened in Middle Eastern affairs and become the target of terrorist groups. That could always change, and travelers concerned about security can register with the **Smart Traveler Enrollment Program** (www.step.state.gov) to receive the latest alerts and allow the U.S. embassy to contact them in case of emergency.

buying your ticket, and consider a very early or very late flight, to limit exposure. Flights may be more infrequent, with increased cancellations.

- Check the website of any museums and other venues you wish to patronize to confirm that they're open, if their hours have been adjusted, and to learn about any specific visitation requirements, such as **mandatory reservations** or **limited occupancy.** Major sights in Rome and Florence require advance reservations during COVID outbreaks, and occupancy is limited. This is less the case in Venice, where advance reservations are only required at the Guggenheim Museum.

- Pack **hand sanitizer,** a **thermometer,** and plenty of **face masks. Cell phones** are also necessary for reading the QR Codes most restaurants now use to reduce contact with printed menus.

- **Assess the risk** of entering crowded spaces, joining tours, and taking public transit.

- Expect **general disruptions.** Events may be postponed or cancelled, and some tours and venues may require reservations, enforce limits on the number of guests, be operating during different hours than the ones listed, or be closed entirely.

RESOURCES

- The latest travel updates are available from the **Italian Foreign Ministry** (www.esteri.it) and **U.S. Embassy in Italy** (https://it.usembassy.gov/covid-19-information). Information can change quickly depending on the situation and it's worth checking them regularly.

- **COVID Info** (https://infocovid.viaggiaresicuri.it), another excellent resource, walks potential visitors through a questionnaire based on where you're traveling from, what countries you've recently visited, and other factors that determine what actions you are required take when entering Italy.

- The **Italian Civil Protection Agency** (www.protezionecivile.gov.it) and **Italian Health Ministry** (www.salute.gov.it) publish a list of the latest emergency decrees and procedures to follow should you become infected with the coronavirus while in Italy.

Travel Tips

WHAT TO PACK

What to pack depends on season and length of stay, but beware of overpacking—traveling to three cities means you'll be unpacking and repacking frequently. Plus, you want to leave plenty of room for souvenirs.

In addition to the below, if you're traveling during the coronavirus pandemic, make sure to pack plenty of standard surgical **facemasks** (at least enough to have a fresh, or freshly laundered, one every day) and **zip lock bags** for storing them when not in use. (Although you can find them at pharmacies,

they have been known to run out during peak infection periods.) A **thermometer** could be handy. Small bottles of **hand sanitizer** are also essential and should be used frequently.

Luggage: A wheeled suitcase makes getting around airports and to hotels easier. Backpacks or handbags are good for daily excursions and should have zippers to dissuade pickpockets. A money belt can be useful for storing cash and valuables.

Paperwork: You'll need your passport and a driver's license if you plan on renting a moped or car. An international permit is not required but can prevent confusion if you're pulled over. Email yourself any important credit card codes or customer service numbers as backup in case you lose your wallet.

Clothing, shoes, and accessories: Select comfortable clothes that can be mixed and matched. Layers are important in spring and fall when mornings are chilly and temperatures vary throughout the day. Formal clothes may be necessary if you plan on any fine dining or clubbing. Remember that knees and shoulders must be covered when entering religious buildings. Flip-flops are fine for the beach but aren't permitted inside the Vatican. Sunglasses are essential during the summer, especially if you'll be doing any driving, and hats are useful. You'll probably do a lot of walking, so bring at least two comfortable pairs of shoes.

Toiletries and medication: A high-SPF sunscreen is vital during summer. If you take medication, make sure to bring enough and have a copy of your prescription in case you need a refill. If you forget something, pharmacies in Italy are useful for replacing lost toiletries or picking up aspirin. Most hotels provide hair dryers, but if you're staying in a B&B or a hostel you may want to pack one. It should be adaptable to Italy's 220 voltage.

Electronics: Voltage is 220 volts in Italy and plugs have two round prongs. Electronic devices that need recharging require an adaptor. Simple U.S.-to-European **travel adapters** are available for under $10 at electronic stores and double that at airports. They're harder to find in Italy but many hotels supply them to guests free of charge. An extra memory card is useful for digital photographers and a portable battery charger can prevent phones and other devices from going dark.

Extra: Binoculars are useful for observing the ceiling of the Sistine Chapel and birdwatching in the Venice lagoon. A good **book** will help pass the time on high speed trains and a **diary** or **sketch pad** are great for capturing your impressions of Italy.

MONEY
Currency
The **euro** replaced the *lire* and has been Italy's currency since 2000. Banknotes come in denominations of €5, €10, €20, €50, €200, and €500 (which is currently being phased out). Bills are different colors and sizes to facilitate recognition. Coins are available in €0.01, €0.02, €0.05, €0.10, €0.20, €0.50, €1, and €2; these also vary in color, shape, texture, and size. The euro is used in 19 nations across Europe, and each country decorates and mints its own coins. Take time to familiarize yourself with the different values, and count your change after each purchase for practice. A fun way to get acquainted with coins is to flip them to the head side and guess the value (which is not visible on the head side) or the country where each coin was minted.

Currency Exchange
Fluctuation between the dollar and euro can have a major impact on expenditures. Over the last decade exchange rates haven't favored U.S. travelers, since 2020 the dollar has weakened and is now worth €0.84.

There are several options for obtaining euros. You can exchange at your local bank before departure, use private exchange agencies located in airports and near major monuments, or simply use ATM machines in Italy. Banks generally offer better rates but charge commission, while agencies charge low commission but offer poor rates. Exchange agencies like **Forexchange** (Rome, Termini Station; tel. 800/305-357; daily 8am-7:30pm) in Piazza Barberini are another option, and automated exchange machines operate nonstop at Fiumicino Airport and inside many bank branches. Look for the *cambio* (exchange) sign in bank windows. When changing money request different denominations and count bills at the counter before leaving.

ATMs and Banks
ATM machines are easy to find and are located inside or outside all Italian banks. They

accept foreign debit and credit cards, and exchange rates are set daily. Before withdrawing cash in Italy, ask your bank or credit card company what fees they charge. Most have an international processing fee that can be a fixed amount or a percentage of the total withdrawal. Italian banks also charge a small fee for cardholders of other banks using their ATMs.

The maximum daily withdrawal at most banks is €500. ATMs provide instructions in multiple languages. Be aware of your surroundings when withdrawing cash late at night or on deserted streets. If the card doesn't work, try another bank before contacting your bank back home. Italian banks are generally open weekdays 8:30am-1:30pm and 2:30pm-5:30pm. They often have lockers at the entrance for storing keys, coins, and anything else that might activate the metal detectors at the entrance.

Debit and Credit Cards

Before your departure, inform your bank and/or credit card company of your travel plans, as many will block cards after unexpected foreign activity.

Debit cards are a ubiquitous form of payment in Italy, and recent legislation meant to encourage cashless transactions has removed monetary limits. You can therefore buy a coffee, museum ticket, or a pair of shoes with Maestro- or Cirrus-equipped cards. Newsstands are about the only place that don't accept plastic, and cash-only restaurants are rare. Most Italian smart cards use a chip-and-PIN system but touchless payment is rapidly spreading. If your card requires old-fashioned swiping, you may need to alert cashiers.

Credit cards are also widely accepted. **Visa** (tel. 800/877-232) and **MasterCard** (tel. 800/870-866) are the most common. **American Express** (tel. 06/4211-5561) comes a distant third, and Discover is unknown. Cards provide the most advantageous exchange rates and a low 1-3 percent commission fee is usually charged on every transaction.

Sales Tax

The Italian government imposes a value-added tax (IVA) of 22 percent on most goods. Visitors who reside outside the European Union are entitled to **tax refunds** (www.taxrefund.it) on all purchases over €155 within stores that participate in the tax-back program. Just look for the **Euro Tax Free** or **Tax Free Italy** logo, have your passport ready, and fill out the yellow refund form. You'll still have to pay tax at the time of purchase but are entitled to reimbursement at airports and refund offices. Forms must be stamped by customs officials before check-in and brought to the refund desk, where you can choose to receive cash or have funds wired to your credit card. Lines move slowly and it's usually faster to be refunded at private **currency exchange agencies** such as **Forexchange** (www.forexchange.it), **American Express** (www.americanexpress.com), **Interchange** (www.interchange.eu), or **Travelex** (www.travelex.com) in Rome, Florence, and Venice. They facilitate the refund process for a small percentage of your refund. All claims must be made within three months of purchase.

COMMUNICATIONS

Telephones

To call Italy from outside the country, dial the **exit code** (011 for the U.S. and Canada) followed by **39** (Italy country code) and the number. All large Italian cities have a 2 or 3-digit **area code** (06 Rome, 055 Florence, and 041 Venice) and numbers are 6-11 digits long. Landline numbers nearly always start with a zero, which must be dialed when making calls in Italy or calling Italy from abroad. Cell phone numbers have a 3-digit prefix (347, 390, 340, etc.) that varies according to the mobile operator and are 7-digits long total.

To call the United States or Canada from Italy, dial the 001 country code followed by area code and number. For collect calls to the United States dial 172-1011 (AT&T), 172-1022 (MCI), or 172-1877 (Sprint).

Numbers that start with 800 in Italy are toll-free, 170 gets you an English-speaking operator, and 176 is **international directory assistance.** Local calls cost €0.10 per minute and public phone booths are slowly disappearing. Fees for calling cell phones are higher.

CELL PHONES

Your smartphone will work in Italy if it uses the GSM system, which is the mobile standard in Europe. All iPhones, Samsung Galaxy, and Google Nexus devices function, although rates vary widely between operators. Voice calls to the United States can vary from as much as $1.79 (Verizon) to $0.20 (T-Mobile) per minute depending on your plan. Most companies offer international bundles that include a certain amount of text messaging, data transfer, and voice traffic. If you don't want any unexpected bills, compare offers and choose one that meets your needs.

You can also purchase a SIM card in Italy at any mobile shop and use it in your phone. **Wind3** (www.windtre.it), **Tim** (www.tim.it), and **Vodafone** (www.vodafone.it) are the most common operators, with stores in all three cities and at airports. This option will require a passport or photo ID and may take a little longer, but it can be the cheapest and most useful if you plan on making many domestic and international calls.

If your phone doesn't use GSM you can rent or buy one in Italy. Rentals are available at the airport but are expensive. New phones are a cheaper option and available from the European telecom operators mentioned above. A basic flip phone can cost as little as €29 and be purchased with prepaid minutes. ID is required and some operators have special deals for foreign travelers.

You can save on telephone charges altogether if you have access to Wi-Fi. Many hotels and bars have hot spots, and using Facetime, Skype, or other VOIP apps is free.

PAY PHONES

The advent of cell phones has led to a steady decline in public pay phones. Those still standing operate with coins or phone cards that can be purchased at *tabacchi* or newsstands. Ask for a *scheda telefonica* (phone card), which can be inserted into a slot in the telephone.

Wi-Fi

Getting online is easy in Italy. Rome, Venice, and Florence all have Wi-Fi networks that make it simple to stay connected throughout a journey. Access is free; however, registration is required and there are time and traffic limits. Both Trenitalia and Italo train operators provide onboard Wi-Fi, as do most Italian airports and hotels.

Postal Services

Francobolli (stamps) for standard-size postcards and letters can be purchased at *tabacchi* shops. Larger parcels will require a trip to the post office. **Poste Italiane** (tel. 800/160-000; www.poste.it) offices are yellow, and larger branches are usually open weekdays 8:30am-7:30pm and Saturdays 8:15am-12:30pm. Grab a numbered ticket at the entrance and prepare for a short wait. A postcard to the United States costs €0.85 as long as it doesn't exceed 20 grams and remains within standard dimensions. The cost of sending letters and other goods varies according to weight; such items can be sent *posta prioritaria* (express) for a couple euros extra. Mailboxes are red and have slots for international and local mail. Travel time varies and it can take weeks for a postcard to reach its destination.

Stamp collectors may be disappointed, as most post office clerks slap computerized stickers onto correspondence. However, there are special philatelic branches in Rome (Piazza San Silvestro 20; tel. 06/6973-7273; Mon.-Fri. 8:20am-1:35pm, Sat. 8:20am-12:35pm) and Venice (Fondamenta del Gaffaro 3510; tel. 041/522-1614; Mon.-Fri. 8:20am-1:35pm, Sat. 8:20am-12:35pm) dedicated to collectors.

WEIGHTS AND MEASURES

Italy uses the **metric system.** A few helpful conversions: 5 centimeters is about 3 inches, 1 kilogram is a little over 2 pounds, and 5 kilometers is around 3 miles. **Celsius** is used to measure temperature, and 20°C (68°F) is a good air-conditioning setting inside hotels and cars. Summers often break the 35°C (95°F) barrier, and it's best to stay indoors when it does.

Italy is on **Central European Time,** six hours ahead of the U.S. East Coast and nine of the West Coast. Military/24-hour time is frequently used. Just subtract 12 from any number after midday so that 13:00 becomes 1pm and 20:15 is 8:15pm.

Italians use commas where Americans use decimal points, and vice versa. That means €10,50 is 10 euros and 50 cents, while €1.000 is a thousand euros. Italians also order dates by day, month, and year—which is important to remember when booking hotels and tours.

ACCESS FOR TRAVELERS WITH DISABILITIES

Special-needs travelers may find visiting Rome, Florence, and Venice challenging. Italy is not famous for its accessibility, and sidewalks throughout historic centers are narrow and uneven. Improvements, however, have been made in all three cities and many museums and monuments are free for special-needs travelers and their companions.

The situation in Rome is gradually improving. All museums are now accessible, and most of the city can be reached with relative ease. The Vatican museums in particular are simple to navigate and provide **tactile tours** (tel. 06/6988-3145; www.mv.vatican.va; free) for the visually impaired. Most subway stations are equipped with elevators, braille maps, and raised-floor trails for safely getting from entrance to platform. Stations on the Metro B line all have lifts, which isn't always the case with Metro A. However, bus 590 follows the same route above ground and is wheelchair accessible, as are many buses in the capital. These are entered from the doors in the center with the assistance of drivers.

Florence is the most accessible of the three cities. The center is flat, pavements are in good condition, and traffic is limited. Many museums are easily navigated and free for the otherly abled and their companions. There's also no need to wait in line to enter the Uffizi or Accademia as long as you have visible or documented proof of medical conditions. You can rent wheelchairs from the tourist office near the train station. There are 14 fully accessible public bathrooms in the city center, and many museums have created special **tactile tours** (tel. 055/268224) for the visually impaired. A group of specialized guides provide tours and the list is available online or from the **tourist office** (Piazza Stazione 4; tel. 055/212-245; Mon.-Sat. 9am-7pm and Sun. 9am-1pm).

Venice may seem impenetrable to special-needs travelers, but 70 percent of the city is actually accessible to all. The city has created a bridge-free itinerary with descriptions in French and English along with a useful accessibility map that highlights options for avoiding urban barriers. Both can be downloaded online (www.comune.venezia.it) or picked up from the *citta per tutti*/**city for all office** (San Marco, Ca' Farsetti 4136; tel. 041/274-8144; Thurs. 9am-1pm) or other tourist offices around the city. Raised **tactile pavements** for the visually impaired have recently been installed along many canals and several flat footbridges and nonslip ramps set up along key routes. Wheelchairs can be rented from **health care stores** (*Sanitaria ai Miracoli,* Cannaregio 6049; tel. 041/520-3513 or Farmacia Morelli, San Marco 5310; tel. 041/522-4196), and up to four at a time can board *vaporetto* lines 1 and 2. Users and companions benefit from reduced fares (€1.50) on all public transportation. There are seven fully accessible public toilets within the city and one in each of the major outlying islands. Museums are free for otherly abled travelers.

Traveling between cities by train is convenient for anyone with reduced mobility. **Italo** (tel. 892929; www.italo.it) goes to great lengths to accommodate passengers. Seat numbers and other signage are written in braille, and two seats in car 8 are reserved for wheelchairs.

These are located next to restrooms and snack machines designed for maximum accessibility. In-station assistance can be arranged up to one hour before departure at Florence SMN and Venezia Santa Lucia stations daily from 8am to 10pm and with 12 hours advance notice in Rome Termini and Tiburtina. **Trenitalia** (tel. 800/906-060) provides similar services and assistance.

Accessible (https://disabledaccessible-travel.com) and **Sage** (www.sagetraveling.com) provide useful recommendations and services for travel throughout Italy.

TRAVELING WITH CHILDREN

Italians go crazy for kids, and if you're traveling with a baby or toddler expect people to sneak peaks inside the stroller or ask for the name, age, and vital statistics of your child. Restaurants and hotels generally welcome young travelers, and some high-end accommodations offer babysitting services for parents who want to sightsee on their own. Many restaurants have children's menus, and most have highchairs. Half-size portions (*mezza porzione*) can also be requested for smaller appetites.

Tickets to museums, amusement parks, and public transportation are discounted for children under 12, and free for kids under 6. **Trenitalia** has several offers geared toward families, who can save up to 20 percent on high-speed rail tickets. **Italo** has similar deals and toddlers sit on laps unless an extra seat is reserved. Trains are roomy and give kids plenty of space to roam or be entertained by the landscape outside. There are diaper-changing facilities, and Italo has a cinema car with eight high-definition screens playing family-friendly movies.

Italian tots are used to taking naps, and a midafternoon break back at the hotel can prevent evening tantrums. Parents may want to intersperse fun and high-octane activities, like horseback riding on the Via Appia or cycling through Villa Borghese in Rome, with visits to monuments and museums.

Most parks are equipped with playgrounds and Roman and Venetian beaches provide a pleasant break from city streets. It's hard for kids not to love Italy and involving them as much as possible in the journey will help leave an impression they'll never forget.

FEMALE AND SOLO TRAVELERS

Women attract the curiosity of Italian men whether traveling alone or in groups. For the most part advances are good-natured and can simply be ignored. If you do feel threatened, enter a shop, bar, or public space. Should harassment persist, call the **police** (113) and remain in a crowded area. At night, it's best to avoid unlit streets and train stations. If you must pass through these areas walk quickly and keep your guard up. Have your cell phone handy as a precaution, and periodically keep in touch with family and friends back home. Pepper spray is legal in Italy as long as active ingredients do not exceed 2.5 percent and range is limited to 3 meters. There are occasional news stories of drinks being spiked in clubs, but rape is rare and severely punished. Hotel staff go out of their way to assist single travelers and will be happy to order a cab or make reservations whenever necessary.

SENIOR TRAVELERS

Italy has a high life expectancy (83) and median age (46), which makes gray hair a common sight and visiting seniors feel young again. There's also a general respect for older people, who are an integral part of economic and social life.

Seniority has benefits. Anyone over age 65 is entitled to discounts at museums, theaters, and sporting events as well as on public transportation and for many other services. A passport or valid ID is enough to prove age, even if these are rarely checked. **Carta Argento** (Silver Card) is available from **Trenitalia** for over-60s traveling by train and provides a 15 percent discount on first- and second-class seating. The card costs €30 but is free for those over 75. It's valid for one year and can be purchased at any train station. Italo offers anyone over 60 a 40 percent discount on all first-class train tickets.

Italy gets very hot in the summer so it's important to remain hydrated and avoid peak temperature times. You'll also walk a lot so take frequent breaks and join bus or ferry tours whenever you need a rest. If you take medication, bring as much as you need as prescriptions can be hard to fill.

LGBT TRAVELERS

Italians in general are accepting and take a live-and-let-live approach to life. It's not uncommon to see same-sex couples holding hands today and the sexual preferences of emperors and Renaissance artists (Michelangelo and da Vinci) are well known. Violence against LGBTs is rare, although cases of physical and verbal harassment do occasionally make headlines. The Roman LGBT community is the most active of the three cities; there's an annual summer **gay village** and **pride march** in June that attracts nearly a million participants. Although there is no dedicated LGBT neighborhood in Rome, **Via di San Giovanni in Laterano** is unofficially known as Gay Street, and many businesses display rainbow stickers in storefronts (rainbow flags also represent peace in Italy) around the city. There are fewer options in Florence and Venice but both cities are LGBT-friendly.

Italian homosexual couples have benefited from the same civil union status as heterosexuals since 2016. Italy was one of the last European countries to enact such legislation, doing so more than 20 years after Denmark. Still, it was a big step, and a sign Italian society (or Italian politicians) is open to change.

Arcigay (www.arcigay.itwww.arcigay.it) is the national association of the Italian LGBT community and the best resource for information on the latest issues, pride events, and activities.

TRAVELERS OF COLOR

Italian demographics have been evolving since the 1980s and the country has become increasingly diversified, with communities of Eastern Europeans, Asians, South Americans, and Africans contributing to the cultural mix. Nevertheless, the country is not without its issues. Incidents of racism against African immigrants (or those perceived as such) have been reported. Racist acts have been committed against Black Italian soccer players as well. Some Black travelers have reported incidents ranging from stares (especially in Venice and Northern Italy) to outright assault, though the latter, fortunately, is rare. If you think you've been discriminated against due to race, report the incident immediately to police or *caribinieri,* who take all acts of racism seriously.

Tourist Information

TOURIST OFFICES

Each of the destination cities have a tourist office where city travel cards, maps, and event information can be obtained. Hours vary but most are open nonstop from 9:30am until 6pm. Staff are multilingual and can help reserve local guides, order tickets, or get directions. Offices are located in airports, train stations, and near major sights such as the Colosseum in Rome, Duomo in Florence, and Piazza San Marco in Venice.

SIGHTSEEING PASSES

City cards provide entry to monuments and museums as well as unlimited access to public transportation for one or more days. They also offer line-skipping privileges at popular sights. Options include the **RomaPass** (www.romapass.it) or **Omniacard** (www.omniakit.org) in Rome, the **Firenzecard** (www.firenzecard.it) in Florence, and **Venezia Unica** (www.veneziaunica.it) in Venice.

Cards are expensive and do not always

guarantee savings. They will save you time entering the Colosseum or Uffizi and are useful for travelers who plan on doing a lot of sightseeing. All cards are available online or directly from tourist offices. They are active upon first entry and meant for individual use only, although there's no real way to prevent cards from being shared.

LOST AND FOUND

Hopefully you'll never need an *oggetti smarriti* (lost and found), but they do exist in Italy. All airports have dedicated offices at baggage claim. If you forget something on board a Trenitalia train, contact the passenger assistance office located inside **Termini** (Rome; 6:35am-midnight), **Santa Maria Novella** (Florence; 7am-10:30am), or **Santa Lucia** (Venice; 6am-9pm). Italo has fewer staff inside stations but you can call **Italo Assistance** (tel. 892/020; daily 6am-11pm) for help finding things. Fortunately, objects lost on high-speed trains have a high recovery rate. Objects lost in the historic centers may wind up at central lost-and-found offices listed in each destination chapter.

MAPS

Maps are available at tourist offices, for a small fee in Rome and Venice and free in Florence. They are also sold at newsstands and bookstores. Examine the selection carefully and choose a map that's easy to read, easy to fold, and small enough to store conveniently. Paper quality varies, and some maps are laminated and come with sight descriptions on the back. Once you have a map, try to orient yourself and memorize major landmarks and rivers. Studying maps and memorizing the layout of each city beforehand will make getting around easier once you arrive.

Finding the name of a street you're standing on is simple, but finding that same street on a map can be tricky. Often, it's quicker to locate a *piazza* or a nearby cathedral, museum, or monument. Also, asking for directions is the best way to start a conversation with a stranger and learn something new. Sometimes it's best to put a map away and rely on your senses to navigate around Rome, Florence, and Venice.

Resources

Glossary

A

aeroporto: airport
albergo: hotel
alcolici: alcohol
alimentari: grocery store
ambasciata: embassy
analcolico: nonalcoholic
aperitivo: appetizer
aperto: open
arrivo: arrival
autista: driver
autobus: bus
autostrada: highway

B

bagaglio: suitcase
bagno: bathroom
banca: bank
bibita: soft drink
biglietteria: ticket office
biglietto: ticket
buono: good

C

calcio: soccer
caldo: hot
calle: street (in Venetian dialect)
cambio: exchange
camera: room
cameriere: waiter
carta di credito: credit card
cartolina: postcard
cassa: cashier
cattedrale: cathedral

centro storico: historic center
chiesa: church
chiuso: closed
città: city
climatizzato: air-conditioned
coincidenza: connection (transport)
consolate: consulate
contante: cash
conto: bill

D E

destinazione: destination
discoteca: disco
dogana: customs
duomo: cathedral
edicola: newsstand
enoteca: wine bar
entrata: entrance
escursione: excursion

F G

farmacia: pharmacy
fermata: bus/subway stop
ferrovia: railway
fontana: fountain
forno: bakery
francobollo: stamp
gratuito: free
grazie: thanks

L

letto: bed
libreria: bookshop
lontano: far

M N O

macchina: car
mare: sea
maschera: facemask
mercato: market
metropolitana: subway
moneta: coin
monumento: monument
mostra: exhibition
museo: museum
negozio: shop
orario: timetable
ospedale: hospital
ostello: hostel

P Q R

palazzo: building
panino: sandwich
parcheggio: parking lot
parco: park
partenza: departure
passeggiata: walk
pasticceria: pastry shop
pasto: meal
periferia: outskirts
piazza: square
polizia: police

ponte: bridge
prenotazione: reservation
prezzo: price
quartiere: neighborhood
ristorante: restaurant

S T

sconto: discount
soccorso: assistance
spiaggia: beach
spuntino: snack
stabilimento: seaside resort
stazione: station
strada: road
tabaccherie: tobacco shop
teatro: theater
termometro: thermometer
traghetto: ferry
trattoria: restaurant (casual)
torre: tower
treno: train

U V

uscita: exit
vaporetto: ferry
via: street
viale: avenue

Italian Phrasebook

Most Italians have some knowledge of English, and whatever vocabulary they lack is compensated for with gesticulation. It can, however, be more rewarding to attempt expression in the melodic vowels of Dante rather than succumb to the ease and familiarity of your own language.

Fortunately, Italian pronunciation is straightforward. There are 7 vowel sounds (one for *a*, *i*, and *u* and two each for *e* and *o*) compared to 15 in English, and letters are nearly always pronounced the same way. Consonants will be familiar, although the Italian alphabet has fewer letters (no j, k, w, x, or y). If you have any experience with French, Spanish, Portuguese, or Latin you have an advantage, but even if you don't,

learning a few phrases is simple and will prepare you for a linguistic dive into Italian culture. Inquiring how much something costs or asking for directions in Italian can be a little daunting but it's also exciting and much more gratifying than relying on English.

PRONUNCIATION
Vowels

a like a in father
e short like e in set
é long like a in way
i like ee in feet
o short like o in often or long like o in rope
u like oo in foot or w in well

Consonants

b like *b* in *boy*, but softer
c before e or i like *ch* in *chin*
ch like *c* in *cat*
d like *d* in *dog*
f like *f* in *fish*
g before e or i like *g* in *gymnastics* or like *g* in *go*
gh like *g* in *go*
gl like *ll* in *million*
gn like *ni* in *onion*
gu like *gu* in *anguish*
h always silent
l like *l* in *lime*
m like *m* in *me*
n like *n* in *nice*
p like *p* in *pit*
qu like *qu* in *quick*
r rolled/trilled similar to *r* in Spanish or Scottish
s between vowels like *s* in *nose* or *s* in *sit*
sc before e or i like *sh* in *shut* or *sk* in *skip*
t like *t* in *tape*
v like *v* in *vase*
z either like *ts* in *spits* or *ds* in *pads*

Accents

Accents are used to indicate which vowel should be stressed and to differentiate between words that are spelled the same.

ESSENTIAL PHRASES

Hi Ciao
Good morning Buongiorno
Good evening Buonasera
Good night Buonanotte
Good-bye Arrivederci
Nice to meet you Piacere
Thank you Grazie
You're welcome Prego
Please Per favore
Do you speak English? Parla inglese?
I don't understand Non capisco
Have a nice day Buona giornata
Where is the restroom? Dove è il bagno?
Yes Sì
No No

TRANSPORTATION

Where is...? Dov'è...?
How far is...? Quanto è distante...?
Is there a bus to...? C'è un autobus per...?
Does this bus go to...? Quest'autobus va a...?
Where do I get off? Dove devo scendere?
What time does the bus/train leave/arrive? A che ora parte/arriva l'autobus/treno?
Where is the nearest subway station? Dov'è la stazione metro più vicina?
Where can I buy a ticket? Dove posso comprare un biglietto?
A round-trip ticket/a single ticket to... Un biglietto di andata e ritorno/andata per...

FOOD

A table for two/three/four... Un tavolo per due/tre/quattro...
Do you have a menu in English? Avete un menu in inglese?
What is the dish of the day? Qual è il piatto del giorno?
We're ready to order. Siamo pronti per ordinare.
I'm a vegetarian. Sono vegetariano
May I have... Posso avere...
The check please? Il conto per favore?
beer birra
bread pane
breakfast colazione
cash contante
check conto
coffee caffè
dinner cena
glass bicchiere
hors d'oeuvre antipasto
ice ghiaccio
ice cream gelato
lunch pranzo
restaurant ristorante
sandwich(es) panino(i)
snack spuntino
to-go da asporto
waiter cameriere

water acqua
wine vino

SHOPPING

money soldi
shop negozio
Do you sell…? Vendete…?
What time do the shops close? A che ora chiudono i negozi?
How much is it? Quanto costa?
I'm just looking. Sto guardando solamente.
What is the local specialty? Quali sono le specialità locali?

HEALTH

drugstore farmacia
pain dolore
fever febbre
headache mal di testa
stomachache mal di stomaco
toothache mal di denti
burn bruciatura
cramp crampo
nausea nausea
vomiting vomitare
medicine medicina
antibiotic antibiotico
pill/tablet pillola/pasticca
aspirin aspirina
mask maschera
thermometer termometro
I need to see a doctor. Ho bisogno di un medico.
I need to go to the hospital. Devo andare in ospedale.
I have a pain here… Ho un dolore qui…
Can I have a facemask? Posso avere una maschera?
She/he has been stung/bitten. È stata punta/morsa.
I am diabetic/pregnant. Sono diabetico/incinta.
I am allergic to penicillin/cortisone. Sono allergico alla penicillina/cortisone.
My blood group is…positive/negative. Il mio gruppo sanguigno è…positivo/negative.

NUMBERS

0 zero
1 uno
2 due
3 tre
4 quattro
5 cinque
6 sei
7 sette
8 otto
9 nove
10 dieci
11 undici
12 dodici
13 tredici
14 quattordici
15 quindici
16 sedici
17 diciassette
18 diciotto
19 diciannove
20 venti
21 ventuno
30 trenta
40 quaranta
50 cinquanta
60 sessanta
70 settanta
80 ottanta
90 novanta
100 cento
101 centouno
200 duecento
500 cinquecento
1,000 mille
10,000 diecimila
100,000 centomila
1,000,000 un milione

TIME

What time is it? Che ora è?
It's one/three o'clock. E l'una/sono le tre.
midday mezzogiorno
midnight mezzanotte
morning mattino

afternoon pomeriggio
evening sera
night notte
yesterday ieri
today oggi
tomorrow domani

DAYS AND MONTHS

week settimana
month mese
Monday lunedi
Tuesday martedi
Wednesday mercoledi
Thursday giovedi
Friday venerdi
Saturday sabato
Sunday domenica
January gennaio
February febbraio
March marzo
April aprile
May maggio
June giugno
July luglio
August agosto
September settembre

October ottobre
November novembre
December dicembre

VERBS

to have avere
to be essere
to go andare
to come venire
to want volere
to eat mangiare
to drink bere
to buy comprare
to need necessitare
to read leggere
to write scrivere
to stop fermare
to get off scendere
to arrive arrivare
to return ritornare
to stay restare
to leave partire
to look at guardare
to look for cercare
to give dare
to take prendere

Suggested Reading

CULTURE

Barzini, Luigi. *The Italians: A Full Length Portrait Featuring Their Manners and Morals*. This classic semi-sociological work may be over 50 years old, but many of Barzini's observations still hold true. He provides detailed portraits of Italians that are often quite hilarious and examine the origins of everyday rituals that have left travelers baffled for generations.

Hofmann, Paul. *That Fine Italian Hand*. With an outsider's perspective and an abundance of curiosity, Hofmann reveals the paradoxes of his adopted country.

Severgnini, Beppe. *La Bella Figura: A Field Guide to the Italian Mind*. Severgnini has made a living out of explaining Italians to the rest of the world. He does it with humor and manages to dissect and explore many of the habits that are uniquely Italian without condescension or oversimplification.

Stille, Alexander. *The Sack of Rome*. Few individuals have influenced modern Italy as much as Silvio Berlusconi. Stille takes an objective look at the consequences of life under a media tycoon and tracks how Italians have changed under his reign.

TRAVELOGUES

James, Henry. *Italian Hours.* A collection of essays about Rome and Venice that balance romantic vision and the realities Henry James wasn't afraid to write about.

Morton, H. V. *A Traveller in Rome.* Morton was a pioneer traveler at a time when tourism was still in its infancy. This diary-like account is filled with impressions of the Eternal City told in an erudite yet easy-to-read style.

Doerr, Anthony. *Four Seasons in Rome.* Before Doerr won the Pulitzer prize for *All the Light We Cannot See* in 2015, he wrote this lighthearted book recounting his adventures with wife and infant son during a yearlong stay in the eternal city. It's a funny and accurate exploration of Italian culture and a pleasant introduction to the city.

HISTORY

Crowley, Roger. *City of Fortune: How Venice Ruled the Seas.* A historical page-turner recounting Venice's rise as a naval power and the lasting repercussions trade had on the city.

D'Epiro, Peter, and Mary Desmond Pinkowish. *Sprezzatura: 50 Ways Italian Genius Shaped the World.* The authors detail how advances in politics, banking, and music—and many other innovations taken for granted today—originated in Italy. After a few pages it becomes evident how different the world would be without Italian ingenuity.

King, Ross. *Brunelleschi's Dome.* The Duomo in Florence may appear like a forgone conclusion today, but in 1418 building the dome on top was anything but certain. The story of its completion is a tale of how a Renaissance genius solved the greatest engineering challenge of his day and reinvented architecture in the process.

McGregor, James H. S. *Rome From the Ground Up.* A concise study of Rome's evolution through the millennia. Each chapter describes a different epoch and the city's gradual transformation. The book's clear prose, color photos, engravings, historical maps, architectural plans, and drawings help make sense of Rome.

Scirocco, Alfonso. *Garibaldi: Citizen of the World: A Biography.* Garibaldi was the George Washington of Italy and one of the most extraordinary figures of the 19th century. A soldier, politician, farmer, and one of the founding fathers of modern Italy, he played a vital role in the country's unification. His story reads like a novel—except it's all true.

ART AND ARCHITECTURE

Kemp, Martin. *Leonardo da Vinci: The Marvelous Works of Nature and Man.* Kemp takes readers on a revealing journey across Leonardo's long and improbable life, describing the artistic, scientific, and technological achievements at various stages of his monumental career.

King, Ross. *Michelangelo and the Pope's Ceiling.* The behind-the-scenes story of the Sistine Chapel and how an egotistical artist and manipulative pontiff created the most famous fresco in history. King's prose reads like fiction but is well documented. It paints a colorful picture of the political drama of the time and how the ceiling came to be.

Murray, Peter. *The Architecture of the Italian Renaissance.* A comprehensive illustrated guide to the art and architecture of the Renaissance. Leonardo, Raphael, Michelangelo, Palladio, and Brunelleschi are the protagonists of this ambitious work that segues between Rome, Florence, and Venice.

Ruskin, John. *The Stones of Venice.* This 19th-century best seller recounts Ruskin's obsession with Venetian art and architecture. It significantly boosted the city's reputation and established Venice as a must-see destination among generations of tourists.

Vasari, Giorgio. *Lives of the Artists.* Vasari (1511-1574) was a well-known painter and architect but this book is his lasting legacy. It contains short biographies of Italy's greatest Renaissance artists and traces the development of art and architecture across three centuries.

FICTION

Forster, E. M. *A Room with a View.* Although the novel is set in Florence, this love story of a young Englishwoman torn between two suitors provides few descriptions of the city. It does offer a jolt of romanticism, which is an essential part of any visit to Italy.

Preston, Douglas. *The Monster of Florence.* For something contemporary and more plausible than Dan Brown, try this thriller about an author's quest to solve a Florentine mystery. The plot traces Preston's semiautobiographical investigation into the city's most infamous double homicide

and has kept readers up at night since it was published.

KIDS

Collodi, Carlo. *The Adventures of Pinocchio.* Kids all over the world have heard about this puppet who came to life over a century ago but the book is more complex than the film and full of lesser-known episodes that capture the attention of children. The author was born and is buried in Florence. Ages 5 and up.

Macaulay, David. *Rome Antics.* The story of Rome as told by a vagabond pigeon who takes readers on a journey through time. Illustrations will fascinate young minds and prepare their eyes for the cobblestone streets and surprises the city has to offer. Ages 7-12.

Sasek, Miroslav. *This is Rome.* A wonderfully illustrated book that explains the past and present of Rome. Landmarks and everyday life are unveiled in a playful narrative that keeps kids tuned in and builds their expectations for the real thing. *This is Venice* also available by the same author. Ages 7-12.

Suggested Films

ROME

Open City (1945) Roberto Rossellini. One of the first films released in Italy after World War II recounts the chaotic days between German occupation and Allied liberation. The film launched the neorealism movement and won the Grand Prize at Cannes.

Bicycle Thieves (1948) Vittorio De Sica. All-time classic that depicts the mood of a country still recovering from war. Different strata of Roman society are depicted along with an epic relationship between a desperate father and loyal son.

La Dolce Vita (1959) Federico Fellini. This film marks a turning point in Italian cinema away from the past and toward a rapidly brightening future. The good life, however, is tainted for the protagonist played by Marcello Mastroianni. He spends his days following fading aristocrats, second-rate movie stars, and aging playboys and remains trapped in an empty life of lonely dawns. The film coined the word *paparazzi* and earned Fellini the second of four Oscars. Every scene is iconic and the midnight dip in the Trevi Fountain is ingrained in popular culture.

Ben Hur (1959) William Wyler. This film was shot at Rome's Cinecetta studios and set the standard for sword-and-sandal epics. It may not have held up as well as Fellini, but the chariot scene climax provides an idea of what racing was like at the Circus Maximus.

Caro Diaro (1993) Nanni Moretti. Moretti is as close as any Italian actor/director gets to Woody Allen. *Caro Diaro* is a cinematic triptych that begins with a meandering moped ride through the deserted streets of Rome, accompanied by a Keith Jarrett soundtrack and an itinerant monologue pondering cinema, sociology, and urban planning.

To Rome with Love (2012) Woody Allen. After New York, Paris, and Barcelona, Woody Allen couldn't resist making a film in Rome. Although the plot may be forgettable the setting isn't.

La Grande Bellezza (2013) Paolo Sorrentino. In this Oscar winner for Best Foreign Film, Rome appears highly stylized and there are plenty of day and night scenes revealing its majestic beauty. The hedonistic storyline may divide opinion but the cinematography is beyond repute.

Lo Chiamavano Geeg Robot (2016). Gabrielle Mainetti. Science fiction meets the working class suburbs of Rome in this film about a man who accidentally gains superhuman strength. It's a love story complicated by criminal intrigue and a reluctant hero who must come to terms with himself and the world around him. Rome isn't meant to look good and it doesn't, but it does offer a fresh

perspective on the city and the film won numerous awards.

FLORENCE

A Room with a View (1985) James Ivory. Florence never attracted the film crews of Rome or had a chance to make the cinematic impact of Venice. The most famous film shot in the city was James Ivory's *A Room with a View*.

VENICE

The Talented Mr. Ripley (1999) Anthony Minghella. This book-based film is set in the late 1950s and was shot in southern Italy and Rome but climaxes in Venice. There are scenes of the Grand Canal and a final confrontation inside Café Florian in Piazza San Marco.

Merchant of Venice (2004) Michael Radford. The *Merchant of Venice* may have flopped at the box office but it wasn't because of the Venetian cityscapes, which feature heavily in the period drama based on Shakespeare's play.

007. James Bond is a frequent visitor to Italy, and there are scenes of Venice in *From Russia with Love* and *Moonraker*. The city gets more extensive screen time during *Casino Royale* when Bond sails down the Grand Canal past the Rialto Bridge. He returns to Rome in *Spectre* for a long car chase and a short-lived romance.

Mozart in the Jungle (2016) Season 3. Venice features prominently in the first five episodes of this series dedicated to classical music starring Monica Bellucci.

Internet and Digital Resources

TRAVEL AND TOURIST TIPS

www.italia.it
The official Italian tourism website is a good place to start browsing. You'll find information about upcoming events along with links to regional and local tourist info sites.

www.travelforkids.com
Discover hundreds of activities for kids.

www.viator.com
Global guide platform that satisfies a wide range of interests and facilitates the purchasing of tickets to museums and monuments.

izi.Travel
Free audio platform with hundreds of narrated explanations and extended tours through Rome, Florence, and Venice. An accompanying app includes offline maps.

TRANSPORTATION

www.skyscanner.net, www.kayak.com, www.hipmunk.com
These flight aggregators help find the cheapest fares. Hipmunk is one of the latest and has paid a little more attention to design and practical features like timelines and maps that simplify planning. They also offer hotel and car-rental services.

www.rome2rio.com
Door-to-door transportation details with distances, departures times, and prices for planes, trains, buses, and ferries. There's also a carbon emissions estimate for the ecologically inclined.

www.seatguru.com
Learn your legroom options and read unbiased advice on where to sit on a flight. The database includes all major airlines along with diagrams, photos, and descriptions of Airbus and Boeing interiors.

www.jetlagrooster.com
Avoid jet lag by creating a personalized sleep plan for a smooth transition between time zones. Just log on 3-4 days before departure and follow their recommended bedtimes.

www.italo.com, www.trenitalia.com
Italy's high-speed rail operators. Tickets can be printed out at home or saved on mobile devices. If your trip is still months away, sign up for the Italo newsletter and receive monthly travel offers.

www.autostrade.it
Drivers can calculate mileage (in kilometers) and toll costs for planned routes. Rest areas are listed, as are the cheapest gas stations. It's also useful for traffic alerts and brushing up on the rules of the Italian road.

ACCOMMODATIONS

www.airbnb.com, www.slh.com, www.tablethotels.com
Search for B&Bs, apartments, or boutique hotels. Sites include realistic visuals and advice from people who have traveled before you.

www.tripadvisor.com
Get feedback and user ratings on sights, services, and hotels. Comments are detailed and often highlight inconveniences like a bad view or small bathroom.

www.xe.com
Calculate what a buck is worth and know exactly how much you're spending. The site's sister app is ideal for the financially conscious and allows travelers to track expenditures on the go.

APPS

There are plenty of well-designed apps for locating restaurants, mastering public transportation, learning Italian, and getting the best deals in Rome, Florence, and Venice. They're available for all operating systems and a search in any app store will turn up a plethora. The following have English versions and are free, although some may incur roaming charges and it's wise to check with your carrier before using them. Many of the larger museums and monuments such as the Vatican, Duomo, and Uffizi have official apps that include maps and detailed descriptions of their collections.

ADR Roma
Real-time flight, boarding, and baggage claim info for both of Rome's airports.

Alitalia
Provides flight, boarding, and baggage claim info for Italy's national airline.

Trenitalia, Italo
Purchase tickets for high-speed trains. Italo also provides departure times, track numbers, and updated info.

Rome2Rio
Transportation alternatives and prices for getting from A to B by plane, train, bus, ridesharing or car.

Enjoy, Share Now
Car-sharing apps that locate and open vehicles in Rome and Florence.

Nugo
All the tickets you need (ferry, bus, train, car, bicycle, etc.) in a single app.

Trainline
Bus and train comparison app.

AppTaxi
Italian taxis at your fingertips.

Autovelox
Helps avoid speed traps.

Muoversi a Roma
Official transportation app of Rome. Provides real-time planning, suggested routes, and expected arrival times.

AVM Venezia
Official transportation app of Venice.

Moovit
Public transportation tips for Rome, Florence, and Venice.

Wikiloc
Social hiking app with hundreds of well-indicated walks to choose from

Komoot
Essential altitude, incline, street-type, and surface paving information for cyclists

Maps.me
Good source of offline maps.

Duolingo
Perfect for brushing up on Italian language vocabulary.

Word Reference
Decipher (and learn to pronounce) Italian on the go.

Index

NO

P

List of Maps

Photo Credits

Craft a personalized journey through the top national parks in the U.S. and Canada with Moon Travel Guides.

MOON

USA NATIONAL PARKS

THE COMPLETE GUIDE TO ALL 62 PARKS

BECKY LOMAX

MOON

ACADIA
NATIONAL PARK

HILARY NANGLE

MOON

ARCHES & CANYONLANDS
NATIONAL PARKS

W. C. McRAE & JUDY JEWELL

MOON

BANFF NATIONAL PARK

HIKE·CAMP SEE WILDLIFE

ANDREW HEMPSTEAD

MOON

DEATH VALLEY
NATIONAL PARK

JENNA BLOUGH

MOON

GLACIER
NATIONAL PARK

HIKING·CAMPING
LAKES & PEAKS

BECKY LOMAX

MOON

GRAND CANYON

HIKE·CAMP RAFT THE COLORADO RIVER

TIM HULL

MOON

GREAT SMOKY MOUNTAINS
NATIONAL PARK

HIKING·CAMPING
SCENIC DRIVES

JASON FRYE

MOON

MOUNT RUSHMORE
& THE BLACK HILLS

EXPLORING THE DAKOTAS

LAURA A. KINIRY

MOON

ROCKY MOUNTAIN
NATIONAL PARK

HIKE·CAMP
SEE WILDLIFE

ERIN ENGLISH

MOON

SEQUOIA & KINGS CANYON

HIKING·CAMPING
WATERFALLS & BIG TREES

LEIGH BERNACCHI

MOON

YELLOWSTONE & GRAND TETON

HIKE, CAMP, SEE WILDLIFE

BECKY LOMAX

MOON

YOSEMITE
SEQUOIA & KINGS CANYON

ANN MARIE BROWN

MOON

ZION & BRYCE

W. C. McRAE, JUDY JEWELL

Trips to Remember

BALI & LOMBOK
CHARINE TAN

ECUADOR
& THE GALÁPAGOS ISLANDS
BETHANY PITTS

GREEK ISLANDS & ATHENS
SARAH SOULI

ICELAND
JENNA GOTTLIEB

TRIP OF A LIFETIME
MACHU PICCHU
EXPLORE THE INCA HEARTLAND
RYAN DUBÉ

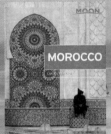

MOROCCO
LUCAS PETERS

NEW ZEALAND
JAMIE CHRISTIAN DESPLACES

OAXACA
ANDREW COLLINS

TRIP OF A LIFETIME
PATAGONIA
EXPLORE THE FJORDS AND GLACIERS
WAYNE BERNHARDSON

PRAGUE, VIENNA & BUDAPEST
JOHANNA BAILEY & AUBURN SCALLON

ROME, FLORENCE & VENICE
ALEXEI J. COHEN

Epic Adventure

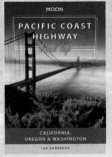

PACIFIC COAST HIGHWAY
Road Trip
CALIFORNIA, OREGON & WASHINGTON
IAN ANDERSON

ROUTE 66
Road Trip
JESSICA DUNHAM

YELLOWSTONE TO GLACIER NATIONAL PARK
Road Trip
JACKSON HOLE, CODY, THE GRAND TETONS & THE ROCKY MOUNTAIN FRONT
CARTER G. WALKER

MAP SYMBOLS

Expressway	City/Town	Information Center	Park
Primary Road	State Capital	Parking Area	Golf Course
Secondary Road	National Capital	Church	Unique Feature
Unpaved Road	Highlight	Winery/Vineyard	Waterfall
Trail	Point of Interest	Trailhead	Camping
Ferry	Accommodation	Train Station	Mountain
Railroad	Restaurant/Bar	Airport	Ski Area
Pedestrian Walkway	Other Location	Airfield	Glacier
Stairs			

CONVERSION TABLES

°C = (°F – 32) / 1.8
°F = (°C x 1.8) + 32
1 inch = 2.54 centimeters (cm)
1 foot = 0.304 meters (m)
1 yard = 0.914 meters
1 mile = 1.6093 kilometers (km)
1 km = 0.6214 miles
1 fathom = 1.8288 m
1 chain = 20.1168 m
1 furlong = 201.168 m
1 acre = 0.4047 hectares
1 sq km = 100 hectares
1 sq mile = 2.59 square km
1 ounce = 28.35 grams
1 pound = 0.4536 kilograms
1 short ton = 0.90718 metric ton
1 short ton = 2,000 pounds
1 long ton = 1.016 metric tons
1 long ton = 2,240 pounds
1 metric ton = 1,000 kilograms
1 quart = 0.94635 liters
1 US gallon = 3.7854 liters
1 Imperial gallon = 4.5459 liters
1 nautical mile = 1.852 km

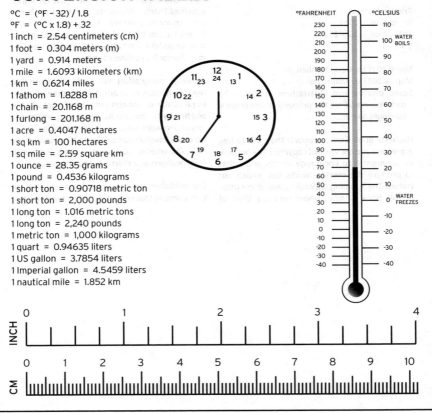

MOON ROME, FLORENCE & VENICE
Avalon Travel
Hachette Book Group
1700 Fourth Street
Berkeley, CA 94710, USA
www.moon.com

Editor: Nikki Ioakimedes
Managing Editor: Hannah Brezack
Graphics and Production Coordinator: Darren Alessi
Cover Design: Faceout Studio, Charles Brock
Interior Design: Domini Dragoone
Moon Logo: Tim McGrath
Map Editor: Kat Bennett
Cartographers: Mark Stroud Moon Street
  Cartography, Kat Bennett, John Culp
Proofreader: Megan Anderluh

ISBN-13: 978-1-64049-467-1

Printing History
1st Edition — 2017
3rd Edition — July 2021
5 4 3 2 1

Front cover photo: Church of St. Ignatius of Loyola
at Campus Martiu in Rome © David J. Green /
Alamy Stock Photo
Back cover photo: sunset over the Grand Canal in
Venice © Shaiith | Dreamstime.com

Printed in China by RR Donnelley

For when your friends want your recommendations.
Keep track of your favorite...

Restaurants and Meals

Neighborhoods and Regions

Cultural Experiences

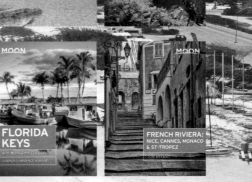